LOGISTIC REGRESSION

LOGISTIC REGRESSION

From Introductory to Advanced Concepts and Applications

Scott Menard
Sam Houston State University

Los Angeles | London | New Delhi
Singapore | Washington DC

For information:

SAGE Publications, Inc.
2455 Teller Road
Thousand Oaks, California 91320
E-mail: order@sagepub.com

SAGE Publications India Pvt. Ltd.
B 1/I 1 Mohan Cooperative Industrial Area
Mathura Road, New Delhi 110 044
India

SAGE Publications Ltd.
1 Oliver's Yard
55 City Road
London EC1Y 1SP
United Kingdom

SAGE Publications Asia-Pacific Pte. Ltd.
33 Pekin Street #02-01
Far East Square
Singapore 048763

Printed in the United States of America.

Library of Congress Cataloging-in-Publication Data

Menard, Scott W.
Logistic regression: From introductory to advanced concepts and applications/Scott Menard.
Includes bibliographical references and index.
ISBN 978–1–4129–7483—7 (hardcover)
   1. Logistic regression analysis. 2. Logistic distribution. I. Title.

HA31.3.M46 2009
519.5'36—dc22   2008049935

Printed on acid-free paper

09   10   11   12   13   10   9   8   7   6   5   4   3   2   1

Acquiring Editor:	Vicki Knight
Associate Editor:	Sean Connelly
Editorial Assistant:	Lauren Habib
Production Editor:	Sarah K. Quesenberry
Copy Editor:	QuADS Prepress (P) Ltd.
Proofreader:	Annette Pagliaro Sweeney
Typesetter:	C&M Digitals (P) Ltd.
Cover Designer:	Glenn Vogel
Marketing Manager:	Stephanie Adams

Contents

Preface

This book is a logical extension of my logistic regression monograph in the SAGE Quantitative Applications in the Social Sciences Series (Menard 2002a). This book begins in much the same place as the monograph, but goes deeper and farther into the technical details and practical applications of logistic regression. While no background beyond basic statistics through ordinary least squares regression is assumed, readers with some background in multiple regression analysis at the level of Lewis-Beck (1980) and Berry and Feldman (1985), and log-linear analysis at the level of Knoke and Burke (1980) or Fienberg (1980) will no doubt find the subject matter of this book quicker and easier to comprehend than readers without such a background. Readers interested in a more limited introduction to logistic regression analysis, either instead of or prior to reading this book, should consider Menard (2002a). One reason for writing this book is to provide a bridge between the reader who is perhaps somewhat less experienced or sophisticated mathematically, but who is interested in more advanced topics in using logistic regression analysis, and the reader who is more sophisticated mathematically but may be unfamiliar with some of the applications of logistic regression analysis.

Over the years, I have noticed that many aspects of logistic regression analysis are treated as "common knowledge" (or ignored altogether), particularly in texts treating topics beyond the simple logistic regression model for a dichotomous dependent variable. Alternatively, topics of interest in logistic regression analysis are relegated to a chapter in a book on another topic such as multilevel analysis. In this book, I have tried to provide thorough coverage of the use of logistic regression analysis, including a number of topics the reader is unlikely to find in a book, much less a chapter, on logistic regression elsewhere. I have also tried as much as reasonably possible to avoid the mathematical shorthand that makes the exposition quicker and perhaps easier for the more advanced reader (and the writer!), but more difficult for others who do not read mathematical notation every day for a living. In my best judgment, some of the more technical sections, such as the discussion of maximum likelihood estimation in Appendix A, would be unbearably tedious and not appreciably clearer without recourse to matrix notation, but for most of the book, the worst the reader will experience is an occasional summation (Σ) sign, and I have even avoided this shorthand when I thought it would make the exposition clearer for less advanced readers.

Each chapter of the book follows a basic outline. First, I try to present the background, sometimes including material that is more methodological than statistical, in as much mathematical detail as is necessary, but always with a translation of the mathematics into something resembling English. Reference is made, mainly in notes at the end of the chapter, to specific software packages, but material specific to both general purpose and more specialized statistical software goes quickly out of date, and in the main body of the text I have tried to avoid tying the presentation to any specific version of any specific software package. I have also indicated where I think that existing statistical software would benefit from supplementary calculation, sometimes best done by hand. Once the basic material has been presented, I then use examples to illustrate the application of different types of logistic regression to different types of substantive problems. A central theme in the examples is again translation into English, this time of the numbers typically output by statistical software (or calculated by hand from that output). A second recurrent theme is that there may be ambiguity in both the selection of specific techniques and the interpretation of the results, and that sometimes statistics is as much art as it is science.

OUTLINE OF THE BOOK

The first two chapters of the book introduce logistic regression analysis from two different perspectives, ordinary least squares linear regression analysis and log-linear analysis. Linear regression and log-linear analysis focus on different criteria for judging how well a model works, and have different problems with the inclusion of categorical dependent variables (problematic for linear regression) or continuous predictors (problematic for log-linear analysis). For Chapter 1, the suggested minimum prerequisite is an introduction to ordinary least squares regression analysis at the level of Chapter 9 in Agresti and Finlay (1997); better would be Chapters 10 to 14 in Agresti and Finlay (1997), or something at the level of the monograph by Lewis-Beck (1980). For Chapter 2, a brief review of contingency table analysis is provided at the beginning of the chapter, but a suggested minimal prerequisite is an introduction to contingency table analysis as in Chapter 8 of Agresti and Finlay (1997); better would be an introduction to log-linear analysis at the level of Knoke and Burke (1980). Either chapter could stand alone as an introduction to logistic regression, but the two combined give a more complete picture of the problems logistic regression was designed to solve, and the reason for the inclusion of various statistics in much logistic regression software (and differences between software packages in what is or is not included). The bottom line message of the first two chapters is that logistic regression provides a more useful tool than some other techniques for the analysis of dichotomous dependent variables. Chapter 1 draws heavily from Menard (2002a); Chapter 2 is entirely new to this book. My own preference is to approach logistic regression from the perspective of ordinary least squares linear regression, but others may feel more comfortable approaching logistic regression from the perspective of logit models for contingency table analysis.

The next two chapters deal with global model statistics, including measures of model fit (comparison with a theoretically "best" model), improvement over a model with no predictors, explained variation in the dependent variable, and inferential statistics. Chapter 3 focuses on measures of quantitative prediction comparing observed values with continuous predicted probabilities, while Chapter 4 focuses on qualitative prediction in the form of prediction or classification tables. Quantitative measures of explained variation with broad applicability include the likelihood ratio coefficient of variation, here and elsewhere (Hosmer and Lemeshow 1989; Menard 1995) designated R_L^2, and the squared correlation between the continuous predicted probabilities and the observed dichotomous dependent variable, here designated R_O^2. In particular, over the past decade, evidence has accumulated to support the use of R_L^2 as the coefficient of variation most appropriate for maximum likelihood logistic regression for dichotomous dependent variables. Qualitative measures of explained variation include the indices of predictive efficiency λ_p, τ_p, and φ_p, along with the appropriate tests for statistical significance, for 2×2 contingency tables of predicted and observed dichotomous scores on the dependent variable. Chapters 3 and 4 build on my previous work in this area, including Menard (2002a) and Menard (2000), but also include previously unpublished material, and Chapter 4 is supplemented with more mathematical detail on the indices of predictive efficiency in Appendix B. No prerequisites beyond either or (preferably) both of the first two chapters in this book are needed for the material in Chapters 3 and 4. The placement of Chapters 3 and 4 reflect my perspective that one should first evaluate the overall model before considering the details regarding specific predictors, and my assessment that it is easier to present tests of statistical significance for individual predictors (particularly the likelihood ratio test) if one has first discussed statistical significance for the whole model; but for those wishing to cover individual coefficients prior to evaluation of the overall model, Chapter 5 can be covered prior to Chapters 3 and 4 with little or no loss.

Chapter 5 discusses interpretation of coefficients and inferential statistics for individual predictors in logistic regression. Unique to this book is a detailed examination of different ways of coding the predictors ("contrasts" for the predictors) and the calculation and use of standardized coefficients in logistic regression analysis. Here, different approaches to calculating standardized logistic regression coefficients are examined, the importance of using standardized logistic regression coefficients to compare the strengths of the relationships of differently scaled predictors with the dependent variable is emphasized, and interpretations of unstandardized coefficients, standardized coefficients, and odds ratios are contrasted. Also of concern here is the use of different tests for the statistical significance of logistic regression coefficients, with a preference for the likelihood ratio test over the Wald statistic, the latter of which is the more common default option in logistic regression output. Chapter 5 represents an expansion of material previously presented in Menard (2002a) and Menard (2004a). No prerequisites beyond either or (preferably) both of the first two chapters in this book are needed for the material in Chapter 5.

Chapters 6 and 7 deal with the diagnosis of and remedies for problems in the dichotomous logistic regression model. Chapter 6 focuses on model building and model specification, including testing for nonlinearity and nonadditivity, and the use of stepwise methods to select variables for inclusion in the model. Chapter 7 focuses on problems in inference, including overdispersion, collinearity, and the presence of outliers and influential cases, and ends with a suggested protocol for logistic regression diagnostics. Chapters 6 and 7 also represent an expansion of material presented in Menard (2002a). No prerequisites beyond Chapter 1 or 2, and Chapters 3 to 5 of this book are necessary for Chapters 6 and 7, but readers who have some prior familiarity with diagnostics for multiple linear regression at the level of Berry and Feldman (1985) and Fox (1991) will find much of the material in Chapters 6 and 7 familiar.

The focus on standardized coefficients returns in Chapter 8, which details how path analysis can be applied in the logistic regression framework with categorical dependent and intervening variables as well as predictors. Some of the material in this chapter was first presented in Menard (2004b), but the coverage of path analysis with logistic regression is substantially expanded from that earlier paper and is unique to this book. Alternatively, path analysis with logistic regression could be covered immediately following the discussion of standardized logistic regression coefficients (which play a central role in path analysis) in Chapter 5, before the material on logistic regression diagnostics. Chapter 8 can be skipped altogether if one also skips (a) the second-to-last section in Chapter 9 on path analysis with polytomous nominal logistic regression and (b) the second-to-last section in Chapter 13 on multiwave logistic regression panel models, both of which may be omitted from less advanced coverage of logistic regression analysis; otherwise, Chapter 8 should be covered prior to those sections. A reasonable prerequisite for Chapter 8 would be Chapters 1, 3, 4, and 5 of this book; better would be coverage at the level of Asher (1983) or Lewis-Beck (1980). The message of Chapter 8 is that logistic regression can be used like multiple linear regression, either separately or in combination with linear regression, to obtain meaningful quantitative estimates of indirect as well as direct effects of predictors on (or through) dichotomous dependent variables.

Chapters 9 and 10 provide extended discussions of logistic regression for polytomous dependent variables. Unique to these chapters is a more detailed consideration of techniques involving separate estimation of logistic functions for polytomous dependent variables than is found in most books on logistic regression analysis; consideration of alternative contrasts for the dependent variable in polytomous logistic regression; and consideration of alternative measures of explained variation for ordinal dependent variables in polytomous logistic regression models. For polytomous nominal dependent variables, the same measures of explained variation as are used in dichotomous logistic regression are applicable. For polytomous ordinal logistic regression, however, for reasons presented in more detail in Appendix C, it is suggested that it is more appropriate to assess explained variation using Kendall's τ_b^2, a measure of explained variation that takes full advantage of the information about the ordering of the categories of the dependent variable, and which has an intuitively reasonable interpretation as a proportional reduction in error measure. No prerequisites beyond Chapters 1 to 8 of this book are necessary, and if one omits the sections (particularly the second-to-last section in Chapter 9) on path analysis, Chapter 8 is not a necessary prerequisite.

Chapters 11 and 12 discuss adjustments to the logistic regression model when data involve clustered or otherwise dependent samples, including contextual dependencies. Chapter 11 compares bootstrap, jackknife, generalized estimating equation (GEE), and multilevel modeling approaches to dealing with dependencies within samples based on clustering within primary sampling units or other contexts. These approaches are not mutually exclusive. Where possible, given the data, the multilevel modeling approach (which may incorporate GEE or be supplemented by bootstrap or jackknife estimation) has some features that make it particularly attractive for the analysis of dependent data. Chapter 12 focuses on conditional logistic regression analysis in retrospectively paired or matched samples. As the examples in Chapter 12 indicate, the constraints imposed by conditional logistic regression may produce results that are more problematic in some types of studies (particularly when there is an interest in the effects of both time-varying and time-invariant predictors on the outcome) than in others (e.g., epidemiological analysis of the impact of exposure on disease). These chapters are entirely new to this volume. No prerequisites beyond Chapters 1 or 2 and Chapters 3 to 5 (and marginally Chapters 6 and 7) of this book are needed for Chapters 11 and 12. Having read Chapters 11 and 12, however, one may wish to pursue the references listed in those chapters for more detailed or advanced treatment of these topics beyond the confines of logistic regression analysis.

Chapters 13 and 14 focus on the use of logistic regression analysis for longitudinal data with few (Chapter 13) and many (Chapter 14) repeated measurements. Chapter 13 parallels discussions of linear panel analysis, with extended consideration of the measurement and modeling of change for categorical dependent variables, and returns to the topic of path analysis with logistic regression first considered in Chapter 8. This chapter provides substantially expanded treatment of topics presented in Menard (2008a), provides some cautionary material on the limitations of the two-wave fixed effects conditional logistic regression model, and suggests that serious consideration be given to the use of the lagged endogenous variable model in panel analysis with logistic regression. Chapters 1 to 12 should be considered prerequisite to Chapter 13. There are no other prerequisites, but readers may wish to follow or accompany Chapter 13 with more detailed discussion of linear panel analysis outside the confines of logistic regression analysis (e.g., Finkel 1995; Kessler and Greenberg 1981).

Chapter 14 represents a substantial expansion of Menard (2008b), and focuses on multilevel change models and also event history analysis using the proportional odds logistic regression model to model the relationship between categorical dependent variables and time dimensions (chronological time and age). Multilevel modeling presently appears to offer the most promise for the analysis of longitudinal data with categorical or dichotomous dependent variables, although an alternative, the latent change model, is also considered in Chapter 15. For event history analysis, however, the logistic regression model is typically not the technique of choice. Instead, the complementary log-log model, with its proportional hazards interpretation, may be preferable, insofar as the assumptions underlying the complementary log-log model are more often consistent with the way in which the data are actually generated. There are no prerequisites to Chapter 14 other than the previous chapters in this book (Chapters 1 to 13), but the use of logistic regression models in event history and multilevel analysis represents a small part of those more general topics, and readers may wish to get more detail on event history analysis (e.g., Allison 1995; Box-Steffensmeier and Jones 2004), multilevel modeling (e.g., Raudenbush and Bryk 2002; Snijders and Bosker 1999) or both (e.g., Singer and Willett 2003).

Chapter 15, completely new here, concludes with a brief comparison of logistic regression analysis to other methods of analysis, including probit models, discriminant analysis, and in the context of event history analysis, complementary log-log models. Consideration is also given to the use of structural equation modeling for panel analysis with logistic regression and to model patterns of intraindividual (or more generically intracase or intraunit) change using latent change models. While structural equation modeling appears to be a viable option for two-wave and multiwave panel analysis with logistic regression, there are both conceptual and technical issues in the application of latent *growth curve* analysis (or, with a dichotomous dependent variable, latent *change* analysis) that suggest that, as indicated above, multilevel modeling for longer series of data may be more tractable and useful in the context of logistic regression analysis. This book began with an explanation of how logistic regression may be better than other techniques for the analysis of dichotomous dependent variables. The point of Chapter 15 is to indicate when the logistic regression model might *not* be the best approach, and what alternatives may be available. There are no prerequisites to Chapter 15 beyond the previous chapters in this book, but one may wish to pursue the references in Chapter 15 for more detailed coverage of the alternatives to logistic regression mentioned in that chapter.

SOFTWARE AND NOTATION

Throughout the book, I have followed certain notational conventions. Variables, which represent vectors of values for the individual cases in the sample, are presented in uppercase: Y is a (usually dependent) variable, X is a (usually independent) variable, a series of subscripted variables $X_1, X_2, \ldots, X_K$ represents a series of K (usually independent) variables. Values of a variable for an individual case are presented in lowercase, practically always subscripted: y_i is the value of Y for case i, x_j is the value of X for case j, and if there is a series of subscripted variables $Z_1, Z_2, \ldots, Z_K$ for which there are $j = 1, 2, \ldots, J$ cases then a doubly subscripted z_{jk} indicates the value of a specific variable Z_k for a specific case j, and the order in which the subscripts are represented should be clear from the context. The mean of a variable will be presented in uppercase, for example, $\bar{Y}$. These notational conventions do not apply to the log-linear models in Chapter 2, because log-linear analysis has its own special notations (and the use of the plural here is deliberate). A vector of subscripted variables $X_1, X_2, \ldots, X_K$ is sometimes presented as **X**, boldface and unsubscripted. For the most part, I try to avoid vector and matrix notation, but it is useful in some parts of the book; see, for example, Appendix A on maximum likelihood estimation. Examples were calculated primarily using SAS, SPSS, and Stata. These three software packages were chosen because they are general purpose statistical packages in wide use, with all of which I am familiar, and each of which has different features in its logistic regression routines. In Chapters 11 and 14, I have also used HLM for contextual and longitudinal multilevel models in the logistic regression framework. For the most part, I have tried to keep the software issues in the background, and to make reference to software-specific issues in endnotes specifically designated as "Software Notes" at the end of each chapter.

ACKNOWLEDGMENTS

Shortly after the publication of my article on R^2 analogs for logistic regression (Menard 2000), I was contacted by a publisher who will remain nameless with the suggestion that I submit a prospectus for a book on logistic regression. When I mentioned this to C. Deborah Laughton, my erstwhile editor for the Quantitative Applications in the Social Sciences series, she suggested that I should instead submit the prospectus to SAGE. Her encouragement (not to mention her patience over the years) convinced me to do so. I feel fortunate to have had the support and patience—a lot of patience— from her and from all of the people at SAGE Publications with whom I have worked over the past decade or so, including Stephanie Adams, Eileen Carr, Sean Connelly, Margo Beth Crouppen, Vicki Knight, Alison Mudditt, Veronica Novak, Sarah Quesenberry, and Lisa Cuevas Shaw. Special thanks also to Michael Lewis-Beck, the editor of the SAGE Quantitative Applications in the Social Sciences series, and to the reviewers of the first and second editions of my two monographs in that series, and to Shankaran Srinivasan and Rajeswari Krithivasan at QuADS Prepress for copyediting the manuscript.

I have also had the pleasure of working in the Institute of Behavioral Sciences at the University of Colorado, which has given me the freedom and intellectual stimulation necessary for the work on this book. My special thanks in this regard to Delbert S. Elliott, then Director of the Center for the Study and Prevention of Violence, for his support and mentoring over the years, particularly in the area of longitudinal research, and to Jarron Saintonge and Jani Little at the Institute of Behavioral Science at the University of Colorado for help in playing with the (endlessly time-consuming) quadrature estimation approach for complex mixed models in SAS and **gllamm**.

I would like to thank everyone whose comments, corrections, questions, and interest in logistic regression have helped me either in understanding logistic regression, or in presenting more clearly what I understand about logistic regression: Kadry Ulas Akay, Mohammed Al-Jerash, Imad A. Alsuwaih, Lisa Barron, Jason Boardman, Paul Boxer, Marta Brown, Sarah Brown-Schmidt, Jim Cofer, Richard Congdon, Mars Cramer, Diana Draghici, Dennis Gene Fischer, Adrienne Freng,

Stephen Giff, Bob Green, Jennifer Grotpeter, Steven Gumerman, Mohammad Habibi Doost, Dina Hardiana, Talia Harmon, Frank Harrell, John Hater, Susan Helmet, Ben Heylen, David Huizinga, Quee-Young Kim, Drew Kingston, Thomas Knapp, Thanittha Kumsri, Shawkat Q. Lafi, Roy Levy, Chung-Tung Jordan Lin, J. Scott Long, Randall MacIntosh, Gillian Marks, S. R. Millis, Diego Mosquera, Christian Neuerburg, David Nichols, Tom Nolan, Gary Pallet, Paul A. Palugod, Fred Pampel, Joanne Peng, Ashley Pica, Daniel Powers, Anantha Rao, Lorraine B. Read, Luis Ribeiro Chorão, Debra Ross, Hidetoshi Saito, Stephen Sands, Volker Schlecht, David Shannon, Tony Smith, Tom Snijders, Irina Soderstrom, Dave Sorenson, Paul Squillace, Tina Stamou, Andy Strowig, Robert Svensson, Robert H. Tai, Rosana P. Thrasher, Will Turner, Mike Veall, Katrine Vej-Hansen, Martin Voracek, John Waller, Dan Waschbusch, Zhigang Wei, Susan Schoenberger White, Julie Wolf, several people for whom I have only e-mail addresses and not full names, and all the students who have applied themselves so diligently in my intermediate statistics classes to the study of logistic regression. My apologies to anyone I have left off this list who should be on it; and as always, no one on this list is responsible for any errors or misinterpretations on my part.

This seems the appropriate place to acknowledge a longstanding intellectual debt. When I was a sophomore engineering student at Cornell University in the late 1960s and early 1970s, there was a lot of "consciousness raising" going on. We engineering students were, much to our annoyance, required to take electives in the liberal arts, and one of the electives I took was an introductory sociology course, which was taught as a series of two-week "mini-courses" in different areas of sociology. Professor Robert McGinnis taught a session on mathematical sociology that opened my eyes to the utility and promise of quantitative techniques in the social sciences, and led me to change my major from engineering to sociology. In subsequent courses I took from him, he further whetted my interest and helped me develop an understanding of mathematical and statistical techniques that went beyond the "cookbook" approaches I was exposed to in other courses in statistics. The work I have done on R^2 analogs, particularly indices of predictive efficiency, and on standardized logistic regression coefficients and path analysis using logistic regression, can be traced directly to insights from his courses. To the extent that I have been able to do something worthwhile with those insights, Bob McGinnis deserves much of the credit; but if I have somehow failed in this attempt, the blame is all my own.

There are other debts of a more personal nature I must also acknowledge. Throughout the writing of this and other books, monographs, and articles, I have had the love and support of my wife Laura and our two wonderful daughters, Jessica and Valery. It is to them that I dedicate this book.

About the Author

Scott Menard is a professor of Criminal Justice at Sam Houston State University and a research associate in the Institute of Behavioral Science at the University of Colorado, Boulder. He received his AB at Cornell University and his PhD at the University of Colorado, Boulder, both in Sociology. His interests include quantitative methods and statistics, life course criminology, substance abuse, and criminal victimization. His publications include *Longitudinal Research* (second edition, 2002), *Applied Logistic Regression Analysis* (second edition, 2002), *Good Kids From Bad Neighborhoods* (2006, with Delbert S. Elliott, Bruce Rankin, Amanda Elliott, William Julius Wilson, and David Huizinga), *Youth Gangs* (2006, with Robert J. Franzese and Herbert C. Covey), and the *Handbook of Longitudinal Research* (2008), as well as other books and journal articles in the areas of criminology, delinquency, population studies, and statistics.

Introduction

Linear Regression and Logistic Regression

In a broad range of scientific disciplines, a common problem is how to predict a categorical outcome when there are two or more *predictors,* which may or may not be *causes* of that outcome. Examples of the use of logistic regression include the prediction of lightning strikes at Kennedy Space Center and Cape Canaveral Air Force Station (Lambert 2007; Lambert and Wheeler 2005), landslide hazards in Kansas (Ohlmacher and Davis 2003), ventilator-associated pneumonia and mortality in premature births (Apisarnthanarak et al. 2003; Elward et al. 2002), environmental conservation attitudes in Nepal (Mehta and Heinen 2001), detection of the filing of false financial statements in Greece (Spathis 2002), the adoption of outside boards of directors by small private firms in the United States (Fiegener et al. 2000), long-term functional outcomes of burn injuries to the hand (van Zuijlen 1999), the impact of school-based arts instruction on attendance at museums and the performing arts (Kracman 1996), self-medication management in older adults (Maddigan et al. 2003), the impact of demographic, family, and individual variables on educational expectations (Trusty and Harris 1999), first-year student attrition rates (Patrick 2001), the choice of walking for transportation and recreation (Lee and Moudon 2006), the formation of high concentrations of trihalomethanes in drinking water (Milot et al. 2000), and wildlife-vehicle collisions in the Canadian Rocky Mountains (Gunson et al. 2003). As should be evident from these examples, from rocket science to roadkill, logistic regression is a statistical technique that spans the "hard" and "soft" sciences in its applicability and usefulness.

Logistic regression blends two very different statistical traditions. One is the analysis of contingency tables (cross-tabulations or crosstabs), in which all the variables are measured at either the dichotomous (two categories), nominal (more than two categories with no inherent order among the categories), or ordinal (more than two categories with some inherent greater-than-or-less-than order among the categories), and in which the variables usually have relatively few (usually less than 10, almost always less than 20) distinct categories. (For a review of levels of measurement, see, e.g., Agresti and Finlay 1997:12–17.) Expanding from two-way or bivariate contingency tables (two variables) to three-way or trivariate (three variables) to multiway or multivariate (multiple variables) contingency tables led to the development of log-linear analysis to deal with the complexity of multidimensional contingency tables. The second tradition is ordinary least squares (OLS) multiple regression analysis, in which the variables are typically measured at the interval or ratio level, or are incorporated as *dummy variables* (a set of several dichotomous variables used to represent a single, multiple-category variable, usually a nominal variable such as ethnicity represented by separate variables for African American, Hispanic/Latino, etc.). The original techniques used in log-linear analysis did not handle predictors measured at a continuous interval or ratio scale level very well, and OLS regression did not handle dichotomous, nominal, or ordinal dependent variables very well.

In logistic regression analysis, the dependent variable may be dichotomous (two categories), unordered polytomous or polytomous nominal (three or more categories with no natural ordering among the categories), or ordered polytomous or polytomous ordinal (three or more categories with a natural ordering among the categories). Examples of dichotomous dependent variables include almost anything that has a simple "yes" or "no" interpretation: whether one uses illicit drugs, uses a computer, wins the lottery, or gets struck by lightning. Examples of polytomous nominal variables include political party affiliation (Democrat, Republican, Libertarian, Socialist, Independent) and type of car owned (American, European, Japanese, other). Examples of polytomous ordinal variables include political orientation (not party, but left-right ideology: fascist, conservative, moderate, liberal, communist) and level of agreement (strongly disagree, disagree somewhat, neutral, agree somewhat, strongly agree). Independent variables or predictors may, as in OLS multiple regression, be interval/ratio variables, or may be dummy variables used to represent variables with a limited number of categories that are measured at less than the interval or ratio level of measurement.

A PREVIEW OF EXAMPLES USED IN THIS BOOK

The examples I will use in this book include personal computer use, illicit drug use, political affiliation, and gun ownership. There are others, but these account for the bulk of the discussion. Broadly, these examples fall under the general category of social science. The intention is not to exclude other fields from consideration, but apart from reflecting my own background and training, these examples do not require technical knowledge in any specific field, and therefore should be accessible to the broadest readership. Based on experience with previous work in this area, there should be little or no difficulty in translating the general principles in this book to applications specific to more technical fields such as medicine and meteorology. Here, let me briefly describe the applications to be addressed in the examples of the book.

Example 1: Friends' behavior, personal beliefs, gender, ethnicity, and illicit drug use. Data for this example are taken from the National Youth Survey (NYS), a nationally representative sample of individuals who were 11 to 17 years old when first interviewed in 1976–1977 and who were in their late thirties and early forties when last interviewed in 2002–2003. The sample includes both delinquent and nondelinquent adolescents. Here, we look at the extent to which their reports of having used illicit drugs are predicted by (a) the general involvement of one's friends in illegal behavior, not limited to illicit drug use; (b) personal beliefs about how wrong it is to violate the law, again not limited to illicit drug use; (c) whether one is male or female; and (d) whether one is a member of an ethnic majority or ethnic minority group. To illustrate logistic regression with a dichotomous outcome, we focus on whether or not the respondents have used marijuana. For logistic regression with a polytomous outcome, we examine different levels of substance use, ranging from no use to alcohol use to marijuana use to hard drug use. NYS data on the predictors of illicit drug use are also used to illustrate the application of logistic regression analysis to longitudinal research. For details on the NYS, see Elliott et al. (1989). Data from a related study analyze outcomes in a clustered sample, with clusters of individuals sampled from the same neighborhoods. Using data from the Denver Neighborhood Survey (Elliott et al. 1996, 2006), we investigate whether it is not only the behavior of one's friends and one's own personal beliefs but also the more general neighborhood environment in which one lives that is predictive of illicit drug use.

Example 2: Income, education, gender, ethnicity, and personal computer use. Data for this example are taken from the General Social Survey (GSS) conducted by the National Opinion Research Center (NORC). For this example, we look at the impact of education and income on whether individuals use personal computers at work or at home, and also whether there are differences in the probability of personal computer use depending on whether one is male or female, or whether one is a member of an ethnic majority or ethnic minority group, once we allow for the influences of education and income. GSS data on computer use are also used to illustrate estimation procedures for logistic regression in samples in which the data are clustered, that is, when the sampling method results in some observations being more closely related than others. Detailed information on the GSS may be found in Davis et al. (2000, 2005), and in a briefer introduction by Smith (2008). Two other examples are based on the GSS.

Example 3: Gun ownership. To what degree are education, income, ethnicity, and gender predictive of gun ownership? Is it just those uneducated citizens living in economic despair who are clinging to their guns for comfort? (OK, if you didn't follow the 2008 Democratic presidential primaries, that may not register—but the suggestion has been made that gun ownership is more prevalent among poorer, less-educated White males.) Data for this example are also taken from the GSS, and education, income, gender, and ethnicity are again used as predictors this time to illustrate the use of conditional logistic regression.

Example 4: Political party preference and voting in the presidential election. In this third example from the GSS, the dependent variables, in separate analyses, are (a) political party affiliation, with income, education, gender, and ethnicity as predictors and (b) whether one voted for Clinton, Perot, or Dole in the 1988 presidential election, with political party affiliation, income, education, gender, and ethnicity as predictors. Here we examine the extent to which political party preference and presidential vote are linked directly to gender and ethnicity, as opposed to having the effects of gender and ethnicity operating indirectly, via their impacts on education and income, to influence party and presidential choice. The 1988 election was chosen because it included a third-party candidate who received a substantial percentage of the vote, so analysis of this election provides a good illustration of polytomous logistic regression analysis.

Other examples are used briefly to illustrate specific aspects of logistic regression analysis, but the focus on the NYS and GSS data sets, and on repeatedly revisiting the same substantive problems, is deliberate. First, both data sets are publicly available through the Inter-University Consortium for Political and Social Research (ICPSR), allowing the reader to not only replicate the results here but also go beyond them with relatively familiar data sets. Second, by returning repeatedly to the same substantive themes, it becomes possible to compare the results of different approaches within the logistic regression framework when they are used to analyze the same problem. It is hoped that having a smaller number of common substantive threads will also make it easier to concentrate on the statistics as opposed to the specific substantive problem under consideration. In each of these examples, we are trying to predict a variable with two or more categories measured on something less than an interval or ratio scale of measurement, using predictors that combine dichotomous, polytomous, and continuous (in principle, interval or ratio) levels of measurement. This is the specific problem for which logistic regression was designed.

One could begin the discussion of logistic regression from either the OLS multiple regression perspective or from the log-linear analysis perspective. Here, we begin with an approach from the multiple regression perspective. From past experience, that seems to be the perspective with which most readers will be familiar to begin with, and one also in which the notation may be a bit less confusing than the notation used in log-linear analysis. The approach from the perspective of log-linear analysis will be deferred until the next chapter. It may be possible to get everything one really needs to apply logistic regression to substantive problems from either chapter, but viewing logistic regression from both perspectives should give a clearer idea of the relationship of logistic regression to other statistical approaches, and also provide a more thorough understanding of logistic regression as a statistical technique.

BIVARIATE ORDINARY LEAST SQUARES LINEAR REGRESSION AND LOGISTIC REGRESSION

In linear regression analysis, it is possible to test whether two variables are linearly related, and to calculate the strength of the linear relationship, if the relationship between the variables can be described by an equation of the form $Y = \alpha + \beta X$, where Y is the variable being predicted (the dependent, criterion, outcome, or endogenous variable), X is a variable whose values are being used to predict Y (the independent, exogenous, or predictor variable), and α and β are population parameters to be estimated. Although the relationship being modeled often represents a causal relationship, in which the single predicted variable is believed to be an effect of the one or more predictor variables, this is not always the case. One can as easily predict a cause from an effect (e.g., predict whether different individuals are male or female based on their income) as predict an effect from a cause (e.g., predict income based on whether someone is male or female). Throughout this book, the emphasis is on predictive rather than causal relationships, although the language of causal relationships is sometimes employed. Describing a variable as independent or dependent, therefore, or as an outcome or a predictor, does not necessarily imply a causal relationship. Instead, all relationships should be regarded as definitely predictive but only possibly causal in nature.

The parameter α, called the *intercept,* represents the value of Y when X is 0. The parameter β represents the change in Y associated with a one-unit increase in X, or the *slope* of the line that provides the best linear estimate of Y from X. In *multiple regression,* there are several predictor variables. If K = the number of independent variables, the equation becomes $Y = \alpha + \beta_1 X_1 + \beta_2 X_2 + \cdots + \beta_K X_K$ and $\beta_1, \beta_2, \ldots, \beta_K$ are called *partial* slope coefficients, reflecting the fact that any one of the K predictor variables $X_1, X_2, \ldots, X_K$ provides only a partial explanation or prediction for the value of Y. The equation is sometimes written in a form that explicitly recognizes that prediction of Y from X may be imprecise: $Y = \alpha + \beta X + \varepsilon$, or for several predictors, $Y = \alpha + \beta_1 X_1 + \beta_2 X_2 + \cdots + \beta_K X_K + \varepsilon$, where ε is the error term, a random variable representing the error in predicting Y from X. For an individual case j, $y_j = \alpha_j + \beta X_j + \varepsilon_j$, or $Y_j = \alpha_j + \beta_1 X_{1j} + \beta_2 X_{2j} + \cdots + \beta_K X_{Kj} + \varepsilon_j$, and the subscript j indicates that the equation is predicting values for specific cases, indexed by j ($j = 1$ for the first case, $j = 2$ for the second case, etc.). Each of the lowercase letters y_j, x_{1j}, $x_{2j} \cdots$, x_{kj}, refers not to the variables themselves but instead to the specific value of the dependent and independent variables for a particular case. This last equation is used to calculate the value of Y for a particular case, j, rather than describing the relationship among the variables for all the cases in the sample or the population.

Estimates of the intercept, α, and the regression coefficients, β (or $\beta_1, \beta_2, \ldots, \beta_K$) are obtained mathematically using the method of OLS estimation, which is discussed in many introductory statistics texts (e.g., Agresti and Finlay 1997; Bohrnstedt and Knoke 1994). These estimates produce the equation $\hat{Y} = a + bX$, or in the case of several predictors, $\hat{Y} = a + b_1 X_1 + b_2 X_2 + \cdots + b_K X_K$, where $\hat{Y}$ is the value of Y predicted by the linear regression equation, a is the OLS estimate of the intercept α, and b (or $b_1, b_2, \ldots, b_K$) is the OLS estimate for the slope β (or the partial slopes $\beta_1, \beta_2, \ldots, \beta_K$). Residuals for each case, e_j, are equal to $(y_j - \hat{y}_j)$, where $\hat{y}_j$ is the estimated value of y_j for case j. For bivariate regression, they can be visually or geometrically represented by the vertical distance between each point in a bivariate scatterplot and the regression line. For multiple regression, visual representation is much more difficult because it requires several dimensions.

An example of a bivariate regression model is given in Figure 1.1.[1] In Part A of Figure 1.1, the dependent variable is FRQMRJ5, the annual frequency of self-reported marijuana use ("How many times in the last year have you smoked marijuana?") and the independent variable is EDF5, an index of exposure to delinquent friends, for 16-year-old respondents interviewed in 1980, in the fifth wave of the NYS, described earlier in this chapter. The exposure to delinquent friends scale is the sum of the answers to eight questions about how many of the respondent's friends are involved in different types of delinquent behavior (theft, assault, drug use). The responses to individual items range from 1 (none of my friends) to 5 (all of my friends), resulting in a possible range from 8 to 40 for EDF5. From Part A of Figure 1.1, there appears to be a positive relationship between exposure to delinquent friends and marijuana use, described by the equation

$$(\text{FRQMRJ5}) = -49.2 + 6.2(\text{EDF5}).$$

In other words, for every one-unit increase in the index of exposure to delinquent friends, frequency of marijuana use increases by about six times per year, or about once every 2 months. The coefficient of determination, or R^2, indicates how much better we can predict the dependent variable from the independent variable than we could predict the dependent variable without information about the independent variable. Without information about the independent variable, we would use the mean frequency of marijuana use as our prediction for all respondents. Knowing the value of exposure to delinquent friends, however, we can base our prediction on the value of EDF5 and the relationship, represented by the regression equation, between FRQMRJ5 and EDF5. Using the regression equation reduces the sum of the squared errors of prediction, $\sum e_j^2 = \sum(\hat{y}_j - y_j)^2$, by $R^2 = .116$, or about 12%.

FIGURE 1.1   **Bivariate Regression Plots**

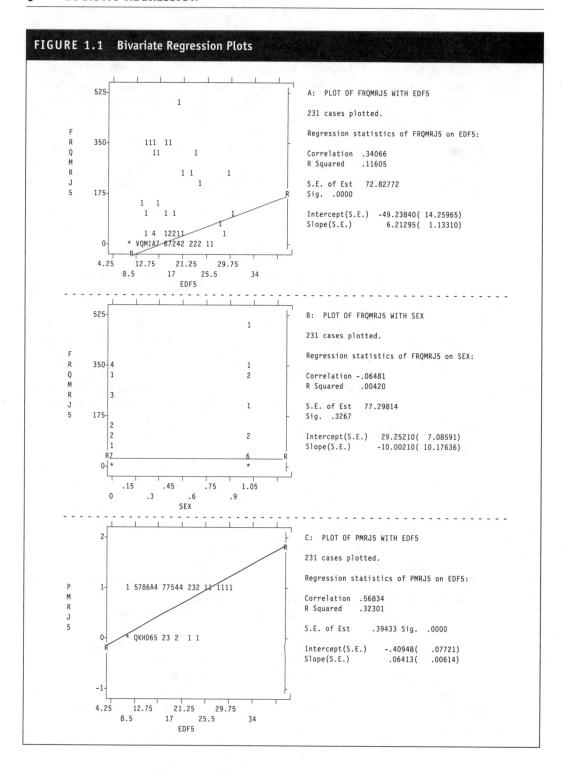

It is necessary to interpret the results to consider the actual values of the dependent and independent variables. The intercept indicates that for an individual with 0 as the value of exposure to delinquent friends, the frequency of marijuana use would be negative. This seemingly impossible result occurs because exposure, as noted above, is measured on a scale that ranges from a minimum of 8 (no exposure at all; none of one's friends involved in any of 8 delinquent activities) to 40 (extensive exposure; all of one's friends involved in all of 8 delinquent activities). Thus, for individuals with the minimum possible exposure to delinquent friends (a value of 8, representing no exposure), the expected frequency of marijuana use is $-49.2 + 6.2(8) = 0.4$, close to 0 but indicating that even some individuals with no exposure to delinquency may use marijuana at least occasionally. The maximum value of EDF5 in this sample is 29, which corresponds to an expected frequency of marijuana use equal to $-49.2 + 6.2(29) = 130.6$, or use approximately every 3 days. This result makes sense substantively, in terms of real-world behavior, as well as statistically, in terms of the regression equation.

REGRESSION ASSUMPTIONS

To use the OLS method to estimate and make inferences about the coefficients in linear regression analysis, a number of assumptions must be satisfied (Berry 1993; Berry and Feldman 1985; Lewis-Beck 1980:26–47). Specific assumptions include the following:

1. *Measurement:* All independent variables are interval, ratio, or dichotomous; the dependent variable is continuous, unbounded, and measured on an interval or ratio scale. All variables are measured without error.

2. *Specification:* (a) All relevant predictors of the dependent variable are included in the analysis, (b) no irrelevant predictors of the dependent variable are included in the analysis, and (c) the *form* of the relationship (allowing for transformations of dependent or independent variables) is linear.

3. *Expected value of error:* The expected value of the error, ε, is 0.

4. *Homoscedasticity:* The variance of the error term, ε, is the same, or constant, for all values of the independent variables.

5. *Normality of errors:* The errors are normally distributed for each set of values of the independent variables.

6. *No autocorrelation:* There is no correlation among the error terms produced by different values of the independent variables. Mathematically, $E(\varepsilon_i, \varepsilon_j) = 0$, where $E(\varepsilon_i, \varepsilon_j)$ represents the *expected value* of the association (correlation or covariance) between ε_i and ε_j.

7. *No correlation between the error terms and the independent variables:* The error terms are uncorrelated with the independent variables. Mathematically $E(\varepsilon_i, x_j) = 0$.

8. *Absence of perfect multicollinearity:* For multiple regression, none of the independent variables is a perfect linear combination of the other independent variables; mathematically, for any i, $R_i^2 < 1$, where R_i^2 is the variance in the *independent* variable X_i that is explained by all the other independent variables $X_1, X_2, \ldots, X_{i-1}, X_{i+1}, \ldots, X_K$. If there is only one predictor, multicollinearity is not an issue.

VIOLATIONS OF THE MEASUREMENT ASSUMPTION: DICHOTOMOUS VARIABLES IN LINEAR REGRESSION

The linear regression model can easily be extended to accommodate dichotomous predictors, including sets of dummy variables (Berry and Feldman 1985:64–75; Hardy 1993; Lewis-Beck 1980:66–71). An example is presented in Part B of Figure 1.1. Here, the dependent variable is again self-reported annual frequency of marijuana use, but the independent variable this time is sex or gender (coded 0 = female, 1 = male). Mathematically, this is equivalent to an analysis of variance (ANOVA) with frequency of marijuana use as the dependent variable and sex as the factor. Cohen's (1968) observation that multiple regression and ANOVA are simply different ways of presenting the same mathematical model (the OLS model) has become common knowledge, as reflected by statistical textbooks that present regression techniques for ANOVA (e.g., Agresti and Finlay 1997). The point is that the comparison of logistic regression to OLS regression here applies equally to the comparison between logistic regression and analysis of variance and covariance (ANOVA and ANCOVA). The regression equation here is

$$FRQMRJ5 = 29.3 - 10.0(SEX).$$

The resulting diagram consists of two columns of values for frequency of marijuana use, one representing females and one representing males. With a dichotomous predictor, coded 0–1, the intercept and the slope have a special interpretation. It is still true that the intercept is the predicted value of the dependent variable when the independent variable is 0 (substantively, when the respondent is female), but with only two groups, the intercept now is the *mean* frequency of marijuana use for the group coded as 0 (females). The slope is still the change in the dependent variable associated with a one-unit change in the independent variable, but with only two categories, that value becomes the *difference in the means* between the first (female) and second (male) groups. The sum of the slope and the intercept, 29.3 − 10.0 = 19.3 is therefore the *mean* frequency of marijuana use for the second group (males). As indicated in Part B of Figure 1.1, then, females report a higher (yes, higher) frequency of marijuana use than males, but the difference is not statistically significant (as indicated by sig. = .3267). In Part B of Figure 1.1, the regression line is simply the line that connects the mean frequency of marijuana use for females and the mean frequency of marijuana use for males, that is, the *conditional means*[2] of marijuana use for females and males, respectively. The predicted values of Y over the observed range of X lie well within the observed (and possible) values of Y. Again, the results make substantive as well as statistical sense.

When the *dependent* variable is dichotomous, the interpretation of the regression equation is not as straightforward. In Part C of Figure 1.1, the independent variable is again exposure to delinquent friends, but now the dependent variable is the *prevalence* of marijuana use: whether (yes = 1 or no = 0) the individual used marijuana at all during the past year. In Part C of Figure 1.1, with a dichotomous dependent variable, there are two rows (rather than columns, as in Part B). The linear regression model with a dichotomous dependent variable, coded 0–1, is called a *linear probability model* (Agresti 1990:84; Aldrich and Nelson 1984). The equation, from Part C of Figure 1.1, is

$$PMRJ5 = -.41 + .064(EDF5).$$

When there is a dichotomous dependent variable, the mean of the variable is a function of the probability that a case will fall into the higher of the two categories for the variable. Coding the values of the variable as 0 and 1 produces the result that the mean of the variable is the proportion of cases in the higher of the two categories of the variable, and the predicted value of the dependent variable (the conditional mean, given the value of X and the assumption that X and Y are linearly related) can be interpreted as the *predicted probability* that a case falls into the higher of the two categories on the dependent variable, given its value on the independent variable. Ideally, we would like the predicted probability to lie between 0 and 1, since a probability cannot be less than 0 or more than 1.

As is evident from Part C of Figure 1.1, the predicted values for the dependent variable may be higher or lower than the possible values of the dependent variable. For the minimum value of EDF5 (EDF5 = 8), the predicted prevalence of marijuana use (i.e., the predicted probability of marijuana use) is $-.41 + .064(8) = .10$, a reasonable result; but for the maximum value of EDF5 (EDF5 = 29), the predicted probability of marijuana use becomes $-.41 + .064(29) = 1.45$, or an impossibly high probability of about one and one half. In addition, the variability of the residuals will depend on the numerical value of the independent variable (Aldrich and Nelson 1984:13; Schroeder et al. 1986:79–80). This condition, called *heteroscedasticity,* implies that the estimates for the regression coefficients, although unbiased (not systematically too high or too low), will not be the best estimates in the sense of having a small standard error. There is also a systematic pattern to the values of the residuals, depending on the value of X. For values of X greater than 23.5 in Part C of Figure 1.1, all the residuals will be negative because $\hat{y}_j$ will be greater than y_j (because for X greater than 23.5, $\hat{y}_j$ is greater than 1 but y_j is less than or equal to 1). Also, residuals will not be normally distributed (Schroeder et al. 1986:80) and sampling variances will not be correctly estimated (Aldrich and Nelson 1984:13–14); therefore, the results of hypothesis testing or construction of confidence intervals for the regression coefficients will not be valid.

A BRIEF INTRODUCTION TO PROBABILITY: DEFINITIONS AND PROPERTIES

The development and explanation of logistic regression from the perspective of linear regression is the movement, step by step, from predicting a dichotomous outcome, which may be expressed as a *probability,* to a continuous outcome with no upper or lower limit, the natural logarithm of the ratio of one probability to another related probability; and to get from here to there, we need to begin with a discussion of probabilities, then conditional probabilities, conditional means, and nonlinear relationships.

The probability of an event is estimated by its relative frequency in a population or sample. For example, if $n_{Y=1}$ is the number of cases for which $Y = 1$ in a sample, and N is the total number of cases in the sample, then

(a) We can denote the probability that Y is equal to 1 as Probability$(Y = 1)$, $\Pi(Y = 1)$, or $P(Y = 1)$; the notation "$P(Y = 1)$" seems sufficiently clear and is also concise, and will be the preferred notation for the remainder of this book.

(b) $P(Y = 1) = n_{Y=1}/N$.

(c) The probability that Y is *not* equal to 1 is $P(Y \neq 1) = 1 - P(Y = 1) = 1 - (n_{Y=1}/N) = (N - n_{Y=1})/N$.

(d) The minimum possible value for a probability is 0 ($n_{Y=1} = 0$ implies $n_{Y=1}/N = 0$).

(e) The maximum possible value for a probability is 1 ($n_{Y=1} = N$ implies $n_{Y=1}/N = 1$).

The *joint probability* of two independent events (occurrences that are unrelated to one another) is the product of their individual probabilities. For example, the probability that both X and Y are equal to 1, if X and Y are unrelated, is $P(Y = 1 \text{ and } X = 1) = P(Y = 1) \times P(X = 1)$. If X and Y are related (e.g., if the probability that Y is equal to 1 depends on the value of X), then $P(Y = 1 \text{ and } X = 1)$ will not be equal to $P(Y = 1) \times P(X = 1)$. Instead, we will want to consider the *conditional probability* that $Y = 1$ when $X = 1$, or $P(Y = 1|X = 1)$.

The conditional probability that $Y = 1$ is the probability that $Y = 1$ *for a given value of some other variable*. In this context, we may sometimes refer to $P(Y = 1)$, the probability that $Y = 1$ regardless of the value of any other variable, as the *unconditional* probability that $Y = 1$. For example, the probability that the prevalence of marijuana use is equal to 1 for the data in Figure 1.1 is $P(PMRJ5 = 1) = .35$ (for males and females combined; detailed data not shown). The conditional probability that prevalence of marijuana use is equal to 1 is $P(PMRJ5 = 1|SEX = 0) = .45$ for females and $P(PMRJ5 = 1|SEX = 1) = .25$ for males. For a dichotomous variable, coded as 0 or 1, the probability that the variable is equal to 1 is equal to the mean for that variable, and the conditional probability that the variable is equal to 1 is equal to the conditional mean for the variable.

NONLINEARITY, CONDITIONAL MEANS, AND CONDITIONAL PROBABILITIES

For continuous dependent variables, the regression estimate of Y, $\hat{Y}$, may be thought of as an *estimate* of the conditional mean of Y for a particular value of X, *given that the relationship between X and Y is linear*. In bivariate regression, for continuous independent variables, the estimated value of Y may not be exactly equal to the mean value of Y for those cases, because the conditional means of Y for different values of X may not lie exactly on a straight line. For a dichotomous predictor variable, the regression line will pass exactly through the conditional means of Y for each of the two categories of X. If the conditional means of FRQMRJ5 are plotted against the dichotomous predictor, SEX, the plot consists of two points (remember, the cases are aggregated by the value of the independent variable), the conditional means of Y for males and females. The simplest, most parsimonious description of this plot is a straight line between the two conditional means, and the linear regression model appears to work well.

The inherent nonlinearity of relationships involving dichotomous dependent variables is illustrated in Figure 1.2. In Figure 1.2, the observed conditional mean of PMRJ5, the *prevalence* of marijuana use, is plotted for each value of the independent variable EDF5. The 21 cases indicated at the bottom of Figure 1.2 are the 21 separate valid values for the predictor, EDF5. The observed conditional mean is symbolized by the letter C. Since PMRJ5 is coded as either 0 or 1, the conditional means represent averages of zeros and ones, and are interpretable as conditional probabilities. Figure 1.2 is therefore a plot of *probabilities* that PMRJ5 = 1 for different values of EDF5. All the *observed* values of Y lie between the two vertical lines at 0 and 1, respectively, in Figure 1.2. *Predicted* probabilities, however, can, in principle, be infinitely large or small, if we use the linear probability model.

FIGURE 1.2 Conditional Probabilities Observed (C) and Predicted by Linear Regression (R)

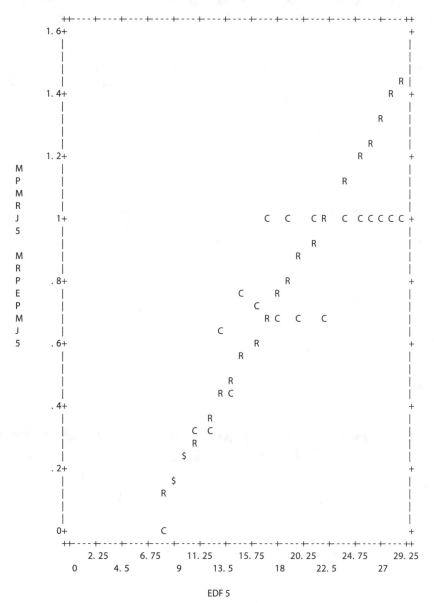

C: Observed Mean Prevalence of Marijuana Use (MPMRJ 5) WITH EDF 5 (Exposure to Delinquent Friends)

R: Linear Regression Prediction of Prevalence of Marijuana Use (MRPEPMJ 5) WITH EDF5

$: Multiple Occurrence (Linear Regression Prediction and Observed Value Coincide)

21 Cases

The plot of *observed* conditional probabilities (C) in Figure 1.2 is overlaid with the plot of *predicted* conditional probabilities based on the regression equation (R) in Part C of Figure 1.1. For values of EDF5 greater than 23.5, the observed value of the conditional mean prevalence of marijuana use stops increasing and levels off at PMRJ5 = 1. The predicted values from the regression equation, however, continue to increase past the value of 1 for PMRJ5, to a maximum of 1.45, and the error of prediction increases as EDF5 increases from 23.5 to its maximum of 29.

Two points need to be made about Figure 1.2. First, although a linear model appears to be potentially appropriate for a continuous dependent variable, regardless of whether the independent variables are continuous or dichotomous, it is evident that a nonlinear model is better suited to the analysis of the dichotomous variable PMRJ5. In general, for very high values of X (or very low values, if the relationship is negative), the conditional probability that $Y = 1$ will be so close to 1 that it should change little with further increases in X. This is the situation illustrated in Figure 1.2. It is also the case that for very low values of X (or very high values if the relationship is negative) the conditional probability that $Y = 1$ will be so close to 0 that it should change little with further decreases in X. The curve representing the relationship between X and Y should therefore be very shallow, with a slope close to 0, for very high and very low values of X, if X can, in principle, become indefinitely large or indefinitely small. If X and Y are related, then between the very high and very low values of X, the slope of the curve will be steeper, significantly different from 0. The general pattern is that of an "S-curve" as depicted in Figure 1.3.

Second, for prevalence data, the observed conditional mean of Y is equal to the observed conditional probability that $Y = 1$, and the predicted value of Y is equal to the predicted conditional probability that $Y = 1$. The actual values used to identify the two categories of Y are arbitrary, a matter of convenience. They may be 0 and 1, for example, or 2 and 3 (in which case the predicted values of Y are equal to two plus the conditional probability that $Y = 3$, still a function of the conditional probability that Y has the higher of its two values for a given value of X). What is substantively important is not the numerical value of Y, but the probability that Y has one or another of its two possible values, and the extent to which that probability depends on one or more independent variables.

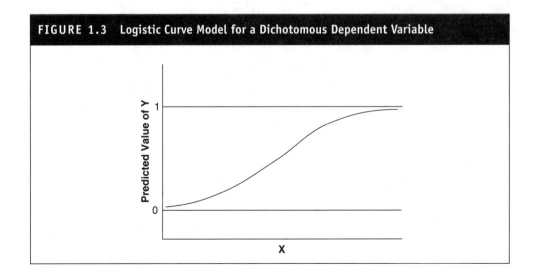

FIGURE 1.3   Logistic Curve Model for a Dichotomous Dependent Variable

The distinction between the arbitrary numerical value of Y, on which OLS bases its parameter estimates, and the probability that Y has one or the other of its two possible values, is problematic for OLS linear regression, and leads us to a consideration of alternative methods for estimating parameters to describe the relationship between X and Y. First, however, we address the issue of nonlinearity. For continuous independent and dependent variables, the presence of nonlinearity in the relationship between X and Y may sometimes be addressed by the use of nonlinear transformations of dependent or independent variables (Berry and Feldman 1985). Similar techniques play a part in estimating relationships involving dichotomous dependent variables.

NONLINEAR RELATIONSHIPS AND VARIABLE TRANSFORMATIONS

When a relationship appears to be nonlinear, it is possible to transform either the dependent variable or one or more of the independent variables so that the *substantive* relationship remains nonlinear, but the *form* of the relationship is linear, and can therefore be analyzed using OLS estimation. Another way of saying that a relationship is substantively nonlinear but formally linear is to say that the relationship is *nonlinear in terms of its variables but linear in terms of its parameters* (Berry and Feldman 1985:53). Examples of variable transformations to achieve a linear form for the relationship are given in Berry and Feldman (1985:55–72) and Lewis-Beck (1980:43–47).

In Figure 1.2, there was some evidence of nonlinearity in the relationship between frequency of marijuana use and exposure to delinquent friends. One possible transformation that could be used to model this nonlinearity is a logarithmic transformation of the dependent variable, FRQMRJ5. This is done by adding 1 to FRQMRJ5 and then taking the natural logarithm. (Adding 1 is necessary to avoid taking the natural logarithm of 0, which is undefined.) The logarithmic transformation is one of several possibilities discussed by Berry and Feldman (1985:63–64), Lewis-Beck (1980:44), and others to deal with relationships that are nonlinear with respect to the variables, but may be expressed as linear relationships with respect to the parameters. After the logarithmic transformation is applied, the regression equation has the form $\ln(Y + 1) = \alpha + \beta X$, or equivalently, $(Y + 1) = e^{\alpha+\beta X}$, or $Y = e^{\alpha+\beta X} - 1$, where $e = 2.72$ is the base of the natural logarithm. Specifically for prevalence of marijuana use and exposure to delinquent friends,

$$\ln(\text{FRQMRJ5} + 1) = -1.7 + .23(\text{EDF5}); R^2 = .32.$$

Comparing the results of the model using the logarithmic transformation with the untransformed model in Part A of Figure 1.1, it is evident that the slope is still positive, but the numerical value of the slope has changed (because the units in which the dependent variable is measured have changed from frequency to logged frequency). The coefficient of determination for the transformed equation is also larger (.32 instead of .12), reflecting a better fit of the linear regression model when the dependent variable is transformed. This is evidence (not conclusive proof, just evidence) that the relationship between the frequency of marijuana use and exposure to delinquent friends is substantively nonlinear. A similar result occurs for the relationship between the dichotomous predictor, SEX, and frequency of marijuana use. With the logarithmic transformation of the dependent variable, the explained variance increases (from a puny .004 to an unimpressive .028), and the relationship between gender and frequency of marijuana use is statistically significant ($p = .011$) in the transformed equation. It appears that the relationship between frequency of marijuana use and both the predictors considered so far is substantively nonlinear, but we are still able to use a formally linear model to describe those relationships, and we can still use OLS to estimate the parameters of the model.

PROBABILITIES, ODDS, AND THE LOGIT TRANSFORMATION FOR DICHOTOMOUS DEPENDENT VARIABLES

As noted earlier, for a dichotomous dependent variable, the numerical value of the variable is arbitrary, a matter of convenience, and is not intrinsically interesting. What is intrinsically interesting is whether the classification of cases into one or the other of the categories of the dependent variable can be predicted by the independent variable. Instead of trying to predict the arbitrary value associated with a category, then, it may be useful to reconceptualize the problem as trying to predict the probability that a case will be classified into one as opposed to the other of the two categories of the dependent variable. Since the probability of being classified into the first or lower-valued category, $P(Y = 0)$, is equal to 1 minus the probability of being classified into the second or higher-valued category, $P(Y = 1)$, if we know one probability we know the other: $P(Y = 0) = 1 - P(Y = 1)$.

We could try to model the probability that $Y = 1$ as $P(Y = 1) = \alpha + \beta X$, but we would again run into the problem that although observed values of $P(Y = 1)$ must lie between 0 and 1, predicted values may be less than 0 or greater than 1. A step toward solving this problem would be to replace the *probability* that $Y = 1$ with the *odds* that $Y = 1$. The *odds* that $Y = 1$, written "odds$(Y = 1)$" or "$\Omega(Y = 1)$" [$\Omega(Y = 1)$ will be the preferred notation for the remainder of this book], is the ratio of the probability that $Y = 1$ to the probability that $Y \neq 1$. The odds that $Y = 1$ is equal to $P(Y = 1)/[1 - P(Y = 1)]$. Unlike $P(Y = 1)$, the odds has no fixed maximum value, but like the probability, it has a minimum value of 0.

One further transformation of the odds produces a variable that varies, in principle, from negative infinity to positive infinity. The *natural logarithm of the odds*, $\ln\{P(Y = 1)/[1 - P(Y = 1)]\}$, is called the *logit* of Y. The logit of Y, written "logit(Y)" or "$\Lambda(Y)$" [for the sake of clarity, logit(Y) will be the preferred notation for the remainder of this book] becomes negative and increasingly large in absolute value as the odds decreases from 1 toward 0, and becomes increasingly large in the positive direction as the odds increases from 1 to ∞. If we use the natural logarithm of the odds that $Y = 1$ as our dependent variable, we no longer face the problem that the estimated probability may exceed the maximum or minimum possible values for the probability. The equation for the relationship between the dependent variable and the independent variables then becomes

$$\text{logit}(Y) = \alpha + \beta_1 X_1 + \beta_2 X_2 + \cdots + \beta_K X_K. \tag{1.1}$$

We can convert logit(Y) back to the odds by *exponentiation*, calculating $\Omega(Y = 1) = e^{\text{logit}(Y)}$. This results in the equation

$$\text{odds}(Y = 1) = \Omega(y = 1) = e^{\ln[\Omega(Y=1)]} = e^{\alpha + \beta_1 X_1 + \beta_2 X_2 + \cdots + \beta_K X_K} \tag{1.2}$$

and a change of one unit in X multiplies the odds by e^β. We can then convert the odds back to the probability that $(Y = 1)$ by the formula $P(Y = 1) = [\Omega(Y = 1)]/[1 + \Omega(Y = 1)]$, that is, the probability that $Y = 1$ is equal to the odds that $Y = 1$ divided by 1 plus the odds that $Y = 1$. This produces the equation

$$\text{Probability}(Y=1) = P(Y=1) = (e^{\alpha+\beta_1 X_1+\beta_2 X_2+\cdots+\beta_K X_K})/(1+e^{\alpha+\beta_1 X_1+\beta_2 X_2+\cdots+\beta_K X_K}). \qquad (1.3)$$

It is important to understand that the probability, the odds, and the logit are three different ways of expressing exactly the same thing. Table 1.1 summarizes how to calculate each directly from the other. The main diagonal in Table 1.1 defines the notation used in the other cells of the table. The first column includes the notation for probabilities, and how to calculate probabilities from odds or logits. The second column similarly defines odds and shows how to compute odds from probabilities or logits, and the third column defines logits and how to compute logits from odds or probabilities. Of the three measures, the probability or the odds is probably the most easily understood. Mathematically, however, the logit form of the probability is the one that best helps us to analyze dichotomous dependent variables. Just as we took the natural logarithm of the continuous dependent variable, frequency of marijuana use, to correct for the nonlinearity in the relationship between frequency of marijuana use and exposure to delinquent friends, we can also take the logit of the dichotomous dependent variable, prevalence of marijuana use, to correct for the nonlinearity in the relationship between prevalence of marijuana use and exposure to delinquent friends.

For any given case, j, logit(Y) is infinitely large and positive or infinitely large and negative, or expressed mathematically, logit(Y_j) $= \pm\infty$. This insures that the probabilities estimated for the probability form of the model (Equation 1.3) will not be less than 0 or greater than 1, but it also means that since the linear form of the model (Equation 1.1) has infinitely large or small values of the dependent variable, OLS cannot be used to estimate the parameters. Instead, *maximum likelihood* techniques (see Appendix A) are used to maximize the value of a function, the *log-likelihood* function, which indicates how likely it is to obtain the observed values of Y, given the values of the independent variables and parameters, $\alpha, \beta_1, \ldots, \beta_K$. Unlike OLS, which is able to solve directly for

TABLE 1.1 Equivalences Among Probabilities, Odds, and Log Odds (Logits)

Definition: **Probability that** $(Y=1) = \Pi(Y=1) = P(Y=1)$	Probabilities to Odds: $\Omega(Y=1) = P(Y=1)/$ $[1 - P(Y=1)]$	Probabilities to Logits: logit($Y=1$) $= \ln[P(Y=1)/$ $[1 - P(Y=1)]$
Odds to Probabilities: $P(Y=1) = \Omega(Y=1)/$ $[1 + \Omega(Y=1)]$	**Definition:** **Odds that $(Y=1) = \Omega(Y=1) =$** **Odds($Y=1$)**	Odds to Logits: logit($Y=1$) $= \ln[\Omega(Y=1)]$
Logits to Probabilities: $P(Y=1) = e^{\text{logit}(Y=1)}/$ $[1 + e^{\text{logit}(Y=1)}]$	Logits to Odds: $\Omega(Y=1) = e^{\text{logit}(Y=1)}$	**Definition:** **Logit that $(Y=1) =$** $\Lambda(Y=1) = \text{logit}(Y=1)$

NOTE: As indicated in the text, the preferred notation in this book is $P(Y=1)$ for probabilities, $\Omega(Y=1)$ for odds, and logit($Y=1$) for logits.

the parameters, for the logistic regression model the solution is found by beginning with a tentative solution, revising it slightly to see if it can be improved, and repeating the process until the change in the likelihood function from one step of the process to another is negligible. This process of repeated estimation, testing, and reestimation is called *iteration,* and the process of obtaining a solution from repeated estimation is called an *iterative* process. When the change in the likelihood function from one step to another becomes negligible, the solution is said to *converge.* All this is done by means of computer-implemented numerical algorithms designed to search for and identify the best set of parameters to maximize the log-likelihood function. When the assumptions of OLS regression are met, however, *the OLS estimates for the linear regression coefficients are identical to the estimates one would obtain using maximum likelihood estimation* (Eliason 1993:13–18). OLS estimation is in this sense a special case of maximum likelihood estimation, one in which it is possible to calculate a solution directly, without iteration.

Logistic Regression and Predicted Probabilities: A First Look From an OLS Regression Perspective

Part C of Figure 1.1 showed the results of an OLS linear regression analysis of the relationship between prevalence of marijuana use (PMRJ5) and exposure to delinquent friends (EDF5). If we calculate the relationship using logistic regression software, the equation for the logit of the prevalence of marijuana use is logit(PMRJ5) = −5.487 + .407(EDF5). Figure 1.4 plots the predicted and observed conditional probabilities (or equivalently the conditional means) for the logistic regression equation. The observed conditional probabilities are represented by the letter "C" and the predicted conditional probabilities by the letter "L" for logistic regression. In Figure 1.2, the predicted probabilities from linear regression analysis represented a straight line, and for values of EDF5 greater than 23.5, the predicted conditional probabilities of being a marijuana user were greater than 1. The observed conditional probabilities, unlike the predicted conditional probabilities, leveled off at 1. In Figure 1.4, the conditional probabilities predicted by logistic regression analysis all lie between 0 and 1, and the pattern of the predicted probabilities follows the curve suggested by the observed conditional probabilities, a curve similar to the right half of the curve in Figure 1.3. Just from looking at the pattern, there appears to be a closer correspondence between the observed and predicted conditional means when logistic regression is used to predict the dependent variable. If we calculate the squared correlation between the observed and predicted values of the dependent variable for the logistic regression model in Figure 1.4, we obtain $R^2 = .34$, slightly higher than the R^2 of .32 obtained in the OLS regression model. Both visually and numerically, it appears that the logistic regression model fits the data better than the OLS model.

SUMMARY

OLS regression analysis is inappropriate for the analysis of dichotomous dependent variables, whether in a bivariate model with a single predictor or a more complex model with multiple predictors. The dichotomous scale of the dependent variable results in the violation of assumptions of interval/ratio level of measurement and homoscedasticity of residuals, and also appears to violate

FIGURE 1.4   Conditional Probabilities Observed (C) and Predicted by Logistic Regression (L)

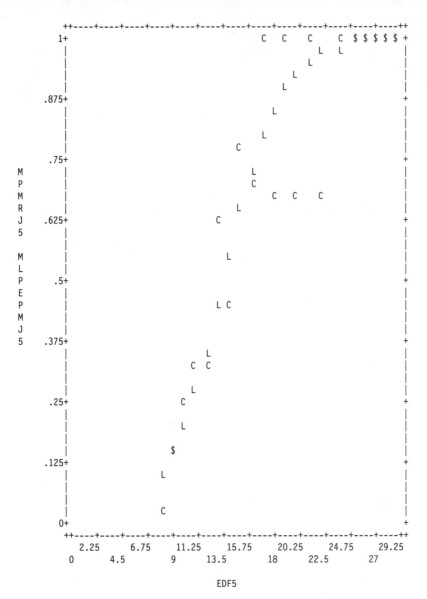

C: Mean Prevalence of Marijuana Use (MPMRJ5) WITH EDF5 (Exposure to Delinquent Friends)

L: Logistic Regression Prediction of Prevalence of Marijuana Use (MLPEPMRJ5) WITH EDF5

$: Multiple Occurrence (Logistic Regression Prediction and Observed Value Coincide)

21 Cases

the assumption that the model is properly specified as a linear model. The linear probability model assigns values of 0 and 1 to the two categories of the dependent variable, and treats these numerical codes as probabilities; it then uses one or more independent variables to predict the value of the dependent variable, interpreted as a probability of membership in the category coded "1" (as opposed to the category coded as "0"). In the logistic regression model, it is not the numerical code for the categories of the dependent variables that matters (as in the linear probability model); the numerical code itself is arbitrary, and it is the actual probability of being in one or the other of the categories that is modeled. It seems evident from the discussion in this chapter that the resulting nonlinear probability model, as represented in Figure 1.3, better represents the relationship between the independent variables and the probability of being in one or the other of the categories of the dependent variable.

NOTES

1. In Figure 1.1, the number of cases at a particular point is indicated by numbers $1 = 1, 2 = 2, \ldots, 9 = 9$, letters $A = 10, B = 11, \ldots, Z = 35$, and $* =$ more than 35 cases at a given point.

2. The *unconditional mean* of Y is simply the familiar mean, $\bar{Y} = \Sigma y/N$. The *conditional mean* of Y for a given value of X is calculated by selecting only those cases for which X has a certain value, and calculating the mean for those cases. The conditional mean can be denoted $\bar{Y}_{X=i} = \Sigma y_{ij}/n_i$, where i is the value of X for which we are calculating the conditional mean of Y; y_{ij} are the values of Y for the cases ($j = 1, 2, \ldots, n_i$) for which $X = i$; and n_i is the number of cases for which $X = i$.

CHAPTER 2

Log-Linear Analysis, Logit Analysis, and Logistic Regression

Log-linear analysis was developed to analyze complex multivariate (or, using an alternative term, multidimensional) contingency tables. A contingency table is simply a table involving two or more categorical variables, in which each cell contains the number of cases having one unique combination of values on the two or more variables. Here, we begin with a brief review of the analysis of bivariate contingency tables in order to lay the groundwork for the discussion of the more complicated log-linear analysis approach to analyzing multivariate contingency tables. More detailed discussion of elementary contingency table analysis may be found in many introductory statistics textbooks (e.g., Agresti and Finlay 1997, chap. 8), and more detailed discussion of log-linear and logit analysis may be found in Knoke and Burke (1980) or Fienberg (1980). As will be seen in this chapter, the development of the foundations of logistic regression analysis owes every bit as much to log-linear and logit analysis as it does to ordinary least squares (OLS) linear regression analysis, and an understanding of log-linear and logit analysis provides a fuller understanding of the logistic regression model.

A REVIEW OF ELEMENTARY BIVARIATE CONTINGENCY TABLE ANALYSIS

Table 2.1, based on data from the National Opinion Research Center (NORC) General Social Survey (GSS),[1] presents a simple bivariate contingency table involving ethnicity and computer use. The first column of cells identifies the categories of the variable Ethnicity (White, Black, Other) and, in the last row, indicates that the last row consists of the totals for each column. The second and third columns indicate the two values for the variable Computer Use (No and Yes, nonuse and use of computers), and contain the total number of computer users and nonusers in each category of ethnicity (and likewise the total number in each ethnic category who are and are not computer users). The number of cases in each cell is called the *observed frequency* of cases in that cell and is represented by f_{ij}, where f stands for (observed) frequency, i represents the row variable, and j represents the column variable (the two are interchangeable). For the first row (White), we can designate $i = 1$, for the second (Black) $i = 2$, and for the third (Other) $i = 3$; for the first column (nonusers) $j = 1$, for the second column (computer users) $j = 2$; and any given cell in the table can be identified by the unique combination of i and j. In parentheses in each cell are the number of cases E_{ij} we would expect for that cell based on the marginal distribution of computer use and ethnicity (the row and column totals) and the assumption that computer use and ethnicity are unrelated or independent of each other, while outside the parentheses we have the actual number of cases observed in each cell. The formula for the expected number of cases in each cell E_{ij} depends on the sum of the cases for that particular row, the sum of the cases for that particular column, and the total number of cases N represented in the table: $E_{ij} = $ (total cases in row i)(total cases in column j)/N. In Table 2.1, we have $f_{11} = 695$ individuals who are White and who do not use computers, $f_{12} = 1,081$ who are White and do use computers, $f_{21} = 186$ who are Black and do not use computers, $f_{22} = 160$ who are Black and do use computers, $f_{31} = 44$ who are "Other" (than White or Black) ethnicity and do not use computers, and $f_{32} = 75$ who are other ethnicity and do use computers.

TABLE 2.1 Ethnicity and Computer Use

Variable B: Ethnicity	Variable C: Computer Use		Row Totals
	No	Yes	
White	695 (733)	1,081 (1,043)	1,776
Black	186 (143)	160 (203)	346
Other	44 (49)	75 (70)	119
Column totals	925	1,316	Grand total 2,241

NOTES: Pearson $\chi^2 = 26.26$, $df = 2$, $p = .000$.
Likelihood ratio $\chi^2 = 26.122$, $df = 2$, $p = .000$.

Odds of being a computer user:

White : $\Omega = 60.9/39.1 = 1.5575$ or 1.56.
Black: $\Omega = 46.2/53.8 = 0.8587$ or 0.86.
Other: $\Omega = 63.0/37.0 = 1.7027$ or 1.70.

Odds ratios:

White to Black: OR = 1.5575/0.8587 = 1.8138.
White to Other: OR = 1.5575/1.7027 = 0.9147.
Black to Other: OR = 0.8587/1.7027 = 0.5043.

Lambda:

With computer use dependent: $\lambda_{yx} = .028$.
With ethnicity dependent: $\lambda_{xy} = .000$.

Goodman and Kruskal's tau:

With computer use dependent: $\tau_{yx} = .172$.
With ethnicity dependent: $\tau_{xy} = .399$.

From Table 2.1, it can be seen that the observed and the expected frequencies in each cell are not identical. To see whether the difference is greater than we would expect by chance alone, we can calculate Pearson's chi-square statistic (χ^2) as the sum of the squared differences between the observed and expected frequencies in each cell, divided by the expected frequencies in each cell: $\chi^2 = [(695 - 733)^2/733] + [(1,081 - 1,043)^2/1,043] + [(186 - 143)^2/143] + [(160 - 203)^2/203] + [(44 - 49)^2/49] + [(75 - 70)^2/70] = 26.26$. For any bivariate table, the number of degrees of freedom is $df = (r - 1)(c - 1)$ where r is the number of categories in the row variable and c is the number of categories in the column variable. In a 3×2 table (3 categories for ethnicity, 2 categories for computer use), there are $(3 - 1)(2 - 1) = 2$ degrees of freedom. The degrees of freedom represent the minimum number of cells we need to know in order to know all of the cells in the table, if we already know the marginal distribution. For example, in Table 2.1, if we know the first two cells in Column 1 (White and Black computer nonusers), then we can subtract the sum of the two from the column total to obtain the number of "Other" computer nonusers, and once we have the first column filled in, we can subtract each cell in the first column from the row total for that row to obtain the frequencies in the cells in the second column. To illustrate, if we know that the first two cells in the first column have frequencies of 695 and 186, and the column total is 925, then the third cell in that column must be $925 - 695 - 186 = 44$. Similarly, knowing that in the first row, the row total is 1,776 and the frequency in the first cell in that row is 695, we know that the frequency in the second cell in that row must be $1,776 - 695 = 1,081$, and the process is the same for the next two rows. Looking up the result in a table for critical values of the chi-square statistic (or letting the computer do the work), we find that for $\chi^2 = 26.26$ with 2 degrees of freedom, $p = .000$. Table 2.1 also includes the likelihood ratio χ^2 for the table, to be discussed in the next section (multivariate contingency table analysis).

From the frequencies in Table 2.1, one can calculate the percentage of each ethnic group that uses computers: 60.9% for Whites, 46.2% for Blacks, and 63.0% for Others. This corresponds to probabilities of computer use of .609 for Whites, .462 for Blacks, and .630 for Others. From these probabilities, we can calculate the odds of computer use for each ethnic group by dividing the probability of computer use by (1 − probability of computer use), thus $.609/(1 - .609) = 1.5575$ for Whites, $.462/(1 - .462) = .8587$ for Blacks, and $.630/(1 - .630) = 1.7027$ for Others. For the odds, values less than 1 correspond to probabilities less than .5, and values greater than 1 correspond to probabilities greater than .5. Like probabilities, the minimum value of the odds is 0, but unlike probabilities, there is no maximum value for the odds, which can be infinitely large (e.g., if the probability is equal to 1, which results in $1 - 1 = 0$ in the denominator for calculating the odds).

In comparing the odds of an outcome for two different groups, the ratio of the odds for the two groups, or simply the odds ratio (OR) is often used. The odds ratio for computer use for Whites as opposed to Blacks would thus be $OR = 1.5575/.8587 = 1.8138$; for Whites as opposed to Others $OR = 1.5575/1.7027 = .9147$; and for Blacks as opposed to Others $OR = .8587/1.7027 = .5043$. An odds ratio of less than 1 indicates that the outcome is less likely for the first group than for the second. Thus in the foregoing example, the odds of Whites using computers is about 91% as high as the odds of Others using computers, and the odds of Blacks using computers is about half as high (.5043 or 50.43%) as the odds of Others using computers. An odds ratio greater than 1 indicates that the odds of the outcome is higher for the first group than for the second, by a percentage equal to the odds ratio minus 1, or $OR - 1$. Thus in the preceding example, the odds of Whites using computers is $(OR - 1) = (1.8138 - 1) = .8138$ or 81.38% higher than the odds of Blacks using computers.

One can switch the categories by dividing 1 by the odds ratio; thus, instead of saying that Whites have an odds of using computers that is 81.38% higher than Blacks, one could say that the odds of Blacks using computers is $1/1.8138 = .5513$ or 55.13% as high as the odds of Whites using computers. Although it lacks some desirable properties for a measure of association (in particular, it does not vary between 0 and 1 but instead has no upper bound), the odds ratio is sometimes used as a measure of association or of the strength of an effect, particularly in experimental or epidemiological research, in which the outcome variable may be the presence or absence of an illness or other characteristic and the predictor may be a treatment (either presence vs. absence, or two or more treatment conditions that may or may not include the absence of any treatment).

Other measures of the strength of the relationship between two variables in a contingency table include Goodman and Kruskal's tau and Goodman and Kruskal's lambda. The latter measure is typically referred to simply as lambda, or λ_{yx} (with one variable dependent) and λ_{xy} (with the other variable dependent), but the former measure is usually referred to as Goodman and Kruskal's tau or τ_{yx} and τ_{xy} to distinguish it from Kendall's tau (τ_a, τ_b, and τ_c), a set of measures of association we will consider later, in conjunction with polytomous ordinal logistic regression models. Goodman and Kruskal's tau and lambda are *asymmetric* measures of association; their value depends on which variable is being treated as the predictor and which is being treated as the outcome, and are also *proportional reduction in error* (PRE) measures of association, having the general form

Association = [(Errors without model) − (Errors with model)]/(Errors without model).

Errors without the model are the number of errors we would make in predicting one variable (the outcome) from the other (the predictor) when we do not know the values of the predictor, but we do know the number of cases in each category of the outcome, and we apply some rule for predicting the values of the outcome. Errors with the model are the errors we get when we predict the outcome based on the value of the predictor. Because there are different rules we can use for predicting the outcome when we do not know the value of the predictor, there are different possible measures of association. PRE measures vary between 0 and 1, and have an intuitively appealing interpretation as the proportion (or multiplied by 100, the percentage) improvement in prediction with as opposed to without the predictor.

The simplest measure of association for contingency tables involving nominal variables is lambda. The prediction rule when we do not know the value of the predictor is to predict the modal category of the outcome for all cases. If we are predicting computer use from ethnicity in Table 2.1, this means that we predict "yes" for all cases; if we are predicting ethnicity from computer use in Table 2.1, this means predicting "White" for all cases (remember, in a purely predictive analysis, we can just as reasonably try to predict a cause from an effect as predict an effect from a cause). For computer use, this results in a total of 925 errors (the number of cases outside the modal category); for ethnicity, this results in a total of $346 + 119 = 465$ errors (the number of cases outside the modal category, White: 346 Black and 119 Other). Next, we use information about the predictor to predict the outcome. For computer use, we predict "yes" for White and Other, but "no" for Black. This is because more White and Other respondents use computers than do not (1,081 vs. 695 for White; 75 vs. 44 for Other), but more Black respondents do not use computers than do (186 vs. 160). The total number of errors with the model for computer use is equal to the number of cases in the nonmodal category *within* each ethnic group: 695 ("no") for White, 160 ("yes") for Black, and 44 ("no") for Other, for a total of $695 + 160 + 44 = 899$ errors. Lambda is thus equal to [(errors without model) − (errors with model)]/(errors without model), or, substituting the numbers above, [(925) − (899)]/(925) = .028, indicating a proportional reduction in error of about 3% when predicting computer use from ethnicity. If we try to predict ethnicity from computer use, however, we get a different result. For both users and nonusers of computers, the modal ethnic category is White, so for both users and nonusers, we predict the same (modal) category with the predictor (computer use) as without it; the number of errors remains the same (465); and lambda is equal to [(465) − (465)]/465 = 0. Again, lambda is an asymmetric measure whose value depends on which variable is the predictor and which is the outcome.

The rule for errors without the model is different for Goodman and Kruskal's tau. Instead of predicting the modal category and counting the errors (the number of cases that are not in the modal category), Goodman and Kruskal's tau assumes that prediction of the outcome will be made at random, but in such a way as to produce the same number of predicted as observed cases for each row or column (something that does not happen with lambda, which predicts that *all* cases will be in *one* row or column). For each row or column, the *expected* number of errors from this random prediction process is the number of cases in that row, multiplied by the number of cases not in that row, and divided by the total number of cases. For computer use in Table 2.1, this is equal to (a) for Column 1, (925)(1,316)/(2,241) = 543.195, and (b) for Column 2, (1,316)(925)/(2,241) = 543.195, for a total expected error without the model of 543.195 + 543.195 = 1,086.39. Predicting ethnicity from computer use, (a) for Row 1, (1,776)(346 + 119)/(2,241) = (1,776)(465)/(2,241) = 368.514, (b) for Row 2, (346)(1,776 + 119)/(2,241) = (346)(1,895)/(2,241) = 292.579, and (c) for Row 3, (119)(1,776 + 346)/(2,241) = (119)(2,122)/(2,241) = 112.681; and the total number of expected errors without the model is 368.514 + 292.579 + 112.681=773.774. Errors with the model are the same as for lambda (we predict the mode within each category), so for computer use as the outcome, Goodman and Kruskal's tau = (1,086.39) − (899)/(1,086.39) = .172, and for ethnicity as the outcome, Goodman and Kruskal's tau = (773.774)−(465)/(773.774) = .399. Predicting computer use from ethnicity results in a 17% reduction in error compared with predicting computer use at random; and predicting ethnicity from computer use results in a 40% reduction in error compared with predicting ethnicity at random. That Goodman and Kruskal's tau is larger than lambda is not unusual, particularly when cases are heavily concentrated in one row or column. In Chapter 4, we will examine parallels to Goodman and Kruskal's tau and lambda as measures of proportional reduction in error for prediction tables.

MULTIVARIATE CONTINGENCY TABLE ANALYSIS: LOG-LINEAR AND LOGIT ANALYSIS

The basic formulation of the log-linear and logit models begins with the assumption that we are dealing with a contingency table of two or more dimensions, representing two or more variables, each of which has two or more categories, which may be ordered but which are usually assumed to be unordered. As illustrated above, analysis of a contingency table with only two variables is relatively straightforward and easy. When contingency tables contain three or more categorical variables, however, it quickly becomes cumbersome to consider all the different ways of arranging the multidimensional tables in the two-dimensional space of a page. Log-linear models summarize three-way and higher-dimensional contingency tables in terms of the effects of each variable in the table on the frequency of observations in each cell of the table, and show the relationships among the variables in the table. As described, for example, by Knoke and Burke (1980:11), the *general log-linear model* makes no distinction between independent and dependent variables, but in effect treats all variables as dependent variables, and models their mutual associations. The expected cell frequencies based on the model, F_{ijk} for a three-way contingency table, are modeled as a function of all the variables in the model. The *logit model* is mathematically equivalent to the log-linear model, but one variable is considered a dependent variable, and instead of modeling the expected cell frequencies, the *odds* of being in one category (as opposed to any of the other categories) of the dependent variable is modeled as a function of the other (independent) variables.

Consider, for example, Table 2.2, a three-way contingency table, also based on the GSS. Variable A is sex (0 = male, 1 = female), Variable B is race (1 = White, 2 = Black, 3 = Other), and Variable C is computer use, whether (0 = no, 1 = yes) the respondent uses a personal computer. The categories of each variable are indexed by i = 0, 1 for Variable A; j = 1, 2, 3 for Variable B; and k = 0, 1 for Variable C. The cell contents in Table 2.2 include f_{ijk}, the observed frequency in each cell; E_{ijk}, the expected frequency in each cell, based on the marginal distributions (the number of cases in each category) of the variables in the table and assuming independence (no relationship) among the variables; and the standardized residual, the standardized difference between the observed (f_{ijk}) and expected (E_{ijk}) cell frequencies, which can be treated as a z statistic to test whether the difference between the observed and expected cell frequencies is statistically significant. Note that E_{ijk} is *not* the same as F_{ijk}, the expected frequency in each cell *if the log-linear model is true*. For E_{ijk}, only the marginal distribution is used to predict cell frequencies. For F_{ijk}, the model is more complex, as detailed below. Based on the data in Table 2.2, it is readily apparent (as it was in the previous example) that Black respondents, both male and female, are less likely to be computer users than White or other respondents. Although it is not directly apparent from Table 2.2, the bivariate relationships indicate that both sex and race are statistically significantly related to computer use, with females less likely to use computers than males and, as in Table 2.1, Black respondents less likely to use computers than White or other respondents.

Table 2.2 has 5 degrees of freedom, and we can calculate the usual χ^2 statistic as $\chi^2 = \Sigma(f_{ijk} - E_{ijk})^2/E_{ijk}$. For Table 2.2, $\chi^2 = 23.01$ with 5 degrees of freedom ($df = 5$), and $p < .001$. This means that the observed values are statistically significantly different from the expected values, which in turn means that computer use is not independent of sex and race. (If it were, then the expected cell frequencies, based on the marginal frequencies, would be the same as the observed cell frequencies). Having a nonzero number of degrees of freedom is a requirement for estimating the statistical significance of a relationship (e.g., a difference or a measure of association). If the number of degrees of freedom is 0, this implies that all the frequencies or other quantities of interest are known, that there is no difference between the observed and expected values of these quantities, and that inferential tests are not appropriate or informative. This issue of zero as opposed to nonzero degrees of freedom becomes important when considering saturated and unsaturated log-linear models described in the next section.

WARNING: Notation from this point forward can be difficult to follow. This is because there is an overlap in the symbols used in log-linear analysis (λ and τ) and the measures of association (λ_{yx}, τ_{yx}) just discussed and because there is no single standard for log-linear and logit model notation. Goodman (1973b) presents two notations, one of which expresses the row and column variables as exponents to the coefficients, and has come to be more frequently used in log-linear analysis, as exemplified by Knoke and Burke (1980), and the other of which is more similar to the OLS regression

TABLE 2.2   Three-Way Contingency Table

Variable A: Sex	Variable B: Race	Variable C: Computer Use		Row Totals
		No (k = 0)	Yes (k = 1)	
Male (i = 0)	White (j = 1)	Observed $f_{010} = 292$ Predicted $E_{010} = 313$ Std. residual $= -1.2$	Observed $f_{011} = 518$ Predicted $E_{011} = 497$ Std. residual $= 0.9$	$f_{01.} = 810$
	Black (j = 2)	Observed $f_{020} = 64$ Predicted $E_{020} = 46$ Std. residual $= 2.7^*$	Observed $f_{021} = 55$ Predicted $E_{021} = 73$ Std. residual $= -2.1^*$	$f_{02.} = 119$
	Other (j = 3)	Observed $f_{030} = 24$ Predicted $E_{030} = 21$ Std. residual $= 0.7$	Observed $f_{031} = 30$ Predicted $E_{031} = 33$ Std. residual $= -0.5$	$f_{03.} = 54$
Female (i = 1)	White (j = 1)	Observed $f_{110} = 403$ Predicted $E_{110} = 419$ Std. residual $= -0.8$	Observed $f_{111} = 563$ Predicted $E_{111} = 548$ Std. residual $= 0.7$	$f_{11.} = 966$
	Black (j = 2)	Observed $f_{120} = 122$ Predicted $E_{120} = 98$ Std. residual $= 2.4^*$	Observed $f_{121} = 105$ Predicted $E_{121} = 129$ Std. residual $= -2.1^*$	$f_{12.} = 227$
	Other (j = 3)	Observed $f_{130} = 20$ Predicted $E_{130} = 28$ Std. residual $= -1.5$	Observed $f_{131} = 45$ Predicted $E_{131} = 37$ Std. residual $= 1.3$	$f_{13.} = 65$
Column totals		$f_{..0} = 925$	$f_{..1} = 1,316$	Grand total: $f_{...} = 2,241$

$\chi^2 = 23.01$, $df = 5$, $p < .001$.

*Statistically significant ($p < .05$).

format, in which the row and column variables of the table are expressed as dummy variables X_1, $X_2, \ldots, X_K$, and which is used in Hutcheson and Sofroniou (1999) and Powers and Xie (2008). To facilitate the transition from log-linear and logit models to logistic regression models for readers with a background in log-linear and logit models, I begin with something close to the first notation, with a few minor changes to avoid confusion later [e.g., following Lindeman et al. 1980, the use of V_{ijk} instead of G_{ijk} for $\ln(F_{ijk})$, the natural logarithm of the expected cell frequency, to avoid potential confusion with the later use of G to represent the model chi-square statistic]. Fitted marginals notation, involving the use of "curly" brackets to specify effects (e.g., representing the saturated model as {A}{B}{C}{AB}{AC}{BC}{ABC} for Table 2.2) is not really relevant in the present context.

THE GENERAL LOG-LINEAR MODEL

For a trivariate contingency table, the *saturated model* is the model that includes the effect of each variable, plus the effects of all possible interactions among the variables in the model. The equation for the saturated model for Table 2.2 is, in the notation used in this book,

$$F_{ijk} = \eta \, \tau_i^A \tau_j^B \tau_k^C \tau_{ij}^{AB} \, \tau_{ik}^{AC} \, \tau_{jk}^{BC} \, \tau_{ijk}^{ABC}, \tag{2.1}$$

where each term on the right-hand side of the equation is multiplied by the other terms, and

F_{ijk} = frequency of cases in cell (i, j, k) that is expected if the model is correct;

η = geometric mean of the number of cases in each cell in the table; in Table 2.2, $\eta = (f_{010} f_{020} f_{030} f_{110} f_{120} f_{130} f_{011} f_{021} f_{031} f_{111} f_{121} f_{131})^{1/12}$;

τ_i^A = effect of Variable A on cell frequencies (one effect for each category of A; one category is redundant); similarly, τ_j^B and τ_k^C are the respective effects of Variables B and C; *note that this is not Goodman and Kruskal's tau* (a potential source of confusion in the present context);

τ_{ij}^{AB} = effect of the interaction between Variables A and B; effects that occur to the extent that Variables A and B are not independent; similarly, τ_{ik}^{AC} and τ_{jk}^{BC} are the respective interaction effects of Variables A with C and B with C; and

τ_{ijk}^{ABC} = effect of the three-way interaction among Variables A, B, and C.

In the multiplicative model of Equation 2.1, any $\tau > 1$ results in more than the geometric mean number of cases in a cell, while $\tau < 1$ results in less than the geometric mean number of cases in the cell. When any $\tau = 1$, the effect in question has no impact on the cell frequencies (it just multiplies them by one; this is analogous to a coefficient of zero in OLS regression). Since the saturated model includes all possible effects, including all possible interactions, it perfectly reproduces the cell frequencies, but it has no degrees of freedom. As effect parameters (τ) are constrained to equal one (in other words, they are left out of the model), we gain degrees of freedom and are able to test how well the model fits the observed data.

Taking the natural logarithm of the saturated model for Table 2.2 results in the equation

$$\ln(F_{ijk}) = \ln(\eta) + \ln(\tau_i^A) + \ln(\tau_j^B) + \ln(\tau_k^C) + \ln(\tau_{ij}^{AB}) + \ln(\tau_{ik}^{AC}) + \ln(\tau_{jk}^{BC}) + \ln(\tau_{ijk}^{ABC}) \tag{2.2}$$

or

$$V_{ijk} = \theta + \lambda_i^A + \lambda_j^B + \lambda_k^C + \lambda_{ij}^{AB} + \lambda_{ik}^{AC} + \lambda_{jk}^{BC} + \lambda_{ijk}^{ABC}, \tag{2.3}$$

where $V_{ijk} = \ln(F_{ijk})$, $\theta = \ln(\eta)$ and each $\lambda = \ln(\tau)$ for the corresponding effect. Equations 2.2 and 2.3 convert the multiplicative model of Equation 2.1 to an additive model, more similar to the OLS regression model. In Equation 2.3, the absence of an effect is indicated by $\lambda = 0$ for that effect; and the λ *here is not Goodman and Kruskal's λ* (again, a potential source of confusion in the present context). For example, if the interaction between Variables A and B has no impact on the cell frequencies, $\lambda_{ij}^{AB} = 0$, corresponding to $\ln(\tau_{ij}^{AB}) = 0$ because $\tau_{ij}^{AB} = 1$ and $\ln(1) = 0$. The additive form of the model has several advantages, as described in Knoke and Burke (1980), including ease of calculating standard errors and thus of determining the statistical significance of the parameters.

THE LOGIT MODEL

In the log-linear model described in Equations 2.1, 2.2, and 2.3, all three variables have the same conceptual status. Computer use is treated no differently from sex or race. Substantively, however, we may be interested specifically in the impact of race and sex on computer use. The logit model is a version of the log-linear model in which we designate one variable as the dependent variable and the other variables as predictors or independent variables. For the dichotomous dependent variable C (computer use) in Table 2.2, in which the saturated model is the model specified in Equation 2.1, we can express the expected *odds* that a respondent is a computer user as the ratio between the expected frequency of being a computer user, F_{ij1}, and the expected frequency of not being a computer user, F_{ij0}:

$$
\Omega_C = \frac{F_{ij1}}{F_{ij0}} = \frac{\eta \tau_i^A \tau_j^B \tau_1^C \tau_{ij}^{AB} \tau_{i1}^{AC} \tau_{j1}^{BC} \tau_{ij1}^{ABC}}{\eta \tau_i^A \tau_j^B \tau_0^C \tau_{ij}^{AB} \tau_{i0}^{AC} \tau_{j0}^{BC} \tau_{ij0}^{ABC}}
$$
$$
= \frac{\tau_1^C \tau_{i1}^{AC} \tau_{j1}^{BC} \tau_{ij1}^{ABC}}{\tau_0^C \tau_{i0}^{AC} \tau_{j0}^{BC} \tau_{ij0}^{ABC}},
$$

(2.4)

where η, τ_i^A, τ_j^B, and τ_{ij}^{AB} cancel out of the numerator and the denominator of the equation, and all the remaining terms include Variable C. If we take the natural logarithm of Equation 2.4, the dependent variable becomes the log-odds of computer use, or the *logit* of the probability that the respondent is a computer user:

$$
\ln(\Omega_C) = \ln\left(\frac{\tau_1^C \tau_{i1}^{AC} \tau_{j1}^{BC} \tau_{ij1}^{ABC}}{\tau_0^C \tau_{i0}^{AC} \tau_{j0}^{BC} \tau_{ij0}^{ABC}}\right)
$$
$$
= \ln(\tau_1^C) + \ln(\tau_{i1}^{AC}) + \ln(\tau_{j1}^{BC}) + \ln(\tau_{ij1}^{ABC})
$$
$$
- \ln(\tau_0^C) - \ln(\tau_{i0}^{AC}) - \ln(\tau_{j0}^{BC}) - \ln(\tau_{ij0}^{ABC})
$$
$$
= \lambda_1^C + \lambda_{i1}^{AC} + \lambda_{j1}^{BC} + \lambda_{ij1}^{ABC} - \lambda_0^C - \lambda_{i0}^{AC} - \lambda_{j0}^{BC} - \lambda_{ij0}^{ABC}.
$$

Now the λ parameters across the two categories of computer use sum to zero (i.e., $\lambda_{ij1} = -\lambda_{ij0}$), so $\ln(\Omega_C) = 2\lambda^C + 2\lambda_i^{AC} + 2\lambda_j^{BC} + 2\lambda_{ij}^{ABC}$, or re-expressing $\beta = 2\lambda$ and $\text{logit}(C) = \ln(\Omega_C)$,

$$
\text{logit}(C) = \beta^C + \beta^{AC} + \beta^{BC} + \beta^{ABC}.
$$

(2.5)

An alternate form of this equation described by, among others, Goodman (1973b), Hutcheson and Sofroniou (1999), and Powers and Xie (2008), breaks each variable into dummy variables (including one reference category, typically either the first or the last category for the variable), and casts Equation 2.5 in the familiar OLS regression format:

$$\text{logit}(C) = \beta_0 + \beta_1 X_{A=1} + \beta_2 X_{B=2} + \beta_3 X_{B=3} + \beta_4 X_{A=1} X_{B=2} + \beta_5 X_{A=1} X_{B=3}. \tag{2.6}$$

The subscripts on the X variables here indicate that Male (A = 0) is the reference category for Variable A, White (B = 1) is the reference category for Variable B, $X_{A=1}$ is the dummy variable for being female, $X_{B=2}$ and $X_{B=3}$ are the dummy variables for being Black and Other, respectively, and the last two terms in the equation represent the interaction between sex and race (A and B).[2] Equations 2.5 and 2.6 represent exactly the same model; they are just two different ways of showing which effects are included in the model. Equation 2.5 is in the form most commonly used in logit analysis based on the log-linear approach; Equation 2.6 is more similar to the OLS regression format. All the marginal effects included in the log-linear model are included in the logit model, although not all are explicitly listed (because of the cancellation of some terms from the numerator and the denominator in Equation 2.4). For the saturated model, the β parameters exactly reproduce the observed odds.

REDUCED MODELS AND THE INDEPENDENCE MODEL

The saturated model, as noted above, includes all possible effects, up to and including the highest possible order interaction effect. In some cases, however, we may believe that not all of the effects matter, and that therefore the model can be simplified by excluding one or more of the terms in the saturated model. For example, we may believe that the three-way interaction of sex, race, and computer use in the log-linear model, corresponding to the effect of the interaction between sex and race on computer use in the logit model, really adds nothing to our ability to predict or explain the cell frequencies. In this case, we may calculate a *reduced* model, $\text{logit}(C) = \beta^C + \beta^{AC} + \beta^{BC}$, in which the value of β^{ABC} is assumed to be zero. Alternatively, we may believe that race, but not sex, has an impact on computer use, in which case we would eliminate all terms with sex from the model, obtaining the reduced model $\text{logit}(C) = \beta^C + \beta^{BC}$. Finally, if neither sex nor race is really related to computer use, we would say that computer use is independent of sex and race, and construct a model in which all terms containing either A or B or both were eliminated, $\text{logit}(C) = \beta^C$, the *independence* model, in which the only predictor of computer use is its geometric mean. This corresponds to an OLS regression model in which there are no predictors, only the intercept, which corresponds to the arithmetic mean of the dependent variable in OLS regression. Reduced models and the independence model are both *unsaturated* or *restricted* in the sense that they do not include all the possible effects that could be included, but instead exclude some possible effects, and there is no guarantee beforehand that they will do as well as the saturated model in reproducing the cell frequencies in the contingency table.

For an unsaturated logit model, in which one or more of the β parameters is assumed to be zero, the observed odds may not be exactly reproduced. The *fit* of the unsaturated model is calculated as

$D = 2\sum_{ij}(f_{ij})[\ln(f_{ij}/F_{ij})]$, which has a χ^2 distribution. The model parameters (β) are selected to mini-mize D, using an iterative maximum likelihood or generalized least squares algorithm (Eliason 1993; King 1989; see also Appendix A). In the saturated model, $D = 0$ with no degrees of freedom, and it makes no sense to try to assess the fit of the saturated model. The unsaturated or restricted model is typically compared with the saturated model, and a statistically significant χ^2 indicates that the restricted model fits the data statistically significantly *worse* than the saturated model. D here is used as a *goodness-of-fit* statistic, a measure of the extent to which the model departs from the ideal or perfectly fitting model (here, the saturated model). For researchers used to statistical sig-nificance in other contexts (e.g., OLS regression), it sometimes seems counterintuitive at first that statistical significance of the goodness-of-fit statistic indicates a model that does *not* do a good job of explaining the dependent variable. As an alternative to D, it is possible to calculate the Pearson goodness-of-fit χ^2 statistic: $\chi^2 = \sum(y_i - m_j p_j)^2/[m_j p_j(1 - p_j)]$, where (a) there are $j = 1, 2, \ldots, M$ cova-riate *patterns* (cells in a two-way or higher-order cross-tabulation that includes all of the predictors but not the dependent variable, corresponding to the separate and distinct possible combinations of values of the predictors); (b) m_j is the number of cases having the covariate pattern j; (c) p_j is the probability of a "positive" outcome (in a dichotomous variable having values zero and one, the probability of having a one) in covariate pattern j; (d) the product $m_j p_j$ is thus the expected number of cases with covariate pattern j, corresponding to E_{ijk} in Table 2.2; and (e) y_i is the total *number* of positive responses among cases with covariate pattern j, corresponding to f_{ijk} in Table 2.2. Another way of writing the formula for the Pearson's χ^2 goodness-of-fit statistic is the familiar $\chi^2 = \sum(\text{observed} - \text{expected})^2/\text{expected}$, where the "observed" and "expected" refer to the observed and expected cell frequencies, given the logit model (SPSS 1991). D is generally more widely used than the Pearson's goodness-of-fit χ^2, however, and is generally preferable to the Pearson χ^2 since D and not χ^2 is the criterion being minimized by the maximum likelihood estimation procedure for the model.

It is also possible to compare two models, neither of which is the saturated model, if one model is *nested* within the other. One model is nested within another if the nested model is the same as the model within which it is nested, except that the nested model omits one or more of the parameters in the model within which it is nested. For example, the model logit(C) = $\beta^C + \beta^{ABC}$ is nested within the saturated model, logit(C) = $\beta^C + \beta^{AC} + \beta^{BC} + \beta^{ABC}$, but not within the model logit(C) = $\beta^C + \beta^{AC} + \beta^{BC}$. The model logit(C) = $\beta^C + \beta^{ABC}$ has fewer parameters than the model logit(C) = $\beta^C + \beta^{AC} + \beta^{BC}$, but the term β^{ABC} is included in the model logit(C) = $\beta^C + \beta^{ABC}$ but not in the model logit(C) = $\beta^C + \beta^{AC} + \beta^{BC}$. Most commonly, we will want to compare a saturated model with an independence model, or either a saturated model or an independence model with some other reduced model. Comparison of a saturated model or a reduced model to the independence model indicates whether the hypothesis of independence (no relationship among the variables) can be rejected, and in this instance, a statistically significant result has the more familiar substantive con-clusion that the alternative (saturated or reduced) model provides a *better* fit than the independence model. This comparison is closely akin to the F test in OLS regression, analysis of variance, and analysis of covariance. It is also fairly common to compare alternative models in sequence, begin-ning with either the saturated or the independence model and moving toward the other extreme, gradually working through successively more (or less) complex models, to ascertain which model is the most parsimonious while still providing an adequate fit to the data.

THE LOGIT MODEL FOR CATEGORICAL VARIABLES: COMPUTER USE, SEX, AND RACE

Table 2.3 presents the logit model for computer use as a dependent variable and race and sex as predictors. The model represented in Part A of Table 2.3 is a saturated model (all possible effects are included), so goodness-of-fit statistics cannot be calculated. Part B of Table 2.3 presents an unsaturated model in which the interaction effects between sex and race have been eliminated from the model. As is standard in log-linear and logit analyses, the *last* category for each variable is used as the reference category (the omitted category). Thus, the reference category for race is "White" (Category 3), and the reference category for sex is "male" (Category 2). Computer use has been coded so that the coefficients in Table 2.3 correspond to the dummy variable notation described earlier; thus, the equation represented by Part A of Table 2.3 is logit(computer use) = .57 − .24(female) − .72 (Black) − .35(Other) + .24(female)(Black) + .82(female)(Other), and the equation from Part B is logit(computer use)= .53 − .16(female) − .58(Black) +.09(Other).

From both Parts A and B of Table 2.3, it appears that females are less likely to be computer users than males; that Black respondents are less likely to be computer users than White respondents (but there is no statistically significant difference between White respondents and respondents who are other than White or Black); and from Part A only (since there are no interaction effects in Part B) that there is no statistically significant interaction effect of being both Black and female; and that there is a statistically significant interaction effect of being both "Other" race and female. The last two conclusions are based on the interaction terms between sex and race. The absence of a significant interaction between being Black and female means that while both being Black and female reduces the likelihood of using a computer, being both Black and female has no additional impact on the likelihood of using a computer, beyond the separate effects of race and sex. The statistically significant interaction effect between being other race and female can be interpreted in either of two ways. One can say either (a) for "Other" females, in contrast to White or Black females, the relationship between being female and using a computer is positive rather than negative or (b) for "Other" females, in contrast to "Other" males, the statistically nonsignificant relationship between computer use and "Other" race becomes statistically significant and positive. Combining the two interpretations, because the interaction effect is both greater in magnitude and opposite in sign (positive instead of negative) from the coefficients for both other race and female sex, it indicates that the relationship of computer use to both race and sex is reversed for "Other" females, who are relatively more likely to use computers than either (a) Black or White females or (b) "Other" males.

For Table 2.3, the χ^2 statistic for the difference between the independence model and the saturated model, found by running a standard log-linear routine to calculate the independence model, is 34.4461 with 5 degrees of freedom (one for each category of sex plus one for each category of race), $p = .000$, indicating that the independence model fits statistically significantly worse than the saturated model. The likelihood ratio χ^2 statistic for the difference between the saturated model and the unsaturated model with only sex and race, but not the interaction between sex and race, as predictors of computer use is the likelihood ratio χ^2 statistic in the lower part of Part B of Table 2.3, which also includes the Pearson χ^2. Both the likelihood ratio χ^2 and the Pearson χ^2 are marginally statistically significant ($p = .08$) with 2 degrees of freedom (compared with 5 degrees of freedom in the independence model, with 1 degree of freedom lost by the inclusion of the dummy variable for sex and 2 degrees of freedom lost by the inclusion of two dummy variables for race), indicating that the fit

TABLE 2.3   Logit Analysis of Computer Use by Race and Sex

A. Saturated Model

Predictor	Coefficient (β)	Z Statistic	Significance (p)
Sex: Female	−0.24	−2.43	.015

Race:
  Black
  Other
	−0.72
	−0.35
		−3.67
		−1.26
			.000
			.208

Sex by race:
  Black female
  Other female
	0.24
	0.82
		0.97
		2.08
			.332
			.038

Intercept	0.57	7.83	.000
	Coefficient		

Analysis of dispersion
  Entropy R^2
  Concentration coefficient
	0.01
	0.01		

B. Unsaturated Model

Predictor	Coefficient (β)	Z Statistic	Significance (p)
Sex: Female	−0.16	−1.83	.067

Race:
  Black
  Other
	−0.58
	0.09
		−4.85
		0.47
			.000
			.638

Intercept	0.53	7.72	.000
Model Fit/Explanatory Power	*Coefficient*	*Degrees of Freedom*	*Significance (p)*

Goodness of fit
  Pearson χ^2
  Likelihood ratio χ^2
	4.9873
	5.0056
		2
		2
			.083
			.082

Analysis of dispersion
  Entropy R^2
  Concentration coefficient
	0.01
	0.01		

of the unsaturated model is marginally (here defined as $.10 < p < .05$) statistically significantly worse than the fit of the saturated model, but not to the same degree as the fit of the independence model. The difference between the independence model and the unsaturated model can be calculated as the difference between the likelihood ratio χ^2 statistics, with the degrees of freedom equal to the difference between the degrees of freedom of the two models, because the independence model is nested within the unsaturated model: $\chi^2 = (34.4461 - 4.9873) = 29.4588$ with $(5 - 2) = 3$ degrees of freedom, $p = .000$. This indicates that the independence model fits statistically significantly worse than the unsaturated model or, more positively, that the unsaturated model fits statistically significantly better than the independence model. In log-linear and logit analysis, the difference between an unsaturated model and the independence model is frequently ignored. In logistic regression, however, the independence model rather than the saturated model is usually the standard against which other models are compared.

In addition to the goodness-of-fit statistics, Part B of Table 2.3 presents an "analysis of dispersion" section. The analysis of *dispersion* (SPSS 1991:136) or *variation* (Nagelkerke 1991) is similar to the analysis of variance in OLS regression analysis. Sums of squared errors do not have the same conceptual status in log-linear or logit analysis that they do in OLS regression, however, and instead of sums of squared errors, the quantities analyzed are quantities derived from information theory (Haberman 1982; Krippendorf 1986; Shannon 1948). Briefly, the information theory measures attempt to separate the informative bits of data (information) from the uninformative bits of information such as random error (noise). The entropy coefficient is based on the log likelihood, and calculates the ratio of information to the sum of information plus noise, with the log likelihood as the measure of dispersion or variation. The concentration coefficient has similar conceptual underpinnings. Both can be regarded as analogs of the R^2 measure for explained variance in OLS regression, but the entropy and concentration coefficients are measures of explained variation, not explained *variance,* the latter having a more specific, restricted meaning. We shall return to the entropy coefficient in Chapter 3. Here, we may simply note that the low values for both the entropy coefficient and the concentration coefficient indicate that sex and race, in both Parts A and B of Table 2.3, appear to explain little (only about 1%) of the variation in computer use.

CONTINUOUS VARIABLES, LOG-LINEAR AND LOGIT MODELS

Log-linear analysis is not restricted to the analysis of nominal variables. Variables with ordered categories may be ordinal, interval, or ratio scaled, and information about the ordering of the categories of the variable, and the distances between different sets of adjacent and nonadjacent categories, can be used to construct unsaturated log-linear analysis models that may be tested against saturated and independence models. In the model with categorical variables, the effect for one category (typically the last) is redundant. For an ordered variable, when the effect of any contrast between adjacent categories is equal to the effect between any other two adjacent categories, then all effects after the first are redundant with the first. Thus, for a five-category categorical variable, we must calculate four effects, and thus lose 4 degrees of freedom, to fully account for the effect of the variable. For a five-category ordered variable, when the effect of a change between any two adjacent categories is the same, regardless of which specific categories are considered, we only need to calculate one effect for the difference between adjacent categories (since it will be the same regardless of which two adjacent categories are considered), and hence we lose only 1 degree of freedom. To calculate the effect of a difference between nonadjacent categories, we simply combine the effects across all categories from the first to the last.

Suppose we have a saturated model with two variables, R (row) and C (column): $V_{ij} = \theta + \lambda_i^R + \lambda_j^C + \lambda_{ij}^{RC}$. (Models with more variables are possible, but for purposes of exposition, the bivariate case works best.) It is possible that either R or C or both are at least ordinal, in which case (a) we may have a relatively small or a relatively large number of categories (order does not matter for a dichotomous variable) and (b) instead of examining the effect of each category separately, we can examine the effect of the *order* of the category relative to the other categories of the variable. The first question is how to code or score the categories of the ordered variables. Two common approaches are integer scoring, in which the categories of the ordered variable are assigned consecutive integers, usually beginning with 1, from the lowest to the highest. Alternatively, midrank scoring (Hutcheson and Sofroniou 1999) may be used, in which, with typically more than one case in each category, the starting rank and the finishing rank for each category of the variable are averaged and the average is the score assigned to that category. Hutcheson and Sofroniou note that repeating the same analysis using both midrank scoring and integer scoring is one way to test for the sensitivity of the results to the scoring procedure.

Once a decision has been made on how to score the ordered variable(s), a model is constructed to take advantage of the information about the ordering of the variable. If both variables are ordered, the usual approach is to construct a *linear-by-linear* model, of the form $V_{ij} = \theta + \lambda_i^R + \lambda_j^C + \beta x_i y_j$, where x_i is the score assigned to the ith category of the row variable, y_j is the score assigned to the jth category of the column variable, and the parameter β indicates the strength of the relationship between the row and the column variables. [Once again, notation for log-linear models, including the linear-by-linear model and the row effects and column effects models discussed below, is not standard; compare, for example, Hutcheson and Sofroniou (1999), Ishii-Kuntz (1994), and Powers and Xie (2008).] If integer scoring is used, we have a *uniform association* model, a special case of the linear-by-linear model, in which i and j index the integer scores used for the row and column variables, and the model can alternatively be written as $V_{ij} = \theta + \lambda_i^R + \lambda_j^C + \beta ij$, where i and j are no longer subscripts but instead integer values of the categories of the row and column variables, (i.e., $x_i = i$ and $y_j = j$). The linear-by-linear model is unsaturated, with $[(I-1)(J-1)-1]$ degrees of freedom. If only the row variable is ordered, we have the *column effects* model in which $V_{ij} = \theta + \lambda_i^R + \lambda_j^C + \beta \psi_j x_i$, where x_i is again the score assigned to the row variable, β is once again the parameter indicating the relationship between R and C, and ψ_j is the column effect. As described by Powers and Xie (2008:96), the column effect ψ_j is latent, and needs to be normalized, and it is not possible to separate ψ_j from β; therefore, we set $\beta = 1$ to normalize the scale of ψ_j, use dummy variable coding with one category (typically the first) as a reference category to normalize the location of ψ_j (i.e., $\psi_1 = 0$), and rewrite the equation in the form $V_{ij} = \theta + \lambda_i^R + \lambda_j^C + \psi_j x_i$. The column effects model has $(I-2)(J-1)$ degrees of freedom. If the column variable is instead the only one of the two variables that is ordered, we have instead a *row effects* model, and the equation for the model becomes $V_{ij} = \theta + \lambda_i^R + \lambda_j^C + \varphi_i y_j$, with an interpretation parallel to the column effects model just described. The row effects model has $(I-1)(J-2)$ degrees of freedom. The column effects and row effects correspond, respectively, to separate equations for each category of the row or column variable.

The linear-by-linear, row effects, and column effects models can also be expressed in terms of log-odds models or logit models (see, e.g., Powers and Xie 2008). For the linear-by-linear uniform association model, the equation for comparing any two categories is $\ln[F_{ij}F_{i'j'}/F_{ij'}F_{i'j}] = \beta(i - i')(j - j')$, and for adjacent categories, $\ln[F_{(i)(j)}F_{(i+1)(j+1)}/F_{(i)(j+1)}F_{(i+1)(j)}] = \beta$; in other words, β is the log-odds of the difference between adjacent categories. Correspondingly, the odds of being in the first as opposed to the second of two adjacent categories is e^β, where e is the base of the natural logarithm and $e = 2.72$. For the row effects model, again assuming integer coding, $\ln[F_{ij}F_{i'j'}/F_{ij'}F_{i'j}] = (\varphi_i - \varphi_{i'})$ $(j - j')$, and for adjacent categories, $\ln[F_{(i)(j)}F_{(i+1)(j+1)}/F_{(i)(j+1)}F_{(i+1)(j)}] = (\varphi_i - \varphi_{i'})$. Similarly, again with integer coding for the column effects model, $\ln[F_{ij}F_{i'j'}/F_{ij'}F_{i'j}] = (\psi_j - \psi_{j'})(i - i')$, and for adjacent categories, $\ln[F_{(i)(j)}F_{(i+1)(j+1)}/F_{(i)(j+1)}F_{(i+1)(j)}] = (\psi_j - \psi_{j'})$. If the unordered variable in a row or column effects model is dichotomous (only two categories), then because the first row or column effect is set to zero (as noted above, to normalize the location of the row or column effect), then we have only one row or column effect, ψ or φ. In this special case, if we use β instead of ψ or φ to represent the row or column effect, we get the equation $V_{ij} = \theta + \lambda_i^R + \lambda_j^C + \beta y_j$ for the row effects model or $V_{ij} = \theta + \lambda_i^R + \lambda_j^C + \beta x_i$ for the column effects model, and the corresponding logit equations are (again, with only two categories, there is only one log-odds that can be computed) $\ln[F_{ij}F_{i'j'}/F_{ij'}F_{i'j}]$ $= \beta$, where β represents φ_2 for the row effects model or ψ_2 for the column effects model. In other words, in a model with one ordered and one dichotomous variable, the results look very similar to the linear-by-linear model, and in particular, the column effects model begins to look very similar in form to the OLS regression model.

CONTINUOUS VARIABLES AND LOGIT MODELS: EDUCATION, INCOME, AND COMPUTER USE

Tables 2.1 and 2.2 deal with the case in which all the variables are categorical, either *dichotomous* (having only two categories; e.g., computer use and sex) or *polytomous* (having more than two categories; e.g., race). There may, however, be other variables that we would like to use to predict computer use. For example, more educated respondents may have both more ability, in terms of intellectual skills, and more reason, in terms of occupational requirements, to use computers. Also, respondents with higher incomes may be better able to afford to own and therefore use computers. Education may be measured in number of years of schooling completed, and income may be measured in dollars, both ratio scale variables, with income having more categories and a more continuous-appearing distribution than education. Even when income is collapsed into categories, as it is in the GSS, the number of categories for income is large, and there may be few cases in any one category. If we combine this in the same analysis with education, there are many possible combinations of values for the two predictors, and many combinations (or cells in the contingency table) with no cases or only one case.

In the NORC GSS, education can be coded as number of years of school completed, from 1 to 20 or more. The category numbered 20 includes all cases with 20 or more years of schooling, and the frequencies in Categories 1 to 6 are so small that they are combined into Category 7 (now representing 7 or fewer years of schooling). This produces 14 categories for the variable Education. Income is coded in 23 categories, from less than $1,000 per year to $110,000 or more per year. If we treat each category as a dummy variable in the logit model, with one category omitted as the reference category, the saturated model has not only the 13 dummy variables or categories for education plus the 22 categories for income but also 286 possible interaction terms between income and education, a total of 321 predictors for computer use. The resulting equation for Computer Use expressed as C, Income expressed as D, and Education expressed as E, is, in the more usual format, $C = \beta^C + \beta^{AC} + \beta^{BC} + \beta^{ABC}$, or in the dummy variable format, omitting the last category,

$$C = \beta_1 X_{E=7} + \beta_2 X_{E=8} + \cdots \beta_{13} X_{E=19} + \beta_{14} X_{D=1} + \beta_{15} X_{D=2} + \cdots + \beta_{35} X_{D=21}$$
$$+ \beta_{36} X_{D=22} + \beta_{37} X_{(E=7,D=1)} + \beta_{38} X_{(E=7,D=2)} + \cdots + \beta_{321} X_{(E=19,D=22)}. \tag{2.7}$$

This model is cumbersome to interpret (321 total coefficients), and typically most cells in the 3×3 contingency table will contain either no cases or one case. In this situation, the goodness-of-fit statistic, D, no longer has an asymptotic χ^2 distribution (DeMaris 1992:44). Moreover, there is information about the predictors, namely, the ordering of their categories, that we are ignoring by constructing the model with 321 dummy variables. At this point, treating the data as a contingency table breaks down as a strategy for analysis. Because there are too few cases per cell, it is no longer reasonable to calculate the log likelihood for the model as $D = 2\sum_{ij} f_{ij}[\ln(f_{ij}/F_{ij})]$, which assumes sufficient cases per cell to produce reliable estimates of F_{ij}. Instead, we move from the prediction of frequencies in cells of the contingency table to predictions of the value of the dependent variable for individual cases. For this purpose, a different likelihood function is used:

$$D = -2\sum \left\{ (Y_i)\ln\left[(e^{\beta_0 + \Sigma \beta_m X_m})/(1 + e^{\beta_0 + \Sigma \beta_m X_m})\right] + (1 - Y_i)\ln\left[1 - (e^{\beta_0 + \Sigma \beta_m X_m})/(1 + e^{\beta_0 + \Sigma \beta_m X_m})\right]\right\}, \tag{2.8}$$

where y_i is the observed value of Y, coded as either 0 or 1 for a dichotomous dependent variable, the X_m are the $m = 1, 2, \ldots, M$ predictors in the equation for Y, and the β are the coefficients in the logit model. When there are no predictors in the model, we have the independence model. The saturated model is the model described in Equation 2.7 for C, in which all possible predictors are in the model (one dummy variable for each category of each of the predictors).

As DeMaris (1992:42) notes, when continuous explanatory variables are used, the contingency table format is appropriate only with grouped or "replicated" data, not in the sense of replicating a research study but in the sense of having multiple cases for each possible combination of values of the predictors. When logit modeling is used with *unreplicated* data, data for which there may be no cases or only a single case for any given combination of values for the predictors, the analysis shifts from an aggregate analysis at the level of the cells of the contingency table to an individual level analysis, more similar to OLS linear regression. For DeMaris and others, this marks the boundary between the logit analysis and logistic regression.[3] In terms of the form of the mathematical model, however, logit analysis and logistic regression analysis are identical. Any data that can be analyzed with one can also be analyzed with the other.[4] The difference is more one of presentation of results and selection of specific statistical algorithms and software routines than of the underlying mathematical model. Some of the statistics associated with the model, however, must be calculated differently, or may not have the same distribution, when individual as opposed to grouped data are used. This distinction between grouped and individual data will be important in the discussion of logistic regression primarily with regard to choice of software and selection of statistics to evaluate the logistic regression model.

There are different ways to incorporate continuous or interval/ratio scale variables into logit analysis. Parallel to linear regression analysis, the continuous predictor may be entered directly into the model and treated identically to any categorical predictors in the model. Another commonly available option is to include the continuous variables as "covariates," adjusting expected cell frequencies based on the value of the covariate, similar to the use of covariates in analysis of covariance when the primary interest is in the effects of the factors (the categorical variables), and the covariates are controlled as "nuisance" variables. When all the predictors are continuous, however, there are no other expected cell frequencies to adjust. When there is a mix of continuous and categorical predictors, the results of treating continuous predictors as cell covariates will not generally be the same as if the continuous predictors were used to directly predict the probability of category membership on the outcome variable. Special contrasts can be used in some software to specify continuous predictors that are to be treated identically to the categorical predictors (i.e., as a nominal variable), or in a way that takes into account the ordering of the categories in the predictor (e.g., by assigning consecutive integer values to the successive categories of the predictor and defining the predictor as having 1 degree of freedom, effectively defining the variable as an interval-scaled variable).

DIGRESSION: A GENERALIZED LINEAR MODELING APPROACH TO LOGIT ANALYSIS

Up to this point, the focus has been on what might be called the "classical" or contingency table approach to logit models. An alternative, more consistent with OLS regression and with the use of continuous predictors, is the general linear modeling or GLM approach (e.g., Hutcheson and Sofroniou 1999; McCullagh and Nelder 1989). In GLMs, linear parametric methods such as OLS regression are extended to data in which the dependent variable may be something other than a continuous, normally distributed, interval or ratio-scaled variable, and to variables that, at least in their original units of measurement, may not be linearly related to the predictors in the model. GLMs can be described as having three components: (1) the random component, a probability distribution assumed to describe the distribution of the dependent variable; (2) the systematic component, usually a linear function of the explanatory variables; and (3) a link function specifying the relationship of the dependent variable in its original metric to the linear function of the explanatory variables. The systematic component may be written as $\eta = \beta_0 + \beta_1 X_1 + \beta_2 X_2 + \ldots + \beta_m X_m$, where $X_1, X_2, \ldots, X_m$ are $m = 1, 2, \ldots, M$ predictors, β_0 is the intercept or constant, $\beta_1, \beta_2, \ldots, \beta_m$ are the coefficients associated with the respective predictors $X_1, X_2, \ldots, X_m$, and η is some transformation of the dependent variable Y. The function $g(Y) = \eta$ is the link function, which transforms the dependent variable Y into a variable η, η being the variable that is linearly related to the predictors.

In data for which the OLS regression model is appropriate, no transformation of Y is really necessary, and $\eta = g(Y) = Y$, the *identity* link function, or more simply the *identity link,* serves as the link function, bringing OLS regression within the set of GLMs. Similarly, if Y is not linearly related to the predictors, but the natural logarithm of Y is linearly related to the predictors, then $\eta = g(Y) = \ln(Y)$, the *logarithmic link,* is used. In the case of logit models, we may model not the value of the dependent variable, but the expected frequency, based on the model, for each cell in the contingency table, as the dependent variable. If F represents the expected frequency, and if the random component is assumed to follow a Poisson distribution, then $g(F) = \ln(F)$ and the log-linear model can be expressed as $\ln(F) = \eta = \beta_0 + \beta_1 X_1 + \beta_2 X_2 + \ldots + \beta_m X_m$. GLMs with the natural logarithm as the link function are generally called *log-linear models* (e.g., Hutcheson and Sofroniou 1999:171), but the log-linear model with which we have been dealing to this point in this chapter is not the only model of this form, as indicated above. There is some potential for confusion because of similarity in the terminology here, and in general, it may be best to reserve the term *log-linear models* for the broader category of models encompassed within the GLMs, in which the logarithmic transformation of the dependent variable is used regardless of the original scale of the dependent variable; and the term *log-linear analysis* or *log-linear analysis models* to describe the iterative procedures used to analyze log-linear models when the dependent variable is, in fact, the predicted frequency of a cell in a contingency table. Similarly, in logit models, if π represents the probability of a certain outcome, then we may use the logit transformation to specify the logit model $g(\pi) = \text{logit}(\pi) = \eta = \beta_0 + \beta_1 X_1 + \beta_2 X_2 + \ldots + \beta_m X_m$.

The previous chapter essentially took a GLM approach (without naming it as such) to make the transition from OLS multiple regression to logistic regression analysis. The main reason for describing these GLM variants of the log-linear and logit models in the present context is to show how readily the log-linear and logit analysis models in this chapter can be expressed in the same form as the OLS models in the previous chapter, and thus to make clearer the transition from log-linear and logit models to the logistic regression models in the remainder of the book. It is also perhaps helpful to think of log-linear and logit models more in the GLM context when considering logit models with continuous independent variables, at least with respect to the form of the model.

LOGISTIC REGRESSION FOR LOGIT ANALYSIS WITH CATEGORICAL AND CONTINUOUS PREDICTORS

Table 2.4 presents the results of running logistic regression analysis[5] of computer use (a) by sex and race, including the interaction between sex and race, thus including all possible predictors in the model, resulting in a saturated model; (b) by sex and race but without the interaction term, resulting in an unsaturated model; (c) by education and income, including an interaction term; and (d) by education and income with no interaction term. Computer use is coded $0 = $ No, $1 = $ Yes; sex is coded $1 = $ female, $2 = $ male (with male as the reference category); race is coded $1 = $ Black, $2 = $ Other, and $3 = $ White (with White as the reference category); and education and income are coded, with modifications to the original coding, as described earlier. Because education and income are treated as continuous variables, each consumes only 1 degree of freedom, and the models involving only education and income are unsaturated regardless of whether the interaction between education and income is included in the model.

In the first model in Table 2.4, the model $\chi^2 = 34.446$ with 5 degrees of freedom, $p = .000$, indicating a statistically significant improvement over the intercept-only model when we include sex and race as predictors of computer use. Since this is a saturated model, both the Pearson and log-likelihood χ^2 statistics are zero (there is no difference between the saturated model and itself), there are 0 degrees of freedom (as indicated in a warning at the beginning of the output used to produce this table), and significance levels cannot be calculated for the difference between the full model and the saturated model (since they are the same). The entropy R^2 indicates relatively weak explanation of the dependent variable (only about 1%). Compare the coefficients in the first model in Table 2.4 with the saturated logit model coefficients (β) in Table 2.3, the latter of which were calculated from a log-linear rather than a logistic regression analysis routine. Within rounding error in the last digit, they are the same as the coefficients in Table 2.3. As long as we use β (as opposed

TABLE 2.4 Logistic Regression Analysis of Computer Use

Model	Predictor	Coefficient (β)	Standard error (degrees of freedom)	Significance (p)
1	Intercept	0.577	.073 (1)	.000
	Sex: Female	−0.239	.098 (1)	.015
	Race: African American	−0.725	.198 (1)	.000
	Other	−0.350	.283 (1)	.217
	Gender by ethnicity:			
	African American female	0.240	.247 (1)	.786
	Other female	0.827	.396 (1)	.037
	Model χ^2	34.446	(5)	.000
	Pearson χ^2	0	(0)	–
	Likelihood ratio χ^2	0	(0)	–
	Entropy R^2	0.011	–	(same as model χ^2)
2	Intercept	0.529	.108 (1)	.000
	Sex: Female	−0.160	.138 (1)	.248
	Race: African American	−0.575	.187 (1)	.002
	Other	0.092	.310 (1)	.766
	Model χ^2	29.459	(3)	.000
	Pearson χ^2	5.006	(2)	.082
	Likelihood ratio χ^2	4.987	(2)	.083
	Entropy R^2	0.010	–	(same as model χ^2)
3	Intercept	−8.128	1.050 (1)	.000
	Education	0.537	0.081 (1)	.000
	Income	0.279	0.065 (1)	.000
	Education × Income	−0.014	0.005 (1)	.004
	Model χ^2	525.043	(3)	.000
	Pearson χ^2	300.906	(258)	.034
	Likelihood ratio χ^2	298.174	(258)	.043
	Entropy R^2	0.173	–	(same as model χ^2)
4	Intercept	−5.363	.330 (1)	.000
	Education	0.322	.024 (1)	.000
	Income	0.097	.011 (1)	.000
	Model χ^2	515.271	(2)	.000
	Pearson χ^2	307.022	(259)	.022
	Likelihood ratio χ^2	307.946	(259)	.020
	Entropy R^2	0.170	–	(same as model χ^2)

to τ or λ) coefficients for the logit model, and as long as any multiple category nominal variables are coded the same way, and as long as the same algorithm (e.g., Newton-Raphson or iteratively reweighted least squares; see Appendix A) is used to calculate both the logit and the logistic regression model, the coefficients should be identical.

The second model in Table 2.4 is a simpler model involving the same dependent variable and the same predictors, but this time without the interaction between sex and race. Missing, therefore, are the last two coefficients from the saturated model. The resulting unsaturated model has 2 degrees of freedom for testing model fit, corresponding to the two parameters that are possible but not included in the model. The model χ^2 statistic has changed slightly, from 34.446 to 29.459, now with only 3 degrees of freedom (only three more parameters in the full model than in the intercept-only model, two fewer parameters than in the saturated model), but the unsaturated model is still a statistically significant improvement over the intercept-only model. With 2 degrees of freedom, it is now possible to assess model fit using the Pearson and log-likelihood statistics, and both indicate a marginal fit ($.10 < p < .05$) for the model, not quite statistically significantly (at the .05 level) different from the saturated model, but close. Note that the goodness-of-fit statistics in the second model are comparing the second model with the saturated model. There are also slight changes in the coefficients, as would be expected for a different model. The entropy R^2 statistic for the second model is nearly the same as for the first.

The third and fourth models present the results of running a logistic regression analysis of computer use with education and income as predictors. In the third model, the interaction term is included, and in the fourth model, the interaction term is excluded. Substantively, there is little difference between the two models, and the discussion here will focus on the third model, with the same comments generally applying to the fourth as well. To begin with, for both the third and the fourth models, there are 112 cells, 21% of the total cells, that have zero frequencies—that is, are empty. This is the issue raised earlier with respect to the logit model for continuous predictors, and it suggests that the goodness-of-fit statistics, in particular, may not really have a χ^2 distribution, rendering the inferential statistics about model fit invalid. Thus, although the Pearson and log-likelihood statistics for these models indicate that the models are statistically significantly different from a theoretically best possible model (one in which, for instance, the predictors are treated as categorical, nominal variables rather than continuous, interval/ratio variables), we cannot be sure that the inference based on these goodness-of-fit statistics is correct. The model χ^2, however, should be unaffected, and indicates a statistically significant improvement over the intercept-only model. It may be tempting to compare the -2 log likelihood or model χ^2 statistics for the first and second models (with sex and race as predictors) with those for the third and fourth models (with education and income as predictors), but since neither of the sex-and-race models nor the education-and-income models are nested within each other, such a comparison would not be appropriate. The entropy R^2 statistics for the respective models, however, suggest that education and income are better predictors of computer use than sex or race.

SUMMARY

The linear regression model is designed to analyze two or more continuous variables, when one of the variables is designated as a dependent variable and the other variables are designated as predictors. The log-linear model is designed to analyze two or more categorical variables when none of the variables is designated as a dependent variable or a predictor. The logit model is a variant of the log-linear model in which one of the variables is designated as a dependent variable and the others as predictors. The linear regression model was inappropriate when the dependent variable was dichotomous. The log-linear model is well suited to handle a dichotomous dependent variable but less well suited to handle continuous predictors. Sometimes a distinction is made between logistic regression as a method for dealing with continuous predictors, as opposed to logit analysis as a method for dealing with categorical predictors, but this distinction is artificial. Instead, logistic regression handles continuous and categorical predictors with equal facility. Rather than being a special case of the log-linear or logit model (as it is sometimes presented), it is a hybrid between the logit model and the OLS regression model.

Just as it was possible to trace the development of logistic regression from OLS regression in Chapter 1, the development of logistic regression from log-linear analysis via the logit model was traced in the present chapter. For OLS regression, the use of a dichotomous dependent variable forced us to consider a nonlinear transformation of the dependent variable, which in turn led us to abandon OLS in favor of iteratively reweighted least squares (IRLS) or maximum likelihood as the method of estimating the model parameters. For log-linear analysis, the use of continuous predictors of the dichotomous dependent variable led us to consider a contingency table with many empty cells, which in turn led us to a different formula for calculating the likelihood to be maximized in the logit model. Thus, adaptations to the problems of dichotomous dependent variables in OLS regression and continuous predictors in log-linear analysis and logit models converged, in a sense, on the same solution, the logistic regression model. To oversimplify the contrast, the logistic regression model *is* the OLS regression model, estimated differently but presented in the same way; and it *is* the log-linear/logit analysis model, estimated in the same way but presented differently. A strength of logistic regression analysis is its flexibility: Properly constructed, it deals equally well with the individual case data on which the OLS regression model is based and the grouped data on which the log-linear analysis model is based.

NOTES

1. For a general description of the NORC General Social Survey, see Davis and Smith (1992). GSS data are publicly available from the Inter-University Consortium for Political and Social Research (ICPSR). The terms *sex* and *race* and, for the latter variable, the categories "White," "Black," and "Other," are used here to be consistent with the variable naming in the GSS, although I prefer "gender" for the female versus male distinction and "ethnicity" for distinctions (such as Hispanic/Latino and African American) in place of origin in general practice. Based on bivariate contingency analysis of ethnicity and gender, gender is statistically significantly related to ethnicity for these data. While the ratio of females to males is roughly 55:45 for White and Other respondents, it is 66:33 for Black respondents. In other words, while a little over half of the White and Other respondents are female, about two-thirds of the Black respondents are female. This underrepresentation of Black males raises questions about the representativeness of the GSS sample and suggests that some form of sample weighting to compensate for the missing Black male respondents might be appropriate, but that is beyond the scope of the present discussion.

2. For a discussion of the construction and use of dummy variables and their interactions in regression analysis, see Hardy (1993).

3. Software Note: For the Stata software package (Versions 7–10), however, that boundary is marked by the use of odds ratios as opposed to logit coefficients.

4. Software Note: It helps to know exactly what coefficients the statistical routine is outputting, however. For example, SPSS (Versions 11–16) **loglinear** and SAS (Version 8) **catmod** output β coefficients (see Equation 2.5) for continuous (single degree of freedom) predictors, but for categorical predictors they output λ coefficients (see Equation 2.3 and the discussion immediately preceding Equation 2.5), which are half as large in magnitude as the β coefficients output by SAS **logistic** and SPSS **logistic** (using comparable contrasts, either Simple or Deviation, in SPSS **logistic** and **loglinear**); while SPSS **genlog** outputs coefficients comparable to those output by SAS **logistic** (the latter using indicator contrasts). The different contrasts and their use in logistic regression will be discussed in greater detail in Chapter 5, but the points here are (a) the output using the default options in different software routines may not always look the same, but (b) with appropriate tweaking, the same results can be obtained from log-linear routines to calculate logit models as can be obtained from logistic regression routines. This latter point had greater practical value prior to the turn of the millennium, when statistical routines for certain types of analyses (ordered and unordered polytomous logistic regression among them) were less readily available in general purpose statistical packages, but now it only serves to underscore the point that the logit and logistic regression models are essentially the same, differing in presentation of results and software implementation but not in the mathematical model. The distinction between individual level data and "replicated" or grouped data is more important and will be discussed further in later chapters. It does not change the model, however, but only the computation of some statistics associated with the model.

5. Software Note: The models in Table 2.4 can be calculated with any number of routines designed specifically for logistic regression as opposed to log-linear or logit analysis, including SAS (Version 8) **logistic** with the AGGREGATE option, SAS **catmod** with single degree of freedom predictors in the case of education and income, SPSS (Versions 11–16) **nomreg**, and Stata (Versions 7–10) **logistic** or **logit**. Stata **blogit** also calculates logit models for grouped data, but it expects data in a format different from that provided by the GSS. Output format and other features will be different for log-linear analysis routines such as SAS **catmod** and SPSS **loglinear** or **genlog**.

CHAPTER 3

Quantitative Approaches to Model Fit and Explained Variation

The first thing we want to know about any logistic regression model is whether we can do a better job of predicting the dependent variable with the independent variables in the model than without them. There are two main components to the question of whether the independent variables, taken as a group, help us to improve our ability to predict the dependent variable. First, how sure are we that any improvement in our ability to predict the dependent variable is not attributable to just "getting lucky" with the particular data we are using, or phrased a little differently, not attributable to chance or to random sampling variation? Second, if we can be reasonably sure that the improvement in our ability to predict the dependent variable is not attributable to chance, how much of an improvement is it really?

To determine whether any improvement in prediction of the dependent variable can reasonably be attributed to chance, we use tests of statistical significance. In ordinary least squares (OLS) regression, the analysis of variance (ANOVA) F statistic is commonly used for this purpose. As described in Chapter 2, for log-linear analysis, the same test is performed using the log likelihood χ^2 statistic to test for the significance of the difference between the model with the predictors and the *independence* model (no predictors). A parallel question from log-linear analysis is whether the model fits statistically significantly *worse* than the best model available from the data, the question of goodness of fit. In log-linear analysis, the question regarding the goodness of fit of the model to the data is answered using the log likelihood χ^2 statistic for the comparison between the model with the predictors and the *saturated* model, assuming that the model with the predictors omits at least one possible effect (otherwise, it *is* the saturated model).

The second question is how much of an improvement in prediction we get with the predictors instead of without them. In its most general terms, this question involves the analysis of *variation* or dispersion in the dependent variable, as introduced in Chapter 2. Variation can be measured in different ways for both qualitative and quantitative dependent variables; for a good overview, see Weisberg (1992). For interval- or ratio-scaled continuous variables, the *variance* is not the only available measure of variation or dispersion, but it is the one most commonly used because it has certain desirable mathematical properties. In OLS regression the amount of explained and unexplained variation for models with and without the predictors is analyzed by examining the *explained variance* using the R^2 statistic. Again as noted in Chapter 2, there are parallel statistics one can use in log-linear analysis, but they are given less attention in log-linear analysis than R^2 receives in OLS regression analysis. Also, while there is broad consensus on the use of R^2 (or the adjusted R^2, adjusted for the number of predictors in the model to provide an unbiased estimate of a population R^2 from a sample R^2) in OLS regression, no such consensus exists on how to measure the strength of the predictive relationship in log-linear analysis. There is likewise no consensus on the most appropriate measure for explained variation in logistic regression.

One reason is because, as described by Efron (1978), there is only one reasonable residual variation criterion for quantitative dependent variables in OLS, the familiar error sum of squares, $\sum(y_j - \hat{y}_j)^2$, but there are several possible residual variation criteria (entropy, squared error, qualitative difference) for binary dependent variables. Another hindrance to consensus is the existence of numerous mathematical equivalents to R^2 in OLS, which are not necessarily mathematically (same formula) or conceptually (same meaning in the context of the model) equivalent to R^2 in logistic regression. Logistic regression also adds the twist that some of the more appropriate measures of explained variation are not (at least as of this writing) directly available from some of the more commonly used statistical packages for calculating logistic regression models. Moreover, in logistic regression we must choose whether we are more interested in *qualitative* prediction (*whether* predictions are correct or incorrect), *quantitative* prediction (*how close* predictions are to being correct), or both, because different measures of explained variation are appropriate for these two different types of prediction.

Logistic regression predicts a probability of group membership, the probability of a "yes" as opposed to a "no" answer, and this predicted probability can be compared with the observed group membership to see how far we are from a correct or an incorrect prediction. The predicted probability can also be used to qualitatively classify or assign cases. For example, a case with a probability of .50 or greater can be assigned to the category we are trying to predict (typically coded $Y = 1$), and a case with a probability of less than .50 can be assigned to the reference category (typically coded $Y = 0$). This allows us to construct a *prediction table*, in which observed category membership is compared with predicted category membership. The results for quantitative prediction (how close?) are not necessarily the same as or even consistent with the results for qualitative prediction (right or wrong?), as will be detailed in the next chapter. Therefore, different tests of statistical significance and different measures of the strength of the predictive relationship are appropriate, depending on whether we are interested in qualitative or quantitative accuracy of prediction. The present chapter addresses the issue of quantitative prediction; the next chapter examines qualitative prediction and compares the results of assessing qualitative and quantitative prediction.

CRITERIA FOR GOOD MEASURES OF EXPLAINED VARIATION

In the context of OLS regression analysis, Kvålseth (1985:281) proposes eight properties for a "good" R^2 statistic: (1) R^2 must possess utility as a measure of accuracy of prediction[1] and have an intuitively reasonable interpretation; (2) R^2 ought to be dimensionless, that is, independent of the units of measurement of the model variables; (3) the potential range of values of R^2 should be well defined with endpoints corresponding to perfect prediction and complete lack of improvement in prediction when the predictors are included in the model, such as $0 \leq R^2 \leq 1$, where $R^2 = 1$ corresponds to a perfect prediction and $R^2 \geq 0$ for any reasonable model specification; (4) R^2 should be sufficiently general to be applicable to any type of model, whether the predictors are random or nonrandom variables, and regardless of the statistical properties of the model variables (including residuals); (5) R^2 should not be confined to any specific model fitting technique—that is, it should only reflect the accuracy of prediction for the model *per se*, irrespective of the way in which the model has been derived; (6) "R^2 should be such that its values for different models fitted to the same data set are directly comparable"; (7) relative values of R^2 ought to be generally compatible with those derived from other acceptable measures of fit such as standard error of prediction and root mean squared residual; and (8) positive and negative residuals should be equally weighted by R^2.

Of these eight criteria, Criteria 1 (intuitively reasonable interpretation) and 3 (endpoints corresponding to perfect prediction and complete lack of any improvement in prediction as a result of adding the predictors) are central to the discussion that follows. Costner (1965), among others, has suggested that measures of association with a *proportional reduction in error* (PRE) interpretation are to be preferred over other measures, because we intuitively understand the concept of reducing prediction error by some percentage. An R^2 measure is, among other things, a measure of association, and a PRE interpretation is one obvious way to satisfy the first criterion. At the same time, the question may also arise whether the specific measure of error being reduced is reasonable in the sense of being the error we are actually most interested in reducing. Put another way, are we getting a proportional reduction in the errors with which we are most concerned? Criterion 7 is usually considered by comparing alternative coefficients of determination, but for a logistic regression model, some of the usual "other" acceptable measures of accuracy of prediction (standard error of prediction, root mean squared residual) may not be appropriate. This is especially true if the focus is on discrete as opposed to continuous predicted values, as typically presented in the classification tables that are included in most logistic regression output (e.g., in SAS, SPSS, or Stata). Criteria 2, 4, 5, and 8 are generally satisfied by the coefficients of determination that have been proposed for logistic regression, and thus are not considered in detail here.[2]

Criterion 6 is somewhat vague as stated, but is here interpreted or extended, following Menard (2000), to suggest that a "good" coefficient of determination should be such that its values for different models should be comparable whether the models differ in one or more predictors (as implied in the criterion as stated) *or* in the dependent variable *or* in whether the models are specified as being different for different subsets of the data set. This includes but is not limited to the question of whether the measure is applicable to both dichotomous (two categories) and *polytomous* (more than two categories) dependent variables. It is sometimes the case in practical applications that we are unsure which of two or more alternative codings of the dependent variable is more useful (are two nominally different categories *really* different in terms of the impact of independent variables on membership in one as opposed to the other of the two categories?). Having an index that is comparable across different codings of the dependent variable would be useful in deciding whether an alternative coding is reasonable. Similarly, we may want to know whether a model works as well for one group, however groups are defined, as for another. Suggesting that the coefficient of determination should be comparable across not only different predictors, but also different dependent variables and different subsets of the data set, probably constitutes an extension of the criterion proposed by Kvålseth, but the extension is a reasonable one. It allows us to answer certain questions that may arise in practical, empirical research, such as comparisons of the adequacy of models across subgroups defined in terms of gender or ethnicity, or models with different but related dependent variables, such as more or less serious outcomes (e.g., more or less serious forms of crime or substance use, or more or less serious illness or injury, with the expectation that the percentage or proportion of people engaging in the specific behavior may be higher for the less serious forms and lower for the more serious forms).[3]

One criterion *not* used here is the behavior of the measure of explained variation when the dichotomous dependent variable represents a latent continuous dependent variable. This criterion has been used by several authors in comparing alternative measures of explained variation for logistic regression (Cox and Wermuth 1992; Hagle and Mitchell 1992; Veall and Zimmerman 1996). If we assume a latent continuous dependent variable, however, there are several other alternatives, including the possibility of calculating a linear probability model (since the restriction of predicted values to vary between 0 and 1 is really artificial for a latent interval scale), and using R^2 itself to measure the strength of the association between the observed and predicted values of the dependent variable, or using polychoric correlation and weighted least squares estimation in the context of a more complex structural equation model (Jöreskog and Sörbom 1993). One of these alternatives may be more appropriate than logistic regression if the dichotomous dependent variable *really* represents a latent interval- or ratio-scaled variable. For most of this book, the working assumption is that the assumptions of logistic regression, including the assumptions of proportional odds and a truly discrete, usually dichotomous dependent variable, are met. Discrete polytomous nominal and ordinal models will be considered in more detail in later chapters. In this chapter, however, some consideration will be given to whether different proposed measures of qualitative and quantitative accuracy of prediction are applicable to discrete polytomous as well as dichotomous dependent variables, in the context of Kvålseth's sixth criterion.

THE *F* STATISTIC AND SUMS OF SQUARED ERRORS IN THE LINEAR REGRESSION MODEL

In linear regression analysis, evaluation of the overall model is based on two sums of squares. If we were concerned with minimizing the sum of the squared errors of prediction, and if we knew only the values of the dependent variable (but not the cases to which those values belonged), we could minimize the sum of the squared errors of prediction by using the mean of Y, $\bar{Y}$, as the predicted value of Y for all cases. The sum of squared errors based on this prediction would be $\Sigma(y_j - \bar{Y})^2$, the *total sum of squares* or *SST*, where y_j is the value of Y for case j. If the independent variables are useful in predicting Y, then $\hat{y}$, the vector of predicted values of Y based on the regression equation (the conditional mean of Y) will be a better predictor than $\bar{Y}$ of the values of Y, and the sum of squared errors $\Sigma(y_j - \hat{y}_j)^2$ where $\hat{y}_j$ is the value of Y that is estimated by the model for case j, which will be smaller than the sum of squared errors $\Sigma(y_j - \bar{Y})^2$. $\Sigma(y_j - \hat{y}_j)^2$ is called the *error sum of squares* or *SSE*, and is the quantity OLS selects parameters ($\beta_1, \beta_2, \ldots, \beta_K$) to minimize. A third sum of squares, the *regression sum of squares* or *SSR* is simply the difference between *SST* and *SSE*: $SSR = SST - SSE$.

It is possible in a sample of cases to get an apparent reduction in error of prediction by using the regression equation instead of $\bar{Y}$ to predict the values of Y, even when the independent variables are really unrelated to Y. This occurs as a result of sampling variation, random fluctuations in sample values that may make it appear as though a relationship exists between two variables when there really is no relationship. The multivariate F ratio is used to test whether the improvement in prediction using $\hat{Y}$ instead of $\overline{Y}$ could reasonably be attributed to random sampling variation. Specifically, the multivariate F ratio tests two equivalent hypotheses: H_0: $R^2 = 0$ and H_0: $\beta_1 = \beta_2 = \ldots = \beta_K = 0$. For OLS linear regression, the F ratio with N cases and K independent variables can be calculated as

$$F = [SSR/K]/[SSE/(N - K - 1)] = (N - K - 1)SSR/(K)SSE.$$

The *attained statistical significance* (p) associated with the F ratio indicates the probability of obtaining an R^2 as large as the observed R^2, or β coefficients as large as the observed β coefficients, *if the null hypothesis is true*. If p is small (usually less than .05, but other values of p may be chosen), then we reject the null hypothesis, and conclude that there is a relationship between the independent variables and the dependent variable that cannot be attributed to chance. If p is large, then we "fail to reject the null hypothesis," and conclude that there is insufficient evidence to be sure that the variance explained by the model is not attributable to random sample variation. This does not mean that we conclude that there is no relationship, only that if there is a relationship, we have insufficient evidence to be confident that it exists.

The coefficient of determination, or R^2, or "explained variance" (really, the *proportion* of the variance that is explained) is an indicator of *substantive* significance—that is, whether the relationship is "big enough" or "strong enough" for us to be concerned about it. R^2 is a *proportional reduction in error* statistic. It measures the proportion (or, multiplied by 100, the percentage) by which use of the regression equation reduces the error of prediction, relative to predicting the mean, $\overline{Y}$. R^2 ranges from 0 (the independent variables are no help at all) to 1 (the independent variables allow us to predict the individual values y_j perfectly). R^2 is calculated as $R^2 = SSR/SST = (SST - SSE)/SST = 1 - (SSE/SST)$. The F ratio and R^2 can also be expressed as functions of one another: $F = [R^2/K]/[(1 - R^2)/(N - K - 1)]$ and $R^2 = KF/(KF + N - K - 1)$.

It is possible for a relationship to be statistically significant ($p \leq .0001$), but for R^2 not to be substantively significant (e.g., $R^2 \leq .005$), for a large sample. If the independent variables explain less than one half of 1% of the variance in the dependent variable, we are unlikely to be very concerned with them, even if we are relatively confident that the explained variance cannot be attributed to random sample variation. It is also possible for a relationship to be substantively significant (e.g., $R^2 \geq .4$) but not statistically significant (e.g., $p > .25$) for a small sample. Even though the relationship appears to be moderately strong (an explained variance of .40, or equivalently a 40% reduction in errors of prediction), there may not be enough cases for us to be confident that this result cannot be attributed to random sampling variation.

THE G_M STATISTIC AND THE −2 LOG LIKELIHOOD FUNCTION IN LOGISTIC REGRESSION

Close parallels to F and R^2 exist for the logistic regression model. Just as the sum of squared errors is the criterion for selecting parameters in the linear regression model, the *log likelihood* is the criterion for selecting parameters in the logistic regression model. Some software presents information on the log likelihood itself; however, other software presents not the log likelihood itself, but the log likelihood multiplied by −2, which forms the basis of calculating χ^2 statistics based on the likelihood ratio, as described in Chapter 2. For convenience, the log-likelihood multiplied by -2 will be abbreviated as $-2LL$ in general, with subscripts to identify specific $-2LL$ statistics. Since the log likelihood is negative, $-2LL$ is positive, and larger values indicate worse prediction of the dependent variable. The intercept-only or independence model or initial $-2LL$, sometimes designated $-2LL_0$ or D_0 to indicate that it is the -2 log likelihood statistic with none (zero) of the independent variables in the equation, is analogous to the total sum of squares, SST, in linear regression analysis. The use of "D" for "$-2LL$" is based on the terminology of McCullagh and Nelder (1989), who called the $-2LL$ statistic comparing the hypothesized model with the saturated model the "deviance" statistic. For a dichotomous dependent variable (coded as 0 or 1), if $n_{Y=1}$ is the number of cases for which $Y = 1$, N is the total number of cases, and $P(Y = 1) = n_{Y=1}/N$ is the probability that Y is equal to 1, then for individual or casewise data,

$$D_0 = -2LL_0 = -2\{n_{Y=1}\ln[P(Y=1)] + (N - n_{Y=1})\ln[1 - P(Y=1)]\}$$
$$= -2\{(n_{Y=1})\ln[P(Y=1)] + (n_{Y=0})\ln[P(Y=0)]\}.$$

Following Nagelkerke (1991), the quantity $D_0 = -2LL_0 = -2[\ln(L_0)]$ represents the "error variation" of the model with only the intercept included.

For the full logistic regression model including all of the predictors plus the intercept (if any), a conditional log likelihood statistic is calculated, in which $P(Y = 1)$ is replaced by the conditional probability $P(Y = 1|X_1, X_2, \ldots, X_K)$, where $X_1, X_2, \ldots, X_K$ is a vector of independent variables or predictors of Y. [In the leftmost side of the equation above, correspondingly, we would replace $P(Y = 0)$ with $P(Y = 0|X_1, X_2, \ldots, X_K)$.] The value of $-2LL$ for the logistic regression model that includes the independent variables will hereafter be referred to as $-2LL_M$ or D_M for the full model. D_M is analogous to the error sum of squares, SSE, in linear regression analysis. Again following Nagelkerke (1991), $D_M = -2LL_M = -2[\ln(L_M)]$ is the "error variation" for a model with all of the predictors included. Just as OLS attempts to minimize the error sum of squares, maximum likelihood logistic regression seeks to minimize the -2 log likelihood statistic (or equivalently, to maximize the likelihood function). The most direct analog in logistic regression analysis to the regression sum of squares, SSR in linear regression, is the difference between D_0 and D_M, that is $(D_0 - D_M)$. This difference, often termed the "model chi-square" or something similar, will be referred to as G_M, or the Model χ^2. A comment on notation: since D_M and G_M represent χ^2 statistics, some authors use D^2 or G^2 instead, but there is no consensus on this point.

As noted in Chapter 2, in logistic regression (and in other general linear models), the difference between two log likelihoods, when multiplied by -2, can be interpreted as a χ^2 statistic if they come from two different models, one of which is *nested* within the other (see McCullagh and Nelder 1989). G_M can be straightforwardly interpreted as the difference in the $-2LL$ statistics between a first model that contains only an intercept, and a second model that contains the intercept plus one or more variables as predictors. Treated as a chi-square statistic, G_M provides a test of the null hypothesis that $\beta_1 = \beta_2 = \ldots = \beta_K = 0$ for the logistic regression model. If G_M is statistically significant (typically $p \leq .05$), then we reject the null hypothesis and conclude that information about the independent variables allows us to make better predictions of $P(Y = h)$ (where h is some specific value, usually 1, usually for a dichotomous dependent variable) than we could make without the independent variables. G_M is thus analogous to the multivariate F test for linear regression, in addition to being analogous to the regression sum of squares.

R_L^2: THE LIKELIHOOD RATIO R^2

If we maintain the analogy between the $-2LL$ statistics for logistic regression and the sums of squares for linear regression analysis, the most natural choice for a parallel in logistic regression, directly analogous to SSR/SST, is the likelihood ratio R^2, $R_L^2 = G_M/(D_0) = G_M/(G_M + D_M)$ (McFadden 1974; see also Agresti 1990:110–111; DeMaris 1992:53–54; Hosmer and Lemeshow 1989:148–149; Knoke and Burke 1980:40–41; Maddala 1983:40; Menard 2000). R_L^2 may equivalently be calculated as the difference between the initial and model $-2LL$ statistics, divided by the initial $-2LL$ statistic: $R_L^2 = -2[\ln(L_0) - \ln(L_M)]/-2[\ln(L_0)] = [\ln(L_0) - \ln(L_M)]/\ln(L_0) = 1 - [\ln(L_M)/\ln(L_0)] = G_M/-2[\ln(L_0)]$, where G_M is the model chi-square statistic and $-2[\ln(L_0)]$ is the initial $-2LL$ statistic, both commonly provided in the output from logistic regression software. Just as R^2 in OLS regression analysis can be interpreted as the proportional reduction in the error sum of squares, R_L^2 can be interpreted as the proportional reduction in the $-2LL$ statistic. R_L^2 is thus a *proportional reduction in $-2LL$* or a *proportional reduction in the absolute value of the log likelihood* measure, where the $-2LL$ or the absolute value of the log likelihood, the quantity being minimized to select the model parameters, is taken as a measure of "variation" (Nagelkerke 1991) or "dispersion" (SPSS 1991:136), not necessarily identical but analogous to the variance in OLS regression. Actually, as noted by Hosmer and Lemeshow (1989:14), the $-2LL$ statistic is identically equal to the sum of squared errors when computed for OLS. The parallel for logistic regression is thus close conceptually as well as mathematically. The treatment of the total and regression sum of squared errors to construct R^2 in OLS is directly parallel to the treatment of the total and regression "error variation" to construct R_L^2 in the logistic regression equation, including R_L^2 naturally varying between 0 and 1, and having a proportional reduction in error interpretation. R_L^2 is applicable to models with both dichotomous and polytomous dependent variables.

R_L^2 is also the *information theory* measure of association (Hauser 1978) derived from Shannon's (1948) entropy measure (see Eliason 1993; Haberman 1982; SPSS 1991:136) and presented in some log-linear routines.[4] R_L^2 indicates how much the inclusion of the independent variables in the model reduces the variation, as measured by D_0. It varies between 0 (for a model in which $G_M = 0$, $D_M = D_0$, and the independent variables are useless in predicting the dependent variable) and 1 (for a model in which $G_M = D_0$, $D_M = 0$, and the model predicts the dependent variable with perfect accuracy). An earlier version of SAS **logistic**, SAS (SUGI) **proc logist** (Harrell 1986) included a variant of R_L^2, adjusted for the number of parameters in the model. This measure is analogous to the adjusted R^2 in linear regression, $R_a^2 = R^2 - [k(1 - R^2)/(n - k - 1)]$ (using the formula from Hutcheson and Sofroniu 1999:76), and we may denote it as R_{LH}^2, to indicate its connection with R_L^2 and to distinguish it from other R^2-type measures. $R_{LH}^2 = (G_M - 2K)/(D_0)$, where K is the number of independent variables in the model. A similar adjusted R_L^2 measure, here designated $R_{LBL}^2 = (G_M - K)/(D_0)$, cited by Long (1997), was suggested by Ben-Akiva and Lerman (1985), which does not penalize as heavily for the number of parameters in the model as R_{LH}^2. A nearly identical adjusted R_L^2 measure, $R_{LMS}^2 = (G_M - K)/(D_0 + 1)$, was suggested by Mittlböck and Schemper (1996); Shtatland et al. (2002) have suggested an Akaike information criterion (AIC)-based adjustment, $R_{LSKC}^2 = 1 - (D_M - K - 1)/(D_0 - 1)$, which they indicate works exactly the same as the AIC as a goodness-of-fit measure, but is more easily interpretable as an explained variation measure.

Liao and McGee (2003) suggested a more complex formulation with no closed form solution but instead using Monte Carlo estimation, R_{LLM}^2. R_{LLM}^2 is based on the use of what Liao and McGee called inherent prediction error (IPE) as a criterion. In simulations based on this criterion with a small number of cases ($n = 50$, $n = 100$) and a large number of predictors relative to the number of cases ($K = 10$), R^2_{LMS} performed nearly as well as R^2_{LLM}, and both R^2_{LLM} and R^2_{LMS} were both less likely than R^2_{L} to overestimate the explained variation, based on the inherent prediction error criterion. The PRE interpretation of all these adjusted R^2 measures derives from their interpretation as sample estimates of the true population value of R^2_{L}. They may be especially appropriate for large numbers of predictors relative to sample size, or more generally for small samples, which is when R^2_{L} is most likely to overestimate the explained variation. Even for larger samples and smaller numbers of predictors, R^2_{LH} and the other adjusted R^2_{L} measures may have some utility as a diagnostic similar to the adjusted R^2 in OLS regression, in the sense that if there is a large difference between R^2_{LH} and R^2_{L}, that difference suggests that some of the apparent accuracy of prediction in the model may just be the result of adding predictors to the model and capitalizing on random covariation between the additional predictors and the dependent variable.

Hosmer and Lemeshow (1989) express reservations about the use of R^2_{L} as a goodness-of-fit measure for logistic regression, noting that

> R^2_{L} is nothing more than an expression of the likelihood ratio test and, as such, is not a measure of goodness-of-fit. This likelihood ratio test compared fitted values under two models rather than comparing observed values to those fitted under one model. (p. 149; see also Hosmer and Lemeshow 2000:164)

Shtatland et al. (2002), however, disagree, because R^2_{L}, unlike other R^2 analogs for logistic regression, also compares the estimated model with a saturated model. As noted earlier, the term *goodness of fit* seems best applied to the difference between the observed model and the best possible model (all possible predictors, including interactions), given the data, and given the consideration raised by Shtatland et al., it seems that one can argue either way about the appropriateness of R^2_{L} as a measure of goodness of fit; but its more important use is as a measure of explained variation. R^2_{L} is based on the comparison of the observed model with a model in which there are *no* predictors. This comparison of fitted values for the observed model and an intercept-only model is also one conceptual interpretation of the OLS R^2. The parallel here is between $R^2 = 1 - (SSE/SST)$ for OLS and $R^2_{\text{L}} = 1 - [\ln(L_{\text{M}})/\ln(L_0)]$ for logistic regression. Hagle and Mitchell (1992) note that R^2_{L} tends to underestimate the strength of the relationship between the predictors and the dependent variable *when the dichotomous dependent variable represents an underlying continuous variable*. As DeMaris (1992:56) notes, however, this criticism of R^2_{L} is invalid whenever the dependent variable is truly dichotomous. It is also noteworthy that the results unfavorable to the use of R^2_{L} are limited to the case in which the residuals are truly normally distributed. For skewed and bimodal distributions, R^2_{L} was numerically closest to the OLS R^2 of all the measures compared by Hagle and Mitchell (1992:772–773).

R^2_{M} AND R^2_{N}: THE UNADJUSTED AND ADJUSTED GEOMETRIC MEAN R^2

Another proposed R^2 analog, described in Maddala (1983:39–40), Cox and Snell (1989), Magee (1990), and Ryan (1997:267) is $R^2_{\text{M}} = 1 - \exp\{-(2/N)[\ln(L_{\text{M}}) - \ln(L_0)]\} = 1 - (L_0/L_{\text{M}})^{2/n}$ where the subscript "M" refers to the use of the geometric mean squared improvement per observation interpretation of the statistic. Like R_L^2, R_M^2 is based on the likelihood statistic for the logistic regression model. Unlike R_L^2, however, it cannot have a value of 1 even when the model fits the data perfectly, as noted by Maddala (1983), Nagelkerke (1991), and Ryan (1997): (maximum R_M^2) = $1 - \exp[2 \ln(L_0)/N] = 1 - L_0^{2/N}$ (Nagelkerke 1991). An alternative considered by Cragg and Uhler (1970), Maddala (1983:40), and Nagelkerke (1991) is to adjust R_M^2 by its maximum to produce $R_N^2 = [1 - (L_0/L_M)^{2/N}]/[1 - L_0^{2/N}]$, where the *subscript* N here refers to Nagelkerke, as contrasted with the sample size N. Like R_L^2, R_M^2 and R_N^2 are applicable to models with both dichotomous and polytomous dependent variables.

In its unadjusted form, R_M^2 may be interpreted in the OLS context in terms of the geometric mean improvement (or reduction in error) per observation produced by the full model as opposed to the model with only the intercept (Cox and Wermuth 1992). Geometric mean squared error is not, however, the criterion being minimized in maximum likelihood logistic regression models, so at best R_M^2, like the OLS R^2, only partially satisfies the criterion of having an intuitively meaningful interpretation. Even this partial advantage is lost for the adjusted R_N^2. Given the dependence noted by Ryan (1997) of R_M^2 on the *base rate,* $n_{Y=1}/N$ (the proportion of cases for which $Y = 1$), it should be comparable in both adjusted and unadjusted forms for different models on the same data set, but not necessarily for the same model on different data sets, different dependent variables, or different subsamples, since the base rate may vary from one data set to another. Menard (2000) found that both R_M^2 and R_N^2 appeared to be more dependent on the base rate than R_L^2, R_N^2 less so than R_M^2. As the base rate increases, so do R_M^2 and R_N^2. Shtatland et al. (2002), using different notation, offer a proof of why this is the case, showing how R_M^2 and R_N^2 are both functions of R_L^2 and the base rate; and they indicate that for $.2 < Y < .8$, $R_M^2 > R_L^2$, but for $.2 > Y$ or $.8 < Y$, $R_M^2 < R_L^2$ because of the base rate dependency of R_M^2 (and a parallel consideration applies to R_N^2).

CONTINGENCY COEFFICIENT TYPE R^2 MEASURES

A family of alternatives to R_L^2 includes (a) the pseudo-R^2 or contingency coefficient $R_C^2 = G_M/(G_M + N)$, proposed by Aldrich and Nelson (1984) in their discussion of logit and probit models, and the subscript C is used to indicate that this is a variant of the contingency coefficient (see, e.g., Reynolds 1984:47 or Chen and Popovich 2002:81–82); (b) the Wald $R_W^2 = W/(W + N)$, where W is the multivariate Wald statistic (Magee 1990); and (c) the McKelvey and Zavoina (1975) $R_{MZ}^2 = S_{\hat{Y}}^2 / (S_{\hat{Y}}^2 + 1)$ for the probit model (the context in which it was originally developed), or $R_{MZ}^2 = S_{\hat{Y}}^2 / (S_{\hat{Y}}^2 + \pi^2/3)$ for a logit or logistic regression model, where $S_{\hat{Y}}^2$ is the variance in $\hat{Y}$, the predicted value of Y, and 1 and $\pi^2/3$ are the standard deviations for the standard normal and standard logistic distributions, respectively. R_C^2 at least has the advantage of being based on a quantity the model tries to maximize, and it is readily applicable to both polytomous and dichotomous dependent variables. However, R_C^2 shares with the other two measures the common feature that they cannot attain a value of 1, even for a perfect model fit, because of the inclusion of the sample size N in the denominator for R_C^2 and R_W^2, and because of the inclusion of the constant $\pi^2/3$ for the logistic regression model (or 1 for the probit model) in R_{MZ}^2. Moreover, the dependence of R_C^2 and R_W^2 on the sample size N means that the upper bound varies from one subsample or data set to another.

Like the original contingency coefficient, and just as R_M^2 may be adjusted to calculate R_N^2, any of these measures can be adjusted by dividing them by their maxima, with the result that they vary between 0 and 1. As in the case of adjusting any coefficient of determination, this raises the possibility that for comparisons across models or subsamples, the adjusted and unadjusted measures may produce contradictory conclusions about which of the models or subsamples produces the better fit. Hagle and Mitchell (1992) also noted that the corrected R_C^2 provided a good approximation for the OLS regression R^2, and Veall and Zimmerman (1996) noted the same with respect to the McKelvey-Zavoina R_{MZ}^2, *when the dichotomous dependent variable represented a latent interval scale.* As noted above, there are several alternatives to logistic regression that may be more appropriate in this instance. In brief, then, the unadjusted contingency coefficient type measures (a) do not really satisfy the criterion of an intuitively reasonable interpretation, at least in the sense of being describable as a coefficient that minimizes a reasonable measure of model variation, and (b) also fail to satisfy the criterion of fixed points corresponding to perfect fit and perfect lack of fit. The adjusted measures (a) are even worse with respect to lacking an intuitively reasonable interpretation, but (b) do have fixed end points corresponding to perfect fit or complete lack of fit. As with R_N^2, however, there is reason to question their suitability for comparing models with different dependent variables or subsamples.

THE BRIER INDEX

In OLS regression and ANOVA, the mean squared error, defined as $MSE = \Sigma(o - p)^2/df$, where o is the observed value of the dependent variable, p is the expected value of the dependent variable, and df is the degrees of freedom in the model for the dependent variable, is used in calculating the F statistic that tests whether the model represents a statistically significant improvement over a model in which one simply predicts the mean value of the dependent variable for all cases (see, e.g., Agresti and Finlay 1997). In some disciplines including meteorology (e.g., Brier 1950; Livezey 1995) and biomedical sciences (e.g., Biagotti et al. 1999), in studies using logistic regression or related methods, a variant of the mean squared error defined as $MSE = \Sigma(o - p)^2/n$, where o and p are defined as before and n is the number of cases, has been designated the *Brier index* and used as a measure of multiple association (either in this original form or in some variant thereof). Because the observed (o) and predicted (p) values are probabilities, numerically lying between 0 and 1, each squared error $(o - p)^2$ also lies between 0 and 1, and the sum divided by the number of cases also lies between 0 and 1, with 0 representing complete agreement (no error of prediction) and 1 representing complete disagreement. If we calculate the quantity $1 - \Sigma(o - p)^2/n$, then, we obtain a quantity that behaves very much like a nominal measure of association (e.g., Goodman and Kruskal's tau or lambda), with a value of 0 for perfect disagreement and 1 for perfect agreement. The Brier index by itself, however, is not a PRE measure of association. Although it can be used to compare the predictive accuracy of different models, it cannot by itself indicate whether, given the distribution of the dependent variable, that predictive accuracy is statistically or substantively significantly different from what would be expected by chance. In this respect, it is more like a percentage correctly classified than a true measure of association. PRE measures, in contrast, provide information about both the relative accuracy of prediction of different models *and* whether the predictive accuracy of a model is statistically and substantively different from what would be expected by chance. For this reason, there seems to be little reason to recommend the use of the Brier index in preference to a PRE measure of association.

IF YOU WANT R^2, WHY NOT USE R^2?

The use of R^2, the familiar coefficient of determination from OLS linear regression analysis, has been discussed in Agresti (1990:111–112, 1996:129), Maddala (1983:38–39), Menard (2000, 2002a:26–27), and Mittlböck and Schemper (1996), among others; see also Cramer (1999). Two methods of calculating R^2 have been considered. One corresponds to what Kvålseth (1985) designated $R_1^2 = 1 - [\Sigma(y_j - \hat{y})^2 / \Sigma(y_j - \overline{Y})^2] = 1 - (SSE/SST) = (SST - SSE)/SST = SSR/SST$, expressed in terms of sums of squared errors. The second corresponds to what Kvålseth designated $R_6^2 = r_{\hat{Y}Y}^2 =$ the squared correlation between Y and $\hat{Y}$. While these two measures may not be precisely equal to each other under certain circumstances, as described by Kvålseth, in the bivariate case to be discussed here, involving only the observed and predicted values of Y, they are equal, and both versions will be designated R_O^2, the O representing the OLS derivation of the measure. Note that R_O^2 can be calculated for both dichotomous and polytomous dependent variables. For a polytomous dependent variable, membership in each category (coded as 0 or 1) can be compared with the predicted probability of membership in each category (coded as a continuous probability), with each category of the dependent variable providing one observation (the observed classification plus the predicted probability) per case. The easiest computational approach is to simply calculate what Kvålseth (1985) designates as R_6^2, the squared correlation between the predicted probabilities and observed membership or nonmembership in each category.[5]

The rationale for using R_O^2 is (a) it is the identical measure that is used in OLS regression, (b) it is interpretable as the proportional reduction in error variance in the dependent variable in the original metric, (c) it varies in principle from 0 for complete lack of fit to 1 for perfect fit, and (d) it makes possible direct comparisons between logistic regression and models based on OLS. With regard to the first rationale, it seems superficially reasonable to use R_O^2 as its own analog (it is, after all, mathematically equal to R_O^2 for OLS), but R_O^2 in OLS is based on the quantity actually being minimized to select the model parameters. The same is not true for maximum likelihood logistic regression. OLS and maximum likelihood logistic regression are based on minimizing two different quantities, which may be described following Efron (1978) as a squared error measure of residual variation for OLS and an entropy measure of residual variation for maximum likelihood logistic regression. R_O^2 in maximum likelihood logistic regression is thus *mathematically* equivalent (same formula) but not *conceptually* equivalent (in the sense of being based on the quantity that is being minimized, and being interpretable as a proportional reduction in that quantity) to R_O^2 in OLS regression. R_O^2 in logistic regression may actually decrease when additional variables are added to the model, unlike R_O^2 in OLS regression, which cannot decrease as a result of adding additional variables to the model (Agresti 1996:129). Also, if the dichotomous dependent variable is assumed to be an indicator for an unmeasured latent variable, R_O^2 actually provides a downward-biased estimate of the explained variance (Cox and Wermuth 1992), and the McKelvey-Zavoina R_{MZ}^2 (Veall and Zimmerman 1996) or the adjusted Aldrich-Nelson R_C^2 may be preferable. Once again, however, as noted earlier, the assumption of a continuous latent dependent variable raises several other possibilities. It is also the case that the sample R^2 in OLS regression may overestimate the explained variance, and the same is true for R_O^2 in logistic regression (Liao and McGee 2003). Liao and McGee examined adjusted versions of the OLS R^2 for logistic regression but found that they did not perform as well as adjusted versions of R_L^2 in reducing the bias toward overestimation of explained variation in the presence of irrelevant predictors in small samples.

With regard to the second rationale for using R_O^2 in logistic regression, it is not the (arbitrary) observed numerical values of the (dichotomous) dependent variable themselves that are of concern, but rather the *probability* that the dependent variable has one or the other of these values. In this sense, R_O^2 only partially satisfies the criterion of being intuitively meaningful; it has a clear intuitive interpretation in logistic regression (in terms of the numerical values of the dependent variable), but it is not really the interpretation in which we are most interested. The third rationale is more applicable, but would usually not be a compelling reason for selecting R_O^2 over other R^2 analogs for logistic regression. It is true that R_O^2 varies in principle between 0 and 1, with 0 indicating complete lack of fit and 1 indicating perfect fit. In practice, R_O^2 is usually less than 1 (just as it is in OLS regression). Given the inherent inaccuracy of using a symmetric measure of association to measure the strength of the bivariate relationship between one dichotomous variable (the observed Y) and one continuous variable (the predicted $\hat{Y}$), this is to be expected.

With regard to the fourth rationale, comparing R_O^2 for a linear probability model and a logistic regression model may be useful at least for didactic purposes (see, e.g., Chapter 1), but it is unclear that it has any practical utility. Staying with the consideration of practical utility for a moment, however, R_O^2 does not depend on the method used to estimate the model, but only on whether one has both observed and predicted values of the dependent variable to compare. If the model is estimated by other than a maximum likelihood method of estimation, then measures of explained variation based on maximum likelihood estimation ($R_L^2, R_M^2, R_N^2, R_C^2$) may not be available, making a variance-based measure of explained variation such as R_O^2 or R_{MZ}^2, or the Wald R_W^2, potentially useful simply because they can be estimated for models using methods other than maximum likelihood estimation (e.g., IRLS). This consideration is relevant to the fifth criterion suggested by Kvålseth (1985) described at the beginning of this chapter, but only becomes relevant for models involving dependencies in the data, to be discussed in later chapters.

Agresti (1996) characterizes the correlation between the observed and predicted values of Y as "a crude index of predictive power," which nevertheless "is useful for comparing fits of different models to the same data set" (p. 129). Stronger advocacy for the use of R_O^2 in logistic regression comes from Mittlböck and Schemper (1996). Cox and Wermuth (1992) criticized R_O^2 on the basis that (a) R_O^2 depends on the range and distribution of explanatory factors and (b) with a binary response, R^2 tends to be low even for an underlying perfect regression relationship. Mittlböck and Schemper responded by arguing (see also Korn and Simon 1991) that these criticisms apply only to R_O^2 as a measure of goodness of fit, not as a measure of explained variation. They acknowledge the argument that R_O^2 is not the quantity being optimized in logistic regression, but assert that its interpretation is intuitively clearer than the likelihood ratio R^2 analogs ($R_L^2, R_M^2,$ and R_N^2), and that R_O^2 (in both the R_1^2 and R_6^2 forms described by Kvålseth) are numerically closer to R^2 for a general linear model, using the same variables, than are other measures in their simulation results. The conditions for their simulation were, however, restrictive, limiting the range of predictors to ensure that $.2 < P(Y = 1) < .8$, the range over which the logistic function tends to be nearly linear, but effectively cutting off 40% (or more, for predictions based on a linear probability model) of the potential range of predicted values. Moreover, the R^2 from the general linear model is a questionable criterion for comparison, since it, like R_O^2, is not the quantity being optimized in logistic regression, and in empirical research it may be based on a misspecified model (linear instead of logistic). The whole point of using logistic regression, after all, is that it is *not* restricted to situations appropriate to a simpler linear model.

With respect to Mittlböck and Schemper's (1996) critique of the intuitive interpretability of R_L^2, this seems true only if one finds the explanation of sums of squared errors more *intuitively* appealing than the explanation of differences in likelihoods. As long as we recognize that there are different possible ways to measure error, variation, or dispersion (see Haberman 1982; Nagelkerke 1991; Weisberg 1992), the interpretation of R_L^2 is intuitively clear. From my own perspective, proportional reduction in error makes the same intuitive sense, regardless of how the errors are measured, but especially when the error in question is the error actually being minimized by the model estimation process. I suspect that the issue here is less one of intuition than of greater familiarity with the more widely used R^2 statistic. With respect to the numerical differences between R_L^2 and R_O^2, Mittlböck and Schemper (1996:1993) themselves note the difference between the log likelihood and sum of squares measure in their construction, and warn that they should not necessarily be expected to be numerically comparable.

COMPARISONS AMONG R^2 ANALOGS

Table 3.1 summarizes some of the considerations for choosing an R^2 analog for logistic regression with respect to several of the measures that have been considered in this chapter. Based on research on the properties of the different proposed measures, I have elsewhere suggested (Menard 2000, 2002a) and here continue to suggest that R_L^2 is the most appropriate for logistic regression, based on several considerations. First and most important, R_L^2 is conceptually closest to the OLS R^2, insofar as it reflects a proportional reduction in the quantity actually being minimized ($-2LL$; equivalently, the log likelihood is being maximized). This is also true of the Aldrich-Nelson R_C^2, but not of the other measures considered here. In particular, the other likelihood ratio measures R_M^2 and R_N^2 are based on the geometric mean log likelihood, R_O^2 and R_{MZ}^2 are based on variances, and R_W^2 is based on the multivariate Wald statistic. Second, unlike measures that are calculated based on the sample size as well as the log likelihood, or calculated based on some measure of variation other than the log likelihood (R_M^2, R_W^2, R_C^2, R_{MZ}^2), R_L^2 depends *only* on the quantity being maximized or minimized. Third, R_L^2 does not appear to be sensitive to the base rate (the proportion of cases that have the attribute, e.g., being or not being a marijuana user) of the phenomenon being studied. Evidence indicates that R_M^2, R_N^2, R_C^2, and R_O^2 all have the undesirable property that their value increases as the base rate (whichever is smaller, $n_{Y=1}/N$ or $n_{Y=0}/N$) increases from 0 to .50, absurdly implying that one could, in effect, substitute the base rate itself for one of these coefficients of determination as a measure of explained variation (Menard 2000:23)[6]. Fourth, R_L^2, unlike the unadjusted versions of R_W^2, R_C^2, and R_{MZ}^2, varies between 0 and 1, with 0 representing no predictive utility for the independent variables and 1 representing perfect prediction. The adjusted R_C^2 and R_N^2 solve the problem that R_C^2 and R_M^2 do not vary between 0 and 1, but raise a new problem of not being comparable across different models, for example, models for males and females calculated separately. Fifth, as noted by Veall and Zimmerman (1996), R_L^2 works as well for polytomous nominal or ordinal dependent variables as for dichotomous dependent variables, in contrast to the variance-based measure R_{MZ}^2 (and also R_O^2 if it is calculated as Kvålseth's R_1^2 as opposed to R_6^2). Particularly for smaller samples or analyses with a large number of predictors relative to the number of cases, it also seems reasonable to report an adjusted measure of R_L^2 in addition to, not instead of, R_L^2, as a diagnostic for overprediction. The limited research to date suggests that the more complicated R_{LLM}^2 suggested by Liao and McGee (2003) may have some small advantage over the R_{LMS}^2 suggested by Mittlböck and Schemper (1996),

TABLE 3.1 Comparisons Among R^2 Analogs for Logistic Regression

Coefficient of Determination	Residual Variation Criterion (From Efron 1978)	Correlation With Base Rate (From Menard 2000)	Interpretation as Proportional Reduction in Residual Variation (or Some Comparable Measure)	Fixed Interval With Maximum = Perfect Fit and Minimum = No Relationship	Comparability Across Models (e.g., $R^2 = .5$ Has the Same Meaning in Different Models for the Same Data Set and in the Same Model Across Different Data Sets)
R_O^2	Squared error	.834	Partially; proportional reduction in squared error (numeric values)	Yes, but for some models, only if adjusted	Problematic; base rate dependent; but permits comparisons with OLS models and calculation of explained variation for models not based on maximum likelihood estimation
R_L^2	Entropy	.002	Yes; proportional reduction in $-2LL$ statistic	Yes, for all models	Yes
R_M^2	Entropy	.910	Partially; geometric mean improvement per observation in likelihood	Only if adjusted (see R_N^2)	Problematic; base rate dependent
R_N^2	Entropy	.597	No	Yes	Problematic; base rate dependent
R_C^2	Entropy	.903	No	Only if adjusted	Problematic; base rate dependent

and the R^2_{LH} suggested by Harrell (1986) has not been adequately investigated. Further research is needed before a clear preference among these measures can be made, but at present the Liao and McGee R^2_{LLM} seems preferable for calculation by computer, if one has access to the software, while the Mittlböck and Schemper R^2_{LMS} seems preferable for calculation by hand, based on simulation results to date.

The limitations to R^2_O acknowledged that there do appear to be certain advantages to the use of R^2_O not instead of R^2_L, but as a supplemental measure of association between the independent variables and the dependent variable. First, using R^2_O permits direct comparison of logistic regression models with linear probability, ANOVA, and discriminant analysis models if predicting the observed value (instead of predicting the observed probability that the dependent variable is equal to that value) is of interest. Second, R^2_O is useful in calculating standardized logistic regression coefficients, a topic to be covered in Chapter 5. In the context in which there really is a latent continuous dependent variable in which we are concerned, and in which the dichotomous coding of the dependent variable *truly*[7] represents crudeness of measurement, while there are other options for analysis, it may be reasonable to use R^2_{MZ} or the adjusted R^2_C, but there are other reasonable alternatives. Third, R^2_O can be used in models using methods other than maximum likelihood estimation for the logistic regression model, particularly IRLS, and also robust methods of estimation that will be covered in later chapters.

For proportional hazards models (as opposed to the proportional odds model assumed in logistic regression), R^2_N may be more appropriate than R^2_L because R^2_N is less sensitive to censoring in that context (Schemper 1990, 1992). Note, however, that both the latent continuous dependent variable assumption and the proportional hazards assumption contradict the assumptions for which the logistic regression model is designed (proportional *odds* rather than proportional *hazards*, and a truly dichotomous dependent variable), and (one last repetition) suggest that it may be preferable *not* to use logistic regression in precisely those circumstances in which the use of R^2_L is questionable.

GOODNESS OF FIT REVISITED

The *goodness of fit* of a model, as described earlier, indicates by how much the model deviates from an ideal model. For grouped data, the Pearson χ^2 statistic (as described in Chapter 2) or more commonly D_M (the likelihood ratio deviance statistic, calculated as described in Chapter 2 for grouped models) can be used as a measure of goodness of fit, essentially a test for the statistical significance of the variation *unexplained* by the logistic regression model. This is analogous to testing for the statistical significance of unexplained variance in an OLS regression model, a procedure practically never performed in conjunction with OLS regression. While G_M compares the intercept-only model with the full model (the model that includes all the predictors), D_M compares the full model with a *saturated* model (a model that includes all predictors, plus all possible interactions among them). The problem with using D_M as a χ^2 statistic lies in the fact that there are different ways to define a saturated model, resulting in different values for D_M and different degrees of freedom (Simonoff 1998).

As explained by Simonoff (who uses the notation G^2 instead of D_M), one approach is to consider each case as independent (*casewise* approach), and contributing 1 degree of freedom. This is the approach most appropriate for continuous predictors, when there are few cases with any one combination of values of the predictors (i.e., lying in any one cell of a contingency table). The alternative approach is to consider each combination of values of the predictors, or each *covariate pattern*

(Hosmer and Lemeshow 1989) or *covariate class* (McCullagh and Nelder 1989) as a separate cell in a cross-tabulation (the *grouped* data approach, or in Simonoff's terminology, the *contingency table* approach), and to calculate degrees of freedom based on the number of covariate patterns (cells in the table) rather than the number of individuals. In either approach, if the number of cases per covariate pattern (cell) is too small, or if there are many empty cells, neither D_M nor the Pearson χ^2 statistic will generally have a χ^2 distribution, and it would be inappropriate to use either as a χ^2 statistic to test goodness of fit (McCullagh and Nelder 1989:120–121; Simonoff 1998). If there is a large number of cases relative to the covariate patterns, and sufficient cases per covariate pattern, it is possible to define an appropriate saturated model, as in Chapter 2, and to calculate a D_M statistic that will have a χ^2 distribution, and the correct degrees of freedom based on the contingency table approach. Clogg and Shihadeh (1994:162) and Stokes et al. (2000:197) note that if the Pearson and likelihood χ^2 statistics have dissimilar values, it suggests that the sample sizes in the groups are not large enough to support their use as goodness-of-fit statistics.

Other possible goodness-of-fit indices include the Score statistic, the Akaike Information Criterion (AIC), and the Schwartz criterion (SC, a modification of the AIC). The Score statistic is, like G_M, a test of the statistical significance of the combined effects of the independent variables in the model. The AIC and the Schwartz criterion, briefly discussed in Bollen (1989), are two related indices used for comparing models rather than providing absolute tests of adequacy of fit. AIC = $D_M + 2k$, and SC = $D_M + (k)\ln(N)$, where D_M is the model $-2LL$ statistic, k is the number of estimated parameters in the model, and N is the number of cases. As noted by Shtatland et al. (2002), AIC takes arbitrary values that are hard to interpret. It is possible to compare the AIC or the Schwartz criterion for the fitted model with the AIC or Schwartz criterion for the model with only the intercept, but this provides no more information than G_M. As Simonoff notes, there is no reason to report D_M as a goodness-of-fit statistic when the casewise approach is being used. If the researcher is concerned about goodness of fit, however, there are other possible options for models with continuous predictors.

One commonly available index for dichotomous dependent variables is Hosmer and Lemeshow's (1989) goodness-of-fit index, $\hat{C}$. Hosmer and Lemeshow's goodness-of-fit index was designed primarily as an alternative to avoid the problems associated with using D_M as a goodness-of-fit index for casewise data. It proceeds by collapsing the data into a finite number of groups, g, usually g = 10 deciles, which are constructed based on the predicted probability (according to the logistic regression model) of having the characteristic of interest. For example, if the outcome of interest is the prevalence of marijuana use, the first decile would contain the 10% of cases with the lowest predicted probabilities of marijuana use, the next decile would contain the 10% of cases with the next lowest predicted probabilities of marijuana use, and so forth, to the tenth decile, which would contain the 10% of cases with the highest predicted probabilities of marijuana use. Other quantiles can also be used, or may arise naturally, if there are fewer than 10 distinct covariate patterns. Hosmer and Lemeshow (1989:144) caution that with too few groups, $\hat{C}$ will not be sensitive enough to distinguish observed from expected frequencies, and they report that with fewer than 6 groups or quantiles, it will almost always indicate a good fit for the model. The statistic (Hosmer and Lemeshow 1989:141) is calculated as $\hat{C} = \sum_g (o_g - n_g \bar{\pi}_g)^2 / [n_g \bar{\pi}_g (1 - \bar{\pi}_g)]$, where the summation is taken over g = 1, 2,..., G groups, n_g is the number of covariate patterns in the gth group, $\bar{\pi}_g$ is the average estimated probability for the gth group, and o_g is the observed number of "positive" responses (e.g., the number of cases with a value of 1 for a dichotomous dependent variable coded 0 for "failure" and 1 for "success") in the gth group. $\hat{C}$ has an approximate χ^2 distribution with

($G - 2$) degrees of freedom, where G is the number of groups. Hence, to have at least 1 degree of freedom, the statistic requires that there be at least three groups. DeMaris (1992:47) suggests that the Hosmer-Lemeshow statistic is too liberal and "tends to confirm almost any model," and recommends focusing instead on measures of explained variation ("predictive efficacy" in his description) such as R_L^2. Regardless of whether $\hat{C}$ is liberal, explained variation will usually be of more interest than goodness of fit in logistic regression analysis.

Goodness-of-fit statistics are used extensively in log-linear analysis, as described in Chapter 2, and in structural equation modeling (e.g., Bollen 1989). There is less consensus on their use in logistic regression analysis, and if anything, there appears to be an emerging consensus that goodness-of-fit statistics need not be presented for logistic regression analysis, particularly when individual or casewise data, as opposed to grouped data, are being analyzed. At issue is whether we are more concerned with how much better the model is than a model with no predictors, or with how much worse the model is than a saturated model. For theoretical purposes, at least, and consistent with the log-linear model, it seems reasonable to consider D_M or goodness of fit as one element in evaluating a logistic regression model. From a more applied perspective, and consistent with OLS regression, it seems essential to consider G_M as an important criterion for whether the model is worthwhile. On balance, it seems more important to focus on G_M, because a model whose predictors have no value in predicting the dependent variable is of no interest for theoretical or applied research. D_M may or may not be of some interest, but with respect to G_M, even an imperfect model that significantly improves our ability to predict the dependent variable of interest is of both theoretical and practical interest.

EXAMPLES

In Chapter 1, a model was presented in which exposure to delinquent friends was used to predict the prevalence of marijuana use, using data from the National Youth Survey (NYS). For that model, $G_M = 85.39$ with 1 degree of freedom, $p = .000$, and $R_L^2 = G_M/D_0 = .285$. To calculate R_O^2 we must (a) generate predicted values in the original scale (between 0 and 1), (b) calculate the zero-order correlation between the observed and predicted values, and (c) square the result. As noted for the model in Chapter 1, $R_O^2 = .34$, slightly higher than $R^2 = .32$ from Part C of Figure 1.1 on page 6. The explained variance is slightly higher for the logistic regression model, despite the fact that OLS linear regression is set up to try to maximize R^2 by minimizing the sum of squared errors. (It will not always be the case that logistic regression produces a higher R^2 than linear regression for a dichotomous dependent variable; in a parallel analysis of theft for the full NYS sample, R^2 for linear and logistic regression were .255 and .253, respectively.) Calculating the Hosmer-Lemeshow test for the model results in a Hosmer-Lemeshow test statistic that is not statistically significant. It appears that the logistic regression model fits the data well, indicates a moderately strong relationship between the predictor and the dependent variable, and does a fairly good job of predicting the classification of the cases.

Table 3.2 presents summary statistics for a model in which the dependent variable is again the prevalence of marijuana use (0 = nonuse, 1 = use), and the predictors are sex (SEX: 0 = male, 1 = female), ethnicity (ETHN3: 1 = non-Hispanic European or White, 2 = African American or Black, 3 = other than non-Hispanic European and African American, or Other), exposure to delinquent friends (EDF5: an index of the extent to which the respondent's friends are reported by the

TABLE 3.2 Model Fit and Explained Variation for Marijuana Use			
Statistic	*SAS*	*SPSS*	*Stata*
D_0 (Intercept-only -2 log likelihood)	294.616	294.616	294.616
D_M (Model -2 log likelihood)	186.359	186.359	186.359
G_M (Model χ^2)	108.257	108.257	108.26
Degrees of freedom	5	5	5
Statistical significance (p)	<.0001	.000	.0000
Hosmer-Lemeshow χ^2	8.755	8.754	4.04
Degrees of freedom	8	8	8
Statistical significance $(p)^a$	.363	.363	.854
Pearson χ^2	261.37	261.44	261.44
Degrees of freedom	151	151	151
Statistical significance $(p)^b$	<.0001	.000	.000
Deviance χ^2	158.27	158.27	–
Degrees of freedom	151	151	–
Statistical significance $(p)^b$	.326	.326	–
R_L^2 (Likelihood ratio R^2)^c	.37	.37	.37
R_M^2 (Geometric mean R^2)	.38	.38	–
R_N^2 (Adjusted geometric mean R^2)	.52	.52	–
R_O^2 (Ordinary least squares R^2)	.44	.44	.44

NOTES: a. Stata 7 used a different method from SAS 8 and SPSS 11 for partitioning cases for the Hosmer-Lemeshow χ^2 test, resulting in a more even partition (20 to 25 cases per decile for Stata, compared with 15 to 25 cases per decile for SAS and SPSS).

b. The Pearson and deviance χ^2 statistics were obtained in SAS using the "scale=" none, deviance, or Pearson specification; in SPSS **nomreg** and **plum** as standard output using the "fit" option; and the Pearson (but not the deviance) goodness-of-fit χ^2 was obtained from Stata using the "lfit" command following Stata **logistic** or **logit**.

c. For SAS and SPSS **logistic**, R_L^2 was not provided directly, but had to be calculated from information provided in the output. For SPSS **nomreg** and **plum** and Stata **logistic**, **logit**, **mlogit**, and **ologit** (all of which can be used for dichotomous dependent variables), R_L^2 was included in the output. For all three packages, $D_0 = 294.616$, $D_M = 186.359$, $G_M = 108.257$ with 5 degrees of freedom and $p = .000$, $R_L^2 = .37$, and $R_O^2 = .44$, indicating agreement among the different routines for estimating the logistic regression model, statistically significant improvement over the intercept-only model, and moderately good explanation of the variation in the dependent variable. For the Hosmer-Lemeshow test statistic, however, SAS and SPSS differ noticeably from Stata. The difference arises because Stata uses a different method to partition the cases into deciles, resulting in deciles that all have 20 to 25 cases, as opposed to SPSS and SAS in which each decile contains 15 to 25 cases, not as evenly distributed as in Stata. SAS produces a Pearson χ^2 goodness-of-fit statistic that is very slightly different from the SPSS and Stata estimates for the same statistic. The SAS and SPSS estimates of the deviance χ^2 statistic, R_M^2, and R_N^2 (none of which are included in Stata) are consistent with one another. The apparent differences in the models thus arise in the comparison of goodness-of-fit statistics. With respect to the statistics in which we are most likely to be interested (G_M, R_L^2, R_O^2), and also with respect to the actual estimates of the coefficients, exponentiated coefficients (odds ratios), their standard errors, and their statistical significance (to be discussed in detail in Chapter 5, but presented here in Table 3.3 to complete the example), there are very slight differences (the last decimal place differs by 1) between SPSS on one hand and SAS and Stata on the other (and hence separate rows in the table) in the coefficient for gender and the intercept, but not in their standard errors and statistical significance, and no differences for the other predictors. In general, there is consistency across the general purpose statistical packages used to estimate logistic regression models.

TABLE 3.3 Logistic Regression Coefficients Associated With Table 3.2

Predictor	b	e^b (Odds Ratio)	Standard Error of b	Wald Statistic (χ^2)	p
Intercept (SAS)	−1.750	0.174	2.028	0.744	.388
(SPSS)	−1.749	0.174	2.028	0.744	.388
(Stata)[a]	−1.750	0.174	2.028	0.744	.388
Gender: Male (SAS)	−1.515	0.220	0.405	14.011	.000
(SPSS)	−1.514	0.220	0.405	14.008	.000
(Stata)	−1.515	0.220	0.405	14.011	.000
Ethnicity: African American	0.245	1.277	0.508	0.233	.630
Ethnicity: Other	0.772	2.164	0.745	1.075	.300
Exposure to delinquent friends	0.407	1.502	0.069	34.345	.000
Belief that law violation is wrong	−0.118	0.889	0.060	3.903	.048

NOTE: a. Stata used a Wald z instead of a Wald χ^2 statistic; the results have been converted to a Wald χ^2 for Stata.

60

respondent as being involved in illegal behavior), and belief that it is wrong to violate the law (BELIEF4: an index of how wrong the respondent believes it is to engage in several specific law-violating behaviors). The first column lists the statistics being compared, while the second, third, and fourth columns present the results from SAS (Version 8) **logistic**, SPSS (Version 11) **logistic**, and Stata (Version 7) **logit**, respectively. The purpose here is to both illustrate the interpretation of the statistics and also note some differences in the results that can be produced by different statistical packages.

SEMI-CONCLUSION: ONLY HALFWAY THERE

The quantitative indicators of model fit, statistical significance of the model improvement over chance prediction, and explained variation presented in this chapter represent only one half of the issue of how well the model works. If quantitative prediction is our only concern, as is so often assumed, the focus should be on the measures presented in this chapter. If, however, qualitative prediction is an additional or even a primary concern, as may be the case especially in applied research, then we need to focus on the prediction tables rather than the comparison of predicted probabilities with observed outcomes or probabilities. This other half of the issue of assessing the quality of prediction of logistic regression models is taken up in the next chapter, in which we continue with a consideration of the results in Table 3.2, and compare the results of quantitative and qualitative prediction. As we shall see in the next chapter, the two approaches do not always yield consistent results, and there are good reasons why they should not be expected to do so.

NOTES

1. Kvålseth uses the term *goodness of fit* instead of *accuracy of prediction* here, but in this book, goodness of fit is used to refer specifically to the difference between the observed model and the model with the best possible fit, given the data, not to the difference between the observed model and the model with no predictors.

2. Criterion 5 is not a consideration in the context of maximum likelihood logistic regression, but may, as indicated later in the chapter, be relevant once one considers alternative methods of estimation for the logistic regression model.

3. Comparisons of performance across different data sets make sense only if the explanatory variables have a meaningfully defined distribution, for example, estimates of population distributions. Otherwise, the criteria are highly sensitive to the dispersion of the explanatory variables actually encountered in the set of data, and this may be somewhat arbitrary by explicit choice or by design. Comparisons may thus be reasonable across random probability samples from the same population, but not across samples from different populations or nonprobability samples from the same population.

4. For example, as the entropy measure of association in SPSS Versions 11 to 16 **genlog** and earlier SPSS versions of **loglinear**.

5. Zheng and Agresti (2000) suggest using R_O^2, possibly modified by a jackknife estimator for bias. DeMaris (2002) suggests a measure very similar to R_O^2, $\Delta = 1 - N^{-1} \sum [\hat{\pi} \cdot (1 - \hat{\pi})|x]/p(1 - p)$, where the denominator $p(1 - p)$ is the observed binomial variance in the dependent variable and the numerator (in which $\hat{\pi}$ represents probability corresponding to p predicted by the model) differs from the binomial variance of $\hat{\pi}$ by $N^{-1}[\sum (\hat{\pi})^2 - N^{-1}(\sum \hat{\pi})^2]$. Simulation results presented by DeMaris indicate that the performance of Δ is very similar to that of R_O^2; that both appear to be slightly better than R_L^2 for estimating "explained risk" when the

dependent variable is considered to be a true dichotomy, rather than a latent continuous variable (in contrast, R^2_{MZ} appears to be best at explaining "explained variance" when the dependent variable represents a latent continuous variable that has been measured as a dichotomy); but that R^2_L also performs reasonably well, and better than measures of "explained risk" other than Δ and R^2_O. In practical terms, Δ is an adjusted R^2_O measure based on binomial variances of the observed and predicted probabilities of being in one or the other category of the dependent variable, and is not considered separately in the present chapter.

6. Further evidence of the dependence of R^2_O on the base rate is offered by Allen and Le (2008). Their simulation study indicates that "among the R^2 analogs, R^2_L appears to be most invariant to the base rate" (and that most of that dependence, small as it is, occurs for base rate below .05 or above .95). They also suggest the use of the *overall odds ratio* (OOR) as a measure of effect size that gives results in an intuitively appealing metric (odds), parallel to the odds ratios for individual effects. The OOR also appears to be independent of the base rate, but they note that the OOR cannot be interpreted as a measure of proportional reduction in error.

7. Based on observations of published research, however, I am concerned that methodological preference sometimes drives conceptualization. It seems that sometimes even when conceptually the variable of interest is a manifest variable (an observable behavior rather than an unobservable "tendency" or other truly unmeasurable variable), whether coded dichotomously or otherwise, researchers sometimes appear to pretend the variable of interest is a latent variable in order to justify the use of, for example, structural equation modeling (SEM) techniques or, in this instance, the use of a measure of explained variation based on the assumption that the dichotomous dependent variable represents a latent continuous dependent variable.

CHAPTER 4

Prediction Tables and Qualitative Approaches to Explained Variation

$\mathbf{I}$n addition to statistics regarding goodness of fit and R^2 analogs, logistic regression programs commonly print classification tables that indicate the predicted and observed values of the dependent variable for the cases in the analysis. These tables resemble the contingency tables, similar to those discussed at the beginning of Chapter 2, which can be produced by standard statistical subroutines such as SAS **freq**, SPSS **crosstabs**, and Stata **tabulate**. In most instances, we will be more interested in how well the model predicts probabilities, $P(Y = 1)$. In other cases, however, we may be more interested in the accurate prediction of group membership, and the classification tables may be of as much or more interest than the overall fit of the model. There is no consensus at present on how to measure the association between the observed and predicted classification of cases based on logistic regression or related methods such as discriminant analysis. There are, however, several good suggestions that can easily be implemented for providing summary measures for classification tables. The best options for analyzing the prediction tables provided by logistic regression packages involve measures of the form

$$\text{Predictive efficiency} = \frac{(\text{Errors without model}) - (\text{Errors with model})}{(\text{Errors without model})} \tag{4.1}$$

which is a *proportional change in error* formula. If the model improves our prediction of the dependent variable, this is the same as a *proportional reduction in error* (PRE) formula. It is possible under some circumstances, however, that a model will actually do worse than chance at predicting the values of the dependent variable. When that occurs, the predictive efficiency is negative, and we have a proportional *increase* in error. The errors with the model are simply the number of cases for which the predicted value of the dependent variable is incorrect. The errors without the model differ for different indices and depend on whether we are using a prediction, classification, or selection model. The distinctions among these three types of models are illustrated in Table 4.1 and described on page 65.

TABLE 4.1	**Prediction, Classification, and Selection Models**	
Type of Model	*Constraints on Prediction*	*Examples*
Prediction	None; all cases may, in principle, belong to a single group; marginal frequencies should be the same for predicted and observed classification.	Who will succeed in college? (Maybe everyone, maybe no one.)
		Which convicted felons will commit additional crimes if they are released on probation or parole? (Maybe none, maybe all.)
		Which eligible enlistees or conscripts will have serious emotional or behavioral problems in the military? (Maybe none, maybe all.)
Classification	Cases should, in principle, belong to two or more distinct groups; marginal frequencies should be the same for predicted and observed classification.	How can we distinguish between individuals who succeed and individuals who fail in college? (Some will succeed, some will fail, and there is no fixed number or proportion in either category.)
		How can we distinguish between individuals who will and will not commit crimes if released on probation or parole? (Some will, some will not, and there is no fixed number or proportion.)
		How can we distinguish between individuals who will and will not have emotional or behavioral problems in the military? (Some will, some will not, and there is no fixed number or proportion.)
Selection	Cases should, in principle, belong to two or more distinct groups; marginal distributions of observed and predicted classifications need not be, and in fact probably will not be, equal; that is, the base rate and the selection ratio will probably be unequal.	Which 5,000 students shall we select for admission to our freshman class? (There may be too many or too few who look like they will succeed, but we have 5,000 slots to fill.)
		Which convicted felons should we place in our 500 prison cells, and which shall we release on probation or parole, even though we know some may fail on probation or parole? (We only have so many prison beds we can fill.)
		Which 25% of eligible enlistees should we reject for military service? (There may be more or fewer that we expect to succeed or fail, but we have a fixed number of slots to fill).

PREDICTION, CLASSIFICATION, AND SELECTION MODELS

In prediction models, the attempt is made to classify cases according to whether they satisfy some criterion: success in college, absence of behavioral or emotional problems in the military, involvement in illegal behavior after release from prison. In prediction models, there are no a priori constraints on the number or proportion of cases predicted to have or not to have the specified behavior or characteristic. In principle, it is possible (but not necessary) to have the same number of cases *predicted* as "positive" (having the behavior or characteristic; e.g., "successes") and "negative" (not having the behavior or characteristics, e.g., "failures") as are *observed* to be positive or negative. That is, there is nothing that constrains the *marginal distributions* (the number or proportion of cases in each category, positive or negative) of predicted and observed frequencies to be equal or unequal. In particular, all cases may be predicted to belong to the same category, that is, the sample or population may be *homogeneous*. In practical terms, prediction models are appropriate when identical treatment of all groups ("lock 'em all up" or "let 'em all go") is a viable option.

In classification models, the goal is similar to that of prediction models, but there is the added assumption that the cases are truly heterogeneous. Correspondingly, the evaluation of a classification model imposes the constraint that the model should classify as many cases into each category as are actually observed in each category. The proportion or number of cases *observed* to be in each category (the base rate) should be the same as the proportion or number of cases *predicted* to be in each category (the *selection ratio*). To the extent that a model fails to meet this criterion, it fails as a classification model. Complete homogeneity is an unacceptable solution for a classification model. Practically speaking, classification models are appropriate when heterogeneity is assumed, and identical treatment of all groups is not a viable option.

In selection models (Wiggins 1973), the concern is with "accepting" or "rejecting" cases for inclusion in a group, based both on whether they will satisfy some criterion for success in the group and on the minimum required, maximum allowable, or specified number of cases that may (or must) be included in the group. In selection models, the base rate may or may not be equal to the selection ratio. For example, a company may need to fill 20 positions from a pool of 200 applicants. The selection ratio will be $20/200 = .10$ (10%) regardless of whether the base rate (the observed probability of success on the job) is 5% or 20%, half or twice the selection ratio. The classification tables provided in logistic regression packages may naturally be regarded as prediction or classification models. They may be used to construct selection models, but they must be altered (unless, purely by coincidence, the selection ratio turns out to be equal to the base rate) to ensure that the correct number of cases is selected, most typically by selecting a cutoff point greater than or less than .5 to decide which cases are assigned to which category, based on the predicted probability of membership in that category. Either the base rate or the selection ratio may be fixed, the former by sampling on the dependent variable or by sampling a population with a known base rate, the latter as a matter of policy or of a decision by the researcher regarding the number of proportion of cases to be assigned by the model to each category of the dependent variable. Once a cutoff is set (other than the default value of .500), the model effectively becomes a selection model. The logistic regression model itself, however, remains the same, still maximizing the likelihood function. In principle, there is nothing to prevent changing the calculation of the model to maximize some other criterion, including, for example, φ_p (discussed below) or some other index of predictive efficiency if the explicit goal is accuracy of qualitative prediction.

COMMON MEASURES OF ASSOCIATION FOR CONTINGENCY TABLES AS INDICES OF PREDICTIVE EFFICIENCY

Among the various measures that have been considered as indices of predictive efficiency are several measures of association that are commonly employed to analyze contingency tables: phi, Goodman and Kruskal's gamma, kappa, the contingency coefficient, Pearson's r, and the odds ratio (Farrington and Loeber 1989; Mieczkowski 1990; Ohlin and Duncan 1949). The problem with using common contingency table measures of association to analyze 2×2 or larger prediction tables lies in the distinction between (a) the strength of a relationship between an independent variable X and a dependent variable Y and (b) the strength of the relationship between predicted group membership $\hat{Y}$ and observed group membership Y. These differences are illustrated in Figure 4.1. Table A in Figure 4.1 represents the general format to be used throughout this section in designating cell and marginal frequencies in 2×2 tables; Table B represents the hypothetical relationship between ethnicity and political orientation; and Table C illustrates the hypothetical relationship between predicted and observed political orientation.

Although Tables B and C are numerically identical, the inferences to be drawn from them are very different. In Table B, knowledge of ethnicity allows us to predict political orientation with a proportional reduction in error or PRE (Bohrnstedt and Knoke 1994:164; Costner 1965) of .20 according to Goodman and Kruskal's lambda or .04 according to Goodman and Kruskal's tau. In Table C, the PRE is the same—but only if we predict the *opposite* of what the hypothetical model predicts. Actually, the model does *worse* than chance in predicting political orientation (a situation that may arise naturally with skewed data, or with the application of a prediction model developed from one set of data to another set of data). If every case were *misclassified,* both lambda and tau would have a value of 1.00 for Table C; they would make no distinction between perfectly accurate classification and perfect *misclassification.* Pearson's r and its equivalents for 2×2 tables, Kendall's tau, and phi when phi is calculated as,

$$\phi = \frac{(ad - bc)}{\sqrt{(a+b)(a+c)(b+d)(c+d)}},$$

could indicate misclassification with a negative sign and may be interpreted as PRE measures when squared. For larger tables with unordered categories, however, Pearson's r and Kendall's tau cannot be used, and phi becomes Cramer's V, which no longer has a PRE interpretation. The odds ratio may also be used for 2×2 tables, but for larger tables, two or more odds ratios must be calculated, and the odds ratio no longer provides a single summary measure of accuracy of prediction. On the whole, it does not appear that the application of common measures of association for contingency tables to predictive tables provides a straightforward or general solution to the problem of estimating accuracy of prediction. Pearson's r and r^2, or φ and φ^2, are reasonable indices for use with 2×2, but not larger, tables, as long as we remember to interpret them contingent on the sign of r or φ.

λ_p, τ_p, AND φ_p

Equation 4.1 provides a basic form for indices of predictive efficiency. Errors with the model for all of the indices is simply the number of cases misclassified when we use the model and is analogous

FIGURE 4.1   Association Versus Prediction

Table A: Standard format for prediction tables

		Predicted Y:		
		Positive (success)	Negative (failure)	
Observed Y:	Positive (success)	a	b	a+b
	Negative (failure)	c	d	c+d
		a+c	b+d	a+b+c+d

Table B: Ethnicity and Political Orientation

		X: Ethnicity:		
		European	Non-European	
Political Orientation:	Conservative	20	30	50
	Liberal	30	20	50
		50	50	100

Table C: Predicted and Observed Political Orientation

		Predicted Political Orientation:		
		Conservative	Liberal	
Observed Political Orientation:	Conservative	20	30	50
	Liberal	30	20	50
		50	50	100

For Tables B and C, Goodman and Kruskal's $\lambda = 0.20$;
Goodman and Kruskal's $\tau = \varphi^2 = r^2 = 0.04$.

to the error sum of squares. It may be calculated as $N - \Sigma f_{ii}$ where N is the sample size, f_{ij} is a case for which i is the predicted value and j is the observed value, $i \neq j$, and f_{ii} represents a case for which the predicted value equals the observed value. This is equal to the sum of the cells $b + c$ in Table A of Figure 4.1. Errors without the model is analogous to the total sum of squares and depends on whether we are using a prediction model, a classification model, or a selection model. For a prediction model, the approach most closely analogous to linear regression (with an interval level dependent variable) is to use the mode of the dependent variable as the predicted value for all cases (analogous to using the mean in linear regression). The number of errors without the model is thus $N - n_{mode}$, where n_{mode} is the number of cases observed to have the modal value of the dependent variable. This method of defining errors without the model is the same as the one used in defining Goodman and Kruskal's λ for contingency tables with nominal variables (see Chapter 2), and it gives us an index first proposed by Ohlin and Duncan (1949). Because of the similarity to Goodman and Kruskal's λ, the index is here referred to as lambda-p or λ_p, where the subscript p refers to its use with prediction tables, and $\lambda_p = [(N - n_{mode}) - (N - \Sigma f_{ii})]/(N - n_{mode})$. Lambda-p is a PRE measure like R^2 when it is positive, but if the model does worse than predicting the mode, λ_p may be negative, indicating the proportional *increase* in error. The possible values of λ_p vary depending on the marginal distributions. In general, the full range of possible values for λ_p in all tables with N cases is from $1 - N$ to 1 (see Appendix B).

For a classification model, an appropriate definition of the expected error without the model is

$$\text{Errors without model} = \sum_{i=1}^{N} f_i[(N - f_i)/N],$$

where N is the sample size and f_i is the number of cases observed in category i. This is the same formula for error without the model as is used for Goodman and Kruskal's τ, discussed in Chapter 2. An index based on this definition of errors without the model was proposed by Klecka (1980) for use with discriminant analysis models. Parallel to λ_p, Klecka's index will be referred to as tau-p (τ_p), or tau for prediction tables, and $\tau_p = [(\Sigma f_i(N - f_i)/N) - (N - \Sigma f_{ii})]/(\Sigma f_i(N - f_i)/N)$.

Like λ_p, τ_p is a measure of change. Unlike λ_p, τ_p requires that even in the estimation of error without the model, cases must be separated into distinct groups or categories and not all placed in the same category. In effect, τ_p adjusts the expected number of errors for the base rate. Accuracy of prediction is thus secondary, subject to the a priori assumption of heterogeneity. As with λ_p, a value of 1 for τ_p indicates that all cases are correctly classified, and a negative value for τ_p indicates that the prediction model does worse than expected (based on the observed marginal distribution) in predicting the classification of cases. Secondary properties of τ_p, as detailed in Appendix B, include the fact that $\tau_p \geq \lambda_p$ because the number of errors without the model for τ_p will be equal to or larger than the number of errors without the model for λ_p. For tables with equal marginal distributions, τ_p varies between -1 and $+1$, but the maximum value of τ_p is < 1 when the marginal distributions are unequal. In the worst possible case, with extremely skewed and inconsistent marginal distributions, the minimum value of τ_p is equal to $1 - N^2/[2(N - 1)]$. The range of τ_p is not constant but varies from 1 to 2 for different marginal distributions. A smaller range occurs for models in which τ_p is negative and large in absolute value.

It is also possible to construct a proportional change in error measure of accuracy of prediction for selection models. For such a measure, the error with the model will be $(N - \Sigma f_{ii})$, or from Figure 4.1, the sum of the cells $b + c$, just as it is for λ_p and τ_p. Error with the model should depend on both the base rate, $B = (a + b)/N$, and the selection ratio, $S = (a + c)/N$. Given B, S, and N, we know the expected value of cell *a* (Table A, Figure 4.1): $E(a) = BSN$. Because a 2×2 prediction table has only 1 degree of freedom, once the expected value of *a* is known, then given the marginal distribution, the expected value of all the other cells is known and is identical to the expected values used in calculating the χ^2 statistic. The expected error is $E(b + c) = [(a + b)(b + d)/N + (c + d) (a + c)/N]$. Plugging these values into the PRE formula, we obtain a proportional change in error measure, φ_p, so named because φ_p like φ is based on comparisons between observed and expected values for individual cells, rather than rows or columns as with λ_p and τ_p, because the numerical value of φ_p is typically close to the numerical value of φ for tables with consistent marginals, and φ_p and φ have the same sign because they have the same numerator; and

$$\varphi_p = [(a + b)(b + d)/N + (c + d)(a + c)/N - (b + c)]/[(a + b)(b + d)/N + (c + d)(a + c)/N]$$
$$= [(a + b)(b + d) + (c + d)(a + c) - N(b + c)]/[(a + b)(b + d) + (c + d)(a + c)]$$
$$= (ad - bc)/.5[(a + b)(b + d) + (c + d)(a + c)].$$

For tables with equal marginal distributions, φ_p has a maximum value of +1. In general, it varies between −1 and +1, but the actual maximum, minimum, and range depend on the marginal distributions. As long as errors without the model are calculated as the sum of the expected frequencies for cells off the main diagonal based on the base rate and the selection ratio, and errors with the model are calculated as the sum of the observed frequencies in those same cells, φ_p can be extended to tables larger than 2×2 and still retain a proportional change in error interpretation. For 2×2 tables, it can be shown (see Appendix B) that $|\varphi_p| \leq |\varphi|$ and that φ_p has the same sign as φ and Pearson's *r* (the numerator is the same, $ad - bc$, as for φ). When all cases are correctly predicted, $\varphi_p = 1$. Otherwise, $\varphi_p < 1$, even when the maximum possible number of cases for a given set of marginals is correctly classified.

Phi-p can be adjusted by adding the minimum number of errors, $|(a + b) - (a + c)| = |b - c|$, to the expected number of errors without the model. This results in a coefficient that (a) retains the proportional change in error interpretation (because the adjustment is built into the calculation of the expected error) and (b) still may have negative values if the model is pathologically inaccurate. For extremely poor models, the revised index still has maximum values less than one, even when the maximum number of cases is correctly classified, and the increment over φ_p is small. Based again on similarities with φ, we may designate this adjusted φ_p as φ_p'. Note, however, that φ_p' cannot be calculated as $\varphi_p/\max(\varphi_p)$; to do so would destroy the proportional change in error interpretation for the measure and would leave the measure undefined when the maximum value of φ_p was zero.

STATISTICAL SIGNIFICANCE OF λ_p, τ_p, AND φ_p

Lambda-p, tau-p, and phi-p are analogous to R^2 as measures of substantive significance. For statistical significance, an analog to the *F* test is the binomial test for small *N* or the normal approximation to the binomial test for larger *N*. Let N = total sample size, P_e = (errors without model)/N, and p_e = (errors with model)/N. The binomial statistic *d* may then be computed as

$$d = (P_e - P_e)/\sqrt{P_e(1 - P_e)/N},$$

and d is approximately normally distributed (Bulmer 1979). Note that what is being compared is not the proportion of cases in each category but the *proportion of cases correctly or incorrectly classified* by the model. This test is the same for λ_p, τ_p, and φ_p, for predictive, classification, and selection models. Only the definition of errors without the model differs.

For a two-tailed test, the null hypothesis is that there is no difference between the proportion of errors with and without the prediction model, and the alternative hypothesis is that the proportion of errors with the prediction model is not equal to the proportion of errors without the prediction model. For a one-tailed test specifying that the model results in increased accuracy of prediction of the dependent variable, the null hypothesis is that the proportion of errors with the prediction model is no smaller than the proportion of errors without the prediction model, and the alternative hypothesis is that the proportion of errors with the prediction model is less than the proportion of errors without the prediction model. If we want to know whether the prediction model improves our ability to predict the classification of the cases, the one-tailed test is more appropriate, and a negative value of λ_p, τ_p, or φ_p will result in a negative value for d and failure to reject the null hypothesis.

In the binomial d test of statistical significance, the value of the observed classification is taken as a given; the test indicates whether the proportion predicted incorrectly with the model (which, by assumption, depends on the model, and is thus variable) differs significantly from the proportion incorrectly predicted without the model (which depends only on the marginal distribution, not on the model, and is assumed to be fixed). This form of the binomial test, which explicitly uses the expected number of errors as the criterion by which the number of errors generated by the model is to be judged, is preferable to the binomial test for a *difference* of two proportions (Bulmer 1979:145), which assumes that the two proportions (errors with the model and errors without the model) are based on separate samples (possibly of unequal size), a condition that is clearly not met when comparing observed and predicted classifications taken from the classification tables generated by logistic regression, or expected and actual errors, both of which are derived from these tables. The binomial test for the difference of two proportions may, however, be useful if we want to test whether the overall predictive accuracy (percent correctly predicted) is statistically significantly different for two *separate* prediction models. Even in this situation, however, we would want a separate test to indicate whether either or both of the prediction models was significantly better than chance in reproducing the observed classification of cases.

OTHER PROPOSED INDICES OF PREDICTIVE EFFICIENCY

Maddala (1983:76–77) reviewed three indices of predictive efficiency proposed in the econometric literature. He appropriately dismissed one as being unable to distinguish a perfectly accurate model from a perfectly inaccurate model, a characteristic it shares with many of the measures of association commonly used in the analysis of contingency tables. A second, which considered both "first best" and "second best" guesses was more akin to R^2 analogs than to indices of predictive efficiency, insofar as a "near miss" (the second most likely category, according to the prediction model) was credited as an accurate choice. The third typically varied from -1 to $+.50$, depending on the marginal distribution, and produced values similar to φ and Pearson's r. Because it lacks a PRE interpretation, it appears to have little or no advantage over φ or Pearson's r.

Loeber and Dishion (1983), Copas and Loeber (1990), and Farrington and Loeber (1989) proposed a measure they called Relative Improvement Over Chance, or RIOC. Although Loeber and his colleagues applied the RIOC to the analysis of prediction and classification tables, the measure corrects for differences between the base rate and the selection ratio, an approach appropriate for selection models rather than classification or prediction models. This measure is identical to the coefficient φ', the φ coefficient corrected for the marginal distribution. Unlike φ, φ' has no PRE interpretation. The measure varies between -1 (for perfectly inaccurate prediction, *if cells b and c in Table A of Figure 4.1 are both nonzero*) and $+1$. If *either one* of the cells (b or c) containing incorrect predictions is equal to zero, RIOC $= 1$, *regardless of how small a proportion of the cases are correctly classified* (a problem it shares with Yule's Q, a measure of association sometimes used for contingency tables). Even if more than 90% of the cases are misclassified, RIOC may have a value of 1. Copas and Loeber (1990) noted this property and indicated that in this situation it would be a misinterpretation to regard a value of 1 as indicating perfect prediction. This leads to two questions. How *should* we interpret the value of RIOC in this situation? What value *does* indicate perfect prediction for RIOC? Ambiguity of interpretation is an undesirable quality in any measure of change, and there are enough better alternatives that the use of the RIOC measure should be avoided.

Cohen's kappa, as described for example in Liebetrau (1983), was constructed specifically as a measure of agreement between two judges, but can be more generally interpreted as a measure of agreement between two methods of classifying cases. In this respect, kappa differs from other measures of association for contingency tables. If p_{ij} is the probability that an item is classified into category i by one method and j by another, where i and j range from 1 to M (M representing the number of categories), $\theta_1 = \Sigma_i p_{ii}$ (the proportion of cases on which the two methods agree) and $\theta_2 = \Sigma_i p_{i+} p_{+i}$ (representing the proportion of cases on which the two methods would be expected to agree purely by chance, where p_{i+} represents the row sum and p_{+i} represents the column sum for category i), then $\kappa = (\theta_1 - \theta_2)/(1 - \theta_2)$. Values of κ can range from $-\theta_2/(1 - \theta_2)$ if the two methods disagree completely to 1 if the two methods agree completely for a given set of marginal totals. A maximum likelihood estimator for κ under the multinomial sampling model is $\hat{\kappa} = [N\Sigma_i N_{ii} - \Sigma_i N_{i+} N_{+i}]/[N^2 - \Sigma_i N_{i+} N_{+i}]$. For sufficiently large samples, $\hat{\kappa}$ has sampling variance $\sigma_{\hat{\kappa}}^2 = \{1/[n(1 - \theta_2)^2]\} [\theta_2 + (\theta_2)^2 - \Sigma_i p_{i+} p_{+i}(p_{i+} + p_{+i})]$ (under the assumption of independence) and is approximately normally distributed with mean κ, allowing us to calculate inferential statistics for κ. A related measure is the Coleman-Light measure of conditional agreement, κ_i, in which probabilities are calculated conditionally with respect to a particular rating of one of the methods. As described by Liebetrau (1983), $\kappa_i = (p_{ii} - p_{i+} p_{+i})/(p_{i+} - p_{i+} p_{+i})$; the maximum likelihood estimator of κ_i under the multinomial sampling model is $\kappa_i = (NN_{ii} - N_{i+} N_{+i})/(NN_{i+} - N_{i+} N_{+i})$. For large samples, κ_i is approximately normally distributed with mean κ_i and variance (under independence) $\sigma_{\kappa}^2 = [p_{+i}(1 - p_{+i})]/Np_{i+}(1 - p_{+i})$. A disadvantage to κ is that it can be 0 even if the two classifications are not completely independent; unlike κ, however, κ_i is 0 only when the classifications from the two methods are independent. Neither κ nor κ_i has a PRE interpretation, and neither makes any distinction among prediction, classification, and selection models. I am unaware of any dependency of κ or κ_i on the base rate. Clearly, κ_i, conditioning on the observed classification seems preferable to κ, and it may be a reasonable alternative to λ_p, τ_p, and φ_p as an index of predictive efficiency if a PRE interpretation is not a consideration. More generally, however, I believe λ_p, τ_p, and φ_p should be preferred to κ_i.

COMPARING INDICES OF PREDICTIVE EFFICIENCY

Table 4.2 takes Table 3.1 on page 55 from the previous chapter and expands it to include λ_p, τ_p, and φ_p. Menard (2000) provided empirical evidence that when the base rate alone is manipulated, λ_p and φ_p are highly correlated with the base rate, but τ_p is not. Soderstrom and Leitner (1997) compared λ_p, τ_p, and φ_p, and also the RIOC and percentage correct, for models in which both base rate and selection ratio, plus sample size and reliability of predictors, were manipulated. Based on Monte Carlo simulations, they found that φ_p was least affected by the base rate, followed by τ_p and then λ_p, for models including continuous predictors. For models involving only dichotomous predictors, however, τ_p was less sensitive than φ_p to changes in the base rate (and RIOC often could not be calculated at all, for reasons noted above). They concluded that across a broad range of conditions, φ_p and τ_p were the most appropriate choices as indices of predictive efficiency. Taken together, these results reinforce the suggestion that the index should be selected consistent with the nature of the model and, in particular, that τ_p is most appropriate for classification models, and φ_p is most appropriate for selection models. These indices may also be applied to prediction tables generated by procedures other than logistic regression and are not limited to dichotomous variables; they are applicable to any prediction table in which correct predictions can be distinguished from incorrect predictions.

COMPARING R^2 ANALOGS WITH INDICES OF PREDICTIVE EFFICIENCY

One reason for the lack of consensus about indices of predictive efficiency may be the fact that researchers are more often interested in the question of quantitative prediction or explained variation of the model, as indicated by R^2 analogs, than in qualitative prediction or how accurately the model qualitatively classifies cases into the discrete categories of the dependent variable, as indicated by the classification table and indices of predictive efficiency. Especially for theory testing, "how close" the predicted value is to the correct value is simply regarded more important than "right or wrong" accuracy of predicted classification. Often the two approaches, goodness of fit and accuracy of prediction, will produce consistent results. It is entirely possible, however, to have a model in which qualitative prediction is good but quantitative prediction is poor, or vice versa.

Figures 4.2 and 4.3 illustrate how R^2 analogs and indices of predictive efficiency may lead to very different substantive conclusions about how well the model predicts the dependent variable. In Figure 4.2, hypothetical data are presented for a single dependent variable, TRUE, and a single predictor, P1. The SPSS output has been edited to include R_L^2, R^2, λ_p, and τ_p. For the 40 cases analyzed in Figure 4.2, the model fits well. G_M = Model χ^2 = 20.123 and is statistically significant (significance $p = .0000$), leading us to reject the null hypothesis that the independent variable, P1, is not related to the dependent variable, TRUE. $R_L^2 = .363$ suggesting a moderate association between TRUE and P1. The binomial d is the same for both λ_p and τ_p (50% expected error for both): $d = 5.060$, with statistical significance $p = .000$. Both τ_p and λ_p are equal to .80, indicating that the independent variable allows us to classify the cases with a very high degree of accuracy, as reflected in the classification table. Overall, the accuracy of qualitative prediction, the ability of the model to correctly classify cases into discrete categories, is considerably higher than the accuracy of quantitative prediction, the ability of the model to predict the precise value of the probability, $P(y_j = 1)$. The plot of observed groups and predicted probabilities at the bottom of Figure 4.2 indicates that

TABLE 4.2 Comparison of Coefficients of Determination for Logistic Regression Analysis

Coefficient of Determination	Residual Variation Criterion (From Efron 1978)	Interpretation as Proportional Reduction in Residual Variation (or Some Comparable Measure)	Fixed Interval With Maximum = Perfect Fit and Minimum = No Relationship	Comparability Across Models (e.g., $R^2 = .5$ Has the Same Meaning in Different Models for the Same Data Set and in the Same Model Across Different Data Sets)
R_O^2	Squared error	Partially; proportional reduction in squared error (numeric values)	Yes, but for some models, only if adjusted	Problematic; base rate dependent; but permits comparisons with OLS models
R_L^2	Entropy	Yes; proportional reduction in −2 log likelihood statistic	Yes, for all models	Yes
R_M^2	Entropy	Partially; geometric mean improvement per observation in likelihood	Only if adjusted (see R_M^2)	Problematic; base rate dependent
R_N^2	Entropy	No	Yes	Problematic; base rate dependent
R_C^2	Entropy	No	Only if adjusted	Problematic; base rate dependent
λ_p	Qualitative difference	Yes; proportional change in error of prediction based on predicting the mode	Partially; 1 = perfect fit, 0 = no relationship, but can be negative	Problematic; base rate dependent; but appropriate for pure prediction models
τ_p	Qualitative difference	Yes; proportional change in error of prediction based on predicting proportional to the base rate	Partially; 1 = perfect fit, 0 = no relationship, but can be negative	Yes; not completely uncorrelated with base rate, but less so than other indices of predictive efficiency
φ_p	Qualitative difference	Yes; proportional change in error of prediction based on marginal frequencies	Partially; 1 = perfect fit, 0 = no relationship, but can be negative	Problematic but potentially useful; results from Menard (2000) indicate problems in one specific application, but simulation results from Soderstrom and Leitner (1997) do not indicate problems with correlation with base rate

---

FIGURE 4.2 SPSS Logistic Regression Output for Hypothetical "Good Prediction" Data

Classification Table(a)

			Predicted		
			TRUE		Percentage Correct
	Observed		0	1	
Step 0	TRUE	0	18	2	90.0
		1	2	18	90.0
	Overall Percentage				90.0

a The cut value is .500

Omnibus Tests of Model Coefficients

		Chi-square	df	Sig.
Step 1	Step	20.123	1	.000
	Block	20.123	1	.000
	Model	20.123	1	.000

R_L^2 = .363
R^2 = .408
τ_p = .80
λ_p = .80

Model Summary

Step	-2 Log likelihood	Cox & Snell R^2	Nagelkerke R^2
1	35.329	.395	.527

Variables in the Equation

		B	S.E.	Wald	df	Sig.	Exp(B)
Step 1(a)	P1	8.203	2.894	8.035	1	.005	3653.109
	Constant	-4.102	1.505	7.432	1	.006	.017

a Variable(s) entered on step 1: P1.

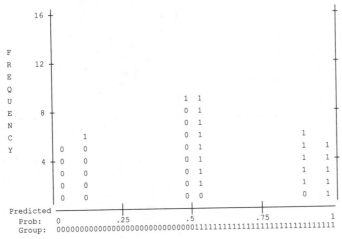

Observed Groups and Predicted Probabilities

```
         16 +                                                   +
              
    F
    R
    E
    Q    12 +                                                   +
    U
    E         8 +                 1 1                           +
    N                             0 1
    C                             0 1
    Y                   1         0 1             1
              4 +   0   0         0 1             1   1         +
                    0   0         0 1             1   1
                    0   0         0 1             1   1
                    0   0         0 1             1   1
                    0   0         0 0             0   1
Predicted  --------------------------------------------------------
  Prob:    0        .25          .5         .75          1
  Group:   0000000000000000000000000000011111111111111111111111111111

              Predicted Probability is of Membership for 1
              The Cut Value is .50
              Symbols: 0 - 0
                       1 - 1
              Each Symbol Represents 1 Case.
```

FIGURE 4.3   SPSS Logistic Regression Output for Hypothetical "Poor Prediction" Data

Classification Table(a,b)

			Predicted		
			TRUE		Percentage Correct
	Observed		0	1	
Step 0	TRUE	0	11	9	.55
		1	9	11	.55
	Overall Percentage				.55

a Constant is included in the model.
b The cut value is .500

Model Summary

Step	-2 Log likelihood	Cox & Snell R^2	Nagelkerke R^2
1	37.477	.362	.483

Omnibus Tests of Model Coefficients

		Chi-square	df	Sig.
Step 1	Step	17.974	1	.000
	Block	17.974	1	.000
	Model	17.974	1	.000

R_L^2 =   .324
R^2 =   .356
τ_p =   .10
λ_p =   .10

Variables in the Equation

		B	S.E.	Wald	df	Sig.	Exp(B)
Step 1(a)	P2	7.193	2.497	8.299	1	.004	1329.985
	Constant	-3.596	1.311	7.527	1	.006	.027

a Variable(s) entered on step 1: P2.

Observed Groups and Predicted Probabilities

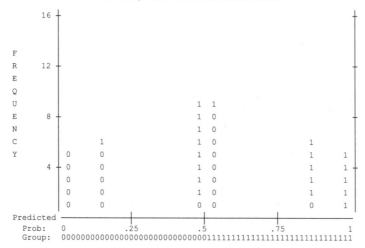

Predicted Probability is of Membership for 1
The Cut Value is .50
Symbols: 0 - 0
          1 - 1
Each Symbol Represents 1 Case.

the predicted probabilities are sometimes very high, and sometimes close to .5, the cutoff for classification into $(Y = 1)$ or $(Y = 0)$. Accuracy of prediction is very high, even for cases whose predicted probability of belonging in $(Y = 1)$ is close to .5.

In Figure 4.3, G_M is again statistically significant, and both R_L^2 and R^2 indicate a moderately strong relationship between the dependent variable, TRUE, and the new predictor, P2. However, tau-p and lambda-p indicate no more than a weak relationship between the observed and predicted classification of the cases, and the binomial $d = .632$, with statistical significance $p = .264$ (one-tailed), suggests that the classification on the dependent variable is not statistically significantly related to the values of the independent variable. The plot of observed groups and predicted probabilities indicates why. Now, instead of accurate prediction when the predicted probability is close to .5, predictions close to .5 are nearly all inaccurate. For 26 of the 40 cases, the predicted probabilities are the same for P1 and P2. For the other 14, the predicted probability changed by .02, either from .49 to .51 or from .51 to .49. This had little impact on R_L^2, R^2, and G_M, but it had a tremendous impact on the indices of predictive efficiency. While the data in Figures 4.2 and 4.3 were artificially constructed, it is not uncommon in practical applications with real data to find similar (though usually not so extreme) discrepancies in the evaluation of the model based on R^2 analogs as opposed to indices of predictive efficiency.

SENSITIVITY, SPECIFICITY, AND RECEIVER OPERATING CHARACTERISTICS (ROC) CURVES

Consider a dichotomous dependent variable coded such that 0 represents failure and 1 represents success. In making qualitative predictions, we may be interested separately in the *sensitivity* of our predictions, the probability of observing a success when success is the predicted outcome, or the "true positive" rate, and the *specificity* of our predictions, the probability of observing a failure (i.e., *not* observing a success) when failure is the predicted outcome, or the true negative rate. If we always predict success, we have 100% sensitivity but 0% specificity, and conversely, if we always predict failure, we have 0% sensitivity but 100% specificity. In between predicting 0% and 100% success lies a continuum of possible cutoff points, with different associated levels of sensitivity and specificity. These cutoff points correspond to the cutoff points used in the prediction tables commonly available in logistic regression routines in SAS, SPSS, and Stata.

By default, logistic regression prediction tables typically use .5 as the cutoff. If the predicted probability of success is .5 or larger, the case is qualitatively predicted to be a success; if the predicted probability is less than .5, the case is predicted to be a failure. As noted above, however, there are alternatives to the default cutoff for classification and selection models. A second possibility, appropriate to selection models, is to set the cutoff to achieve some minimally acceptable value of *either* the specificity *or* the sensitivity. Since sensitivity and specificity are inversely related, it is impossible to maximize both at the same time, but selecting a cutoff that corresponds to the *minimum* acceptable value of one maximizes the other, subject to the requirement that the first be greater than or equal to some specific value. For example, one might choose a cutoff with a sensitivity of 67% (67% of those who succeed in treatment are predicted to do so). Subject to this requirement, specificity (the percent of those predicted to fail in treatment who actually fail in treatment) will be maximized when sensitivity is set to 67%, the minimum allowable value for sensitivity. As suggested by the example, the selection of a specific cutoff may be motivated by practical considerations such as selecting individuals for treatment.

A third possibility, appropriate for classification models, is to make the cutoff point equal to the base rate, thereby setting the selection ratio equal to the base rate. This has the virtue of counteracting the tendency of logistic regression to overpredict the modal category and is the logical procedure for selection (as opposed to prediction or classification) models. Similar results can be obtained graphically by selecting the cutoff point at which sensitivity and specificity are equal, as suggested by Hosmer and Lemeshow (2000:161). If we plot sensitivity and specificity on the same graph, relative to different cutoffs from 0 to 1, the result is a pair of curves, one for sensitivity that starts at 1 (100%) for a cutoff of 0 and declines to 0 (0%) for a cutoff of 1, and one for specificity that starts at 0 (0%) for a cutoff of 0 and increases to 1 (100%) for a cutoff of 1. The point at which the two curves cross is the point at which sensitivity is equal to specificity. This crossover occurs close to where the cutoff is equal to the base rate. It is possible to calculate this point precisely but may be operationally easier and conceptually more straightforward to just select the base rate as the cutoff point.

Sensitivity and specificity may also be used as a basis for calculating a measure of explained variation. In this approach, sensitivity is used to define the y-axis and the quantity $(1 - \text{specificity})$ is used to define the x-axis, producing a single curve called the *receiver operating characteristic curve,* or *ROC curve*. The ROC curve has been used in information theoretical studies of signal processing and psychological studies of perception but has been most extensively used and developed in conjunction with biomedical studies of diagnostic tests (Pepe 2002). The ROC curve is also closely related to the Lorenz curve and its associated indices, used long and extensively in the study of income and wealth inequality (Allison 1978). For both the ROC and the Lorenz curve, the "null" situation (no effect of the predictors for the ROC curve, no inequality for the Lorenz curve) can be represented by a straight line from the point (0, 0) to the point (1, 1), a diagonal line 45° from the horizontal.

The area under the ROC curve, or AUC, is sometimes used as a measure of explained variation. If AUC = .5, this represents the area under the 45° line, and it corresponds to the situation in which the independent variables have no predictive utility. If AUC is used as the measure of explained variation, it is possible to calculate standard errors and confidence intervals (Stata 2003), but the proper test is whether AUC is significantly different from .5, not from 0 (agreement beyond chance). Alternatively, we can define $R^2_{ROC} = 2\,(\text{AUC} - .5 = 2)\,A_R$, where A_R is the area between the ROC curve and the 45° line. This parallels the construction of the Gini coefficient, which can be calculated as $G = 2A_L$, where A_L is the area between the Lorenz curve and the 45° line. R^2_{ROC} varies between 0 and 1, and if we define the area between the 45° line and the ROC curve as the variation to be explained, then R^2_{ROC} can be interpreted as a PRE measure of explained variation. R^2_{ROC} so defined combines elements of an index of predictive efficiency and an R^2 analog and should probably be considered a third, separate class of measure of explained variation. Like an index of predictive efficiency, it is based on qualitative prediction. Because it represents the full range of specificity and sensitivity, however, it encompasses the full range of indices of predictive efficiency, instead of being dependent on a particular cutoff, in contrast to the indices of predictive efficiency described earlier, all of which depend on the specific cutoff used in a particular prediction table. In this respect, then, it more closely resembles the R^2 analogs, which are likewise independent of the specific cutoff used in the prediction tables.

Although derived from sensitivity and specificity, the ROC curve masks the distinction between the two, and it may be useful to present sensitivity and specificity in addition to R^2_{ROC} if the decision is made to use the ROC curve to assess explained variation. Because the ROC curve is defined specifically for a dichotomous outcome such as success or failure, it is not directly applicable to models for polytomous dependent variables. Subjecting R^2_{ROC} to the same analysis used for the other R^2 analogs and indices of predictive efficiency used in Menard (2000), it appears that, as one would expect, R^2_{ROC} was positively correlated (Pearson's $r = .65$, $r^2 = .42$) with the percentage of cases correctly classified by the model with a .5 cutoff. In addition, it was modestly negatively correlated (Pearson's $r = -.57$, $r^2 = .32$) with the base rate and highly correlated (Pearson's $r = .78$, $r^2 = .61$) with R^2_L. These results, like the parallel results in Menard (2000), are exploratory, but they suggest that further attention to the extent to which R^2_{ROC} is systematically correlated with the base rate in multiple replications is warranted.

EXAMPLE

Table 4.3 presents the prediction table for the logistic regression model described in the last chapter, with prevalence of marijuana use as the dependent variable and exposure, belief, gender, and ethnicity as predictors. For λ_p, the predicted number of errors without the model is equal to the number of errors in the smaller of the two observed categories (yes), 80. For τ_p, the expected number of errors is equal to the product of the row totals multiplied by 2 and divided by the total number of cases: $2(147)(80)/227 = 103.612$. For φ_p, it is necessary to calculate the expected frequency for each cell and add the expected frequencies for the cells indicating incorrect classification, using the row and column totals for the calculation. For all three coefficients, the error with the model is the sum of the cases incorrectly classified, 41. Using the data in the prediction table (Table 4.3),

$$\lambda_p = (80 - 41)/80 = .49,$$

$$\tau_p = \{[2(147)(80)/227] - 41\}/2(147)(80)/227 = .60, \text{ and}$$

$$\varphi_p = 2[(134)(52) - (28)(13)]/[(147)(65) + (80)(162)] = .59, \text{ or equivalently,}$$

$$\varphi_p = \{[(147)(65)/227] + [(80)(162)/227] - 41\}/[(147)(65)/227] + [(80)(162)/227] = .59,$$

for Table 4.3. The test for each coefficient, subscripted with that coefficient, is

$$d_\lambda = (.352 - .181)/\sqrt{(.352)(.648)/227} = 5.39,$$

$$d_\tau = (.228 - .181)/\sqrt{(.456)(.544)/227} = 8.32, \text{ and}$$

$$d_\phi = (.437 - .181)/\sqrt{(.437)(.563)/227} = 7.78.$$

In these formulas, .181 is the proportion observed to be wrong based on the model (41/227); and .352 for λ_p, .456 for τ_p, and .437 for φ_p are the proportions of expected errors calculated according to the formulas presented earlier. All these statistics are statistically significant ($p < .001$). However, here φ_p is really not appropriate because we have used the default selection ratio of .50 rather than specifying a selection ratio (which could still be .50) for theoretical or substantive reasons. Whether λ_p or τ_p is the more appropriate index depends on whether we assume that marijuana users are qualitatively different from nonusers or whether we believe that there may be no real difference between users and nonusers. Absent any other reason for accepting or rejecting the possibility of a homogeneous population, it seems most reasonable to assume that the population is indeed hetero-geneous, and to use τ_p as the index of predictive efficiency, particularly given the insensitivity of τ_p to the base rate. Based on this, it appears that we have moderately good quantitative prediction ($R_L^2 = .37$), and fairly strong ($\tau_p = .60$) qualitative prediction, in this model for the prevalence of marijuana use. Figure 4.4 presents the sensitivity-specificity curve and the ROC curve for the model for prevalence of marijuana use. Based on the sensitivity-specificity graph, the cutoff at which sensi-tivity = specificity appears to occur at about .30 (give or take a little), close to the observed 35% base rate for marijuana use in the data. For the ROC curve, $R_{ROC}^2 = 2(.8828 - .5) = .77$, suggesting that by the ROC curve criterion, prevalence of marijuana use is indeed very well explained by the model.

TABLE 4.3	Prediction Table for Marijuana Use	
	Predicted	
Observed	*No*	*Yes*
No	134	13
Yes	28	52

$\lambda_p = .49$, $d = 7.36$, $p = .000$.
$\tau_p = .60$, $d = 8.32$, $p = .000$.
$\varphi_p = .59$, $d = 7.78$, $p = .000$.

CONCLUSION: SUMMARY MEASURES FOR EVALUATING THE LOGISTIC REGRESSION MODEL

The distinctions among R^2 analogs, indices of predictive efficiency, and measures of goodness of fit may be summarized as follows:

(1) R^2 analogs and their associated tests of statistical significance (usually G_M, but possibly the multivariate Wald statistic for R_W^2 or the ANOVA F statistic for R_O^2) indicate the extent to which *quantitative* prediction is improved when the predictors are added to the model; *how much closer* the predicted probabilities are to the observed classification or group membership of the cases in the sample. The R^2 analogs themselves measure the strength of the predictive relationship; the asso-ciated tests of statistical significance indicate how likely it is that the predictive relationship can be reasonably attributed to random sample variation.

FIGURE 4.4   Sensitivity-Specificity and ROC Curves

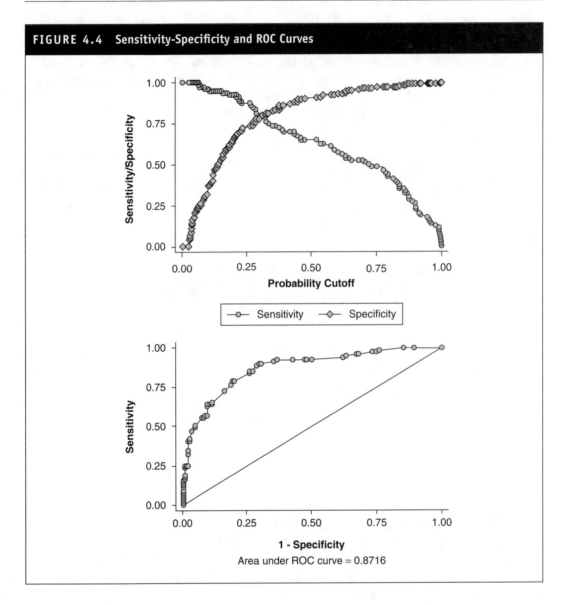

(2) Indices of predictive efficiency and their associated tests of statistical significance (the binomial d for λ_p, τ_p, and φ_p; the normal z test for the Coleman-Light index of agreement κ_j) indicate the extent to which *qualitative* prediction is improved when the predictors are added to the model; *how many more correct predictions* about classification or group membership are made for the cases in the sample relative to the total number of cases in the sample. The indices of predictive efficiency measure the strength of the predictive relationship; the associated tests of statistical significance indicate how likely it is that the predictive relationship can reasonably be attributed to random sample variation.

(3) Goodness-of-fit statistics indicate whether the quantitative predictions are statistically significantly different from the observed values in the model when the model is *not* a saturated model. Put another way, goodness-of-fit statistics indicate whether the unsaturated model, with its more *limited* or *constrained* set of predictors, does a statistically significantly worse job of prediction than a saturated model, with no limitations or constraints, but instead with all possible interactions among predictors, as well as main effects of predictors, included in the model.

It should be clear from this discussion that there is no equivalence among R^2 analogs, indices of predictive efficiency, and goodness-of-fit statistics. One will not necessarily give the same results as another, or even necessarily produce results consistent with another. Using one as a proxy for another is a mistake, but the literature on logistic regression seems replete with examples treating (or more encouragingly, in some cases trying to emphasize that one cannot treat) one type of measure as though it were another.

In linear regression, we use the F statistic and R^2 to test statistical significance and substantive significance, respectively, of the relationship between the dependent variable and the independent variables. Both are based on the total and error sums of squares, SST and SSE. The protocol of presenting R^2, the associated F statistic, and the attained significance level of the F statistic as summary measures of how well the model predicts the dependent variable, is standard and generally accepted. Other information, including regression diagnostics, may also be presented, but almost always in addition to and almost never instead of R^2, F, and the statistical significance of F.

In logistic regression, there is at present no such standard protocol. If our principal concern is with quantitative prediction (e.g., in the context of theory testing), we use G_M and R_L^2, based on $-2LL$, to test for statistical and substantive significance. If we are more concerned about the accuracy with which the model predicts actual category membership on the dependent variable, the binomial d and one of the three indices of predictive efficiency (λ_p, τ_p, or φ_p) are best used to assess the statistical and substantive significance of the model. Since λ_p, τ_p, and φ_p are not provided in logistic regression routines, they must be computed by hand. An alternative that may be used in addition to both R_L^2 and the indices of predictive efficiency is R_{ROC}^2, calculated from the AUC. It may also be informative, particularly when comparing results from the linear probability model and logistic regression, to calculate R_O^2.

Absent good reason to omit one or more of these indices, I would recommend as a standard protocol the presentation of

(1) G_M along with its degrees of freedom and attained significance level (from which, if one so desires, one can derive a qualitative decision whether the result is significant at some prespecified level such as .05) for models when maximum likelihood estimation is used (an alternative to G_M when maximum likelihood estimation is not used is the multivariate Wald statistic);

(2) R_L^2 and R_O^2 when maximum likelihood estimation is used (R_L^2 will not be available for models using other than maximum likelihood estimation, but R_O^2 will be available for any model);

(3) the three indices of predictive efficiency (or at least the most appropriate of the three) plus the classification table on which they are based;

(4) the binomial d for each of the indices of predictive efficiency presented along with the attained level of statistical significance of the binomial d; and

(5) the adjusted version of R_O^2, $R_a^2 = R_O^2 - [k(1 - R_O^2)/n - k - 1]$, and at least one adjusted version of R_L^2. For the latter, there is no one adjusted R_L^2 measure that has been shown to be superior to the others, but the logic behind the AIC-based $R_{LSKC}^2 = 1 - (DM - K - 1)/(D_0 - 1)$, described in Chapter 3, is appealing; if a more conservative measure is desired to penalize more heavily for the inclusion of additional parameters, the $R_{LH}^2 = (G_M - 2K)/(D_0)$ measure suggested by Harrell (1986) appears to be a reasonable choice. The purposes of including the adjusted measures of explained variation are (a) to obtain more reasonable estimates of population parameters for R_O^2 and R_L^2 (which may be overestimated relative to their true population values in any given sample) and (b) as a diagnostic, since large differences in adjusted and unadjusted R_O^2 and R_L^2 would suggest that the apparent explained variation in the model may reflect a large degree of capitalizing on chance covariation with a large number of predictors in the model.

Clearly, in some models, there will be good reason to omit one or more of the indices of predictive efficiency, and without maximum likelihood estimation, alternatives to G_M and R_L^2 will be necessary. The five categories of indices for the overall utility of the model should be considered a minimum set of indices, and other measures (such as the ROC curve and AUC, the Hosmer-Lemeshow or other goodness-of-fit test, or other R^2 analogs) should not be presented instead of, but may be included in addition to, R_L^2 R_O^2, the indices of predictive efficiency, and their associated tests for statistical significance.

Logistic Regression Coefficients

$\mathbf{I}$f the overall model works well, how important is each of the independent variables? Is the relationship of the dependent variable to any of the independent variables attributable to random sample variation? If not, how much does each independent variable contribute to our ability to predict the dependent variable? Which variables are stronger or weaker, better or worse predictors of the dependent variable?

In logit analysis, it is common to consider only the statistical significance of the log-linear coefficients. The logit coefficients themselves may be used for prediction in an equation relating the outcome to the predictors, but they are practically never used to decide whether the impact of a predictor in the model is relatively large or small. If substantive significance is considered at all, it is typically evaluated in terms of odds ratios, usually with only discrete, usually dichotomous or nominal level, predictors in the analysis, to see how much a difference between being one category and another of the predictor increases or decreases the odds of being in any particular category, relative to some other category, of the dependent variable. For example, odds of mortality may be modeled as an outcome with medical treatment alternatives as predictors.

In linear regression analysis, in contrast, we evaluate the contribution of each independent variable to the model by testing for its statistical significance, then examining the substantive significance of its effect on the dependent variable. Statistical significance is evaluated using an F or t statistic to produce an attained significance level (p) representing the probability that we would find this strong a relationship in a sample this large if there really were no relationship between the independent variable and the dependent variable. Substantive significance may be evaluated in one of several ways. We may examine the unstandardized regression coefficient to see whether the difference or change in the dependent variable associated with or caused by a given difference or change in the independent variable is large enough to be concerned about. To apply this test, we must have some idea beforehand how big a change needs to be before we are concerned with it, and equivalently how big a change we are willing to ignore. Unstandardized linear regression coefficients are especially useful for comparing the effects of the same variable in different samples and for evaluating the practical impact of one variable on another when either all predictors have a natural metric (natural units of measurement such as kilometers, dollars, or numbers of people, even if the metrics are different for different predictors), or if all of the predictors are measured in the same metric, even if it is not a natural metric (e.g., if all predictors are measured on the same 5-point Likert scale).

Alternatively in linear regression, especially when there are no clear criteria for deciding "how big is big enough," and when some variables are not measured in natural units of measurement but are instead scale scores (an example of this would be the variable EDF5, exposure to delinquent friends, or BELIEF5, belief that it is wrong to violate the law, as used in the examples in previous chapters), we may focus on a *standardized* regression coefficient, which indicates how many *standard deviations* a dependent variable changes in response to a one standard deviation change in the independent variable. Use of standardized coefficients is especially appropriate for theory testing, and when the focus is on comparing the relative strengths of the effects of different variables with either different metrics or no natural metric for the same sample. Categorical predictors are incorporated into linear regression using "dummy" variables or *design* variables (Hardy 1993; Lewis-Beck 1980), with separate regression coefficients for each category. In the most commonly used *contrasts* (ways of coding the categorical predictor), the code for one category, the *reference* category, is set to zero for all of the design variables included in the analysis, but in some contrasts, particularly *deviation* contrasts, it may have a nonzero value with a meaningful substantive interpretation.

In logistic regression, there are two types of unstandardized coefficients, the unstandardized logistic regression coefficient, which closely parallels the unstandardized coefficient in ordinary least squares (OLS) regression and is the same as the logit coefficient in logit analysis, and the exponentiated logistic regression coefficient or odds ratio, e^β. Several possible ways of calculating a standardized coefficient for logistic regression analysis have been suggested. The numeric value and the interpretation of the standardized and unstandardized logistic regression coefficients may, for nominal predictors with more than two categories, depend on the specific contrasts used to represent the predictor. The statistical significance of an independent variable may be measured in one of several possible ways, including the likelihood ratio test, the Wald test (which comes in two forms, one with an approximate normal distribution and one with an approximate χ^2 distribution), and the Score test. The issue of which of these tests and coefficients are most useful in logistic regression analysis is the focus of this chapter, along with interpreting the different types of logistic regression coefficients. We begin with a discussion of unstandardized logistic regression coefficients and their interpretation in terms of the probability of the outcome for different values of the predictors. Next, we move to standardized logistic regression coefficients, comparing the importance of independent variables with different metrics for predicting the dependent variable. Then, we examine the use (and misuse) of odds ratios in logistic regression analysis. Next, we consider alternative ways of coding categorical predictors, and how that affects the interpretation but not the overall results of the model. Finally, we conclude with a discussion of statistical inference for logistic regression coefficients.

We return here to the example of computer use first introduced in Chapter 2 using data from the National Opinion Research Center (NORC) General Social Survey (GSS) with computer use (COMPUSX, coded 1 = nonuser, 2 = user) as the dependent variable. The predictors are ethnicity (in the GSS, RACE, coded 1 = White, 2 = Black, 3 = Other), an unordered categorical variable; gender (SEXFM coded 1 = female, 2 = male), a dichotomous predictor; and educational attainment (EDUCNEW, originally coded 0 to 20 years of education but recoded 7 to 20, with 7 = 7 or fewer years of education because of the small number of cases with 7 or fewer years of education and 20 including cases with 20 or more years of education), an ordered predictor which is an interval variable at all except its end points; and income (INCNEW98, coded 1 to 23, with 1 = less than $1,000 per year, 2 = $1,000 to $2,999, etc., up to 22 = $90,000 to $109,999, 23 = $110,000 per year or more), an ordinal categorical predictor with a large enough number of categories to be treated as continuous (and thus treated as an interval or ratio variable). For income, there was a substantial number of refusals (229, or 8% of the sample) in addition to the "don't know" and "not applicable" responses, which constituted another 5% of the sample. The refusals, rather than being dropped from the analysis, were assigned the mean value for income for purposes of analysis.

UNSTANDARDIZED LOGISTIC REGRESSION COEFFICIENTS

The unstandardized logistic regression coefficient is simply the coefficient used in the equation to predict the dependent variable, logit(Y).[1] Expressing the equation in terms of estimates (a and b) rather than parameters (α and β), logit(Y) = $a + b_1X_1 + b_2X_2 + \ldots + b_KX_K$ where the dependent variable is logit(Y), the predictors are $X_1, X_2, \ldots, X_K$, a is the estimate for the intercept α, and $b_1, b_2, \ldots, b_K$ are the estimates for the coefficients $\beta_1, \beta_2, \ldots, \beta_K$. The model estimated here is

$$\text{logit(Computer use)} = a + b_1(\text{Male}) + b_2(\text{Black}) + b_3(\text{Other}) + b_4(\text{Education}) + b_5(\text{Income}).$$

The results of estimating this logistic regression model are summarized in Table 5.1. Based on the data in Table 5.1, the equation for the log odds of computer use is Logit(COMPUSX) = −5.281 − .029(SEXFM) −.133(BLACK) + .228(OTHER) + .321(EDUCNEW) + .097(INCNEW98). Ignoring the issue of statistical significance for the moment, the negative coefficients for SEXFM and BLACK indicate that computer use, controlling for the other variables in the model, is lower among males than among females (this is evident because SEXFM is coded 1 for females and 2 for males), lower among Black individuals than among non-Black individuals, and higher among individuals of Other (than Black or White) ethnicity than among individuals not of "Other" ethnicity (non-Other). The relationship between gender and computer use may seem surprising, particularly because if one looks only at gender and computer use without the other variables in the model, being male is positively associated with computer use. More will be said on this in the discussion of

TABLE 5.1 Logistic Regression Analysis of Computer Use

Dependent Variable	$R^2_L[p(G_M)]$	Independent Variable	b	Odds Ratio (e^b)	Significance (Likelihood Ratio)
Computer use	.170 (.000)	Intercept	−5.281	—	—
		Gender (Male)	−0.029	0.971	.767
		Ethnicity Black	−0.133	0.876	.323
		Other	0.228	1.256	.310
		Education	0.321	1.379	.000
		Income	0.097	1.101	.000

statistical significance later in this chapter. The positive coefficients for education, income, and Other ethnicity indicate that computer use is more likely to occur for more- rather than less-educated individuals, for higher- rather than lower-income individuals, and for individuals who are other than White or Black. Because the variables are measured in different units, it is not possible based on these coefficients to say that one variable has a "stronger" influence on computer use than another.

Verbally, with some variation in phrasing, we can say that (a) a one-unit "increase" in gender (i.e., being male as opposed to being female) is associated with a change of −.029 (a reduction of .029, since the sign is negative) in the logit (or log odds) of being a computer user; (b) a one-unit "increase" in Black ethnicity (i.e., being Black as opposed to being non-Black) is associated with a change of −.133 (a reduction of .133) in the logit of computer use; (c) a one-unit "increase" in Other ethnicity (i.e., being Other as opposed to being non-Other) is associated with a change of .228 (an increase of .228, since the sign is positive) in the log odds (or logit) of being a computer user; (d) a one-unit (except at the end points, one year) increase in education is associated with an increase of .321 in the logit of being a computer user; and (e) an increase of one unit (remember, these are ordinal categories, not dollars) in income is associated with a .097 change in the log odds of computer use. One could phrase all of the results in terms of the logit or the log odds, of computer use or of being a computer user; these are just equivalent ways of saying the same thing. Talking about the logit or log odds lacks some intuitive appeal, but it is just being precise about the nature of the dependent variable in logistic regression.

INTERPRETING UNSTANDARDIZED LOGISTIC REGRESSION COEFFICIENTS

Digressing for a moment from the discussion of Table 5.1, if we calculated the bivariate relationship between education and computer use using logistic regression, we would obtain the equation logit(COMPUSX) = −4.654 + 0.380(EDUCNEW). When EDUCNEW has its minimum value, this becomes logit(COMPUSX) = −4.654 + 0.380(7) = −1.994; when EDUCNEW has its maximum value, logit(COMPUSX) = −4.654 + 0.380(20) = 2.946; and when EDUCNEW has its mean value, logit(COMPUSX) = −4.654 + 0.380(13.3) = 0.400. Translating the logits into probabilities using Table 1.1 on page 15 from Chapter 1, the probability of computer use for individuals with 7 or fewer years of education is $e^{-1.994}/(1 + e^{-1.994}) = .12$, or about 12%; the probability of computer use for someone with 20 or more years of education is $e^{2.946}/(1 + e^{2.946}) = .95$, or about 95%; and the probability of computer use for individuals with about a year beyond high school is $e^{0.400}/(1 + e^{0.400}) = .60$, or about 60%. All of these values lie within a reasonable range and would be consistent with our expectations about the likelihood of computer use by individuals with different levels of education. The mean value for COMPUSX is .578, indicating that about 58% of the sample use computers, a figure close to the predicted value of computer use for individuals with the mean level of education. For respondents who have completed high school, logit(COMPUSX) = −4.654 + 0.380(12) = −.094, and the probability of computer use is $e^{-.094}/(1 + e^{-.094}) = .48$, or about 48%. This is the modal pattern in the GSS sample.

Like the linear regression coefficient, the logistic regression coefficient can be interpreted as the difference or change in the dependent variable, logit(Y), associated with a one-unit difference or change in the independent variable. The change in $P(Y = 1)$, however, is *not* a linear function of the independent variables. The slope of the curve varies depending on the value of the independent variables. It is possible to calculate the slope of the curve for different pairs of points by examining the change in $P(Y = 1)$ between those points. For example, returning to the bivariate relationship between education and computer use, going from 15 years of education (some college) to 16 years of education (usually meaning college graduation) results in a change in probability of computer use from .740 to .806, implying a slope of (.806 − .740 =) .066; while going from 18 to 19 years of education results in a change of probability from .899 to .929, implying a slope of .030, only about half as large as the slope between some college and college graduation. In general, changes between adjacent values for the predictor result in larger slopes in the middle of the distribution than toward either of the extremes.

Returning to Table 5.1, if we hold constant the contributions of the other predictors to computer use, by using only the intercept and the coefficient for education, then when EDUCNEW has its minimum value, we obtain logit(COMPUSX) = −5.281 + 0.321(7) = −3.034; when EDUCNEW has its maximum value, logit(COMPUSX) = −5.281 + 0.321(20) = 1.139; and when EDUCNEW has its mean value, logit(COMPUSX) = −5.281 + 0.321(13.3) = −1.0117. Translating the logits into probabilities, the probability of computer use for individuals with 7 or fewer years of education is $e^{-3.034}/(1 + e^{-3.034}) = .05$, or about 5%; the probability of computer use for someone with 20 or more years of education is $e^{1.139}/(1 + e^{1.139}) = .76$, or about 76%; and the probability of computer use for individuals with about a year beyond high school is $e^{-1.0117}/(1 + e^{-1.0117}) = .27$, or about 27%. Controlling for the other variables in the model, the impact of education on computer use is not as high as it was in the bivariate equation. In particular, it is reasonable to suspect that at each given level of education, individuals who have higher incomes (and thus are better able to purchase personal computers) may be more likely to be computer users. Because education and income are correlated with one another, their impacts on computer use may be *confounded,* that is, it may not be possible to *completely* disentangle the effects of education from the effects of income. Logistic regression, like linear regression, attempts to partition the effects of education and income, statistically controlling for the possible overlap in the effects of education and income on computer use.

STANDARDIZED LOGISTIC REGRESSION COEFFICIENTS AND SUBSTANTIVE SIGNIFICANCE

Increases in years of education, and even in ordinally coded income categories, may make good intuitive sense, but what does a one-unit increase in exposure to delinquent friends really mean? Since, as described earlier, exposure items are measured on a 5-point scale, and belief items are measured on a 4-point scale, and since the number of items is larger for exposure (8) than for belief (7), is a one-unit increase in belief really equivalent to a one-unit increase in exposure? Should we regard a one-unit change in belief (which has, in principle, a range of 7 to 28) as equivalent to a one-unit change in gender (which has a range of only one unit, 0 to 1)? Similarly, to return to computer use, can we regard a one-unit change in years of education as equivalent to a one-unit change in the ordered categories of income or a one-unit change in gender? These questions could be asked in the context of either linear regression, with frequency of marijuana use or computer use as a dependent variable, or logistic regression, with prevalence of marijuana use or computer use as a dependent variable. When independent variables are measured in different units or on different scales and we want to compare the strength of the relationship between the dependent variable and different independent variables, we often use standardized regression coefficients in linear regression analysis. For the same reasons, we may want to consider using standardized coefficients in logistic regression analysis.

In the usual sense used in regression analysis, a standardized coefficient is a coefficient that has been calculated for variables measured in standard deviation units. A standardized coefficient indicates how many standard deviations of change in a dependent variable are associated with a 1 standard deviation increase in the independent variable. In linear regression, a standardized coefficient between a dependent variable Y and an independent variable X, b^*_{YX}, may be calculated from the unstandardized coefficient between Y and X, b_{YX}, and the standard deviations of the two variables, s_Y, and s_X: $b^*_{YX} = (b_{YX})(s_X)/(s_Y)$. Alternatively, standardizing both X and Y prior to regression by subtracting their respective means and dividing by their respective standard deviations, to obtain $Z_Y = (Y - \bar{Y})/s_Y$ and $Z_X = (X - \bar{X})/s_X$, produces a standardized regression coefficient between Y and X.

For a variable that is approximately normally distributed, 99.9865% of all cases will lie in a range of 6 standard deviations (3 standard deviations on either side of the mean), and 99.999999713 will lie within a range of 10 standard deviations. Thus, a 1 standard deviation change in an independent variable typically means a change of about one-eighth of the range of its possible values (one-sixth in a small sample, one-tenth in a very large sample). According to Chebycheff's inequality theorem (Bohrnstedt and Knoke 1994:82–83), for *any* distribution, even for a very nonnormal distribution, *at least* 93.75% of all cases will lie within 8 standard deviations of the mean, and 96% within 10 standard deviations. Thus, a change of 1 standard deviation seems intuitively to be a large enough change that its effect should be felt (if the independent variable has any impact on the dependent variable) but not so large that a trivial relationship should appear to be substantial, even in a distribution that departs considerably from a normal distribution. By measuring the relationship of all of the independent variables to the dependent variables in common units (standard deviations, or roughly about one-eighth to one-tenth of their range), the relative impact on the dependent variable of independent variables measured in different units can be directly compared.

In logistic regression analysis, the calculation of standardized coefficients is complicated by the fact that it is not the value of Y, but the probability that Y has one or the other of its possible values, that is predicted by the logistic regression equation. The actual dependent variable in logistic regression is not Y, but logit(Y), whose observed values of logit(0) = $-\infty$ and logit(1) = $+\infty$ do not permit the calculation of means or standard deviations. Although we cannot directly calculate the standard deviation for the observed values of logit(Y), we can calculate the standard deviation indirectly, using the predicted values of logit(Y) and the explained variance, R^2. Recall from Chapter 3 that $R^2 = SSR/SST$. Dividing both the numerator and the divisor by N ($N - 1$ for a sample), we get $R^2 = SSR/SST = (SSR/N)/(SST/N) = s^2_{\hat{Y}}/s^2_Y$. Rearranging this equation to solve for S^2_Y produces the equation $s^2_Y = s^2_{\hat{Y}}/R^2$, and substituting logit(Y) for Y and logit($\hat{Y}$) for $\hat{Y}$, we are able to calculate the variance of logit(Y) based on the standard deviation of the predicted values of logit(Y) and the explained variance. Since the standard deviation is the square root of the variance, we can estimate standardized logistic regression coefficients as

$$b_{YX}^* = (b_{YX})(s_X)/\sqrt{s_{\text{logit}(\hat{Y})}^2/R^2} = (b_{YX})(s_X)(R)/s_{\text{logit}(\hat{Y})}, \qquad (5.1)$$

where b_{YX}^* is the standardized logistic regression coefficient, b_{YX} is the unstandardized logistic regression coefficient, s_X is the standard deviation of the independent variable X, $s_{\text{logit}(\hat{Y})}^2$ is the variance of logit($\hat{Y}$) [in other words, the variance of the estimated values of logit(Y)], $s_{\text{logit}(\hat{Y})}$ is the standard deviation of logit($\hat{Y}$), R^2 is the coefficient of determination, and R is just the square root of R^2.

The standardized logistic regression coefficient is not, as of this writing, commonly available in logistic regression software, but can be calculated using the following steps:

Step 1. b: Calculate the logistic regression model to obtain the unstandardized logistic regression coefficient, b. Save the predicted value of Y, $\hat{Y}$, from the logistic regression model.

Step 2. R: Use the predicted value of Y to calculate the zero-order correlation, R, between the observed and predicted values of the dependent variable, Y and $\hat{Y}$. R here is really a multiple correlation coefficient, the square root of Kvålseth's (1985) R_6^2 or equivalently the square root of the R_O^2 statistic introduced in Chapter 3.

Step 3. Use the predicted value of Y to calculate the predicted value of logit(Y), using the equation logit($\hat{Y}$) = $\ln[\hat{Y}/(1 - \hat{Y})]$.

Step 4. $S_{\text{logit}(\hat{Y})}$: Calculate descriptive statistics for logit($\hat{Y}$), including the standard deviation.

Step 5. S_X: If you have not already done so, calculate the standard deviations of all the independent variables in the equation. Be sure that you calculate them only for the cases actually included in the model.

Step 6. Enter b, R, s_X, and $s_{\text{logit}(\hat{Y})}$ into Equation 5.1 above to calculate b^*.

In calculating the standardized coefficient, it is important to select only those cases on which the model was actually computed; usually this will mean only those cases with valid values on all the variables included in the model.[2] Using the formula in Equation 5.1,
$b_{\text{sexfm}}^* = (-.029)(.496)(.468)/(1.170) = -.006$; $b_{\text{black}}^* = (-.133)(.361)(.468)/(1.170) = .019$;
$b_{\text{other}}^* = (.228)(.224)(.468)/(1.170) = -.020$; $b_{\text{educnew}}^* = (.321)(2.762)(.468)/(1.170) = -.355$; and
$b_{\text{incnew98}}^* = (.097)(5.032)(.468)/(1.170) = .195$. Table 5.2 includes the information from Table 5.1, plus the standardized coefficients, R_O^2, and indices of predictive efficiency.

The interpretation of the standardized logistic regression coefficient, calculated as $b^* = bs_X R/s_{\text{logit}(\hat{Y})}$, is straightforward, and closely parallels the interpretation of standardized coefficients in linear regression: a 1 standard deviation increase in X produces a b^* standard deviation change in logit(Y). (Recall that a *one-unit*, including a *one standard deviation unit*, change in X will produce a variable change in Y, depending on the location of X relative to the logistic distribution of Y.) For the model in Table 5.2, the relationship between the dependent variable and the independent variables is statistically significant: $G_M = 517.58$ with 5 degrees of freedom, $p = .000$. Measures of the strength of association between the dependent variable and the independent variables, $R_L^2 = .170$ and $R_O^2 = .219$, indicate a modest relationship between the dependent variable and its predictors.

TABLE 5.2 **Logistic Regression for Computer Use Including Standardized Coefficients and Indices of Predictive Efficiency**

Dependent Variable	Independent Variable	Unstandardized Coefficients (b)	Standardized Coefficients (b*)	Odds Ratio (e^b)	Significance (Likelihood Ratio)
Computer use (COMPUSX)	Intercept	−5.281	—	—	—
	Gender (Male)	−0.029	−0.006	0.971	.767
	Ethnicity:				.324
	Black	−0.133	−0.019	0.876	.323[a]
	Other	0.228	0.020	1.256	.310[a]
	Education	0.321	0.355	1.379	.000
	Income	0.097	0.195	1.101	.000

$G_M = 517.58$ (5 df), $p = .000$.

$R_L^2 = .170$; $R_O^2 = .219$; $R_O = .468$.

Standard deviations (for use in calculating standardized coefficients):

$s_{Gender} = 0.496$; $s_{Black} = 0.361$; $s_{Other} = 0.224$; $s_{Education} = 2.762$; $s_{Income} = 50.32$.

a. Statistical significance for the individual categories of ethnicity (the design variables BLACK and OTHER) are based on the Wald statistic.

	Predicted	
Observed	0	1
0	544	381
1	244	1,072

$\lambda_p = .324$, $d = 16.776$, $p = .000$.

$\tau_p = .425$, $d = 19.502$, $p = .000$.

$\varphi_p = .411$, $d = 14.982$, $p = .000$.

ALTERNATIVE APPROACHES TO CONSTRUCTING STANDARDIZED LOGISTIC REGRESSION COEFFICIENTS

Other approaches that have been proposed to calculating standardized logistic regression coefficients have been reviewed in Menard (2004a). One approach (Agresti 1996; Menard 1995; see also Kaufman 1996, who discusses standardized coefficients that vary across different observed values of the dependent variable) standardizes only the predictors: $b_A^* = (b)(s_x)$. (Recall that standardizing the dependent variable makes no difference because the numerical value of the dependent variable does not enter into the calculation of the logistic regression coefficients.) A second approach, implemented in SAS **logistic**, and presented as the "Standardized Estimate" in SAS output, takes b_A^* and divides by the standard deviation of the standard logistic distribution, $\pi/\sqrt{3}$, regardless of the actual variation in the dependent variable: $b_{SAS}^* = (b)(s_X) / (\pi/\sqrt{3}) = (b)(s_X) / 1.8138$. A third approach, suggested by Long (1997), takes b_A^* and divides by the standard deviation of the standard logistic distribution plus the standard deviation of the predicted values of the dependent variable: $b_{Long}^* = (b)(s_X)/\sqrt{s_{logit(\hat{Y})}^2 + \pi^2/3}$. It should be noted that based on the formula for Long's (1997) proposed coefficient, the standard deviation and variance of the dependent variable do vary across different dependent variables, but it also varies for the same cases with the same dependent variable, because inclusion of different predictors produces different values of $s_{logit(\hat{Y})}$, and these are not adjusted for the relationship between the variance in the predicted value of the dependent variable (the explained variance in an absolute sense) and the ratio of explained to total variance, R^2. This adjustment is made in the fully standardized logistic regression coefficient, and hence for that coefficient the estimated variance in the dependent variable should be a constant.

None of these standardized coefficients will generally be equal to the fully standardized coefficient $b^* = (b)(s_X)(R)/s_{logit(\hat{Y})}$ and none of them really takes into account the empirical variation in the dependent variable. Because of this, they may be considered *partially standardized coefficients,* as opposed to the *fully standardized coefficient* $b^* = (b)(s_X)(R)/s_{logit(\hat{Y})}$, which also takes into account the empirical variation in the dependent variable. They will, however, produce the same ranking of effects of independent variables on the dependent variables, since all contain the quantity $(b)(s_X)$ in the numerator, multiplied or divided by a constant [divided by 1 for b_A^*, 1.8138 for b_{SAS}^*, the square root of $(s_{logit(\hat{Y})} + 1.8138)$ for b_{Long}^*, and, for the fully standardized coefficient, divided by $s_{logit(\hat{Y})}/R$ or equivalently multiplied by $R/s_{logit(\hat{Y})}$, which varies across models and samples but is constant within a given model for a given sample]. Limited experience, however, suggests that the three partially standardized coefficients are more likely than the fully standardized coefficient b^* to be greater than 1 or less than -1 even when there are no problems of collinearity or other problems (see Chapter 7). The principal reasons favoring the use of the fully standardized coefficient are (a) construction and interpretation that directly parallel the standardized coefficients in linear regression, and correspondingly (b) the ability to apply the same standards used to interpret standardized coefficients in linear regression to standardized coefficients in logistic regression.

Yet another procedure for constructing standardized coefficients is possible based on information theory and R_L^2 rather than R_O^2, but this procedure is (a) mathematically more complex to present, (b) very tedious to implement with all but the simplest logistic regression models, and (c) still not adequately developed conceptually (Menard 2004a). Briefly, it involves calculating each step of every possible sequence of entering the predictors into the model, examining the change in R_L^2 at each step in every model, then averaging the change in R_L^2 for every possible order of entry for every predictor. The result at each step is then divided by the square root of the change in R_L^2 that occurs when the variable is the first to be entered into the model. The practical problem with the method is that if the number of predictors is K, there are $K!$ (K factorial) possible orderings of the predictors, 2^{K-1} of which are unique with respect to the ordering of each variable relative to the variables that precede it in entry into the equation. The conceptual problem is that the resulting standardized coefficients cannot be described in terms of "a one $\underline{?}$ unit change in the predictor results in a one $\underline{?}$ unit change in the dependent variable," because the variables themselves are not, strictly speaking, being standardized to any well-defined unit, in contrast to the application of the same procedure in OLS multiple linear regression, in which case the result is the familiar standardized coefficient which can be described in terms of standard deviation units. It will be interesting to see whether further developments in both conceptualization and computation will result in a stronger case being made for this approach to constructing standardized coefficients for logistic regression. Having compared this and the various approaches to constructing standardized logistic regression coefficients, however, the fully standardized coefficients described above appear to be preferable to any of the alternatives.

If we naively evaluate the strength of the relationships of the independent variables to computer use based on the unstandardized coefficients, education appears to have the strongest effect, followed by the two design variables for ethnicity, Other at .228 and Black at −.133, then income at .097 and gender at −.029, even though ethnicity and gender are not statistically significant. Based on the standardized coefficients, however, education still has the strongest effect ($b^* = .355$), but income has the second strongest effect ($b^* = .195$). The statistically significant effects of income as well as education are much larger in magnitude than the statistically nonsignificant effects of ethnicity and gender. A 1 standard deviation increase in education is associated with a .355 standard deviation increase in logit(computer use), and a 1 standard deviation increase in income is associated with a .195 standard deviation increase in logit(computer use). Changes of 1 standard deviation unit in gender or ethnicity are associated with changes of only one or two hundredths of a standard deviation in computer use.

ISSUES IN THE USE OF STANDARDIZED LOGISTIC REGRESSION COEFFICIENTS

For gender and ethnicity, a "one standard deviation increase" is not as intuitively meaningful as the difference between males and females, or between respondents from different ethnic backgrounds, as reflected in the unstandardized logistic regression coefficient. The real utility of the standardized logistic regression coefficient here is to compare the magnitude of the effects of the different predictors by converting them to a common scale of measurement. In presenting substantive results, it may make sense to focus on standardized coefficients primarily for unitless scales such as exposure to delinquent friends and belief that it is wrong to violate the law, in the analysis of marijuana use, on unstandardized coefficients for variables with a natural metric (inches, kilograms, dollars, number of occasions) or close to a natural metric such as education in the analysis of computer use, and, as discussed in the next section, on exponentiated coefficients or odds ratios for categorical variables such as ethnicity and gender (corresponding to realistic differences in ethnicity and gender). For a variable like INCNEW98, which is an ordinal categorical variable based on an underlying natural metric (dollars), one could reasonably argue for the use of any of the three types of coefficients, but particularly for purposes of comparing the relative strengths of different variables in the same sample, when the variables are measured on different scales, standardized coefficients offer an intuitively plausible basis of comparison.

Although standardized coefficients are quite useful for comparing the *relative strength of influence of two different independent variables on the dependent variable in a single sample*, there are well-known problems with using standardized coefficients to compare the *strength of the influence of the same (single) independent variable on the same dependent variable across different samples or populations* (see, e.g., Achen 1982:68–77; Blalock 1971b; Duncan 1971, 1975; Heise 1975). Heise (1975:126–127) gives a particularly nice summary of the advantages and disadvantages of standardized coefficients under different circumstances. Because the standardized coefficient depends on the distribution in the population or sample on which it is calculated, when we have variables measured in the same natural metric across different samples or populations, the standardized coefficient can vary even when the unstandardized coefficients, again in the natural metric, are the same, indicating the same impact (e.g., dollar profit per dollar invested) in the two populations or samples. For this reason, critics of standardized coefficients emphasize that they cannot be used to compare the same relationship across different populations or samples or even across time within the same population or sample when the distribution of the variables in the sample changes over time. Blanket criticisms of the use of standardized coefficients, however, invariably focus on comparisons of the *same effect across samples,* and fail to adequately address the issue of comparing the *relative impacts of two different predictors, each measured on a different scale,* especially when they are measured on an arbitrary scale rather than a natural metric.

Consider three research questions. (1) Is the impact of X on Z the same across two different samples or populations? (2) Is the impact of X on Z greater than or less than the impact of Y on Z? (3) Is the impact of X on Z greater than (or less than) the impact of Y on Z in both (or all) of two (or more) samples or populations? If X, Y, and Z are all measured in the same natural metric, it does not matter whether we use standardized or unstandardized coefficients; the results will be identical. If, however, X and Y, in particular, are measured on different scales, especially if neither is a natural metric, then which coefficient we should use depends on which question we are asking. For Question 1, comparison of the same effect (implying the same variables measured the same way) across samples, we should use the unstandardized coefficient to avoid the problem of random variation in the standardized coefficient as a result of random sampling variation in the sample variance. For Question 2, the standardized coefficient is an equally obvious choice, since it assigns the same units to X and Y and makes them directly comparable in terms of their effect on Z. For Question 3, the answer may not be as obvious, but because our focus is not on the precise value of a single parameter, but rather on the *comparison of two different parameters* (again, with two different predictors measured on two different scales), the unstandardized coefficients fail to tell us which of the two predictors has the stronger influence on the dependent variable in *either* sample. Comparing the *relative* strength of the two variables, even across samples, requires the use of standardized coefficients to give any reasonable answer to the question.

Briefly, then, unstandardized and standardized coefficients convey different information about the relationships in the model. Standardized but not unstandardized coefficients reduce all variables to a common metric (standard deviation units), while unstandardized but not standardized coefficients are independent of the vicissitudes of random sample variation. Properly used and interpreted, both can be informative. When deciding whether to focus on standardized or unstandardized coefficients, as a general guideline, *the rule that (a) standardized coefficients should be used for comparing the effects of different predictors measured on different scales takes precedence over the rule that (b) unstandardized coefficients should be used for comparisons of predictors across different samples or populations.*

EXPONENTIATED COEFFICIENTS OR ODDS RATIOS

In addition to unstandardized logistic regression coefficients, odds ratios are also typically included in the output for most logistic regression software. The *odds ratio* is the number by which we would multiply the odds of being a computer user for each one-unit increase in the independent variable. An odds ratio greater than 1 indicates that the odds of being a computer user increase when the independent variable increases; an odds ratio of less than 1 indicates that the odds of being a computer user decrease when the independent variable increases. For example, a one-unit increase in education (here measured in a natural metric, years, for years 8 to 22, but not for 7 or 20, which aggregate 7 and fewer years of education and 20 and more years of education, respectively) results in a 37.9% increase in the odds of being a computer user (the odds of being a computer user is multiplied by 1.379). A one-unit increase in income (not measured in the natural metric of dollars but measured instead in ordinal income categories) increases the odds of being a computer user by 10.1% (the odds of being a computer user is multiplied by 1.101).

Hosmer and Lemeshow (2000:52) suggest that the odds ratio "is usually the parameter of interest in a logistic regression due to its ease of interpretation." While this may be true in biometric research, or research involving only or primarily categorical predictors, in social science research and in any research involving primarily continuous or interval/ratio scaled predictors, for which the interpretation of the odds ratio depends on the scale on which the predictor was measured, the odds ratio does not generally seem preferable to the simple unstandardized coefficient. For categorical variables such as gender and ethnicity, however, the odds ratio may provide a more intuitively appealing description than the unstandardized logistic regression coefficient. Based on the coefficients in Table 5.1, (a) the odds of computer use for males are only 97% (odds ratio = .971) of the odds for females for being a computer user, or to put it another way, the odds of being a computer user are 3% lower (.971 − 1 = −.029; that this is equal to the unstandardized logistic regression coefficient is coincidental here) for males than for females; (b) the odds of computer use for individuals of Black ethnicity are only 88% (odds ratio = .876) of the odds for non-Blacks, or to put it another way, the odds of being a computer user are 22% lower (.876 − 1 = −.224) for Blacks than for non-Blacks; and (c) the odds of computer use for individuals of Other ethnicity are 1.256 times the odds of non-Others, or to put it another way, the odds of being a computer user are 26% higher (1.256 − 1 = +.256) for Others than for non-Others. For many people, it may seem more understandable to phrase the differences in computer use for different genders or different ethnic groups in terms of odds than in terms of the log odds or logit, and it is in conjunction with categorical variables such as gender and ethnicity that presentation in terms of odds ratios rather than standardized coefficients seems most helpful.

Because the odds ratio is between 0 and 1 when the unstandardized logistic regression coefficient is negative, and between 1 and +∞ when the unstandardized logistic regression coefficient is positive, it is awkward to compare the relative magnitudes of odds ratios without putting them into a canonical form, either all greater than or equal to 1 (by taking the inverse of any odds ratios less than 1) or all between 0 and 1 (by taking the inverse of any odds ratios greater than 1). In the latter case, it is the odds ratios that are smallest in magnitude that indicate the greatest impact on the dependent variable, assuming a common metric for all the independent variables. Unless the predictors are all measured in a common metric (or perhaps if they are all categorical variables), however, there is as little point in comparing the magnitude of odds ratios as there is in comparing the magnitude of unstandardized regression coefficients.

FURTHER INTERPRETATION (AND MISINTERPRETATION) OF ODDS RATIOS

As described in Chapter 2, the odds ratio is sometimes advocated and used as a measure of association in contingency table analysis and in log-linear analysis (see, e.g., Bohrnstedt and Knoke

1994:178–181; Reynolds 1984:45–46). For an extended discussion of odds ratios and their use, primarily in the context of log-linear models, see also Rudas (1998). To review, the odds ratio does provide a single measure of the strength of the relationship between two dichotomous variables, as does the unstandardized logistic regression coefficient or the standardized logistic regression coefficient. Even for the relationship between two dichotomous variables, however, (a) the odds ratio does not vary between 0 and 1 but, instead, varies between 0 and $+\infty$, and (b) the odds ratio is not a proportional reduction in error measure. In a contingency table or log-linear analysis involving variables with more than two categories, there will be two or more odds ratios (just as there are two or more unstandardized logistic regression coefficients, e.g., the coefficients for the dummy variables BLACK and OTHER when ethnicity is a predictor), and the use of odds ratios cannot provide a single summary measure of the relationship between the two variables. The odds ratio still, however, provides a measure of the strength of one *part* of that relationship (e.g., the relationship between being Black and computer use, ignoring all other ethnic categories) in the original (unstandardized coefficient) or transformed (standardized coefficient) metric of the predictor. In this respect, the odds ratio may be regarded as a partial measure of association, but still with the undesirable properties of not being a PRE measure and not varying between 0 and 1. Once we introduce continuous variables into the model, a third undesirable property of the odds ratio as a measure of association becomes evident: the odds ratio is not scale invariant, but depends on the scale on which the continuous variable is measured. Rescale the continuous variable, for example, by dividing by 100 and the odds ratio increases; multiply by 100 and the odds ratio decreases.

The description of the odds ratio as a measure of association may (perhaps; this is speculation on my part) be at the root of two mistaken uses of the odds ratio I have occasionally seen in publications or publications involving logistic regression analysis: the use of the odds ratio as either a "sort of" standardized coefficient or as a measure of effect size, which, as the term is used in applied research (see, e.g., Lipsey 1998; Rosenthal et al. 2000), is a different type of standardized measure. The odds ratio, just like the unstandardized logistic regression coefficient, is neither a standardized coefficient nor a measure of effect size. It contains the same information as the unstandardized logistic regression coefficient or the probability. All that is different is the way in which the information is presented. In particular, the odds ratio cannot take the place of a standardized logistic regression coefficient for evaluating the strength of the influences of the independent variables on the dependent variable, relative to one another, because the odds ratio will provide exactly the same ordering, from strongest to weakest, as the unstandardized logistic regression coefficient, once all the odds ratios are put into canonical form, as described above. The odds ratio provides no additional information beyond what is provided by the unstandardized logistic regression coefficient; it just provides the same information as the unstandardized logistic regression coefficient in a different way.

In logistic regression analysis with a dichotomous dependent variable, I have also repeatedly seen the mistake of equating the *odds ratio* (a ratio of two odds) with a *risk ratio* (a ratio of two probabilities), sometimes with the justification that the two are "approximately" equal under certain fairly restrictive conditions (a base rate less than .10). In general, the use of an odds ratio to "represent" a risk ratio will overstate the strength of the relationship. In the example for this chapter, the .971 ratio for computer use for males as opposed to females indicates that the odds of computer use for males is 97% as high as the odds of computer use for females, or inverting the odds ratio, the odds of computer use for females is (1/.971 =) 1.030 as high as for males or 3% higher for females than for males. This does not mean that females are 3% more *likely* to use computers than males or that the *probability* of computer use is 3% higher for males than for females; the actual difference in probability or likelihood is 2%, not 3%. Since gender is not a statistically significant predictor of computer use, however, and since the difference between 2% and 3% may seem small, let us consider also the relationship between gender and marijuana use from Chapters 3 to 4, as illustrated in Table 3.3.

The odds ratio of about .22 for males in Table 3.3 does not mean that the *risk* of marijuana use is only a little over one-fifth as high for males as for females (or, dividing 1 by the odds ratio for males, we obtain the odds ratio for female marijuana use, 4.5; but again, this does not mean that females are nearly five times as likely to use marijuana as males). To compare the *relative risk* of marijuana use for males and females, it is necessary to use the model to calculate the probabilities for each, assuming values of the other predictors. For White males and females with average levels of EDF5 (12) and BELIEF4 (27), the respective probabilities are for females $e^{0.407(12)-.118(27)-1.749}/$ $(1+e^{0.407(12)-.118(27)-1.749})=.487$ and for males $e^{0.407(12)-.118(27)-1.514-1.749}/(1+e^{0.407(12)-.118(27)-1.514-1.749})=.173$, for example, and the relative risks for males and females differ by a factor of about 3 (2.8:1 for females:males or .35:1 for males:females), not by a factor of 4 or 5. *Suggestion:* Do the math. There is no excuse here for approximations that can so easily be misleading. Odds ratios are best used subject to the following six guidelines:

1. Odds ratios are *not* standardized coefficients.

2. Odds ratios are *not* risk ratios in logistic regression with a dichotomous dependent variable (but see Chapter 9 for polytomous nominal dependent variables).

3. Odds ratios are *not* effect sizes as that term is commonly used in applied research.

4. Odds ratios are most informative for categorical predictors with fewer, rather than more, categories, for example, gender and ethnicity.

5. Odds ratios are least informative for ordinal, interval, ratio, or continuous predictors with no natural metric. In this instance, a standardized coefficient is more informative.

6. Odds ratios can be multiplied to ascertain the cumulative effect of two or more categorical predictors. For example, if gender is coded as male or female, and ethnicity is coded as Black or non-Black, and if being female increases the odds of voting Democratic by a factor of 1.3, and being Black increases the odds of voting Democratic by a factor of 2.2, and if there is no interaction effect between gender and ethnicity, then being a Black female increases the odds of voting Democratic by $1.3 \times 2.2 = 2.86$, compared with being a non-Black male.

CATEGORICAL PREDICTORS AND CONTRASTS

In the example given in Table 5.1, gender is a dichotomous variable coded 1 for females and 2 for males. Ethnicity in its original form is a nominal variable coded 1 for White, 2 for Black, and 3 for Other. Because these values are meaningless (one could just as easily have used 1 for Black, 2 for Other, and 3 for White), it makes no sense to use the nominal variable with these values as a predictor in either linear or logistic regression. Instead, a nominal variable is represented by a set of dichotomous *dummy variables* (Hardy 1993; Lewis-Beck 1980). The most common scheme for translating a nominal variable into a set of dummy variables is to construct a dummy variable for each category, and code the case as 0 if the case lacks the attribute represented by that category or code it 1 if the case possesses the attribute represented by that category, then exclude one category (the reference category) to avoid collinearity (to be discussed in Chapter 7). In Table 5.1, it is the dummy variable White that is excluded; so White is the reference category for the dummy variables representing ethnicity.

In effect, this sets the value of the unstandardized logistic regression coefficient for the reference category to 0 (and equivalently, the odds ratio to 1); we then compare the other two ethnic categories with the omitted category. Since the coefficient for Black is less than 0 (−.133), Black respondents have a lower log odds of being computer users than White respondents, and since the coefficient for Other is greater than 0 (+.228), Other respondents have a higher log odds of being computer users than White respondents. This method of coding the dummy variables for ethnicity is sometimes called *indicator* coding, because each variable "indicates" the presence of the characteristic in question, here the characteristic for which the variable is named. Indicator coding is the most commonly used coding for categorical predictors in OLS regression analysis and in logistic regression analysis.[3] This coding scheme is used so often that it may be considered by some to be *the* coding scheme for categorical predictors. Not quite true.

Indicator coding is only one of several ways of creating dummy variables (also called design variables) for categorical predictors (including dichotomous as well as nominal variables) in logistic regression analysis. One alternative to indicator coding is the *simple* contrast, comparing each category to a single reference category, for example, Black to White (rather than Black to non-Black) and Other to White (rather than Other to Non-Other). Another useful alternative is called *deviation* coding or *effect* coding.[4] In logistic regression, the deviation contrast measures the deviation of the logit for each group from the unweighted average logit for the entire sample. With deviation coding, the reference category no longer has an arbitrary coefficient of 0. Instead, its coefficient is equal to the negative of the sum of the coefficients for the other categories. If computer time is more expensive than human labor, calculation of the omitted coefficient by hand may be reasonable. In a personal computer or free computing environment, however, it makes more sense to calculate two models, with different reference categories, to obtain not only the estimates for the coefficients of all three categories but also the standard error and statistical significance of the otherwise omitted category. (Mathematically, the omitted category is redundant, of little or no interest. In both theory testing and applied research, however, it makes more sense to provide full information about the coefficients and their statistical significance for all three categories, rather than leave one for pencil-and-paper calculation.) Other than the two alternative reference categories in the two models, with deviation coding, the coefficients for the remaining (nonreference) categories will remain the same across the two models, a characteristic not shared with other contrasts, in which changing the reference category changes all of the coefficients. Table 5.3 on page 98 presents the same model as in Table 5.1, but with deviation coding for ethnicity and gender.

Other than the changes in the individual coefficients for ethnicity and gender, the use of a different coding scheme for the indicator variables has not changed the substantive results of the analysis. The explained variation (R_L^2) remains the same, as do the coefficients for education and income. The constant has changed, as will normally be the case when the design variables are changed (e.g., by changing contrasts, or by changing the reference category in an indicator or simple contrast). This change occurs because the constant itself has a different meaning. In the present example, with the indicator contrast, it was the adjustment needed to make the model fit for White

TABLE 5.3   Logistic Regression Analysis of Computer Use With Deviation Coding of Race

Dependent Variable	$R^2_L[p(G_M)]$	Independent Variable	b	Odds Ratio (e^b)	Significance (Wald z)
Computer use (COMPUSX)	.170 (.000)	Intercept	−5.293	—	—
		Gender:			
		Female	−0.015	0.971	.767
		Male	0.015	1.015	.767
		Ethnicity:			.325
		White Non-Hispanic	−0.032	0.969	.728
		Black	−0.164	0.848	.136
		Other	0.196	1.217	.196
		Education	0.321	1.379	.000
		Income	0.097	1.101	.000

females (the combined reference categories with the indicator contrast); now it is the adjustment needed to make the model fit for the unweighted mean of males and females and the unweighted mean of the different ethnic groups. For gender, with only two categories, the coefficient for one category is simply the negative of the coefficient for the Other category. For ethnicity, the coefficients indicate that being White as opposed to Black or Other is negatively associated with computer use (but more on this when we get to statistical significance). The coefficients for Black and Other in Table 5.1 can be reconstructed from the coefficients in Table 5.3 (within the limits of rounding error) by subtracting −.032, the coefficient for White, from the coefficients for the other dummy variables in Table 5.3 (in other words, adding .032, since we are subtracting a negative number). Deviation coding thus gives us the same information as indicator coding, but with a comparison to an "average" effect instead of a reference category. Odds ratios for deviation coding are not based on the comparison of the category for which the odds ratio is calculated with the reference category; instead, they compare the category for which the odds ratio is calculated with the unweighted mean odds of all the categories. To obtain the odds ratio for the category in question relative to the reference category, it is necessary to exponentiate not b_k, but $2b_k$, that is, twice the unstandardized coefficient (Hosmer and Lemeshow 2000:55; Stokes et al. 2000:200–201). This may be done automatically in some software, and one should check the exponentiated coefficients to see whether they represent e^b or e^{2b} when using deviation coding for categorical predictors.

Other contrasts available for logistic regression analysis in one or more software packages include Helmert, reverse Helmert, polynomial (or orthogonal polynomial), repeated, GLM (a variant of reference cell coding applicable when the measured categories are not exhaustive of all the possible codes for the variable), and special, user-defined contrasts.[5] Orthogonal polynomial contrasts test for linear and nonlinear effects and will be illustrated in Chapter 12. Helmert, reverse Helmert, and repeated contrasts are appropriate for testing whether the effects of different categories of an ordinal predictor are consistent with the ordering of the categories. The use of different contrasts for ordinal variables has no effect on the model fit or on the statistical significance of the categorical ordinal variable. The results may, however, suggest an appropriate recoding of the variable to take advantage of any apparent linearity, monotonicity, or any natural breaks between categories. The simplest ordinal contrast is the repeated or profile contrast, in which each category of the independent variable except the first (the reference category) is compared with the previous category (and a reverse repeated or profile contrast would compare each category except the last with the subsequent category). Helmert and reverse Helmert contrasts, instead of comparing each category to the *one* preceding or subsequent category, compare each category with *all* the preceding or subsequent categories. By examining the coefficients for the categories, it is possible to see whether a monotonic or linear relationship exists between the independent variable and the dependent variable. If there is a nonsystematic pattern of positive and negative coefficients, a nonlinear, nonmonotonic relationship is indicated, and the independent variable is best treated as though it were nominal rather than ordinal.

STATISTICAL SIGNIFICANCE OF LOGISTIC REGRESSION COEFFICIENTS

Of the several methods that have been used to evaluate the statistical significance of the contribution of an independent variable to the explanation of a dependent variable in maximum likelihood logistic regression analysis, one stands out as being clearly the best, in the sense of being the most accurate with respect to the criterion used for selecting the coefficients in the model: the likelihood ratio test. In the likelihood ratio test, the logistic regression model is calculated with and without the variable being tested. The likelihood ratio test statistic is equal to (G_M for the model with the variable) minus (G_M for the model without the variable). The result, which we can call G_k (G_1 when we test X_1, G_2 when we test X_2, ..., G_k when we test X_k), has a chi-square distribution with degrees of freedom equal to the degrees of freedom in the model with X minus the degrees of freedom in the model without X. For example, if we designate G_{M1} to represent the model chi-square with X_k in the model, and G_{M2} to represent the model chi-square with X_k not in the model, $G_k = G_{M1} - G_{M2}$, and if X is a continuous, interval or ratio variable, then G_k has 1 degree of freedom.

The only drawback to the use of the likelihood ratio statistic is that it requires more time to compute than alternative tests for statistical significance. If you are paying for every second on a mainframe computer, this may be a serious concern, but for many users with access to relatively fast personal computers and workstations, this is irrelevant except for very large samples. Nonetheless, statistical packages are often written to use a less computationally intensive alternative to the likelihood test, the Wald statistic, to test for the statistical significance of individual coefficients. The Wald statistic may be calculated as $W_k^2 = [b_k /(\text{Standard error of } b_k)]^2$, in which case it is asymptotically distributed as a chi-square distribution, or as $W_k = b_k /(\text{Standard error of } b_k)$, in which case it follows a standard normal distribution (Hosmer and Lemeshow 1989:31; SAS Institute 1989:1097; SPSS, Inc. 1991:140–141) and its formula parallels the formula for the t ratio for coefficients in linear regression. The disadvantage of the Wald statistic is that for large b, the estimated standard error is inflated, resulting in failure to reject the null hypothesis when the null hypothesis is false (Hauck and Donner 1977; see also Jennings 1986). This is sometimes called a "Type II" error or a false negative (failure to detect a relationship that exists), as opposed to a "Type I" error or a false positive (concluding that there is a relationship when there really is none). The use of the Wald statistic as the default option in most logistic regression software despite its known shortcomings is largely dictated by the fact that it can be computed in a single step, using only the unstandardized coefficient and its standard error.

As noted by Hosmer and Lemeshow (2000:52–53), the odds ratio has a skewed distribution, and when one wants to make inferences based on the odds ratio, one returns to the unstandardized coefficients. To construct a confidence interval for the odds ratio, one first calculates the end points of the confidence intervals for the unstandardized logistic regression coefficient, then exponentiates the result, so if the confidence interval for b_k is $b_k \pm z_{1-\alpha/2}SE(b_k)$ then the confidence interval for the odds ratio associated with b_k is $\exp[b_k \pm z_{1-\alpha/2}SE(b_k)]$, where b_k is the unstandardized coefficient for the predictor X_k, $z_{1-\alpha/2}$ is the two-tailed z test (based on the z distribution version of the Wald test), and $SE(b_k)$ is the standard error of the estimate b_k.

Whenever design variables are used to represent the effect of a single *nominal* variable, it is probably best that the design variables be treated as a group, rather than as individual variables. The statistical significance of the individual design variables should be considered *only* if the design variables *as a group* have a statistically significant effect on the dependent variable. The statistical significance of the individual design variables should be interpreted as whether the effects of being in a certain category is statistically significantly different from being in the reference category (for indicator coding) or from the average effect of the categorical variable (in deviation coding), *given that the categorical variable has a statistically significant effect to begin with.* For ordinal contrasts, the overall statistical significance of the design variable indicates only whether the categorical variable, *treated as a nominal variable,* has a statistically significant effect on the dependent variable. For ordinal contrasts, the statistical significance of the individual coefficients may provide important information about the form of the relationship between the categorical predictor and the dependent variable, even when the categorical variable does not appear to have a statistically significant effect on the dependent variable.

A GENERAL NOTE ON THE PRESENTATION AND DISCUSSION OF STATISTICAL SIGNIFICANCE

There are three substantially distinct approaches to the presentation and discussion of information on statistical significance. One is essentially a qualitative approach: Does the result meet some prespecified criterion for rejecting the null hypothesis? A level of statistical significance designated as "α" (typically $\alpha = .05$) is selected and if the attained significance level (p) is less than or equal to .05 (e.g., $p = .049$), the null hypothesis is rejected, but if it is greater than .05 (e.g., $p = .056$), we fail to reject the null hypothesis. In this approach, it is commonplace to report only rejection of or failure to reject the null hypothesis and not the attained significance level. As with indices of predictive efficiency (Chapter 4), close doesn't count. This approach is sometimes used both for overall tests of the model, such as F statistics in OLS multiple regression and G_M in logistic regression, and for testing the statistical significance of individual predictors. Diametrically opposed to this approach is the presentation of attained significance levels, without specific indication of whether we reject or fail to reject the null hypothesis at any specific level. This allows the researcher to discuss the results in terms of some prespecified criterion (or not), and it also allows the reader to interpret the results in terms of a different criterion (e.g., .01 or .10) if he or she so chooses. The second approach, also used both for overall tests of the model and for testing the statistical significance of individual predictors, provides more information, allows for the possibility that we may not want to attribute too much importance to a difference between $p = .049$ and $p = .056$, and is generally to be preferred to the first approach.

A third approach preselects a level of statistical significance (again designated "α" and again typically .05) and constructs confidence intervals around the point estimate. This approach, used almost exclusively for testing statistical significance of individual predictors and almost never for overall tests of the model, conveys the information necessary for the first approach, the fixed cutoff, because if the confidence interval contains the value (usually 0) against which the test statistic is being compared, we fail to reject the null hypothesis. It also provides additional information in the form of a range of plausible values for a parameter at the prespecified level of statistical significance; in respect of this additional information, it is preferable to the first approach. It is incorrect, however, to suggest that the third approach conveys all the information of the second approach. Implicit in the second approach is the orientation that the difference between an attained significance level of .04 and .06 should *not* be treated as enormously more consequential than a difference between .06 and .08 or between .02 and .04, but that these are all quantitative, not qualitative, differences in statistical significance. The first and third approach reify .05 as a "magic" number; the second approach treats it as just one more number on the continuum from .00 to 1.00. The second and third approaches are essentially complementary and can reasonably be used together. A mix of the first and second approaches, in which attained significance levels are presented, and those meeting some criterion are "flagged" (commonly with one or more asterisks, *, depending on the attained significance level) as meeting one of one or more levels of statistical significance (e.g., * for $p \leq .05$, ** for $.05 < p \leq .01$) is also sometimes used.

There is some disagreement about which approach is best. My own preference is to include sufficient information for the reader to implement *any* of the approaches, without overdoing it by providing too much information (e.g., multiple confidence intervals for three or more different levels of significance). This leads me to recommend the presentation of (a) the attained significance level (possibly using asterisks to flag different levels of significance) for both overall model tests and for tests of individual predictors, allowing the reader to select whatever cutoff for rejecting or failing to reject the null hypothesis the reader deems appropriate, and (b) for individual predictors (but not for overall tests of the model), the standard error of the parameter estimate, allowing the reader to construct confidence intervals at whatever level of significance the reader deems appropriate. This approach does not preclude providing additional information (e.g., 95% confidence intervals) or discussing the results in terms of a prespecified cutoff (e.g., .05) for rejecting or failing to reject the null hypothesis, but it does allow the reader to easily explore the consequences of applying different criteria of statistical significance to the results.

A NOTE ON STATISTICAL SIGNIFICANCE AND STATISTICAL POWER

While the greatest emphasis is given to the probability of rejecting the null hypothesis when it is true, or Type I error, increasing attention is given (especially in applied research) to the probability of failing to reject the null hypothesis when it is false, or Type II error. The Greek letter α is frequently used to represent the probability of Type I error and, confusingly, to represent the intercept (as a population parameter) in an OLS or logistic regression model. Equally confusingly, the Greek letter β is frequently used to represent the probability of Type II error; one just needs to pay attention to the context here. The quantity $(1 - \beta)$, or one minus the probability of Type II error, is called the *statistical power* of a given model for a particular sample. For a given sample size, the probabilities of Type I and Type II errors are inversely related. As one reduces the probability of a Type I error by making the cutoff value for α smaller, the value of β increases and, correspondingly, statistical power decreases. In general discussions of statistical power, the focus is usually on how large the sample size needs to be to reach a given level (often .80) of statistical power. In such discussions, it is often assumed (unrealistically) that one knows a great deal about (a) exactly how large or small an effect needs to be before we can decide whether to ignore it and (b) the variance of the variables in the sample. In empirical research, one can sometimes make educated guesses about these quantities in advance of drawing a sample, but it is more often the case that there is insufficient information to make more than a relatively uneducated guess. An alternative approach, less frequently applied, is to take the results from an analysis on a particular sample and calculate the statistical power for a particular relationship.

With respect to statistical power, as noted by Hosmer and Lemeshow (2000:339), "There has been surprisingly little work on sample size for logistic regression." Discussions of statistical power analysis and sample size (e.g., Agresti 2002:240–245; Hosmer and Lemeshow 2000:339–347) typically present formulas for calculating the appropriate size for logistic regression with (1) a single dichotomous predictor, (2) a single quantitative predictor, and (3) multiple predictors. In the case of a single dichotomous predictor, one can use the formula for sample size for a difference in proportions, $n = (z_{\alpha/2} + z_\beta)^2 [\pi_1(1 - \pi_1) + [\pi_2(1 - \pi_2)]/(\pi_1 - \pi_2)^2$, where π_1 is the first proportion and π_2 is the second proportion, both assumed to be known; α is the desired significance level (the probability of Type I error); $(1 - \beta)$ is the desired level of statistical power and β is the corresponding maximum acceptable probability of Type II error; and $z_{\alpha/2}$ and z_β are the z (normal distribution) statistics associated with the respective levels of $\alpha/2$ (two-tailed α) and β. For a continuous predictor, the desired sample size (given here for a one-tailed test) depends on the probability of "success" at the mean of the predictor, denoted $\tilde{p}$, and the natural logarithm comparing the odds of success at the mean of the predictor to the odds of success 1 standard deviation above the mean of the predictor, denoted λ: $n = [z_\alpha + (z_\beta) \exp(-.25\lambda^2)]^2 (1 + 2\tilde{p}\delta)/(\tilde{p}\lambda^2)$, where $\delta = [1 + (1 + \lambda^2)\exp(1.25\lambda^2)]/[1 + \exp(-.25\lambda^2)]$, and "exp" is the exponential function $\exp(Y) = e^Y$.

Hsieh et al. (1998) suggested a modification of the formula for a single quantitative predictor to calculate the desired sample size for multiple predictors. In this formula, R_X^2 is the squared multiple correlation between the predictor of interest and all the other predictors in the model (and can be calculated by making the predictor of interest the dependent variable in an OLS regression analysis with all of the other predictors as independent variables), $\tilde{p}$ is the probability of "success" when *all* of the predictors are at their mean values, and λ remains the same, with the qualification that all of the other predictors in the model are taken at their mean values for the calculation of λ. Then $n = [z_\alpha + (z_\beta) \exp(-.25\lambda^2)]^2 (1 + 2\tilde{p}\delta)/[(\tilde{p}\lambda^2)(1 - R_X^2)]$. Hosmer and Lemeshow (2000:346) suggest that this formula overestimates the needed sample size for the given α and β. Agresti (2002:243), however, notes that although this formula provides only a rough estimate, in most instances we are only guessing at the values of R_X^2 and $\tilde{p}$ prior to drawing the sample. Thus for purposes of empirical research, the formula may be adequate. Based on the above formula, it is also possible to estimate the statistical power for a given sample size and α, algebraically rearranging the formula to

$$z_\beta = \left[-z_\alpha + \sqrt{(N\tilde{p}\lambda^2)/(1 + 2\tilde{p}\lambda^2)} \right] / (-25\lambda^2).$$ Looking up z_β in a standard table for the normal distribution gives the value for β (the measure of Type II error), and hence statistical power $(1 - \beta)$, for a given effect size (represented by $\tilde{p}$) and a given level of statistical significance (α). This is most relevant as a diagnostic when an expected relationship fails to attain statistical significance.

SUMMARY

Table 5.2 is the general format in which I would recommend presenting the basic results of a logistic regression analysis, except that I would also include the standard errors for the coefficients and the Wald statistic if those were being used instead of the likelihood ratio statistic to assess the statistical significance of the predictors. The summary measures at the bottom indicate how well the model predicts the dependent variable quantitatively and qualitatively. In Table 5.2, the quantitative prediction, indicated by R_L^2 (and, if one is interested, R_O^2), indicates a weak to moderate relationship between the dependent variable and the set of predictors in the model. The prediction table and the indices of predictive efficiency indicate a somewhat stronger qualitative relationship between the observed and predicted values of the dependent variable, a pattern which, as we have seen in Chapter 4, may occur when the predicted probabilities tend to be close to .50 and not close to 0 or 1, but tend to be on the "correct" side of .50 for purposes of classifying individuals, in this case, as computer users or nonusers. The statistical significance presented in Table 5.2 is based on the likelihood ratio statistic, which in this case gives the same results as the Wald z statistic.

Two of the variables in the analysis, ethnicity and gender, are not statistically significant. If they were, the odds ratios would indicate that the odds of computer use are 97% as high for males as for females; 88% as high for individuals who identify themselves as Black as for individuals who identify themselves as non-Black; and 26% higher for individuals who identify themselves as neither Black nor White as compared with individuals who identify themselves as either Black or White. Education is statistically significant, and the unstandardized coefficient indicates that an increase of 1 year of education (between the lowest value of 7 and the highest value of 20) increases the logit of computer use by .321. Income is also statistically significant, and the standardized coefficient indicates that a 1 standard deviation increase in the ordinally scaled measure of income results in a .195 standard deviation increase in the logit of computer use. My use of all three types of coefficients in both the table and the verbal description is, of course, a deliberate attempt to illustrate the point that different types of coefficients may be the most intuitively appealing or informative for different types of predictors.

The standardized coefficients also indicate that, measured in the same units (standard deviations), education has the strongest influence on computer use, followed by income. Also, like the standardized coefficients from OLS regression, these standardized logistic regression coefficients can be greater than 1 in magnitude, but they tend not to be unless there are problems, particularly collinearity, in the model. This is not true, however, of the other approaches to constructing standardized coefficients, which were described earlier, all of which have a greater tendency to produce standard coefficients greater than 1, even when there are no problems in the model. It is also the case, especially with large samples, that smaller and larger standardized coefficients for statistically significant predictors can provide a quick visual clue to effects that may be statistically significant but of little or no practical significance. Finally, the fully standardized coefficients presented in this chapter and in Table 5.2 in particular are especially well suited to path analytic models with logistic regression, a topic to be discussed in detail in Chapter 9.

There is a broader principle at work in the decision to provide three different types of coefficients for individual predictors and several different summary measures for the model in Table 5.2. Logistic regression analysis is much younger in its development than OLS regression analysis, and also younger than log-linear analysis. Some of the discussion in this and the preceding two chapters reflects the still unsettled state of the art regarding which measures are most appropriate for assessing the overall model and the individual predictors. The summary statistics and statistics associated with individual predictors in Table 5.2 should be regarded as something close to a minimal set, to which other information may be added. The most sensible general approach, given the state of the art in presenting logistic regression analysis results, is to be inclusive rather than exclusive, to present more rather than less information. Even beyond hedging one's bets on what will become the accepted standards in the field, however, it does seem that logistic regression as an analytical framework is broad enough that the different summary statistics and different coefficients for individual predictors will have their uses for different purposes in different situations.

NOTES

1. Software Note: As with the model for marijuana use, there is a slight difference between output obtained from SPSS (here, Version 11) and output from SAS (here, Version 8) and Stata (here, Version 7) in the precise estimate for the intercept. In this example the intercept from the SAS and Stata output is used. To make the results compatible across different statistical packages, it may be necessary to recode some of the predictors or the dependent variable, depending on the default option used by the software to select the reference category for a categorical variable. Even with this recoding, in the example used in this chapter, the intercepts for SAS and Stata as opposed to SPSS are identical to only two significant digits (5.3) and diverge at the third significant digit (5.31 for SAS and Stata vs. 5.28 for SPSS). This may be a result of the fact that the default convergence criteria were more restrictive in SAS 8 and Stata 7 than in SPSS 11. For example, by default in SPSS, iteration terminated when parameters changed by less than .001, or the log likelihood decreased by less than .01; but by default in Stata (using maximum likelihood estimation), iteration terminated when the coefficients changed by less than .000001 or when the log likelihood decreased by less than .0000001. The point is that different algorithms, regardless of the version of the software, may produce differences in estimates.

2. Software Note: This is accomplished by using appropriate selection statements when computing the correlations and standard deviations on which the standardized coefficients are based, including, for example, the use of the "miss=list" option for SPSS **corr** and **descriptives** and the "casewise" option in Stata **tabstat**. Note carefully that it is the standard deviation of the predicted value of logit(Y), not the predicted value of Y, that is used in the equation for the standardized coefficients.

3. Software Note: The use of 0s and 1s to represent the different possible values of the variable ethnicity is called indicator coding in SPSS and reference cell coding in SAS. Indicator coding is the coding produced in Stata when the "xi.logit" option is used.

4. Software Note: This type of coding is called deviation coding in SPSS and effect coding in SAS, and is the default option in SPSS **logistic** and (when the "class" statement is used) in SAS **logistic.**

5. Software Note: Both SPSS and SAS offer orthogonal polynomial contrasts. SPSS offers the Helmert, reverse Helmert, repeated, and special contrasts; SAS includes the GLM contrast (a variant of reference cell coding applicable when the measured categories are not exhaustive of all the possible codes for the variable). Contrasts in Stata, other than the indicator contrast, must be constructed prior to analysis.

Model Specification, Variable Selection, and Model Building

Statistics textbooks are often written as though we were using statistics merely to confirm what we already believe we know, to test well-formulated theories with a simple examination of statistical influence and strength of association. Realistically, in many disciplines, this is more the exception than the rule. The "theory" being tested is often no more than a set of best guesses developed just before (or, even less desirably, just after) the data analysis; the mathematical form of the relationships specified in the theory is driven more by software availability (Can I analyze a complementary log-log model with the software I am using?) than by considerations of the likely functional form of the relationship. We are not sure whether some variables that are in the model should be removed, or whether some variables that are not in the model should be included. Even when we have a reasonably well-formulated theory, the question remains whether there may be problems in the data that make our examination of the statistical significance and strength of relationship, either for the model as a whole (Chapters 3 and 4) or for individual variables (Chapter 5), questionable. At its most basic level, the diagnosis and correction of problems in the model boils down to one of three basic questions. First, are the variables in the model correct? Do we need to add variables to the model, or should we consider removing variables from the model or combining some variables in the model? Second, is the form of the model correct? Are there nonlinear or nonadditive elements that need to be added or removed, or, more remotely, do we need to change the assumptions about the distribution of errors in the model? Third, are the cases in the data appropriate for the analysis? In particular, do we need to consider removing some cases, or adjusting the model to better account for some observations in the data? The first two questions revolve around the inclusion of variables in the model and are addressed in this chapter in discussing variable selection and model building. The third question revolves around the cases included in the analysis and are addressed in the discussion of logistic regression diagnostics in the next chapter.

SPECIFICATION ERROR

Most generally, the question is whether the assumptions underlying the use of logistic regression analysis are being met. The assumptions for using ordinary least squares multiple regression were listed in Chapter 1. Some but not all of these assumptions are the same or parallel in logistic regression analysis. Here, we focus on one of the first and most important of the assumptions common to both ordinary least squares linear regression and logistic regression: the assumption that the model is correctly specified. (Issues relative to other assumptions underlying logistic regression analysis will be considered in the next chapter.) When the assumption of correct model specification is violated, the result is that the coefficients calculated for the model are biased, systematically too high or too low, too close to or too different from zero, compared with the true value of the coefficients. (In some instances, coefficients may be biased but *consistent*, meaning that although they are consistently underestimated or overestimated, the estimated coefficients approach the true values of the population parameters as the sample size increases toward infinity.)

Correct specification has two components: (1) the functional form of the model is correct and (2) the model includes all relevant independent variables and no irrelevant independent variables. With regard to the functional form of the model, it is assumed that the logistic function is the correct function to use and that the form of the relationship between the dependent variable and the independent variables, allowing for transformations of the *independent* variables, is *linear in the logit*. Misspecification as a result of using the logistic function, as opposed to a different S-shaped function, is unlikely to be a problem. Aldrich and Nelson (1984) demonstrated that logit models (based on the logistic distribution) and probit models (based on the normal distribution) produce highly similar results. Hosmer and Lemeshow (1989:168) note that logistic regression models are highly flexible and produce results very similar to other models in the range of probabilities between .2 and .8. There is usually little theoretical basis for preferring an alternative model. Nonetheless, some software readily allows the computation of models with probit or other specifications as alternatives to the logistic regression model.

"Linear in the logit" simply means that logit(Y) is linearly related to the predictors, as specified in Equation 1.1 from Chapter 1 (p. 14): logit(Y) $= a + \beta_1 X_1 + \beta_2 X_2 + \ldots + \beta_K X_K$. Even if the logistic function is the correct function, there are ways in which the assumption of linearity in the logit may be violated. First, logit(Y) may be a function of a nonlinear combination of the independent variables. Second, the relationship among some or all of the independent variables may be multiplicative or interactive, rather than additive. These issues parallel issues of linearity and additivity in ordinary least squares multiple linear regression. In linear regression, allowance was made for transformations in both the independent and the dependent variables, and transformation of the values of the dependent variable was meaningful because the dependent variable was assumed to be measured on a continuous/interval/ratio scale. In logistic regression, however, the values of the dependent variable are themselves meaningless; they only reflect assignment to one or the other of two categories. It is not those values, but rather the probability of membership in one of the two categories, that matters. Transformation of the dependent variable has no impact on the analysis; whatever values are assigned to the dependent variable are simply ignored.

The discussion of specification error is inextricably intertwined with the discussion of model selection. For some purposes, stepwise methods are used to evaluate the contribution of variables to the regression equation, in particular to avoid inclusion of irrelevant predictors. In some instances, the stepwise inclusion or exclusion of variables or cases is decided entirely by the researcher. This is especially the case when we test for nonlinearity (e.g., by including quadratic terms) or nonadditivity (e.g., by including interaction terms) in the regression equation. The decision about whether the inclusion of nonlinear or nonadditive terms is justified is typically based on the magnitude and statistical significance of the change in the explained variance, R^2, in linear regression and, in parallel, the magnitude and statistical significance of the change in explained variation (most likely R_L^2, although other criteria including R_O^2 or one of the indices of predictive efficiency could also be used) in logistic regression. Alternatively, stepwise methods may proceed automatically, using selection criteria specified by the researcher, but then allowing the statistical routine to add or remove variables without further direct intervention by the researcher. Automatic stepwise methods are typically used in exploratory analysis, when we are more concerned with theory development than theory testing. Such research may occur in the early stages of the study of a phenomenon, when neither theory nor knowledge about correlates of the phenomenon is well developed. Criteria for automatic stepwise inclusion or removal of variables for a model generally involve tests that are similar to but less restrictive than the tests used in theory testing.[1]

OMITTING RELEVANT VARIABLES

Omitting relevant variables from the equation in logistic regression results in biased coefficients for the independent variables, to the extent that the omitted variable is correlated with the independent variables in the logistic regression equation. As in linear regression (Berry and Feldman 1985), the direction of the bias depends on the parameter for the excluded variable, the direction of the effect of the excluded variable on the dependent variable, and the direction of the relationship between excluded and included variables. The magnitude of the bias depends on the strength of the relationship between the included and the excluded variables. If the excluded variable is completely uncorrelated with the included variables, the coefficients may be unbiased, but in practice this is unlikely to occur. Bias is generally regarded as a more serious problem than inefficiency, but a small amount of bias may be preferable to massive inefficiency.

Omitted variable bias may occur because available theories have failed to identify all the relevant predictors or causes of a dependent variable, or because theoretically relevant variables have been omitted. The pattern characteristic of omitted variable bias may also occur if the functional form of the model is misspecified. A linear specification of a nonlinear model may be computationally equivalent to the omission of a variable representing a nonlinear component of the relationship between the dependent variable and an independent variable. An additive specification of a nonadditive model may be equivalent to the omission of a variable, specifically a variable constructed as the interaction of two other variables, from the model. When the omitted variable is neither a nonlinear term nor an interaction term, only theory (or perhaps a disappointingly low R_L^2) offers much hope of identifying and remedying the problem. When the excluded variable is really a nonlinear term or an interaction term, a function of variables already in the equation, the detection and correction of the problem can be considerably easier.

NONLINEARITY IN THE LOGIT AS AN OMITTED VARIABLE PROBLEM

In a linear regression model, the change in the dependent variable associated with a one-unit change in the independent variable is constant, equal to the regression coefficient for the independent variable. If the change in Y for a one-unit change in X depends on the value of X (as it does when Y is a dichotomous variable), the relationship is nonlinear. Correspondingly, when logit(Y) is the dependent variable, if the change in logit(Y) for a one-unit change in X is constant, and does not depend on the value of X, we say that the logistic regression model has a linear form, or that the relationship is *linear in the logit*, and the change in logit(Y) for a one-unit change in X is equal to the logistic regression coefficient. If the relationship is not linear in the logit, the change in logit(Y) for a one-unit change in X is not constant but depends on the value of X.

There are several possible techniques for detecting nonlinearity in the relationship between the dependent variable, logit(Y), and each of the independent variables (Hosmer and Lemeshow 1989:88–91). One technique is to treat each of the independent variables as a categorical variable, and use an orthogonal polynomial contrast to test for linear, quadratic, cubic, and higher-order effects in either bivariate logistic regression or in a multiple logistic regression model. If the independent variable has a large number of categories (e.g., 20), the standard errors tend to be large, and neither the linear nor any of the nonlinear effects may appear to be statistically significant, even when a statistically significant linear effect exists. A second possibility is to use the Box-Tidwell transformation (Fox 1991:70–73; Hosmer and Lemeshow 1989:90; Ryan 1997:74–76). This involves adding a term of the form $(X)\ln(X)$ (X multiplied by the natural logarithm of X) to the equation. If the coefficient for this variable is statistically significant, there is evidence of nonlinearity in the relationship between logit(Y) and X. The estimate of the power to which X needs to be raised is equal to one plus the coefficient of the term $(X)\ln(X)$ divided by the coefficient of X in the original equation; that is, if the coefficient of X in the original equation is b, and the coefficient for $(X)\ln(X)$ in the new equation is designated γ, then the power δ to which X needs to be raised is $\delta = 1 + (b/\gamma)$. We can then substitute the new power of X, X^δ, for X in the equation.

As Ryan (1997) notes "the Box-Tidwell approach is geared toward detecting the need for a nonlinear term *instead* of the corresponding linear term" (p. 76), that is, using a higher or lower power of the predictor X in place of, not in addition to, X. The process can then be repeated, again adding $(X)\ln(X)$ terms to the equation, to see whether further transformation is necessary, until the estimated value of δ stabilizes. Hosmer and Lemeshow (1989) note that this procedure is not sensitive to small departures from linearity. Additionally, this procedure does not specify the precise form of the nonlinearity. If the relationship is nonlinear, further investigation may be necessary to determine the pattern of the nonlinearity. Finally, in applying this procedure, some balance may need to be struck between simplicity and adopting the precise estimates of δ that minimize the deviation of the model from linearity (in the transformed power of X). If δ is estimated to be 2.21 or 0.57 for X_1 and X_2, for example, one may want to use $(X_1)^2$ and $\sqrt{X_2}$ rather than $(X_1)^{2.21}$ and $(X_2)^{0.57}$ because the latter terms may, in their apparent precision, merely be capitalizing on chance variation while the former, simpler terms are more intuitively understandable and may in fact better reflect reality (which, in the laws of physics at least, rarely produces an exponent that cannot reasonably be expressed as an integer or the ratio of single-digit integers).

A third procedure suggested by Hosmer and Lemeshow (1989) is to aggregate cases into groups defined by the values of the independent variable X, calculate the mean of the dependent variable Y for each group, and then take the logit of the mean of Y for each group and plot it against the value of the independent variable. For each value I of the independent variable X, the mean of Y is the conditional probability $P(Y = 1|X = I)$. One problem with this procedure arises if, for any value of X, Y is always either 1 or 0. If it is, then we cannot calculate logit($\overline{Y}$), which would in this circumstance be equal to $\pm\infty$, either infinitely large or infinitely small. It may be possible to overcome this problem by grouping adjacent categories with similar but unequal probabilities. This could conceal some of the nonlinearity in the relationship, however. Another possible option would be to assign an arbitrarily large mean (e.g., 0.99) to groups with a mean of 1, and an arbitrarily small mean (0.01) to groups with a mean of 0, in order to implement this method. An important advantage to this method is that, like graphical techniques generally, it helps identify the pattern of the nonlinearity. In addition, examination of the plot may help identify cases with unusual values on the independent variable or combinations of values on the dependent and independent variables.

Table 6.1 presents the results of a Box-Tidwell test for nonlinearity in the model for marijuana use. In the first part of Table 6.1, the two nonlinear terms BTEDF = (EDF5)ln(EDF5) and BTBEL = (BELIEF4)ln(BELIEF4) are added to the model. Taken together, the effects of the two nonlinear interaction terms are statistically significant (change in G_M = 15.065 with 2 degrees of freedom; p = .001), but based on the G_X, the likelihood ratio statistic for each of the nonlinear terms, only BTBEL is statistically significant (G_X = 9.932 with 1 degree of freedom, p = .002 for BTBEL; G_X = 2.226 with 1 degree of freedom, p = .136 for BTEDF). When BTEDF is removed from the model, the coefficient for BTBEL is still statistically significant (G_X = 12.839, 1 degree of freedom, p = .000), and inclusion of BTBEL in the equation increases R_L^2 by .034, 3.4%.

Figure 6.1 (p. 111) shows why the relationship between PMRJ5 and BELIEF4 appears to be nonlinear. The mean of PMRJ5 was calculated for each value of BELIEF4, and since the mean of PMRJ5 was either 0 or 1 for several values of BELIEF4, values of 1 were recoded as .99 and values of 0 were recoded as .01. Next, the logit of each mean was taken, and plotted in Figure 6.1 against the values of BELIEF4. In the lower-left quadrant of the plot, there are two outliers, respondents with very weak mean beliefs that it is wrong to violate the law, but who report no marijuana use. Each mean, as it turns out, is based on a single case. Except for these two cases, the plot does not appear to depart substantially from linearity. The second half of Table 6.1 confirms this assessment. With the two cases deleted from the analysis, BTEDF and BTBEL, separately and in combination, have no statistically significant effect on the logit of PMRJ5. Whether these cases should be deleted or retained will receive further consideration in Chapter 7.

A second example of the use of the Box-Tidwell test is presented in Table 6.2 (p. 112). In this table, the model for computer use with gender, ethnicity, education, and income as predictors has been augmented by $(x)\ln(x)$ terms for education and income. In the first half of the table, both the change in R_L^2 and the individual $(x)\ln(x)$ coefficients are statistically significant, indicating nonlinearity in the model. To further explore this nonlinearity, the mean probability of computer use is calculated for each value of education and income, and then the mean probability of computer use is plotted as the dependent variable with education and income, respectively, as predictors. The results are presented in Figure 6.2 (p. 113).

The two plots suggest two different reasons for the apparent nonlinearities with respect to education and income. For education, the plot appears somewhat S-shaped around the regression line, but perhaps more important, the impact of education on computer use appears to level off after 16 years of education (college graduation). This suggests three possible strategies: (1) modeling the effect of a function of education that has at least two points of inflection, perhaps a cubic function of education; (2) using separate logistic regressions for different parts of the continuum represented by education, and in particular trying a separate regression for education less than or equal to 16 years and education greater than 16 years; and (3) recoding education so that college and above is collapsed into a single category. The first option, not shown in detail, does produce a better fit, but suggests an accelerating rate of decrease in the probability of computer use as the number of years of education increases, a result that seems to make little sense. The second option would be reasonable for a bivariate relationship but is complicated by the inclusion of the other predictors in the model. The third option is presented in the second part of Table 6.2, where the recoding of education

TABLE 6.1   Box-Tidwell Tests for Nonlinearity in the Model for Marijuana Use

Dependent Variable	Association/ Predictive Efficiency	Independent Variable	Unstandardized Logistic Regression Coefficient (b)	Standard Error of b	Statistical Significance of b (Based on Likelihood Ratio G_X)	Standardized Logistic Regression Coefficient
PMRJ5 $n = 227$	$G_M = 123.322$ ($p = .000$)	EDF5	2.415	1.191	0.076	3.073
		BELIEF4	3.620	1.421	0.002	−4.272
	$R^2_L = .418$					
		SEX (Male)	−1.660	0.428	0.000	−0.249
	Change in G_M from base model (Table 3.1) = 15.065 ($p = .001$)	ETHN (Black) (Other)	0.333 0.859	0.536 0.817	0.516 0.535* 0.293*	0.036 0.063
		BTEDF	−0.551	0.325	0.136	−1.620
	Change in R^2_L from base model = .051	BTBEL Intercept	−0.891 −29.210	0.340 8.733	0.002 0.001*	−4.172 —
PMRJ5 $n = 225$	$G_M = 125.195$ ($p = .000$)	EDF5	2.411	1.184	0.076	3.012
		BELIEF4	1.380	2.812	0.644	−1.503
	$R^2_L = .427$					
		SEX (Male)	−1.676	0.436	0.000	−0.249
	Change in G_M from base model ($n = 225$) = 2.561 ($p = .278$)	ETHN (Black) (Other)	0.342 0.823	0.534 0.814	0.530 0.522* 0.312*	0.036 0.060
		BTEDF	−0.555	0.323	0.137	−2.551
	Change in R^2_L from base model ($n = 225$) = .009	BTBEL Intercept	−0.371 −15.541	0.660 17.134	0.599 0.364*	−1.716 —

*Statistical significance based on the likelihood ratio statistic is not available for individual categories of categorical independent variables or for the intercept; for these, the Wald statistic is used to determine statistical significance.

FIGURE 6.1   Logistic Regression Diagnostics: Test for Nonlinearity

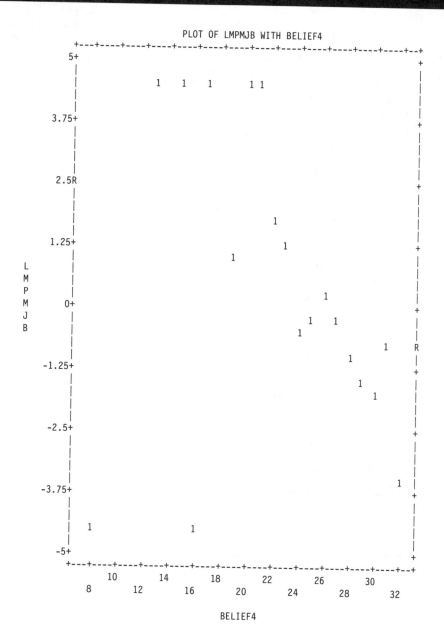

LMPMJB = Logit of Mean of Prevalence of Marijuana Use for Each Value of BELIEF4

BELIEF4 = Belief That It Is Wrong to Violate the Law

TABLE 6.2   Box-Tidwell Tests for Nonlinearity in the Model for Computer Use

Dependent Variable	Association/ Predictive Efficiency	Independent Variable	Unstandardized Logistic Regression Coefficient (b)	Standard Error of b	Statistical Significance of b (Based on Likelihood Ratio G_X)	Standardized Logistic Regression Coefficient
COMPUSX $n = 2,241$	$G_M = 545.476$ $(p = .000)$	INCNEW98	−0.353	0.118	0.003	−0.332
		EDUCNEW	2.503	0.584	0.000	1.293
	$R_L^2 = .180$					
		SEX (Male)	−0.010	0.100	0.918	−0.001
	Change in G_M from base model = 27.895 $(p = .000)$	RACE (Black) (Other)	−0.158 0.219	0.135 0.227	0.276 0.243* 0.334*	−0.011 0.009
		BTEDUC	−0.610	0.162	0.000	1.130
	Change in R_L^2 from base model = .010	BTINC	0.128	0.034	0.000	0.427
		Intercept	−11.750	8.733	0.000*	—
COMPUSX $n = 2,241$	$G_M = 823.095$ $(p = .000)$	INCNEW98	−0.351	0.118	0.003	−0.340
		EDUC17	0.532	0.110	0.000	0.256
	$R_L^2 = .180$					
		SEX (Male)	−0.013	0.100	0.895	−0.001
	Change in G_M from base model = 16.028 $(p = .000)$	RACE (Black) (Other)	−0.145 0.203	0.135 0.225	0.333 0.283* 0.369*	−0.010 0.009
		BTEDUC	−0.048	0.028	0.095	−0.091
	Change in R_L^2 from base model = .010	BTINC	0.127	0.034	0.000	0.436
		Intercept	−4.959	0.666	0.000*	—

*Statistical significance based on the likelihood ratio statistic is not available for individual categories of categorical independent variables or for the intercept; for these, the Wald statistic is used to determine statistical significance.

FIGURE 6.2 Plots of Mean Probability of Computer Use With Education and Income

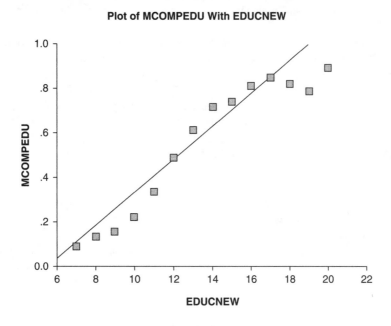

Plot of MCOMPEDU With EDUCNEW

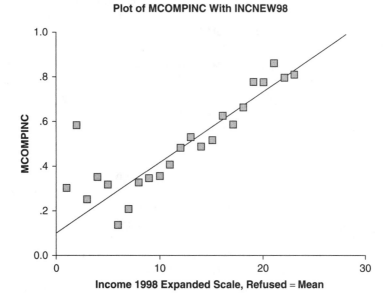

Plot of MCOMPINC With INCNEW98

results in a substantial reduction in the standardized coefficient for (education)ln(education) and a change in the p value from .000 to .095 according to the likelihood ratio statistic (.084 according to the Wald statistic). The change in the coding of education thus reduces the nonlinearity to marginal statistical significance and arguably below the level at which we would consider the nonlinearity substantively significant.

The apparent nonlinearity in the relationship between computer use and income appears to be the result of relatively poor discrimination among income categories at the lower end of the scale. In particular, the mean probability of computer use appears to be particularly high (.583) for the second category of annual income ($1,000 to $2,999) and low (.138) for the sixth category of income ($6,000 to $6,999). The plots suggest that it may be appropriate to collapse the lower categories of income like the higher categories of education, because below a certain threshold for income, the model no longer discriminates accurately among the existing categories. Doing so, however, does not eliminate the nonlinearity in the relationship between income and computer use. Alternatively, the apparent nonlinearity in income may be the result of nothing more than random error and unreliability in the estimates of computer use below a certain income level. Unlike education, for which the mean probability of computer use clearly appeared to level off and fluctuate only slightly about the mean probability of computer use for 16 years of education, the mean probability of computer use fluctuates wildly for the lowest six or seven categories of income. Given the failure to eliminate the nonlinearity in the relationship between computer use and income by collapsing the lowest categories of income, nothing has been changed about income for Table 6.2. The apparent nonlinearity may, in fact, be no more than apparent, attributable to random error.

NONADDITIVITY AS AN OMITTED VARIABLE PROBLEM

Nonlinearity occurs when the change in the dependent variable associated with a one-unit change in the independent variable depends on the value of the independent variable. Nonadditivity occurs when the change in the dependent variable associated with a one-unit change in the independent variable depends on the value of one of the other independent variables. For example, a one-unit change in exposure to delinquent friends may produce a larger change in the frequency or prevalence of marijuana use for individuals with weak to moderate beliefs that it is wrong to violate the law (who may be more susceptible to peer influence) than in individuals who strongly believe that it is wrong to violate the law (who may be less susceptible to peer influence). Detection of nonadditivity is not as straightforward as detection of nonlinearity in either linear or logistic regression. Unless theory provides some guidance, one is commonly left with the choice between assuming an additive model, testing for interaction effects that seem intuitively plausible, or testing for all possible interaction effects. This last option is feasible for relatively simple models, but becomes progressively more tedious and carries increasingly more risk of capitalizing on random sampling variation as the number of variables in the model increases.

Interaction effects may take several different forms, depending on the scale on which the variables thought to interact are measured. For two categorical variables, dummy variable coding eliminates one category from each variable from the model, and the remaining dummy variables are multiplied so that each category of the first variable is multiplied by each category on the second variable. If there are H nonredundant categories for the first variable and I nonredundant categories for the second, the result is a set of $H \times I$ dummy variables representing the interaction effect. For example, if we believe that there is an interaction between sex (one nonredundant category and one reference category) and ethnicity (two nonredundant categories and one reference category), we get $1 \times 2 = 2$ dummy variables for the interaction, one representing females of African American ethnicity and one representing females of Other ethnicity. For two continuous variables, such as exposure and belief, the usual procedure is to assume a linear interaction and to multiply the two variables, usually after *centering* the variables by subtracting their means. Centering helps avoid problems of collinearity between the interaction term and the original variables in the model. For a continuous and a categorical variable, each nonredundant category of the categorical variable is multiplied by the continuous variable.

An example of an interaction effect involving a categorical (really dichotomous) and a continuous variable is given in Table 6.3. In Table 6.3, two interaction terms are added to the model. The interaction terms are formed by multiplying the dummy variable for gender by each of the two continuous variables. The interaction terms, representing the interaction between SEX and EDF5 and the interaction between SEX and BELIEF4, test whether the effects of belief that it is wrong to violate the law and exposure to delinquent friends are different for males and females. This is a test

TABLE 6.3   Testing for the Interaction of Sex With Belief and Exposure

Dependent Variable	Association/ Predictive Efficiency	Independent Variable	Unstandardized Logistic Regression Coefficient (b)	Standard Error of b	Statistical Significance of b	Standardized Logistic Regression Coefficient
PMRJ5	$G_M = 112.913$ $(p = .000)$	EDF5	0.549	0.126	0.000	0.662
		BELIEF4	−0.161	0.088	0.067	−0.180
	$R_L^2 = .383$ $(R_L^2$ change = .016)	SEX (Male)	−1.516	0.408	0.000	−0.215
		ETHN			0.459	
	$R^2 = .435$ (no change)	(Black)	−0.303	0.516	0.558	−0.032
		(Other)	0.891	0.761	0.242	0.063
	$\lambda_p = .463$ (change = −.025)	SEX $\times Z_{EDF}$	−0.919	0.638	0.150	−0.187
		SEX $\times Z_{BELIEF}$	0.451	0.491	0.358	0.084
	$\tau_p = .585$ (change = −.019)	Intercept	−2.132	3.122	0.495	—

NOTE: EDF5 and BELIEF4 were standardized for inclusion in the interaction terms to avoid collinearity.

for differences in the partial slopes of the curves representing the relationship of PMRJ5 to EDF5 and BELIEF4 for males and females. Individually, neither of the interaction terms is statistically significant. The addition of the two interaction terms together results in a marginally significant change in G_M (4.656, $p = .098$), a small increase in R_L^2 (.016), and *decreases* in λ_p (−.025) and τ_p (−.019) because there are two more false negatives in the prediction table when the interaction terms are added. The most reasonable conclusion from this result would be that the effects of belief that it is wrong to violate the law and exposure to delinquent friends have the same effects on the prevalence of marijuana use for males and females.

Linear interactions involving only two variables, as described above, are the most commonly calculated types of interactions, but it is also possible to have (a) higher-order interactions, in which three or more variables are combined, possibly by multiplication, to obtain a three-way or higher-order interaction and (b) nonlinear interactions, in which a nonlinear function of one variable is multiplied by a linear or nonlinear function of one or more other variables to produce the interaction term. For a more extensive discussion of interactions in logistic regression, see Jaccard (2001). It is rare that nonlinear interaction terms, or terms involving more than two or three variables will be needed, and the inclusion of more complex interaction terms runs the risk of capitalizing on random variation.

In some statistical software, one need only specify the interaction term to be included and the software calculates the interaction term, includes it in the equation, and provides information about its statistical significance and the strength of its relationship to the dependent variable. In other software packages, it is necessary to separately calculate the interaction term (or terms, if the interaction involves a nominal variable with more than two categories) and add it (or them) to the model. The only complication here is when the interaction involves a nominal variable with more than two categories, in which case it may be necessary to compare the model with and without *all* the interaction terms to determine whether the interaction is statistically and substantively significant. In linear regression, statistical significance of the interaction effect is equal to the statistical significance of the change in R^2 that results from adding the interaction effect to the model, and substantive significance is best evaluated as the magnitude of the change in R^2 (how much does the interaction add to our ability to predict the dependent variable?). In logistic regression, the corresponding criteria are the statistical significance of the change in G_M and the magnitude of the change in R_L^2.

INCLUDING IRRELEVANT VARIABLES

Including one or more irrelevant variables has the effect of increasing the standard error of the parameter estimates, that is, of reducing the efficiency of the estimates, without biasing the coefficients. The degree to which the standard errors are inflated depends on the magnitude of the correlation between the irrelevant included variable and the other variables in the model. If the irrelevant included variable is completely uncorrelated with the other variables in the equation, the standard errors may not be inflated at all, but this condition is extremely unlikely in practice.

As noted earlier, the term *stepwise regression* could, in principle, be applied to the analysis of interaction effects or nonlinear effects, insofar as that analysis involved a two-step procedure for testing whether interaction terms were appropriate in the model for prevalence of marijuana use. More often, the term refers to the use of decisions made by computer algorithms, rather than choices made directly by the researcher, to select a set of predictors for inclusion or removal from a linear or logistic regression model. Some authors defend stepwise techniques in this latter sense as a useful tool for exploratory research (Agresti and Finlay 1997:527–534; Hosmer and Lemeshow 1989:106); others criticize it as an admission of ignorance about the phenomenon being studied (Studenmund and Cassidy 1987). Without going too deeply into the arguments about the use of stepwise procedures, there appears to be general agreement that the use of computer-controlled stepwise procedures to select variables is inappropriate for theory testing because it capitalizes on random variations in the data and produces results that tend to be idiosyncratic, difficult to replicate in any sample other than the sample in which they were originally obtained.

Proponents of the use of stepwise procedures suggest that they may be useful in two contexts: purely predictive research and exploratory research. In purely predictive research, there is no concern with causality, only with identifying a model, including a set of predictors, that provides accurate predictions of some phenomenon. For example, a college admissions office may want to know what variables are good predictors of college success, not for theoretical development, but purely for the practical purpose of selecting students likely to succeed in college. In exploratory research, there may be a concern with theory construction and development to predict and explain a phenomenon, when the phenomenon is so new or so little studied that existing "theory" amounts to little more than empirically unsupported hunches about explanations for the phenomenon. An example of the use of stepwise techniques in exploratory research is provided by Wofford et al. (1994).

Wofford et al. (1994) studied the continuity of domestic violence in the National Youth Survey for young men and women, 18 to 27 years old. Twenty-six predictors, based on the domestic violence literature, were included in their analysis. As part of the study, respondents who had reported being victims or perpetrators of domestic violence in 1984 were reinterviewed in 1987, to see whether the domestic violence had continued or been suspended since the 1984 interview. A total of 108 women (out of 807 in the original sample) reported being victims of domestic violence in 1983 and were reinterviewed in 1986. Wofford et al. constructed a logistic regression model that included all 26 predictors. Because theory in this area was not well developed, and because the number of cases was small relative to the number of explanatory variables suggested in the literature, stepwise logistic regression was used.

Backward elimination rather than forward inclusion was selected as the method of stepwise regression. In some cases, a variable may appear to have a statistically significant effect only when another variable is controlled or held constant. This is called a *suppressor* effect (Agresti and Finlay 1997:368). One disadvantage to forward inclusion as a method for stepwise regression is the possible exclusion of variables involved in suppressor effects. With backward elimination, since both variables will already be in the model, there is less risk of failing to find a relationship when one exists. Usually, the results of backward elimination and forward inclusion methods of stepwise linear (and logistic) regression will produce the same results, but when the results differ, backward elimination may uncover relationships missed by forward inclusion.

To further prevent the failure to find a relationship when one exists, the usual .05 criterion for statistical significance should probably be relaxed. Bendel and Afifi (1977), based on their studies of forward stepwise regression, suggested that .05 is too low, and often excludes important variables from the model. Instead, they recommended that the statistical significance criterion for inclusion be set in a range from .15 to .20 for forward inclusion, and about half that for backward elimination. This results in an increased risk of rejecting the null hypothesis when it is true (finding a relationship that is not really there), but a lower risk of failing to reject the null hypothesis when it is false (not finding a relationship that really is there). In exploratory research, as opposed to theory testing, there tends to be a greater emphasis on finding good predictors than on eliminating bad ones. Wofford et al. (1994) examined three models: (1) a full model with all the variables in the logistic regression equation, (2) a reduced model with all variables for which $p > .10$ were eliminated (in practice, this produced the same result as using a .15 or .20 cutoff), and (3) a further reduced model with all variables for which $p > .05$ eliminated. Table 6.4 presents the results.

The first part of Table 6.4 compares the three models. For the full model, G_M is not statistically significant, indicating that the predictor variables contribute no more than chance to the explanation of the dependent variable. Part of the reason for the failure of the model chi-square to attain

TABLE 6.4 Continuity of Marital Violence Victimization (Women)			
$N = 108$	*Model 1: All Variables Included*	*Model 2: Maximum p = .100*	*Model 3: Maximum p = .050*
Model chi-square G_M (degrees of freedom)	30.254 (28 *df*)	21.284 (7 *df*)	4.472 (1 *df*)
Statistical significance of G_M	0.351	0.003	0.034
D_M	119.429	128.298	145.211
Change in G_M from previous model (degrees of freedom)	—	8.870 (21 *df*)	16.812 (6 *df*)
Statistical significance of change in G_M from previous model	—	0.99	0.010
R_L^2	0.202	0.150	0.030
τ_p	0.481	0.509	0.145
Individual Predictor Results for Model 2			
Independent Variables	*b*	*Standard Error*	*p (Based on Likelihood Ratio Statistic)*
Welfare recipient	1.88	.95	.03
Social class background	−0.03	.02	.05
Prior minor assault	1.24	.53	.02
Prior felony assault	−1.07	.62	.08
Witnessed parental violence	−1.70	.64	.00
Frequency of serious violence in relationship	0.12	.06	.05
Sought professional assistance	0.88	.53	.09

statistical significance is the small sample size; another may be the large number of variables included in the model. Model 2, including only predictors with coefficients significant at $p < .10$, has a smaller, but statistically significant G_M, as does Model 3, which includes only predictors with coefficients significant at $p < .05$, and which has only one predictor satisfying this criterion in the model. The change in the model chi-square (or equivalently the change in D_M) from Model 1 to Model 2 and from Model 1 to Model 3 is not statistically significant; however, the change in G_M from Model 2 to Model 3 is statistically significant at the .01 level. For the full model, R_L^2 is .20; for Model 2, it decreases to .15, and for Model 3 it is only .03. Model 1 has a τ_p of .48; τ_p actually increases to .51 for Model 2, but for Model 3 it is only .14.

Model 2 was selected for further analysis because (1) G_M was statistically significant for the reduced models but not the full model, (2) Model 2 provided a statistically significantly better fit than Model 3, and did not fit statistically significantly worse than the full model, and (3) the change in R_L^2 and τ_p were relatively small (and in opposite directions) for Model 1 compared with Model 2, but R_L^2 and τ_p were much lower for Model 3 than for Model 2. The results of Model 2 are presented in the second half of Table 6.4. Substantively, they indicate that women who are welfare recipients, from a *higher* social class background, who have committed minor assaults but who have *not* committed felony assaults, who have *not* witnessed parental violence, who have experienced higher frequencies of serious violence in the relationship, and who have sought professional assistance are more likely to experience continuity rather than suspension of domestic violence. Full discussion of the substantive results is left to Wofford et al. (1994).

Several methodological points regarding stepwise logistic regression are illustrated in Table 6.4. Probably, the most important methodological point is that these results must be regarded as very tentative and inconclusive. This is a search for plausible predictors, not a convincing test of any theory. Second, an important element of the stepwise procedure is the comparison of the full and reduced models. As suggested by Bendel and Afifi (1977), the .05 criterion for inclusion appears to be too severe; based on the comparisons of goodness-of-fit and predictive efficiency statistics, more reasonable results are obtained with a more liberal cutoff point for statistical significance. Third and finally, the variables identified in Model 2 are good candidates for use in the prediction of domestic violence, but some may as easily be effects (e.g., seeking professional assistance) as causes. Further development and testing of theory may be based on these results, but would require replication with other data and explanation (preferably in the form of a clear theoretical justification) of why these variables appear as predictors of continuity of domestic violence.

MODEL BUILDING AND SELECTION

The use of mechanically applied, software-driven stepwise selection of variables is one approach to deciding what variables to include in a model when theoretical guidance is limited. Another approach sometimes used in research is, as a first step, to examine the bivariate relationship of each predictor to the dependent variable and then, in the second step, to include only those predictors satisfying some criterion (typically a statistically significant relationship with the dependent variable) in the model. Subsequent steps may further modify the model, possibly including the use of backward stepwise elimination to further reduce the model. This approach has the same drawback as stepwise logistic regression using forward inclusion: It misses any suppressor effect, thereby potentially excluding one or more variables which, not in the bivariate relationship but in the presence of other variables, might have a statistically and substantively significant effect on the dependent variable. For this reason, this approach seems to be generally inferior to stepwise logistic regression using backward elimination (and little or no better than stepwise logistic regression with forward inclusion), and is therefore not recommended.

It has also been suggested (Hosmer and Lemeshow 2000:92–96) that examination of bivariate relationships prior to calculation of the full model may be used to help identify variables for which transformations may be appropriate. A concern with this approach is that while examination of bivariate relationships is useful to supplement diagnostics for the full model, apparent nonlinearities in the logit for bivariate models may be symptoms of more than one problem, not only nonlinearity in the logit but also nonadditivity or the presence of outliers. Allowing the bivariate data to drive the functional specification of the model runs the risk of capitalizing on chance variation, overfitting the data and producing an excessively complex model that cannot be generalized beyond the sample at hand, a result with very little practical and even less theoretical usefulness. By all means, one should use the bivariate analysis to inform the diagnostics for the full model, but it would be unwise to allow the bivariate diagnostics rather than theory (or at least informed speculation), plus perhaps consideration of the diagnostics of the full model, to drive the specification of the model.

A third approach is to construct models with different sets of predictors and to compare those models with one another. When the models are nested, comparison is straightforward, and the usual tests for statistical and substantive significance of changes in G_M and R_L^2 can be performed for the model overall. Other indices used to compare models include the Akaike information criterion, AIC = $D_M + 2K$ and the Schwartz criterion, SC = $D_M + (2)\ln(N)$ (which has also been called the Schwartz-Bayes criterion, SBC, and is one of at least two measures to have been called the Bayesian information criterion, BIC), where $D_M = -2LL_M$ is the deviance statistic, K is the number of parameters estimated in the model, and N is the number of cases. As with D_M on which AIC and SC are based, smaller numbers for AIC and SC indicate better models. For non-nested models, it is not possible to directly compare model χ^2 statistics across models, but there are other comparisons that can be made. First, although one cannot assess the statistical significance of the differences in the models using G_M, one can use the prediction tables to compare the percentage of cases correctly classified, and test whether the difference is statistically significant, using the binomial $d = (p_1 - p_2)/\sqrt{(P)(1 - P)(2/N)}$, where p_1 is the percentage correct in the first model, p_2 is the percentage correct in the second model, N is the number of cases in the sample (assuming the model is being calculated over the same set of cases; otherwise one must use separate numbers of cases n_1 for the first sample and n_2 for the second sample; and in the denominator, $2/N$ must be replaced by the sum $1/n_1 + 1/n_2$), $P = (p_1 + p_2)/N$ is the average percentage correct, and d is approximately normally distributed for large samples (Bulmer 1979:144–145). This comparison is most appropriate when the interest is more in qualitative than quantitative accuracy of prediction. Second, although one cannot directly compare G_M across models, there is nothing to prevent comparison of the ratio of G_M to $-2LL_0$, that is, R_L^2, across models, and more generally, one can compare measures of multiple association (R_L^2, R_O^2, λ_p, τ_p, φ_p) to see whether different nested *or* non-nested models differ in explained variation. The limitation here is that one does not know whether a given difference in measures of explained variation is statistically as well as substantively significant, but large differences can be accepted as evidence (not proof) that the model with the higher explained variation may be preferable to the alternative model.

A related approach sometimes taken in logistic regression analysis is to begin with a simple model and to add variables, not mechanically using software-driven stepwise inclusion, but instead with the researcher sequentially adding blocks of related variables to a model to see how the addition of different sets of variables changes the explanatory power of the model or the influence of specific variables in the earlier blocks. For example, for computer use, we could begin with variables involving ascribed sociodemographic characteristics (gender, ethnicity, and age, over which the individual has little or no control) to examine the impact of those variables in the absence of other variables, then add achieved characteristics (education and income, over which the individual typically has some control or some ability to change) to see (a) by how much the addition of achieved characteristics improves the model that includes only ascribed characteristics, (b) by how much the addition of the ascribed characteristics improves the model that includes only the achieved characteristics, and (c) by how much the inclusion of both ascribed and achieved characteristics changes the relationships of the ascribed and achieved characteristics, respectively, to computer use, relative to the models including one or the other but not both. This is a simple two-step process (first calculating the separate models, then calculating the combined model); it is possible to expand this approach to include multiple steps when there are more than two blocks of variables to be considered. Table 6.5 presents the example described above using ascribed characteristics (Model 1), achieved characteristics (Model 2), and the combination of both (Model 3) as predictors of computer use.

Typically, the first question in this sort of sequential approach to model building is whether the additional variables added on subsequent steps offer any substantial improvement over the model with those variables excluded. The first criterion is whether there is a statistically significant change in the model χ^2 statistic, followed by a consideration of whether the increase in the explained variation is substantively significant. If both these criteria are met, the focus moves to the individual predictors to see which of the old predictors remain statistically and/or substantively significant as predictors, and which of the new predictors are statistically and/or substantively significant. If neither of the first two criteria are met, the only real point in examining the statistical and substantive significance of the individual predictors is exploratory, to see whether yet another alternative model could be constructed and tested, based on which of the variables appear to be useful in predicting the outcome in the more inclusive model, a procedure that parallels the ideas behind the more mechanical application of stepwise techniques. In Table 6.5, the first and second models are not nested, so although we know that the achieved characteristics (income and education, $R_L^2 = .17$) in Model 2 explain 5% more of the variation in computer use than the ascribed characteristics (sex, race, and age, $R_L^2 = .12$) in Model 1, we do not know whether these differences are statistically significant. Using the information on the percent of cases correctly classified, the binomial d statistic was calculated for each comparison and is presented in Table 6.5. It appears that the difference between Model 1 and Model 2 is marginally significant ($p = .06$).

We can, however, compare Model 3 with both Model 1 and Model 2, since Model 1 and Model 2 are both nested within Model 3. For the comparison with Model 1, the difference in G_M is 394.48 with 2 degrees of freedom (two parameters that are estimated in Model 3 but not Model 1), $p = .000$; and for the comparison with Model 2, the difference in G_M is 270.45 with 4 degrees of freedom, $p = .000$. Model 3 is also statistically significantly different from both Model 1 ($p = .000$) and Model 2 ($p = .004$) in the percent of cases correctly classified. It appears, then, that achieved characteristics explain more of the variation in computer use than ascribed characteristics, but the combination of ascribed and achieved characteristics explains statistically significantly ($p = .000$ in both comparisons of G_M, $p = .000$ and $p = .004$ in comparisons of percent correctly classified) and substantively significantly (difference in R_L^2 of .14 for the comparison between Model 3 and Model 1, .09 for the comparison between Model 3 and Model 2) more than either set of characteristics by itself.

TABLE 6.5   Sequential Model Building

Dependent Variable: COMPUSX (N = 2,237)	Association/ Predictive Efficiency	Independent Variable	Unstandardized Logistic Regression Coefficient (b)	Standard Error of b	Statistical Significance of b (Likelihood Ratio Test)
Model 1	$G_M = 355.57$ (p = .000)	SEX (Male)	−0.076	0.094	0.420
$D_0 = 2678.278$	$R_L^2 = .12$	RACE (Black) (Other)	−0.878 −0.450	0.128 0.209	0.000 0.031
AIC = 2688.28					
SC = 2716.84	% Correctly classified = 69.9	AGE	−0.051	0.003	0.000
		Intercept	3.443	0.321	0.000
Model 2	$G_M = 514.21$ (p = .000)	EDUCNEW	0.322	0.022	0.000
$D_0 = 2519.640$	$R_L^2 = .17$	INCNEW98	0.097	0.011	0.000
AIC = 2525.64		Intercept	−5.358	0.302	0.000
SC = 2545.78	% Correctly classified = 72.0				
Model 3	$G_M = 785.72$ (p = .000)	SEX (Male)	0.153	0.106	0.151
$D_0 = 2248.136$	$R_L^2 = .26$	RACE (Black) (Other)	−0.444 −0.328	0.144 0.229	0.002 0.153
AIC = 2262.14					
SC = 2302.13	% Correctly classified = 75.5	AGE	−0.052	0.003	0.000
		EDUCNEW	0.313	0.023	0.000
		INCNEW98	0.107	0.012	0.000
		Intercept	−2.836	0.477	0.000

NOTES: Model 1 versus Model 2: $d_{12} = (.720 − .699)/[(.7095)(.2905)(2/2237)]^{.5} = 1.55, p = .061$.

Model 1 versus Model 3: $d_{13} = (.755 − .699)/[(.7270)(.2730)(2/2237)]^{.5} = 4.20, p = .000$.

Model 2 versus Model 3: $d_{23} = (.755 − .720)/[(.7375)(.2625)(2/2237)]^{.5} = 2.66, p = .004$.

The AIC and SC statistics are also consistent with this conclusion. The bottom line, then, would be that Model 3 appears to be statistically and substantively significantly better than either of the two alternative models. Because multiple models are considered here, however, precise levels of statistical significance are somewhat suspect (just as they are in stepwise logistic regression).

Moving to a consideration of the coefficients in the model, sex is not a statistically significant predictor in either Model 1 or Model 3; Other ethnicity is statistically significant in Model 1 but not Model 3. This suggests that the association between Other ethnicity and computer use can be explained by education and income; it also raises the question of whether sex may have an indirect effect on computer use (as suggested in Table 6.5) with income and education as mediating variables. One use to which sequential model building has been put is to examine the possibility of such indirect relationships. Another approach to the examination of indirect relationships, path analysis with logistic regression (PALR), will be described in Chapter 8. PALR makes it possible not only to infer the existence of, but also to quantify, such indirect relationships. The sequential model building approach adds information by indicating not only that the effect of Other ethnicity is mediated by income and education, but also that in the absence of the mediating variables it appears to be statistically significantly related to computer use; and also that sex does not appear to have any direct effect on computer use, controlling for other sociodemographic variables, even excluding the achieved characteristics. The sequential model building approach thus appears to be informative beyond just the concerns of exploratory model building and selection.

SUMMARY OF MODEL BUILDING AND SELECTION APPROACHES

In building and selecting a model when theoretical reasons for including or excluding variables provide insufficient guidance, there are several criteria to be considered. For nested models, it is possible to test for the statistical significance of differences in the model χ^2 statistic. For both non-nested and nested models in which the emphasis is on qualitative prediction, it is possible to test for the statistical significance of differences in the proportion of cases correctly predicted by the model. Besides statistical significance, one can focus on the strength of the relationship between the predictors and the outcome and see whether the appropriate measure of explained variation changes enough to conclude that one model is substantively significantly different from another. It may also be appropriate to consider whether, for two models that may not be substantively or statistically significantly different, the diagnostic statistics (described in the next chapter) are markedly better for one than for the other, a criterion which calls for considerable subjective judgment. Finally, there may be other criteria based on outside information, including a straightforward assessment of the plausibility of the model. This can be the most subjective (and hence the most dangerous) criterion, and particularly for theory testing it runs the risk of tautology (this model is best because it most closely conforms with my theory), but it is sometimes necessary in order to avoid utterly nonsensical conclusions. Of the general approaches to model building and model selection, one can often get away with stepwise logistic regression with forward inclusion or with selecting predictors based on their bivariate relationship with the dependent variable, in the sense that these procedures may produce the same result as other, preferable procedures. However, because of the danger of missing suppressor effects, backward stepwise elimination is to be preferred over either of these strategies. Sequential model building, while no longer the only approach to investigating indirect or mediated effects, is still potentially informative, above and beyond PALR, and represents a useful strategy in model comparison and selection.

NOTE

1. Software Note: SAS **logistic** (Version 8) uses the statistical significance of the Wald statistic as the criterion for backward or forward stepwise selection of predictors. It can also produce a list of the best subsets of $1, 2, \ldots, K - 1$ predictors based on the score statistic. SPSS **logistic** (Versions 11 to 16) allows forward or backward stepwise selection of predictors, based on either the Wald, score (conditional), or likelihood ratio statistic. In general, it is preferable to use the likelihood ratio statistic, which compares the change in G_M for each alternative model, because this is the criterion actually being maximized by the estimation process. SPSS **nomreg** as of Version 12 also allows stepwise selection of variables.

CHAPTER 7

Logistic Regression Diagnostics and Problems of Inference

$\mathbf{I}$n the previous chapter, one of the potential violations of the assumptions underlying the use of logistic regression analysis, misspecification, was addressed as a problem in selecting variables for inclusion in the model, including the addition of independent variables transformed to address problems of nonlinearity and nonadditivity. In this chapter, we broaden the scope to address other potential violations of logistic regression assumptions. The assumptions for using ordinary least squares (OLS) multiple regression were listed in Chapter 1. Some but not all of these assumptions are the same or parallel in logistic regression analysis, and it may be useful to detail them here:

1. *Measurement:* All independent variables are interval, ratio, or dichotomous (nominal variables can be represented, as indicated in Chapter 5, by dichotomous dummy variables; ordinal categorical variables can be treated the same as nominal variables if there are few categories, but may be treated as interval variables if there are many categories); the dependent variable is dichotomous. This can be addressed prior to analysis, and is not considered in detail here. Note the material in Chapter 5 on contrasts for categorical predictors.

2. *Specification:* (a) All relevant predictors of the dependent variable are included in the analysis, (b) no irrelevant predictors of the dependent variable are included in the analysis, and (c) the *form* of the relationship (allowing for transformations of the *independent* variables) is linear in the logit. This assumption was the focus of the previous chapter.

3. *Expected value of error:* The expected value of the error is 0.

4. *Normality of errors:* Errors (in the original metric) have a binomial distribution, which in large samples is approximated by a normal distribution (Agresti 2002:220–221; Hosmer and Lemeshow 2000:7).

5. *Absence of perfect multicollinearity:* None of the independent variables is a perfect linear combination of the other independent variables. There are two related issues, zero cell count and perfect separation, to be discussed in this chapter, whose effects are similar to the effects of multicollinearity.

When the assumptions of logistic regression analysis are violated, calculation of a logistic regression model may result in one of three problematic effects: biased coefficients, inefficient estimates, or invalid statistical inferences. *Bias* refers to the existence of a systematic tendency for the estimated logistic regression coefficients to be too high or too low, too far from zero or too close to zero, compared with the true values of the coefficients. In some instances, coefficients may be biased but *consistent*, meaning that although they are consistently underestimated or overestimated, the estimated coefficients approach the true values of the population parameters as the sample size increases toward infinity. *Inefficiency* refers to the tendency of the coefficients to have large standard errors relative to the size of the coefficient. This makes it more difficult to reject the null hypothesis (the hypothesis that there is no relationship between the dependent variable and the independent variable) even when the null hypothesis is false. *Invalid statistical inference* refers to the situation in which the calculated statistical significance of the logistic regression coefficients is inaccurate. In addition, *high-leverage* cases, cases with unusually high or low values on the independent variables (not on the dependent variable, which has only two values), or *outliers* with unusual combinations of values on the dependent and independent variables, may be *influential cases* that exert a disproportionate influence on the estimated parameters. This chapter focuses on the consequences of violations of logistic regression assumptions and on methods for detecting and correcting violations of logistic regression assumptions. Also considered here are methods for detecting outliers, high-leverage cases, and influential cases in logistic regression, and alternative approaches to dealing with those cases.

PROBLEMS OF INFERENCE

Problems of inference in logistic regression can sometimes arise when variables in the model are so closely related that their effects cannot be clearly separated; when the dependent variable is invariant for one or more categories of a categorical independent variable; when there are no cases for one or more categories of a categorical independent variable; and when grouped data are treated as though they were independent observations of individual cases, resulting in variances that are larger or smaller than expected based on the distributional assumptions of the model. The first three problems—collinearity, complete separation, and zero cell counts—all have the common symptom of very large standard errors and, often but not always, large coefficients as well. All, therefore, result in inefficient estimation of the parameters in the model, but none are known to result in biased parameters or in inaccurate (as opposed to inefficient) inferences. The fourth problem, overdispersion or underdispersion, results in incorrect standard errors and thus incorrect inferential statistics. All of these problems may be addressed by data screening prior to the analysis but are sometimes detected only during the course of the analysis.

COLLINEARITY

Collinearity (or colinearity, or multicollinearity) is a problem that arises when independent variables are correlated with one another. *Perfect collinearity* means that an independent variable is a perfect linear combination of the other independent variables. If we treated each independent variable in turn as the dependent variable in a model with all of the other independent variables as predictors, perfect collinearity would result in an R^2 of 1 for each of the independent variables. When perfect collinearity exists, it is impossible to obtain a unique estimate of the regression coefficients; any of an infinite number of possible combinations of linear or logistic regression coefficients will work equally well. Perfect collinearity is rare, except as an oversight: The inclusion of three variables, one of which is the sum of the other two would be one example. Inclusion of *all* of the dummy variables representing a nominal variable, instead of excluding one reference category (e.g., including WHITE as well as BLACK and OTHER in the analysis of computer use) would be another.

Less than perfect collinearity is fairly common. *Any* correlation among the independent variables is indicative of collinearity. As collinearity increases among the independent variables, linear and logistic regression coefficients will be unbiased and as efficient as they can be (given the relationships among the independent variables), but the standard errors for linear or logistic regression coefficients will tend to be large. More efficient unbiased estimates may not be possible, but the level of efficiency of the estimates may be poor. Low levels of collinearity are not generally problematic, but high levels of collinearity (perhaps corresponding to an R^2 of .80 or more for at least one of the independent variables) may pose problems, and very high levels of collinearity (perhaps corresponding to an R^2 of .90 or more for at least one of the independent variables) will almost certainly result in coefficients that are not statistically significant in typical samples, even though they may be quite large. Collinearity also tends to produce linear and logistic regression coefficients that appear to be unreasonably high: As a rough guideline, standardized logistic or linear regression coefficients greater than 1, or unstandardized logistic regression coefficients greater than 2, should be examined to determine whether collinearity is present.

For linear regression, detection of collinearity is straightforward. Most standard regression routines in widely used software packages provide optional information on R^2, or some function of R^2, for each of the independent variables, when it is treated as the dependent variable with all of the other independent variables as predictors. For example, the *tolerance* statistic is simply $1 - R_X^2$, where R_X^2 is the variance in each independent variable X, explained by all of the other independent variables. Corresponding to the rough guidelines outlined above, a tolerance of less than .20 is cause for concern; a tolerance of less than .10 almost certainly indicates a serious collinearity problem. Tolerance is typically not available in logistic regression software, but it can easily be obtained by calculating a linear regression model using the same dependent and independent variables as you are using in the logistic regression model. Since the concern is with the relationship among the *independent* variables, the functional form of the model for the dependent variable is irrelevant to the estimation of collinearity.

In Table 6.1 on page 110 in the previous chapter, here duplicated as Table 7.1, for both of the models with the nonlinear terms BTEDF and BTBEL, the logistic regression coefficients were somewhat high, and the standardized logistic regression coefficients for EDF5, BELIEF4, BTEDF, and BTBEL were all greater than 1. This suggests that there may be a problem of collinearity in the nonlinear model. Table 7.2 on page 129 presents collinearity statistics, produced by an OLS regression routine, for two models. The first model, labeled "Basic Model" (second-to-last column) is the logistic regression model for marijuana use from Chapter 3 (Tables 3.2 and 3.3, pp. 59–60). The second model, labeled "Nonlinear Model" (last column) is the model from the first half of Table 7.1 with the nonlinear terms BTEDF and BTBEL included. In both models, "BLACK" and "OTHER" are design variables for ETHN. For the basic model, all of the tolerances exceed .70, indicating no serious problem of collinearity. For the nonlinear model, Table 7.2 confirms what the standardized coefficients in Table 7.1 suggested: The tolerances for SEX and the two design variables for ETHN remain high, but BTEDF and BTBEL are severely collinear with EDF5 and BELIEF4, as indicated by tolerances less than .01.

TABLE 7.1 Box-Tidwell Tests for Nonlinearity in the Model for Marijuana Use

Dependent Variable	Association/ Predictive Efficiency	Independent Variable	Unstandardized Logistic Regression Coefficient (b)	Standard Error of b	Statistical Significance of b (Based on Likelihood Ratio G_X)	Standardized Logistic Regression Coefficient
PMRJ5	$G_M = 123.322$ ($p = .000$)	EDF5	2.415	1.191	0.076	3.073
$n = 227$		BELIEF4	3.620	1.421	0.002	−4.272
	$R^2_L = .418$	SEX (Male)	−1.660	0.428	0.000	−0.249
	Change in G_M from base model (Table 3.1) = 15.065 ($p = .001$)	ETHN (Black) (Other)	0.333 0.859	0.536 0.817	0.516 0.535* 0.293*	0.036 0.063
		BTEDF	−0.551	0.325	0.136	−1.620
	Change in R^2_L from base model = .051	BTBEL	−0.891	0.340	0.002	−4.172
		Intercept	−29.210	8.733	0.001*	—
PMRJ5	$G_M = 125.195$ ($p = .000$)	EDF5	2.411	1.184	0.076	3.012
$n = 225$		BELIEF4	1.380	2.812	0.644	−1.503
	$R^2_L = .427$	SEX (Male)	−1.676	0.436	0.000	−0.249
	Change in G_M from base model ($n = 225$) = 2.561 ($p = .278$)	ETHN (Black) (Other)	0.342 0.823	0.534 0.814	0.530 0.522* 0.312*	0.036 0.060
		BTEDF	−0.555	0.323	0.137	−2.551
	Change in R^2_L from base model ($n = 225$) = .009	BTBEL	−0.371	0.660	0.599	−1.716
		Intercept	−15.541	17.134	0.364*	—

*Statistical significance based on the likelihood ratio statistic is not available for individual categories of categorical independent variables or for the intercept; for these, the Wald statistic is used to determine statistical significance.

TABLE 7.2 Testing for Collinearity			
Dependent Variable	Independent Variable	Tolerance: Basic Model	Tolerance: Nonlinear Model
PMRJ5	EDF5	.717	.00249
	BELIEF4	.707	.00148
	SEX (Male)	.994	.994
	ETHN		
	(Black)	.959	.958
	(Other)	.983	.974
	BTEDF	—	.00253
	BTBEL	—	.00147

The good news about collinearity is that it is easy to detect. The bad news is that there are few acceptable remedies for it. Deleting variables involved in collinearity runs the risk of omitted variable bias. Combining collinear variables into a single scale, for example, by factor analysis, suggests that the theory (if any) used in constructing your model or the measurement process used in collecting your data was faulty, casting doubt on any further inferences you may draw from your analysis. *Ridge regression* (Schaefer 1986) allows the user to produce somewhat more biased but substantially more efficient estimates by increasing the estimated variance of the variables (thereby decreasing the proportion of the variance that is explained). Perhaps the safest strategy is to focus on the combined effects of all of the variables in the model and to recognize the precariousness of any conclusions about individual predictors in the presence of high collinearity. For a more detailed discussion of remedies to collinearity, see Berry and Feldman (1985:46–50) or Fox (1991). Briefly, though, there is really no satisfactory solution to high collinearity.

NUMERICAL PROBLEMS: ZERO CELLS AND COMPLETE SEPARATION

When collinearity exists, it does not necessarily indicate that there is anything wrong with the model or the theory underlying the model. Instead, problems arise because of empirical patterns in the data (the high correlation among independent variables). Two related problems, with similar symptoms, are zero cell count and complete separation. Zero cell count occurs when the dependent variable is invariant for one or more values of a categorical independent variable. If, for example, all of the respondents in the "Other" category for ethnicity reported using marijuana (or if they all reported *not* using marijuana), we would have a problem with a zero cell in the contingency table for the relationship between prevalence of marijuana use and ethnicity. The odds of marijuana use for respondents "Other" than White and Black would be $1/(1 - 1) = 1/0 = +\infty$, and the logit $= \ln(\text{odds})$ would also be $+\infty$, infinitely large. [If the prevalence of marijuana use were 0 for this group, the odds would be $0/(1 - 0) = 0$, and the logit would be $\ln(0) = -\infty$, infinitely small.] When the odds is 0 or 1 for a single individual or case, this is not a problem; when it is 0 or 1 for an entire group of cases, as defined by the value of a categorical independent variable, the result will be a very high estimated standard error for the coefficient associated with that category (including coefficients for which that category serves as a reference category).

The problem of zero cell count applies specifically to categorical variables, and particularly nominal variables. For continuous variables, and for ordinal categorical variables, it is common to have means of 0 or 1 for some values of the independent variables. The reason that this is not a problem is that we assume a certain pattern to the relationship between the dependent variable and the continuous predictor (linear in linear regression, logistic in logistic regression), and we use that pattern to "fill in the blanks" in the distribution of the dependent variable over the values of the independent variable. For categorical variables, we are unable to assume such a pattern. Instead, when we find problems of zero cell count for categorical predictors, we must choose among (1) accepting the high standard errors and the uncertainty about the values of the logistic regression coefficients, (2) recoding the categorical independent variable in a meaningful way (either by collapsing categories or by eliminating the problem category) to eliminate the problem of zero cell count, or (3) adding a constant to each cell of the contingency table to eliminate zero cells.

The first option may be acceptable if we are concerned more with the overall relationship between a set of predictors and a dependent variable than with the effects of the individual predictors. The overall fit of the model should be unaffected by the zero cell count. The third option has no serious drawbacks, but Hosmer and Lemeshow (1989:127) suggest that it may not be adequate for complex analyses. The second option results in cruder measurement of the independent variable, and may bias the strength of the relationship between the predictor and the dependent variable toward zero. However, if there is a conceptual link between some categories of the independent variable, and if the distribution of the dependent variable across those categories appears similar, this may be a reasonable option. Usually, this will be done during univariate and bivariate screening of the data. A hidden example of this has been followed throughout this book to this point: the coding of ethnicity. In the original data from the National Youth Survey, ethnicity was divided into six categories: (1) non-Hispanic European American, (2) African American, (3) Hispanic American, (4) Native American, (5) Asian American, and (6) Other. The last four categories were collapsed into a single category, "Other," because of the small number of cases. Had they been retained in their original form, problems of zero cell count would have plagued the analyses.

If you are too successful in predicting the dependent variable with a set of predictors, you have the problem of complete separation. Both the logistic regression coefficients and their standard errors will tend to be extremely large. The dependent variable will be perfectly predicted: $G_M = D_0$, $D_M = 0$, $R_L^2 = 1$. As Rindskopf (2002) describes, complete separation may indicate that the appropriate functional form for the relationship between the dependent variable and the predictor(s) should be a step function, rather than the logistic curve. If separation is less than complete (sometimes called *quasi-complete* separation), logistic regression coefficients and their standard errors will still be extremely large. An example of quasi-complete separation is given in Figure 7.1, based on artificially constructed data. If complete separation occurs in a bivariate logistic relationship, the logistic regression model cannot be calculated. Although there is nothing intrinsically wrong with complete separation (after all, perfect prediction is what we are trying to achieve), as a practical matter it should arouse our suspicions, as it almost never occurs in real-world research. Complete or quasi-complete separation may instead indicate problems in the data or the analysis, for example, having almost as many variables as there are cases to be analyzed.

FIGURE 7.1   Quasi-Complete Separation

Model Summary

Step	-2 Log likelihood	Cox & Snell R Square	Nagelkerke R Square
1	13.003	.654	.872

Omnibus Tests of Model Coefficients

		Chi-square	df	Sig.
Step 1	Step	42.448	1	.000
	Block	42.448	1	.000
	Model	42.448	1	.000

Classification Table(a)

			Predicted		
			TRUE		Percentage Correct
	Observed		0	1	
Step 1	TRUE	0	19	1	95.0
		1	1	19	95.0
	Overall Percentage				95.0

a The cut value is .500

Variables in the Equation

		B	S.E.	Wald	df	Sig.	Exp(B)
Step 1(a)	P3	219.720	74.535	8.690	1	.003	2.65E+95
	Constant	-109.860	37.275	8.687	1	.003	.000

a Variable(s) entered on step 1: P3.

Step number: 1

Observed Groups and Predicted Probabilities

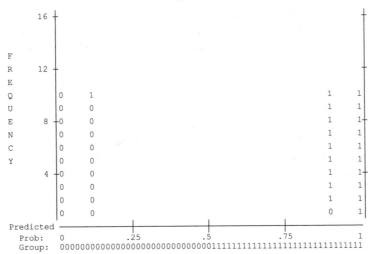

Predicted Probability is of Membership for 1
The Cut Value is .50
Symbols: 0 - 0; 1 - 1
Each Symbol Represents 1 Case.

As noted earlier, collinearity, zero cells, and complete separation have the common symptom of very large standard errors, and often but not always large coefficients as well (Hosmer and Lemeshow 1989). All, therefore, result in inefficient estimation of the parameters in the model. None, however, are known to result in biased parameters or in inaccurate (as opposed to inefficient) inferences. Problems with zero cell counts can be averted by careful univariate and bivariate analysis before logistic regression is used. Complete separation may either indicate an error that needs to be corrected or a brilliant breakthrough in theory and analysis. (Congratulations!) Most likely, it indicates a problem. Collinearity is the most bothersome of the three problems, because it indicates either a flaw in the theory, a flaw in the operationalization of the theory, or a problem in the empirical data that confounds the testing of the theory, insofar as the theory is concerned with the effects of individual predictors rather than with the combined effect of a set of predictors. Like zero cell counts, collinearity can be detected (with the help of a good multiple regression package) before logistic regression analysis begins. What to do about it if it is detected is problematic, more art than science.

OVERDISPERSION AND UNDERDISPERSION[1]

Logistic regression with a dichotomous dependent variable assumes binomial errors, and thus it is assumed that the variance $\sigma_Y^2 = P_{Y=1}(1 - P_{Y=1})$. This theoretical variance is called the *nominal* variance. For casewise data, when there is only one case per covariate pattern, this condition is satisfied. For grouped data, however, when cases are aggregated by covariate pattern and the covariate patterns are treated as the "cases," this assumption may be violated for one of several reasons, including the omission of an important predictor, clustering within the sample (sometimes for known reasons, such as a cluster sampling design or repeated observations on the same cases) resulting in correlated observations, or because the underlying distribution of the population is different from the assumed distribution, including the case in which there is a mixture of different distributions in the data. Overdispersion refers to the case in which σ_Y^2 is larger than expected, and underdispersion refers to the case in which σ_Y^2 is less than expected. For grouped data, if we calculate $\delta = D/df$, where D is the deviance statistic calculated by covariate pattern and df is the degrees of freedom associated with the deviance statistic (and reported in the same table), then *overdispersion* is indicated by $\delta > 1$ and *underdispersion* is indicated by $\delta < 1$.

Underdispersion and overdispersion result in incorrect standard errors and thus incorrect inferences, but it is possible to adjust the standard error by multiplying by the square root of δ: Adjusted Standard Error = Standard Error $\times \sqrt{\delta}$. When the source of the overdispersion is unknown, correction of standard errors using a scaling factor may be the most reasonable approach; however, when the source of the overdispersion is known, as in the case of a clustered sampling design or longitudinal data, the use of generalized estimating equations (Hardin and Hilbe 2003; Liang and Zeger 1986) may be more appropriate.

ANALYSIS OF RESIDUALS[2]

In linear regression, the residual is commonly denoted e, and $e_j = Y_j - \hat{y}_j$ is the difference between the observed and predicted values of Y for a given case, j. This should be distinguished from the error of prediction, denoted ε_j, which represents the difference between the true value of Y_j in the population (a value that may be different from the observed value of Y in the sample, e.g., as a result of measurement error) and the estimated value of y_j, $\hat{y}_j$ (Berry 1993). In linear regression, certain assumptions about errors (zero mean, constant variance or homoscedasticity, normal distribution, no correlation of error terms with one another, no correlation of error terms with independent variables) are necessary if we are to draw statistical inferences from a sample to a larger population. These assumptions may sometimes be tested by using the residuals, e_j, as estimates of the errors, ε_j. Violations of some assumptions (zero mean, normal distribution) may have relatively minor consequences. Violation of others is more problematic. Heteroscedasticity inflates standard errors and renders tests of statistical significance inaccurate and may itself be a symptom of nonadditivity or nonlinearity. Correlation between the independent variable and the error term generally indicates misspecification, whose effects may include bias, inefficiency, or inaccurate statistical inference.

In linear regression, the residuals are straightforwardly computed from the regression equation. In logistic regression, several different residuals are available, corresponding to the different levels (probability, odds, logit) at which the analysis may be conceptualized. The principal purpose for which residuals analysis is used in logistic regression is to identify cases for which the model works poorly, or cases that exert more than their share of influence on the estimated parameters of the model.

The difference between the observed and the predicted probability is $e_j = P(Y_j = 1) - \hat{P}(Y_j = 1)$, where $\hat{P}(Y_j = 1)$ is the estimated probability that $Y = 1$ based on the model. As Hosmer and Lemeshow (1989) explain, in linear regression, we can assume that the error is independent of the conditional mean of Y, but in logistic regression, the error variance is a function of the conditional mean. For this reason, residuals (estimates of error) are standardized by adjusting them for their standard errors. The Pearson (Hosmer and Lemeshow 1989) or chi (SAS), standardized (SPSS) or rs (Stata) residual is equal to

$$r_j = z_j = \chi_j = \frac{P(Y_j = 1) - \hat{P}(Y_j = 1)}{\sqrt{\hat{P}(Y_j = 1)[1 - \hat{P}(Y_j = 1)]}}.$$

This is just the difference between the observed and estimated probabilities divided by the binomial standard deviation of the estimated probability. For large samples, the standardized residual, hereafter z_j, should be normally distributed with a mean of 0 and a standard deviation of 1. Large positive or negative values of z_j indicate that the model fits a case j poorly. Since z_j should have a normal distribution, 95% of the cases should have values between −2 and +2, and 99% of cases should have values between −2.5 and +2.5.

An alternative or supplement to the Pearson residual is the deviance residual, which is equal to plus or minus the square root of the predicted probability of being in the correct group. For casewise data (only one case per covariate pattern), the deviance residual $d_j = -\sqrt{2|\ln(1 - \hat{y}_j)|}$ when $Y = 0$ and $d_j = \pm\sqrt{2|\ln(1 - \hat{y}_j)|}$ when $Y = 1$, where $|\ln(\hat{y}_j)|$ is the absolute value of the natural logarithm of the predicted value of Y, and $|\ln(1 - \hat{y}_j)|$ correspondingly is the absolute value of 1 minus the predicted value of Y. For data in which there are multiple cases per covariate pattern, the formula is more complicated; for each covariate pattern j,

$$d_j = \pm\sqrt{\{2\{(y_j)\ln[y_j/(m_j\hat{y}_j)] + (m_j - y_j)\ln[(m_j - y_j)/(m_j - m_j\hat{y}_j)]\}\}},$$ where j indexes the covariate patterns, m_j is the number of cases with covariate pattern j, y_j is the number of cases for

which $Y = 1$ in covariate pattern j, and the sign of d_j is the same as the sign of the quantity $[y_j - m_j \hat{y}_j]$ (Agresti 2002:220; Hosmer and Lemeshow 2000:145–147). The deviance residual d_j, available in SAS, SPSS, and Stata, is the contribution of each case to D_M. Like z_j, d_j should have a normal distribution with a mean of 0 and a standard deviation of 1 for large samples. One reason for using the deviance residual instead of or in addition to the Pearson residual is that the Pearson residual tends to be unstable when $P(Y = 1)$ is close to either 0 or 1 (Pregibon 1981). A third residual, the logit residual, is equal to the residual e_j divided by its variance (instead of its standard deviation, as in the standardized residual). This may be written,

$$l_j = \frac{P(Y_j = 1) - \hat{P}(Y_j = 1)}{\hat{P}(Y_i = 1)[1 - \hat{P}(Y_i = 1)]}$$

NONNORMALITY OF RESIDUALS

In OLS regression, it is usually assumed that the errors are normally distributed. In small samples, if this assumption is violated, it renders statistical inference based on the regression equation (e.g., the statistical significance of the regression coefficients) inaccurate. In large samples, inaccuracy of statistical inference is considered inconsequential because of the results of the Central Limit Theorem, which, briefly, indicates that the distribution of the regression coefficients in repeated sampling for large enough samples will approach a normal distribution with known mean (equal to the population mean) and variance. In logistic regression, the errors are *not* assumed to have a normal distribution. Instead, it is assumed that the distribution of the errors follows a binomial distribution, which approximates a normal distribution only for large samples. If the residuals are used to estimate the errors, and if they are normally distributed (for a large sample), we can be more confident that our inferential statistics are correct, because normal (the distribution we are considering) and binomial (the assumed distribution) distributions are about the same for large samples. Contrary to the situation in linear regression analysis, however, if we find that the residuals are not normally distributed for small samples, we need not necessarily be concerned about the validity of our statistical inferences.

We can test for normality by plotting the standardized or deviance residuals against a normal curve, or in a normal probability plot; see, for example, SPSS (1999b). More important, we can use the standardized and deviance residuals to identify cases for which the model fits poorly, cases with positive or negative standardized or deviance residuals greater than 2 or 3 in absolute value.[3] This may help us identify not only cases for which the model fits poorly but also cases that exert a disproportionately large influence on the estimates for the model parameters.

DETECTING AND DEALING WITH UNUSUAL AND INFLUENTIAL CASES

For OLS regression, Belsley et al. (1980:3) define *unusual* data as observations that lie outside patterns set by other data, and *influential* data as data that strongly influence the regression results. Agresti and Finlay (1997:310) similarly define observations as influential if removing them results in a large change in the prediction equation. Commonly, in small samples, an observation can have a strong influence on the slope if it is unusual, that is, if its value on one or more of the predictors is much lower or higher than the values for other cases in the data; in other words, it is an outlier with respect to the predictor X. A variable can also be an outlier with respect to the dependent variable, if its value on the dependent variable is unusual given the value of the independent variable (Fox 1991:21). Fox, somewhat in contrast to Belsley et al. (1980) and Agresti and Finlay (1997), defines influence in terms of *leverage* (to be described in the next paragraph) and *discrepancy* (being an outlier): Influence = Leverage × Discrepancy, and high leverage by itself does not necessarily imply high influence, according to Fox. This definition essentially drops the distinction between unusual (discrepancy) and influential (leverage) data, combining the two in a single definition of influential data.

Cases that potentially have a large influence on the parameters of the logistic regression model may be identified in part[4] by high values of the leverage statistic, or hat value, h_i. In linear regression, the leverage statistic is derived from the equation $\hat{y}_j = h_{1j}y_1 + h_{2j}y_2 + \cdots + h_{nj}y_n = \Sigma h_{ij}y_i$, and it expresses the predicted value of Y for a case j as a function of the observed values of Y for case j and for all of the other $i = 1, 2, \ldots, n - 1$ cases as well (Fox 1991). Each coefficient h_{ij} captures the influence of the observed variable y_i on the predicted value $\hat{y}_j$. It can be shown that $h_{ii} = \Sigma(h_{ij})^2$, so if we designate $h_i = h_{ii}$, we have a measure of the overall influence of y_i on the predicted values of Y for all of the cases in the sample. The leverage is similarly derived in logistic regression (Hosmer and Lemeshow 1989:150–151), and it varies between 0 (no influence) and 1 (it completely determines the parameters in the model). In an equation with K independent variables (including each design variable as a separate variable) or, equivalently, in an equation in which there are K degrees of freedom associated with G_M, the sum of the values of h_i is equal to $K + 1$, and the mean value of h_i, $\Sigma h_i/N = (K + 1)/N$. Technically, cases with hat values larger than $(K + 1)/N$ are high-leverage cases, but the suggested cutoff for leverage is set at $2K/N$ (Belsley et al. 1980:17) or $3K/N$ (Agresti and Finlay 1997:539) for OLS regression. Agresti and Finlay note that leverage tends to decrease as the sample size increases, so inordinately large leverage for an observation occurs primarily in small to moderate size samples. SAS, SPSS, and Stata all provide leverage values as part of their diagnostic output for logistic regression.

Other indices of the influence of an individual case include the change in the Pearson χ^2 statistic and the change in D_M attributable to deleting the case from the analysis. The change in the Pearson χ^2 attributable to deleting a case j is $\Delta\chi_j^2 = z_j^2/(1 - h_j)$, where z_j is the standardized residual and h_j is the leverage statistic for case j. The change in D_M is equal to $\Delta D_j = d_j^2 - z_j^2 h_j/(1 - h_j) = d_j^2 - h_j(\Delta \chi^2)$, where d_j is the deviance residual, z_j is the standardized residual, and h_j^2 is the leverage statistic for case j. Both ΔD_j and $\Delta\chi_j^2$ have a chi-square distribution, and their values should be interpreted accordingly. Their respective square roots should have an approximately normal distribution; if $\sqrt{\Delta D_j}$ or $\sqrt{\Delta \chi_j^2}$ is large, less than -2 or -3 or greater than $+2$ or $+3$ (Agresti and Finlay 1997:538 suggest a cutoff of ±3), it indicates a case that may be poorly fit, and deserves closer inspection. The quantity $z_j^2 h_j/(1 - h_j)$, sometimes termed *Cook's distance*, is itself an indicator of the overall change in regression estimates attributable to deleting an individual observation. A standardized version of this measure may be obtained by dividing Cook's distance by $(1 - h_j)$; $z_j^2 h_j/(1 - h_j)^2$ = dbeta, the standardized change in the regression coefficients attributable to the deletion of case j. The leverage statistic and the related statistics described above are all summary indicators of the influence of a case on the estimation of the model parameters. More detailed information can be obtained by examining the change in the logistic regression coefficient produced by removing a single case, divided by its standard error for the sample (this is a standardized measure), sometimes termed DBETA or DFBETA, for either the deletion of a single case (when the analysis is based on individual data) or the deletion of *all* cases sharing the same covariate pattern (when the analysis is based on grouped data).

OUTLIERS AND RESIDUAL PLOTS

Table 7.3 on page 138 presents the results of an analysis of residuals for the model of marijuana use from Tables 3.2 and 3.3. Cases with $\sqrt{D_j}$ less than -2 or greater than $+2$ were selected for examination. The table includes the sequential number of the case, the observed and predicted values of the case, the Pearson (ZResid), Studentized (SResid), and deviance (Dev) residuals, the leverage (Lever), and the deleted residuals ΔD_j (DIFDEV), $\Delta \chi^2$ (DIFCHI), and dbeta (DBETA). Part A of Table 7.3 presents the residuals for the model from Chapter 3. Part B presents the results with the most extreme outlier deleted. This case is one of the two identified in the analysis of nonlinearity in Figure 6.1 (p. 111), here duplicated as Figure 7.2. Part C presents the results with both the outliers from Figure 7.2 deleted.

A first comment to be made about Table 7.3 is that several of the indicators are essentially redundant with one another. The change in the Pearson chi-square statistic, DIFCHI ($\Delta \chi^2$), is approximately equal to the Pearson residual, ZResid, squared. The deviance residual, Dev (d_j) is approximately equal to the Studentized residual (SResid), and the change in the deviance residual, DIFDEV (ΔD_j), is equal to the Studentized residual squared. The Pearson χ^2-based residuals are larger than the residuals based on D_M but they provide essentially the same information about the cases. The leverage and DBETA provide information not evident from the other diagnostics, similar to but not redundant with one another. Further analysis of the table focuses on the Pearson residual, the Studentized residual, the leverage, and DBETA.

In Part A of Table 7.3, one case, number 178, stands out. The Pearson residual is an enormous -10.7, the Studentized residual is greater than three in absolute value, and DBETA is greater than 1, all indicators of an extremely poor fit. Deleting this case would result in an improvement in G_M of 9.899 (1 degree of freedom, $p = .003$) and an increase in R_L^2 of .034. Clearly, the model would work better with this case deleted. In Part B, with case 178 deleted, no case stands out as clearly. Case 148 has the highest Pearson residual and the highest Studentized residual, but would produce relatively little change in the logistic regression coefficients if deleted. Case 1 would have more of an effect on the logistic regression coefficients (DBETA = .50), and has the fourth highest Pearson residual and the third highest Studentized and deviance residuals of the six cases selected as outliers. Case 1 has the additional feature that it is one of the two outliers identified in Figure 7.2 as introducing nonlinearity into the model. With Case 1 deleted, G_M improves by 4.478 (1 degree of freedom, $p = .038$), and R_L^2 increases by .015. The improvement that results from deleting Case 1 is considerably smaller than the improvement from removing Case 178.

Should Cases 1 and 178 be removed from the analysis? The answer to this question requires closer examination of the data. The two cases in question are both White, one male and one female. Both report low levels of belief that it is wrong to violate the law, but neither uses marijuana or hard drugs, and both report very low levels of alcohol use as well. Case 1 (female) has a slightly higher level of belief and a substantially lower level of exposure to delinquent friends than Case 178 (male), and is therefore less inconsistent with the model than Case 178. Although unusual, the results are

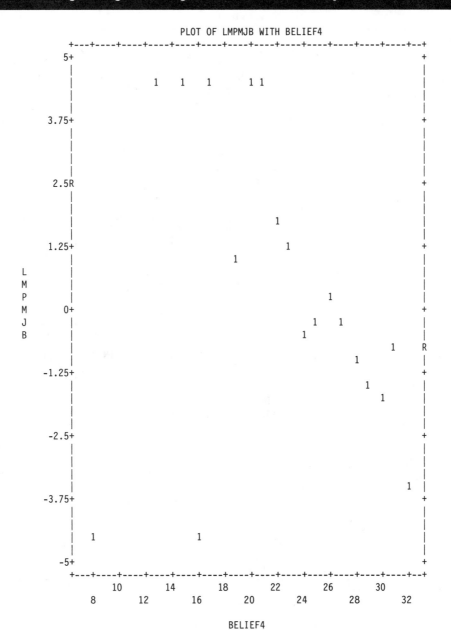

FIGURE 7.2   Logistic Regression Diagnostics: Test for Nonlinearity

LMPMJB = Logit of Mean of Prevalence of Marijuana Use for Each Value of BELIEF4

BELIEF4 = Belief That It Is Wrong to Violate the Law

TABLE 7.3 Logistic Regression Diagnostics for Marijuana Use

A. Full Model

CASE	Observed PMRJ5	Pred	ZResid	Dev	SResid	Lever	DIFCHI	DIFDEV	DBETA
66	1	0.0991	3.0143	2.1500	2.1637	0.0127	9.20	4.68	0.12
94	0	0.8608	−2.4864	−1.9858	−2.0325	0.0455	6.48	4.13	0.31
139	1	0.0815	3.3565	2.2391	2.2668	0.0243	11.55	5.14	0.29
148	1	0.0612	3.9183	2.3641	2.3762	0.0102	15.51	5.65	0.16
178	0	0.9914	−10.7055	−3.0823	−3.0983	0.0103	115.80	9.60	1.21
201	1	0.0650	3.7937	2.3383	2.3526	0.0121	14.57	5.53	0.18

$G_M = 108.257$, 5 df, $p = .0000$, $R_L^2 = .367$.

B. Most Extreme Case Deleted

CASE	Observed PMRJ5	Pred	ZResid	Dev	SResid	Lever	DIFCHI	DIFDEV	DBETA
1	0	.9122	−3.2239	−2.2059	−2.2557	0.0436	10.87	5.09	0.50
66	1	.0894	3.1913	2.1975	2.2116	0.0127	10.32	4.89	0.13
94	0	.8786	−2.6903	−2.0536	−2.0999	0.0436	7.57	4.41	0.34
139	1	.0861	3.2577	2.2146	2.2444	0.0264	10.90	5.04	0.30
148	1	.0510	4.3137	2.4396	2.4515	0.0097	18.79	6.01	0.18
200	1	.0661	3.7601	2.3312	2.3463	0.0129	14.32	5.51	0.19

$G_M = 118.156$, 5 df, $p = .0000$, $R_L^2 = .401$.

C. Outliers From Figure 7.2 Deleted (Cases 178 and 1)

CASE	Observed PMRJ5	Pred	ZResid	Dev	SResid	Lever	DIFCHI	DIFDEV	DBETA
66	1	.0808	3.3732	2.2432	2.2573	0.0125	11.52	5.10	0.15
94	0	.8858	−2.7852	−2.0832	−2.1289	0.0425	8.10	4.53	0.36
133	0	.8675	−2.5584	−2.0105	−2.0506	0.0387	6.81	4.20	0.27
139	1	.0885	3.2099	2.2023	2.2332	0.0275	10.59	4.99	0.30
148	1	.0441	4.6536	2.4982	2.5097	0.0092	21.86	6.30	0.20
200	1	.0675	3.7175	2.3221	2.3378	0.0135	14.01	5.47	0.19

$G_M = 122.634$, 5 df, $p = .0000$, $R_L^2 = .416$.

NOTE: Cases with Studentized residuals greater than 2.0000000 are listed.

plausible, and both cases should probably be retained. It would be useful, however, to extend the model to include variables that might explain why an individual who sees nothing wrong with breaking the law chooses not to use alcohol, marijuana, or other illicit drugs.

Landwehr et al. (1984) and Hosmer and Lemeshow (1989) discuss graphical techniques for logistic regression diagnostics. These techniques offer a visual rather than numerical representation that may be more intuitively appealing to some researchers. For example, Hosmer and Lemeshow (1989) recommend plots of DIFCHI, DIFDEV, and DBETA with the predicted values in order to detect outlying cases. Examples of these plots are provided in the first column of plots in Figure 7.3. Each of the three plots represents two curves, one declining from left to right (cases for which the observed value of PMRJ5 is 1) and one increasing from left to right (cases for which the observed value of PMRJ5 is 0). Cases in the upper left and right corners of the plot are cases for which the model fits poorly. In the plot of the χ^2 change (DIFCHI) with the predicted value, one case is an extreme outlier, with DIFCHI greater than 100. From Table 7.3, we can see that this is Case 178. Similarly, Case 178 is the case in the plot of DIFDEV with a value of DIFDEV greater than 8, and in the plot of DBETA with a value greater than 1. On the scale of the plots in the first column of Figure 7.3, all of the other cases seem to cluster fairly close together. Once Case 178 is deleted, however, the scale of the plots may be changed, and other cases appear as outliers.

The second column of plots in Figure 7.3 presents the same plots with Case 178 deleted. The plots may appear to be more spread out than the plots in the first column, but this is only because the scale has changed (from 0–100 to 0–20 for DIFCHI, from 0–10 to 0–6.25 for DIFDEV, and from 0–1.25 to 0–0.5 for DBETA). The combination of the two curves for PMRJ5 = 1 and PMRJ5 = 0 takes on a characteristic goblet-shaped pattern (especially for DIFDEV), with the outliers again located in the upper right and left corners of the plot, and also in the "cup" of the goblet. In contrast to the first column, there is a relatively smooth transition from the upper corners to the rest of the graph. The most outlying cases are not as sharply separated as Case 178 was in the first column. This is reflected numerically in Table 7.3, Part B, in which none of the Studentized residuals is larger than 2.5 in absolute value, and none of the DBETAs is greater than 1.

Moving to an analysis of residuals for the model for computer use (Table 5.1 from Chapter 5, p. 85), Figure 7.4 on pages 141–142 presents plots of DIFDEV, DIFCHI, and DBETA with the predicted probability of computer use using graphics that allow us to weight the points by their leverage. Larger circles in Figure 7.4 represent higher leverage values. In the plot for deviance, there is one point that stands out with a high leverage and a DIFDEV greater than 10. The plot of DIFCHI is similar, but there are more cases with DIFCHI greater than 10. There are eight cases with DBETA greater than .10. In the plot of the leverage with the Pearson residual, there is one case with a very high leverage and a very small residual, and several cases with leverages greater than .04. Further analysis indicates that there are 64 cases out of 2,241 with leverages greater than 4 times the expected value. There are no cases with Studentized residuals greater than 4, and no more cases than might be expected by chance with standardized residuals greater than 4. Closer examination of the outlying cases indicates that they have relatively high income and education but are not computer users. It seems entirely reasonable that some highly educated individuals with high incomes might not be computer users. While this does suggest that we might consider trying to expand the model to account for these cases (perhaps by adding age as a predictor?), it does not suggest that these cases are in any sense unreasonable or candidates for elimination from the model.

FIGURE 7.3 Logistic Regression Diagnostic Plots

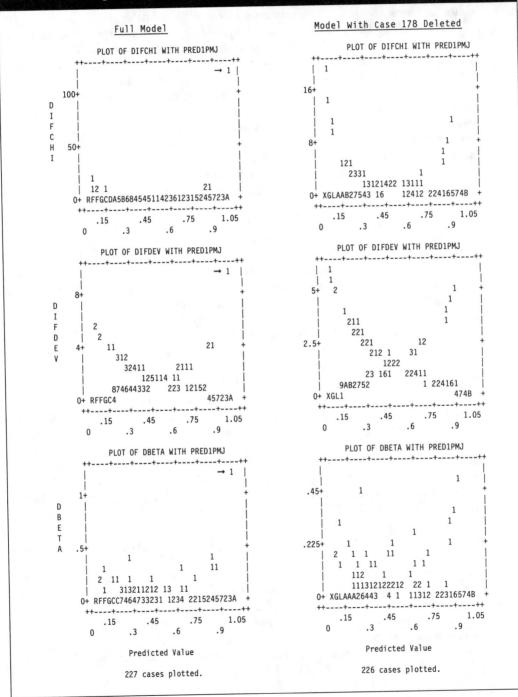

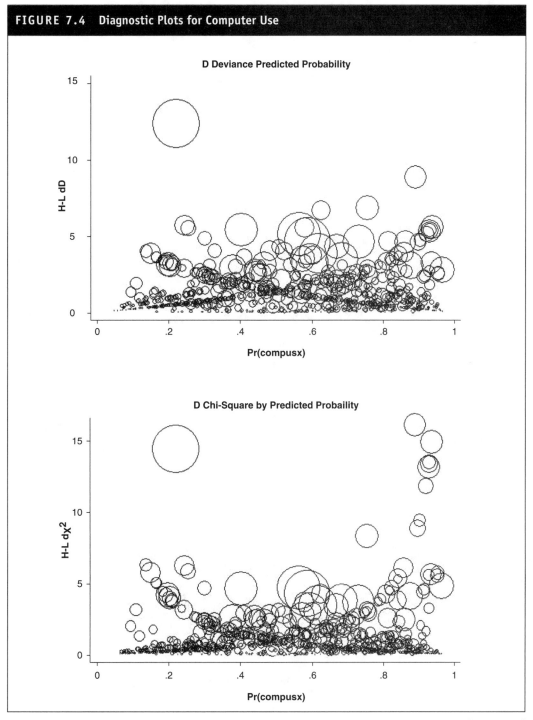

FIGURE 7.4 **Diagnostic Plots for Computer Use**

(Continued)

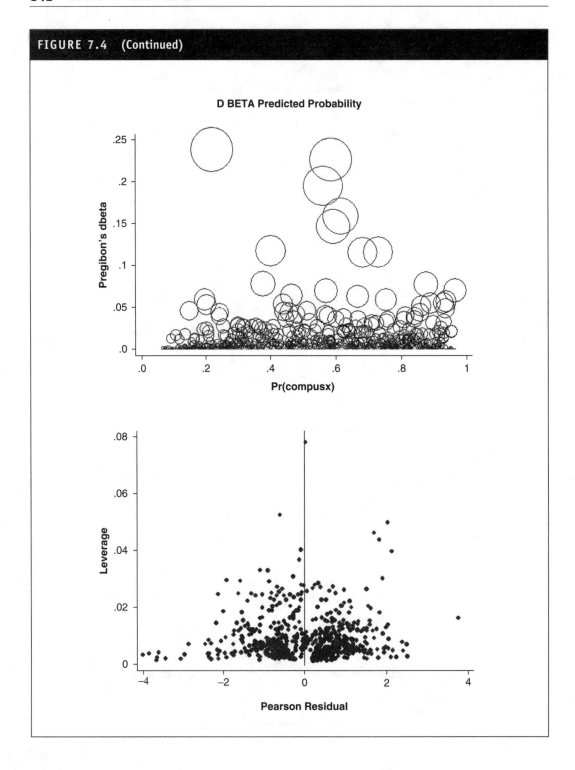

FIGURE 7.4 (Continued)

A SUGGESTED PROTOCOL FOR LOGISTIC REGRESSION DIAGNOSTICS

Testing for collinearity should be a standard part of any logistic regression analysis. It is quick, simple to implement with existing regression software, and may provide valuable information about potential problems in the logistic regression analysis before the analysis is undertaken. The Box-Tidwell test for nonlinearity is quick, easy to perform, and not overly sensitive to minor deviations from linearity, and should also be incorporated as a standard procedure in logistic regression. Whether to test for nonadditivity by modeling interactions among the independent variables depends on whether one has theoretical or other reasons to believe that such interactions exist. Modeling nonlinearity and nonadditivity should be approached with some caution, however. There is a real danger of overfitting a model, building in components that really capture random variation rather than systematic regularities in behavior.

Using logistic regression diagnostics, like using linear regression diagnostics, is more art than science. The diagnostic statistics hint at potential problems, but what those problems are, and whether remedial action is required, can only be decided after closer inspection of the data for the unusual cases. In a sample of 200 to 250, random sampling variation alone will produce 10 to 12 cases with values greater than 2 or less than −2 on standardized, normally distributed variables such as the deviance residual or the Studentized residual. Even cases with very large residuals, such as Case 178 in Table 7.3, do not necessarily indicate problems in the model, insofar as we are dealing with nondeterministic models in which individual human choice and free will may naturally produce less-than-perfect prediction of human behavior.

As a general approach, it seems appropriate to perform at least a limited set of diagnostics on any model, as a precaution against miscoded data and a guide to weaknesses in our conceptual models. A minimal set of diagnostics might include the Studentized residual, the leverage, and DBETA. Studentized residuals less than −3 and greater than +3 definitely deserve closer inspection; values less than −2 or greater than +2 may also warrant some concern. The disadvantage to the Pearson residual is that the information it provides tends to be redundant with the information provided by the deviance and Studentized residuals, and the deviance residual, not the Pearson residual, is the criterion for estimating the parameters of the model and is thus somewhat more pertinent to the analysis of residuals. The advantage to the Pearson residual is that, because it has larger values, outlying cases sometimes stand out more sharply (as does Case 178 in Part A of Table 7.3) than with the deviance or Studentized residuals. Leverage values several times the expected value of $(K + 1)/N$ also deserve close attention. Large values of DBETA, especially values greater than 1 (remember, this is a standardized measure), also deserve closer examination. Whether the information contained in these diagnostics is presented visually is a matter of taste. The critical concern is that extreme values on these diagnostics require closer inspection of the data and, possibly, reconsideration of the model.

NOTES

1. A particularly clear and concise discussion of overdispersion and underdispersion may be found in Hutcheson and Sofroniou (1999). See also McCullagh and Nelder (1989:124–128), Norusis (1999:78), and Stokes et al. (2000:195).

2. Hosmer and Lemeshow (1989) distinguish between analyzing residuals based on individuals, and analyzing residuals based on covariate patterns, the combinations of values of the independent variables that actually occur in the sample. When the number of covariate patterns is equal to the number of cases, or very nearly so, residuals must be analyzed for each case separately. This is the implicit approach taken in this section, and in SAS **logistic** and SPSS **logistic**, but SPSS **nomreg** aggregates cases by covariate pattern and produces the correct predictions, residuals, and goodness-of-fit tests based on those subpopulations (Norusis 1999). When the number of cases is much larger than the number of covariate patterns, or when some of the covariate patterns hold for more than five cases, Hosmer and Lemeshow (1989) recommend aggregating the cases by covariate pattern, because of potential underestimation of the leverage statistic, h_j.

3. In a standard normal distribution with a mean of 0 and a standard deviation of 1, 95% of the cases should have standardized scores (or in this context, standardized residuals) between −2 and +2, and 99% should have scores or residuals between −3 and +3. Having a standardized or deviance residual larger than 2 or 3 does not necessarily mean that there is something wrong with the model. We would expect about 5% of the sample to lie *outside* the range of −2 to +2, and 1% to lie outside the range of −2.5 to +2.5. Values far outside this range, however, are usually indications that the model fits poorly for a particular case, and suggest that there is either something unusual about the case that merits further investigation, or that the model may need to be modified to account for whatever it is that explains the poor fit for some of the cases.

4. As Fox (1991) notes, in linear regression, Influence = Leverage × Discrepancy, where "discrepancy" refers to being an outlier on Y with respect to the predictors. In logistic regression, in contrast with linear regression, as fitted probabilities get close to 0 (less than .1) or 1 (greater than .9), the leverages stop increasing and turn rapidly toward 0 (Hosmer and Lemeshow 1989:153–154).

Path Analysis With Logistic Regression (PALR)

The use of path analysis to examine causal structures among continuous variables was pioneered by Sewall Wright (1918, 1921, 1934, 1971) and popularized in the social sciences through the work of Blau and Duncan (1967), among others. There are several advantages to path analysis that account for its continuing popularity: (1) It provides a graphical representation of a set of algebraic relationships among variables that concisely and visually summarizes those relationships. (2) It allows us not only to examine the direct impact of a predictor on a dependent variable (an issue raised at the end of Chapter 6) but also to see other types of relationships, including indirect and spurious relationships. (3) It indicates, at a glance, which predictors appear to have stronger, weaker, or no relationships with the dependent variable. (4) It allows us to decompose or split up the variance in a dependent variable into explained and unexplained, and also allows us to decompose the explained variance into variance explained by different variables. (5) It allows us to decompose the correlation between a predictor and a dependent variable into direct, indirect, and spurious effects. This chapter begins with a very brief review of path analysis as used with ordinary least squares (OLS) regression analysis to review the terminology and provide a basis for comparison with path analysis as implemented with logistic regression analysis, then moves on to a detailed consideration of path analysis with logistic regression (PALR), something to which we will return in subsequent chapters. Path analysis is used to describe systems of predictive or, more often, causal relationships involving three or more interrelated variables. Because path analysis is most often used in causal rather than purely predictive analysis, the language of causality is adopted throughout this chapter, but it should be borne in mind that causal relationships require more than path analysis for evidence; in particular, questions not only of association and spuriousness but also of causal (and thus implicitly temporal) order must be considered.[1]

In path analysis, more than one variable is typically treated as a dependent variable with respect to other variables in the model. Variables that affect other variables in the model, but are not affected by other variables in the model, are called *exogenous* variables, implying not so much that they are outside the model but that their explanation lies outside the model. A variable that is affected or predicted by at least one of the other variables in the model is considered an *endogenous* variable. An endogenous variable may be the last variable in the causal chain, or it may be an *intervening* variable, one that occurs between an exogenous variable and another endogenous variable. In practice, in any path analytical model, there will be at least one exogenous and one endogenous variable.

The simple patterns of direct, indirect, and spurious relationships are diagrammed in Figure 8.1. Diagram "a" in Figure 8.1 shows a simple relationship in which X and Y are both exogenous variables, and each has a direct effect on the endogenous variable Z. Diagram "b" in Figure 8.1 shows a spurious relationship, in which X is an exogenous variable, Y and Z are endogenous variables, and X has an effect on both Y and Z. From Diagram "b," we would expect that the zero-order correlation between Y and Z would be nonzero, but that the partial correlation between Y and Z, controlling for X, would be zero. Diagram "c" in Figure 8.1 shows a causal chain, in which X is an exogenous variable and has a direct effect on Y but not on Z; Y and Z are endogenous variables; and Y has a direct effect on Z. In Diagram "c," X has an indirect effect on Z, through its effect on Y. We would therefore expect the zero-order correlation between X and Z to be nonzero, but the partial correlation between X and Z, controlling for Y, to be zero. Diagram "d" in Figure 8.1 shows a mixture of direct and indirect effects and incorporates all the effects in the previous three diagrams. X is an exogenous variable that has a direct effect on the endogenous variable Y, a direct effect on the endogenous variable Z, and an indirect effect (via Y) on the endogenous variable Z. Y is an endogenous variable that is related to Z in part through a direct effect, but also in part through a spurious effect, since X is a cause of both Y and Z. In this diagram, we would expect the zero-order correlations among all

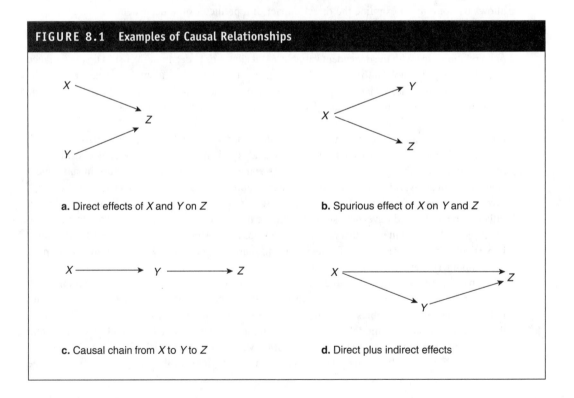

FIGURE 8.1   Examples of Causal Relationships

a. Direct effects of X and Y on Z

b. Spurious effect of X on Y and Z

c. Causal chain from X to Y to Z

d. Direct plus indirect effects

the variables to be nonzero, the partial correlation between X and Z controlling for Y to be nonzero but smaller than the zero-order correlation between X and Z (because part of the zero-order correlation would reflect the indirect effect of X on Z via Y), and the partial correlation between Y and Z controlling for X to be nonzero but smaller than the zero-order correlation between Y and Z (because the zero-order correlation would reflect the spurious relationship between Y and Z resulting from their both being influenced by X).

Diagrams "a" and "b" in Figure 8.1 both represent models that can be described as *weakly ordered recursive* models. If we trace each arrow forward, we never come back to the variable where we started, but there are two variables (X and Y in Diagram "a," Y and Z in Diagram "b") between which there is not a clear causal ordering. In Diagram "a," X and Y occur before Z, but it is not evident from the diagram that either occurs before the other. Similarly in Diagram "b," Y and Z both occur after X, but there is no clear ordering between Y and Z. Diagrams "c" and "d" represent *strongly recursive* or *fully ordered recursive* models, in which it is again the case that if we trace each arrow forward we never come back to the variable where we started, but it is also the case that X is the only exogenous variable in the model, and there is a clear ordering from left to right, with no ambiguity about which variable comes before or after any other variable. It is also possible to have *nonrecursive* models, in which it is possible to start from at least one variable, trace the arrows forward, and come back to the variable where you started. For example, if in Diagram "b" in Figure 8.1 we added two arrows, one from Y to Z and another from Z to Y, we would have a nonrecursive model, with a *nonrecursive loop* between Y and Z. Alternatively, if in Diagram "d" in Figure 8.1 we reversed the direction of the arrow from X to Z so it pointed instead from Z to X, we would have a nonrecursive loop involving all three of the variables (from X to Y to Z and back to X again).

DECOMPOSITION OF VARIANCE IN PATH ANALYSIS

The shared variation among variables can be represented by overlapping circles, as in Figure 8.2. In Figure 8.2, X and Y are predictors of the dependent variable Z, corresponding to Diagram "a" in Figure 8.1. The circle with the horizontal lines represents the variable X, the circle with the vertical lines represents the variable Y, and the circle with no lines represents the variable Z. If X and Y are uncorrelated, there is no overlap between the two circles, but the more usual case is that the variables X and Y are correlated, resulting in the crosshatched section where the circles X and Y overlap. The variance in Z explained by X and Y is represented by the overlap of circles X and Y with circle Z. Notice that within the circle Z (Figure 8.2), there is an area with horizontal lines, another with vertical lines, and a third with crosshatched lines. The area within Z with the horizontal lines represents the variance in Z explained uniquely by X, and the area within Z with the vertical lines represents the variance in Z explained uniquely by Y. The more or less triangular area within Z with crosshatched lines, where all three circles overlap, represents the variance in Z explained jointly by X and Y, but which cannot be uniquely attributed to either X or Y. (It should be readily apparent that as more predictors are added to the model, the problem of representing the model with a diagram like Figure 8.2 becomes increasingly complex.) The white area within Z corresponds to the unexplained variance, $1 - R^2$, the square root of which, $\sqrt{1 - R^2}$, is sometimes explicitly included in a path model as the path coefficient for the "residual" effect, the presumed effect of variables not in the model, which, if included, would explain the endogenous variable perfectly.

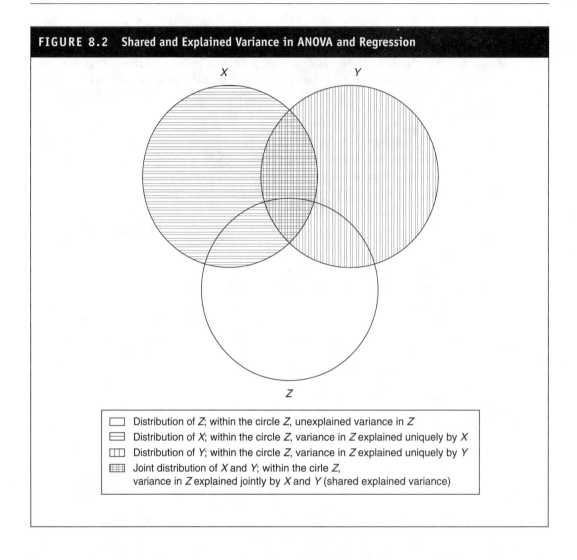

FIGURE 8.2   Shared and Explained Variance in ANOVA and Regression

> ☐ Distribution of *Z*; within the circle *Z*, unexplained variance in *Z*
> ⊟ Distribution of *X*; within the circle *Z*, variance in *Z* explained uniquely by *X*
> ⊞ Distribution of *Y*; within the circle *Z*, variance in *Z* explained uniquely by *Y*
> ▦ Joint distribution of *X* and *Y*; within the cirle *Z*, variance in *Z* explained jointly by *X* and *Y* (shared explained variance)

There are basically two approaches to dealing with the crosshatched area within *Z*. In partial correlation analysis and the usual partitioning of variance in analysis of variance (ANOVA), only the explained variance that can be *uniquely* attributed to one variable or the other is considered variance explained by that variable. In ANOVA, in particular, shared explained variance is typically treated as a category separate from the variance explained uniquely by either variable. The area within *Z* with the horizontal lines thus represents the unique variance in *Z* attributable to *X* in ANOVA, or the partial correlation coefficient between *X* and *Z* controlling for *Y*, $r_{ZX \cdot Y}$. The area within *Z* with the vertical lines represents the unique variance in *Z* attributable to *Y* in ANOVA, or the partial correlation coefficient between *Y* and *Z* controlling for *X*, $r_{ZY \cdot X}$. The area within *Z* with the crosshatched lines represents variance attributed directly to the joint effect of *X* and *Y*, but not specifically to either *X* or *Y*.

In contrast to partial correlation or ANOVA, OLS regression analysis and similar techniques (including logistic regression) effectively take the crosshatched area and, rather than treating it as a separate component of the variance, split it up between the two predictors, X and Y. Without going into excessive detail, the relative proportions of the crosshatched area going to X and Y correspond to the relative magnitude of the variance in Z uniquely explained by X and Y. Thus, in Figure 8.2, more of the crosshatched area would be "assigned" to X than to Y, because the area within Z with horizontal lines (corresponding to variance uniquely explained by X) is larger than the area within Z with vertical lines (corresponding to Y). *All* of the explained variance in Z is thus attributed to one or the other of the two variables separately, not jointly. This is indicated in Figure 8.3 by placing "x"s in the crosshatched area within the circle Z, corresponding to the shared explained variance in Z that

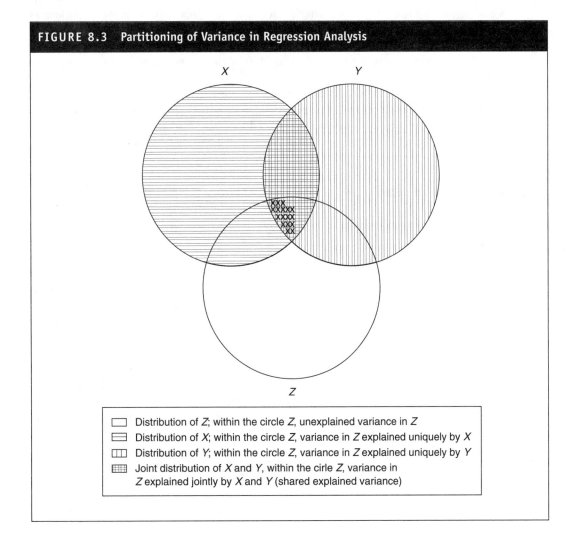

FIGURE 8.3 Partitioning of Variance in Regression Analysis

Distribution of Z; within the circle Z, unexplained variance in Z
Distribution of X; within the circle Z, variance in Z explained uniquely by X
Distribution of Y; within the circle Z, variance in Z explained uniquely by Y
Joint distribution of X and Y, within the cirle Z, variance in Z explained jointly by X and Y (shared explained variance)

would be attributed to X instead of Y. Path analysis, which is based on multiple linear regression analysis (although not necessarily on the use of OLS), likewise partitions all of the explained variance in Z among the predictors. According to this method of partitioning the variance, the proportion of the variance in Z that is estimated to be *directly* (but not *uniquely*, since we are splitting up shared explained variance among the predictors) explained is equal to the product of the standardized regression coefficient and the zero-order correlation between the dependent variable and the predictor, for example, $r_{ZX}b^*_{ZX}$ or $r_{ZY}b^*_{ZY}$. The sum of the products of all the standardized path coefficients and their associated zero-order correlations is known to be equal to the total proportion of the variance that is explained or R^2, that is, $\sum(b^*)(r) = R^2$; for a proof, see Tatsuoka (1971:31–34). In this sense, the explained variance can be partitioned *completely,* but again not *uniquely,* among the predictors in the model, without specific reference to a separate shared effect.

Several authors have been harshly critical of the use of this product, rb^*, to represent the proportion of the variance in the dependent variable that is uniquely attributable to a predictor. As long as one keeps in mind the distinction between the proportion of explained variance that can be uniquely ascribed to a predictor (the square of the partial correlation coefficient) and the proportion of the variance that can be directly (but not really uniquely) attributed to that variable (the product of the zero-order correlation and the path coefficient), it can be informative not only to compare the magnitude of the path coefficients, as is commonly done, but also to examine the proportion of the variance directly attributed to each of the predictors, along with the proportion of the variance that is unexplained by any of the predictors. For further discussion of rb^* and other indices of relative importance in linear and logistic regression, see Grömping (2007) and Menard (2007).

DECOMPOSITION OF ZERO-ORDER CORRELATIONS IN PATH ANALYSIS

Figure 8.4 presents the model from Diagram "d" of Figure 8.1 with coefficients assigned to each of the causal paths. One approach to calculating the coefficients for path analysis models is to first regress the last variable in the causal order (Z) on the prior two variables, then to regress each endogenous variable in turn, working back from the last to the second variable in the sequence, on the variables that precede it in the model. In this approach, the path coefficients (the numbers associated with each of the arrows) are the identical standardized regression coefficients produced by OLS regression analysis. In the model in Figure 8.4, X has a direct effect (a path coefficient or standardized regression coefficient) on Z of .200, and a direct effect on Y of .100, while the direct effect of Y on Z is .300. The *indirect* effect of X on Z can be found by multiplying the path coefficients that connect X to Z via other variables. In this simple model, there is only one such path, and the indirect effect of X on Z is equal to $(b^*_{XY})(b^*_{YZ}) = (.100)(.300) = .030$. Alternatively, one can follow the common practice of using "p" in place of "b^*" to designate the path coefficients, and rewrite this as $(p_{XY})(p_{YZ}) = .030$. The *total* effect of X on Z is equal to the *direct* effect plus the sum of all the *indirect* effects (of which there is only one in this example):

$$(p_{ZX}) + (p_{XY}p_{YZ}) = (.200) + (.100)(.300) = .230.$$

The fundamental theorem of path analysis states that the correlation between any pair of variables, such as X and Z or Y and Z, can be expressed as the sum of all the nonredundant paths between the two variables. For a fully ordered recursive model, this is the sum of the direct plus indirect plus spurious causal paths between the two variables (i.e., the total effect plus the sum of the spurious effects) when the path coefficients are expressed as standardized regression coefficients.[2] For a weakly ordered recursive model, this may also include paths involving correlations between exogenous variables, as described, for example, by Asher (1983:34–35). It must also be the case that all nonzero paths are included in the model. When some paths are defined to be zero a priori, one test of how well the model works is to compare the *observed* correlation with the *implied* correlation (the latter calculated based on the path coefficients) between each of the predictors and the endogenous variables.

The total effect of X on Z in the present example will be equal to the zero-order correlation between X and Z. Because Y has no indirect effect on Z, the direct effect of Y on Z is the same as the total effect, .300, but there is also a spurious effect, equal to the product of the path from X to Y and the path from X to Z: (.100)(.200) = .020, implying a zero-order correlation between Y and Z of (.300) + (.020) = .320. Finally, the only relationship between X and Y is the direct effect of X on Y, and the zero-order correlation should in this instance be equal to the path coefficient for that direct effect, .100. Because the path coefficients in Figure 8.4 are standardized regression coefficients, it is reasonable to conclude that the impact (measured in terms of the total effect) of Y on Z is stronger than the impact of X on Z, even when we include direct as well as indirect effects.

Now consider some possible changes in the model. If the path coefficient between X and Z were .280 instead of .200, then the total effect of X on Z would be (.280) + (.030) = .310, and the total effect of X on Z (.310) would be slightly larger than the total effect of Y on Z (.300), even though the zero-order correlation between Y and Z (.320, equal to the direct plus spurious effect) is larger than the zero-order correlation between X and Z (.310, equal to the direct plus indirect effect). Second, if the direct effect of X on Z were 0 instead of .200, X would still have the indirect effect, .030, on Z, and because it had only an indirect effect, the indirect effect would be equal to the total effect (and to the zero-order correlation) between Z and X. Third, if the direct effect of X on Y were 0, then the direct effect of X on Z would be equal to the total effect of X on Z, .200, and moreover, with X and Y uncorrelated, the path coefficients would be equal not only to the standardized regression coefficients but also to the zero-order correlations for the relationship between X and Z and the relationship between Y and Z. All these are relatively simple examples. In general, it will not usually

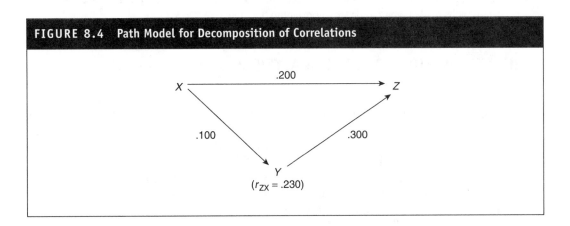

FIGURE 8.4   Path Model for Decomposition of Correlations

be the case that the zero-order correlation coefficient will be equal to the standardized regression coefficient, that predictors will be completely uncorrelated, or that the total effects will be equal to either the direct or the indirect effect.

METHODS OF ESTIMATING PATH COEFFICIENTS

In the earlier years of path analysis, when computer time was costly and the memory and processing speed on a mainframe computer was puny compared with the memory and processing time on even low-end personal computers today, the usual method of calculating path coefficients was to run separate regression analyses on each of the endogenous variables in the model. Increasingly, however, as the sophistication of both computers and statistical programmers increased, the accepted practice has shifted to the use of software that simultaneously estimates all of the relationships in the model, including not only the path coefficients but also involving oblique factor analysis to estimate the values of latent variables (not directly measured, but estimated on the basis of observed indicator variables in the model), correlations among residuals, and other technical features of the model. The term *structural equation modeling (SEM)*[3] has come to refer less to the model itself than to the more sophisticated techniques for estimating simultaneous equation causal models. It is worth noting that OLS estimates or, for nonrecursive models, two-stage least squares (2SLS)[4] estimates are used as a first step in these more sophisticated SEM estimation techniques, which, like logistic regression analysis, rely on iterative algorithms to improve the fit of the model to the data.

As described by Heise (1975), one major advantage of full-information maximum likelihood simultaneous equation methods for estimating path models is that they make more efficient use of valid theory, incorporating all such knowledge into the estimate of each system parameter, resulting in more precise estimates. The major disadvantage, correspondingly, is that they similarly incorporate any erroneous theory into the calculations, so if part of the model has been misspecified, all coefficient estimates may be affected instead of just a few. In general, Heise recommends the use of full-information methods in the latter stages of research, when there is a high level of confidence in the specification of the model. Estimation of a single equation at a time may be more appropriate in the earlier stages of model testing, when the emphasis is less on precise estimation of coefficients for causal paths that are known with some certainty to belong in the model than on deciding *which* causal paths really belong in or are important to the model.

EARLY EXPLORATIONS OF PATH ANALYSIS WITH LOGIT MODELS

Leo Goodman (1972, 1973a, 1973b) did much to pioneer and popularize log-linear and logit analysis. As part of his work in this area, he attempted to develop a causal path analytic model for dichotomous variables using logit analysis. Goodman (1972) describes a "standardized" coefficient that is really the normal distribution version of the Wald test statistic for logistic regression: "By dividing each estimated β parameter by its estimated standard deviation s_β, we obtained the corresponding 'standardized value' of the estimate" (p. 36). Note 17 on the same page cautions against confusing this standardized value with "other things," presumably including the analog of a standardized OLS regression coefficient. Goodman (1973a) later uses this same standardized value or

(Goodman 1973b) the unstandardized value in calculating a series of logit models that are then combined into a single path model.

The limitations of Goodman's standardized coefficient, and correspondingly of path analysis in log-linear and logit analysis, have been detailed, for example, in Fienberg (1980:chap. 7) and Knoke and Burke (1980:42–47); see also Maddala (1983:108–113). As they observe, the path coefficients, either unstandardized or standardized using Goodman's suggested method, cannot legitimately be multiplied to calculate the indirect effects. The magnitude of numerical relationships is thus problematic, and they recommend limiting the presentation of the path analysis results using Goodman's method to noting the signs of the direct and indirect effects. This permits us to ascertain whether the indirect effects have the same or different signs, but when the separate indirect effects do not have the same sign, it does not allow us to determine whether the sum of the indirect effects is positive or negative. Fienberg (1980:129) further observes that fitting recursive systems of logit models, using the single-equation estimation technique described above, is not always equivalent to fitting a single log-linear model to the full set of variables. Taken altogether, then, the limitations of Goodman's approach to causal path analysis with logit models are that (1) the relative magnitude of direct and indirect effects cannot be calculated;[5] (2) because the magnitudes of different effects cannot be calculated, it is similarly not possible to calculate the relative magnitude of differently signed indirect effects; (3) because the relative magnitude of differently signed indirect effects cannot be calculated, it is not possible even to calculate whether the indirect effect of one variable on another is positive or negative if the indirect effect must be traced over two or more paths; and (4) because the magnitude of the different effects cannot be computed, it is not possible to calculate total effects, to partition variation in the dependent variable, or to partition correlations between predictors and the dependent variable, as in path analysis for continuous variables. Probably because of these limitations, causal path analysis using log-linear and logit models is rarely if ever used in empirical research.

STRUCTURAL EQUATION MODELING (REVISITED) AND PATH ANALYSIS WITH LOGISTIC REGRESSION

An alternative to Goodman's approach based on log-linear analysis has been the attempt to incorporate categorical variables in the SEM framework. Kupek (2005, 2006) has summarized the current state of the field regarding the path analysis of categorical variables in the SEM framework as involving four main strategies. One is the use of asymptotic distribution free estimators that adjust for nonnormality by taking into account the kurtosis in a joint multivariate distribution (Browne 1984). A second is the use of robust maximum likelihood estimation or resampling techniques (to be covered in the context of logistic regression analysis but outside the context of SEM in Chapter 14) to obtain standard errors for SEM parameters, because these are most affected by the departure from multivariate normality (Bollen and Stine 1993). A third strategy is to calculate polyserial, tetrachoric, or polychoric correlations, then incorporate these correlations as input for the structural equation model (Jöreskog and Sörbom 1988). This is the strategy used in the statistical package LISREL and its companion PRELIS. The fourth approach is to calculate probit or logit model scores for observed categorical variables and then use these scores as input for the structural equation model (Muthén 1995). Eshima et al. (2001), using only categorical variables in their analysis, approach this problem by using a combination of log-odds ratios, uncertainty differences, and an inner product of explanatory variables and a response variable.

All these approaches treat the dichotomous variable not as an inherent dichotomy, but as a manifestation of an underlying continuous variable, and it is only by doing so that they are able to produce path models with categorical variables. If there truly is justification for assuming that the dichotomous variable in question represents an underlying latent variable, then SEM approaches to the problem make sense. The assumption of a latent variable, however, typically seems to be driven by the method, rather than by the substance of the problem. On a slightly different track, in the statistical package MPlus (Muthén and Muthén 2007), it is possible to include categorical variables as such, but MPlus has no provision for calculating standardized coefficients for categorical variables as dependent variables and cannot provide indirect or total effects. What is missing here is an approach that (a) treats dichotomous and (see Chapter 9) unordered categorical variables in a way that preserves their inherent nature as dichotomies or categorical variables, without trying to recast them as representing continuous latent variables, and (b) allows the inclusion of categorical and continuous variables as both exogenous variables and as endogenous variables at any stage in causal or temporal order in the model. In the following sections, path analysis with logistic regression will be approached as a problem for which separate regressions are presently the most viable strategy (given existing software), but there is nothing in principle that would preclude the implementation of PALR in simultaneous equation, maximum likelihood algorithms.

BIVARIATE PALR

The simplest case of PALR occurs when we have a dichotomous dependent variable and a dichotomous predictor. Substantively, this model is uninteresting, but it provides a good starting point for building a method of path analysis with logistic regression and illustrating the parallels between PALR and path analysis as commonly used in multiple linear regression. Table 8.1 presents the bivariate logistic and linear regression results for gender as a predictor of (a) marijuana use and

TABLE 8.1 PALR With a Dichotomous Dependent Variable and a Dichotomous Predictor

Dependent Variable	Method of Analysis	Predictor	Standardized Coefficient	Predicted Values of the Dependent Variable	
				Minimum	Maximum
Marijuana use $R^2 = .042$ $R_O^2 = .042$	Linear regression	Gender (Female)	.205	.25000	.44538
	Logistic regression	Gender (Female)	.205	.25000	.44538
Computer use $R^2 = .003$ $R_O^2 = .003$	Linear regression	Gender (Male)	.055	.56677	.61343
	Logistic regression	Gender (Male)	.055	.56677	.61343

(b) computer use, using the same data as in earlier chapters. The standardized coefficients presented are the fully standardized coefficients suggested by Menard (1995) and presented in Chapter 5. For both dependent variables, the linear and logistic regression standardized coefficients are identical to each other and to the zero-order correlation between the two variables. This property is only true of the fully standardized logistic regression coefficient suggested by Menard (1995), and not of the other standardized coefficients proposed elsewhere as described in Chapter 5. Henceforth, the term *standardized logistic regression coefficient* will, unless otherwise noted, refer to this fully standardized logistic regression coefficient. Predicted minimum and maximum values of the dependent variables are also identical for linear and logistic regression, although predicted means may diverge at higher levels of precision.

For marijuana use, the predicted minimum and maximum values are the same for linear and logistic regression, the means are trivially different (.3506494 for linear regression and .3506495 for logistic regression; the observed mean is .3506), the predicted values from linear and logistic regression are perfectly correlated ($r = 1.000$), and the standardized coefficients for both linear and logistic regression are equal to the zero-order correlation between sex and marijuana use. For computer use, the predicted mean from linear regression is .5869974 for linear regression and .5869966 for logistic regression (the observed mean is .57799), again trivially different, and the correlation between the values predicted by linear and logistic regression is again perfect, $r = 1.000$. The standardized linear and logistic regression coefficients are again equal to each other, and to the zero-order correlation coefficient. The reason for the almost identical result is that for a dichotomous predictor with a dichotomous dependent variable, there should really be no difference between the linear and the logistic model: for both OLS and maximum likelihood prediction, the best prediction is to predict the conditional mean of the dependent variable for each of the two categories of the predictor.

The case of a single continuous predictor has already been examined in Chapter 1, with the example of predicting marijuana use from exposure to delinquent friends. To further illustrate the case with a single continuous predictor, Table 8.2 presents both the results for marijuana use with exposure as a predictor and computer use with education as a predictor. As shown in Chapter 1, bivariate linear and logistic regression produce different results when a single continuous predictor is used to predict a dichotomous dependent variable. In particular, linear regression can predict minimum or maximum values for the dependent variable that lie outside the range (0, 1). For both marijuana use and computer use, this is the case in Table 8.2, with a predicted maximum value for the probability of marijuana use equal to 1.45, and for computer use equal to 1.08. We would likewise not expect the explained variance, measured by R_O^2 to be the same for the logistic and linear regression models, particularly if the logistic regression model provides a better fit to the data. For education as a predictor of computer use, $R^2 = .17$ for linear regression and $R_O^2 = .18$ for logistic regression; and for exposure to delinquent friends as a predictor of marijuana use, $R^2 = .32$ for linear regression and $R_O^2 = .34$ for logistic regression. The marijuana use example indicates that the standardized coefficient is larger for logistic than for linear regression for marijuana use. Similarly, the standardized coefficient for the effect of education on computer use is larger for logistic than for linear regression. As is evident from this example, it will not generally be the case that the standardized coefficients produced by linear and logistic regression will be equal when the predictor is a continuous variable. Note also that the standardized logistic regression coefficient is approximately equal to r_O (the square root of R_O^2), or $b* = r_O$, or equivalently $(b*)^2 = R_O^2$, paralleling the relationship between the standardized coefficient and the zero-order correlation (or the squared standardized coefficient and R^2) for bivariate OLS regression. The equality is not generally exact, however, only close.

TABLE 8.2   PALR With a Dichotomous Dependent Variable and a Continuous Predictor

Dependent Variable	Method of Analysis	Predictor	Standardized Coefficient	Predicted Values of the Dependent Variable	
				Minimum	Maximum
Marijuana use $R^2 = .32$ $R_O^2 = .34$	Linear regression	Exposure to delinquent friends	.568	.10	1.45
	Logistic regression	Exposure to delinquent friends	.587	.11967	.94975
Computer use $R^2 = .17$ $R_O^2 = .18$	Linear regression	Education	.417	.11	1.08
	Logistic regression	Education	.430	.09687	.99819

TWO OR MORE DICHOTOMOUS PREDICTORS

A situation similar to the case of the single continuous predictor arises once we have a nominal predictor with three or more categories, or equivalently two or more dichotomous variables. The case of an unordered categorical predictor is identical to the case of having two or more dichotomous predictors because two or more dummy variables would be used to represent the three or more categories of the single nominal predictor, as illustrated in Table 8.3. Three examples are given in Table 8.3. Ethnicity is used as a predictor of both marijuana use and computer use, following the examples we have been using up to this point. Ethnicity, however, is a weak predictor of both marijuana use and computer use. In the interest of providing a comparison in which the relationships involved were stronger, a third dependent variable, hard drug use, has been included in the last third of Table 8.3, with marijuana use and gender as predictors. The data on hard drug use, marijuana use, and gender were taken from the National Youth Survey, and the equation describing the relationship involving drug use and the two (dichotomous) predictors is logit(hard drug use) = .348(marijuana use) + .071(gender) −.096, where gender is coded 1 = male and 2 = female, so the positive coefficient for gender indicates that females in this sample had higher rates of hard drug use as well as marijuana use than males. In the model for hard drug use, $R_L^2 = .367$ ($G_M = 66.906$ with 2 df, $p = .000$) and $R_O^2 = .282$ (as compared with $R^2 = .270$ for the linear regression model for the same variables).

As indicated in Table 8.3, for the prediction of marijuana use, the linear and logistic regression models produced similar standardized coefficients and identical predicted minimum and maximum values, and the predicted mean values were identical (and equal to the observed mean) as well at .3506 but this may be attributable to the fact that neither model did very well in predicting marijuana use. For the linear regression model, $R^2 = .010$, and for the logistic regression model $R_O^2 = .010$ as

TABLE 8.3   PALR With a Dichotomous Dependent Variable and Two Dichotomous Predictors

Dependent Variable	Method of Analysis	Predictor	Standardized Coefficient	Predicted Values of the Dependent Variable	
				Minimum	Maximum
Marijuana use $R^2 = .010$ $R_O^2 = .010$	Linear regression	Black Other	−.075 .055	.26316	.46667
	Logistic regression	Black Other	−.078 .051	.26316	.46667
Computer use $R^2 = .012$ $R_O^2 = .011$	Linear regression	Black Other	−.107 .010	.46243	.63025
	Logistic regression	Black Other	−.102 .010	.46243	.63025
Hard drug use $R^2 = .270$ $R_O^2 = .282$	Linear regression	Marijuana Gender (Female)	.488 .104	−.02462	.39495
	Logistic regression	Marijuana Gender (Female)	.497 .111	.00402	.44032

well; $R_L^2 = .008$ ($G_M = 2.242$ with 2 df, $p = .324$). Ethnicity is little better as a predictor of computer use. For the linear regression model, $R^2 = .012$ ($p = .000$, thanks to the larger sample size), $R_L^2 = .009$ ($G_M = 26.122$, with 2 df, $p = .000$) and $R_O^2 = .011$. The predicted minimum and maximum values of the probability of computer use are identical once again, the predicted means differ trivially (.5866604 for linear and .5866592 for logistic regression), and the calculated standardized coefficients are once again similar for linear and logistic regression. At least when the model predicts the dependent variable poorly, linear regression seems little worse than logistic regression for producing in-range predicted values.

In a model in which the prediction of the dependent variable is predicted well by the independent variables, however, we once again run into the problem of predicted values that lie outside the possible range of values for the dependent variable, as illustrated in the OLS regression model for hard drug use. The standardized coefficients are once again similar in the linear and logistic regression models, but the linear regression model produces negative predicted values of the probability of hard drug use. Comparing R^2 for the linear regression model and R_O^2 for the logistic regression model, we see that in this example $R_O^2 > R^2$, which coupled with the negative predicted values in the linear regression model is reminiscent of the results using a single continuous predictor, as illustrated in Chapter 1.

For anything but the simplest models involving a single dichotomous predictor of a dichotomous outcome, then, linear regression and logistic regression may differ in the explained variance, the values of the standardized coefficients, and whether the predicted values are in range. With respect to this last comparison, logistic regression is clearly to be preferred to linear regression. With respect to the second comparison, results vary, but logistic regression often produces slightly higher explained variance than linear regression for a dichotomous dependent variable. That the first comparison in the simple models considered so far indicates that the fully standardized logistic regression coefficients appear to be comparable in magnitude to the standardized coefficients from linear regression hints that the two may be used similarly in path analysis, a suggestion that we now explore in greater detail.

A FULLY ORDERED RECURSIVE LOGISTIC REGRESSION PATH MODEL

The simplest models with only a single continuous or dichotomous predictor, or two or more dichotomous predictors of which all are exogenous variables, do not exploit the full potential of path analysis. Figure 8.5 and Table 8.4 present a fully ordered recursive model for computer use, with education, income, and gender as predictors. The model was constructed using the single equation method, that is, the models for computer use (using logistic regression), income, and education (using OLS linear regression) were calculated separately. As indicated in Table 8.4, levels of explained variance are modest: $R_O^2 = .218$ for computer use ($R_L^2 = .170$), $R^2 = .206$ for income, and $R^2 = .064$ for education, all statistically significant at the .002 level or better. The only path coefficient that is not statistically significant, based on the statistical significance of the corresponding unstandardized coefficient, is the coefficient for the direct path from gender to computer use ($b^* = .005, p = .817$). In path analysis with OLS linear regression, the correlations can be precisely reproduced from the path coefficients only if all nonzero paths are included in the model, and the inclusion of the nonsignificant path in the PALR model for computer use allows us to test whether this is also possible with PALR. The zero-order correlations of the predictors with the dependent variable are presented at the bottom of Table 8.4.

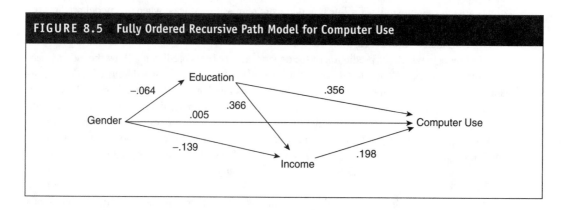

FIGURE 8.5 Fully Ordered Recursive Path Model for Computer Use

TABLE 8.4   Logistic Regression for Computer Use: Fully Ordered Recursive Model

Dependent Variable	Independent Variable	Unstandardized Coefficients (b)	Standardized Coefficients (b*)	Significance (Wald z for Logistic Regression, t for OLS Linear Regression)
Computer use $R_L^2 = .170$ $(p = .000)$ $R_O^2 = .218$	Intercept	−5.381	—	.000
	Gender (Female)	0.023	.005	.817
	Education	0.322	.356	.000
	Income	0.098	.198	.000
Income $R^2 = .206$ $(p = .000)$	Intercept	8.712	—	.000
	Gender (Female)	−1.409	−.139	.000
	Education	0.667	.366	.000
Education $R^2 = .064$ $(p = .002)$	Intercept	13.907	—	.000
	Gender (Female)	−0.356	−.064	.002

NOTES: Zero-order correlations with dependent variable (Pearson's r):

Gender $r = -.055$.

Education $r = .417$.

Income $r = .330$.

The path coefficients in Figure 8.5 are the same as the standardized (linear or logistic) regression coefficients in Table 8.4. From these, we can calculate the direct, indirect, and spurious effects as follows:

(A) Gender

1. Direct effect = .005 (the path coefficient for the direct path from gender to computer use).

2. Indirect effects:
   a. gender to education to computer use = (−.064)(.356) = −.022784
   b. gender to education to income to computer use = (−.064)(.366)(.198) = −.004638
   c. gender to income to computer use = (−.139)(.198) = −.027522
   d. Total indirect effect = (−.022784) + (−.004638) + (−.027522) = −.054944 ≈ −.055

3. Spurious effects: none; gender is exogenous

4. Total direct + indirect + spurious = (.005) + (−.055) + (0) = −.050; $r = -.055$

(B) Education

1. Direct effect = .356

2. Indirect effect = (.366)(.198) = .072468 [education to income to computer use]

3. Spurious effects: These are calculated by tracing back (in the opposite direction of the arrowhead) from the predictor to each prior predictor in the model, then tracing forward (the same direction of the arrowhead) all possible paths that do not include the predictor

   a. Education back to gender to income to computer use: (−.064)(−.139)(.198) = .0017614
   b. Education back to gender to computer use: (−.064)(.005) = −.00032
   c. Total spurious effects: (.0017614) + (−.00032) = .0014414 ≈ .001

4. Total direct + indirect + spurious = (.356) + (.072)+(.001) = .429; r = .417

(C) Income

1. Direct effect = .198

2. Indirect effect = 0 (There is no variable between income and computer use)

3. Spurious effects

   a. income back to education back to gender to computer use:
      (.366)(−.064)(.005) = −.0001171
   b. income back to education to computer use: (.366)(.356) = .130296
   c. income back to gender to computer use: (−.137)(.005) = −.000685
   d. income back to gender to education to computer use:
      (−.139)(−.064)(.356) = .003167
   e. total spurious effects = (−.0001171) + (−.000685) + (.130296) + (.003167) =
      .1326609 ≈ .133

4. Total direct + indirect + spurious = (.198) + (0) + (.133) = .331; r = .330

It is evident from the above calculations that the calculated total effect plus the sum of the spurious effects for each predictor is close to but not precisely equal to the zero-order correlation of that predictor with the dependent variable. Note also, however, that the total effect for Education *is* close to the standardized coefficient, which is equal to the bivariate R_O^2 for the logistic regression model, in Table 8.2. Also recall that in the bivariate analysis of marijuana use with exposure to delinquent friends, the explained variance was different for logistic regression than for linear regression, and consider that in the bivariate case for linear regression, the explained variance is simply the square of the zero-order correlation. The zero-order correlation, like the standardized coefficients in linear regression, is based on the assumption of a *linear* relationship between the predictor(s) and the dependent variable. In contrast, the standardized coefficients in logistic regression analysis are based on the assumption of a *nonlinear* (logistic) relationship between the predictor(s) and the dependent variable. In effect, the sum of the direct, indirect, and spurious effects for a predictor provides an estimate for the nonlinear association[6] under the logistic model between that predictor and the dependent variable. If the logistic model is correct, and if the relationship between the predictor and the dependent variable is significantly different from zero, it will typically be the case that the estimated nonlinear association will be greater in magnitude than the Pearson correlation, but this will not always be the case, particularly when the relationship itself appears to be close to zero. The only instance in which it consistently makes no difference whether linear or logistic regression is used is in the case of a single dichotomous predictor. Nevertheless, it is evident that using the fully standardized logistic regression coefficients suggested in Menard (1995) can produce results very close to what we would expect from path analysis based on linear regression, without the disadvantages associated with linear regression analysis for dichotomous dependent variables.

DECOMPOSITION OF EXPLAINED VARIATION IN PALR

A similar pattern emerges for the decomposition of variance using fully standardized logistic regression coefficients. In linear regression, as noted earlier, the explained variance is equal to the sum of the products of the standardized coefficients for each predictor with the corresponding zero-order correlation between the predictor and the dependent variable: $R^2 = \Sigma(b^*)(r)$. Using the results in Table 8.4, $\Sigma(b^*)(r) = (.005)(-.055) + (.356)(.417) + (.198)(.330) = -.000275 + .148452 + .06534 = .213517 \approx .214$. In addition to the fact that this sum is not equal to R_O^2 (.218), note that the contribution of gender to the explained variance is negative, but very small. This commonly occurs in linear regression when the sign of the zero-order correlation is the opposite of the sign of the (standardized or unstandardized) regression coefficient, and the resulting estimate of the contribution to the explained variance is not only negative, but typically small, because such reversals of sign rarely occur in the absence of collinearity when the predictor is strongly correlated to the dependent variable to begin with. If we want to avoid negative estimates of the direct (again, not unique) contribution of the predictor to the explained variance, one approach is to take the absolute value of each $(b^*)(r)$ product term, sum the results, then multiply each by R^2 divided by the sum of the product terms. This procedure results in (a) all positive estimates of the direct contribution to the explained variance, recognizing that adding variables to the equation never reduces R^2 but can only increase R^2 or leave it unchanged and (b) the sum of the transformed products still adds up to the explained variance.

In the present example, $|(.005)(-.055)| + |(.356)(.417)| + |(.198)(.330)| = .214067 \approx .214$; $R_O^2 = .218$; and so each product term would be normed by $.218/.214 = 1.0186916$. The resulting direct contribution to the explained variance of the predictors then becomes $.00028 \approx .000$ for gender, .151 for education, and .067 for income, totaling .218. R_O^2 is not, however, the only basis for norming the direct contributions of the predictors. One could as easily substitute R_L^2 or one of the indices of predictive efficiency into the equation, in place of R_O^2, if one wished to speak of the direct contribution of the explained variation (R_L^2) or the direct contribution to the predictive efficiency (λ_p, τ_p, or φ_p), since the contribution of the variable without norming remains the same. Typically, the relative strength of the direct contribution to the explained variance (or variation, or predictive efficiency) will be the same as the relative strength of the logistic regression path coefficients, but in some instances, the order between two predictors may be reversed. In general, when we are simply interested in the relative strengths of the different predictors, we will want to rely on the standardized logistic regression coefficients (unless all the predictors are measured in the same metric, in which case even the unstandardized coefficients can be used). If we want to estimate what proportion of the variance is explained by each predictor, however, the estimate of the direct contribution to the explained variance based on the product of the zero-order correlation and the standardized logistic regression coefficient may be preferred.

A WEAKLY ORDERED RECURSIVE LOGISTIC REGRESSION PATH MODEL

Table 8.5 and Figure 8.6 present a weakly ordered recursive path model for computer use. Even the addition of only two dummy exogenous variables for ethnicity increases the density of the paths considerably, and makes it difficult to include the path coefficients in the model, so the coefficients have been excluded from Figure 8.6 and can instead be found in Table 8.5. In this example, we will focus on the direct and indirect effects, rather than repeating the exercise of decomposing the correlations among the variables. As in a fully ordered recursive model, one can estimate direct, indirect, spurious, and total effects from the weakly ordered recursive model, in particular to examine the extent to which a predictor that does not have a statistically or substantively significant direct effect may have an indirect effect of sufficient magnitude to be of interest.

Without presenting the results in the same detail as was done for the fully ordered recursive model, the direct effect of gender (as indicated in Table 8.5) is −.006, and the indirect effects sum

TABLE 8.5   Logistic Regression for Computer Use: Weakly Ordered Recursive Model

Dependent Variable	Independent Variable	Unstandardized Coefficients (b)	Standardized Coefficients (b*)	Odds Ratio (e^b) for Logistic Regression	Significance (Wald z for Logistic Regression, t for OLS)
Computer use	Intercept	−5.281	—	—	.000
$R_L^2 = .170$	Gender (Female)	−0.029	−.006	0.971	.767
$(p = .000)$	Ethnicity				.325
	Black	−0.133	−.019	0.876	.323
$R_O^2 = .219$	Other	0.228	.020	1.256	.310
	Education	0.321	.355	1.379	.000
	Income	0.097	.195	1.101	.000
Income	Intercept	9.350	—	—	.000
$R^2 = .180$	Gender (Female)	−1.305	−.129	—	.000
$(p = .000)$	Ethnicity			—	—
	Black	−1.993	−.143	—	.000
	Other	−0.797	−.036	—	.065
	Education	0.633	.348	—	.000
Education	Intercept	13.970	—	—	.000
$R^2 = .022$	Gender (Female)	−0.296	−.053	—	.011
$(p = .000)$	Ethnicity			—	—
	Black	−1.014	−.133	—	.000
	Other	−0.008	−.001	—	.977

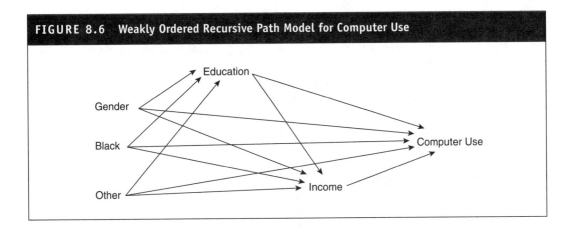

FIGURE 8.6 Weakly Ordered Recursive Path Model for Computer Use

to −.048. The indirect effect of gender on computer use, as it operates via education and income, is thus greater than the direct effect and in the same direction for a total direct plus indirect influence of −.054. For African American ethnicity, a similar pattern holds, with a direct effect of only −.019, but indirect effects sum to −.084, for a total direct plus indirect influence of −.103. For Other ethnicity, the indirect effects sum to only −.007, smaller and of opposite sign than the direct effect. The sum of the direct plus indirect effects, .013, is thus smaller in magnitude than the direct effect. Although spurious effects are of interest in decomposing the correlations between the predictors and the dependent variable, they are not generally of interest when our only concern is with the impact of the predictors on the dependent variable. Their calculation is left as an exercise for the reader.

NONRECURSIVE MODELS

Suppose we believe that not only does income affect computer use (people with higher incomes are better able to afford personal computers) but also that computer use affects income (people with better computer skills are able to obtain higher salaries). In Figure 8.6, this would be represented by the addition to the diagram of an arrow starting at computer use but pointing to income. In other words, there would be two arrows, one pointing in each direction, between computer use and income. A naive approach to estimating the resulting model might be to calculate two equations, one (logistic regression) with income as a predictor and computer use as a dependent variable (as in Table 8.5), and a second (linear regression) equation with income as the dependent variable and computer use as the predictor. As Berry (1984:60–61) explains, we cannot assume the errors are uncorrelated with the predictors in a nonrecursive system, and the estimated coefficients may be biased and inconsistent (where *consistency* refers to the tendency of the value of the estimated parameter to approach the true population value of the parameter, and hence the tendency of the bias of the parameter to approach zero as the sample size increases).

To calculate the parameters for the model, we need to replace the observed variables, when they are used as predictors, with variables that are as similar as possible to the observed variables, but which we can reasonably conclude are uncorrelated with the error terms in the dependent variables.

Three approaches to doing this when all the variables are continuous, in reverse chronological order of their development, are (1) the use of simultaneous equation SEM, using a statistical package such as LISREL, EQS, AMOS, or Mplus; (2) the use of a 2SLS statistical routine in a statistical package such as SAS, SPSS, or Stata, in which all the equations involved in the nonrecursive relationship are estimated in a single step; and (3) the implementation of 2SLS using an OLS multiple linear regression routine in a statistical package such as SAS, SPSS, or Stata, in which each equation is estimated separately. It is worth noting that even in the first option, 2SLS is typically an early step in the estimation of the parameters for the structural equation model.

It is possible to use the simultaneous equations approach to estimate path models with a dichotomous dependent variable, for example, in MPlus (Muthén and Muthén 2007), but as noted earlier, the treatment of dichotomous and categorical variables in SEM is problematic, unless one is willing to assume that the dichotomy represents an underlying or latent continuous variable.[7] Similarly, unless one is willing to assume that the dichotomy represents a latent continuous variable, it is difficult to incorporate dichotomous variables as endogenous variables in nonrecursive loops with existing software. Direct application of 2SLS routines suffers the same problems as OLS regression (violations of assumptions, out-of-range predicted values) when dichotomous variables are involved in the nonrecursive loop. It is, however, possible to follow the third path and to use separate, single-equation estimation techniques, using just logistic regression if all of the variables in the nonrecursive loop are dichotomous, or using a mix of both logistic and linear regression when the variables involved in the nonrecursive loop are themselves mixed, both dichotomous and continuous.

First, however, we need to have a model that is *just identified* or *overidentified*, instead of *underidentified*. Asher (1983:53–72) and Heise (1975) deal with the problem of identification in nonrecursive models at some length, and the reader is referred to those sources for details, but briefly, because all the other variables in Figure 8.6 are assumed to affect both income and computer use, we lack sufficient information to separate the effect of income on computer use from the effect of computer use on income. What we need for the model to be identified is at least one reasonably good predictor of each variable that is not directly related to the other. Examining the coefficients and their significance in Table 8.5, it appears that gender and ethnicity have no statistically significant direct effects on computer use (at least not with income in the equation), so it may be reasonable to exclude them from the equation for computer use. We still, however, lack a variable that is a predictor of computer use but not income. One possibility is age, on the assumption that there are well-paid younger as well as older workers (no relationship with income), but that older people are less likely to adopt the use of personal computers than younger people. In fact, if we run a quick regression of income on age, sex, race, and education, age is not statistically significant as a predictor of income, but if we include it in the analysis for computer use, it is a statistically significant predictor.[8]

With age as a predictor of computer use but not income, and gender and ethnicity as predictors of income but not computer use, our nonrecursive model is identified, and we may proceed to estimate the nonrecursive relationships. This is done in a two-stage process, parallel to the single equation, two-step process for 2SLS. In 2SLS, the first stage involves using the variables exogenous to the nonrecursive loop to estimate *instrumental variables* (sometimes simply called *instruments*) for the endogenous variables in the nonrecursive loop. The second stage is to take each observed variable in turn and calculate the model for that variable, using the instrumental variables for the other endogenous variables in the nonrecursive loop as predictors. In other words, when a variable in the loop is treated as a dependent variable, we use the observed variable; when it is a predictor, we use the instrumental variable.

The single-equation, two-step estimation process has certain disadvantages compared with the simultaneous equation, single-step estimation process (Asher 1983; Berry 1984; Kritzer 1977). First, because the instrumental variable tends to have less variance than the observed variable, estimates for unstandardized coefficients may be unaffected but estimates for standardized coefficients may be attenuated. In the context of logistic regression, however, two questions about this problem with 2SLS for continuous variables arise. First, if we recode the estimated probabilities from the estimation of the instrumental variable back into the original binary scale (e.g., assign a value of 0 to probabilities less than .5 and a value of 1 to probabilities greater than .5), limited experience suggests that there is little attenuation of variance. This is because all the values are coded to the extremes of the range of the instrumental variable. Second, while extreme values of a predictor tend to be highly influential in linear regression analysis, they tend to be less so for logistic regression analysis. Recall the shape of the logistic curve from Chapter 1. It is the changes in values toward the center of the distribution that produce the greatest change in the dependent variable per unit change in the predictor; at the tails of the logistic distribution, a large increment or decrement in the predictor has a much smaller impact on the value of the dependent variable. Given the very early stage of development of two-stage estimation for nonrecursive models using PALR, it is unclear to what extent this problem of two-stage estimation in 2SLS occurs in two-stage estimation using PALR.

Other problems in two-step, single-equation estimation using 2SLS are that the parameter estimates may be biased, and standard errors and explained variances may be incorrect. For some of these problems, there are potential remedies. Standardized coefficients for instrumental variables can be adjusted by either substituting the variance of the observed variable for the variance of the instrumental variable when calculating the standardized coefficient, or by dividing the standardized coefficient by the square root of the explained variance in the first-stage equation for the instrumental variable. Note that these two options do not necessarily produce the same result. A third option, standardizing the variables prior to estimating the parameters, is of no practical use when the dependent (observed) variable is dichotomous and logistic regression is being used to estimate the impact of the predictors, because as noted in Chapter 5, the logistic regression routine will ignore the coding of the *dependent* variable, resulting in a partially standardized coefficient that lacks some of the desirable properties of the fully standardized coefficient. An alternative estimate of explained variance can be obtained by using the model for the dependent variable from the second stage of estimation to generate predicted values, whose correlation with the dependent value can then be calculated. Again, however, the technique of two-stage PALR estimation for nonrecursive models is in a very early state of development, and further investigation is necessary to determine the extent to which these problems arise in two-step estimation of nonrecursive models using PALR.

TWO-STAGE ESTIMATION OF A NONRECURSIVE MODEL WITH PALR

In the present example, with income and computer use as the endogenous variables in the nonrecursive loop, and with age as a predictor of computer use and not income, and with gender and ethnicity as predictors of income but not computer use, we obtain the model structure diagrammed in Figure 8.7. To estimate the model, we first estimate instrumental variables for the two variables involved in the nonrecursive loop. For income, we regress income on gender, ethnicity, and education, resulting in the predictive equation TSPINC98 = 9.340 − 1.304(SEX) − 1.996(BLACK) − .801(OTHER) + .634(EDUCNEW). For computer use, the predictive equation is logit(TSPCOMP) =

$-2.438 - .047(AGE) + .377(EDUCNEW)$. For computer use, however, we need to decide whether to keep the instrumental variable as a continuous variable scaled in the metric of (predicted) probabilities ranging continuously from 0 to 1, or to recode it back to the original binary metric of the observed variable. The use of two-stage estimation for nonrecursive models involving PALR is not sufficiently well developed to offer a conclusive answer, but my own recommendation until I see solid evidence to the contrary is to recode the instrumental variable into its original metric. This not only preserves the original dichotomous nature of the variable, but from limited experience it also appears to result in less attenuation of variance in the instrumental variable, relative to the observed variable, with the result that it appears likely to result in less attenuation in the corresponding path coefficients, a potential problem in the single equation, two-step approach to 2SLS for continuous variables, as described earlier. The instrumental variables appear to be reasonably good estimates for the observed variables. For computer use, the equation for the instrumental variable has $R^2_L = .22$, $\lambda_p = .34$, and $\tau_p = .44$. For income, $R^2 = .180$. The instrumental variable for computer use has almost the same standard deviation (.475) as the observed variable (.493), once the instrumental variable is recoded to the original binary metric. The instrumental variable for income, however, has a much lower variance (2.139) than the observed variable (5.036), and a reduced range as well (roughly 9 to 21, instead of 1 to 23).

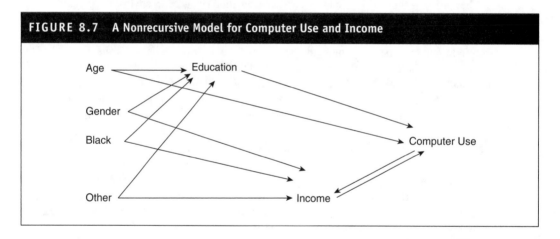

FIGURE 8.7   A Nonrecursive Model for Computer Use and Income

The results of the second stage of estimation for income and computer use are presented in Table 8.6. Note that in this second stage, as well as in the estimation of the instrumental variables, gender and ethnicity are excluded from the equation for computer use and age is excluded from the equation for income. Otherwise, the instrumental variables would be collinear with the other variables in the model. Collinearity is another potential problem in two-stage estimation, for which there is little cure (Berry 1984; Kritzer 1976). A good approach to prevention, however, is to have the predictors unique to each instrumental variable (age for computer use, gender and ethnicity for income) sufficiently strongly related to that variable that the instrumental variables are not dominated by the variables common as predictors to both (or all) of the variables involved in the nonrecursive loop. In the present example, there is no evidence of collinearity.

Comparing the results in Table 8.6 with the results in Table 8.5 for computer use and income, it appears that the removal of gender and ethnicity and the addition of age to the model for computer

TABLE 8.6 Logistic Regression for Computer Use and Income: Nonrecursive Model

Dependent Variable	Independent Variable	Unstandardized Coefficients (b)	Standardized Coefficients (b*)	Significance (Wald z for Logistic Regression, t for OLS)
Computer use	Intercept	−3.551	—	.000
$R^2_L = .233$	Age	−0.049	−.305	.000
$(p = .000)$	Education	0.261	.266	.000
$R^2_O = .283$	Income (Instrument)	0.178	.140	.000
$\lambda_p = .359$			(.260)	
$\tau_p = .445$				
Income	Intercept	9.866	—	.000
$R^2 = .184\ (.191)$	Gender (Female)	−1.288	−.127	.000
$(p = .000)$	Ethnicity			—
	Black	−2.072	−.149	.000
	Other	−0.914	−.041	.035
	Education	0.557	.305	.000
	Computer use (Instrument)	0.762	.072	.003
			(.074)	

use results in an increase in explained variation: from 17% to 23% for R^2_L and from 22% to 28% for R^2_O. The indices of predictive efficiency indicate a strong relationship between observed and predicted classification, with $\lambda_p = .36$ and $\tau_p = .45$. For income, the explained variance is very slightly higher in Table 8.6 than in Table 8.5 (18.4% compared with 18.0%); the figure in parentheses, .191, indicates that if we use the equation for income based on the coefficients in Table 8.6, the squared correlation between the predicted and observed values of income is actually .191, or 19% explained variance, only very slightly higher than the explained variance without adjusting for attenuation in the model. All of the predictors of both dependent variables are statistically significant.

For computer use as a dependent variable, the addition of age appears to reduce both the standardized and unstandardized coefficients for education. The unstandardized coefficient for income is larger, but the standardized coefficient is smaller in Table 8.6 than in Table 8.5. If we apply the suggested adjustment for attenuation, the standardized coefficient for income becomes larger in Table 8.6 than in Table 8.5, but the different adjustments produce different results: $b* = .260$, if we use substitution of the standard deviation of the original variable for the standard deviation of the instrumental variable in calculating the standardized coefficient, but $b* = .329$ if we instead divide the standardized coefficient from Table 8.6 by the multiple correlation coefficient (the square root of the explained variance) from the first stage of the estimation. These different estimates of the standardized coefficient affect the comparison of the impact of income relative to the other variables in the model; a standardized coefficient of .140 makes it the weakest predictor in the model, while a standardized coefficient of .329 makes it the strongest. There is no clear solution here, but given the clear reduction in the variance of the instrumental variable relative to the observed variable, it seems reasonable to adjust the standardized coefficient back to the original metric of the observed variable by using the standard deviation of the observed variable rather than the standard deviation of the instrumental variable to calculate the standardized coefficient for that variable. Doing this results in income still being the weakest predictor in the model ($b* = .260$, noted in parentheses under the standardized coefficient for the instrumental variable). For income as a dependent variable, adjusting the standardized coefficient has little impact, changing $b*$ from .072 to .074. As noted earlier, recoding the instrumental variable back into its original binary metric appears to preserve most of the variation in the predictor. The effects of gender and ethnicity are very similar in Table 8.5 and Table 8.6, but the effect of education appears to be a bit smaller in Table 8.6 than in Table 8.5.

This example suggests that two-stage estimation with PALR may be a viable approach for estimating nonrecursive models in which at least one of the variables in the nonrecursive loop is dichotomous. It also illustrates the possibility of using a dichotomous variable (in this case computer use) as an intervening variable (with respect to income vs. education, gender, and ethnicity in this model) in a causal path model. Of course, a better approach for models that are nonrecursive in terms of the variables included in the model is to render the model recursive by measuring the variables at two or more different times, with measurement intervals corresponding to the time expected for one variable's effect to be felt in the other. This approach will be illustrated in Chapters 12 and 13. Asher (1983) commented more than 20 years ago that this might frequently not be feasible, but with the increasing proliferation of longitudinal data over the past several decades, this limitation is much less frequently a concern than it was earlier. Still, for situations in which longitudinal data are not (yet) available, two-stage estimation with PALR may offer some initial insight into the nature of the nonrecursive relationship.

CONCLUSION

The keys to using PALR are (1) to select an appropriate criterion for variation to be partitioned and (2) to select an appropriate standardized logistic regression coefficient. Keeping the analogy as close as possible to path analysis with OLS regression, the criterion for variation to be partitioned could be the estimate of the explained variance, the traditional R^2 statistic, as given in logistic regression analysis by R_O^2. Alternatively, more in keeping with the logistic regression model itself, the criterion could be R_L^2. Stretching the analogy a little further, if model fit is less important than accurate qualitative prediction, classification, or selection, the criterion for variation to be partitioned could be one of the indices of predictive efficiency discussed in Chapter 4. Unlike OLS regression analysis, there is some ambiguity about the most appropriate criterion. For direct comparison with OLS regression models, and also for models with mixed qualitative and quantitative predictors, especially when the ordering of some of the qualitative predictors is intermediate between some of the quantitative predictors (e.g., a quantitative variable predicting a qualitative variable, which then in turn is used to predict a quantitative variable, the last of which is used to predict a qualitative variable), the logical default would seem to be using R_O^2 as the criterion for variation to be partitioned. Absent the mix of qualitative and quantitative predictors, however, a case could easily be made for R_L^2 or one of the indices of predictive efficiency.

The use of path analysis models involving dichotomous endogenous variables (both as intervening variables and as the final variable in the causal chain) has been relatively rare to date, all the more so when there is no assumption of a continuous latent variable underlying the observed dichotomous variable. More often, the focus has been on presenting models involving only direct effects, and perhaps mentioning the possibility of, but not attempting to quantify, the indirect effects on or through dichotomous endogenous variables. Hopefully the present chapter will provide a basis for the use of path analysis with dichotomous endogenous (including intervening) variables that will encourage the same attention to partitioning of variation and correlations and especially to indirect effects that is commonplace in the analysis of continuous variables.

NOTES

1. Elementary introductions to path analysis are provided in some elementary to intermediate statistics texts, including Agresti and Finlay (1997), Asher (1983), and Bohrnstedt and Knoke (1994). The underlying logic of causal modeling in nonexperimental research, and its description by means of path diagrams, is covered in Asher (1983), Blalock (1964), and Davis (1985). More advanced treatment of causal analysis and path analysis is offered in Blalock (1971a), Duncan (1975), and Heise (1975); see also Pearl (2000). This chapter provides a brief introduction to path analysis at the level of Agresti and Finlay (1997) and Bohrnstedt and Knoke (1994) for the reader of this book who has little or no background in path analysis, and to help draw the parallels between path analysis as typically used for continuous variables and PALR. This is not intended to be a comprehensive review, and the reader unfamiliar with path analysis should consult the sources listed above for more detailed background.

2. It is also possible to assign some other value to the paths represented by the arrows in Figure 8.4, for example, to use unstandardized instead of standardized coefficients, in which case the correlations cannot be directly calculated from the path diagram. Bohrnstedt and Knoke (1994:423–424) give a good description of how to decompose implied correlations by tracing paths in a path diagram for more complex models as well as the simple type of model depicted in Figure 8.4.

3. For an introduction to simultaneous equation structural equation modeling with latent variables, see, for example, Bollen (1989), Hayduk (1987), or Kaplan (2000). There are several different techniques for estimation of simultaneous equation structural equation models (simultaneous equation SEMs), including *weighted least squares* (WLS, of which the IRLS approach sometimes used in logistic regression analysis is one variant) and *full information maximum likelihood* (FIML, of which the Newton-Raphson algorithm is one implementation used in logistic regression). More generally, full information estimation techniques take account of all the relationships in the model and all of the data when estimating each of the individual parameters to maximize the fit of the model by some statistical criterion (minimizing a sum of squares or maximizing a likelihood).

4. See, for example, Asher (1983), Berry (1984), or Heise (1975).

5. Knoke and Burke (1980:46) state that we can compare the magnitudes of the coefficients to judge the relative importance of the causes, since both are in the standard form of odds ratios, but this is true only if all variables in the analysis are dichotomous and, hence, measured on the same scale. More generally, as detailed in Chapter 5, for logistic regression models with predictors having different measurement scales, the unstandardized coefficients cannot be used to compare the relative impact of the different predictors.

6. It may seem somewhat contradictory to be advocating the use of the linear R_O^2 and nonlinear correlations in the same analysis, but we should expect a linear relationship between the predicted and observed values of the dependent variable, even when we do not expect a linear relationship between the observed values of the dependent variable and the observed values of the predictor, as long as we have specified (correctly) the nonlinear model that generates the predicted values. This is a basic assumption of the generalized linear model,

which is used to "linearize" the nonlinear relationship between a dependent variable and one or more predictors (see, e.g., Hutcheson and Sofroniou 1999; McCullagh and Nelder 1989).

7. As noted previously, attempting to justify or rationalize a latent variable conceptualization of a variable, whether dichotomous or ordinal, seems to be a frequent practice, particularly in social science research, and one suspects that the desired method of analysis is driving the conceptualization, rather than (as would be more appropriate) vice versa.

8. If age was an important predictor of computer use, why did we not include it in the model to begin with? (The answer, of course, is that the analyses here are being used to illustrate features of logistic regression, not to try to make a breakthrough in the substantive study of computer use.) If we include computer use as well as age in the regression equation for income, age is statistically significant ($p = .023$), but the standardized coefficient is less than .100. Similarly, with age in the equation for computer use, gender is still not statistically significant, but ethnicity is ($p = .005$); however, the coefficients for Black ($-.060$) and Other ethnicity ($-.027$), like the coefficient for gender ($.028$) are all less than .100, a commonly used cutoff for substantive significance for standardized OLS regression coefficients. Such "artistic license" in eliminating some causal paths at the initial stage of estimation is relatively common in the practical application of 2SLS and the quest for identification of nonrecursive models. Given the low standardized coefficients for all the causal paths being eliminated here, it does seem reasonable in the present example.

Polytomous Logistic Regression for Unordered Categorical Variables

$\mathbf{L}$ogistic regression analysis may be extended beyond the analysis of dichotomous variables to the analysis of nominal or ordinal dependent variables with more than two categories. In the literature on logistic regression, the resulting models have been called polytomous, polychotomous, or multinomial logistic regression models. Here, the terms *dichotomous* and *polytomous* will be used to refer to logistic regression models (and the dependent variables in those models), and the terms *binomial* and *multinomial* will be used to refer to logit models (and the associated distributions) from which polytomous logistic regression models may be derived. For polytomous dependent variables, the logistic regression model may be calculated as a particular form of the multinomial logit model. Mathematically, the extension of the dichotomous logistic regression model to polytomous dependent variables is straightforward. One value (typically the first or last) of the dependent variable is designated as the reference category, $Y = h_0$, and the probability of membership in other categories is compared with the probability of membership in the reference category. For nominal variables, this parallels the "simple" contrast used for independent variables in the logistic regression model for dichotomous variables described in Chapter 5. The resulting model is sometimes called the *baseline category logit model* in the terminology of log-linear analysis. For ordinal variables, contrasts may be made with successive categories, in a manner similar to the repeated or Helmert contrasts for independent variables in dichotomous logistic regression models, also described in Chapter 5. For convenience, throughout the rest of this chapter, polytomous nominal logistic regression, given its frequent recurrence, will be abbreviated to PNLR.

For dependent variables with some number of categories, M, the PNLR model requires the calculation of $M - 1$ equations—one for each category relative to the reference category—to describe the relationship between the dependent variable and the independent variables. For each category of the dependent variable except the reference category, we may write the equation

$$f_h(X_1, X_2, \ldots, X_K) = e^{a_h + b_{h1}X_1 + b_{h2}X_2 + \cdots + b_{hK}X_K} \qquad h = 1, 2, \ldots, M - 1, \qquad (9.1)$$

where the subscript $k = 1, 2, \ldots, K$ refers to specific independent variables $X_1, X_2, \cdots, X_K$, and the subscript h refers to specific values of the dependent variable Y ($Y = 1$, $Y = 2, \cdots$, $Y = M - 1$). For the reference category h_0 (corresponding, e.g., to $Y = 0$ or $Y = M$), all the coefficients $a_h = b_{h1} = b_{h2} = \cdots, = b_{hK} = 0$ by definition and $g_0 (X_1, X_2, \cdots, X_K) = e^0 = 1$. The probability that Y is equal to any value h other than the excluded value, h_0, is

$$P(Y = h | X_1, X_2, \ldots, X_K) = \frac{e^{a_h + b_{h1} X_1 + b_{h2} X_2 + \cdots + b_{hK} X_K}}{1 + \sum_{h=1}^{M-1} e^{a_h + b_{h1} X_1 + b_{h2} X_2 + \cdots + b_{hK} X_K}} \qquad (9.2)$$

$$h = 1, 2, \ldots, M - 1$$

and for the excluded category,

$$P(Y = h_0 | X_1, X_2, \ldots, X_K) = \frac{1}{1 + \sum_{h=1}^{M-1} e^{a_h + b_{h1} X_1 + b_{h2} X_2 + \cdots + b_{hK} X_K}} \qquad (9.3)$$

$$h = 1, 2, \ldots, M - 1$$

Note that when $M = 2$, we have the logistic regression model for the dichotomous dependent variable, the reference category is the first category, and we have a total of $M - 1 = 1$ equations to describe the relationship. The set of equations defined by $\mathrm{logit}(Y) = g_h = \ln(f_h) = a_h + b_{h1}X_1 + b_{h2}X_2 + \cdots + b_{hK}X_K$ are sometimes called the *logistic functions* for the polytomous dependent variable Y.

For a dichotomous dependent variable, the odds of being in one category (call it Category A) as opposed to the other (reference) category (call it Category B) is identically the odds of being in Category A, so exponentiating the logistic function for Category A directly produces the odds of being in Category A (and transforming the odds to a probability gives the probability of being in Category A). For a nominal dependent variable with three or more categories, however, the interpretation of the logistic functions is not as straightforward. If, for example, the third category (call it Category C) is the reference category, then the two logistic functions give us (a) the odds of being in Category A as opposed to Category C and (b) the odds of being in Category B as opposed to Category C. Neither of these is identically the odds of being in Category A or B, respectively, which also depends on (c) the odds of being in Category A as opposed to Category B. This last odds (and the associated probability) can be calculated by simply selecting a different reference category (e.g., Category B). The resulting model will provide (1) the logistic function and thus the odds for being in Category A as opposed to Category B and (2) the logistic function and thus the odds for being in Category C as opposed to Category B. The second logistic function will be equal to -1 times the logistic function for being in Category B as opposed to Category C; in other words, compared with the logistic function described in (b) above, the coefficients for logistic function (2) will have the same absolute value but the opposite sign ($+$ or $-$). The odds or the probability of being in a particular category depends on both of the possible logistic functions for that category, so for example, the probability of being in Category C depends on both the odds of being in Category C as opposed to Category B and also the odds of being in Category C as opposed to Category A: (Probability of being in Category C) = 1 $-$ (Probability of being in Category A as opposed to Category C) $-$ (Probability of being in Category B as opposed to Category C).

In this respect, the logistic functions must be regarded as providing the conditional odds or relative probabilities of being in each category, relative to a particular reference category. The more categories in the dependent variable, the more terms are involved in the calculation of the absolute odds or probability of being in a particular category (i.e., the odds or the probability of being in Category A compared with the odds or probability of being in all the other categories combined, not compared with being in just one of the other categories). As noted by Allison (1999:130–131), this poses some complications in interpreting the sign of the logistic function coefficients relative to the probability of being in a specific category. In particular, the sign of the coefficient for a particular predictor in the logistic function for a particular category does not necessarily correspond to whether the probability of being in that category increases or decreases as the value of the predictor increases or decreases. Instead, there may be a nonlinear pattern of increase, then decrease (or decrease, then increase), because as the probability of being, for example, in Category A as opposed to Category B increases, it is also possible that at the same time the probability of being in Category A as opposed to Category C is decreasing at an even faster rate, resulting in a net decrease in the absolute probability of being in Category A.

As long as we keep the same set of categories and the same predictors for the model, the choice of one category as opposed to any other for the reference category will have no impact on the statistics for the overall model (D_M, G_M, R_L^2). The absolute value of the coefficients for the logistic function comparing any two categories (one of which will, in the baseline category logit model, be the reference category) will always be the same in absolute value but will be reversed in sign if one as opposed to the other of the two categories in question is chosen as the reference category. In principle, one could use contrasts other than the indicator contrast for the dependent variable, but again given the same dependent variable with the same set of categories, plus the same predictors and the same method of estimation, the overall model statistics will remain unchanged. For nominal contrasts (indicator, deviation, or simple contrasts, as opposed to ordered contrasts such as Helmert, difference, and repeated, which are more appropriate for ordinal dependent variables), the predicted probabilities of category membership should also be identical. For user-specified contrasts that do not clearly maintain the same structure of the categories for the dependent variable (e.g., contrasts that collapse two or more categories), the predicted probabilities may be different (simply because they are calculated not for the original individual categories but for sets of categories), but they should be consistent with the categories as originally coded. In short, the baseline category logit model for a polytomous nominal dependent variable contains all of the information that would be provided in a model with a different contrast (preserving the categories themselves) for the dependent variable.

By default in some statistical software, the last category is designated as the reference category. In many instances, this will not be the optimum selection for the reference category, however, and other software defaults instead to the category in which the largest number of cases is classified. Making the largest category the reference category generally makes more sense than setting the first or last category as the reference category, because there is no natural ordering to the categories and coefficients calculated based on the category with the highest number of cases will generally be more reliable than coefficients calculated based on a category with fewer cases as the reference category. In some instances, there will be a theoretical or substantive reason for selecting a particular category as the reference category.[1] For example, one may want to compare both Treatment A and Treatment B with a placebo or no treatment category, in which case it seems logical to use the placebo or no treatment condition as the reference category, regardless of the number of cases in each category.

SIMULTANEOUS ESTIMATION AND SEPARATE ESTIMATION FOR PNLR

Presently, the most common routines available for estimating PNLR models use the simultaneous estimation method to estimate all of the logistic regression equations for the $M-1$ categories of the polytomous dependent variable at once. In the earlier stages of development of logistic regression analysis, one would sometimes instead calculate separate dichotomous logistic regression equations to estimate the model (Begg and Gray 1984). As described by Begg and Gray, the separate estimation approach uses ordinary dichotomous logistic regression routines to estimate each of the logistic functions (the equations) associated with the unordered polytomous dependent variable. According to Begg and Gray, the estimated logistic regression coefficients from the separate estimation approach will be asymptotically unbiased, and their efficiency (relative to the simultaneous estimation method) tends to be high, although Allison (1999:123) notes that improved efficiency is one of the advantages of the simultaneous estimation method over the separate estimation method. Without some adjustment, however, model fit and related statistics will not be the same as in the simultaneous estimation method. If we use the simultaneous estimation and separate estimation approaches to estimate the same logistic regression coefficients for the baseline category logit model, the results are typically not identical but are similar for the two different estimation methods. Begg and Gray (1984) also note that the separate estimation approach makes it possible to eliminate different predictors from the different equations in, for example, a backward stepwise elimination procedure, rather than retaining a variable in the model for all equations only because it is a statistically significant predictor in one of those equations.

Begg and Gray's (1984) examination of the separate estimation approach to analyzing unordered polytomous dependent variables was, as they described, motivated by issues of computer storage, unavailability of statistical routines to analyze unordered polytomous dependent variables, particularly with sparse data (few cases in a particular category or covariate pattern), and inability to selectively include a predictor in one but not all of the equations in the model. The issue of storage is somewhat less likely to arise for existing PNLR routines. Issues that would presently lead one to use the separate estimation approach instead of the simultaneous estimation approach would thus be (a) the desire to exclude one or more predictors from at least one but not all of the logistic regression equations, (b) the greater ease with which one can use logistic regression diagnostic tests, and (c) as will be discussed later in this chapter, the desire to construct path analytic models using PNLR.

EXPLAINED VARIATION AND STATISTICAL INFERENCE IN PNLR

In PNLR, we can calculate measures of explained variation, indices of predictive efficiency, and statistical significance for (a) the model as a whole and *either* (b) each separate equation in the model *or* (c) each category of the dependent variable (bearing in mind that the relationship between the probability of category membership and the logistic function for a particular category relative to the reference category, as discussed earlier, is not entirely straightforward). The routines available for PNLR in general purpose statistical software typically output some combination of G_M, D_0, D_M, and one or more R^2 analogs for the overall model. By generating predicted values, it is possible to calculate statistics for the separate components of the model. One could also use separate estimation to calculate the statistics for the separate components of the model, but there is no guarantee that the statistics so obtained will add precisely to the statistics generated by simultaneous estimation. Calculating the ordinary least squares (OLS) R_O^2 for the separate categories of the dependent variable is useful as a step in calculating the standardized coefficients for the model. To calculate the standardized coefficients for the PNLR model, the explained variance R_O^2 and the standard deviations of both logit$(\hat{Y})$ and the predictors should, like the unstandardized logistic regression coefficients, be calculated separately for each logistic function or each category of the dependent variable. Thus, we have $b_{X1(1)}^* = [b_{X1(1)}][s_{X1(1)}][R_{O(1)}]/s_{\text{logit}[\hat{Y}(1)]}$, $b_{X2(1)}^* = [b_{X2(1)}][s_{X2(1)}][R_{O(1)}]/s_{\text{logit}[\hat{Y}(1)]}$ and so on for the first logistic function; $b_{X1(2)}^* = [b_{X1(2)}][s_{X1(2)}][R_{O(2)}]/s_{\text{logit}[\hat{Y}(2)]}$, $b_{X2(2)}^* = [b_{X2(2)}][s_{X2(2)}][R_{O(2)}]/s_{\text{logit}[\hat{Y}(2)]}$, and so on for the second logistic function; and so forth for the $M - 1$ logistic functions, where the added subscript (in parentheses) refers to the logistic function for which the standardized coefficient is being calculated.

In PNLR as in dichotomous logistic regression, we have a choice between quantitative and qualitative indices of explained variation, and careful consideration should be given as to whether we are more interested in *how close* the predicted probabilities of category membership are to observed category membership or whether we are instead more concerned with *whether* the prediction of category membership is correct or incorrect. My own impression is that, if methodological preferences (and the convenience of avoiding calculating statistics by hand) are not allowed to prevail, the substantive questions for which PNLR is the preferred method of analysis are more often qualitative than quantitative in nature, suggesting that λ_p, τ_p, and φ_p may be preferable to R_L^2 or R_O^2 as measures of explained variation. Naturally, the decision of which quantitative or qualitative measures of explained variation are more appropriate needs to be specific to the analysis, but the question of which is most appropriate deserves careful consideration and should not be made purely on the basis of convenience.

Example: Political Party Identification

The PNLR model can be illustrated with data taken once again from the National Opinion Research Center (NORC) General Social Survey (GSS). The dependent variable in this example is political party identification, PARTYID4, coded as 1 = Democrat, 2 = Independent, 3 = Republican, and 4 = Other. The predictors are once again gender, ethnicity, education, and income. Popular, general, and journalistic impressions that would lead us to believe that these variables are related to political party identification in the United States include (1) the "gender gap," referring to the tendency of women to be more likely to vote for Democrats than for Republicans; (2) the frequently documented tendency of African Americans and other minority group members to vote for Democrats rather than for Republicans; and (3) the common perception that the Republican policies are more favorable than Democratic policies toward wealthy individuals, who in their own self-interest are therefore more likely to identify with the Republican rather than the Democratic party. With respect to education, while I am sure all of the parties would like to claim that they are the party of choice for more educated voters, there is less solid evidence linking education to political party preference. The results of the analysis are summarized in Table 9.1.

A word is in order here about some of the procedures for transforming or restructuring the data that are likely to cut across different software packages. First, depending on the specific software package, we will either want to begin by recoding the dependent variable so that the largest or most

TABLE 9.1 Political Party Preference						
Function	Predictor	b^*	b	e^b	se(b)	p(Wald)
1. Democrat	Gender (Male)	−.106	−0.308	0.735	.095	.001
	Ethnicity (Black)	.226	0.917	2.501	.122	.000
	Ethnicity (Other)	.020	0.126	1.135	.190	.507
	Education	.055	0.029	1.029	.018	.118
	Income	−.009	−0.003	0.997	.010	.785
	Intercept	—	−0.305	(0.737)	.268	.255
2. Republican	Gender (Male)	.030	0.162	1.175	.102	.113
	Ethnicity (Black)	−.182	−1.358	0.257	.242	.000
	Ethnicity (Other)	−.079	−0.924	0.397	.266	.001
	Education	.041	0.039	1.040	.020	.043
	Income	.109	0.057	1.058	.012	.000
	Intercept	—	−4.681	(0.009)	.303	.000
3. Other	Gender (Male)	.013	0.205	1.227	.300	.495
	Ethnicity (Black)	−.034	−0.756	0.470	.610	.215
	Ethnicity (Other)	−.017	−0.581	0.559	.735	.430
	Education	.050	0.143	1.154	.055	.010
	Income	−.026	−0.040	0.961	.030	.192
	Intercept	—	−2.053	(0.128)	.862	.000

$D_M = 2799.843$, $G_M = 285.945$, $df = 15$, $p = .000$.
$R_L^2 = .05$, $R_O^2 = .17$, $R_{O1}^2 = .065$, $R_{O2}^2 = .066$, $R_{O3}^2 = .004$.
[$R_{O4}^2 = .010$ = correlation between observation and predicted probability of being Independent]
Goodness of Fit:
Pearson $\chi^2 = 2136.545$, $df = 2172$, $p = .702$;
Deviance $\chi^2 = 1778.941$, $df = 2127$, $p = 1.000$.

Prediction/Classification Table

	Predicted			
Observed	Democrat	Other	Republican	Independent
Democrat	233	0	62	580
Other	3	0	7	38
Republican	22	0	108	526
Independent	140	0	92	856

$\lambda_p = .07$, $p = .000$; $\tau_p = .17$, $p = .000$; $\varphi_p = .11$, $p = .000$.

theoretically appropriate category is the reference category, or plan on using options in the statistical routine to appropriately define the reference category. In this particular example, the small number of individuals expressing a preference for "Other" political parties could produce very unreliable coefficients, were "Other" selected as the reference category for the dependent variable, as would be the case with some statistical packages (since "Other" is the last category). Second, for PNLR models, it will generally be useful to dichotomize categorical predictors, not necessarily for entry into the model but to calculate the descriptive statistics (specifically the standard deviations) used in calculating the standardized logistic regression coefficients, since the standardized coefficients should be calculated for each logistic function separately. Third, some software packages will provide a warning when the number of zero-frequency cells is large. In the present example, 1,684 cells, or 58% of the total, are empty, commonplace in PNLR with continuous predictors. When the number of empty cells is large, the Pearson and deviance χ^2 goodness-of-fit indices cannot be assumed to have a χ^2 distribution and should not be interpreted in the context of this model as indicative of goodness of fit.

Fourth, when using simultaneous estimation, calculation of R_O^2 for the full model, in most statistical packages, requires a series of statements constructing the observed (OBS) and predicted (PRED) values of the dependent variable for each of the logistic functions, saving each set of observed and predicted values separately and merging the files to obtain a file with the observed and predicted values combined for the four categories of the dependent variable. Each separate file is then treated as a new set of cases, and the files are "stacked": The first 2,667 "rows" (sets of variable values for each single case) contain the observed and predicted values for the first category, the next 2,667 "rows" contain the observed and predicted values for the second category, and so on. The total number of cases in the merged file is four times the number of cases in the original data set, and to obtain an accurate estimate of the statistical significance of R_O^2, we use a weight of ¼ = .25 for all cases (reflecting the fact that each case is replicated four times in the data set). Calculation of the zero-order correlation between OBS and PRED in the merged file produces the global R_O^2 for the entire PNLR model.[2]

Separate R_O^2 statistics are also calculated for each of the categories of the dependent variable for use in calculating the standardized logistic regression coefficients. Here, a decision needed to be made between using R_O^2 (a) for the category probability, as predicted by the full model, or (b) for the logistic function comparing each single category with the reference category. As noted earlier, the logistic functions do not directly provide the absolute or unconditional probability of category membership but instead produce the probability of being in one category as opposed to the reference category. While an argument might be made that the explained variance should be calculated on the same basis as that on which the coefficients are estimated (comparison of a category with a reference category, rather than absolute probability of category membership), this construction of the model is driven by the need to use a workable method of estimation (the baseline category logit model). Our real interest is not in how well a particular logistic function explains the contrast between a category and a reference category but in how well the model explains political party identification, that is, the probability of membership in one category as opposed to all the other categories. With this in mind, the R_O^2 coefficients for each category $[R_{O(1)}^2, R_{O(2)}^2, \cdots, R_{O(M-1)}^2]$ are used in calculating the standardized coefficients here. These R_O^2 statistics do not depend on which category is chosen as the reference category, but the R_O^2 statistic for the reference category (call it $R_{O(0)}^2$) will not be needed in the calculation of the standardized coefficients (since all the coefficients for that category are, by its selection as the reference category, defined as being equal to 0). While this decision seems reasonable at present, the question of whether to use the R_O^2 associated with absolute probability of category membership or an R_O^2 calculated instead on the basis of a logistic function, comparing probability of membership in a particular category with probability of membership in a single reference category, may deserve further consideration in future research on standardized logistic regression coefficients.

The prediction table is now a 4×4 table with observed and predicted frequencies for all four categories of political party identification. Note that no cases are predicted to be in the "Other" category, even though some cases are observed to be in that category. With heavily skewed data (very unequal numbers of cases in the different categories), overprediction of the category with the most observed cases and underprediction of the category with the fewest observed cases is not uncommon. The fact that the column sum for "Other" is 0 poses no particular problems in the present context. Not shown is the calculation of expected category frequencies for each cell, calculated as the product of the row sum (the number to the far right of the row, outside the lines of the table), multiplied by the column sum (the number at the bottom of each column, also outside the lines of the table), and divided by the total ($N = 2,667$), to calculate the index of predictive efficiency φ_p. For this purpose, a zero marginal total for the predicted frequency of any category merely indicates that the selection rate for that category is equal to 0. Using the data from the prediction table in Table 9.1, we can calculate the indices of predictive efficiency for political affiliation as follows. For all three indices of predictive efficiency, the total number of errors with the model is equal to the sum of the frequencies in the off-diagonal cells, so the error with the model, E_2, is

$$E_2 = 62 + 580 + 3 + 7 + 38 + 22 + 526 + 140 + 92 = 1,470.$$

For λ_p, the expected error without the model, E_1, is equal to N minus the number of cases in the modal category (in this case, the 1,088 Independents), or

$$E_1(\lambda_p) = 2667 - 1088 = 1,579;$$

so

$$\lambda_p = (1579 - 1470)/1579 = .0690 \approx .07;$$

and

$$d(\lambda_p) = (1579 - 1470)/\sqrt{(1579)(1088)/2667} = 4.29, \quad p = .000$$

and the 1,088 under the square root sign is equal to N minus the expected error (or equivalently, 1088/2667 is equal to 1 minus the expected proportion of errors), as described in the formula for the binomial d in Chapter 4. For τ_p, the expected error without the model, as described in Chapter 4, is equal to the sum of the products of each category frequency (the row sum) with N minus that frequency, all divided by N:

$$E_1(\tau_p) = [(875)(1792) + (48)(2619) + (656)(2011) + (1088)(1579)]/2667 = 1773.8582;$$
$$\tau_p = (1773.8582 - 1470)/1773.8582 = .1713 \approx .17;$$

and

$$d(\tau_p) = (1773.8582 - 1470)/\sqrt{(1773.8582)(893.1418)/2667} = 12.47, \quad p = .000.$$

For φ_p, the expected error without the model is equal to the sum of the expected values in the off-diagonal cells in the prediction table:

$$E_1(\varphi_p) = 88.2456 + 656.168 + 7.1631 + 4.8414 + 35.9955$$
$$+ \, 97.8958 + 491.9385 + 162.3637 + 109.7383 = 1654.3499;$$
$$\varphi_p = (1654.3499 - 1470)/1654.3479 = .1114 \approx .11;$$

and

$$d(\phi_p) = (1654.3499 - 1470)/\sqrt{(1654.3499)(1012.6501)/2667} = 7.36, \quad p = .000.$$

Of the three indices of predictive efficiency, φ_p is most clearly inappropriate in this instance (there is no preset selection rate), and it is presented here only for illustration. Both λ_p and τ_p tell a similar story of relatively low predictive power, parallel to R_L^2 and R_O^2, but given the large sample size, both are still statistically significant.

EFFECTS OF INDIVIDUAL PREDICTORS ON POLITICAL PARTY PREFERENCE

The standardized coefficients,[3] unstandardized coefficients, exponentiated coefficients,[4] standard errors, and statistical significance of the coefficients for the individual predictors of political party preference are also summarized in Table 9.1. The logistic functions for Table 9.1 may be defined as

g_1 = logit(Probability of Democratic party identification as opposed to being an Independent),

g_2 = logit(Probability of Republican party identification as opposed to being an Independent), and

g_3 = logit(Probability of Other party identification as opposed to being an Independent).

The equations for g_1, g_2, and g_3 using unstandardized coefficients from Table 9.1 are[5]

$g_1 = -.305 - .308(\text{SEXFM}) + .917(\text{BLACK}) + .126(\text{OTHER}) + .029(\text{EDUCNEW}) - .003(\text{INCNEW98});$

$g_2 = -4.681 + .205(\text{SEXFM}) - .756(\text{BLACK}) - .581(\text{OTHER}) + .143(\text{EDUCNEW}) - .040(\text{INCNEW98}); \text{ and}$

$g_3 = -2.053 + .162(\text{SEXFM}) - 1.358(\text{BLACK}) - .924(\text{OTHER}) + .039(\text{EDUCNEW}) + .047(\text{INCNEW98}).$

In Table 9.1, the model chi-square (G_M) is equal to 285.9455 with 15 degrees of freedom (5 predictors in each of the three equations), statistically significant at .000. R_L^2 is only .05, R_O^2 is .17, $\lambda_p = .07$, and $\tau_p = .17$, all indicating that quantitative and qualitative measures of explained variation are statistically significant but weak for this model. Examining R_O^2 for the separate categories of the dependent variable, the model is weakly able to predict (a) being a Democrat and (b) being a Republican, both at about $R_O^2 = .07$, but the model's ability to predict (c) being a member of an "Other" political party is not substantively significant ($R_O^2 = .004$), suggesting that we might consider collapsing "Other" with one of the other categories, possibly Independent, and reanalyzing the model. Because the accuracy of prediction provided by the model is relatively weak, it comes as no surprise that the standardized coefficients are all relatively small in magnitude. All of the predictors, however, are statistically significant in the overall model, as indicated in the likelihood ratio tests for the model.

Turning to the individual logistic functions, the strongest predictor (based on the standardized coefficients) of being a Democrat (as opposed to an Independent) is African American ethnicity, then gender, both in the expected direction, with African Americans and females (note the negative sign associated with male gender) being more likely to be Democrats than Independents. None of the other predictors is statistically significant at the .05 level in the first logistic function. African American ethnicity is also the strongest predictor of being Republican (as opposed to Independent), this time with, as expected, a negative coefficient, followed by Income, with the expected positive coefficient. Except for gender, which is not statistically significant in the second logistic function, all of the other coefficients are statistically significant but weak: "Other" ethnicity is negatively associated with being Republican, but education is positively associated with being Republican. Prediction is poorest for "Other" political party preference (again with Independent as the reference category). In this third logistic function, higher education is statistically significantly but weakly associated with preference for a political party other than Democrat, Republican, or Independent. Notice that all of the coefficients for education are positive (although not statistically significant for being a Democrat), suggesting that lower education is associated with being a political independent. On balance, the results are consistent with the expectations stated earlier about the relationships among political party preference and gender, ethnicity, and income.[6] Bear in mind, however, that all the coefficients in the model are relative to the political "Independent" category.

SEPARATE ESTIMATION FOR POLITICAL PARTY PREFERENCE

There are several differences to note between the use of the simultaneous and separate estimation approaches. In particular, each case will be used more than once in the separate estimation procedure. As a result, although coefficients for individual predictors may be very similar, maximum likelihood summary statistics for the different approaches may be very different. In Table 9.2, unstandardized logistic regression coefficients are presented for simultaneous and separate estimation of the three logit functions in the model of political party preference. Although not identical, the unstandardized coefficients are reasonably similar for the two approaches. If we naively sum D_0, D_M, and G_M statistics across the different logit functions[7] in the separate estimation approach, however, then as indicated at the bottom of Table 9.2, the estimates for these statistics in the separate estimation approach can be very different from the estimates obtained in the simultaneous approach. The point of all this is that the explained variation and the inferential statistics for the global model

TABLE 9.2   Comparison of Simultaneous and Separate Estimation

Equation for g_1: Democrat Versus Independent

	Male	Black	Other	Education	Income
Simultaneous	−0.308	0.917	0.126	0.029	−0.003
Separate	−0.313	0.917	0.130	0.027	−0.003

Equation for g_2: Republican Versus Independent

	Male	Black	Other	Education	Income
Simultaneous	0.162	−1.358	−0.924	0.039	0.057
Separate	0.147	−1.316	−0.937	0.040	0.056

Equation for g_3: Other Versus Independent

	Male	Black	Other	Education	Income
Simultaneous	0.205	−0.756	−0.581	0.143	−0.040
Separate	0.171	−0.731	−0.578	0.135	−0.038

Model Statistics				
	D_0^*	D_M^*	G_M^*	R_L^2
Simultaneous	3085.788	2799.843	285.945	.05
Separate (no adjustment)	5405.398	5211.114	194.284	.04

*Summed across dichotomous models for separate estimation.

may not be that close to the same statistics calculated from a model based on simultaneous estimation of all the logistic functions at once; but the coefficients of the predictors should, because they are sufficiently similar, produce comparable accuracy of prediction and classification across the two different approaches.

DIAGNOSTICS FOR THE PNLR MODEL

Given the state of existing software, Hosmer and Lemeshow (2000:281) recommended that logistic regression diagnostics for the PNLR model be performed by using the separate estimation method and applying the diagnostic tests to each of the separate equations in the model. In view of the results presented in this chapter, this approach seems reasonable, but again, if a high degree of precision is desired, it may be necessary to consider alternative approaches. Although the separate equations approach may be useful for residuals analysis, other diagnostic tests for PNLR models can be performed without resorting to separate equations. High standardized logistic regression coefficients (greater than 1) offer evidence of problems in the data such as collinearity or quasi-complete separation, as described in Chapter 7. Collinearity can be assessed by entering the set of predictors in an OLS regression routine that produces collinearity diagnostics, such as the tolerance or variance inflation factor. Quasi-complete separation can be assessed using multiway contingency tables; also, some software will print out warnings when quasi-complete separation appears to be present. Neither collinearity nor quasi-complete separation appears to be a problem in the present model.

In some instances, there may be a question of whether categories can be combined without adversely affecting the fit of the model. In the present example, for instance, one may wish to know whether the categories "Independent" and "Other" can reasonably be combined. Cramer (2003:122–125) notes that combining categories of the dependent variable is the same as constraining the coefficients of the two categories (relative to the reference category) to be equal to one another. In this context, a reference category other than either of the two categories to be combined needs to be selected. Because the model with the constraint is nested within the model without the constraint, a test of whether the two categories can be combined can be performed by (a) calculating the two models, one with and the other without the constraint, and (b) subtracting D_M for the model with fewer categories from D_M for the model with more categories in the dependent variable. The difference is a χ^2 statistic under the usual assumptions for comparing nested models under maximum likelihood estimation. This procedure can be extended to collapsing more than two categories, using the same basic procedure. The reverse of this, of course, is to split a single category and compare D_M for the two models to see whether the split significantly improves the model. Table 9.3 presents the results of recalculating the model for political party identification with the categories "Independent" and "Other" combined. Comparing R_L^2, R_O^2 for each of the two comparable categories (Democrat and Republican), the indices of predictive efficiency, and the standardized and unstandardized logistic regression coefficients, there appears to be little change from Table 9.1, with the exception that education is no longer a statistically significant predictor based on the likelihood ratio test ($p = .189$) and, at the .05 level, based on the Wald statistics as well, for the model as a whole or for the two logistic functions. As indicated in Table 9.3, however, R_O^2 for the full model has been reduced from .17 to 07, and the change in D_M is statistically significant suggesting that the two categories, "Independent" and "Other," should probably not be combined. The same conclusion is reached if "Other" and "Independent" are combined when a different reference category is selected.

It has been suggested (e.g., Clogg and Shihadeh 1994:162) that the discrepancy between the Pearson and likelihood ratio χ^2 statistics indicates that the sample size is not large enough for the number of cells used, and thus D_M cannot reasonably be used to test the fit of the model. In Table 9.1, the difference between the Pearson and likelihood ratio (deviance) χ^2 statistics is 357.604, calling into question whether model fit can reasonably be assessed by either, particularly since the assumption of a χ^2 distribution is problematic because of the large number of empty cells—a result of the inclusion of the continuous predictors education and income in the model. As described in Chapter 7, overdispersion occurs when the likelihood ratio χ^2 statistic for the full model, D_M, is large relative to its degrees of freedom. In the present model, this does not appear to be the case. If anything, judging from the ratio of D_M to its degrees of freedom, there may be underdispersion in the model, but to reiterate, the assumption of a true χ^2 distribution is questionable in the present instance.

TABLE 9.3	Political Party Preference (Collapsing Categories)				
Function	*Predictor*	b^*	b	*se(b)*	*p(Wald)*
1. Democrat	Gender (Male)	−.112	−0.317	.095	.001
	Ethnicity (Black)	.239	0.941	.122	.000
	Ethnicity (Other)	.024	0.147	.189	.436
	Education	.043	0.022	.018	.216
	Income	−.004	−0.001	.010	.924
	Intercept	—	−0.917	.251	.000
2. Republican	Gender (Male)	.030	0.152	.101	.132
	Ethnicity (Black)	−.186	−1.333	.242	.000
	Ethnicity (Other)	−.080	−0.902	.265	.001
	Education	.036	0.033	.019	.089
	Income	.118	0.059	.012	.000
	Intercept	—	−1.724	.381	.000

$D_M = 2526.422$; Change in $D_M = 2799.843 - 2526.422 = 273.421$ with 5 *df*, *p* = .000.

$G_M = 276.057$ with 10 *df*, *p* = .000.

$R_L^2 = .05$.

$R_O^2 = .07$; $R_{O1}^2 = .065$; $R_{O2}^2 = .066$.

[$R_{O3}^2 = .010$ = correlation between observation and predicted probability of being Independent/Other]

$\lambda_p = .06$, *p* = .000; $\tau_p = .17$, *p* = .000; $\varphi_p = .10$, *p* = .000.

PATH ANALYSIS WITH POLYTOMOUS NOMINAL LOGISTIC REGRESSION

The extension of the use of path analysis with logistic regression (PALR) from dichotomous to polytomous dependent variables is a second problem for which separate logistic regressions may be the solution. In OLS linear regression, dummy variables for a nominal polytomous predictor (or in the more usual language of linear regression analysis, a nominal categorical predictor) are usually constructed based on an indicator contrast (this contrast was discussed in Chapter 5). Each dummy variable is coded 1 for the presence of a characteristic or attribute and 0 for its absence. If political party preference were being used as a predictor, then following this approach we would construct three dummy variables: (1) Democrat = 1 if political party preference is Democrat, 0 if political party preference is Republican, Independent, or Other; (2) Other = 1 if political party preference is Other, 0 if Democrat, Republican, or Independent, and (3) Republican = 1 if political party preference is Republican, 0 if Democrat, Independent, or Other. One category (here, consistent with the analysis to this point, Independent) is excluded because inclusion of all four categories would produce perfect collinearity among the predictors.

Note that the contrast used in modeling political identification as a dependent variable is similar but not identical to the indicator contrast. Instead, the baseline category logit model selects one category as the baseline or reference category, and compares each of the other categories specifically with that baseline category, not (as in the indicator contrast) to all the other categories combined. For the baseline category logit model, operationalizing the contrast in terms of dummy variables would also result in three dummy variables, but somewhat different from those described in the preceding paragraph: (1) Democrat versus Independent, equal to 1 if Democrat, 0 if Independent and excluded or missing if Republican or "Other"; (2) "Other" versus Independent, equal to 1 if "other", 0 if Independent, and excluded or missing if Democrat or Republican; and (3) Republican versus independent, equal to 1 if Republican, 0 if Independent, and excluded or missing if Democrat or "Other." This is the dummy variable construction that was used to produce the results used in the comparison of simultaneous and separate estimation in Table 9.2. Using this set of contrasts for a predictor, however, is problematic. Under the usual practice of listwise deletion of missing cases, (a) the first dummy variable, Democrat versus Independent, would have missing values for everyone with Republican and "Other" as the preferred political party, and (b) the second dummy variable would similarly eliminate Democrats from the analysis. This would effectively eliminate political party preference as a predictor from the model.

For an intervening polytomous nominal variable (an endogenous variable that acts as an effect or outcome with respect to some set of predictors, but is also itself a cause or predictor of one or more variables in the model), if we use one set of contrasts in setting up the dummy variables for the polytomous variable as a predictor and a different set of contrasts for the same polytomous variable as an outcome, then in effect we are using two different sets of variables, and the path coefficients for paths to the intervening variable are really from a model that is operationally different from the model in which the same polytomous variable is being used as a predictor. For us to be able to trace indirect paths through an intervening polytomous nominal variable, we need to use the same contrasts for the intervening variable both as cause and as effect. We cannot do this with the contrasts used in simultaneous estimation of the PNLR model (the baseline category logit model), so the question is whether we can do this instead with indicator contrasts and separate estimation. As noted above, the indicator contrast, instead of comparing a given category with one specific (baseline) category, compares each category, one at a time, with all other categories, thus generating no missing cases as a result of how the dummy variables are constructed.

Here it may be useful to review some points made earlier about alternative contrasts for the dependent variable and the comparison of separate with simultaneous estimation in PNLR. First, the choice of different contrasts does not alter the more important model summary statistics, such as G_M and R_L^2, or the predicted probabilities of category membership, and hence the qualitative prediction of category membership, and hence further the indices of predictive efficiency (λ_p, τ_p, and φ_p), if the identical method of estimation is used for the models with the different contrasts. There may, however, be some differences between separate and simultaneous estimation, and it may be worthwhile to test whether summary statistics that can be calculated for both separate estimation and simultaneous estimation models (R_O^2 for the overall model, and for the individual categories; λ_p, τ_p, and φ_p) appear to be comparable. Second, the different contrasts will typically produce different coefficients for the predictors, so we should not expect logistic regression coefficients for an indicator contrast, however measured, to be identical to coefficients using the contrast for a baseline category logit model. Third, while one category needs to be excluded from the analysis when the intervening polytomous nominal variable is being used as a predictor (to avoid perfect collinearity), all the categories can be modeled when the polytomous nominal intervening variable is being treated as the dependent variable relative to other predictors in the model. Modeling the category that is excluded when the variable is a predictor may be mathematically redundant, but it makes it easier to construct the predicted qualitative classification of the dependent variable.

Taking the polytomous variable as a dependent variable, R_O^2 can be calculated for each of the logistic functions by simply calculating the correlation between the observed and the predicted values for each of the indicator-contrasted dummy variables, and $s_{\text{logit}(\hat{Y})}$ can similarly be calculated for each logistic function (it will be irrelevant for the category excluded when the variable is treated as a predictor) just as in dichotomous logistic regression, thus allowing the calculation of standardized logistic regression coefficients for each logistic function. R_O^2 for the overall model can be calculated by (1) calculating the model for each of the indicator-coded dummy variables, including all the categories (e.g., Democrat, Other, Republican, and Independent, if the variable is political party identification); (2) saving observed and predicted values for each category into four separate files; (3) stacking the files of observed and predicted values into a single merged file; and (4) calculating (with appropriate weighting of cases) the correlation between the observed and predicted values, then squaring the result to obtain R_O^2. To produce classification tables of observed and predicted category membership, after calculating the logistic regression equations for all the indicator-coded dummy variables, assign each case to the category for which it has the highest predicted probability. The observed and predicted classifications can then be cross-tabulated. The resulting table can then be used to calculate λ_p, τ_p, and φ_p, and their statistical significance.

To illustrate this approach, a PNLR model was calculated with presidential choice in 1996 as the dependent variable, and political party preference, income, education, gender, and ethnicity as predictors. The dependent variable was constructed by combining the variables PRES96 and VOTE96 in the NORC GSS data file. The dependent variable was coded as 1 if the respondent voted for Clinton, 2 if the respondent voted for Dole, 3 if the respondent voted for Perot, and 4 if the respondent voted for none of the above (either by not voting or by voting for someone other than Clinton, Dole, or Perot). There is missing data for respondents who refused to answer, did not remember whether they voted or for whom they voted, or for whom the question was inapplicable (e.g., individuals who were ineligible to vote). We begin by comparing the results for simultaneous and separate estimation presented in Table 9.4 for presidential choice and Table 9.5 for political party identification.

In Table 9.4, looking first at the bottom of the table, the summary statistics for the two estimation methods are identical for the indices of predictive efficiency (there is actually a slight difference in the fourth decimal place for φ_p), and R_O^2 is nearly identical for the overall model and the separate logistic functions. The logistic regression coefficients are clearly similar but equally clearly not identical, and examination of one pair of coefficients may serve to reinforce an earlier point. In separate estimation, the coefficient of Republican party membership on voting for Clinton is negative and statistically significant, but in simultaneous estimation, it is positive and not statistically significant. What is going on here? To answer the question, consider to what "voting for Clinton" is being compared. In the separate estimation model, we are looking at "voting for Clinton" compared with all other options (voting for Dole, voting for Perot, and not voting for any of the three major candidates). In the simultaneous estimation model, the baseline category is "not voting" and the nonsignificant coefficient means that Republicans were not significantly more or less likely to vote for Clinton than they were to vote for none of the three major candidates. Here and more generally, one needs to be mindful of the specific comparison being made to correctly interpret the coefficients. In Table 9.5, a similar pattern emerges. The model summary statistics are not quite as close for political party identification as they were for Presidential choice, but they are still close, as are the unstandardized logistic regression coefficients for the two models. The point of all this is that separate estimation appears to be reasonably similar to simultaneous estimation for the purpose of constructing path analysis models with PNLR.

TABLE 9.4   Presidential Vote in 1996, Separate and Simultaneous Estimation

Dependent Variable Category	Predictor	Logistic Regression Coefficient (Statistical Significance)	
		Separate Estimation: Dichotomous Logistic Regression	Simultaneous Estimation: Baseline Category Logit Model
Clinton	Democrat	1.636 (.000)	1.545 (.000)
	Other	−0.387 (.318)	−0.374 (.367)
	Republican	−0.982 (.000)	0.198 (.249)
	Income	0.012 (.247)	0.030 (.009)
	Education	0.083 (.000)	0.141 (.000)
	Male	−0.321 (.001)	−0.283 (.010)
	Black	0.604 (.000)	0.306 (.031)
	Other	−0.654 (.008)	−1.806 (.000)
	Intercept	−1.835 (.000)	−3.008 (.000)
Dole	Democrat	−1.499 (.000)	−0.684 (.008)
	Other	0.005 (.991)	−0.098 (.039)
	Republican	2.149 (.000)	2.401 (.000)
	Income	0.037 (.013)	0.060 (.000)
	Education	0.116 (.000)	0.188 (.000)
	Male	0.274 (.030)	0.165 (.238)
	Black	−1.457 (.000)	−1.485 (.000)
	Other	−0.917 (.019)	−1.568 (.000)
	Intercept	−4.422 (.000)	−4.588 (.000)
Perot	Democrat	−0.904 (.000)	−0.147 (.507)
	Other	0.232 (.613)	0.091 (.853)
	Republican	−0.158 (.351)	0.860 (.000)
	Income	0.036 (.042)	0.061 (.001)
	Education	−0.001 (.967)	0.103 (.001)
	Male	−0.008 (.957)	−0.847 (.773)
	Black	−1.807 (.000)	−1.790 (.000)
	Other	−1.751 (.015)	−2.366 (.000)
	Intercept	−2.437 (.000)	−3.597 (.000)
Summary Statistics		$R_O^2 = 0.257$	$R_O^2 = 0.259$
		$R_O^2 \text{ (Clinton)} = 0.236$	$R_O^2 \text{ (Clinton)} = 0.238$
		$R_O^2 \text{ (Dole)} = 0.331$	$R_O^2 \text{ (Dole)} = 0.331$
		$R_O^2 \text{ (Perot)} = 0.030$	$R_O^2 \text{ (Perot)} = 0.032$
		$R_O^2 \text{ (Nobody)} = 0.140$	$R_O^2 \text{ (Nobody)} = 0.144$
		$\lambda_p = 0.338$	$\lambda_p = 0.338$
		$\tau_p = 0.409$	$\tau_p = 0.409$
		$\varphi_p = 0.294$	$\varphi_p = 0.294$

TABLE 9.5	Political Identification (Model With Presidential Vote in 1996)		
		Logistic Regression Coefficient (Statistical Significance)	
Dependent Variable Category	*Predictor*	*Separate Estimation: Dichotomous Logistic Regression*	*Simultaneous Estimation: Baseline Category Logit Model*
Democrat	Income	−0.026 (.007)	−0.009 (.393)
	Education	0.006 (.715)	0.022 (.257)
	Male	−0.360 (.000)	0.303 (.003)
	Black	1.204 (.000)	0.854 (.000)
	Other	0.446 (.033)	0.150(.498)
	Intercept	−0.076 (.772)	−0.669 (.014)
Other	Income	−0.054 (.093)	−0.042 (.194)
	Education	0.101 (.083)	0.118 (.047)
	Male	0.253 (.426)	−0.197 (.539)
	Black	−0.841 (.169)	−0.743 (.295)
	Other	−0.063 (.732)	−0.213 (.774)
	Intercept	−4.854 (.000)	−3.883 (.000)
Republican	Income	0.064 (.000)	0.059 (.000)
	Education	0.021 (.268)	0.033 (.109)
	Male	0.277 (.007)	−1.480 (.171)
	Black	−1.810 (.000)	−1.387 (.000)
	Other	−1.006 (.001)	−.948 (.002)
	Intercept	−2.593 (.000)	−1.647 (.000)
Summary Statistics		$R_O^2 = .151$ R_O^2 (Democrat) = .064 R_O^2 (Other) = .004 R_O^2 (Republican) = .066 R_O^2 (Independent) = .010 $\lambda_p = .078$ $\tau_p = .165$ $\varphi_p = .117$	$R_O^2 = .148$ R_O^2 (Democrat) = .065 R_O^2 (Other) = .003 R_O^2 (Republican) = .069 R_O^2 (Independent) = .008 $\lambda_p = .083$ $\tau_p = .169$ $\varphi_p = .126$

Table 9.6 presents the results of the path analysis for presidential choice using separate estimation of the logistic functions with the indicator contrast. Drawing a path model based on the standardized coefficients in Table 9.6 would be a complex undertaking, even if we were to use backward stepwise elimination to remove the statistically nonsignificant paths, but with some care and attention to detail, we can still trace indirect effects in the data. Let us consider two examples, the total effects of income and education on voting for Clinton and for Dole. The direct impact of income on voting for Clinton is positive (b = .022) but not statistically significant. Income has direct and at

TABLE 9.6 Path Analysis of Presidential Choice

Dependent Variable or Category	Predictor	b^*	b	p
Presidential Choice: $R_O^2 = .257$, $p = .000$; $\tau_p = .409$, $p = .000$; $\lambda_p = .338$, $p = .000$				
Clinton	Democrat	.286	1.636	.000
	Other Party	−.019	−0.387	.318
$R_O^2 = .236, p = .000$	Republican	−.158	−0.982	.000
	Income	.022	0.012	.247
	Education	.085	0.083	.000
	Gender (Male)	−.059	−0.321	.001
	Ethnicity (Black)	.080	0.604	.000
	Ethnicity (Other)	−.050	−0.654	.008
	Intercept	—	−1.835	.000
Dole	Democrat	−.230	−1.499	.000
	Other Party	.000	0.005	.991
$R_O^2 = .331, p = .000$	Republican	.305	2.149	.000
	Income	.061	0.037	.013
	Education	.105	0.116	.000
	Gender (Male)	.044	0.274	.030
	Ethnicity (Black)	−.169	−1.457	.000
	Ethnicity (Other)	−.061	−0.917	.019
	Intercept	—	−4.422	.000
Perot	Democrat	−.079	−0.904	.000
	Other Party	.006	0.232	.613
$R_O^2 = .030, p = .000$	Republican	−.013	−0.158	.351
	Income	.034	0.036	.042
	Education	−.001	−0.001	.967
	Gender (Male)	−.001	−0.008	.957
	Ethnicity (Black)	−.119	−1.807	.000
	Ethnicity (Other)	−.067	−1.751	.015
	Intercept	—	−2.437	.000

Dependent Variable or Category	Predictor	b^*	b	p
Political Party Preference: $R_O^2 = .151, p = .000; \tau_p = .165, p = .000; \lambda_p = .078, p = .000$				
Democrat	Income	−.063	−0.026	.007
	Education	.008	0.006	.715
$R_O^2 = .064, p = .000$	Gender (Male)	−.086	−0.360	.000
	Ethnicity (Black)	.207	1.204	.000
	Ethnicity (Other)	.044	0.446	.033
	Intercept	—	0.076	.772
Other party	Income	−.038	−0.054	.093
	Education	.040	0.101	.083
$R_O^2 = .004, p = .002$	Gender (Male)	.018	0.253	.426
	Ethnicity (Black)	−.042	−0.841	.169
	Ethnicity (Other)	−.002	−0.063	.732
	Intercept	—	−4.854	.000
Republican	Income	.099	0.064	.000
	Education	.018	0.021	.268
$R_O^2 = .066, p = .000$	Gender (Male)	.042	0.277	.007
	Ethnicity (Black)	−.199	−1.810	.000
	Ethnicity (Other)	−.064	−1.006	.001
	Intercept	—	−2.593	.000
Income	Education	.356	0.643	.000
	Gender (Male)	.142	1.435	.000
$R_O^2 = .190, p = .000$	Ethnicity (Black)	−.143	−2.024	.000
	Ethnicity (Other)	−.018	−0.449	.325
	Intercept	—	5.209	.000
Education	Gender (Male)	.051	0.283	.013
	Ethnicity (Black)	−.133	−1.037	.000
$R_O^2 = .022, p = .000$	Ethnicity (Other)	.023	0.314	.257
	Intercept	—	13.200	.000

least marginally significant effects on political party preference for Democrats ($b = -.063$), Others ($b = -.038$), and Republicans ($b = .099$). Multiplying each of these by the direct effects of each category on voting for Clinton, then adding the direct effect of income, we get $(.286)(-.063) + (-.019)(-.038) + (-.158)(.099) + .022 = -.012$, still not a significant effect, but reversed in sign and diminished in magnitude. For Dole, we get $(-.230)(-.063) + (.000)(-.038) + (.305)(.099) + .061 = .106$, suggesting that the impact of income on voting for Dole involves more than just the direct effect, which itself is statistically significant. To obtain the total effect of education on voting for each candidate, first multiply the total effect of income for each by the effect of education on income ($b = .356$), then calculate the indirect effect of education via political party preference, then add the direct effect of education for each candidate ($b = .085$ for Clinton and $.105$ for Dole). For Clinton, the total effect of education is little different from the direct effect:[8] Total effect = $(.356)(-.012) + (.008)(.286) + (.040)(-.019) + (.018)(-.158) + .085 = .079$. The total effect of education on voting for Dole is $(.356)(.106) + (.008)(-.230) + (.040)(.000) + (.018)(.305) + .105 = .146$, a more substantial change from the direct effect of $.105$, suggesting that the impact of education, like that of income, is underestimated if we consider only its direct effects on voting for Dole.

SUMMARY

PNLR may seem like a straightforward extension of dichotomous logistic regression to the analysis of nominal variables with three or more categories, in which we split up the nominal variable into dummy variables, much as we do in OLS linear regression analysis when we are using nominal variables as predictors. I believe that impression is deceptive and masks some subtle issues of model estimation and interpretation that are sometimes ignored in describing PNLR. The dependent variable contrast chosen for implementation in software packages for estimating the PNLR (or in other nomenclature, the generalized logit, baseline category logit, or multinomial logit) model uses a contrast other than the indicator contrast most often used for predictors both in OLS linear regression and in logistic regression with a dichotomous outcome. The choice of a reference category has an important impact on the substantive interpretation of the logistic regression coefficients, as the example of presidential choice (being Republican having a significant negative impact as opposed to a nonsignificant positive impact on voting for Clinton, depending on whether it is compared with a single alternative, not voting, or with all other alternatives, including but not limited to not voting). For the mechanics of simultaneous estimation of the PNLR model, the baseline category logit model works well, but if our substantive concerns are not adequately reflected in this type of contrast, we may need to consider as alternatives either the cruder approach of separate estimation of the logistic functions, with contrasts that better reflect the substantive question for which the model is being calculated (and the knowledge that the coefficients should be close to what we would obtain from simultaneous estimation), or using the information in the baseline category logistic regression model to calculate (by hand or by spreadsheet, if we do not plan to reprogram existing statistical packages) the appropriate coefficients.

It is instructive to see what is provided by the different general purpose statistical packages for PNLR models and how much additional effort is required when the existing packages do not provide something you want. If one replicates the analyses for this chapter, the sheer length of the output for the models used in this chapter compared with what is needed for preceding chapters (and to later chapters as well) should give some indication of the amount of additional effort required. Given the current state of the art, PNLR more than logistic regression for dichotomous or ordered polytomous dependent variables appears to be an area in which there is considerable potential for the development of more accessible approaches to alternative contrasts for the dependent variable for simultaneous estimation, diagnostics for PNLR, and, parallel to dichotomous logistic regression, inclusion of more features in general purpose software, including calculation of standardized coefficients that can be used not only in the usual PNLR models but also in path analytic models involving polytomous nominal variables, as both dependent variables and predictors. Pending those future developments, existing statistical routines for simultaneous estimation of PNLR models are adequate when (a) our only concern is with modeling direct influences on a polytomous nominal dependent variable, (b) we are not concerned with the regression diagnostics that are not available in existing statistical routines for PNLR models, and (c) we are satisfied with comparisons involving a single reference category with all other categories of the dependent variable. Otherwise, given the present state of statistical software, we may need to supplement existing routines with either separate estimation or hand (or spreadsheet) calculation of the logistic regression coefficients of interest.

When the concern is not with diagnostics or path analysis with PNLR, the simultaneous estimation approach now available in most general purpose statistical software packages is preferable to the approach using separate estimation. Using this simultaneous estimation approach, we can present much the same information we would for a dichotomous dependent variable in logistic regression: G_M and its statistical significance, R_L^2, R_O^2 (for both the overall model and the individual logit functions), and indices of predictive efficiency for the prediction tables as summary statistics; and the unstandardized coefficients with their standard errors, standardized coefficients, exponentiated coefficients (odds ratios), and the statistical significance of the unstandardized coefficients. For path analysis, however, separate estimation presently appears to be the most viable approach, and the likelihood-based model summary statistics do not appear to be comparable to those generated in the simultaneous estimation approach. This also occurs under other circumstances, particularly with data in which the sampling design results in dependencies in the data; however, it may not be that critical in the context of the PNLR model, particularly for practical applications. The reason is that for the PNLR model, we may be more interested in accuracy of qualitative prediction, as indicated by the indices of predictive efficiency associated with the prediction table, than with the likelihood-based evaluation of the model (i.e., we may be more concerned with whether our predictions are "correct or incorrect" than with "how close" they are to being correct).

If we are willing to live with the limitations imposed by separate estimation, then we can take advantage of PALR to quantitatively examine indirect and total effects using PNLR; and if the concerns of PALR with indirect and total effects are not an issue (and if we are not terribly concerned with diagnostics for PNLR), then we can take advantage of the simultaneous estimation approach, including the likelihood-based summary statistics. Given the present state of the art, there is a trade off here, but one we can probably live with, pending future progress in PNLR.

NOTES

1. Software Note: SAS **logistic** defaults to the last category as the reference category but permits specification of a reference category other than the last using the "REF =" specification on the CLASS statement, and a reference category other than the last on the original dependent variable can also be specified by recoding the dependent variable (e.g., using "if" statements in the data step). In SPSS **nomreg**, the last category is also the default as the reference category, and as of this writing there is no provision for selecting a category other than the last as the reference category, and selection of a different category as the reference category requires recoding the dependent variable prior to running SPSS **nomreg**. Stata **mlogit** defaults to the largest category

as the reference category but permits specification of a reference category other than the one with the highest frequency using the "basecategory(#)" option.

2. Correspondence with J. S. Cramer helped me clarify my thoughts on the use of all four categories to calculate R_O^2. While I am grateful for the intellectual stimulation provided by our correspondence, any errors in the conclusions I have drawn based on that correspondence are entirely my own. The use of all four categories in this example is justified by the fact that the squared errors represented in the calculation of R_O^2 are independent. It can be shown, for example, that given the same R_O^2 for the first three categories, it is possible to have different values of R_O^2 for the fourth category, in different PNLR models for a four-category dependent variable.

3. Software Note: It should be noted once again that the SAS "Standardized Estimate" is not equal to the fully standardized logistic regression coefficient. In this example, for the first logistic function, the fully standardized coefficients are consistently larger than the SAS standardized estimates, but for the other two logistic functions, the fully standardized coefficients are consistently smaller than the SAS standardized estimates, suggesting that the variance in the dependent variable is in some instances underestimated and in other instances overestimated by $\pi^2/3$, the variance of the standard logistic distribution.

4. Software Note: SAS uses the term *odds ratio*, SPSS merely uses "Exp(B)," and Stata uses the term *relative risk ratio* to describe the exponentiated logistic regression coefficient in the PNLR model. In view of the distinction between relative risk ratios and odds ratios made earlier, this terminology may seem a bit confusing; see the explanation in Stata (2003:506–507), Hardin and Hilbe (2001:177–178), and also Allison (1999:131). Briefly, the terminology is based on the observation (made earlier in the text) that the logistic functions do not directly transform into absolute probabilities (risks) of category membership but rather to relative (to a reference category) probabilities (risks) of category membership. It is in this sense that an odds ratio in the PNLR model is a relative risk ratio, but the terminology still leaves ample room for misinterpretation, since the relative risk is really derived from, not equal to, the exponentiated logistic regression coefficient. Note that none of the three statistical packages actually provide the exponentiated coefficient for the intercept (nor is it really of any great importance that they do not do so), but the exponentiated coefficients have been calculated by hand and are included in parentheses in Table 9.1.

5. Software Note: In the analysis for Table 9.1, SPSS produces estimates for the intercept, its standard error, and its statistical significance, which are different from the estimates produced by SAS or Stata. This is true even when variables are recoded to produce the identical model in SAS, SPSS, and Stata. The source of this discrepancy, which appears to have no effect on any of the other statistics, is unclear but may be the result of slightly different convergence criteria in SPSS as opposed to SAS and Stata. In Table 9.1, the estimates from SAS and Stata for the intercept, its standard error, and its statistical significance are used. Note that the estimation of $\text{logit}(\hat{Y})$ is done for the purpose of obtaining the standard deviation of $\text{logit}(\hat{Y})$ to calculate the standardized coefficients for each logistic function, and this will be unaffected by differences in the constant in the equation.

6. Again, when the interest is in comparing the strengths of several predictors within a logistic function, standardized coefficients are most appropriate. If, however, the interest is in comparing the strength of a single predictor across logistic functions, the unstandardized coefficients should be used. For example, based on the unstandardized coefficients, being African American is a stronger predictor of being an Independent rather than a Republican (notice the sign of the coefficient) than it is of being a Democrat rather than an Independent, and it is not a statistically significant predictor of being "Other" (than Democrat or Republican) rather than being an Independent.

7. This is not as far-fetched as it seems; see the discussion of the continuation ratio logit model in the next chapter.

8. In case this is unclear, the first product is the effect of education on income times the total effect of income; the second is the effect of education on being a Democrat times the effect of being a Democrat on voting for Clinton; the third is the effect of education on being an "Other" political party member times the effect of being an "other" political party member on voting for Clinton; the fourth product is the effect of education on being Republican times the effect of being Republican on voting for Clinton; and the final term, .085, is the direct effect of education on voting for Clinton.

CHAPTER 10

Ordinal Logistic Regression

Ordinal variables are in some respects the most difficult to deal with analytically. Most often (arguably always), ordinal variables represent either (1) crude measurement of a variable that could be measured on an interval or (more often) a ratio scale or (2) measurement of an abstract characteristic or concept for which there is no natural metric or unit of measurement, which cannot be "counted" in the way we count physical quantities, but for which the assumption is made that there is relatively continuous variation in the degree to which a case possesses the characteristic or manifests the concept. Examples of the first situation, crude measurement, occur when, for example, different ages or incomes or other measurable quantities with natural metrics are grouped. For example, ages may be grouped in 5-year intervals (0–4, 5–9, 10–14, etc.) or incomes may be grouped in intervals of $10,000 ($0–$9,999, $10,000–$19,999, etc.). Sometimes, the groupings involve unequal intervals, perhaps based on external considerations. For example, education may be measured not in years of school completed, but in level of schooling completed: some grammar school, completion of grammar school, some high school, completion of high school, some college, completion of college, some graduate school, completion of a master's degree, completion of a doctoral degree. This sort of crudeness of measurement often arises in survey research, and may accurately reflect the precision with which respondents are able to answer some questions. How many respondents, for example, know their income or net worth down to the last dollar?

Abstract characteristics or concepts may include political orientation (conservative or liberal), happiness, propensities or tendencies toward certain types of behavior (such as drug use or violence), or attitudes, the last often measured as the extent of agreement with a set of statements, where agreement is categorized as, for example, (a) strongly disagree, (b) disagree, (c) neutral or not sure or neither agree nor disagree, (d) agree, and (e) strongly agree, or in which the respondent is asked to score the extent of her or his agreement on a numerical scale (e.g., 1 to 10) that has no metric referent (i.e., the scores 1, 2, etc., are interpreted in a purely subjective way, typically differently by different respondents). There is a sense in which we generally believe that there is an underlying "quantity" of agreement or happiness or tendency, which is in nature like centimeters, kilograms, or numbers of dollars that should be measurable on an interval or ratio scale, if only we could conceptualize the right units of measurement. It is in this sense that ordinal variables representing abstract concepts usually represent an underlying or latent interval or ratio-scaled variable, and we should be able to describe one case (e.g., one person) as being twice as happy, liberal, conservative, or inclined toward drug use as another.

Another way to think of this is that a nominal variable simply indicates whether two cases have equal or unequal values; an ordinal variable indicates not only equality or inequality but also whether one case has a larger or smaller value than another; an interval variable, in addition to the information conveyed by a nominal or ordinal variable, indicates how much more or less of some attribute one case has than another; and a ratio variable, in addition to the information conveyed by nominal, ordinal, and interval variables, indicates how many times more or less of some attribute one case has than another. For categorical nominal and ordinal variables, different values can legitimately only be compared as equal or unequal (= or ≠) for nominal and ordinal variables, or greater than or less than (> or <) for ordinal but not nominal variables. Values of (in principle, continuous) interval variables can legitimately be subjected to the same comparisons, and also can be added to or subtracted from one another (+ or −) but not multiplied or divided, while ratio variables can be subjected to the same comparisons and also can be multiplied or divided (× and ÷). For truly ordinal variables, addition, subtraction, multiplication, or division cannot legitimately be performed.

There are two fundamentally different approaches to scaling an ordinal variable. The first and most common approach is to assign consecutive integers, beginning with 0 or 1, to each of the successive categories of the ordinal variable, from lowest to highest. In the case of agreement, this would result in 1 = strongly disagree, 2 = disagree, 3 = neither agree nor disagree, 4 = agree, and 5 = strongly agree. The numeric codes make computer processing easier, but it would be wrong to think that they convey anything more than order. One could as easily use 1 = strongly disagree, 5 = disagree, 6 = neither agree nor disagree, 10 = agree, and 37 = strongly agree. Although it is commonplace with consecutive integer coding to treat the numbers as though they really represented an interval or ratio scale (e.g., by adding them to form scales), there is often little justification for doing so. With consecutive integer coding, treating the variable as an interval (or ratio) variable by adding different variables with this coding to form a scale implies that we regard the differences between ranks as being equal. Doing the same with a numeric coding other than consecutive integers implies that we regard the numbers as corresponding to a true interval scale, but not necessarily equal spacing between the different categories.

Following this logic, the second approach to coding ordinal variables is to select numbers for the ordinal categories to try to approximate an interval scale, albeit one that is crudely measured. For crudely measured variables with a natural metric, the *midpoint of the range of the category* is sometimes used. For age coded in 5-year intervals, this would entail using the numbers 2, 7, 12, and so on, to represent the categories, and for income, the median income in the category might be used. When there is no known underlying metric, and when the data cannot be regarded as grouping a range of values on an underlying interval or ratio scale, another option, described in Hutcheson and Sofroniu (1999:183), is the use of *midranks*. In this approach, scores are constructed by first adding the total number of cases in each category of the ordinal variable, then adding the starting rank to the final rank for each category *and* for all the categories lower in rank than the selected category, and finally, dividing the resulting sum by 2. This is similar to using the midpoint of the range of the category, except that now the ranks of the cases in the category, rather than some underlying metric, are being used to scale the variable. Powers and Xie (2008:222–224) describe a normal score transformation for ordinal variables that calculates the score on an ordinal scale based on an underlying normal distribution. This transformation also represents an attempt to convert the ordinal scale into a ratio scale, but whether it conveys any more information than simple consecutive integer scaling depends on whether the assumption of an underlying normal distribution is true. Most often, when there is not a known metric underlying the ordinal scale, there will be no evidence, much less any guarantee, that any alternative coding procedure will really convey any more information about the variable than consecutive integer coding.

ALTERNATIVE TREATMENTS OF ORDINAL VARIABLES IN REGRESSION-TYPE ANALYSIS

When the dependent variable is measured on an ordinal scale with more than two categories (with only two categories, of course, it reduces to the dichotomous case), many possibilities for analysis exist, including but by no means limited to logistic regression analysis. Briefly, the options available include

1. ignoring the ordering of the categories of the dependent variable and treating it as nominal;

2. ignoring the fact that the numeric values assigned to the variable are artificial (in the sense that one cannot legitimately use addition, subtraction, multiplication, or division, and the ordered values could just as easily be represented nonnumerically) and treating the variable as though it were measured on an interval or ratio scale (in which case the ordinal variable may be coded using the midpoint of the range, midrank, or normal score transformations described above);

3. treating the variable as though it were measured on an ordinal scale, but the ordinal scale represented crude measurement of an underlying interval/ratio scale; and

4. treating the variable as though it were measured on a true ordinal scale.

When we want to analyze the ordinal dependent variable, these different options suggest different statistical procedures. One possibility consistent with the first option is the use of a polytomous nominal logistic regression model, as described in the previous chapter. Also possible under Option 1 would be the use of discriminant analysis (Klecka 1980). In this instance, the information about the ordering of the categories of the dependent variable is ignored and thus lost.

The second option, treating ordinal variables as interval or ratio variables, might be implemented by using ordinary least squares (OLS) regression with an ordinal dependent variable. This approach has several disadvantages. First, especially for ordinal scales representing abstract concepts such as happiness or agreement, the scoring system is often arbitrary, and the assignment of different (but equally valid, insofar as they correctly reflect the ordering of the variables) sets of ordered scores can lead to different substantive and inferential results in regression analysis. Second, as described in some detail by Clogg and Shihadeh (1994:142–143) and McKelvey and Zavoina (1975:104–105), (a) the analysis cannot be fully efficient (in a minimum variance sense); (b) unless certain conditions (including a relatively large number of ordered categories for the dependent variable) prevail, the assumption of homoscedasticity is likely to be violated; and (c) distributional assumptions about the dependent variable (and regression residuals) are likely to be incorrect. In particular, the error term is unlikely to have a mean of 0 and a constant variance across all values of the predictors. These problems are less likely with a large number of categories, or when the ordinal variable actually represents an underlying interval/ratio variable with a normal distribution (Bollen and Barb 1981), but if either a small number of categories or a skewed distribution (e.g., log-normal) is present, it tends to produce bias in coefficients based on a linear model (Henry 1982; O'Brien 1979). Third, the meaning of a "one-unit increase" or, with respect to regression coefficients, a "b-unit increase" in the dependent variable is unclear. With integer coding, a one-unit increase refers to a one-unit increase in the rank of the dependent variable, but what does it mean to have a fractional (e.g., .38) or a partially fractional (e.g., 1.38) increase in the rank of the variable? What is 38/100 of a rank? Similarly, because addition, subtraction, multiplication, and division are required to calculate the variance of a variable, the variance of the ordinal variable is arbitrary, and the meaning of explained variance in an ordinal dependent variable is unclear in the ordinary least squares regression context.[1] All this is mitigated, to some extent, when the number of ordered categories is large, in which case the behavior of the ordinal dependent variable may approximate that of an interval or ratio-scaled variable; but a large number of categories alone may not be sufficient to justify the treatment of an ordinally scaled variable as though it were an interval or ratio variable when the distribution is heavily skewed. Treating the dependent variable as though it were measured on an interval or ratio scale effectively assumes that the data are measured more precisely than they really are; but for ordinal variables with a large number of categories, it may produce reasonable results.

The third option, treating the ordinal variable as a crude measurement of an underlying interval or ratio variable in the context of regression-type models, could be implemented in structural equation modeling packages such as LISREL by using weighted least squares (WLS) analysis of polychoric correlations (Jöreskog and Sörbom 1988), which for reliable estimates requires a large number of cases (Hu et al. 1992); or by using an ordinal logistic regression model consistent with the assumption of an underlying interval or ratio-scaled variable. The use of WLS with polychoric correlations appears to be a better option than using OLS regression; it can be used with both large and small numbers of categories, and for most ordinal variables, the assumption of imprecise measurement of a quantity that is really continuous (political conservatism, seriousness of drug use) is inherently plausible.

An example of the fourth option would be the use of an ordinal logistic regression or similar model[2] in which the transformation of the dependent variable incorporated information about the order of the categories, without assuming an underlying interval or ratio-scaled variable. Use of ordinal logistic regression techniques is also possible with both large and small numbers of categories, and may or may not involve the assumption of an underlying interval or ratio-scaled variable. There are four principal arguments for this approach. First, it makes use of exactly as much information as we actually have about the variables, neither ignoring the ordering of the variables (as would be the case using a polytomous nominal logistic regression model) nor reading more into the numeric codes for the values of the variable than is really there for a truly ordinal dependent variable. Second, unlike the approach of simply treating the ordinal variable as though it were measured (albeit crudely) on an interval or ratio scale, the substantive and inferential outcomes do not depend on the specific scores selected for the dependent variable. Third, it does not make the (usually false) assumptions regarding homoscedasticity and distribution of the dependent variable that typically plague OLS regression for ordinal dependent variables. Fourth and finally, it does not generally impose the same demands on the data, particularly for large numbers of cases that are commonplace in structural equation modeling.

MODELS FOR ORDINAL LOGISTIC REGRESSION

Ordinal logistic regression models all explicitly incorporate the ordering of the categories of the dependent variables without regard to anything about the numerical codes other than their order.

Different models, however, have different ways of incorporating that order through the use of different contrasts for the ordinal dependent variable, much like the alternative contrasts for predictors described in Chapter 5 and also mentioned in conjunction with polytomous nominal dependent variables in Chapter 9. For each different contrast, one must further consider whether all, some, or none of the coefficients of the predictors are equal across levels of the dependent variable, or whether each predictor may have a different coefficient for each level of the predictor in each of $I-1$ logistic functions, where I is the number of categories in the ordinal dependent variable. Some descriptions of ordinal logistic regression restrict themselves to the *equal slopes model,* in which it is assumed that the coefficient for each respective predictor is the same across the $I-1$ logistic functions; however, in principle, *any* ordinal logistic regression model may be formulated with either equal or unequal slopes, *without* ignoring the ordering of the categories of the dependent variable. In addition, different models make different implicit or explicit assumptions about whether the dependent variable is intrinsically ordinal or reflects an underlying continuous interval or ratio variable. Models proposed for the analysis of ordinal dependent variables in the logistic regression framework include (1) the cumulative logit model, (2) the continuation ratio logit model, (3) the adjacent categories logit model, and (4) the stereotype model.

The *cumulative logit model* is the most widely implemented ordinal logistic regression model.[3] The cumulative logit model is motivated by the assumption that the ordinal dependent variable represents crude measurement of an underlying continuous interval or ratio variable, call it η, where $\eta = \alpha + \beta_1 X_1 + \beta_2 X_2 + \cdots + \beta_K X_K$. We cannot directly observe η, but we believe that η can be transformed into Y, an ordinal variable, according to the rules (1) Y is in the first category, or to abbreviate numerically $Y = 1$, whenever η is less than some threshold value, here represented as θ_1. More concisely $\eta < \theta_1$, and θ_1 simply represents a single value of the variable η. (2) $Y = 2$ whenever η is greater than or equal to the first threshold value, but less than some second threshold value θ_2, that is, $Y = 2$ when $\theta_1 \leq \eta < \theta_2$; (3) $Y = 3$ whenever $\theta_2 \leq \eta < \theta_3$, where θ_3 is a third threshold value; and so forth until we reach the final category, I, and $Y = I$ whenever $\theta_{I-1} < \eta$. Now, for each category of Y (and thus for each range between two consecutive threshold values of η), the effect of the predictors is assumed to be the same in the equal slopes model. Between two thresholds, the value of η increases gradually, but the value of Y does not change; and as each threshold is crossed, there is the same gradual increase in the value of η, but a "jump" in the value of Y. This "jump" at each threshold, if plotted on a graph, would look like a set of stairs, as in Figure 10.1. The straight line from the lower left to the top right of the graph represents the relationship between η and X; the "stepped" line represents the observed relationship between Y and X. In Figure 10.1, the thresholds are about equally spaced, but this does not necessarily occur in practice.

For the cumulative logit model, all categories at or below a given cutoff are compared with all categories above that cutoff. Notation for the cumulative logit model varies. In intercept format, we would use the equation $\ln[P(Y > i)/P(Y \leq i)] = \alpha_i + \beta_{i1}X_1 + \beta_{i2}X_2 + \cdots + \beta_{iK}X_K$. Using the format that incorporates the thresholds, however, the equation is commonly written $\ln[P(Y \leq i)/P(Y > i)] = \theta_i - (\beta_{i1}X_1 + \beta_{i2}X_2 + \cdots + \beta_{iK}X_K)$. In these equations, the subscripts $k = 1, 2, \cdots, K$ index the predictors, and the subscripts $i = 1, 2, \cdots, I$ index the categorical values of the dependent variable. In the equal slopes model, the subscript i is dropped from the β coefficients. Geometrically, the assumption of equal slopes but unequal intercepts corresponds to a model involving a set of parallel lines, one for each split ($Y > i$ vs. $Y \leq i$) in the cumulative logit model. Equivalently, the odds of being in one category as opposed to the next are equal regardless of which two categories are being compared (as implied by having the same coefficient, and thus the same odds ratio, for all of the logistic

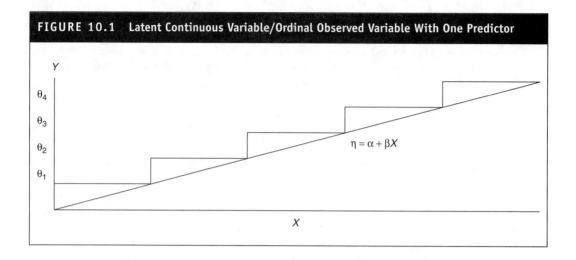

FIGURE 10.1   Latent Continuous Variable/Ordinal Observed Variable With One Predictor

functions), for which reason the equal slopes model is also called the *proportional odds* model. The different formulas (intercept vs. threshold) affect the numerical values of the thresholds or intercepts, but not the magnitude of the ordinal logistic regression coefficients, or the predicted values or predicted probabilities of category membership of the dependent variable.

In the cumulative logit model, collapsing or splitting categories of the dependent variable has no effect on the coefficients in the model other than (1) if two categories are combined, the coefficient associated with the split between those two categories is eliminated, or (2) if one category is split, a new coefficient is added for the split between the two newly constructed categories. This is illustrated in Figure 10.2. Because all of the comparisons include *all* cases on both sides of each split, the comparison of Categories 4 and 5 with Categories 1, 2, and 3 is the same in both the top and the bottom panels in Figure 10.2 (hence, no change is expected in the coefficients associated with this comparison). An advantage to the cumulative logit model, then, is that it is invariant to the crudeness or precision with which the ordered categories are measured. If the coefficients are the same across categories in one model, they should be the same across categories if the categories are expanded or collapsed in another model, because the comparisons themselves do not change (other than to be included or excluded, based on whether categories are split or collapsed into a more or less precise set of ordered categories). Although the cumulative logit model is motivated by the assumption of a latent continuous variable, that assumption is not necessary to justify its application (McCullagh and Nelder 1989:154).

In the *continuation ratio logit model,* the contrast for the dependent variable is based on the assumption that only cases or individuals who have attained a certain level (e.g., Category 3) are at risk of or are eligible to attain a subsequent level (e.g., Category 4) on the dependent variable. A common example of this is educational attainment, in which only individuals who have completed high school are considered to be "at risk" of or eligible for completion of 1 or more years of college (occasional exceptions notwithstanding). The equation for the model is $\ln[P(Y \geq i)/P(Y = i)] = \sum \alpha_i + \beta_{i1}X_1 + \beta_{i2}X_2 + \cdots + \beta_{iK}X_K$ in intercept format. The continuation ratio logit model can also be expressed in threshold format (e.g., Long 1997:146) and can be written as $\ln[P(Y = i)/P(Y \geq i)] = \theta_i - (\beta_{i1}X_1 + \beta_{i2}X_2 + \cdots + \beta_{iK}X_K)$. The basic assumption of the model seems more consistent with the

FIGURE 10.2   Contrast for the Cumulative Logit Model

Category 1	2	3	4	5	
0	1	1	1	1	1 vs. 2, 3, 4, 5
0	0	1	1	1	1, 2 vs. 3, 4, 5
0	0	0	1	1	1, 2, 3 vs. 4, 5
0	0	0	0	1	1, 2, 3, 4 vs. 5

Threshold   1   2   3   4

Category 1	2 + 3	4	5	
0	1	1	1	1 vs. 2, 3, 4, 5
NA	NA	NA	NA	(1, 2 vs. 3, 4, 5)
0	0	1	1	1, 2, 3 vs. 4, 5
0	0	0	1	1, 2, 3, 4 vs. 5

Threshold   1   3   4

assumption of an intrinsically ordinal variable rather than crude measurement or the categorical manifestation of an underlying interval/ratio variable. As with the cumulative logit model, equal slopes may be assumed for the continuation ratio logit model (and the subscript i may be dropped from the β coefficients) if it is assumed that the process of transition from one ordered category to the next is uniform across categories. Operationally, the continuation ratio logit model is often calculated in a series of steps (see, e.g., Agresti 2002:289; Allison 1999:151–155; Clogg and Shihadeh 1994:149; SPSS, Inc. 1999a:233–239). First, using all the cases, the model is calculated for the difference between cases in the initial category compared with cases in all of the other categories (and hence that have *at least* entered the second category) of the dependent variable. Second, excluding those cases in the initial category, the model is calculated for the difference between cases in the second category compared with cases in all categories higher than the second (and hence have entered at least the third category). This continues until the final model comparing the second-to-last and last categories is calculated. This process of separate estimation yields a model in which neither the slopes nor the intercepts are constrained to be equal across the separate logistic functions.

Because this process involves the calculation of a series of separate equations, it has all the concerns associated with the use of the separate estimation technique for nominal categorical dependent variables described in the previous chapter; however, as indicated in Agresti (2002:289) and SPSS, Inc. (1999a:234), because the logit functions are independent, the D_M statistics for the separate logit functions can not only be used specifically for the functions for which they were calculated but can also be added to provide a test of fit for the total model. In practice, this allows calculation of D_0 statistics for each logit function separately and using their sum as D_0 for the full model, plus the calculation of the corresponding D_M, G_M, and R_L^2 statistics. Alternatively, some software allows estimation of the continuation ratio logit model with equal slopes in a single step.

The pattern for the contrast implied by the continuation ratio logit model parallels the reverse Helmert (or, working backward from the highest category, the Helmert) contrast introduced in Chapter 5. Starting with the last category and working backwards results in a different set of parameter estimates. This pattern for the contrast used in the continuation ratio logit model is illustrated in Figure 10.3. In the first part of Figure 10.3, there are five categories, and the contrast coefficients reflect comparisons of (a) Category 1 with Categories 2, 3, 4, and 5 combined; (b) Category 2 with Categories 3, 4, and 5 combined and Category 1 excluded; (c) Category 3 with Categories 4 and 5 combined and Categories 1 and 2 excluded; and (d) Category 4 with Category 5, and Categories 1, 2, and 3 excluded. Unlike the cumulative logit model, collapsing or splitting categories in the continuation ratio logit model will change parameter estimates. In the second half of Figure 10.3, Categories 2 and 3 have been combined. As can be seen from the summary of which categories are being compared (on the right of the table in each part of the figure), not only is the comparison between the two combined categories excluded but the comparison with Categories 4 and 5 combined is also directly affected. Hence, if all of the coefficients for the predictors in the first part of Figure 10.3 were equal (indicating equal slopes across the different comparisons), we could expect the coefficients, and thus the equality of slopes, to change with the different coding for the dependent variable indicated in the second part of Figure 10.3. In particular, since we are no longer comparing Category 3 with Categories 4 and 5, but instead comparing the *combination* of Categories 2 (more separated from 4 and 5 than 3) and 3 with Categories 4 and 5, we would expect the slope for the comparison of Categories 2 and 3 combined compared with Categories 4 and 5 combined to be steeper (larger in magnitude) than the slope for the comparison of Category 3 with Categories 4 and 5 combined.

The *adjacent category logit model* compares each category with each subsequent category, using the equation (in intercept format) $\ln[P(Y = i)/P(Y = i - 1)] = \alpha_i + \beta_{i1}X_1 + \beta_{i2}X_2 + \cdots + \beta_{iK}X_K$. As with the cumulative and continuation ratio logit models, this equation can also be written in threshold format as $\ln[P(Y = i - 1)/P(Y = i)] = \theta_i - (\beta_{i1}X_1 + \beta_{i2}X_2 + \cdots + \beta_{iK}X_K)$, and in the equal slopes model the subscript i can be deleted from the β coefficients. This suggests that the process of progression from one ordered category to the next is the same for each pair of adjacent categories. The pattern for the contrast for the adjacent category logit model is illustrated in Figure 10.4 (p. 202). The same comments regarding the impact of collapsing or combining categories as applied to the continuation ratio logit model apply as well to the adjacent category logit model, as illustrated again by comparison of the first and second halves of Figure 10.4, in the latter of which Categories 2 and 3 are once again collapsed. Once again, as an example, if there were equal slopes across the comparisons of the original categories, then collapsing categories would again result in a finding of unequal slopes across categories. Use of the adjacent category logit model or the continuation ratio logit model suggests that the dependent variable is *intrinsically* ordinal, rather than representing a latent or crudely measured interval/ratio variable. For both the continuation ratio and the adjacent categories logit models, in contrast to the cumulative logit model, the selection of specific categories

---

FIGURE 10.3   Contrasts for the Continuation Ratio Logit Model

Category 1	2	3	4	5	
0	1	1	1	1	1 vs. 2, 3, 4, 5
Excluded	0	1	1	1	2 vs. 3, 4, 5
Excluded	Excluded	0	1	1	3 vs. 4, 5
Excluded	Excluded	Excluded	0	1	4 vs. 5

Threshold   1   2   3   4

Category 1	2 + 3	4	5	
0	1	1	1	1 vs. 2, 3, 4, 5
NA	NA	NA	NA	(2 vs. 3)
Excluded	0	1	1	[2 + 3] vs. 4, 5 *
Excluded	Excluded	0	1	4 vs. 5

Threshold   1   3   4

matters substantively insofar as it affects the parameter estimates. As Clogg and Shihadeh (1994) put it for the adjacent category logit model, "*choice of categories should be taken seriously if this modeling approach is used*" (p. 149). They go on to suggest further (Clogg and Shihadeh 1994:152) that when equal spacing of the categories of Y cannot be assumed, the equal slopes adjacent categories logit model may be inappropriate.

The adjacent category logit model can be calculated in some specialized software using simultaneous estimation.[4] Alternatively, separate bivariate logistic regressions (with all of the qualifications noted earlier regarding separate estimation) can be used to estimate the adjacent categories logit model even when the number of continuous predictors is relatively large. As with the continuation ratio logit model, the logistic functions may be regarded as independent. Some of the appeal of the adjacent category logit model may come from its equivalence to other models. Agresti (2002:286–287) and Hosmer and Lemeshow (2000:289) note that the adjacent category logit model is equivalent to a baseline category logit model with constraints on the parameters, and Clogg and Shihadeh (1994:151) indicate that the standard Poisson regression model can be viewed as a special case of the adjacent category logit model. These parallels, however, do not seem sufficient to recommend

FIGURE 10.4 Contrasts for the Adjacent Category Logit Model (and the Stereotype Model)

Category 1	2	3	4	5	
0	1	Excluded	Excluded	Excluded	1 vs. 2
Excluded	0	1	Excluded	Excluded	2 vs. 3
Excluded	Excluded	0	1	Excluded	3 vs. 4
Excluded	Excluded	Excluded	0	1	4 vs. 5

Threshold   1   2   3   4

Category 1	2 + 3	4	5	
0	1	Excluded	Excluded	1 vs. [2 + 3] *
NA	NA	NA	NA	(2 vs. 3)
Excluded	0	1	Excluded	[2 + 3] vs. 4 *
Excluded	Excluded	0	1	4 vs. 5

Threshold   1   3   4

the use of the adjacent category logit model in preference to either the cumulative logit model (with its advantage of being invariant to collapsing or splitting categories) or, when the ordered categories represent a clear progression, the continuation ratio logit model.

Anderson's (1984) *stereotype model* can be regarded as a special case of the adjacent category logit model, and thus uses the same contrast as the adjacent categories logit model (illustrated in Figure 10.4). The stereotype model, however, like the cumulative logit model, assumes that the ordinal dependent variable reflects a latent continuous interval/ratio variable, and involves the assignment of latent scores $\eta = \mu_0, \mu_1, \cdots, \mu_I$ to the (typically integer) scores $Y = 0, 1, \cdots, I$. This means that the latent scores as well as the parameters must be estimated in the model $\ln[P(Y = i)/P(Y = i - 1)] = \sum_{ik}[\alpha_i + \beta^*(\mu_i - \mu_{i-1})X_k]$ (in intercept format), where the summation sign indicates summation over all values of the predictors (k) and all values of the ordinal categorical dependent variable (i). Alternatively, in threshold notation, the model may be written $\ln[P(Y = i - 1)/P(Y = i)] = \theta_i - \sum_{ik}[\alpha_i + \beta^*(\mu_i - \mu_{i-1})X_k]$. As described in Clogg and Shihadeh (1994:155), the stereotype model is a generalization of the row effects association model in log-linear analysis, with the dependent variable as the row variable. We expect that if the model assumptions are correct, we will find that $\mu_0 \le \mu_1 \le \cdots \le \mu_I$. Another way to represent this model is $\eta = \theta_i - \varphi_i(\beta_{i1}X_1 + \beta_{i2}X_2 + \cdots + \beta_{ik}X_k)$, where

φ_i is a scale parameter. If it is assumed that the β coefficients are completely independent across categories of the dependent variable, $\varphi_i = 1$ for each logistic function, and the resulting equation produces the same results as the polytomous nominal baseline category logit model. If, however, it is assumed that the β coefficients differ across categories of the dependent variable only by some multiple that is constant within that category, then the category index i is dropped from the β coefficients and the equation becomes $\eta = \theta_i - \varphi_i(\beta_1 X_1 + \beta_2 X_2 + \cdots + \beta_K X_k)$, where for each category, all the β coefficients are multiplied by the same scale parameter φ_i. Written another way, the equation becomes $\eta = \theta_i - \varphi_i \beta_1 X_1 + \varphi_i \beta_2 X_2 + \cdots + \varphi_i \beta_k X_k$. If the categories of the dependent variable are truly ordered, then the φ coefficients should also be monotonically ordered. Until recently, the stereotype regression model was unavailable in general purpose statistical packages, but it became available in Stata Version 9. It remains to be seen, however, whether this will result in more extensive use of the stereotype regression model. Compared with the other models discussed here, the stereotype model is somewhat more complicated to implement and interpret, and seems to have little to recommend its use over the other models for ordinal logistic regression.

TESTS FOR EQUALITY OF COEFFICIENTS ACROSS LOGISTIC FUNCTIONS

The usual assumption in the cumulative logit model (and an assumption sometimes examined in other models) is that the coefficients β for the predictors are equal across logistic functions and across cases, resulting in the equation (described above for the cumulative logit model but here written with estimates rather than parameters) $\ln[P(Y > i)/P(Y \le i)] = a_i + b_1 X_1 + b_2 X_2 + \cdots + b_K X_K$, where the "$a$" coefficients are the estimates of the intercepts $\alpha_1, \alpha_2, \cdots, \alpha_{J-1}$ (or in threshold notation $\ln[P(Y \le i)/P(Y > i)] = \theta_i - b_1 X_1 - b_2 X_2 + \cdots - b_K X_K$) and the "$b$" coefficients are the coefficients by which the predictors are multiplied to obtain the predicted values of the dependent variable. Three alternatives to this assumption may be considered. First, the slopes may not be equal across logistic functions, but may instead vary by logistic function. For example, the impact of gender may be different for each of the logistic functions, implying an interaction between gender and the specific logistic function being estimated. Second, slopes may not be equal across cases because there is an interaction between two or more predictors in the model. Here, for example, the impact of gender on the outcome may depend on ethnicity, with majority females, majority males, minority females, and minority females all having different slopes. Third, in a variation on the second possibility, the model may include a *scale* component. In all of the models discussed to this point, an equation has been specified only for what is sometimes called the *location* component of the model, the linear predictor of the central tendency or mean response. As described in McCullagh and Nelder (1989:154–155), a more general model may include, in addition to the location component, a scale component, which can be written $\exp(\tau_1 Z_1 + \tau_2 Z_2 + \cdots + \tau_M Z_M)$, "$\exp(Z)$" is the exponential function e^Z, $\tau_1, \tau_2, \cdots, \tau_M$ are a set of $m = 1, 2, \cdots, M$ coefficients, and $Z_1, Z_2, \ldots, Z_M$ are a set of predictors, which may be a subset of the predictors in the location component. The more general model may be written in the form $\text{logit}(Y) = (\theta_i - \beta_1 X_1 - \beta_2 X_2 + \cdots - \beta_K X_K)/\exp(\tau_1 Z_1 + \tau_2 Z_2 + \cdots + \tau_M Z_M)$, and just as $\theta_i - \beta_1 X_1 - \beta_2 X_2 + \cdots - \beta_K X_K$ is the linear predictor for the central tendency, $\exp(\tau_1 Z_1 + \tau_2 Z_2 + \cdots + \tau_M Z_M)$ is the linear predictor for the dispersion or variance in the model. Another way of viewing this is as an interaction term: each coefficient β is divided by the quantity $\exp(\tau_1 Z_1 + \tau_2 Z_2 + \cdots + \tau_M Z_M)$ or, equivalently, multiplied by its inverse. The difference between this and a simpler interaction term is that *every* coefficient in the model, including each of the thresholds, is multiplied by a nonlinear function of at least one variable (Z_1 if there is only one variable involved in the scaling component of the model). The number of different slopes depends on the number of covariate patterns produced by the combination of the predictors $Z_1, Z_2, \cdots, Z_M$.

Three tests for equality of slopes are the likelihood ratio test, the Score test, and the Wald test. The likelihood ratio test is not merely a comparison of the ordinal cumulative logit model with the nominal baseline category logit model. As noted by Clogg and Shihadeh (1994), "It is very difficult to estimate the cumulative logit model with nonparallel slopes; it is not the case that the regular multinomial logit model is equivalent to this more general model" (pp. 170–171). A parallel caution is offered in Stata (2003) that "goodness of fit for ologit can be evaluated by comparing the likelihood value with that obtained by fitting the model with mlogit" is "only suggestive because the ordered logit model is not nested within the multinomial logit model"(Volume 3, p. 102). Strictly speaking, the cumulative logit model is not nested within the baseline category logit model, so differences between the D_M or G_M statistics cannot be assumed to have a χ^2 distribution. As a practical matter, even though the likelihood ratio test should (as noted by Clogg and Shihadeh) be the most powerful of the available tests for unequal slopes, absent availability in existing general purpose software packages, its use may require substantial programming, in lieu of which either the Wald or the Score test is likely to be preferred.

Paralleling the presentation in SAS Institute (1999), the Score test is constructed as follows. Let $\mathbf{U}(\boldsymbol{\gamma})$ be the vector of first partial derivatives of the log likelihood with respect to the parameter vector $\boldsymbol{\gamma}$ (the gradient vector). Let $\mathbf{H}(\boldsymbol{\gamma})$ be the matrix of second partial derivatives of the log likelihood with respect to $\boldsymbol{\gamma}$ (the Hessian matrix). Let $\mathbf{I}(\boldsymbol{\gamma})$ be either $-\mathbf{H}(\boldsymbol{\gamma})$ or the expected value of $-\mathbf{H}(\boldsymbol{\gamma})$. Let $\hat{\boldsymbol{\gamma}}_0$ be the maximum likelihood estimate of $\boldsymbol{\gamma}$ under some null hypothesis H_0. The χ^2 statistic for testing H_0 is defined by $S = \mathbf{U}'(\hat{\boldsymbol{\gamma}}_0)\boldsymbol{I}^{-1}(\hat{\boldsymbol{\gamma}}_0)\mathbf{U}(\hat{\boldsymbol{\gamma}}_0)$, and has an asymptotic χ^2 distribution with degrees of freedom under H_0 equal to the number of restrictions imposed on $\boldsymbol{\gamma}$ by H_0. The procedure for applying the Score test can be described as follows. First, fit the reduced model. Second, calculate the Score function for the additional parameters in the full model. If L_F is the log likelihood function for the full model, then the Score function for the jth element of the vector of additional parameters $\boldsymbol{\gamma}$ is $u_j = \partial L_F/\partial \gamma_j$ for $j = 1, 2, \cdots, q$. Let $\mathbf{U}_S$ be the vector of Score functions $(u_1, u_2, \cdots, u_q)$, and let $\Sigma_R(\mathbf{U})$ be the $q \times q$ variance-covariance matrix of the Score statistics calculated under the reduced mode. Then the Score statistic is defined as[5] $S = \mathbf{U}_S[\Sigma_R(\mathbf{U})]^{-1}\mathbf{U}'_S$. A major advantage to the Score test is the ease with which it can be calculated, not requiring the actual calculation of a full model with the additional slope coefficients. The major disadvantage to the Score test is that it tends to be highly sensitive and not very powerful, indicating apparent statistical significance when the number of covariate patterns is large (either because the model includes a large number of dichotomous or nominal variables or because it includes continuous variables with a large number of categories) and when the number of cases is large (see, e.g., Allison 1999; Clogg and Shihadeh 1994; Peterson and Harrell 1990).

The multivariate Wald test is similar in construction to the Score test. If $\mathbf{S}(\hat{\boldsymbol{\gamma}})$ is the variance-covariance matrix for the estimated values of $\boldsymbol{\gamma}$ in the full model, then the Wald statistic $W = (\hat{\boldsymbol{\gamma}})'[\mathbf{S}(\hat{\boldsymbol{\gamma}})]^{-1}(\hat{\boldsymbol{\gamma}})$. As noted by Clogg and Shihadeh (1994:169–171), the likelihood test will generally be the most powerful of the tests, and the values of the Wald test will generally be intermediate between the Score and the likelihood ratio tests. Clogg and Shihadeh also emphasize that the use of the likelihood ratio test (and implicitly the multivariate Wald test) is based on the assumption that the full model is in some sense the "true" model, and we are testing whether it can be simplified without compromising its fit. If the full model is seriously inadequate (e.g., badly misspecified), then the test procedure is invalid because it is based on a full model, which itself is not appropriate. The three tests should produce similar results in large samples, but not necessarily in smaller samples.

The Score test has the advantage of convenience, both in eliminating the necessity to estimate a separate model (as is necessary for the likelihood ratio and Wald tests) and in the fact that it is readily available in some statistical routines for estimating the ordinal logistic regression model. It is also informative when it fails to reject the hypothesis of proportional odds or parallel slopes (given its tendency not to do so), but as noted earlier, the hypothesis of proportional odds generally should not be rejected based solely on the results of the Score test. For all of these tests, inclusion of interaction terms between predictors in the ordinal logistic regression model negates the assumption of equal slopes and renders tests for proportional odds irrelevant, since the whole point of interaction terms is that the slope for one variable will not be constant, but will depend on the value of another variable.

INTERPRETING COEFFICIENTS IN THE ORDINAL LOGISTIC REGRESSION MODEL

The interpretation of the unstandardized coefficients in the ordinal logistic regression model seems at first to be straightforwardly parallel to the interpretation of coefficients in the polytomous nominal or dichotomous logistic regression model: a one-unit increase in the predictor X_k is associated with a b_k increase in logit(Y). Of what, however, is logit(Y) the log odds? It depends on which ordinal logistic regression model is being used. (1) For the cumulative logit model, logit(Y) is the natural logarithm of the odds of being in a higher category as opposed to being in *any* of the lower categories. (2) For the continuation ratio logit model, logit(Y) is the natural logarithm of the *conditional* odds, *given* that the case is *at most* in a certain category, of being in that category as opposed to being in a lower category; or if the contrast is reversed, the conditional odds, *given* that the case is *at least* in a certain category, of being in that category as opposed to being in a higher category. (3) For the adjacent category logit model, logit(Y) is the natural logarithm of the odds of being in one category as opposed to being in the *next lowest* category, without reference to any category lower than the next lowest category. Note that the unstandardized coefficients do not indicate that a one-unit increase in X_k is associated with a b_k increase in the *rank* of Y (for which the difficulty of interpretation was noted earlier); that interpretation would apply if we were using OLS regression with an ordinal dependent variable treated as an interval/ratio variable. The interpretation of standardized logistic coefficients has the usual parallel to the interpretation of the unstandardized logistic regression coefficients: a 1 standard deviation increase in X_k is associated with a b_k* standard deviation increase in logit(Y), again with the qualification that the precise meaning of logit(Y) depends on which ordinal logistic regression model we are estimating.

Another issue in the interpretation of coefficients in the ordinal logistic regression model is how, exactly, they are to be used to generate predicted values of the dependent variable. In dichotomous and polytomous nominal logistic regression, there is little to decide about how to predict values from the logistic regression model. The logistic regression equation in dichotomous logistic regression, or the separate logistic functions in polytomous nominal logistic regression, can be used to calculate a unique probability of membership in each category of the dependent variable. For ordinal logistic regression, in this as in other matters, the issue is a little more complicated. As in nominal polytomous and dichotomous logistic regression, one can generate continuous or categorical predicted values of the dependent variable, but continuous predicted values in ordinal logistic regression need to be approached differently because of the information contained in the ordering of the categories. For categorical predicted values, the process is identical to the process used to calculate predicted values in polytomous nominal logistic regression. For each case, the $I - 1$ logistic functions are calculated, then transformed to produce the probability of being in each category other than the reference category (the first or last category). The sum of the probabilities for each of the nonreference categories is then subtracted from 1 to obtain the probability of being in the reference category. The case is classified into the category for which it has the highest probability.[6]

For continuous predicted values, prediction depends on whether we are using the equal slopes or unequal slopes model. In the equal slopes model, we could similarly construct $I - 1$ predictions for each case, using the separate intercepts, but it makes more sense to simply ignore the intercepts and use only the predictors with their coefficients to calculate a predicted value of Y as $\text{pred}(Y) = \hat{Y} = b_1 X_1 + b_2 X_2 + \cdots + b_K X_K$. The reason this makes sense is because the dependent variable is ordinal, and it is not the precise value of $\hat{Y}$, Y, or $\text{pred}(Y)$ but rather the ordering of the cases on $\hat{Y}$, Y, or $\text{pred}(Y)$ that is informative.[7] For the unequal slopes model, using separate logistic regressions to estimate the model, we actually calculate as many predicted values for each case as there are logistic functions, using the slopes plus the thresholds or intercepts of each function to calculate the predicted values. There is thus not a single, unique *continuous* predicted value for each case the unequal slopes model, but instead there is one predicted value for each logistic function.[8]

Which of the approaches to prediction is preferable may be decided on the conceptual basis for the ordinal categories used in the analysis. One possibility is that the ordinal values of the dependent variable may themselves be meaningful independent of (and possibly excluding) any assumption of a continuous latent dependent variable. An example here might be academic attainment, in which the explicit assumption may be made that the dependent variable of interest is *not* continuous (e.g., years or some other measure of time spent in school) but instead that it is inherently discrete (partial or full completion of successive levels of education, where no distinction is made and no distinction should be made between different degrees of partial completion). In this instance, even with the equal slopes model, we may be less interested in the continuous predicted value of the dependent variable than in the predicted category (some high school, high school graduation, some college, college graduation, etc.) of the dependent variable, and it would be more appropriate to use the predicted category membership than the continuous predicted value of the dependent variable.

There seems to be little to recommend the use of multiple continuous predicted values for the dependent variable; therefore, in the separate slopes model, categorical prediction again appears to be the best option. In the equal slopes model, when an ordinal variable represents crude measurement of a continuous latent variable such as happiness or agreement, it seems reasonable to use the continuous predicted scores rather than categorical scores, although doing so may imply more precision in prediction than is really justified by knowledge of the manifestly ordinal categorical dependent variable. The predicted values can and should still be treated as ordinal rather than interval or ratio, but if the underlying dependent variable is assumed to be continuous, one may question whether they should be collapsed into the same categories as the observed categories on the dependent variable. An argument for using the categorical predicted values, even when an underlying interval/ratio scale is assumed and seems reasonable, is that we should not suggest more precision for the predicted values than was present for the observed values of the dependent variable. The adequacy or accuracy of the assumption of an underlying interval/ratio variable can also be questioned. On balance, even with an assumed latent interval/ratio variable, there seems to be little to argue against the use of the categorical predicted scores, either in addition to or instead of the continuous predicted scores.

MEASURES OF EXPLAINED VARIATION, STATISTICAL SIGNIFICANCE, AND GOODNESS OF FIT

Goodness of fit of the ordinal logistic regression model can be assessed with the same G_M and fit statistics (Pearson, deviance) that are used for dichotomous and nominal polytomous dependent variables. These statistics are commonly printed out as part of the standard output in ordinal logistic regression routines in the major general purpose statistical packages. R_L^2 is still a quantitative measure of association that indicates how much of the variation in the dependent variable, as measured by the likelihood ratio statistic ($-2LL$), is explained by the model, but it does not take into account the ordering of the categories of the dependent variable. Use of R_O^2 as a measure of explained variation may be based on the assumption of an underlying interval or ratio variable, and R_O^2 remains useful for the calculation of standardized logistic regression coefficients, but it is in the context of an ordinal dependent variable assumed to reflect an underlying interval/ratio dependent variable that the justification for the use of the McKelvey-Zavoina R_{MZ}^2 in place of R_O^2 is conceptually strongest. Besides R_L^2, R_O^2, and R_{MZ}^2, other R^2 analogs discussed in Chapter 3 are no more justified or useful in the ordinal logistic regression context than for dichotomous logistic regression.

For calculating the correlation between categorical observed and categorical or continuous predicted values of an ordinal dependent variable, without making assumptions associated with a truly quantitative variable (an interval or ratio scale), ordinal logistic regression poses additional considerations. It is generally the case that nominal measures of association can be used with ordinal predictors, and in particular, λ_p, τ_p, and φ_p can be used for ordinal dependent variables; but like all nominal measures of association, they ignore and thus lose the information contained in the ordering of the categories of the dependent variable. Measures that incorporate the information about the ordering of the categories include the asymmetric measure Somers' d_{yx} and the symmetric measures Spearman's ρ_s (rho), Goodman and Kruskal's γ (gamma), and Kendall's τ (tau), of which there are three varieties, τ_a, τ_b, and τ_c, τ_b being most relevant to the present discussion. Readers not thoroughly familiar with ordinal measures of association (and maybe some who think they are) should refer at this point to Appendix C. For reasons detailed there, it seems most appropriate to use τ_b^2, the squared Kendall's tau-b ordinal correlation coefficient, as the PRE[9] (proportional reduction in error) measure of explained variation for an ordinal dependent variable, regardless of whether the correlation is being calculated between categorical or continuous predicted values. The statistical test for Kendall's τ_b is $z = 3\tau_b\sqrt{N(N-1)/[2(2n+5)]}$, which has an approximate normal distribution for large ($N > 40$) samples.

Calculation of τ_b^2 will produce different results, depending on whether categorical or continuous predicted values of the dependent variable are used. In particular, since τ_b^2 can reach its maximum value of 1 only for a table in which the number of categories of the two variables is equal, and there is likely to be a relatively large number of different predicted values of the dependent variable whenever we have continuous predictors, the method of classifying predicted scores into the observed categories of the dependent variable (thus producing a square table with equal numbers of categories for the observed and predicted values of the dependent variable) can generally be expected to produce potentially higher values for τ_b^2 than the method of simply using the (potentially continuous) predicted values calculated directly from the equation $\text{logit}[F(Y)] = b_1X_1 + b_2X_2 + \cdots + b_KX_K$. When the data are heavily skewed, with very few cases in all but one category, all of the cases may be predicted to lie in a single category, and τ_b^2 for categorical prediction may thus be equal to 0, while τ_b^2 for continuous prediction will be nonzero for the same analysis. With heavily skewed data (the vast majority of cases in a single category), it is even possible to obtain a *negative* value for τ_b, indicating that the model does worse than chance for categorical prediction.

EXAMPLE: THE CUMULATIVE LOGIT MODEL FOR ORDINAL LOGISTIC REGRESSION

To examine models for ordinal logistic regression, we return to the data from the National Youth Survey (NYS). The dependent variable will be drug user type, DRGTYPE, an ordinal variable with four categories. *Nonusers* report that they have not used alcohol, marijuana, heroin, cocaine, amphetamines, barbiturates, or hallucinogens in the past year. *Alcohol users* report having used alcohol, but no illicit drugs, in the past year. *Marijuana users* report having used marijuana (and except in one case using alcohol as well), and *Polydrug users* report illicit use of one or more of the "hard" drugs (heroin, cocaine, amphetamines, barbiturates, hallucinogens). Polydrug users also report using alcohol and, except in one case (a respondent who reported a single incident of hard drug use), marijuana as well. The four categories can reasonably be regarded as being ordered from least serious to most serious drugs, in terms of legal consequences. Alternatively, with respect to the nonlegal consequences of the drugs, the scale could arguably be regarded as nominal. One additional change is made from the previous models for marijuana use. Because the dependent variable has four categories, and because of the small number of cases in the category "Other" on the variable ethnicity (ETHN), ethnicity was recoded into two categories, White and non-White, for the following analyses. Failure to do this would have resulted in problems with zero cells, and instability in estimates of coefficients and their standard errors.

For comparison, DRGTYPE was also analyzed as a nominal polytomous dependent variable, with adjustment for underdispersion based on the deviance statistic; the results are presented in Table 10.1. Table 10.1 compares, in succession, (a) nonusers with alcohol users, (b) nonusers with marijuana users, and (c) nonusers with polydrug users. The resulting functions, $g_1(X)$, $g_2(X)$, and $g_3(X)$ may be defined as

$g_1 = \text{logit (Probability of using some alcohol vs. nonuse of drugs)}$,

$g_2 = \text{logit (Probability of using marijuana vs. nonuse of drugs)}$, and

$g_3 = \text{logit (Probability of using other illicit drugs vs. nonuse of drugs)}$.

The equations for g_1, g_2, and g_3 using unstandardized coefficients are, from Table 10.1,

$g_1 = 0.165(\text{EDF5}) - 0.271(\text{BELIEF4}) + 0.505(\text{SEX}) + 1.616(\text{WHITE}) + 5.085$,

$g_2 = 0.506(\text{EDF5}) - 0.285(\text{BELIEF4}) - 0.920(\text{SEX}) + 0.357(\text{WHITE}) + 2.503$, and

$g_3 = 0.633(\text{EDF5}) - 0.360(\text{BELIEF4}) - 2.224(\text{SEX}) + 2.209(\text{WHITE}) + 0.768$.

TABLE 10.1	Polytomous Nominal Logistic Regression for Drug User Type			
Logistic Function	*Predictor*	*Standardized Coefficient*	*Unstandardized Coefficient*	*P(Wald) for Unstandardized Coefficients Separately by Logistic Function*
Function 1:	EDF5	.209	0.165	.069
Nonuser vs.	BELIEF4	−.319	−0.271	.000
Alcohol user	SEX (Male)	.075	0.505	.136
$R^2_O = .189$	ETHN (White)	.202	1.616	.000
	Intercept	—	5.085	.039
Function 2:	EDF5	.671	0.506	.000
Nonuser vs.	BELIEF4	−.350	−0.285	.000
Marijuana user	SEX (Male)	−.143	−0.920	.036
$R^2_O = .149$	ETHN (White)	.047	0.357	.440
	Intercept	—	2.503	.349
Function 3:	EDF5	.677	0.633	.000
Nonuser vs.	BELIEF4	−.357	−0.360	.000
Polydrug user	SEX (Male)	−.279	−2.224	.000
$R^2_O = .337$	ETHN (White)	.233	2.209	.009
	Intercept	—	0.768	.801

Global model statistics:

$G_M = 169.348$, 12 *df*, *p* = .000; $R^2_L = .282$; $R^2_O = .303$; $\lambda_p = .300$, *p* = .000; $\tau_p = .399$, *p* = .000.

Proportion correctly classified = .57.

Global likelihood ratio tests for individual predictors:

EDF5 *p* = .000; BELIEF4 *p* = .001; SEXFM *p* = .000; NONWHITE *p* = .000.

In Table 10.1, the model works fairly well, as indicated by the statistically significant model χ^2 and $R^2_L = .28$. The explained variance in logit(Y) varies by the category of the dependent variable, and is highest for g_3 (polydrug use) and lowest for g_2 (marijuana use). In the overall model, as indicated by the likelihood ratio tests, all four of the predictors are statistically significant. For alcohol use, the standardized coefficients indicate that the best predictor is belief that it is wrong to violate the law, followed by ethnicity. (White respondents are more likely to use alcohol than non-Whites.) Exposure to delinquent friends is marginally significant according to the Wald statistic (*p* = .069), and gender is not statistically significant. For both marijuana and polydrug use, the best predictor is exposure to delinquent friends, followed by belief, then gender. Ethnicity is not a statistically significant predictor for marijuana use, but White respondents are more likely than non-White respondents to be polydrug users. Based on the classification table (not shown), the indices of predictive efficiency $\lambda_p = .300$ and $\tau_p = .399$ are both statistically significant and moderately strong.

Table 10.2 illustrates the cumulative logit model and the difference in approach using thresholds as opposed to intercepts with drug user type as a dependent variable. The results include fully standardized coefficients (which were, as usual, calculated by hand) and the threshold estimates, which are standard in some software for ordinal regression models. Summary statistics for the overall model are presented at the bottom of the table. The table of coefficients is followed by a prediction table. The intercepts and thresholds should essentially be regarded as nuisance parameters here; the focus is really on the coefficients for the predictors and the summary statistics for the overall model.

TABLE 10.2 Polytomous Ordinal Logistic Regression (Proportional Odds)

Dependent Variable: Drug User Type

Predictor	b^*	b	$SE(b)$	Wald χ^2 (1 df)	p
Exposure	.438	0.270	0.042	40.540	.000
Belief	−.267	−0.177	0.043	17.322	.000
Gender (Male)	−.151	−0.790	0.263	9.031	.003
Ethnicity (Non-White)	−.134	−0.834	0.317	6.939	.008
Cutpoint/Threshold (1)	—	−3.823	1.436	7.163	.007
Cutpoint/Threshold (2)	—	−1.450	1.412	1.062	.303
Cutpoint/Threshold (3)	—	0.527	1.423	0.139	.709

$D_0 = 600.600$ $D_M = 471.626$ $G_M = 128.975, df = 4, p = .000$ $R^2_L = .21$; $R^2_O = .41$; $R^2_{MZ} = .48$

Score test: $\chi^2 = 32.569, df = 8, p = .000$

Prediction Table

Observed	Predicted			
	1	2	3	4
1 Nonuser	27	31	1	0
2 Alcohol	16	62	7	2
3 Marijuana	2	22	19	11
4 Hard drugs	0	6	14	11

$\tau^2_b = .32, p = .000$ Proportion correctly classified = .52.

The model does a moderately good job of explaining the dependent variable: τ_b^2 indicates that about one-third of the variation in the dependent variable is explained, based on the classification table. R_O^2 (primarily of interest for calculating standardized logistic regression coefficients) is larger, and R_L^2 is smaller, but both also indicate moderate levels of explained variation. The McKelvey-Zavoina R_{MZ}^2, which in the present context can be considered a better estimate of the true value of R_O^2 for the population when the dependent variable represents a crude categorization of a continuous latent variable, was also calculated. $R_{MZ}^2 = .48$, indicating a stronger association than either $R_O^2 = .44$ or $\tau_b^2 = .32$ for categorical prediction and $\tau_b^2 = .28$ for continuous prediction.

It appears that all four predictors are statistically significant, and that exposure has the strongest effect on the dependent variable, followed in turn by belief, gender, and ethnicity. Being involved in a higher (no pun intended; well maybe . . .) stage or category of substance use is positively associated with exposure to delinquent friends, and negatively associated with beliefs that it is wrong to violate the law, being male (parallel to the results for marijuana use in earlier chapters), and being non-White, for the 16-year-old respondents in this sample. There is, however, an apparent problem: the Score test statistic indicates that the proportional odds, equal slopes assumption appears to be violated in the model. Examination of Table 10.2 suggests why this may be so. The unstandardized coefficient for EDF5 appears to be considerably smaller in the equation for alcohol use than in the other two logistic functions, the coefficient for SEX is positive for alcohol use but very large and negative for polydrug use, and the coefficients for ethnicity are higher for marijuana and polydrug use than for alcohol use. Even though Tables 10.1 and 10.2 are not based on the same contrasts, this hints that we should seriously consider an unequal slopes model.

A SCALED ORDINAL MODEL

Given the statistically significant departures from proportional odds or parallel slopes in Table 10.2, three alternative models deserve consideration: a model with a scale component, a model with separate slopes for each logistic function, and a model with an interaction effect between specific predictors in the model. The third alternative is one that would normally have been tested before applying the test for proportional odds, based on prior research or theoretical consideration. With the hypothesized interaction term in the model, the slopes would not be assumed to be parallel, and a test for proportional odds or parallel slopes would thus not be appropriate. The second alternative in principle could involve calculation of an ordinal model with unequal slopes, but in practice the easiest course is to revert to the polytomous nominal logistic regression baseline category logit model. A variation on the second alternative would be a model in which only some of the slopes were constrained to be equal and others were permitted to differ across logit functions, sometimes termed a *partial proportional odds model* (Peterson and Harrell 1990; see also Stokes et al. 2000:533–554).

For the first alternative, the model with the scale component, all the predictors were included in the scale component of the model and nonsignificant predictors ($p > .10$) in the scale component were deleted using backward stepwise elimination, beginning with the least statistically significant effect, until only exposure (EDF5; $p = .024$) remained in the scale component. Table 10.3 presents the results for this model, including the prediction table. Note that for calculation of the standardized coefficients, the correlation between DRGTYP5 and the continuous predicted value of the dependent variable, logit($\hat{Y}$), was used, since logit($\hat{Y}$) is the value used in the calculation of standardized coefficients for dichotomous and polytomous nominal models, and the value most consistent with a variance-based conceptualization of the standardized coefficients. For calculating the variation explained by the model, however, as discussed earlier, Kendall's τ_b^2 based on the predicted category rather than the predicted continuous value of the dependent variable, is probably most appropriate, and $\tau_b^2 = (.584)^2 = .34$ for the scaled model, compared with .32 for the unscaled model. Similarly, there are slight increases in R_O^2, R_L^2, and the percentage of cases correctly classified. The change in the model χ^2 (G_M) is statistically significant at $p = .034$ (and this comparison is valid because the model without the scale component is nested within the model that includes the scale component). The scaled ordinal logistic regression model does, in this instance, appear to represent an improvement over the unscaled model.

TABLE 10.3   Polytomous Ordinal Scaled Logistic Regression

Dependent Variable: Drug User Type

Predictor	b^*	b	SE(b)	Wald χ^2 (1 df)	p
Exposure	.959 (.534)	0.606	0.202	9.034	.003
Belief	−.443 (−.247)	−0.302	0.108	7.796	.005
Gender (Male)	−.206 (−.115)	−1.110	0.534	4.320	.038
Ethnicity (Non-White)	−.215 (−.120)	−1.379	0.635	4.716	.030
Scale factor (EDF)	(mean = 1/1.791)	.049	0.022	5.095	.024
Threshold (1)	—	−4.975	2.892	2.960	.085
Threshold (2)	—	−0.814	2.698	0.091	.763
Threshold (3)	—	3.129	3.000	1.088	.297

$D_0 = 600.600$ $D_M = 467.130$ $G_M = 133.470, df = 5, p = .000$ $R_L^2 = .22$ $R_O^2 = .43$

$\Delta G_M = 4.495, df = 1, p = .034$ $\Delta R_L^2 = .01$

Prediction Table

	Predicted			
Observed	1	2	3	4
1 Nonuser	33	24	2	0
2 Alcohol	16	60	7	4
3 Marijuana	2	21	14	13
4 Hard drugs	0	6	10	15

$\tau_b^2 = .34, p = .000, \Delta\tau_b^2 = .02$ Proportion correctly classified = .54.

Using the predicted continuous value of the dependent variable in the calculation of τ_b^2 results as expected in a slightly lower estimate of explained variation: $\tau_b^2 = (.546)^2 = .30$ for the scaled model, .28 for the unscaled model. The use of the predicted category rather than the predicted continuous value of the dependent variable here would be justified by the conceptualization of alcohol, marijuana, and other drug use, respectively, as separate and successive stages in substance use (a conceptualization supported in the literature on substance use; see, e.g., Elliott et al. 1989; Kandel and Faust 1975). An alternative conceptualization of substance use as a "propensity" or "tendency," or of substance use as more of a continuum rather than a set of relatively discrete states, is less supported by the literature, but if supported could be used to argue for the use of the predicted continuous values rather than the predicted categories of the dependent variable.

The standardized coefficients indicate that the strongest predictor of being in a higher drug user type category is exposure to delinquent friends, followed by belief that it is wrong to violate the law, then ethnicity, and finally gender, a reversal of order for gender and ethnicity relative to the unscaled model. The standardized coefficients as first calculated, based on the unstandardized coefficients plus R_O^2 and the standard deviations of the predictors, appear to be close to twice as large as the coefficients in the unscaled model, but this is a little misleading. Remember that each coefficient will be divided by the scaling factor, in this case $e^{(.049)(EDF5)}$. The mean value for EDF5 is 11.8987, so the mean value of $e^{(.049)(EDF5)} = e^{(.049)(11.8987)} = 1.791$, so each coefficient will be divided *on average* by 1.791. The resulting average coefficients, taking into account the scaling component of the model, would thus be 0.534 for exposure, -0.247 for belief, -0.115 for gender, and -0.120 for ethnicity. These average standardized coefficients are indicated in parentheses (along with the average adjustment for the scaling factor in the column for standardized coefficients in the table). Bearing in mind that these are *average* coefficients, which vary with the value of EDF5, and therefore will not be the same for every respondent in the sample, it appears that in the scaled model, the magnitude of the effect of exposure relative to the other predictors has increased on average, but the standardized coefficients are otherwise similar in magnitude to the standardized coefficients in the unscaled model, in comparison with the coefficients in Table 10.2.

EXAMPLE: THE CONTINUATION RATIO LOGIT MODEL

One reasonable alternative to the cumulative logit model for drug user type would be the continuation ratio logit model. As noted earlier, the literature on substance use (Elliott et al. 1989; Kandel and Faust 1975) suggests that alcohol, marijuana, and harder drugs represent successive stages in substance use, and in the NYS data, with only two exceptions, individuals who have progressed to a later stage have also used the substances in the earlier stages as well. Table 10.4 presents the results of estimating an equal slopes/proportional odds continuation ratio logit model with the same set of predictors as was used for the cumulative logit model. $D_M = 473.05$ for the model. $G_M = 127.55$ (4 df, $p = .0000$), $D_0 = D_M + G_M = 600.60$, $R_L^2 = .21$, $R_O^2 = .45$, $\tau_b^2 = .30$ for the categorical predicted value and $\tau_b^2 = .28$ for the continuous predicted value of the dependent variable. The global model statistics are thus quite similar to the global model statistics for the cumulative logit model. One difference, however, is that the proportion of cases for which the observed and predicted category is the same is higher than in the cumulative logit models, and in each row of the prediction table, the plurality of cases is predicted to belong in the correct category; yet τ_b^2 is higher for the cumulative logit model than for the continuation ratio logit model. There is no contradiction here; remember that for ordinal variables, it is not just "right or wrong" but "how close" (in rank) the predicted classification is to the observed classification. As in the cumulative logit model, all the predictors are statistically significant, with parameters close in value to those in the cumulative logit model. Based on the standardized coefficients in the equal slopes model in Table 10.4, the strongest influence on progression to higher levels of substance use is again exposure, followed by belief, then gender, then ethnicity. The prediction table indicates the modal category, alcohol user, is somewhat overpredicted, as is typically the case in logistic regression.

Table 10.5 presents the continuation ratio logit model with unequal slopes, using separate logistic regressions. If we sum the initial −2 log likelihood statistics (−2 times the log likelihood at iteration 0 for each equation), we obtain $D_0 = -2(-130.063 - 116.342 - 53.896) = 600.60$, identical to

TABLE 10.4   Simultaneous Estimation Continuation Ratio Logit Model

Dependent Variable: Drug User Type

Predictor	b^*	b	SE(b)	Wald χ^2 (1 df)	p
Exposure	.447	0.239	0.039	6.15	.000
Belief	−.258	−0.148	0.039	−3.84	.000
Gender (Male)	−.169	−0.766	0.231	−3.31	.001
Ethnicity (Non-White)	−.119	−0.642	0.279	−2.30	.021
Threshold (1)	—	−3.218	1.294	−2.49	.006
Threshold (2)	—	−1.343	1.267	−1.06	.145
Threshold (3)	—	0.121	1.295	0.09	.463

$D_0 = 600.600$ $D_M = 473.05$ $G_M = 127.55, df = 4, p = .000$ $R_L^2 = .21$ $R_O^2 = .45$

Prediction Table

Observed	Predicted			
	1	2	3	4
1 Nonuser	25	15	2	0
2 Alcohol	33	63	21	8
3 Marijuana	1	6	19	8
4 Hard drugs	1	5	9	17

$\tau_b^2 = .30, p = .000$ Proportion correctly classified = .55.

D_0 for the model using simultaneous estimation. $D_M = -2(-92.497 - 78.288 - 44.339) = 430.25$, smaller than D_M for the model with equal slopes, as might be expected since the equal slopes model is nested within the model for unequal slopes. The likelihood ratio test for equal slopes is equal to the difference in D_M between the two models: $473.05 - 430.25 = 42.8$ with 8 degrees of freedom (the 8 additional coefficients in the model with unequal slopes), $p = .000$, and we would reject the hypothesis of equal slopes for the continuation ratio logit model. G_M for the unequal slopes model is $600.60 - 430.25 = 170.35$ with 12 degrees of freedom ($p = .000$), and $\tau_b^2 = .28$, .07 higher than the equal slopes model, but Kendall's $\tau_b^2 = .06$, a major drop in explained variation compared with $\tau_b^2 \geq .30$ for the cumulative logit, scaled cumulative logit, and simultaneous estimation continuation ratio logit models. The proportion of cases correctly classified is also considerably lower than in the previous models, only 31% compared with more than 50% for the other models. Here, we have a dilemma. On the one hand, it does appear that the slopes are statistically significantly different; but on the other hand, incorporating that difference into the model makes our predictions worse, not better, when we focus on the ordinal categorical outcome itself, rather than on the likelihood-based model summary statistics. For theory testing, an argument may be made either way; but for practical applications, the equal slopes model, with its superior predictive ability, is clearly to be preferred.

As described in Chapter 5, while standardized coefficients are most appropriate for comparing the effects of predictors within the same model, for comparing the effects of a single predictor across two or more models, the unstandardized coefficient is more appropriate. Comparing the unstandardized coefficients across the three logistic functions, exposure to delinquent friends has its strongest impact on being a marijuana user, and its weakest influence on being a polydrug user; belief that it is wrong to violate the law has its strongest influence on being an alcohol user, and no statistically significant influence on marijuana or polydrug use; gender is not statistically significantly related to being an alcohol user, but females are more likely to progress to marijuana and polydrug use; and non-Whites are *less* likely to progress to alcohol use—but once they are alcohol users, they are *more* likely to go on to marijuana use, and once they are marijuana users, they are *less* likely to go on to polydrug use.

Turning to the standardized coefficients, exposure is the strongest influence on the transitions to alcohol use and to marijuana use, and belief that it is wrong to violate the law is the second strongest predictor of the transition to alcohol use during adolescence, but belief has little impact on later transitions (to marijuana and harder drug use), and the transition to polydrug use among these teenagers is more closely related to being female and White than to exposure to delinquent friends or belief that it is wrong to violate the law. This finding is consistent with a more general research literature that implicates exposure more in the early stages of delinquency, when the influence runs primarily from exposure to illegal behavior, than at later stages, when the influence becomes reciprocal (e.g., Elliott and Menard 1996). Gender is not statistically significant as a predictor of the transition to alcohol use, consistent with widespread use of alcohol by both sexes during adolescence, and ethnicity shows mixed effects, consistently statistically significant, but the second-weakest predictor of the two earlier transitions, in which, as noted earlier, being White is associated with the transition to alcohol use and to polydrug use, but being non-White is associated with the transition to marijuana use. In passing, note that although the level of statistical significance is slightly better for belief than for exposure in the first logistic function, exposure nonetheless has the stronger effect, reinforcing the point that comparison of significance levels does not always produce the same ordering of strength of effect as comparison of standardized coefficients (and this would also be true for partially standardized coefficients).

TABLE 10.5   Separate Estimation Continuation Ratio Logit Model

Dependent Variable: Drug User Type

Function	Predictor	b^*	b	SE(b)	Wald z	p
Function 1:	Exposure	.333	0.314	0.091	3.45	.001
Nonuser vs. Alcohol user	Belief	−.267	−0.271	0.076	−3.55	.000
	Gender (Male)	.008	0.064	0.364	0.17	.861
	Ethnicity (Non-White)	−.137	−1.300	0.410	−3.17	.002
	Intercept	—	5.802	2.637	2.20	.028
Function 2:	Exposure	.548	0.412	0.081	5.11	.000
Alcohol user vs. Marijuana user	Belief	−.020	−0.017	0.063	−0.27	.788
	Gender (Male)	−.263	−1.746	0.431	−4.05	.000
	Ethnicity (Non-White)	.127	1.130	0.535	2.11	.035
	Intercept	—	−4.111	2.237	−1.84	.066
Function 3:	Exposure	.174	0.115	0.063	1.82	.069
Marijuana user vs. Polydrug user	Belief	−.166	−0.118	0.075	−1.59	.112
	Gender (Male)	−.204	−1.141	0.603	−1.89	.058
	Ethnicity (Non-White)	−.256	−1.729	0.872	−1.98	.047
	Intercept	—	1.325	2.294	0.58	.563

$D_0 = 600.60$ $D_M = 430.25$ $G_M = 170.35$, df = 4, p =.000 $R^2_L = .28$

Prediction Table

	Predicted			
Observed	1	2	3	4
1 Nonuser	45	42	9	2
2 Alcohol	3	17	28	27
3 Marijuana	3	5	7	1
4 Hard drugs	9	25	7	1

$\tau^2_b = .06$, $p = .000$ Proportion correctly classified = .31.

EXAMPLE: THE STEREOTYPE REGRESSION MODEL

Table 10.6 illustrates the stereotype regression model. Typically, a single equation model is estimated; but it is possible to specify the number of dimensions or logistic functions to be computed, and setting the number of dimensions to $M - 1$, where M is the number of categories in the dependent variable, will result in the calculation of the (nominal polytomous) baseline category logit model, with some additional parameters. With only one dimension, the results of the stereotype regression model should be similar to the results for the cumulative logit, continuation ratio, and adjacent category logit models. As described in Stata (2005), the test of a one-dimensional model like that in Table 10.6 against the null model (no predictors) does not have an asymptotic χ^2 distribution because of the unconstrained scale (φ) parameters, so likelihood-based statistics are not presented in Table 10.6; but based on the multivariate Wald statistic, the model is statistically significantly better than the null model in predicting drug user type.

The equation being modeled here is $\eta = \theta_i - \varphi_i(\beta_1 X_1 + \beta_2 X_2 + \cdots + \beta_K X_K)$, with, as noted earlier, the expectation that the φ coefficients will be monotonically ordered. From the results in Table 10.6, this equation becomes η (DRGTYP5) $= \theta_i - \varphi_i[(.644)\text{EDF5} - (.335)\text{BELIEF4} - (.335)\text{SEXFM} - (1.461)\text{NONWHITE}]$, where θ_i is equal to -1.922 for the first logistic function, $.471$ for the second logistic function, and $.646$ for the third logistic function (and is 0 for the last logistic function, corresponding to the reference category or base outcome, hard drug use); and φ_i is constrained to equal 1 for the first logistic function (a constraint applied to allow the model to be estimated), is equal to $.549$ for the second logistic function, and is equal to $.204$ for the third logistic function (and for the reference category it is set to 0). The fact that the φ coefficients are monotonically ordered supports the decision to treat drug user type as an ordinal dependent variable. Finally, comparing the coefficients in Table 10.6 to the coefficients in previous models, they tell a similar story: All of the predictors are statistically significantly related to the outcome, with exposure being positively related and the other predictors being negatively related to increasing levels of substance use. For the prediction table in Table 10.6, Kendall's $\tau_b^2 = .33$, and 53% of the cases are correctly classified, results comparable with the cumulative logit and continuation ratio models. Standardized coefficients were calculated and included in Table 10.6, and the results are similar to the results for the previous models, with exposure having the strongest influence, followed by belief, then gender, and finally, ethnicity.

CHOOSING A MODEL FOR DRUG USER TYPE

How do we choose among the different models? As noted in Clogg and Shihadeh (1994:171), the problem with comparing different logit models is that the models are not nested, although tests for comparing nonnested models have been suggested and can be implemented with some effort. The issue here may be more conceptual than technical. Overall, the best prediction is achieved by the baseline category logit model, but not by much, and the baseline category logit model ignores the ordering of the categories for the dependent variable. If we are really talking about a truly ordinal variable, and if the stages described are truly distinct stages with a logical order of *progression* from one stage to the next, then the continuation ratio logit may be preferable. Substantively, the continuation ratio logit model with separate estimation of the different logistic functions may seem

TABLE 10.6 Stereotype Regression Model With One Dimension

Dependent Variable: Drug User Type

Predictor	b^*	Coefficient	Standard Error	Wald z	p
Exposure	.482	0.644	0.109	5.92	.000
Belief	−.232	−0.335	0.095	−3.51	.000
Gender (Male)	−.120	−1.368	0.589	−2.32	.020
Ethnicity (Non-White)	−.108	−1.461	0.668	−2.19	.029
φ_1		1	—	—	—
φ_2		0.549	0.082	6.69	.000
φ_3		0.204	0.066	3.12	.002
φ_4		0	(base outcome)	—	—
θ_1		−1.922	3.106	−0.62	.536
θ_2		0.471	1.688	0.28	.780
θ_3		0.646	0.679	0.85	.342
θ_4		0	(base outcome)	—	—

Wald $\chi^2 = 61.05$, $p = .000$

Prediction Table

Observed	Predicted			
	1	2	3	4
1 Nonuser	36	18	2	0
2 Alcohol	23	60	24	7
3 Marijuana	0	8	18	16
4 Hard drugs	1	3	7	8

$\tau_b^2 = .33$, $p = .000$ Proportion correctly classified = .53.

richer in its distinctions among the effects of the predictors for different stages of the progression in substance use; but it does the poorest job of prediction, based on τ_b^2 and percentage of cases correctly classified, of all the models considered here. At least for some purposes, the practical advantage of better prediction may outweigh the technical consideration of statistical significance. If drug user type really reflects an underlying *continuum* of intensity of involvement in substance use rather than a series of discrete stages, then the cumulative logit model would be more appropriate, and the specific substantive conclusions based on the continuation ratio logit model may be artifactual, since they depend on the precise cut points used to categorize the ordinal dependent variable. The stereotype regression model appears to have no conceptual advantage over the cumulative or continuation ratio logit models in the present context, but may be more applicable to other analytical problems. Put simply, the choice among the different models involves substantive considerations beyond purely technical aspects of the different models.

CONCLUSION

Ordinal logistic regression is in a sense the least "logistic-regression-like" of the logistic regression models. First, more information (ordering) is contained in the values of the dependent variable, and statistics that make use of this information are therefore preferable, in the sense of losing less information, than statistics that do not. This does not really affect the individual coefficient estimates or their statistical significance, but it does suggest that τ_b^2 and its statistical significance (especially but not only for ordinal variables believed to represent a natural ordinal scale, such as academic attainment or substance user type; τ_b^2 may also be of interest for ordinal variables representing latent continuous variables) or the McKelvey-Zavoina R_{MZ}^2 (primarily for ordinal variables representing latent continuous variables) may be of more interest than G_{M} and R_{L}^2, the statistics that seem most appropriate for dichotomous and polytomous nominal variables in logistic regression. Second, the choice between equal slopes and unequal slopes models may not be as straightforward as a simple Score test may imply. The Score test tends to be sensitive to relatively small differences between the equal and unequal slopes model, and while a nonsignificant Score statistic provides reasonable assurance that the equal slopes model fits, it is recommended that the unequal slopes model be calculated using separate logistic regressions to see whether the differences are substantial enough to really warrant using the unequal slopes model instead (e.g., Allison 1999:141; Peterson and Harrell 1990). There may be other reasons, as noted earlier, for violation of the proportional odds assumption. Third, as noted by Allison (1999:142) and Clogg and Shihadeh (1994), diagnostics are not generally available for the cumulative logit model. As with the polytomous nominal logistic regression model, collinearity is easily diagnosed using a linear regression routine that calculates tolerance or the variance inflation factor (VIF), and one can estimate the model using separate dichotomous logistic regressions and perform diagnostics on the logistic functions separately.

Fourth, for path analysis with ordinal logistic regression, if one uses the equal slopes model, there is a single set of standardized coefficients to incorporate into the model, much like OLS regression or dichotomous logistic regression. If, however, the unequal slopes model is used, then the ordinal dependent variable must be treated like a polytomous nominal dependent variable. In particular, if it is an intermediate variable in the causal path, it will need to be split into a set of dichotomous variables to calculate path coefficients to and from the ordinal variable. One must also consider in this context whether it would be better to abandon the logistic regression framework altogether in favor of structural equation modeling with polychoric correlations to estimate the association between the ordinal (assumed to be latent continuous) variable and other variables in the model.

Fifth, while the logit model (best when categories of the dependent variable are evenly distributed) is one reasonable approach to modeling an ordinal dependent variable, there are other distributions that may be used and which are readily available in standard general purpose statistical packages, including the probit, which would be most appropriate for normally distributed categories;

the complementary log-log, when higher categories are more probable; the negative log-log, when lower categories are more probable; and the inverse Cauchy (or cauchit) distribution, for an outcome with many extreme values (SPSS 1999a). Sixth, there remains the option of treating an ordinal variable with a large number of categories as an interval or ratio variable, with diagnostics to test whether doing so results in violations of the model being estimated that are both serious and of practical consequence. The ordinal logistic regression model is particularly well suited to the analysis of ordinal variables with relatively few categories, but as the number of categories increases, so does the number of parameters to be estimated; the model at least requires an additional intercept for each additional category of the ordinal dependent variable.

In general, the cumulative logit model offers a reasonable approach to the analysis of ordinal dependent variables. Its strongest features, relative to other ordinal logistic regression models, are the invariance of its logistic regression coefficients to splitting or combining categories, and its applicability to both truly ordinal variables and to observed ordinal variables that represent latent continuous variables. As a practical matter, it is also the most accessible of the ordinal logistic regression models in presently available general purpose statistical software. The continuation ratio logistic regression model seems promising, partly because it is accessible via some existing software, partly because it is also relatively easy to calculate the alternative model using separate estimation and still produce valid global model statistics, and also partly because there are clearly some variables for which this specific model makes good sense conceptually. There seems to be little to recommend the adjacent category logit model over the cumulative logit model, especially considering the loss of statistical power in comparing only two categories at a time. The stereotype regression model may prove useful in certain specific applications, and possibly as a diagnostic for testing whether the categories of the dependent variable appear to be monotonically ordered relative to a given set of predictors (by examination of the φ coefficients), but once the dimensionality of the model has been established, one may want to adjust the number of categories in the dependent variable accordingly, based on the results of the stereotype regression model, and then apply one of the other ordinal models. For most purposes, the advantages of the cumulative logit model seem likely to make it the model of choice for the analysis of ordinal dependent variables.

NOTES

1. Blair and Lacy (2000) offer an interesting approach to measuring variance in an ordinal variable using the cumulative distribution of the ordinal variable, with an emphasis on the variation *relative* to the maximum possible variation given the number of categories in the variable. They calculate an index of concentration, $d^2 = \sum(F_j - .5)$ where F_j is the cumulative relative frequency for category $j = 1, 2, \cdots, J - 1$ of an ordinal variable with J categories and F_J is necessarily equal to 1 because 100% of the cases are in the (combined or cumulated) J categories of the variable. The maximum possible value of d^2 is $(J - 1)/4$, so if the concentration measure $L^2 = d^2/[(J - 1)/4]$, then the quantity $1 - L^2$ is a measure of dispersion ranging from 0 for minimal dispersion to 1 for maximal dispersion. Note that a variance, unlike L^2, is not typically bounded in the interval $[0, 1]$, and again unlike L^2, a variance represents an absolute rather than a relative quantity.

2. In this approach, the logit transformation of the dependent variable is just one of several possibilities. Others include the probit, complementary log-log, negative log-log, and inverse Cauchy or Cauchit transformations. See, for example, SPSS (1999a:247) for a quick overview of these alternatives.

3. Software Note: The cumulative logit model is the default in SAS **logistic**, SPSS **plum** (for polytomous logit universal model, Stata **ologit** (for ordered **logit**), and in HLM, the latter to be discussed in conjunction with contextual and longitudinal models in Chapters 11 and 13.

4. Software Note: SPSS **loglinear** using a REPEATED contrast, or SAS (Version 8) **catmod** using RESPONSE = ALOGITS, can be used to estimate the adjacent category logit model. As a practical matter, although the DIRECT statement allows SAS **catmod** to easily incorporate continuous predictors, specification of the ALOGITS response forces the use of WLS estimation (which requires several cases per covariate pattern) with the result that models with several continuous predictors are likely to generate error messages indicating that the model cannot be calculated (even when the same model without the ALOGITS specification runs smoothly in SAS **catmod** with the DIRECT specification for the continuous predictors). A similar problem occurs with large numbers of continuous predictors in SPSS **loglinear**.

5. Allowing for differences in notation, this has the same form as the general Score statistic as described in the SAS manual, with $\mathbf{U}_S = \mathbf{U}'(\hat{\gamma})$, $\mathbf{U}'_S = \mathbf{U}(\hat{\gamma}_0)$, $[\Sigma_R(\mathbf{U})]^{-1} = \mathbf{I}^{-1}(\hat{\gamma}_0)$ and in the last equality, consistent with maximum likelihood estimation, the negative of the observed or expected Hessian matrix is the variance-covariance matrix for the parameter estimates.

6. Software Note: This approach is implemented in the PRED = PREDPROBS(INDIVIDUAL) subcommand in SAS **logistic**, the SAVE = PREDCAT(*varname*) option in SPSS, and the "predict *varname(1) varname(2)…varname(I − 1), p*" option in Stata. SAS also has a PRED = PREDPROBS(CUMULATIVE) option, from which the predicted category probabilities can be more indirectly calculated.

7. Software Note: This is the procedure used in the "predict *varname,* xb" option in Stata, and can be implemented with a simple data transformation statement in SAS or SPSS.

8. Software Note: This approach is taken when the SAS **logistic** "pred = *varname*" subcommand is used.

9. Note that in the special case of two dichotomous variables, Kendall's τ_b^2 = Pearsons' r^2 = Goodman and Kruskal's τ_{yx} (see Chapter 3) = φ^2 (again see Chapter 3), an equality not generally shared by other measures of association. Thus, when we reduce the ordinal logistic regression model to the dichotomous case, τ_b^2 remains an intuitively appealing measure of explained variation. Note too that τ_b^2 but not ρ_s can easily be used in partial correlation analysis; the formula for the partial τ_b is the same as the formula for the partial Pearson correlation (with, of course, the substitution of τ_b for r in the equation; see Siegel 1956).

CHAPTER 11

Clusters, Contexts, and Dependent Data

Logistic Regression for Clustered Sample Survey Data

$\mathbf{U}$p to this point, we have tacitly assumed that the data to be used in logistic regression analysis have come from a set of cases generated by simple random sampling with replacement from a single exhaustive listing of the population of interest in which each case is listed only once, or from a procedure that effectively produces results indistinguishable from simple random sampling with replacement. This, in principle, results in a set of cases for which (a) there is only one value of the dependent variable Y and of each of the independent variables $X_1, X_2, \cdots, X_K$ for each case, or to put it another way, there is only one *observation* of the set of variables $\{Y, X_1, X_2, \cdots, X_K\}$ for each case, with the rare exception of those cases chosen more than once (since this is sampling with replacement) for the same sample; (b) the probability of any one case being selected does not depend in any way on whether any other given case is selected for inclusion; and (c) the probability of inclusion for each case is the same as the probability of inclusion for all of the other cases at each step in the selection process.

Each of these conditions may be violated in specific sampling designs. Condition (a), a single observation per case, is commonly violated, for example, in longitudinal research, in which *repeated observations* are used to measure and analyze change over time or age. An example of this is one of the data sets we have been using, the National Youth Survey (NYS), which presently has data on individuals collected repeatedly over a span of 28 years. Condition (b) may be violated, for example, in *paired or related samples*, for instance, by selecting some individuals because another family member (spouse, parent, sibling) is in the sample, or pairing individuals with similar characteristics and assigning them at random to different treatments in an experimental design. An example of this is the Panel Study of Income Dynamics (PSID) (Hill 1992), in which individuals were added to the original sample as a result of marrying or being born to one of the original PSID respondents. Condition (c) is commonly violated, for example, in *disproportionate stratified* sampling, in which some strata may be oversampled to provide sufficient cases for analysis. Examples of this include the 1982 and 1987 oversamples of African Americans in the National Opinion Research Center (NORC) General Social Survey (GSS) (Davis and Smith 1992).

In the present chapter, we consider in more detail the different types of samples commonly used in survey research, the dependencies among observations that can result from deviations from simple random sampling, and alternative procedures for dealing with dependencies in the data that result from sampling designs in which some cases are not sampled independently of others. The discussion progresses, roughly in order of complexity, from (a) using a scaling factor to adjust for overdispersion and underdispersion, to (b) resampling methods, (c) robust estimates of standard errors for clustered data, (d) generalized estimating equations (GEE), and finally to (e) multilevel models.

TYPES OF SAMPLING[1]

In a simple random sample, the assumption is that there exists a complete enumeration or list of all the "elements" (cases) in the "population" of interest, a population that may consist of individuals, households, cities, or other units. In *simple random sampling with replacement*, each element is eligible to be chosen into the sample at each stage in the choice process. If cases are selected one at a time, then once a case has been selected, it becomes eligible to be chosen again. If the sample is very small relative to the population, it is possible but rare that an element will be chosen more than once. In simple random sampling with replacement (1) the probability of being chosen is the same for every element at every step of the selection process (the "step" being the point at which an element is chosen) and (2) the joint probability of any two elements being chosen is the same as the joint probability of any other two elements being chosen.

An alternative, *simple random sampling without replacement*, excludes each sampled element from further consideration once it has been chosen. In simple random sampling without replacement, every element has the same initial probability of being chosen, but the probability of being selected is not the same at each step of the sampling process. This distinction is usually trivial, however, and is commonly ignored in practice. In *systematic random sampling*, it is once again assumed that an enumeration of the elements in the population exists, but instead of randomly selecting an element at each stage in the process, one selects (a) a sampling fraction f, where f is equal to the sample size n divided by the total population size N, $f = n/N$ and (b) a random starting point in the list. The sampling fraction is selected to produce a sample of adequate size to do the desired analysis. There are thus $h = 1/f$ sets of n elements, and the starting point determines which of these sets of n elements is chosen. Once the starting point has been selected, that element and every hth element thereafter is selected for inclusion in the sample.

In *cluster* sampling, instead of an enumeration of the elements in the population, the researcher starts with an enumeration of clusters of elements in the population. Common examples of this involve using lists of counties or census tracts, most often as the first stage in a two-stage or multistage cluster sample. Cluster sampling may involve the sampling of whole clusters of individuals, for example, sampling households from an enumeration of households and including everyone in the household who meets certain eligibility criteria (e.g., age) in the sample. In two-stage sampling, only a sample of elements from each cluster may be included in the final sample, which begins by randomly sampling clusters (in a simple or systematic random sample), then sampling elements (individual cases) from the clusters that were selected in the first stage. In *multistage cluster sampling* (or simply *multistage sampling*), the selection process proceeds in three or more steps. In the first step, a large cluster (e.g., a state or a county) is randomly selected from a list enumerating the large clusters. Next, one or more smaller units (e.g., census tracts or block groups) are randomly chosen from within the selected larger clusters. At any step in multistage sampling, the units to be sampled may need to be enumerated prior to selection, but by eliminating clusters from the sample at each step, the number of units that must be enumerated is eventually much smaller than the total population, resulting in the cost savings that have made multistage sampling a popular approach to obtaining national probability samples. The process continues until the final step, at which point either all elements or a random sample of elements in the smallest cluster (e.g., a household) are selected. In multistage samples, the first (largest) of the clusters sampled is called the *primary sampling unit* or PSU.

In *stratified* sampling, prior to selecting cases, the population is divided into strata, and samples are drawn independently from each stratum. Strata are defined to make sure that people with characteristics of interest (female or male, older or younger, majority or minority ethnicity, higher or lower socioeconomic status, urban or rural residence, etc.) are not underrepresented in the sample, as may occur by chance in unstratified random samples. The variables used in stratification are cross-classified to define the strata, so for example, if we were stratifying the sample based on gender and ethnicity (SEX and RACE in the NORC GSS data), we would have six strata: (1) White males, (2) White females, (3) Black males, (4) Black females, (5) Other males, and (6) Other females. Samples would be drawn independently from each of these six groups if these were the strata on which the sample was based.

In proportional stratified sampling, the sampling fraction is the same in each stratum. In disproportionate stratified sampling, the sampling fraction is different for different strata. Proportional stratified sampling is intended to ensure that the distribution of cases in the sample reflects their distribution in the population on relevant variables. Disproportionate stratified sampling is often employed when one stratum in the population is much smaller than another stratum, and the researcher wants to be able to analyze each stratum separately, as well as providing population estimates of parameters such as means and variances. When disproportionate stratified sampling is used, it is necessary to apply weights inversely proportional to the probability of selection into the sample to obtain unbiased estimates for population parameters. In a *stratified multistage cluster* sampling design, the clusters (including the PSUs) are located within strata, and sampling of clusters occurs separately and independently within each stratum. It is important to bear in mind the difference between strata (none of which are excluded from the sample, and from which the clusters are drawn) and clusters (some of which are excluded from the sample). When the probability of inclusion depends on the stratum, as in disproportionate stratified sampling, or when clusters of unequal sizes are sampled with equal probabilities, complex sampling weights may be needed to produce unbiased parameter estimates. When the probability of sampling for all elements is the same, however, as in the case when the probability of sampling a cluster is proportional to the number of elements in the cluster (probability proportional to size or PPS), we may have a *self-weighting* stratified multistage cluster sample, in which case it is not necessary to weight different strata or clusters differently to obtain unbiased parameter estimates. In some multistage cluster designs, some units may be *self-representing units*, included with certainty in the sample, and more appropriately treated as strata than as PSUs for some analyses.

When the relationships are the same across strata, and oversampling is done only to provide reliable estimates of univariate statistics for subpopulations as well as the total population, stratification has little impact on the analysis. In the most commonly used general purpose statistical packages, cases can be weighted to adjust for oversampling in the estimation of more complex models as well as univariate statistics. A common procedure is to weight each case by the inverse of its probability of being selected, multiplied by a constant such that when all of the weights for all of the cases are added together, the sum is equal to the actual sample size. When the relationships are not assumed to be the same for different strata, however, the analysis needs to test for and (if the test is positive) incorporate into the model any variation across the strata. This can be done most simply by including interaction terms between the stratification variable and each of the predictors in the model and testing for the statistical and substantive significance of the interaction terms (just the same as with any other interaction term) as described in Chapter 6. Finding statistically and substantively significant interaction terms suggests that separate models need to be considered for the different strata.

The GSS data set we have been using to analyze computer use employs a multistage self-weighting cluster sample design. As described in Davis and Smith (1992; see also Kalton 1983; Lee et al. 1989), there were exceptions to this with oversampling of African Americans in 1982 and 1987, but the general format has been a multistage self-weighting sample of PSUs consisting of one or more counties selected at the first stage (Standard Metropolitan Statistical Areas, or later Metropolitan Statistical Areas, and nonmetropolitan counties), and secondary clusters, or segments, consisting of one or more blocks of dwellings (block groups or enumeration districts) at the second stage. The sampling design has also employed stratification of PSUs by region, metropolitan status, and other variables; the precise variables used in stratification have varied across different years of the study. Also, several of the PSUs, representing the largest metropolitan areas, are selected with certainty (hence self-representing units) because of their size, thus effectively being treated as strata in the sampling design. The final stage involved listing all of the housing units in the selected segments, then sampling from those listings. From each household, one adult (over age 18) was randomly selected as the respondent for the household.

The sampling design for the NYS was similar: a multistage cluster sample but without stratification. At the first stage, PSUs consisting of counties or groups of counties across the country were selected, with the probability of selection being proportional to the size of the population of the PSU. The second and third stages involved the selection of progressively smaller geographic areas, and in the fourth stage, all dwelling units within the selected segments were enumerated, and a random sample of the dwelling units was selected. In contrast to the GSS, however, all eligible individuals in each household (adolescents 11 to 17 years old who were physically and mentally able to complete an interview, plus one parent, usually the mother) were included in the sample.

OVERDISPERSION, UNDERDISPERSION, AND INCORRECT STANDARD ERRORS

One possible consequence of complex sampling designs is the presence of overdispersion or underdispersion, discussed in Chapter 7, for which the usual adjustment is the use of a scaling factor to adjust the standard errors. As described in Chapter 7, for grouped data, we calculate $\delta = D/df$, where D is the deviance statistic calculated by covariate pattern and df is the degrees of freedom associated with the deviance statistic (and reported in the same table); or alternatively (and less commonly), using the Pearson χ^2 statistic, we can calculate $\delta = \chi^2/df$. *Overdispersion* is indicated by $\delta > 1$ and *underdispersion* is indicated by $\delta < 1$. It is then possible to adjust the standard errors by *scaling* them,[2] that is, multiplying by the square root of δ: Adjusted standard error = Standard error $\times \sqrt{\delta}$.

Overdispersion may occur for reasons other than clustering in the sample, however, including omission of relevant predictors (misspecification, including omission of nonlinear or interaction terms) or presence of influential cases (high leverage). As described by Hardin and Hilbe (2003:5), the major disadvantage to scaling the standard errors based on overdispersion or underdispersion is that scaling is just an overall adjustment that does not explicitly incorporate or account for the actual clustering in the data. Also at issue is whether the Wald statistics based on the adjusted standard errors are any better than the (flawed, as noted in Chapter 5) Wald statistics based on the unadjusted standard errors.

A second (and related) possible consequence is that the standard errors of population estimates may be overestimated or underestimated by the usual statistics based on simple random sampling. In stratified random sampling, the actual sampling variance of the mean may be reduced if the strata are internally homogeneous (less variance within strata, all of which are sampled). In cluster sampling, similarity of elements within the clusters results in larger sampling variance, because some of the clusters are not sampled, and hence the clusters that are sampled contain cases that may be more different from one another (hence greater variance) on average than might have been the case had all clusters in the population been sampled. In stratified multistage cluster sampling, in which cluster sampling is done within each stratum, both effects occur, but the cluster effect is likely to dominate the stratification effect.

For a given parameter, it is possible to calculate a *design effect*, the quantity by which the variance estimate based on the assumption of simple random sampling needs to be multiplied in order to obtain the correct variance for the design. The design effect will not be the same for all parameters but may vary from one parameter to the next. Prior to the development of software that made calculating adjusted standard errors relatively easy, Kish (1965) suggested using the critical *t* value for standard probability levels to take into account an average or representative design effect, based on calculation of some but not all of the design effects for parameters in the model, to be used in tests of statistical significance. With presently existing software, this approach has largely been supplanted by the use of alternative methods to estimate standard errors, including *resampling methods* and *robust estimators,* to be described below. Presently available approaches to adjusting for clustering in the sample differ according to (a) whether they do or do not involve resampling and (b) whether they adjust only the standard errors of the parameters or involve adjustment of both the parameters and the standard errors.

RESAMPLING METHODS

The common element in resampling methods is that they use the existing sample to create two or more alternative samples, which are then used to estimate standard errors of parameters and possibly the parameters themselves. There are three principal resampling methods for estimating variance in complex samples: *balanced repeated replication (BRR), jackknife repeated replication (JRR or simply jackknife),* and *bootstrapping.*[3] BRR (see, e.g., Kalton 1983:79–80; Lee et al. 1989:27–32), also called half-sample replication, requires a sampling design in which there are strata, each of which has exactly two PSUs. The two PSUs within each stratum are treated as having been sampled independently, and the sample is treated as though it consisted of two separate samples, with one

PSU from each stratum being assigned at random to each of the two samples. If $\hat{\gamma}_1$ represents the estimate of the population parameter γ (which may be, e.g., a mean or a logistic regression coefficient) based on the first half-sample, and $\hat{\gamma}_2$ represents the estimate of the same population parameter based on the second half-sample (or in the terminology of resampling methods, the complement), then a variance estimate for $\bar{\gamma} = (\hat{\gamma}_1 + \hat{\gamma}_2)/2$ is $S_\gamma^2 = [(\hat{\gamma}_1 + \bar{\gamma})^2 + (\hat{\gamma}_2 - \bar{\gamma})^2]/2$. As noted in Kalton (1983), this simple approach to estimating the variance of the parameter produces unstable estimates. The problem of instability is addressed by forming $t = 1, 2, \cdots, T$ half-samples by randomly reassigning PSUs to the first or the second half-sample, then calculating the estimated variance of γ as $S_\gamma^2 = \Sigma[(\hat{\gamma}_1 - \bar{\gamma})^2 + (\hat{\gamma}_2 - \bar{\gamma})^2]/(2T)$. For the replications to be fully balanced, T must be a multiple of 4, which is greater than or equal to the number of strata.

A more general approach to using resampling to estimate the variances of sample parameters is jackknife repeated replication. JRR, or simply "the jackknife" (see, e.g., Efron 1979; Frankel 1971; Lee et al. 1989; Mooney and Duval 1993:232–27), is actually a family of procedures based on dropping one subsample out at each step of the process. Again, let γ be the population parameter of interest, and let $\hat{\gamma}$ (no subscript) be the estimate of that parameter based on the full sample. If there are no strata or clusters in the sample, and with sample size n, construct $I = n$ subsamples by dropping each element in turn from the sample. For each subsample, calculate the estimated population parameter $\hat{\gamma}_i$, $i = 1, 2, \cdots, I$ by the usual methods (e.g., logistic regression for a logistic regression coefficient). The jackknife estimate of the parameter is then $\hat{\gamma} = \Sigma_i \hat{\gamma}_i / I$, and the estimated variance of the sample estimate $\hat{\gamma}$ is $S_\gamma^2 = \Sigma(\hat{\gamma}_1/\bar{\gamma})^2/[I/I - 1)]$. For large samples, it is possible to use fewer than n separate subsamples by randomly selecting $I < n$ elements for deletion. In a more general form, let H be the number of clusters in the data. Then instead of eliminating individual elements at each step, one can proceed by eliminating each of the clusters $h = 1, 2, \cdots, H$ and calculating $\tilde{\gamma}_h = h\hat{\gamma} - (h - 1)\hat{\gamma}_h$ for each subsample; the mean parameter estimate over the subsamples is $\tilde{\gamma} = \Sigma_h \hat{\gamma}_h / h$; and the variance of the parameter estimate is calculated as $S_\gamma^2 = \Sigma_h(\hat{\gamma}_h - \tilde{\gamma})^2/[h/h - 1)]$. Once again, it is possible to sample clusters rather than using all clusters in the analysis. When the sample is stratified, at least one element in a simple stratified sample, or one PSU in a stratified cluster sample, must be dropped in the estimation process. In a stratified multistage cluster sampling design, JRR typically involves dropping each PSU, one at a time; weighting up the other PSUs in the stratum from which the one PSU was dropped to retain the sample distribution across the strata; and calculating the population parameter. A test for the statistical significance of the difference between $\hat{\gamma}$ and a null hypothesis value for the parameter, γ_0, can be performed using a jackknife t statistic, calculated as $t_{\text{jackknife}} = (\hat{\gamma} - \gamma_0)/[\Sigma(\hat{\gamma}_h/\bar{\gamma})^2/(h^2 - h)]$.

Another resampling approach to estimating the standard error of population estimates is the bootstrap method (see, e.g., Efron 1979; Mooney and Duval 1993). In the bootstrap method, each element in the sample is replicated a large number of times (e.g., 100,000), then a large number of samples (smaller than the number of replicated elements, e.g., 10,000) is drawn from the set of replicated cases, and the population parameter is calculated. The variance for the population estimate is then calculated as the variance of the separate estimates for the population parameter. As noted in Lee et al. (1989), the bootstrap is more time-consuming and expensive than the jackknife method, and the jackknife is more commonly used in analyzing complex survey data. Mooney and Duval (1993:25) similarly note that the jackknife appears to perform better than the bootstrap in the analysis of complex samples because of its ability to develop reliable estimates of linear sample statistics by setting up subsamples that parallel the strata and clusters in the sample.

NONRESAMPLING METHODS FOR CALCULATING SAMPLE PARAMETER VARIANCES

Alternatives to resampling methods for the analysis of complex samples include (a) the Huber-White, robust, or sandwich estimator for variance, and (b) the linearization, delta, propagation of variance, or Taylor series expansion method for estimating the variance of sample estimates of population parameters. The sandwich estimator of the variance combines (a) an estimate of the variance based on assumptions used in constructing the likelihood function with (b) an empirical estimate of the variance that does not depend on those assumptions (Hardin and Hilbe 2001:27–31). Some detail on the construction of the sandwich estimator is provided in Appendix A. The likelihood-based component of the sandwich estimator is based on the inverse of the Hessian matrix. The empirical estimate used to adjust the parameter variance estimate varies depending on the model and is selected to produce consistent estimates even when the specification of the variance function is incorrect.

As described in Lee et al. (1989:37–39), Taylor series expansion involves taking the first and higher-order derivatives of the formula for the population parameter $f(x)$, and evaluating each component of the expansion $f'(x)$, $f''(x)$, $f'''(x)$, and so on, where $f'(x)$ is the first derivative of $f(x)$, $f''(x)$ is the second derivative of $f(x)$, and so forth, at the mean or expected value of the variable to which the parameter applies. Then the Taylor series expansion is

$$f(x) = f[E(x)] + f'[E(x)][x - E(x)] + f''[E(x)][x - E(x)]^2/2! + f'''[E(x)][x - E(x)]^3/3! + \cdots,$$

where 2!, 3!, and so on are the factorials of 2, 3, and so on, and the series is calculated to some desired level of precision. It is also possible to calculate the variance of the function at the mean, and to use this estimate of the variance as an estimate for the variance of the sample parameter γ. In contrast to resampling methods, this approach produces a variance estimate in a single calculation based on a single pass through the data. For complex surveys, this method of approximation, as noted by Lee et al., is applied to PSU totals within a particular stratum, and although the formulas are complex, they typically require less computing time than the resampling methods. The global significance of the coefficients can be tested using an F statistic based on an adjustment to the Wald χ^2 statistic (see Appendix A).

GENERALIZED ESTIMATING EQUATIONS

Generalized estimating equations were developed and have been used primarily in the analysis of longitudinal data (Diggle et al. 1994; Hardin and Hilbe 2003; Liang and Zeger 1986) and will be revisited in that context in the following chapters. As noted in Hardin and Hilbe (2003), however, GEE models are applicable to clustered data more generally. Broadly in GEE, observations are clustered within panels. The "panel" often consists of repeated observations on the same case at different times, as in longitudinal data. Alternatively, however, it may consist of single observations of multiple individuals who are members of the same higher-level unit, such as students in schools or residents in neighborhoods. A brief description of GEE is given in Appendix A.

In contrast to robust estimation of standard errors, GEE procedures can use the adjusted variance estimate to iteratively adjust not only the standard error but also the parameter estimates themselves, somewhat parallel to the jackknife approach as discussed above. One element of this process is the selection of a correlation structure for the observations within the panels. Possibilities (as discussed in Appendix A) include exchangeable correlations (no difference in the correlation matrix for observations within the same cluster), when there is no logical ordering for observations within a cluster (as in the case under consideration here, cross-sectionally clustered observations resulting from a complex sampling design) or autoregressive correlations for longitudinal data involving multiple periods. As described in Hardin and Hilbe (2003), GEE models (a) are not maximum likelihood based, but are based instead on generalizing another estimating equation, including the incorporation of a working correlation matrix; (b) do not require specific assumptions about second and higher-order moments; (c) involve introduction of second-order variance components directly into a pooled estimating equation; and (d) produce consistent inferences about mean responses and consistent estimates for mean parameters even if the covariance structure is incorrectly specified.

CLUSTERS, CONTEXTS, AND MULTILEVEL MODELING

Multistage cluster sampling designs are frequently encountered in large-scale national samples. Clustering of observations may also occur, however, in smaller-scale samples, not as a result of a strategy for sampling cases, but because the cases to be studied occur within naturally occurring clusters. Two examples are schools and neighborhoods. In examining the impact of curriculum innovations, for example, a study is sometimes designed to implement the curriculum in some classrooms within a school and not in others, or to implement the changes in some schools but not others. Schools or classrooms may be randomly assigned to treatment and control conditions. Although data are collected from individual students or teachers, the implementation occurs at the classroom or school level, not at the individual level. The data from different students are thus not independent but are naturally clustered within the school or the classroom. Similarly, in studies of neighborhood-level interventions, neighborhoods may be randomly assigned to treatment and control conditions. More generally, if one is interested in the impact of neighborhood conditions on outcomes such as illegal behavior, personal competence, or mental health, a frequently used design is to sample individuals within different types of neighborhoods. Because individuals are clustered within the neighborhood, plausibly subject to a set of common influences that may not be explicitly incorporated in the model, neighborhood-level variables cannot be treated as though they were independently measured for each individual in the study.

Natural clustering within *contexts* such as classrooms, schools, and neighborhoods, like cluster sampling, violates the assumption that cases are selected independently, and some adjustment for the dependence of individual responses on the classroom, school, or neighborhood needs to be considered in the analysis of the data. It would be possible to try to apply some of the same solutions to clustering within contexts as were discussed for sampling clusters, but robust estimates and resampling techniques do not deal directly with the nature of the clustering in the data. Other models, variously termed *mixed models, hierarchical models,* or *multilevel models,* explicitly model (a) the context *itself* as a source of dependence in the observations and (b) *characteristics* of the context as potential influences on outcomes and the relationships between individual-level variables and outcomes.[4] Most common is the two-level model, in which the individual respondent constitutes the first (lower) level and the classroom or neighborhood constitutes the second (higher) level of aggregation, but as implied in the name, multilevel models may include more than two levels (e.g., students clustered within classrooms clustered within schools). Initially, these models were developed for continuous dependent variables, but some software also permits the modeling of dichotomous and both nominal and ordinal polytomous dependent variables.[5]

The general form of the two-level multilevel logistic regression model consists of two equations, each representing a different level of the model. The *Level 1 equation* is at the level of the cases being studied, often but not necessarily individuals, and is the same as the logistic regression equations covered in previous chapters. In general,

$$\eta_{ij} = \text{logit}(Y_{ij}) = \beta_0 + \beta_{1j}X_{1ij} + \beta_{2j}X_{2ij} + \cdots + \beta_{kj}X_{kij} + r_{ij}, \tag{11.1}$$

where the subscript $I = 1, 2, \cdots, n$ refers to the cases; $k = 1, 2, \cdots, K$ refers to the predictors $X_1, X_2, \cdots, X_K$; and $j = 1, 2, \cdots, J$ refers to the specific context for which the parameters $\beta_0, \beta_1, \cdots, \beta_J$ are calculated; and here β_0 is the intercept (instead of α) to simplify the multilevel notation. The dependent variable η is a function of Y in a generalized linear model (GLM). For a dichotomous dependent variable in a logistic regression model, $\eta_{ij} = \text{logit}(Y_{ij})$, and parallel transformations are used for the nominal (baseline category logit) and ordinal (continuation ratio or cumulative logit) polytomous logistic regression models. The term r_{ij} represents a random error at Level 1, and the variance of r_{ij} is the random error variance for Level 1 when the dependent variable is an interval/ratio variable. For nonlinear multilevel models in some software using GLM or GEE estimation, the Level 1 variance may be assumed to be a function of the mean [Level 1 variance = $P(Y = 1)/(1 - P(Y = 1))$ in the case of the logit transformation] and may be dropped from the model (Luke 2004:55; Raudenbush and Bryk 2002:298) by default (and consistent with the GLM/GEE approach, there may also be an option to estimate a correction for overdispersion). In general, when using multilevel logistic regression analysis, the focus is on (a) whether there is a random effect that needs to be modeled, (b) parameter estimates, (c) inferences about the parameters, and (d) how well the model predicts or explains the variation in the dependent variable.

Assuming for the moment that the cases are individual subjects or respondents, the predictors $X_1, X_2, \cdots, X_K$ are individual-level predictors, characteristics of individuals that may vary within a context, in contrast to another set of predictors $W_1, W_2, \cdots, W_Q$ that are characteristics not of individuals but of the contexts themselves (e.g., schools or neighborhoods) within which the individuals are *nested*, that is, each individual is assigned to one unique context $j = 1, 2, \cdots, J$, but each context will typically (but need not always) have more than one individual. At the second or *contextual* level, we can model the individual-level coefficients as a function of an intercept (a contextual mean value) and the $q = 1, 2, \ldots, Q$ contextual predictors:

$$\beta_{kj} = \gamma_{k0} + \gamma_{k1}W_{k1} + \gamma_{k2}W_{k2} + \cdots + \gamma_{kQ}W_{kQ} + u_{kj} \tag{11.2}$$

where u_{kj} is the Level 2 *random effect*. The inclusion of the random effects components u_{kj} is a way of modeling the existence of differences among individuals based on the clusters to which they belong. In a pure *fixed effects* multilevel model, all $u_{kj} = 0$ by definition, and the only random variance occurs at Level 1; this is appropriate when there are no real differences among cases based on the clusters to which they belong. Combining the Level 1 and Level 2 models,

$$\eta_{ij} = (\gamma_{00} + u_{0j}) + [\Sigma_k \Sigma_q (\gamma_{kq} W_{kq} + u_{kj})] X_{kij} + r_{ij}, \tag{11.3}$$

where the respective Level 1 β coefficients have been replaced by their Level 2 equations. The addition of a context-specific random error component (u_{kj}) to the intercept (γ_{00}) reflects the impact of cluster membership on the mean value of the outcome; and the inclusion of the u_{kj} in the slope reflects the impact of cluster membership on the strength and direction of the relationships of predictors to the outcome variable. Possible models include pure fixed effect models (all $u_{kj} = 0$ by definition), *random intercept* models with fixed coefficients ($u_{0j} \neq 0$ but all other $u_{kj} = 0$ by definition), and more broadly *random coefficient* or *random effects* models (random components u_{kj} are included in at least some of the β coefficients, probably including the intercept).[6]

For random effects models, an important distinction needs to be made between *unit-specific* models and *population-averaged* models (for fixed effects models, there is no distinction between the two). In the unit-specific model, the concern is with the extent to which a change in an independent variable for a particular case is associated with a change in the dependent variable for that same case, and the random effects model includes specific random components for each cluster. The random effects themselves are not actually estimated, but the parameters (the variance components) of the assumed distribution of the random effects are incorporated into the model (Hardin and Hilbe 2003:42-49). As described in Raudenbush and Bryk (2002:303), the coefficients in the unit-specific model are interpreted as indicating the expected change in logit(Y) for a one-unit change in the predictor when we hold constant not only the other predictors but also the value of the random effect, u_{kj}. For example, how much of an impact would an increase in income or education for a particular individual have on that individual's computer use?

In a population-averaged model, on the other hand, the concern is with rates or averages in the population. For example, how much of an impact would an increase in average income or average education have on the *average* rate of computer use in the population? A population-averaged model (sometimes also called a marginal model or a marginal effects model) includes within-cluster dependence by averaging effects across all clusters. The coefficients in the population-averaged model are interpreted as indicating the expected change in logit(Y) for a one-unit change in the predictor holding all other predictors constant and taking the *average* of the u_{kj} across (rather than within) the Level 2 units.[7] *When there are no random effects, the unit-specific model and the population-averaged model are the same, no different in principle from the models estimated by the standard logistic regression routines available in general purpose statistical software packages such as SAS, SPSS, and Stata; it is only in the presence of random effects, which the unit-specific and population-averaged models treat differently, that there is a distinction between the two.*

SAMPLING MODEL AND ESTIMATION IN MULTILEVEL LOGISTIC REGRESSION ANALYSIS

For a dichotomous dependent variable in multilevel analysis, we may assume a binomial distribution with n_{ij} trials and probability of success π_{ij}, with Y_{ij} representing the number of successes in n_{ij} trials and the expected value of Y_{ij}, $E(Y_{ij}|\pi_{ij}) = n_{ij}\pi_{ij}$, and variance of Y_{ij}, $\text{Var}(Y_{ij}|\pi_{ij}) = n_{ij}\pi_{ij}(1 - \pi_{ij})$. This is the typical pattern for logistic regression and logit models with grouped data in which there are multiple cases per covariate pattern. When $n_{ij} = 1$, representing ungrouped data (corresponding to the usual situation for logistic regression in which each case or individual within a context is selected randomly and may have a unique covariate pattern), then Y_{ij} is equal to either 0 ("failure") or 1 ("success"). As noted in Raudenbush et al. (2000:115), this results in a special case of the binomial distribution known as the Bernoulli distribution, and $E(Y_{ij}|\pi_{ij}) = \pi_{ij}$. The appropriate link function for this GLM is $\eta_{ij} = \ln[\pi_{ij}(1 - \pi_{ij})]$; or in the notation used earlier in this book, $\eta_{ij} = \ln\{P(Y_{ij} = 1)/[1 - P(Y_{ij} = 1)]\}$. Similarly, for a polytomous dependent variable, a multinomial sampling model is assumed.

Estimation methods available for multilevel GLMs, including but not limited to logistic regression models, include penalized quasi-likelihood (PQL) estimation (Breslow and Clayton 1993) using either restricted or full maximum likelihood estimation; the use of robust standard errors in conjunction with restricted and full PQL models; for dichotomous outcomes, a computationally more intensive algorithm based on the Laplace transform; and Gauss-Hermite or adaptive Gauss-Hermite quadrature. Gauss-Hermite or adaptive Gauss-Hermite quadrature estimation methods are the most accurate over the widest range of data structures (Raudenbush and Bryk 2002:465), but they are computationally intensive and much, much slower than other estimation methods, particularly for relatively complex models with dichotomous or categorical dependent variables.[8]

Restricted PQL estimation has the advantage of being faster and computationally less intensive than other methods; but (a) because it is a restricted maximum likelihood approach, we cannot assume that the use of likelihood-based statistics, such as G_M and R_L^2, is appropriate; and (b) restricted PQL estimation tends to underestimate the standard errors for the coefficients in the model. Full information PQL estimation is almost as fast and computationally less intensive than other methods, but it shares the problem of underestimating standard errors. It is possible, however, using full information PQL to obtain likelihood-based summary statistics (D_0, D_M, G_M, R_L^2) for a fixed effects Level 1 only model that are identical to the estimates produced by (unrestricted) maximum likelihood estimation using logistic regression routines available in standard general purpose statistical software packages such as SAS, SPSS, and Stata. The issue with underestimation of standard errors may be addressed by the use of robust standard errors. Limited experience suggests that the (nonrobust) standard errors produced by full information PQL are, indeed, smaller than those produced in an identical model using unrestricted maximum likelihood estimation, but that robust standard errors with PQL are reasonably close (although not identical) to the standard errors produced in the identical model using unrestricted maximum likelihood. A computationally more intensive but still fairly fast algorithm based on the Laplace transform is available for random effects, unit-specific models in HLM; according to Raudenbush et al. (2000:128), it produces a more accurate approximation to maximum likelihood and "efficient (or nearly efficient) estimates of all parameters."[9]

SUMMARY STATISTICS FOR ALTERNATIVE MODELS FOR DEPENDENT AND CLUSTERED DATA

A general issue in all the above procedures is whether it is reasonable to use likelihood ratio tests or other likelihood-based statistics such as R_L^2. Hardin and Hilbe (2001:28, 194; 2003:33–34, 170) repeatedly and in slightly different contexts emphasize that the use of adjusted standard errors (or equivalently, adjusted variance-covariance matrices) for the logistic regression coefficients implies that the underlying likelihood for the model is not correct and also that the use of maximum-likelihood-based statistics is inappropriate in conjunction with the population-averaged GEE model because there is no likelihood underlying the model. Taken to its fullest extent, this logic implies that any adjustment to the standard errors, including adjustment for overdispersion or underdispersion, invalidates the maximum likelihood basis for the model and hence any maximum-likelihood-based descriptive or inferential statistics associated with the model. According to this reasoning, if one is going to adjust the standard errors, one should adjust the coefficients as well. Mitigating this concern, however, is the knowledge that (1) for maximum likelihood logistic regression analysis generally, even when the model is correct, standard errors are known to be inflated when the unstandardized logistic regression coefficient is large and (2) specific to multilevel modeling with PQL estimation, the standard errors are known to be underestimated. In both of these cases, the use of robust, Taylor series, bootstrapped, or jackknifed standard errors seems reasonable in conjunction with the usual likelihood-based statistics, $-2LL_0$ or D_0, $-2LL_M$ or D_M, G_M, and R_L^2. Note, however, that the likelihood is not the same for fixed effects models (the models discussed in all the previous chapters) as for random effects models (which must account for additional cluster-specific effects).

Full PQL for fixed effects models and Laplace estimation for random effects models in multilevel modeling produce estimates that can reasonably be regarded as maximum likelihood estimates (Raudenbush and Bryk 2002), and allow the use of the usual likelihood-based statistics. Also applicable is the use of the likelihood test for statistical significance of individual coefficients, as an alternative to tests based on standard errors. When GEE, bootstrap, or jackknife estimates are used for coefficients as well as standard errors, however, there does not appear to be adequate justification for the use of likelihood-based statistics. As noted earlier, GEE models are based not on maximum likelihood but on generalizing another estimating equation, including the incorporation of a working correlation matrix. Bootstrap and jackknife estimates are not themselves maximum likelihood estimates but may represent an average of maximum likelihood estimates. Depending on specific software, other summary measures may be available for the nonlikelihood-based methods. In some software, in place of the familiar likelihood ratio χ^2 (G_M) test there may be a multivariate Wald χ^2 test based on the Wald goodness-of-fit statistic for the estimated model compared with the model containing only the intercept. As described in Chapter 10, the Wald statistic $W = (\hat{\gamma})'[\mathbf{S}(\hat{\gamma})]^{-1}$ $(\hat{\gamma})$ where $\mathbf{S}(\hat{\gamma})$ is the variance-covariance matrix for the estimated values of γ in the full model; the equation is the same whether that variance-covariance matrix has been estimated by maximum likelihood or not. For Taylor series linearization, as noted earlier, an F test based on an adjustment to the Wald χ^2 statistic may be used.

Like logistic regression for dichotomous dependent variables, polytomous nominal and polytomous ordinal logistic regression models may incorporate adjustments to standard errors using robust, bootstrapped, or jackknifed standard errors, and adjustments to both coefficients and standard errors using GEE, bootstrap, jackknife, or multilevel estimation techniques. In all the above models, whether likelihood-based (adjusted standard errors only, or multilevel analysis with likelihood-based estimation such as full PQL for fixed effects models and Laplace estimation for random effects models) or not (GEE, bootstrap, and jackknife estimation of coefficients and standard errors), it is possible to use the summary statistics that are not likelihood based: R_O^2, λ_p, τ_p, φ_p, and their associated tests of statistical significance (F or t for R_O^2; the binomial d for λ_p, τ_p, and φ_p) for dichotomous and polytomous nominal dependent variables; and Kendall's τ_b^2 and its associated z test for statistical significance for polytomous ordinal dependent variables. R_O^2 may be less than ideal, as noted in Chapters 3 and 9, as an R^2 analog for dichotomous and polytomous nominal dependent variables, but for nonlikelihood estimation, it may be the best we can do. The other measures, λ_p, τ_p, φ_p, and τ_b^2, are based on the prediction table and are unaffected by the method of estimation.

CHOOSING A METHOD TO ADJUST FOR DEPENDENCIES IN THE DATA[10]

Which of the methods is most appropriate to diagnose or adjust for dependencies in the data depends on which of five combinations of information and concerns best describes our situation: (1) no information about the nature (or existence) of dependency in the data and a concern only with standard errors and not with coefficients; (2) information about the nature of dependency in the data (how cases are related to one another), in particular, knowing to which clusters (neighborhoods, schools, PSUs) cases belong and a concern only with standard errors and not coefficients; (3) no information about the nature of dependency in the data and a concern with both coefficients and their standard errors; (4) information about the nature of dependency in the data, either no information or no concern about the characteristics of the clusters themselves (e.g., population size or density, social cohesion or disorganization, percentage majority or minority ethnicity), and concern with both coefficients and their standard errors; and (5) information about the nature of dependency in the data, information and concern about the characteristics of the clusters in the data, and concern with both coefficients and their standard errors.

1. As noted earlier, in logistic regression, even when the maximum likelihood model is correct and all of the assumptions for the use of that model are met, we have the potential problem of inflation of standard errors when logistic regression coefficients are large. This affects both Wald statistics and confidence intervals for the coefficients associated with individual predictors, and may lead to incorrect inferences and Type II (false-negative) errors. Even in the absence of known dependencies in the data, the potential for inaccurate estimates of standard errors, and correspondingly incorrect inferences suggest that bootstrap, jackknife, or robust Huber-White sandwich estimates of standard errors may be useful as diagnostics; but how concerned are we really about standard errors if we have a better criterion (the likelihood test) to assess statistical significance? The clearest advantage to diagnostic alternative estimates of standard errors would seem to be their use in constructing confidence intervals for unstandardized logistic regression coefficients and odds ratios. Absent clear evidence of the superiority of one technique over another, lower computational burden and greater availability argue in favor of the use of the Huber-White robust sandwich estimator for the standard error, but resampling techniques, which rely on fewer assumptions, may be preferable in cases in which the assumptions for using robust standard errors are clearly not met. If resampling is used, then as noted earlier, jackknife estimates are more widely used than bootstrap estimates, but in the present context (no information about how cases are clustered in the data), the main advantage to the jackknife approach may be its lower computational burden.

2. Similarly, if we know the nature of the dependency in the data, we may use that information and apply bootstrap, jackknife, Taylor series, or Huber-White robust standard error estimation to see whether the standard errors and associated inferences are seriously affected and to adjust standard errors if that appears to be justified. Again, however, the question is whether we are really that concerned with the standard errors of the logistic regression coefficients, given the availability of the likelihood test for those coefficients, and again, it is of interest primarily if we are interested in constructing confidence intervals for our estimates of the logistic regression coefficients. When there is no clear evidence of the superiority of one technique over another, lower computational burden, greater availability, and incorporation of information about dependency in the data are advantages of the Taylor series linearization approach, but if resampling techniques are used, then as noted

earlier, jackknife estimates are more widely used than bootstrap estimates and, when the nature of the clustering in the data is known, perform better because of the ability to develop reliable estimates by setting up subsamples that parallel the strata and clusters in the sample (Mooney and Duval 1993).

3. When we are concerned with logistic regression coefficients instead of or in addition to their standard errors, and when we lack information about the nature of dependencies in the data, the use of bootstrap or jackknife estimates for both coefficients and their standard errors may be justifiable as a diagnostic test not only for unobserved dependencies in the data but also for other problems, including failure to meet the assumptions underlying the use of maximum likelihood logistic regression or the presence of outliers or influential cases that have substantial effects on the parameter estimates. As noted earlier, jackknife estimates are more widely used than bootstrap estimates, but in the present context (no information about how cases are clustered in the data), the main advantage to the jackknife approach may be its lower computational burden.

4. If we know the clusters to which cases belong, but have no data on (or are not concerned with) the characteristics of those clusters, it is possible to use GEE or resampling methods to estimate logistic regression coefficients and their standard errors; but none of these justify the use of likelihood-based summary statistics for the model. Multilevel modeling is an alternative here which does allow the use of likelihood-based summary statistics, and which also allows a wider range of options for modeling the effects of the clusters, even when we have no Level 2 variables (characteristics of the clusters as opposed to the individual cases): not only the random intercept model (sometimes called the random effects model in GEE) but also models that include random slopes may be used. The one advantage to resampling methods (more specifically, jackknife estimation, given its preferability, as noted above, to bootstrap estimation) is that they rely on fewer assumptions; but if the assumptions underlying multilevel modeling are reasonable, then multilevel modeling may be recommended here for its greater flexibility in dealing with the range of possible dependencies (random coefficients as well as random intercepts) in the model and the convenience of being able to use likelihood-based summary statistics.

5. The more information we have and want to use, the more appealing the use of multilevel modeling becomes. If we know the clusters to which cases belong, and have (and are concerned with) the characteristics of those clusters, the use of multilevel modeling to estimate coefficients and their standard errors allows us to test for and, if appropriate, incorporate random intercepts (the random effects model), random slopes, coefficients and standard errors for contextual (Level 2) variables (cluster characteristics) that use correct degrees of freedom for calculating inferential statistics, cross-level interactions, and the possibility of incorporating more than two levels of clustering (e.g., individuals within classrooms within schools). If we are concerned with standard errors (again, this is likely to be the case primarily if we are constructing confidence intervals for the coefficients), then the use of robust standard errors for the population-averaged model using full PQL estimation seems advisable, given the known underestimation of standard errors using PQL; but the standard errors from Laplace estimation in the unit-specific random effects model appear to be reasonable. Here as elsewhere, however, a more appropriate test for statistical significance of individual coefficients may be the likelihood test, as described in Chapter 5. In practice, this may involve the tedious repeated calculation of multilevel models excluding each variable and interaction effect in turn to obtain more precise estimates of the statistical significance of each variable and each interaction term.

EXAMPLE: COMPUTER USE WITHIN PSUS

In principle, there is nothing to prevent the use of multilevel modeling with PSUs as the Level 2 clusters, but this is not common practice at present. It may also be the case that the relevant clustering occurs at a lower level than the PSU, for example, within households within the PSU, but here a true multilevel (three or more levels) model may be appropriate. The application of multilevel modeling with random intercepts and slopes applied to cases clustered in PSUs is illustrated here. Table 11.1 presents results from analyzing (once again) computer use in the NORC GSS, here using the 100 PSUs as the clusters within which observations are nested.

Consider first the likelihood-based explained variation as indicated by R_L^2, and compare it with R_L^2 in Table 5.2 on page 90 from Chapter 5. For the model in Chapter 5 (which does not include random effects), $R_L^2 = .170$; for the random effects model here, $R_L^2 = .07$. The difference lies in the fact that the likelihood function for the present model takes into account random variation across PSUs, variation which is not explained by the model but which is used to adjust the estimates of the coefficients and their standard errors. In contrast, there is a small change from Table 5.2 to Table 11.1 in the model χ^2 (G_M: 517.58 vs. 464.61) and little or no change in R_O^2 (.219 in both tables), λ_p (.324 vs. .325), τ_p (.468 vs. .426), or the percentage of cases correctly classified (72% in both tables). It may be appropriate here to calculate R_L^2 separately for only the fixed effects component in Table 11.1, and this is included below R_L^2 for the full model, including random effects, using the formula $R_L^2 = (G_M)/(D_0)$ for the model excluding random effects. The D_0 for the model excluding random effects in Table 5.2 was 3038.115, so R_L^2 here *only for the fixed effects component of the model in Table 11.1* is equal to 464.609/3038.115 = .153, only slightly lower than $R_L^2 = .170$ in Table 5.2.

Next, consider the statistical significance of the random effects, at the bottom the first part of the Table 11.1. The random component of the intercept is statistically significant ($p = .000$), indicating that there is statistically significant variation across PSUs in the prevalence of computer use. The random effects associated with the slope for education are not statistically significant ($p = .268$), but the random effects are marginally significant ($p = .100$) for the slope for income, indicating that the impact of income may vary across PSUs. There is clear evidence for some impact of dependency in the data. Looking at the classification table, the pattern is different from that of the classification table in Table 5.2, but the percentage of cases correctly classified and the indices of predictive efficiency remain largely unchanged. The coefficients for the individual predictors tell the same story as the coefficients in Table 5.2: The impacts of gender and ethnicity on computer use are not statistically significant, and education has the strongest influence, followed by income. There is some slight difference in the unstandardized and standardized logistic regression coefficients and odds ratios, most notably in the intercept, but the difference in the intercepts reflects the fact that in the multilevel model in Table 11.1, but not in the model in Table 5.2, education and income have been centered at their grand mean, a common practice in multilevel modeling. Besides the multilevel model including random slopes as well as random intercepts, it is also possible to calculate a multilevel model that includes only the random intercept, and this produces estimates of coefficients and their standard errors similar to what we would obtain using GEE or jackknife estimates: unstandardized coefficients of about .319 for education, .096 to .099 for income, and nonsignificant coefficients of −.030 to −.058 for gender, −.113 to −.143 for Black ethnicity, and .190 to .240 for Other ethnicity. In short, while there does appear to be evidence of dependency in the data based on PSU membership, that dependency appears to have little effect on the substantive results.

	b^*	b	Standard Error of b	Odds Ratio	Statistical Significance (p)
TABLE 11.1 Random Intercept and Slopes Model for Computer Use by PSU					
Predictors					
Level 2					
Intercept	—	0.296	0.369	1.344	.425
Level 1					
Education	.356	0.332	0.025	1.394	.000
Income	.193	0.099	0.012	1.104	.000
Gender (Male)	−.011	−0.060	0.124	0.884	.631
Ethnicity: Black	−.017	−0.123	0.164	0.942	.455
Ethnicity: Other	.023	0.266	0.286	1.305	.353
$D_0 = 7184.121$					
$D_M = 6619.512$					
G_M (6 df) = 464.609					
$R_L^2 = .065$ (random effects included in D_0)					.000
$R_L^2 = .153$ (fixed effects only)					.000
$R_O^2 = .219$					.000
Random effects					
Intercept					.000
Education					.268
Income					.100

Prediction/Classification Table

	Predicted	
Observed	0	1
0	515	410
1	214	1,102

$\lambda_p = (925 - 624)/925 = .325$, $d = 12.915$, $p = .000$.

$\tau_p^2 = [2(925)(1316)/2241 - 624]/[2(925)(1316)/2241] = (1086.39 - 624)/1086.39 = .426$, $d = 19.544$, $p = .000$.

Proportion correctly classified = .72.

EXAMPLE: MARIJUANA USE WITHIN NEIGHBORHOODS

To examine the prevalence of marijuana use in a clustered sample, data were taken from the Denver Neighborhood Study or DNS (Elliott et al. 1996, 2006). The DNS includes 33 neighborhoods represented by block groups, within which a total of 838 individuals were sampled. Neighborhood-level information on crime rates, income, and other variables was obtained from U.S. Census data; neighborhood-level information on neighborhood social organization was obtained by aggregating (summing or averaging) responses from individuals living in the neighborhood to construct a single score for each neighborhood; and individual-level data were collected on some now-familiar variables, including gender (YMALE, coded as 0 for females and 1 for males), ethnicity (BLACK, LATINO, and OTHER, with WHITE as the reference category), exposure to delinquent friends (YEXPDEL, with higher scores indicating higher exposure to delinquent friends), and attitudes toward deviance (YATTDEV, with higher scores indicating higher disapproval of deviant behaviors, parallel to the BELIEF measure used in the NYS data analyzed in previous chapters). Here, the prevalence of marijuana use (YPMARIJ) is the dependent variable. YMALE, BLACK, LATINO, OTHER, YEXPDEL, and YATTDEV are the Level 1 (individual level) predictors. At the neighborhood level (Level 2), we include BORGANIZ, a composite index of neighborhood social organization constructed from separate indices of institutional effectiveness, informal networks, normative and value consensus, bonding and social control, illegal opportunity and illegal performance structures in the neighborhoods (Elliott et al. 2006). Better organized neighborhoods should result in more favorable outcomes, and the impact of other predictors of problem behavior may depend on the level of neighborhood organization.

Two sets of results are presented in Table 11.2. For computer use, in Table 11.1, we could compare the results of the random effects model with a previously computed model that did not include random effects. Because we lack that for marijuana use in the DNS, results for marijuana use in a model that does not include random effects are presented in parentheses in Table 11.2, to allow comparison with the results for the random effects model (the numbers outside the parentheses). Turning first to the summary statistics for the model, we once again find that R_L^2 with the random effects included in D_0 is considerably smaller than R_L^2 when we consider only fixed effects; but otherwise, G_M, R_O^2, λ_p, τ_p, and the percentage of cases correctly classified are similar for the models with and without random effects. Notice that the random effects on the intercept in this model are *not* statistically significant ($p = .173$); this may indicate either that there really is no impact of the clustering of cases within neighborhoods, in which case a model with only fixed effects may be appropriate; or that the effects of clustering within neighborhoods are adequately accounted for by the variables in the model. In fact, if we calculate an intercept-only model, the random neighborhood effects are marginally statistically significant at $p = .061$, suggesting that it may be best to stick with the random effects model.

As noted in Table 11.2, the individual predictors, including the cross-level interaction terms, were tested for collinearity prior to analysis (tolerances $>.20$; this was done using a linear regression subroutine, the procedure suggested in Chapter 7). Looking first at the statistical significance of the individual coefficients, there are two noticeable differences between the random effects model (outside parentheses) and the model with no random effects (inside parentheses). For the model without random effects, the interaction between exposure and organization is statistically significant ($p = .003$), but for the model with random effects, it is only marginally significant ($p = .085$); and for the model without random effects, the coefficient for the interaction between organization and Hispanic/Latino

TABLE 11.2   Random Intercept Model for Marijuana Use by Neighborhood

Dependent Variable: Marijuana Use (Full Model)	b^*	b	Standard Error of b	Odds Ratio	Significance (p)
Level 2 predictors					
Intercept	— (—)	−2.806 (−2.827)	0.504 (0.384)	0.060 (0.059)	.000 (.000)
BORGANIZ	.175 (.165)	0.598 (0.564)	0.563 (0.346)	1.818 (1.757)	.297 (.103)
Level 1 predictors					
YEXPDEL	.442 (.409)	0.548 (0.507)	0.098 (0.058)	1.730 (1.661)	.000 (.000)
× BORGANIZ	.132 (.132)	0.182 (0.183)	0.106 (0.062)	1.200 (1.201)	.085 (.003)
YATTDEV	−.260 (−.267)	−0.157 (−0.161)	0.057 (0.029)	0.855 (0.851)	.006 (.000)
× BORGANIZ	.060 (.060)	0.040 (0.041)	0.097 (0.033)	1.041 (1.042)	.677 (.216)
YMALE	−.033 (−.036)	−0.200 (−0.220)	0.447 (0.280)	0.819 (0.803)	.655 (.432)
× BORGANIZ	.004 (.005)	0.018 (0.025)	0.487 (0.300)	1.018 (1.026)	.971 (.933)
Ethnicity:					
BLACK	−.016 (−.029)	−0.131 (−0.237)	0.665 (0.514)	0.877 (0.789)	.844 (.644)
× BORGANIZ	.052 (.056)	0.547 (0.582)	1.073 (0.635)	1.728 (1.790)	.610 (.359)
LATINO	−.044 (−.018)	−0.268 (−0.114)	0.597 (0.434)	0.765 (0.892)	.654 (.792)
× BORGANIZ	−.176 (−.172)	−1.108 (−1.081)	0.835 (0.459)	0.330 (0.339)	.185 (.018)
OTHER	.053 (.053)	0.589 (0.588)	0.750 (0.599)	1.803 (1.801)	.432 (.326)
× BORGANIZ	−.007 (−.007)	−0.097 (−0.088)	1.028 (0.639)	0.908 (0.916)	.926 (.890)
$D_0 = 2069.508\ (616.260)$					
$D_M = 1826.618\ (371.458)$					
$G_M = 242.890\ (244.802)$					.000 (.000)
$R_L^2 = .117$ (—) (random effects included in D_0)					.000 (—)
$R_L^2 = .394\ (.397)$ (fixed effects only)					.000 (.000)
$R_O^2 = .372\ (.371)$					.000 (.000)
Note: tolerances all >.20					
Random effects					
Intercept					.173

Prediction/Classification Table

	Predicted	
Observed	0	1
0	666 (667)	23 (22)
1	54 (58)	50 (46)

$\lambda_p = (104 − 77)/104 = .260$, $d = 2.840$, $p = .0005$. $(\lambda_p = .231, d = 2.525, p = .012)$.

$\tau_p^2 = (180.72 − 77)/180.72 = .574$, $d = 8.781$, $p = .000$. $(\tau_p = .557, d = 8.527, p = .000)$.

Proportion correctly classified = .90.   Proportion correctly classified = .90.

ethnicity is statistically significant (p = .018), but for the model with random effects, it is not statistically significant (p = .185). Focusing on the coefficients that are at least marginally significant ($p \leq .100$), it appears that (1) neighborhood organization does not quite have a significant impact on prevalence of marijuana use (if the impact were significant, neighborhood organization would unexpectedly be associated with higher rates of marijuana use); (2) as in previous analyses with the NYS data set, in the DNS data set, exposure to delinquent friends is positively associated with marijuana use, and based on the standardized logistic regression coefficients, exposure to delinquent friends is the strongest predictor of marijuana use; (3) the impact of exposure to delinquent friends on marijuana use is amplified in more organized neighborhoods ($b*$ = .132, b = .182, p = .085); (4) negative attitudes toward deviance in the DNS (like belief that it is wrong to violate the law in the NYS data) are negatively associated with marijuana use in the DNS sample, and based on the standardized logistic regression coefficients, negative attitudes toward deviance represent the second strongest predictor of marijuana use; and (5) neither gender, nor ethnicity, nor any of the other interaction terms in the model has a statistically significant impact on marijuana use. It appears, then, that the random effects model does account for some (at least marginally significant) variation between neighborhoods in overall levels of marijuana use, and also in the impact of exposure to delinquent friends (through its interaction with neighborhood organization); and that the substantive results are consistent both with our expectations and with results from a different sample.

If our purpose here were theory testing, we might stop at this point. Alternatively, if we wanted to develop the most parsimonious model to predict marijuana use in the DNS, we might instead turn to backward stepwise elimination of statistically nonsignificant effects, as suggested in Chapter 6, to construct a reduced model for marijuana use. Table 11.3 presents the results of calculating a reduced model for marijuana use, developed by first eliminating statistically nonsignificant interaction effects, then eliminating statistically nonsignificant effects of the remaining predictors in the model. As indicated in Table 11.3, the change in G_M from the full to the reduced model is not statistically significant; there are slight reductions in R_L^2, R_O^2; λ_p, τ_p, and the percentage of cases correctly classified. In Table 11.3, it appears that the random effect is statistically significant (p = .027), indicating neighborhood differences beyond the variables included in the model. All the predictors are statistically significant (neighborhood organization only in interaction with exposure to delinquent friends, with p = .043 for the interaction term), and again exposure to delinquent friends has the strongest impact on marijuana use, followed by negative attitudes toward deviance. On balance, the full and reduced models tell much the same story; but the statistical significance of both the random effects component of the model and interaction between neighborhood organization and exposure to delinquent friends are clearly statistically significant in the reduced model, as opposed to statistical nonsignificance for the random effect and marginal significance for the interaction term in the full model. Again, from the viewpoint of testing theory, the model in Table 11.2 may be more appropriate, but from the perspective of developing a parsimonious prediction model, the reduced model in Table 11.3 may be more useful.

CONCLUSION

Regardless of the method of accounting for clustering in the data, it is possible, using the output from the model, (a) to calculate predicted values of logit(Y), from which we can obtain $S_{\text{logit}(\hat{Y})}$, for use in calculating standardized logistic regression coefficients; (b) to calculate predicted values of

TABLE 11.3   Reduced Random Intercept Model for Marijuana Use by Neighborhood

Dependent Variable: Marijuana Use (Reduced Model)	b^*	b	Standard Error of b	Odds Ratio	Significance (p)
Level 2 predictors					
Intercept	—	− 0.766	0.281	0.063	.000
BORGANIZ	.050	0.169	0.249	1.184	.502
Level 1 predictors					
YEXPDEL	.427	0.527	0.078	1.693	.000
× BORGANIZ	.107	0.147	0.072	1.158	.043
YATTDEV	−.270	−0.162	0.032	0.850	.000
$D_0 = 2069.508$					
$D_M = 1838.217$					
$G_M = 231.291$					.000
Change in G_M from full model = 11.599, 9 df					.669
$R_L^2 = .112$ (random effects included in D_0)					.000
$R_L^2 = .375$ (fixed effects only)					.000
$R_O^2 = .346$					.000
Random effects					
Intercept					.027

Prediction/Classification Table

	Predicted	
Observed	0	1
0	663	26
1	59	45

$\lambda_p = (104 − 85)/104 = .183, d = 1.999, p = .046$.

$\tau_p^2 = (180.72 − 85)/180.72 = .530, d = 8.103, p = .000$.

Proportion correctly classified = .89.

Y, the dependent variable in its original metric (ranging from 0 to 1), from which we can calculate R_O as the correlation between the observed and predicted values, and R_O^2 as the squared correlation between the observed and the predicted values of the dependent variable, and the F or t test statistic associated with R_O and R_O^2 (although R_O^2 has some disadvantages as a measure of explained variation in logistic regression models, as described in Chapter 3, for models in which likelihood-based statistics are inappropriate, it may be the best we can do for an R^2 analog); (c) to calculate standardized logistic regression coefficients using the unstandardized logistic regression coefficients, the standard deviations of the predictors, R_O and $S_{\text{logit}(\hat{Y})}$; (d) to use the resulting standardized logistic regression coefficients to construct path analysis with logistic regression (PALR) models; (e) to recode the predicted values of the dependent variable in its original metric to 0 if the predicted value is less than .50 and to 1 if the predicted value is greater than or equal to .50 and to use these recoded predicted values to construct prediction tables; and (f) to use the resulting prediction tables to calculate either λ_p, τ_p, or φ_p, and the associated binomial d test statistic for dichotomous and polytomous nominal dependent variables, or Kendall's τ_b^2 and the associated z test statistic for polytomous ordinal dependent variables. None of this is presently standard practice in any of the models (adjusted standard errors, resampling techniques, multilevel modeling), but it is applicable to all those models.

When the nature of the clustering in the data is known, and especially when there is information on theoretically or empirically relevant characteristics of the clusters themselves, multilevel modeling with logistic regression provides an approach that has the advantages of (a) incorporating information about the characteristics of the clusters, (b) adjusting estimates of the effects of cluster characteristics for their correct degrees of freedom, (c) flexibility in modeling fixed effects, random intercepts, or random coefficient models, and (d) when an appropriate estimation method is used, the ability to use likelihood-based summary statistics for the model. The use of multilevel modeling to account for the impact of clustering of cases into different contexts is very different from the use of resampling methods, robust standard error estimates, or GEE for all but the simplest multilevel models involving only random intercepts and no other random coefficients. With multilevel analysis, we are not merely adjusting coefficients or their standard errors for the same model. Instead, we are almost always testing additional effects, including one or more of random slopes, effects of Level 2 units in which the cases are clustered (effects of Level 2 variables), or cross-level interactions. Multilevel modeling provides more technically appropriate inferential tests of the impact of Level 2 variables, both by adjusting the number of degrees of freedom at Level 2 and, when there are random coefficients, adjusting the appropriate Level 1 coefficients as well.

Other models make adjustments for clustering in the data by only adjusting estimates of standard errors; this is possible with some resampling techniques and with the use of robust standard errors. Yet other approaches, somewhat parallel to multilevel analysis, adjust not only the standard errors but also the logistic regression coefficients themselves; this is possible with some resampling techniques and with the use of GEE. In models in which only the standard errors and not the coefficients themselves are adjusted, it is possible to calculate G_M and other likelihood-based statistics, although some of the models for which they can be calculated are not true maximum likelihood models. The utility of adjusting only the standard errors of the logistic regression coefficients may be questioned. It is known that when the logistic regression coefficient is large, there are problems with standard errors even in samples in which there is no clustering or dependency among the cases, and it is unclear whether the adjusted standard errors are any better than the unadjusted standard errors when it comes to constructing confidence intervals or calculating Wald statistics to test for the statistical significance of individual logistic regression coefficients.

The bottom line question is, "What good are these adjustments, and what is the best approach?" Adjustments for clustering in the data are first and foremost useful as diagnostics to see whether any clustering in the data appreciably affects the substantive conclusions reached in the analysis. If there is evidence of clustering in the data, then which is the best approach depends on the nature of the clustering in the data. When dependence is only suspected but not known, or when the precise nature of the dependence is unknown, the use of robust standard errors, GEE, or resampling techniques as diagnostics may represent the best option. The use of GEE models is more prevalent in the analysis of longitudinal data than clustered cross-sectional data, and the use of resampling methods seems to have increasingly given way to the use of robust standard error estimates in practice. One size may not fit all, but the use of robust standard error estimates can generally be recommended as a diagnostic (a) when there is no clear reason to expect dependence in the data, but when one wants to explore that possibility; (b) when one expects dependence in the data, but the precise nature of the dependence is unclear; and also (c) when it is believed that the likelihood function is correct but the standard error estimates are incorrect to produce better estimates for the confidence intervals of the coefficients. This may be particularly appropriate in the context of multilevel models using PQL estimation for population-averaged models but may also be reasonable in logistic regression models more generally, particularly if there is an interest in constructing confidence intervals for the logistic regression coefficients, given the danger of inflated standard errors for large unstandardized logistic regression coefficients. If contextual effects such as the clustering of observations in PSUs, neighborhoods, or schools are the source of dependence in the data, then the random effects model using multilevel modeling appears to be particularly useful, making the most use of the available information, allowing the use of likelihood-based statistics, providing correct degrees of freedom for variables characteristic of higher-level units, and offering flexibility in modeling different types of random effects.

NOTES

1. For a brief introduction to survey sampling and the effects of different types of sampling on the sampling variance of population parameters, see, for example, Babbie (2001), Kalton (1983), or Lee et al. (1989). For more detailed treatment, see, for example, Kish (1965), Levy and Lemeshow (1999), Sudman (1976), or Thompson (2002).

2. An alternative to the use of the deviance or Pearson χ^2 statistic for adjusting the deviance is to use Williams's procedure (Hardin and Hilbe 2001:121–123), which uses an iterative procedure involving an extra parameter, φ, to scale the variance or the weight function, producing new coefficient and standard error estimates that produce $\delta = 1$.

3. Software Note: BRR, JRR, and bootstrap routines were once primarily the province of specialized stand-alone programs such as SUDAAN and WesVar, but they are increasingly available in general purpose software packages. Stata offers a particularly good array of options for complex samples.

4. See, for example, Goldstein (1991, 1995), Kreft and De Leeuw (1998), Luke (2004); Raudenbush and Bryk (2002), Snijders and Bosker (1999), and Wong and Mason (1985). As noted by Raudenbush (2001), the terminology of covariance components models, hierarchical models, mixed models, and multilevel models generally refers to the same mathematical models but to different software packages (e.g., SAS **varcomp**, HLM, SAS **mixed**, and MLWIN, respectively). Here in preference to the longer term "hierarchical generalized linear models" or the abbreviation HGLM, the shorter term "multilevel models" is used.

5. Software Note: Although multilevel analysis is increasingly being incorporated into general purpose software packages, as this is being written, the best available software for multilevel modeling of discrete (dichotomous, polytomous nominal, and polytomous ordinal) dependent variables is not part of or fully integrated into existing general purpose software packages but exists in specialized multilevel analysis software such as HLM (Raudenbush et al. 2004) and MLwiN (Goldstein et al. 1998).

6. The terms *fixed effects* and *random effects* are used with different meaning in other contexts; see, for example, Chapter 13.

7. Software Note: As indicated by Raudenbush et al. (2004:110), the population-averaged model in HLM is equivalent to the GEE approach.

8. With a moderately complex Bernoulli model, Gauss-Hermite or adaptive Gauss-Hermite quadrature estimation may be painfully slow, taking hours or (literally; no exaggeration) days to converge. For simple models, for relatively small samples of Level 2 units, or for relatively small numbers of Level 1 units per Level 2 unit, Gauss-Hermite or adaptive Gauss-Hermite quadrature estimation may be the best option; but for large numbers of Level 1 cases or Level 2 units (or both) and for more complex models, as a practical matter, other estimation methods may be preferable.

9. Software Note: See Agresti (2002:524), Breslow and Lin (1995), Raudenbush and Bryk (2002: 454–464), and Raudenbush et al. (2000:127–128), all referring directly or indirectly to the PQL approach described in Breslow and Clayton (1993) and implemented in HLM. In HLM6, for example, if one calculates the deviance statistic for the fixed effects model with only the intercept, one obtains $-2LL_0$ (D_0), and the deviance statistic for the full model is equal to $-2LL_M$ (D_M); from which it is possible to calculate G_M and R_L^2 identical to estimates obtained from general purpose statistical packages such as SAS, SPSS, and Stata. As noted by Kleinbaum and Klein (2002:366), the GEE model with independent correlation structure, no adjustment for overdispersion [in the context of HLM, Level 1 variance = $P(Y = 1)/(1 - P(Y = 1))$], and model-based standard errors (see Appendix A) is equivalent to the standard logistic regression model; and, as indicated in Note 7, the population-averaged model in HLM is equivalent to the GEE model. The Laplace estimate is a unit-specific estimate, hence available only when there is at least one random effect in the model, and it may not converge for some more complex models. With the Laplace estimation procedure in HLM6, D_0 and D_M for the random effects model will be quite different from D_0 and D_M for the fixed effects model (as should be expected), but the estimates that result for G_M and R_L^2 that I have produced so far from Laplace estimates appear to be reasonable.

10. Software Note: A note is in order here about precision, or the illusion of precision, in models that adjust for dependencies in the sample. One would expect, and one will find, that estimates of standard errors and, if estimated separately, coefficients will vary across the estimation methods described here. Often, however, that difference is no greater than the difference that would be obtained by estimating the same (mathematically identical) model using the same (e.g., maximum likelihood) estimation technique, but using different software algorithms, or even just different convergence criteria.

Conditional Logistic Regression Models for Related Samples

Chapter 11 began with a review of the assumptions about observations in simple random samples, including the assumptions of (a) a single observation for each case, (b) the independence of the probability of selection for any one case from the probability of selection of any other case in the sample, and (c) equal probability of selection for each case at each step in the sampling process. Chapter 11 then focused on violations of those assumptions in complex sampling designs, the consequences of violating those assumptions, and possible ways to detect, account for, or adjust for violations of those assumptions. The focus was on the clustering of cases in a complex sample in a cross-sectional design.

In this chapter, we consider a special type of nonindependence or clustering in samples involving cases that are included because of their comparability to other cases in the sample (and correspondingly, the exclusion of cases that are not comparable with other cases in the sample) in either matched pairs (*paired samples,* two cases, one selected for some form of comparability with the other) or larger matched groups (*related samples,* again, with cases selected for comparability with one another). As indicated in Chapter 11, paired or related samples violate the assumption that the probability of selection of one case is independent of the selection of any other case, and also, as will be seen, in an indirect way they violate the assumption of a single observation per case. We begin by considering the special case of the unconditional change model in a two-wave longitudinal panel, a topic we will revisit in the next chapter, then turn to case-control studies and the discrete choice model. The principal link among these three models, and the reason for their inclusion together in this chapter, is that all involve the use of *conditional logistic regression* to estimate the parameters of the models.

MATCHED PAIRS IN CROSS-SECTIONAL AND REPEATED MEASURES DESIGNS

When we have matched pairs, each case is really the pair of observations, not a separate case for each observation. That is, what we are observing in each matched pair is not two independent cases but the differences between the two cases within each pair. The pairs often involve cases such as individuals, in which for each pair one member of the pair belongs to one clearly defined group and the other member of the pair belongs to a different clearly defined group: cases as opposed to controls in epidemiological studies, husbands as opposed to wives, and so forth. In other words, one member of each pair is drawn from one stratum, while the other is drawn from another stratum, thus linking this model to the case of stratified sampling described in Chapter 11. If the concern is with the explanation of *how much* of a (quantitative) difference there is between, for example, treatment and control cases or husbands and wives in a matched pair, the common approach is to calculate the differences $\Delta Y = (Y_p - Y_q)$, $\Delta X_1 = (X_{1p} - X_{1q})$, ..., $\Delta X_K = (X_{Kp} - X_{Kq})$, and $\Delta \alpha = (\alpha_p - \alpha_q)$, where the subscript p refers to one group and the subscript q refers to the other group, and Δ indicates that we are taking the difference between the two members of each matched pair. We can then model $\Delta Y = \Delta \alpha + \beta_1 \Delta X_1 + \beta_2 \Delta X_2 + \cdots + \beta_K \Delta X_K$ using ordinary least squares (OLS) multiple regression or related models, where the intercept $\Delta \alpha$ may be 0 and thus drop out of the equation if, as is often (but not always) assumed, it is the same for all cases regardless of stratum. If the concern is with the explanation of *whether* there is a (qualitative) difference between the two members of a matched pair, the dependent variable ΔY can be coded 0 for no difference, 1 for a difference, and the model becomes the familiar logistic regression model with logit$(\Delta Y) = \Delta \alpha + \beta_1 \Delta X_1 + \beta_2 \Delta X_2 + \cdots + \beta_K \Delta X_K$.

The pattern is similar for repeated observations on each case, for example, in a longitudinal design. With repeated measures, each case consists of a pair of observations for each variable $Y, X_1, X_2, \ldots, X_K$, but in longitudinal research, the observations are ordered in time, so in place of the subscripts p and q (for different individuals or different strata) we add a second subscript denoting time: $Y_1, Y_2, X_{11}, X_{12}, \ldots, X_{K1}, X_{K2}$. One approach to the analysis is to parallel the analysis of a paired sample in a cross-sectional study, as described above, by setting $\Delta Y = (Y_2 - Y_1)$, $\Delta X_1 = (X_{12} - X_{11})$, $\cdots$, $\Delta X_K = (X_{K2} - X_{K1})$, where the second subscript again refers to the time for which the variable was measured. In an *unconditional change model* (Finkel 1995) for explaining or predicting quantitative change in Y, we can once again model the relationship $\Delta Y = \Delta \alpha + \beta_1 \Delta X_1 + \beta_2 \Delta X_2 + \cdots + \beta_K \Delta X_K$; and for explaining *whether* the dependent variable changes over time, we can once again use logit$(\Delta Y) = \Delta \alpha + \beta_1 \Delta X_1 + \beta_2 \Delta X_2 + \cdots + \beta_K \Delta X_K$, in both cases bearing in mind that the change scores are very much like, but not quite identical to, the difference scores described in the previous paragraph.

As noted by Finkel (1995), Kessler and Greenberg (1981), and others, however, the unconditional change model is not the only possible model in this instance, nor is it generally considered the best model.[1] An alternative is the *unconditional change model,* in which each individual's prior score on the dependent variable is used as a control, but the strength of the relationship between the prior and the subsequent score on the dependent variable is regarded as a parameter to be estimated. If Y is a quantitative variable to begin with, the model is $Y_2 = \alpha + \beta_1 X_1 + \cdots + \beta_K X_K + \gamma Y_1$, where $(X_1, X_2, \ldots, X_K)$ are measured for an appropriate time relative to Y_2, and γ is used instead of, for example, β_{K+1}, to distinguish the coefficient for the lagged endogenous variable from the coefficients for the other predictors in the model. For a dichotomous dependent variable (e.g., whether an individual used tobacco, alcohol, or illicit drugs at Time 1 and Time 2), the conditional change model becomes logit$(Y_2) = \alpha + \beta_1 X_1 + \cdots + \beta_K X_K + \gamma Y_1$. Other alternatives might include the ΔX_K along with Y_1 as predictors of logit(Y_2), but the point is that modeling differences in Y as a function of differences in the predictors is not the only nor necessarily the preferred approach to modeling change over time, although it is probably the most common approach to modeling differences between members of different groups or strata in the analysis of paired samples.

THE SUBJECT-SPECIFIC MODEL FOR A TWO-WAVE PANEL

Staying with the unconditional change model for the moment, each case (at Time 1) serves as its own control (for Time 2), but the strength of the relationship between the scores at Time 1 and Time 2 is not considered to be a parameter we are interested in estimating. An implicit assumption in this model is that the change process is the same across individuals. In particular, it is assumed that the impact of the independent variables on the outcome, as measured by the β parameters, is the same for each case, and that each case has the same marginal probability, as measured by α. As described by Agresti (2002), this model is called the *marginal* model, because it focuses on the marginal distributions of responses for the observations, and the effects in the marginal model are termed *population-averaged* effects, because the effects are averaged over the entire population or sample, rather than being measured separately for each case. This parallels the population-averaged model for (cross-sectionally) clustered data in Chapter 11. Also, as noted above, if α is the same across cases, it drops out of the equations involving difference terms above.

An alternative assumption is that the process of change is unique for each individual and that we must somehow incorporate this uniqueness into the analysis. In this conceptualization, each of the cases on which we obtain two measurements is its own stratum, and each case consists of two observations on a single stratum. The extreme case would be one in which each parameter varied by individual, producing the model $\text{logit}(Y) = \alpha_i + \beta_{1i}X_1 + \beta_{2i}X_2 + \cdots + \beta_{Ki}X_K$, where the subscript $i = 1$, $2, \ldots, n$ refers to the specific case, and the first subscript on the β coefficients corresponds to the subscript for the $k = 1, 2, \ldots, K$ predictors $X_1, X_2, \ldots, X_K$. With only two observations per case, one cannot realistically estimate this model. A simpler model assumes that the effect parameters are constant across cases, but that the intercepts vary by subject, producing the model $\text{logit}(Y) = \alpha_i + \beta_1 X_1 + \beta_2 X_2 + \cdots + \beta_K X_K$, which differs from the marginal model only in the subscript on the intercept, indicating a different intercept for each case. According to Agresti (2002), this model may be described as a *conditional* model, "since the effect β is defined conditional on the subject.... The effect is *subject-specific*, since it is defined at the subject level" (pp. 414–415). This parallels the (cross-sectional) random intercept model from Chapter 11. Actually, Agresti was referring to a model with only one predictor, and it is only the intercept that is subject specific, hence the parallel is really, more specifically, to the random intercept model from the previous chapter. With more observations per case, it is possible to construct models in which the β parameters as well as the intercept are subject specific (random slopes and intercepts, as in Chapter 11). This model essentially differs from the marginal model by allowing each case to have its own probability distribution, as represented by α_i. In this model, if the α coefficients are large relative to the β coefficients, the (shared) α_i within each case may determine the outcome, resulting in the same value of Y for both time periods or both matched subjects. Alternatively, if α_i is small relative to the β parameters, it is possible to have different outcomes at the two time periods or for the two matched subjects. In this sense, the outcome for one of the paired observations is not necessarily independent of the outcome of the other, and this dependence needs to be taken into account unless all of the α_i are equal.

The large number of parameters α_i is problematic for fitting the model using maximum likelihood, whose fit depends on the number of cases being large relative to the number of parameters. In the marginal model, the number of cases can increase indefinitely while the number of parameters remains small, thus resulting in the large sample properties that make maximum likelihood estimation advantageous. When, instead, with the addition of every new case a new parameter is added to the model as well, the maximum likelihood estimates will be inconsistent (Andersen 1970; Chamberlain 1980; Neyman and Scott 1948). This problem, sometimes called the *incidental parameters problem* (Allison 2005; Kalbfleisch and Sprott 1970) can be resolved if the α_i are treated as "nuisance parameters" in which we have no direct interest. This is done in *conditional logistic regression*. Instead of using a likelihood function that explicitly includes the α_i, conditional logistic regression "conditions" the likelihood function on *sufficient statistics* for the α_i.

A sufficient statistic summarizes the information about a particular population parameter (such as the α_i) such that if some function of the outcome Y depends on the distribution of the parameter, the sufficient statistic incorporates sufficient information about that parameter that the conditional distribution of the sample depends on the sufficient statistic and not, in addition to the sufficient statistic, the parameter itself. In conditional logistic regression, the sufficient statistics for the α_i are their pairwise totals of "successes." If we set $Y_{i1} = 0$ for "failure" and $Y_{i1} = 1$ for "success" at Time 1 (or for the first of two individuals in a matched pair) for case i, and $Y_{i2} = 0$ for "failure" and $Y_{i2} = 1$ for "success" at Time 2 (or for the second of two individuals in a matched pair) for the same case i, then the sum $S_i = Y_{i1} + Y_{i2}$ is the pairwise total of successes for Y_i. Again, focusing on the unconditional change model for repeated effects in a two-wave panel, when the observations are identical on Y, the sufficient statistic S_i is equal to either 2 (both successes) or 0 (both failures); when $S_i = 1$, the outcomes differ. As described by Agresti (2002:416), the distribution of (Y_{i1}, Y_{i2}) depends on β only when the outcomes differ for the two responses, and the conditional distribution is equal to $[\exp(\beta_1 X_1 + \beta_2 X_2 + \cdots + \beta_K X_K)]/[1 + \exp(\beta_1 X_1 + \beta_2 X_2 + \cdots + \beta_K X_K)]$ when $Y_{i1} = 0$ and $Y_{i2} = 1$, and equal to $1/[1+\exp(\beta_1 X_1 + \beta_2 X_2 + \cdots + \beta_K X_K)]$ when $Y_{i1} = 1$ and $Y_{i2} = 0$, where "$\exp(Y)$" represents the exponential function e^Y. Conditioning on sufficient statistics is also used in some estimation procedures for multilevel analysis (Hox 2002; Raudenbush and Bryk 2002).

CASE-CONTROL STUDIES

The terminology of case-control studies stems from its roots in epidemiology, a "case" being someone with a disease (a "case" in the medical sense, not in the sense of being the individual or other unit being studied) and a "control" being someone without the disease, presumably someone more or less similar to the "case" in terms of characteristics other than exposure to one or more risk factors for the disease, such as age and gender (Cramer 2003:99). The use of the word *cases* to designate all units on which observations are made becomes confusing in this context, so here it is replaced by the term *subjects*. In a *prospective* case-control study, the sample is drawn, cases and controls are identified, and one can use logistic regression to see which variables predict or explain which subjects are cases or controls. In a *retrospective* case-control study (Breslow 1996), sampling is done based on the outcome variable.[2] Case-control studies are one, but not the only, type of a retrospective study. The study is called a *retrospective* study, because the value of the dependent variable is known for each subject before the sample is drawn, and predictors are measured retrospectively for a period preferably prior to (but possibly at the same time as) the time at which the sample was drawn.

As noted by Cramer (2003:97), in state-dependent sampling (sampling based on the outcome) in general, and in case-control studies more specifically, the justification for sampling based on the outcome is particularly strong when the outcome is rare, and a prospective sample, unless very large, is unlikely to include a sufficient number of "cases" for analysis, a point echoed by Breslow (1996). More broadly, subjects with a particular characteristic (the cases) are first identified and all of the cases or a sample of cases is selected; then a set of comparison subjects without the disease (the controls) is identified and a sample of controls is selected; and then the cases are contrasted with the controls with respect to a set of predictors to see what might account for whether a given individual does or does not get the disease or has the characteristic in question. In an *unmatched* case-control study, the controls are simply sampled on the dependent variable, not specifically matched to particular cases, and may thus be regarded as having been sampled independently of the cases. In a *matched* case-control study, however, individuals are matched on at least some characteristics thought to be risk or protective factors for the disease or characteristic, and controls are selected to be the same on the matching variables as the cases. The variables actually entered into the analysis are, in epidemiology, typically one or more measures of exposure to the disease; the matching variables may be risk factors other than exposure.

THE 1:1 AND *N:M* RETROSPECTIVE MATCHED CASE-CONTROL STUDIES

In a *one-to-one* or *1:1 matched case-control study*, a single control is selected for each case. The outcome variable is once again Y, typically coded 0 if the disease or other condition is absent and 1 if the disease or other condition is present, and the predictors are again $X_1, X_2, \ldots, X_K$. The predictors $X_1, X_2, \ldots, X_K$ typically represent variables other than the variables on which the cases and controls were matched but which are regarded as potential influences on whether a given individual does or does not become ill or have the condition in question. The matching introduces a dependence between observations similar to the dependence noted above for repeated observations, and once again, some adjustment for this dependence in observations must be made.

One major difference between a 1:1 matched case-control study and other types of analysis considered so far, however, is that the dependent variable, ΔY, is actually a constant. If we assign Y_p for the case and Y_q for the control, then $Y_p - Y_q = 1$ for all pairs of subjects because, by definition, the case has the disease ($Y_p = 1$) and the control does not ($Y_q = 0$) for all case-control pairs. What we are really trying to do here is predict (or "retrodict") the X (predictor) variables from the Y (outcome) variable. In other words, given that a case has a certain set of values on $X_1, X_2, \ldots, X_K$, and a control has a set of values on those same predictors, what does this tell us about the relationship between the predictors and Y, even though it is actually Y that is fixed and the variation in $X_1, X_2, \ldots, X_K$ depends on the fixed values of Y? Because the odds ratios (and hence the coefficients) are the same regardless of whether sampling is done on the predictors or on the dependent variable (Prentice and Pyke 1979), it is possible to write the model in the form $\text{logit}(\Delta Y) = \Delta \alpha_i + \beta_1 \Delta X_{1i} + \beta_2 \Delta X_{2i} + \cdots + \beta_K \Delta X_{Ki}$. As was the case for the two-wave repeated measures unit-specific unconditional change model, the α_i can be conditioned out of the likelihood function by using sufficient statistics. The intercepts then drop out of this model leaving us with $\text{logit}(\Delta Y) = \beta_1 \Delta X_{1i} + \beta_2 \Delta X_{2i} + \cdots + \beta_K \Delta X_{Ki}$. With a little manipulation, this equation can be analyzed with a standard[3] logistic regression or logit model; alternatively, there are routines specifically for conditional logistic regression models.

The basic idea of the retrospective case-control study can readily be extended to the situation in which there may be more than one case, more than one control, or both. In its most general form, the *N:M* case-control study, there are N cases and M controls, with N and M possibly varying within strata (i.e., N and/or M may be different for one set of matched subjects than for another). In this instance, the dependent variable is no longer a constant, but remains fixed within each stratum. As described by Breslow (1996), there are known limitations to retrospective case-control methodology. The limitations include selection bias, possibly caused by high rates of nonparticipation; measurement bias, including differential error in recall among cases and controls; and the possibility that the observed relationships may be the result of unobserved variables rather than the variables included in the model.

THE DISCRETE CHOICE MODEL

In discrete choice models, the question is why a particular choice or selection is made from a particular set of options or alternatives, which may be different for different individuals. The dependent variables are binary choices, either yes or no for a particular option, with only one of the two or more options being coded "yes" and the rest being coded "no". Any one of the yes/no coded outcomes is obviously not independent of the other outcomes, since the same individual is making the choice among the possible options. In structure, the discrete choice model parallels a 1:M case-control study, with the one option that is selected paralleling the one case, and the M options that are not selected paralleling the M controls. Explanatory variables may include characteristics of the choices themselves, characteristics of the individuals or other units making the choice, and interaction terms between the choices and the cases. With multiple choices for each case, each individual becomes the stratum or cluster within which the outcome is observed, and the separate observations (at least two, for a choice between two options; usually, more in the typical discrete choice problem in psychology or economics) are not independent but are clustered within the individual. Once again, this interdependence of observations requires some adjustment to the standard dichotomous or polytomous logistic regression model in order to obtain unbiased estimates of the coefficients for the explanatory variables for each of the possible outcomes.

The basic equation for the discrete choice model is $\text{logit}(Y) = \beta_1 X_1 + \cdots + \beta_K X_K + \gamma_1 Z_1 + \cdots + \gamma_H Z_H$, where the log odds of Y are taken with respect to a reference category (one of the two or more possible choices); the X variables represent characteristics of the individual making the choice; and the Z variables represent characteristics of the choices. In one of the most frequently repeated examples, choice of mode of transportation (e.g., Cramer 2003, chap. 8; Powers and Xie 2008, chap. 8), cost, speed, and convenience may be characteristics of the choices (the Z variables) between personal automobiles as opposed to buses or trains, while income may be a characteristic of the chooser (an X variable). Underlying this model is the assumption of the *independence of irrelevant alternatives,* commonly abbreviated IIA. According to this assumption, the odds of making one choice as opposed to another is unaffected by the introduction or removal of other independent alternative choices, but instead depends only on the characteristics of the two choices in question. In the example offered by Powers and Xie (2008), for instance, the choice is among (a) red bus, (b) blue bus, (c) automobile, and (d) train for transportation. If commuters are indifferent to the color of bus they ride, and initially they have equal preferences (25% for each) among the four possible modes of transportation, the odds ratio of red bus to train is the ratio .25/.25 = 1, but the ratio of (red plus blue) bus to train is .50/.25 = 2. If, however, we eliminate the blue bus (and assume that the red bus picks up the routes previously serviced by the blue bus), and we continue to assume indifference to the color of the bus, then the commuters formerly choosing the blue bus should shift to the red bus, resulting in a (changed) ratio of red bus to train which becomes .50/.25 = 2, violating the assumption that the odds of using one as opposed to another mode of transportation is unaffected by the availability or unavailability of any other option. According to the IIA assumption, former blue bus riders should distribute themselves equally among the other choices, resulting in a 1/3 probability of using each of the three remaining modes of transportation.

In some respects, this example seems flawed, and one can question the details of the example: Does bus availability decrease as a result of the elimination of the blue bus (which might result in the equal distribution of blue bus riders among the other modes of transportation), or does the red bus take over all of the old blue bus routes (in which case we have really not eliminated the blue bus category but instead combined it with the red bus category)? Details aside, however, the example does make the valid point that one needs to examine whether the alternatives are truly mutually independent or whether one is a logical substitute for the other when neither is really a logical substitute for other alternatives. Hausman and McFadden (1984; see also Hardin and Hilbe 2001:175–177; Powers and Xie 2008:262–263) proposed a test of the IIA assumption in which two models are calculated, the first a full or unrestricted model and the second a restricted model in which one or more choices are eliminated. The test statistic $q = [b_u - b_r][\mathbf{V}_r - \mathbf{V}_u]^{-1}[b_u - b_r]$, where b_u is the estimated parameter for the unrestricted model, b_r is the parameter estimate for the restricted model, $\mathbf{V}_u$ is the variance-covariance matrix for the unrestricted model, and $\mathbf{V}_r$ is the variance-covariance matrix for the restricted model. The statistic q has a χ^2 distribution under the null hypothesis $b_u = b_r$. Powers and Xie (2008:264–266) describe several alternatives available when the IIA assumption proves untenable (as indicated by a statistically significant q statistic), including the multinomial probit model, the use of a generalized extreme-value distribution, and an approach based on simulating underlying utilities.

ESTIMATION OF THE CONDITIONAL LOGISTIC REGRESSION MODEL

Although the repeated measures within-subject model, the 1:1 and higher-order case-control studies, and the discrete choice model are conceptually different, estimation for all of them involves the same conditional logistic regression estimation procedure, described briefly here.[4] Let $i = 1, 2, \ldots, n$ denote the strata. Within each stratum, let $t = 1, 2, \ldots, T_i$ denote the observations within the ith stratum (and the subscript i will generally be dropped from T_i for convenience when T_i is used as a subscript or superscript). Let the dependent variable Y take on observed values $y_{i1}, y_{i2}, \ldots, y_{iT}$, where each y_{it} is equal to either zero or one, for the T subjects within each stratum. Let there be K predictors, $X_1, X_2, \ldots, X_K$ (here including the Z variables in the discrete choice model). Let h_{1i} be the number of cases for which $y_{it} = 1$, or equivalently the sum (over t) of the observed values $\sum_t y_{it}$. In the most general case, the number of cases for which $y_{it} = 1$ is h_{1i} and the number of cases for which $y_{it} = 0$ is $h_{2i} = T_i - h_{1i}$ within each stratum. Let $\mathbf{x}_{it}$ represent the vector of values of the predictors X_1, $X_2, \ldots, X_K$, let $\boldsymbol{\beta}$ represent the vector of K coefficients for the predictors, and let $\exp(Y)$ represent the exponential function e^Y. Let S_i be the set of all possible combinations of h_{1i} ones and h_{2i} zeros in stratum i, and let d_i be an element of S_i. The individual components of each (vector) element of S_i are designated d_{it} and correspond to the possible values for each corresponding y_{it} for different possible vectors $\mathbf{y}_i$.

Given these definitions, the probability of a possible set of values for Y, the vector $\mathbf{y}_i = \{y_{i1}, y_{i2}, \ldots, y_{iT}\}$, is equal to $P[\mathbf{y}_i | \Sigma_t y_{it} = h_{it}] = \exp(\Sigma_t y_{it} \mathbf{x}_{it} \boldsymbol{\beta}) / [\Sigma_{d_i \in S_i} \exp(\Sigma_t d_{it} \mathbf{x}_{it} \boldsymbol{\beta})]$. That is, the probability of a particular set of *observed* values for Y for a particular stratum is equal to the exponentiated sum (over all cases in the stratum) of the products involving the *observed* values of Y, the observed values of the predictors, and the coefficients of the predictors, divided by the exponentiated sum (over all possible combinations of values for Y in the stratum) of products of the *possible* values of Y (d_{it}), the observed values of the predictors, and the coefficients of the predictors. The corresponding conditional log likelihood is $L = \Sigma_i \Sigma_t y_{it} \mathbf{x}_{it} \boldsymbol{\beta} - \ln[\Sigma_{d_i \in S_i} \exp(\Sigma_t d_{it} \mathbf{x}_{it} \boldsymbol{\beta})]$. When T_i is fixed, the maximum likelihood estimates for α_i and the β parameters are inconsistent; this difficulty can be circumvented by considering the probability of $\mathbf{y}_i$ conditional on $\Sigma_t y_{it}$. This conditional probability does not involve the α_i, so the α_i are not estimated when the conditional likelihood is used. The conditional likelihood is maximized using essentially the same techniques (described in Appendix A) as are used in estimating the standard logistic regression (SLR) models in Chapters 1 to 9.

A major difference between the case-control study and other types of analysis discussed so far is that in a matched case-control study using conditional logistic regression, it is possible to estimate unstandardized logistic regression coefficients and odds ratios associated with the predictors, and the coefficients should be the same (if the assumptions underlying the case-control study are met)[5] as if they had been estimated prospectively; but except in special circumstances (specifically when the sampling fraction is known) it is not possible to use those coefficients to estimate the log odds, odds, or probabilities (of being a case as opposed to being a control) for individual subjects. As noted above, the intercepts typically drop out of the analysis; and even when an intercept is reported, it is not the usual logistic regression intercept but a parameter of no real interest (Kleinbaum and Klein, 2002:15). The intercept here is a nuisance parameter, for which only sufficient statistics are calculated, and on which estimates of the logistic regression coefficients and their associated odds ratios are based. For this reason, one cannot generally construct prediction tables (since we have no predicted values for individual subjects) for the analysis of case-control data, and we can therefore not calculate any of the indices of predictive efficiency. Likewise, one cannot calculate the correlation between observed and predicted values (R_O), since, again, there are no predicted values; and consequently one cannot calculate fully standardized logistic regression coefficients, because that calculation requires R_O. One can, however, calculate partially standardized coefficients (by standardizing only the predictors) to examine the relative effects of the predictors.

AN UNMATCHED CASE-CONTROL STUDY

As noted above, in an unmatched case-control study, the controls are simply sampled on the dependent variable, not specifically matched to particular cases, and may thus be regarded as having been sampled independently of the cases. Because there is no assignment of cases and controls to different strata, and no matching of cases and controls, there is no basis for calculating difference scores or sufficient statistics for the a_i. The unmatched case-control study can thus take the same form as the SLR model (Prentice and Pyke 1979). To illustrate this, an SLR model was calculated with gun ownership as the dependent variable and gender, ethnicity, income, and education as predictors, using data from the National Opinion Research Center (NORC) GSS data. Individuals were asked whether there was a gun in the household, and if so, whether they personally owned a gun. Taking all of the "no" answers to the first question as indicating nonownership, a variable was constructed indicating whether each individual did or did not own a gun. The results of this model are presented in Table 12.1. The model χ^2 is statistically significant ($p = .000$), $R_L^2 = .15$, and $R_O^2 = .16$. Table 12.1 suggests that gun ownership is more likely among individuals who are male, ethnic majority, with less education and higher incomes. These findings would be consistent with the suggestion that gun owners are disproportionately lower-educated White males but not that they are economically disadvantaged. Both fully standardized coefficients (b^*) and partially standardized coefficients (b_A^*) are included in Table 12.1, the latter to facilitate comparison with results in subsequent tables. The standardized coefficients indicate that the strongest effects on gun ownership are, in descending order, (a) gender, (b) ethnicity, particularly "other" ethnicity, (c) income, and finally (d) education.

From the perspective of a case-control study on the epidemiology of gun ownership, the suggestion would be that the results presented in Table 12.1 fail to adequately capture the dependencies in the data. The model in Table 12.1 assumes that cases are independent; however, an alternative is to assume that they are nonindependent, stratified by age, gender, and ethnicity, and to model the differences between cases and controls matched on these stratification variables using conditional logistic regression.

TABLE 12.1 Standard Logistic Regression Model for Gun Ownership					
Dependent Variable: Gun Ownership	*Independent Variable*	b^*	b_A^*	b	*Statistical Significance of b*
$R_O^2 = .16$	Gender (male)	.308	.855	1.721	.000
$R_L^2 = .15$	Ethnicity (vs. White)				
$G_M = 292.91, df = 5,$	African American	−.094	−.260	−0.736	.001
$p = .000$	Other	−.166	−.462	−2.004	.000
$N = 1,773$	Education	−.047	−.131	−0.047	.047
	Income	.129	.357	0.070	.000
	Constant	—	—	−4.226	.000

A 1:1 MATCHED CASE-CONTROL MODEL

For purposes of illustrating the 1:1 matched case-control model, we again consider gun ownership in the NORC GSS data. For this analysis, individuals were cross-classified by gender (the variable SEX in the NORC GSS), ethnicity (RACE), and age (AGE), forming a large number of groups or strata within which gun ownership varies. Purely for illustrative purposes, a single case (gun owner) and control (nonowner) was selected from each stratum in which there were at least one of each, an owner and a nonowner. This parallels the process in which cases are selected and then matched with appropriate controls in epidemiological studies. Maintaining continuity with the previous example, income and education are again used as predictors. The result, after eliminating missing cases, was a set of 260 matched pairs, of which 252 had complete data on all of the variables in the analysis.

The data were then analyzed using the conditional logistic regression model. Although this example is artificial, it illustrates the method for analyzing 1:1 matched case-control data.

In logistic regression programs not specifically designed for conditional logistic regression, but which can estimate the logistic regression model excluding the intercept, in order to calculate the 1:1 matched case-control model, it is first necessary to assign an identification number to each of the matched pairs. Next, a data file is constructed by (1) saving all cases (i.e., subjects for which the condition is present) using one set of variable names and including all variables to be used in the analysis; (2) saving all controls (i.e., subjects for which the condition is not present) using a second set of variable names and again including all variables to be used in the analysis; (3) merging the two files by adding variables (not adding cases), resulting in a file with two observations for each pair, a case and a control, distinguished by different variable names; and (4) performing subtraction in which the second (control) variable value is subtracted from the first (case) value for the variables to be used in the analysis. In the instance of gun ownership as predicted by education and income, (a) the variable ROWNGUN1 contains the value of the dependent variable, ROWNGUN, for the case, while the second variable ROWNGUN2 contains the value of ROWNGUN, for the control, and their difference, ROWNGUND = ROWNGUN1 − ROWNGUN2, is a constant, equal to one for each pair, and is the dependent variable used in the analysis; (b) EDUC1 is the variable containing the value of EDUCNEW (education) for the case, EDUC2 is the variable containing the value of EDUCNEW for the control, and the difference, EDUCDIFF = EDUC1 − EDUC2 is the predictor used in the analysis; and (c) INC1 is the variable containing the value of INCNEW98 (income) for the case, INC2 is the variable containing the value of INCNEW98 for the control, and the difference, INCDIFF = INC1 − INC2 is the predictor used in the analysis. A new file can then be saved with only the difference variables ROWNGUND, EDUCDIFF, and INCDIFF, along with any of the control variables (e.g., either SEX1 or SEX2, which are both equal; either RACE1 or RACE2, which are also equal [because the subjects have been stratified by gender, ethnicity, and age]; and either AGE1 or AGE2, which are likewise equal) that one wants to use in interaction terms with the other predictors. Using the variables in this file, the conditional logistic regression model for the 1:1 matched case-control study can be run, excluding the intercept from the model. Alternatively, all of this can be avoided by using software specifically designed for conditional logistic regression.

Because gender (SEX) and ethnicity (RACE), along with age (AGE), are included as stratification variables, they are not explicitly included in the 1:1 matched case-control model. Instead, the model calculates the impact of education and income on gun ownership *controlling for gender, ethnicity, and age,* the variables used to construct the strata in the model. As indicated in Table 12.2, only income is a statistically significant predictor of gun ownership ($p = .003$ vs. $p = .381$ for education); and explanatory power is weak with $R_L^2 = .06$. Note, however, that one reason for the lower apparent levels of explained variation in Table 12.2 as opposed to Table 12.1 is that gender and ethnicity, which are controlled but not included as predictors in the 1:1 matched case-control model, are included as predictors in the SLR model in Table 12.1, and both are statistically significant as predictors, with males more likely than females, and both African American and Other ethnic group members less likely than White majority group members, to own guns. The standardized coefficients in Table 12.2 are the partially standardized coefficients based on standardizing only the predictors, and indicate that the (statistically significant) effect of income is stronger than the (statistically nonsignificant) effect of education.[6] Note also that the partially standardized coefficients b_A^* for education and income in Table 12.2 for the 1:1 matched case-control model are similar

				Wald χ^2		
Predictor	b_A^*	b	SE(b)	(df = 1)	p	Odds Ratio
Education	−.136	−.048	.054	0.767	.381	0.954
Income	.517	.102	.035	8.606	.003	1.107

TABLE 12.2 A 1:1 Matched Case-Control Conditional Logistic Regression

Dependent Variable: Gun Ownership

NOTE: $N = 226$, $G_M = 10.107$, $df = 2$, $p = .006$, $R_L^2 = .06$.

Pearson $\chi^2 = 66.795$, $df = 101$, $p = .997$, deviance $\chi^2 = 160.407$, $df = 101$, $p = .000$.

to the b_A^* coefficients in Table 12.1, and the corresponding unstandardized coefficients are statistically significant in Table 12.1. Also in Table 12.2, the Pearson and deviance χ^2 goodness-of-fit statistics are presented. The Pearson χ^2 is not statistically significant ($p = .997$), but the deviance statistic is highly significant ($p = .000$). This discrepancy suggests (see Chapter 3) that the assumptions underlying the use of the goodness-of-fit statistics are violated and that they cannot properly be used to assess goodness of fit in the present model.

AN *N:M* MATCHED CASE-CONTROL MODEL

As noted in the description of the 1:1 matched case-control model for gun ownership, there were a number of gender-ethnicity-age combinations for which there existed two or more of either or both gun owners and nonowners. By selecting a single case and a single control from each gender-ethnicity-age stratum, it was possible to illustrate the 1:1 matched case-control model, but in doing so, information was discarded and statistical power was lost by excluding eligible cases and controls from the analysis. In an *N:M* matched case-control model, it is possible to include all cases and controls for each stratum having at least one case and one control, and the dependent variable is not necessarily a constant across strata, as it is in the 1:1 retrospective matched case-control study. Going back to the original GSS data set and including all of the eligible cases and controls produces the results illustrated in Table 12.3. Once again, the groups are defined by the three-way classification on gender, ethnicity, and age. Multiple positive outcomes within groups are encountered (i.e., more than one case, as opposed to control, per group), and 172 groups containing 544 observations (subjects) were dropped because the dependent variable did not vary within these groups.

Several differences are immediately apparent between the 1:1 and *N:M* case-control models. First, with the increased statistical power afforded by the additional cases and controls, not only the coefficient for income but also the coefficient for education is now statistically significant ($p = .026$), indicating that higher levels of education are statistically significantly associated with lower odds of gun ownership. This is true even though the coefficients for education in the 1:1 and *N:M* case-control models are very similar. Second, the coefficient for income in the *N:M* model is only

TABLE 12.3 N:M Matched Case-Control Conditional Logistic Regression

Dependent Variable: Gun Ownership

Predictor	b_A^*	b	SE(b)	Wald χ^2 (df = 1)	p	Odds Ratio
Education	−.788	−.059	.026	4.93	.026	0.943
Income	1.025	.067	.017	14.75	.000	1.069

NOTE: $N = 1{,}225$, $G_M = 16.45$, $df = 2$, $p = .000$, $R_L^2 = .02$.

about half as large as the same coefficient in the 1:1 model. In addition to these two changes, note that R_L^2 has decreased from .06 in the 1:1 model to .02 ($p = .002$ based on the model χ^2 in Table 12.2) in the N:M model. The (partially) standardized coefficients are substantially larger than the coefficients in Table 12.2, but still indicate that income has a stronger effect on gun ownership than education.[7] To the extent that we can treat the proliferation of firearms as a "disease" (a risk factor for mortality), neither (increased) education nor (reduced) income appears to offer promise as an "intervention" to limit its spread (and gender, ethnicity, and age are not variables which can be manipulated in an intervention). If, however, the goal is to understand the prevalence of gun ownership in the population, the SLR model including gender, ethnicity, and age (rather than stratifying on those variables) appears to offer a reasonable level of explanatory power.

A DISCRETE CHOICE MODEL

The discrete choice model is primarily of interest in marketing research or economic research on consumer preferences and behavior. As noted previously, a common example of the discrete choice model is the choice among different modes of transportation. Another example that has been used is the choice to purchase one of several different types of automobiles. In the choice model, data are arranged so each line includes (a) an identification number; (b) one of the two or more (usually three or more) choices coded as 0 if not chosen or one if chosen; (c) one or more characteristics of that choice, such as availability, convenience, or cost, where the characteristic in question may vary from one case or subject (the "chooser") to another; and (d) one or more characteristics of the "chooser," such as income, education, or other sociodemographic characteristics. In the example of consumer choices of automobiles, the choices in this example are American, Japanese, and European cars; the characteristic of the choices is a measure of availability, the number of dealers for each type of car near the respondent; and the respondent characteristics are income (INCOME) and gender (SEX). The questions are whether respondents are more likely to choose European or Japanese rather than American cars; whether the choice is affected by gender and income; and whether availability (DEALER) has an impact on the choice. The results of the conditional logistic regression analysis for consumer choice of automobiles, based on analysis of the Stata (Version 8) "Choice" data set,[8] are presented in Table 12.4.

TABLE 12.4 Discrete Choice Conditional Logistic Regression

Dependent Variable: Automobile Purchase

Predictor	b^*	b	SE(b)	Wald χ^2 (df = 1)	p	Odds Ratio
Japan	−.355	−1.352	.691	3.84	.050	0.259
Europe	−.618	−2.355	.853	7.62	.006	0.095
GenJap	−.128	−0.535	.314	2.89	.089	0.586
GenEur	.136	0.570	.454	1.59	.209	1.769
IncJap	.414	0.033	.013	6.45	.011	1.033
IncEur	.376	0.032	.014	5.34	.021	1.033
Dealer	.271	0.068	.034	3.92	.048	1.070

NOTE: $N = 885$, $G_M = 146.62$, $df = 7$, $p = .000$, $R_L^2 = .23$.

For details on the programming aspects of this example, see Stata (2003, Reference A–F, pp. 181–183). As indicated in that presentation, explanation of the choice among automobiles with different (American, Japanese, or European) manufacturers is moderately well explained, with $R_L^2 = .23$, the interaction between gender and European manufacture is not statistically significant ($p = .209$), and the interaction between gender and Japanese manufacture is marginally significant ($p = .089$) as a predictor of choice among different types of cars. Going beyond the presentation in the Stata manual, consider the standardized coefficients (these are fully standardized logistic regression coefficients as described in Chapter 5), which indicate the strength of the relationship of each predictor to the dependent variable. The three strongest predictors of the type of car selected are European manufacture ($b^* = −.618$), the interaction between Japanese manufacture and income ($b^* = .414$), and the interaction between European manufacture and income ($b^* = .376$), all consistent with the rank ordering of these predictors on statistical significance. The consistency of the rank ordering of statistical significance and magnitude of standardized coefficients breaks down at this point, however, as the next strongest predictor is Japanese manufacture ($b^* = −.355$), followed by accessibility (dealer; $b^* = .271$), the latter of which is a weaker but slightly more statistically significant predictor than the former; then the interaction between European manufacture and gender, which is not statistically significant ($b^* = .136$, $p = .209$), followed by the interaction between Japanese manufacture and gender, which is marginally statistically significant ($b^* = −.128$, $p = .089$). Substantively, the results indicate a general tendency to prefer American to foreign cars (the negative coefficients for JAPAN and EUROPE), for men not to choose Japanese cars (the negative coefficient for GENJAP), for individuals with higher incomes to purchase foreign cars (the positive coefficients for INCJAP and INCEUR), and for accessibility (DEALER) to have a modest effect on car choice, less than foreign versus domestic manufacture or the interaction between income and foreign versus domestic manufacture, but stronger than the interaction between gender and foreign versus domestic manufacture.

CONCLUSION

In this chapter, three models involving nonindependence in the data were considered: (1) the unit-specific longitudinal two-wave panel model, (2) the retrospective case-control study, with a focus on the 1:1 and N:M matched retrospective case-control studies, and (3) the discrete choice model. Substantively, these models focus on different problems. The unit-specific two-wave panel model is one of many models that may be used in longitudinal or repeated measures analysis across a wide range of disciplines, and it will be considered in that broader context in the next chapter. The retrospective case-control study is of interest primarily in epidemiological research, while the discrete choice model is of interest primarily in economics, marketing research, and psychology. What brings these three disparate models together in the same chapter is the method of estimation, conditional logistic regression, common to all three models. This chapter also marks a transition from consideration of primarily cross-sectional (either purely cross-sectional or at best time-ordered cross-sectional; see Menard 2002b) models, like the retrospective case-control and discrete choice models, to primarily longitudinal models such as the unit-specific two-wave panel model, and correspondingly from a focus on differences between subjects to a focus on change within subjects.

Of the three conditional logistic regression models presented here, the discrete choice model is perhaps the least frequently used in practice across the various scientific disciplines, and the results presented here from this model raise the fewest questions about the adequacy of the model for its intended purpose. Issues regarding the use of the unit-specific two-wave panel model have been foreshadowed here, but a fuller discussion is postponed to the next chapter. The retrospective matched case-control study has received the bulk of the attention in this chapter, and the issues raised with respect to the use of this model are several and serious. In real-world applications, with *prospective* data on cases and controls in which subjects are selected *before* they have been identified as either cases or controls, conditional logistic regression, with its restrictions on the inclusion of variables that may be constant across strata, would not be employed. One would instead rely on the more extensive information provided by SLR in the analysis of the prospective data. It is only when prospective data are not available, when the cases and controls are necessarily known prior to sampling (and subjects are stratified and sampled on the dependent variable, i.e., separate samples are taken of cases and controls) that the use of conditional logistic regression for retrospective case-control data may seem warranted.

In contrast to prospective sampling approaches in which cases are selected prior to knowledge of the outcome (and hence irrespective of the outcome), retrospective matched case-control studies involve "prediction" (or "retrodiction") of predictors from the outcomes using conditional logistic regression to estimate the parameters of the model. Here, we have had the advantage of being able to use a prospective sample but to treat it as if we had a set of cases and controls from which we wanted to draw a 1:1 or N:M matched sample. This "as if" exercise has allowed us to examine more closely the differences between prospective and retrospective sampling with respect to the dependent variable and to identify some potential problems with the analysis of retrospective matched case-control studies, including (a) exclusion of subjects, (b) exclusion of variables, and (c) inconsistency of results across models that should produce similar results for the variables included in the model.

(a) First, the number of cases for the SLR model was $N = 1,773$, utilizing all of the cases with nonmissing data on the variables in the model; for the N:M matched retrospective case-control model, $N = 1,225$, lower than 1,773 because for some strata (age-gender-ethnicity combinations) there were no differences among subjects in gun ownership, and so those strata (and the subjects in them) were dropped from the analysis; and for the 1:1 retrospective case-control analysis, $N = 226$, reflecting the existence of 123 strata with at least one case (gun owner) and one control (nonowner).

(b) Second, variables used to define the strata (in this case, age, gender, and ethnicity) are constant within each stratum, and hence cannot be used as predictors of the dependent variable, even if they otherwise appear to be strongly related to the dependent variable. This is a general problem with the use of conditional logistic regression for the analysis of retrospective matched (but not unmatched) case-control studies. In this particular example, two of the stratification variables (age was not analyzed as a predictor here), gender and ethnicity, appeared in the SLR analysis to have *stronger* effects on gun ownership than either education or income.

(c) Third, if the strata on which the cases and controls could be matched were representative of the larger sample (and by implication of the population from which the sample was drawn) then the results should be fairly similar across the 1:1, N:M, and SLR models, even in the presence of adjustment for nonindependence in the data. Contrary to this expectation, however, the three models produced very different results with regard to the summary statistics for the model (R^2_L) and the statistical significance of the coefficients for the individual predictors. In part, the differences in statistical significance may reflect the aforementioned differences in sample sizes for the different models. One might suspect that the magnitude of the coefficients might reflect exclusion of cases with the highest and lowest values of one or both of the predictors, education and income, but neither the standardized nor the unstandardized coefficients appear to reflect a systematic pattern in this respect. The unstandardized coefficient for income in the SLR model is about midway between the 1:1 and N:M models, and the unstandardized coefficient for education is nearly the same in the SLR and 1:1 models. The large differences in explained variation appear to reflect the exclusion of gender and ethnicity as predictors from the 1:1 and N:M models.

It may be that in some circumstances, analysis of the retrospective matched case-control model using conditional logistic regression is the best we can do. The results presented here do not inspire confidence in this approach. Particular attention needs to be paid to the impact of exclusion of subjects and exclusion of variables, to the extent that it is possible to do so. Exclusion of subjects that have particularly high or low values on the predictors included in the model may be affected by variables used in stratification (e.g., income could have been different in strata defined in terms of majority or minority ethnicity), which could in turn attenuate the apparent relationship of the predictor to the outcome. Variables used in stratification may themselves have statistically and substantively significant impacts on the outcome (and if not, why stratify on variables that do not matter?), and their exclusion from the analysis may attenuate the strength of the overall model, as indicated by measures of explained variation like R^2_L. The potentially severe loss of information in retrospective matched case-control studies is in principle avoidable by using prospective instead of retrospective designs; the issue here is cost, but the limitations of the retrospective matched case-control study suggest that it may be worth the cost to employ a prospective rather than a retrospective design when possible. Qualifying this is the observation that whether a prospective design is that much better than a retrospective design may depend on the substantive problem being studied. For some outcomes, the differences between retrospective and prospective case-control studies may not be as pronounced as those in the example used in this chapter. In particular, where involuntary behavior (catching a disease, exposure to an environmental risk factor) is used instead of voluntary behavior (owning a gun, education), the case-control study may provide more reasonable results. At least part of the issue is whether the advantages to matching cases and controls outweigh the loss of information from matched as opposed to unmatched case control studies, but for true epidemiological studies, the matched case-control study may be the best option.

NOTES

1. The disagreements regarding the relative merits of the conditional and unconditional change models under different conditions are extensive; for a brief review with references to the proponents of the various positions on this issue, see Menard (2002b:71–73). The issue is also addressed in Chapter 13.

2. It has long been known that sampling on the dependent variable does not affect the odds ratio, and hence the coefficient in a logit or logistic regression model, including (Prentice and Pyke 1979) logit models with one or more continuous predictors. The intercept is affected, but (a) usually the intercept is not of interest and (b) if it is, we can correct the intercept using the formula $a_{adj} = a - \ln(p_1/p_0)$, where p_1 is the proportion sampled having the value one on the dependent variable and p_0 is the proportion sampled having the value zero on the dependent variable, a is the unadjusted estimate for the intercept, and a_{adj} is the adjusted estimate for the intercept.

3. There is no set terminology for distinguishing logistic regression models estimated using conditional logistic regression from logistic regression models using the usual maximum likelihood techniques covered in Chapters 1 to 9. Possibilities include "ordinary," "standard," and "unconditional" logistic regression. The use of the terms *conditional* and *unconditional* to describe both (a) a method of estimation and (b) a type of change model is already potentially confusing. If we abbreviate "ordinary" logistic regression to OLR, there is a potential for confusing it with ordinal logistic regression. Here, the term *standard* logistic regression (or SLR) is adopted to refer to dichotomous or polytomous logistic regression (Kleinbaum and Klein 2002:279 actually use the term standard logistic regression or SLR to distinguish dichotomous from polytomous logistic regression), estimated using the usual maximum likelihood techniques, to distinguish it from conditional logistic regression or logistic regression using other estimation techniques, for example, iteratively reweighted least squares (IRLS) logistic regression.

4. The models in this chapter are described in more mathematical detail elsewhere. See, for example, Agresti (2002, chap. 10), Cramer (2003, chap. 8), and Hosmer and Lemeshow (2000, chap. 7). An alternative to the conditional logistic regression model, the truncated logistic regression model, is described by O'Neill and Barry (1995).

5. As noted by Kleinbaum and Klein (2002:12), the conditions under which the logistic regression model can be used with case-control data are mathematically complex and difficult to verify empirically but appear to be characteristic of a large number of situations that occur naturally in epidemiology. For a more detailed discussion that is beyond the scope of this book, see Breslow (1996), Breslow and Day (1980), and Prentice and Pyke (1979).

6. If we ignored the fact that predicted values of gun ownership cannot legitimately be calculated for Table 12.2 and calculated the fully standardized coefficients in the usual way, the resulting standardized coefficients for education (−.047) and income (.129) in Table 12.2 for the 1:1 matched case-control model would be similar to the coefficients in Table 12.1.

7. If we again ignored the fact that we cannot legitimately generate predicted probabilities from this model, we would find (a) that the correlation between observed and predicted probabilities was negative, $R_O = -.0437$, $.10 < p < .05$, and (b) because the correlation is negative, the standardized coefficients would be reversed in sign from the unstandardized coefficients.

8. From www.stata-press.com/data/r8/choice.dta, accessed August 2008.

Longitudinal Panel Analysis With Logistic Regression

There is an extensive and well-developed literature on panel analysis with continuous or quantitative variables, measured on an interval or ratio scale, with models for panel data that include approaches based on pooling longitudinal and cross-sectional data, fixed effects and random effects models, and structural equation modeling; see, for example, Bijleveld et al. (1998), Finkel (1995), Hardin and Hilbe (2003), Hsiao (2003), Kessler and Greenberg (1981), Maruyama (1998), Sayrs (1989), and Wooldridge (2002). Less extensively covered, but not entirely absent from this literature, is the use of panel analysis when the endogenous variables are categorical/qualitative dichotomous, nominal, or ordinal variables. Special problems arise in the use of categorical endogenous variables in panel analysis, including issues of how to measure change and how to model the within-cases dependency in multiwave panel data. Logistic regression is readily adaptable to the analysis of panel data for both dichotomous and polytomous endogenous variables. This chapter provides an applied approach to the use of logistic regression analysis to analyze categorical panel data, beginning with the issue of measuring change, then considering simple two-wave panel models, and ending with a consideration of the use of logistic regression analysis for multiwave panel data, applying techniques used in the previous two chapters to model *longitudinal* dependency in the data.

In the designs for clustered samples and for retrospective matched case-control studies discussed in the previous two chapters, the dependencies in the data are, in principle, avoidable. A retrospective matched case-control study could always, if cost were no object, be replaced by a prospective sampling design in which a sufficiently large number of subjects were followed for a sufficiently long period of time to collect sufficient information to ascertain which variables distinguished subjects who eventually experienced a condition such as a disease from subjects who did not. Again with cost no object, a complete enumeration of all cases of interest (the "universe") for a particular study could be obtained, and either simple or systematic random sampling could be used to avoid clustering of cases within the data. Longitudinal research, in contrast, involves *unavoidable* clustering of observations, not within sampling units but within cases (often but not necessarily individuals). The clustering is not a result of an avoidable weakness in the sampling design but instead results from taking repeated observations on the same case for two or more periods of time.

Although the source of the clustering is different for contextual and longitudinal analysis, some of the approaches are essentially the same as the approaches used with clustered-sample data. In this and the following chapter, we will consider several longitudinal models in some detail. In this chapter, we consider three models, beginning with (1) the *subject-specific two-wave panel model*, introduced in Chapter 12, in which change scores are both predictors and dependent variables, and estimation is done using conditional logistic regression. Next, we move to (2) the *unconditional change model,* similar in form to the unit-specific two-wave model but more general insofar as it may include a combination of change or difference scores and stable characteristics of cases as predictors. Finally, we will consider (3) the *lagged endogenous variable model*, which may or may not include change or difference scores as predictors and in which the dependent variable is modeled as a function of the prior value of the dependent variable, as well as the predictors. The focus will be on two-wave panel models, but extensions to multiwave panel models will also be considered. In the models considered in this chapter, the number of measurement periods is typically small, and time does not necessarily enter the analysis as an independent variable, although it may be used as a predictor. In the models used in the next chapter, the number of measurement periods is typically greater, and either chronological time (history), age (development), or both are practically always included as independent variables.

MODELS IN LONGITUDINAL RESEARCH[1]

Longitudinal research is defined in terms of both the data and the methods of analysis to be used in the research. It is research in which (a) data are collected for each variable for two or more distinct time periods, (b) the subjects or cases analyzed are the same or at least comparable from one period to the next, and (c) the analysis involves some comparison of the data between or among periods. At a minimum, any truly longitudinal design would permit the measurement of change in a variable from one period to another. A distinction must be made between the periods *for* which the data are collected and the periods *at* which the data are collected. In *retrospective* longitudinal research, data may be collected *for* several periods *at* a single (later) period. In *prospective* longitudinal research, data are collected *at* the periods (either at a specific point in time or at the end of a relatively short period requiring limited recall) *for* which they are being collected. Longitudinal research has two primary purposes: to describe patterns of change and to establish the direction (positive or negative, and from Y to X or from X to Y) and magnitude (a relationship of magnitude 0 indicating the absence of a relationship) of causal relationships. Logistic regression can be used in longitudinal research to analyze causal relationships or, setting aside the question of causality, to develop predictive models that can account for the relative contributions of multiple predictors. For reasons described in Menard (2002b:52–54), longitudinal data are generally superior to cross-sectional data for modeling causal relationships. Different logistic regression models are used for longitudinal analysis, depending on the nature of the data and the outcome of interest.

There are four "pure" types of causal (or equally applicable in the present context, predictive or explanatory) models: (1) Model A: $X \to Y$, the value of the dependent variable is expressed as a function of the value of the independent variable; (2) Model B: $\Delta X \to Y$, where ΔX represents a change in X, and the value of the dependent variable is expressed as a function of the change in the independent variable; (3) Model C: $X \to \Delta Y$, where ΔY represents a change in Y and the change in the dependent variable is expressed as a function of the value of the independent variable; and

(4) Model D: $\Delta X \rightarrow \Delta Y$ the change in the dependent variable is expressed as a function of the change in the independent variable. Models in which the independent variables include both level and rate-of-change variables (e.g., population density and population growth rate as influences on economic development) are also possible. Model A requires only cross-sectional data (possibly time-ordered cross-sectional data; see Menard 2002b); the other three models require measurement of at least one of the variables in the model for at least two different times, and Models C and D specifically require repeated measurement of Y. In the simplest instance for longitudinal data analysis, $T = 2$ and we have a two-wave panel model, the case on which we will focus in this chapter.

In Model A, the *level* of X is predictive of the *level* of Y, or to phrase it another way, *differences* in X are predictive of *differences* in Y. Model A is not a change model at all, although it has implications for change, and is often described as though it were a change model. An example of Model A might be the relationship between income and education, with higher education being predictive of higher income. Implicitly, if Model A is correct, changes in X will also be associated with changes in Y (which implies that Model D would also be valid). In Model B, a *change* in X is associated with a *difference* in Y. For example, it is possible that the level of stress is predicted not by absolute income but by the rate of *change* in income, with rapidly increasing income being predictive of lower levels of stress and rapidly decreasing income being predictive of higher levels of stress, regardless of whether the *level* of income is high or low before or after the change. In Model C, the rate of change is influenced not by changes in X but by the level of X. For example, in an ethnically biased society or organization, initial salary *levels* could be based on the specific job or position, independent of ethnicity, but the rate of *change* in salary may depend on ethnicity. Finally, in Model D, changes in X influence or are predictive of changes in Y. For example, in Model, D, to return to the example given for Model A, an increase in education may be predictive of an increase in salary.

In all but Model A, change is explicitly included in the model. Change is typically measured with reference to one of two continua: chronological time or age. Time is measured externally in the cases or subjects being studied, while age is measured internally, relative to the subject or case under study. In one sense, age represents biological time for human subjects. The choice of time or age as the underlying continuum may be important, and for some purposes it may be useful to consider both in the same analysis. Age may be included as a predictor in the short-term models of change considered in this chapter, but in such models the age range for an individual will typically be much less than the age range for the sample as a whole. In a study of the labor force over a 5-year period, for example, the range of ages in the sample could be from 18 to 65, but the age range for any individual in the sample would only be 5 years. In contrast, in a long-term longitudinal study focusing on developmental change, the age range for a single individual may be equal (if the study includes a single birth cohort) or nearly equal (if the study includes several contiguous birth cohorts) to the age range for the sample. In the National Youth Survey (NYS) data to be used in this and the next chapter, the age range of the sample as a whole is from 11 to 33; for individuals in the youngest cohort in the NYS, it is 11 to 27; and for the oldest cohort, it is 17 to 33.

MEASURING ΔY IN LOGISTIC REGRESSION MODELS

Implicit in the notation of ΔY, in the forgoing discussion, is the assumption that we know how to measure continuity and change in the kind of variables that we will be using in logistic regression analysis. For linear regression, the options for measuring change are straightforward, involving subtraction of the earlier value of Y from the later value of Y, where Y is measured on an interval or ratio scale and possibly dividing by some other number (the initial value of Y to obtain a proportional or percentage change, or the time between the first and second measurement of Y to obtain a rate of change over time). Measuring change for qualitative variables requires more careful consideration of what types of change (or continuity) are of interest. These possibilities can be represented in a contingency table, as illustrated in Figure 13.1. Alternatively, by using the percentages for the rows or columns representing the earlier measurement of Y, we can represent the possible patterns of continuity or change in a *transition matrix* that indicates the percentage of cases in each initial category of Y that either remain in that category or switch categories. Figure 13.1 illustrates contingency tables and transition matrices for hypothetical dichotomous and polytomous variables.

Let us begin by assuming that we have a dichotomous dependent variable for which 0 = failure and 1 = success. Part A of Figure 13.1 presents a hypothetical contingency table in which we have 500 successes and 500 failures at Time 1, and 400 successes and 600 failures at Time 2. Part B of Figure 13.1 presents the corresponding transition matrix, indicating that 60% of the Time 1 successes and 20% of the Time 1 failures were successes at Time 2. Now the question arises whether we are interested in each of the four cells of Parts A and B of Figure 13.1 separately or whether we are willing to combine some of the cells, in operationalizing ΔY.

(a) We can consider each cell separately: (1) continuity of failure in the lower left cell, (2) continuity of success in the upper right cell, (3) change from success to failure in the upper left cell, and (4) change from failure to success in the lower right cell. This gives us a four-category polytomous nominal dependent variable ΔY, which can be analyzed using polytomous nominal logistic regression.

(b) We can decide that we are interested in the differences in types of changes but not in the differences in types of continuity. This can be accomplished by subtracting Y at Time 1, abbreviated Y_{t1}, from Y at Time 2, abbreviated Y_{t2}, to obtain a polytomous ordinal dependent variable ΔY coded 0 for continuity, -1 for a change from success to failure, and $+1$ for a change from failure to success, which can be analyzed using polytomous ordinal logistic regression.

(c) We can decide that we are interested only in whether a change occurs and not in whether the change is from success to failure or from failure to success. This gives us a dichotomous dependent variable ΔY, which can be coded 0 for no change and 1 for change. This model can be analyzed using either dichotomous logistic regression or conditional logistic regression.

(d) We can decide that we are interested only in whether one particular change (e.g., the change from failure to success) occurred. This also results in a dichotomous dependent variable ΔY, coded 0 if the change did not occur and 1 if the change did occur. Two alternatives within this coding scheme are (d1) to include all cases, in which instance, cases in all except the bottom-right cell (Time 1 failure, Time 2 success) would be coded 0, and cases in the bottom-right cell would be coded 1; or (d2) exclude those cases in the first row, because they

FIGURE 13.1 Contingency Tables and Transition Matrices

(A) Contingency Table, Dichotomous Variable

Frequencies	Time 2 Failure	Time 2 Success
Time 1 Success	200	300
Time 1 Failure	400	100

(B) Transition Matrix, Dichotomous Variable

Row Percentages	Time 2 Failure	Time 2 Success
Time 1 Success	.4000	.6000
Time 1 Failure	.8000	.2000

(C) Contingency Table, Polytomous Variable

Frequencies	1	2	3	4
1	200	100	75	25
2	100	175	50	25
3	50	75	150	125
4	25	50	125	200

(D) Transition Matrix, Polytomous Variable

Row Percentages	1	2	3	4
1	.5000	.2500	.1875	.0625
2	.2500	.4375	.1250	.0625
3	.1250	.1875	.3750	.3125
4	.0625	.1250	.3125	.5000

could not possibly change from failure to success (they are all classified as successes in Time 1), and consider only the second row, coding cases as 0 for failure and 1 for success at Time 2—an approach typical of event history analysis, to be discussed in the next chapter. This second option, however, effectively changes the dependent variable from ΔY to simply Y_{t2}. In either case, the dependent variable can be analyzed using dichotomous logistic regression.

(e) In the two-wave (or multiwave) conditional logistic regression fixed-effects model, cases that do not change are excluded from the analysis; and every case included in the analysis changes either from 0 to 1 (absence to presence of the characteristic in question) or from 1 to 0 (presence to absence of the characteristic in question). This is like option (b) above, including only those cases whose change scores are −1 or +1 and excluding cases whose change scores are 0. The resulting dependent variable can be represented as a dichotomy (change in one direction as opposed to change in another), and is analyzed using conditional logistic regression, described in the previous chapter.

With a polytomous dependent variable, the options are similar, but with a potentially larger number of categories in the dependent variable ΔY.

(a) We can consider each different possibility for continuity and change separately. If the number of categories in Y is c, then we have c^2 cells in the contingency table and hence c^2 possible values for ΔY.

(b) We can ignore continuities and consider only the possible changes, resulting in $c(c - 1)$ possible values for ΔY.

(c) For ordered but not nominal polytomous dependent variables, we can consider only whether there is no change, coded 0, a change from a higher to a lower category, coded −1, or a change from a lower to a higher category, coded +1, producing a polytomous ordinal dependent variable ΔY (the same as Option b for a dichotomous dependent variable).

(d) We can consider only whether a change occurred, regardless of which specific change occurred, resulting in a dichotomous dependent variable ΔY, which might be coded 0 for no change and 1 for change (the same as Option c for a dichotomous dependent variable).

(e) For ordered but not nominal polytomous dependent variables, we can subtract Y_{t1} from Y_{t2}, treating the differences in ranks the same regardless of the initial rank, for example, treating movement from Category 1 to Category 3 as being equal to the movement from Category 2 to Category 4. This effectively assumes an interval rather than an ordinal scale, and it raises the question of whether polytomous ordinal logistic regression or some other technique such as ordinary least squares (OLS) linear regression is most applicable.

LAGGED ENDOGENOUS VARIABLE MODELS IN LOGISTIC REGRESSION

Models involving ΔY as the dependent variable, including the unit-specific two-wave model are *unconditional change models*. The lagged endogenous variable model, which in the context of OLS multiple regression analysis has also been called the *conditional change model* (Finkel 1995), has Y_{t2} instead of ΔY as a dependent variable but includes Y_{t1} as a predictor in the model. Assuming for the moment that none of the predictors is measured as a change score ΔX (giving us Model C as described above), the unconditional change model for continuous interval or ratio variables may be written $\Delta Y = (Y_{t2} - Y_{t1}) = \alpha + \beta_1 X_1 + \beta_2 X_2 + \cdots + \beta_K X_K$. The lagged endogenous variable model for continuous interval or ratio variables may be written $Y_{t2} = \alpha + \beta_1 X_1 + \beta_2 X_2 + \cdots + \beta_K X_K + \gamma_1 Y_{t1}$, or alternatively $(Y_{t2} - \gamma_1 Y_{t1}) = \alpha + \beta_1 X_1 + \beta_2 X_2 + \cdots + \beta_K X_K$, where γ_1 is the unstandardized regression coefficient for the *lagged endogenous variable* (the dependent variable is Y measured at time t_2; the lagged endogenous or lagged dependent variable is Y measured at the previous time t_1), and the subscript is unnecessary if there is only one lag (but if we include more than one lag, e.g., with Y_{t3} as the dependent variable, including $\gamma_2 Y_{t2}$ and $\gamma_1 Y_{t1}$ as predictors, the subscript may become relevant). Compared with the multiple regression model for cross-sectional data, the lagged endogenous variable model just adds one more predictor, the lagged dependent variable Y_{t1}.

Comparing the unconditional change and the lagged endogenous variable models in terms of the equation for the lagged endogenous variable model, the unconditional change model effectively assumes that $\gamma_1 = 1$, regardless of the other predictors in the model (hence unconditionally), while in the lagged endogenous variable model the value of γ_1 depends in part on or controls for (hence is conditional on) the other predictors in the model. Also, as described above, the unconditional change model for categorical dependent variables raises the issue of how to measure change in the dependent variable. In the lagged endogenous variable model, the issue of how to measure ΔY does not arise. Instead, the usual procedures for estimating dichotomous, nominal polytomous, or ordinal polytomous logistic regression models may be used, the only difference being that the lagged value of the dependent variable (Y_{t1}) is included in the model.

The coefficient of the lagged endogenous variable, γ_1, is sometimes called the "stability coefficient." There are several interpretations of the stability coefficient that are statistically indistinguishable; which interpretation is most appropriate must be decided based on conceptual or theoretical considerations (Davies 1994; Finkel 1995; Kessler and Greenberg 1981; Rogosa 1995). Most commonly, it is interpreted either as a control for prior, unmeasured influences on Y or as the inertial effect of past values of Y on the present value of Y. Alternatively, it may be interpreted as doing several things at once. Davies (1994) indicates that the stability coefficient may represent the impact of a previous state or behavior on a present state or behavior, plus prior impacts of measured variables, plus effects of unmeasured variables, on the dependent variable Y_t. Because the stability coefficient may be incorporating more than a single type of effect, the lagged endogenous variable model typically provides a liberal estimate of inertial effects and a conservative estimate of the effects of other predictors in the model. In this respect, as Davies (1994:36–37) notes, the lagged endogenous variable model is far from perfect; but in light of the observation by the same author (Davies 1994:32) that the impact of interventions is often less than that predicted by statistical models, this characteristic may actually be a desirable feature of the lagged endogenous variable model.

In logistic regression, however, the dependent variable is not Y_{t2} but logit(Y_{t2}), which, as noted in Chapter 1, is not defined for an individual case; and if we were to include a lagged endogenous variable in the same metric as the dependent variable, we would need to write the equation as logit(Y_{t2}) $= \alpha + \beta_1 X_1 + \beta_2 X_2 + \cdots + \beta_K X_K + \gamma_1[\text{logit}(Y_{t1})]$, and the last term, logit(Y_{t1}), is also not defined for the individual case. [For grouped data, however, it may be possible to include logit(Y_{t1}) for each covariate pattern in the analysis.] Thus, for individual data, the best we can do is logit(Y_{t2}) $= \alpha + \beta_1 X_1 + \beta_2 X_2 + \cdots + \beta_K X_K + \gamma_1 Y_{t1}$, which implies that the predictor Y_{t1} and the dependent variable

Y_{t2} are measured in different metrics, so the unstandardized stability coefficient, γ_1, cannot be interpreted in exactly the same way it would be interpreted in an OLS multiple regression panel model, and it is not entirely correct to interpret the rearranged equation $\text{logit}(Y_{t2}) - \gamma_1 Y_{t1} = \alpha + \beta_1 X_1 + \beta_2 X_2 + \cdots + \beta_K X_K$ as a change equation.

Although both Y_{t1} and Y_{t2} *as measured* are dichotomous variables, the relationship $\text{logit}(Y_{t2}) = \alpha + \gamma_1 Y_{t1}$, despite being linear in its parameters, is nonlinear with respect to Y_{t1} and Y_{t2} in their original metric, and the *predicted* values of $\text{logit}(Y_{t2})$ will range continuously in principle between $-\infty$ and $+\infty$. The interpretation of the unstandardized logistic regression coefficient γ_1 is that a change from 0 to 1 in Y_{t1} produces a change of γ_1 in $\text{logit}(Y_{t2})$, and in general γ_1 for the nonlinear relationship implied by logistic regression will not be the same as γ_1 for a linear relationship (e.g., estimated by OLS) for the variables in their original metric, so as noted above the interpretation of the lagged endogenous variable model as a change model has some difficulty here. The interpretation of the standardized logistic regression coefficient γ_1^* is that a 1 standard deviation change in Y_{t1} produces a γ_1^* standard deviation change in $\text{logit}(Y_{t2})$; and as noted earlier (Chapter 8; see especially the discussion of Table 8.1, p. 154) the fully standardized logistic regression coefficient for a dichotomous predictor in a bivariate binary logistic regression model *is* identical to the standardized OLS regression coefficient for the same pair of variables. Because γ_1^* is independent of the units of measurement, it should accurately reflect the relationship of Y_{t1} to *both* Y_{t1} *and* $\text{logit}(Y_{t2})$ in standard deviation units. Given this, it *is* reasonable to interpret the lagged endogenous variable model *in standard deviation units* (using *fully* standardized logistic regression coefficients) as a change model, and to interpret the stability coefficient (whether standardized or unstandardized) in logistic regression as one or more of (a) the impact of a previous state or behavior on a present state or behavior, (b) prior impacts of measured variables, plus (c) effects of unmeasured variables on the dependent variable $\text{logit}(Y_{t2})$.

In both the unconditional change and lagged endogenous variable models, the predictors may or may not be cast as change scores, either X or ΔX. If in the unconditional change model, all of the predictors are also change scores, ΔX, so change scores are used for the predictors as well as the dependent variable, we have a *first difference* model, one version of Model D described above. The first difference model is so named because it takes the difference between adjacent measurement periods (the first difference, in time series terminology), but not differences between first differences (the second difference) or higher-ordered differences. In first difference and higher-order difference models, in addition to the usual issues involved in change models, predictors that do not change from one period to the next (stable individual characteristics) are eliminated from the model, potentially, as noted by King (1989) in the context of time series models, leaving more variation attributable to error. Depending on whether we want to estimate a marginal model or a case-specific model, the first difference form of the unconditional change model may be estimated by either standard logistic regression, possibly within the generalized estimating equation (GEE) framework (the population-averaged model), or conditional logistic regression for the unit-specific two-wave panel model. The paradox in terminology (using conditional logistic regression to estimate the unconditional change model) simply reflects the different things being conditioned in the change model and the estimation technique.

A consideration in both the unconditional change and lagged endogenous variable models is when to measure the predictors relative to the dependent variable. Measuring the predictors and the dependent variable for the same time introduces ambiguity in the time ordering of cause and effect, and may produce overestimates of the impact of the predictor on the dependent variable when there are spurious time-specific effects. Measuring the predictors for a time prior to the time for which the dependent variable is measured helps eliminate this ambiguity in temporal ordering (but does not remove it completely; see, e.g., Menard 2002b:18–21) but raises the possibility that the time lag between cause and effect may be too long, resulting in an underestimation of the impact of the predictor on the dependent variable.

In the context of linear regression models with interval or ratio scale dependent variables, there has been considerable disagreement in the social and behavioral sciences about the relative appropriateness of unconditional change as opposed to lagged endogenous variable models when the purpose is to analyze change in panels with a small number of periods. This debate is relevant primarily to (a) the analysis of short term change *within* individuals and (b) when the dependent variable is measured as $\Delta Y = Y_{t2} - Y_{t1}$ on an interval or ratio scale. Arguments against the use of the unconditional change model are that change scores ΔY are systematically related to any random error of measurement, that they are typically less reliable than the raw scores of the variables from which they are calculated, and that the unreliability of change scores may lead to fallacious conclusions or false inferences (Cronbach and Furby 1970). Arguments in favor of the use of change scores, usually cast in the context of the unconditional change model, are based on the assumption that we are interested in explaining intraindividual change rather than in causal analysis of differences among individuals, that the number of periods is small (typically no more than 3), and that certain other assumptions are met. Liker et al. (1985) demonstrated that the unconditional change model may be superior to both cross-sectional models and the lagged endogenous variable model when (a) regression parameters remain constant from one period to another, (b) there are unmeasured variables that influence the dependent variable but do not change over time, (c) there is autocorrelated error in the measurement of those variables that both influence the dependent variable and vary over time, and (d) the panel data give more reliable measurement of *changes* in predictor variables over time than of the level or value of predictor variables at any given time, as may be the case if interindividual differences in change are large relative to interindividual differences in initial scores.

The conditions under which the unconditional change model is preferable to the lagged endogenous variable model are quite restrictive, unlikely to be met in most observational research, and difficult to meet even in experimental or quasi-experimental research (Bijleveld et al. 1998; Cronbach and Furby 1970; Finkel 1995). In addition, the lagged endogenous variable model may be more appropriate when there is a true causal effect of Y_{t-1} on Y_t. As Davies (1994) explains, "positive temporal dependence, or inertia, is to be expected of most social behaviour" (p. 33). Finkel (1995:7) notes that the previous value of Y may influence the current value of Y, and the influence of Y_{t-1} on Y_t may be misspecified by an unconditional change model. On balance, it appears that the lagged endogenous variable model mathematically subsumes (for $\gamma_1 = 1$, which produces the unconditional change model) and is more generally valid than the unconditional change model. In addition, in the present context of qualitative dependent variables, it is easier to decide what model to estimate for the lagged endogenous variable model. As noted earlier, there are several possibilities for operationalizing the measurement of ΔY in the unconditional change model, each of which requires a different method of calculation and different interpretation of the results. In the lagged endogenous variable model, however, the dependent variable, as modeled, has the same coding as the dependent variable (if standardized logistic regression coefficients are used, implying measurement in standard deviation units), the approach to estimating and interpreting the model is the same as for the different types of logistic regression (dichotomous, polytomous nominal, and polytomous ordinal) covered to this point, and the model uses at most c (the number of categories in the dependent variable) sets of coefficients for predicting assignment to the different categories of a polytomous dependent variable (and possibly only one set of coefficients for the predictors in an equal slopes/ unequal intercepts model for a polytomous ordinal dependent variable).

MULTIWAVE PANEL DATA STRUCTURES AND MODELS

There are two distinct approaches to the analysis of panel data. In one, most commonly implemented in structural equation modeling, repeated measures of the same concept at different times are treated as separate variables. In this approach, for example, if prevalence of marijuana use (the dependent variable, appropriately measured one time period later than its predictors) is measured at three periods (or three *waves*), we have three variables—call them Marijuana3, Marijuana4, and Marijuana5. Similarly, the predictors exposure to delinquent friends (Exposure2, Exposure3, Exposure4) and belief that it is wrong to violate the law (Belief2, Belief3, Belief4), here measured one wave prior to the respective dependent variables they will be predicting, will be represented by different, time-specific variables; but invariant characteristics such as gender and ethnicity (here implicitly measured at Wave 1) will be measured only once. For analysis, we construct three separate equations for prevalence of marijuana use; represented in the general format using Y as the dependent variable and X for the predictors: (a) $\text{logit}(Y_{t3}) = \alpha_{t2} + \beta_{t2,1}X_{t2,1} + \beta_{t2,2}X_{t2,2} + \cdots + \beta_{t2,K}X_{t2,K}$; (b) $\text{logit}(Y_{t4}) = \alpha_{t3} + \beta_{t3,1}X_{t3,1} + \beta_{t3,2}X_{t3,2} + \cdots + \beta_{t3,K}X_{t3,K}$; and (c) $\text{logit}(Y_{t5}) = \alpha_{t4} + \beta_{t4,1}X_{t4,1} + \beta_{t4,2}X_{t4,2} + \cdots + \beta_{t4,K}X_{t4,K}$. The first subscript on the predictors X and on the β coefficients (and the only subscript on α) refers to the time period, and will typically be written without the explicit "t"; and the second subscript on the β coefficients refers to the predictor. The time subscripts here are kept consistent with the predictors across the right side of each of the three equations, but alternative notation is possible (e.g., matching the time subscripts of the slope and intercept coefficients to the dependent variable instead of matching them to the predictors), especially if the predictors on the right side of the equation are measured at different times (e.g., one could be measured for the prior time period and another could be measured for the same time period as the dependent variable). In the present context, we will call the data structure with separate variable names for the same variable measured at different time periods the *multiwave panel* data structure and the model that includes separate equations for the dependent variable measured at different periods the *multiwave panel model*.

Figure 13.2 illustrates the structure of a multiwave panel model, in which the dependent variable at each time is regressed on the predictors at the previous time. As in previous path diagrams (see Chapter 8), each arrow represents the effect of a predictor (at the tail of the arrow) on an outcome (at the head of the arrow). For simplicity, in Figure 13.2, the effects of gender and ethnicity are only represented for the first time period, or *wave*, of data; but it is also possible that ethnicity affects each of the variables at each time period. Also notice that in Figure 13.2, reciprocal effects are modeled; not only do belief and exposure affect marijuana use but also (a) belief and exposure influence each other and (b) marijuana use affects belief and exposure. The model here is recursive (again, refer to Chapter 8), so there is no issue of simultaneity bias in the model depicted in Figure 13.2. Instead, the longitudinal nature of the data and the multiwave panel analytic approach allow us to estimate reciprocal effects controlling both for other variables in the model and for past values of the dependent variable itself. This is one of the major advantages to multiwave panel analysis.

In Figure 13.2, there are two exogenous variables (variables not predicted by any of the other variables in the model)—gender and ethnicity. The influences of gender and ethnicity are drawn as

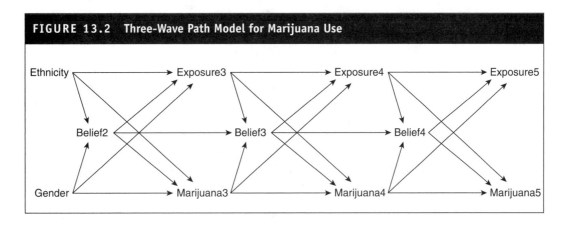

FIGURE 13.2   Three-Wave Path Model for Marijuana Use

though they only influence the initial levels of belief, exposure, and marijuana use in the model, but the model could be extended to include influences of gender and ethnicity on later values of the endogenous variables as well. Instead of prevalence of marijuana use being the only dependent variable, however, now in addition to marijuana use, exposure and belief are also treated as dependent (*endogenous*) variables, each influencing the other at a lag of one wave. The time ordering of belief with respect to marijuana use and exposure reflects the fact that in each wave of the panel, belief is an attitudinal variable, measured at a single point in time, at the end of each measurement period, while exposure and marijuana use are behavioral variables, measured for an interval beginning 1 year prior and ending at the same time as the point at which belief is measured. Because the primary concern is with marijuana use, it and exposure are the last variables in the sequence (at the far right of the model). In principle, it would be possible to use change scores for each of the endogenous variables in Figure 13.2, but more common practice is to use levels of the dependent and independent variables in what amounts to a multiwave lagged endogenous variable model for all three of the endogenous variables in the model. As with path models in logistic regression analysis generally, it may be desirable (see the discussion of separate estimation and propagation of error in simultaneous estimation in Chapter 9) to estimate the nine equations (three each for marijuana, belief, and exposure) separately; but structural equation modeling software also allows simultaneous estimation of the equations implied in the three-wave panel model.

An alternative to assuming a 1-year lag from cause to effect would be to assume instantaneous causation. This strategy is not followed in Figure 13.2 for two reasons. First, the 1-year lag is a conservative strategy with respect to the magnitude of the effect of each variable on each other variable. If there are influences that would lead to a spurious correlation between variables measured at the same time, the 1-year lag should reduce this problem of time-dependent spurious correlation. Second, with respect to causal order, although it is never totally unambiguous unless we measure the precise instant at which each behavioral and attitudinal change occurs, the lagged relationship between cause and effect offers stronger evidence that the two are placed in the correct temporal order. One could also model contemporaneous mutual influence between marijuana use and exposure using the two-stage path analysis with logistic regression as described in Chapter 8, and introduce additional complexities into the model, but the relatively simple model in Figure 13.2 should serve to indicate that the structure of a panel analysis model for logistic regression is fundamentally the same as a path model for panel analysis using linear regression.

POOLED TIME SERIES CROSS-SECTIONAL (TSCS) DATA STRUCTURES AND MODELS

In the *pooled time series cross-sectional* (TSCS) approach, another approach to the analysis of longitudinal data employed particularly in econometrics, each conceptual variable is measured at multiple time periods, but each time-specific measurement of the variable is treated more as if it were a separate case (designated an *observation*) with the same variable than as a separate variable for the same case. Technically, whenever we have measurement of the same variable for more than two separate time periods, we have a time series, although the term *time series* in common statistical usage is often reserved for longer series of, for example, 20 or more periods, as distinguished from short-term panel data or simply *panel data* that typically involves five or fewer periods.[2] The pooling of time series and cross-sectional data needs to be understood in two distinct ways: as a data structure and as a method of analysis. As a data structure, it is illustrated diagrammatically in Figure 13.3, in which periods are "stacked" as though they were part of the same cross-section. Each X in the table represents an observation on a particular case at a particular time for a particular variable, with $i = 1, 2, \ldots, N$ cases, $t = 1, 2, \ldots, T$ periods, and $k = 1, 2, \ldots, K$ variables (represented by the subscripts to each X). The table in Figure 13.3 has the familiar rows-as-cases, columns-as-variables structure used in spreadsheets and statistical packages, except that the cases (rows) are repeated T times. With only one dependent variable, Y, there is no need for the third subscript, but in principle there could be more than one dependent variable. In the model for marijuana use parallel to the multiwave panel model in the last section but examined from the TSCS approach, this would result in only three variables besides gender and ethnicity: Marijuana (measured at multiple times), Exposure (measured at multiple times), and Belief (measured at multiple times), with nothing in the variable designation to indicate the time for which the variable was measured.

When the same cases are measured repeatedly, as in a longitudinal panel design, the pooled TSCS data structure offers the advantage of greater statistical power and greater reliability of estimation, coupled with the disadvantage that in any analysis, parameter estimation may be confounded by correlations between either or both of true scores or errors (a) *within* cases over time or (b) *between* cases measured at the same time. Sayrs (1989) describes several models for such pooled TSCS data, the simplest of which, the *constant coefficients* model, assumes that the measurements for the predictors and the outcome are independent even though they are measured for the same case more than once (at different periods). The form of the constant coefficients model is simply the same as the standard logistic regression model: at the individual case level, $\text{logit}(y_{it}) = \alpha_{it} + \beta_{it1}x_{it1} + \beta_{it2}x_{it2} + \cdots + \beta_{itK}x_{itK} + \varepsilon_{it}$, where $i = 1, 2, \ldots, N$ indexes the cases, $t = 1, 2, \ldots, T$ indexes time, and $k = 1, 2, \ldots, K$ indexes the predictors $X_1, X_2, \ldots, X_K$; and the error term ε_{it} for the individual i at time t is explicitly included here in the equation. It is unlikely, however, that the observations of the same case at one time are totally unrelated to the observations of the same case at a different time. An alternative to the constant coefficients model is the least squares dummy variable regression model, $y_{it} = \alpha_{it} + \beta_{it1}x_{it1} + \beta_{it2}x_{it2} + \cdots + \beta_{itK}x_{itK} + \theta_1 i_1 + \theta_2 i_2 + \cdots + \theta_{N-1}i_{N-1} + \delta_1 t_1 + \delta_2 t_2 + \cdots + \delta_{T-1}t_{T-1} + \xi_{it}$, in which the dummy variables $i_1, i_2, \ldots, i_{N-1}$ are dummy variables indexing cases, multiplied by coefficients $\theta_1, \theta_2, \ldots, \theta_{N-1}$ respectively; $t_1, t_2, \ldots, t_{T-1}$ are dummy variables indexing time, multiplied by coefficients $\delta_1, \delta_2, \ldots, \delta_{T-1}$, respectively; and ξ_{it} is the error component, which is independent of the effects of case (cross-section) or period (time). For logistic regression, the dummy variable regression model potentially runs into the incidental parameters problem described in Chapter 12: The

FIGURE 13.3	Data Structure for Pooled Cross-Sectional/Time Series Data				
		Variable 1: X_1	Variable 2: X_2	... Variable K: X_K	Dependent Variable: Y
Time 1	Case 1	X_{111}	X_{112}	X_{11K}	Y_{11}
	Case 2	X_{211}	X_{212}	X_{21K}	Y_{21}
	.				
	.				
	.				
	Case N	X_{N11}	X_{N12}	X_{N1K}	Y_{N1}
Time 2	Case 1	X_{121}	X_{122}	X_{12K}	Y_{12}
	Case 2	X_{221}	X_{222}	X_{22K}	Y_{22}
	.				
	.				
	.				
	Case N	X_{N21}	X_{N22}	X_{N2k}	Y_{N2}
.					
.					
.					
Time T	Case 1	X_{1T1}	X_{1T2}	X_{1TK}	Y_{1T}
	Case 2	X_{2T1}	X_{2T2}	X_{2TK}	Y_{2T}
	.				
	.				
	.				
	Case N	X_{NT1}	X_{NT2}	X_{NTK}	Y_{NT}

inclusion of a new dummy variable for each case added to the model violates the large-sample assumptions of maximum likelihood estimation and results in inconsistent estimates of the model parameters. As the number of time periods increases, however, this becomes progressively less of a concern, because the number of time-specific observations (and thus observations per parameter) increases without significantly increasing the number of parameters that need to be estimated.[3] Sayrs (1989) also describes more complex models, including generalized least squares, random coefficients, and structural equation models. The generalized estimating equation models in Chapter 11 are one such extension of generalized least squares estimation applicable to (and most often used in the context of) longitudinal data.

Much econometric literature on panel models, including, for example, Chamberlain (1984) and Hamerle and Ronning (1995), focuses on models in which the coefficients β_k do not vary across the time dimension in the model. This assumption can be dropped, either by adding interactions between the coefficients and the periods for which they are estimated (in other words, interaction of each predictor with time in a pooled TSCS model) or by simply using separate estimation of each equation in a longitudinal data file that has not been converted to a TSCS structure (in other words, it is not simply Y but Y_t, that is, Y for a specific time, that is modeled in each equation). This essentially reverts to the multiwave panel model described in the previous section. Also commonplace in econometric models is the assumption of a latent variable η that is observed as a dichotomy but reflects an underlying continuous variable. In these models, period effects are collected into the dummy variables t, and individual effects dummy variables i may be either fixed or random, paralleling the fixed and random effects discussed in Chapter 11, and additional constraints are required if both the case and the time dummy variables are estimated from the same model. The intercept α is commonly dropped from the model and replaced by the dummy variables for cases (sometimes written as intercepts indexed by case, α_i, instead). In the fixed effects model, the α_i parameters are typically regarded as nuisance parameters to be indirectly incorporated into the model using sufficient statistics, as discussed in Chapters 11 and 12 in conjunction with conditional and random effects logistic regression. An alternative approach would be to estimate a population-averaged model with no dummy variables for cases; a single intercept α, and possibly coefficients that vary over the time dimension in the model (implying an interaction of coefficients for other predictors with age and/or time in the model). In multilevel change models, to be discussed in the next chapter, the dummy variables for the cases may be influenced by individual characteristics that do not vary over time, which would be modeled as Level 2 influences as described in Chapter 11. The dummy variables for time are appropriate only if we expect the dependent variable to be influenced by unmeasured time-varying variables. This is most relevant for longer series of data (more periods), rather than short 1 to 5 wave panel models.

In practice, the distinction between the multiwave panel *data structure* (the same conceptual variable at different times is treated as different variables) and the pooled TSCS *data structure* (the same conceptual variable at different times is treated as the same variable) is not critical to the selection of a multiwave panel *model* or a pooled TSCS *model*. A multiwave panel model can be estimated from a pooled TSCS data structure by (a) incorporating interaction terms between time and each of the predictors, thus producing a separate equation for the dependent variable at each wave of the data, and (b) for the lagged endogenous variable model, constructing each panel of the pooled cross-sectional time series to include the lagged value of the endogenous variable, or (c) for the unconditional change model, constructing each panel of the pooled cross-sectional time series to include appropriate change variables. The multiwave panel data structure can be used to estimate a constant coefficients model by constraining the estimates of the coefficients to be constant across waves; and dummy variables for cases, parallel to the least squares dummy variable regression model for continuous data, can be incorporated if the number of observations per parameter is sufficiently large. As a practical matter, heterogeneity across time is more easily incorporated into pooled TSCS data structures and models than heterogeneity across cases is incorporated into multiwave panel data structures and models. In the pooled TSCS approach, heterogeneity may be averaged across cases in a population-averaged GEE model, or left specific to each case in a random effects model. The pooled TSCS data structure allows estimation of any multiwave panel model if the appropriate interaction terms are included. In general, while the pooled TSCS data structure is more flexible and easier to use across a wider range of possible models, the choice between the two data structures likely depends at least as much on the software being used as on the model being estimated.

THE FIXED EFFECTS MODEL USING
CONDITIONAL LOGISTIC REGRESSION

In Chapter 12, the conditional logistic regression model was described for observations clustered within strata. The equation for the model was $logit(\Delta Y) = \Delta\alpha_i + \beta_1\Delta X_{1i} + \beta_2\Delta X_{2i} + \cdots + \beta_K\Delta X_{Ki}$, where i indexes the strata within which the observations are clustered. The unit-specific intercepts are assumed to be constant within the strata, so $\Delta\alpha_i = 0$ and drops out of the equation. In longitudinal research the strata within which the observations are clustered are cases, and each observation for a case is taken at a different time. Estimating this model using full maximum likelihood results in inconsistent estimates for the α_i and the β_k (Andersen 1970; Chamberlain 1980). Although the conditional logistic regression model most closely parallels Model D at the beginning of this chapter (the unconditional change model with change scores as predictors, $\Delta X \rightarrow \Delta Y$), it is different from the model obtained using standard (as opposed to conditional) logistic regression in several respects: (1) strata for which Y is a constant (and hence $\Delta Y = 0$) are dropped from the analysis, thus potentially excluding cases for which the predictors have consistently high or consistently low values within the stratum over time; (2) predictors that were constant within strata were also dropped from the model, thus potentially excluding predictors that might, although constant, affect the probability of change; (3) it includes the assumption of fixed within-case effects, α_i, and if the within-case effect is not fixed, then the model is misspecified; and (4) the model is actually retrodicting the independent variables from the dependent variable. All of these differences may lead to results that may be different from the results produced using other methods of estimation for longitudinal models.

Conditional logistic regression is used in Table 13.1 to estimate the two-wave panel model for marijuana use from Time 1 to Time 2 using the NYS data set for the years 1979 and 1980, and once again using exposure and belief as predictors. The data used in Table 13.1, however, are not restricted to the 16-year-old subsample used in previous analyses, but instead they include the full sample, with an age range of 15 to 21 in 1980. Because they do not vary over time, gender and ethnicity are necessarily excluded from the model. In principle, conditional logistic regression is not limited in the number of time periods that can be incorporated into the model, but use of a large number of time periods makes it important to consider nonlinear relationships between the dependent variable and the time dimension, if the time dimension (age or period) is included in the model. Also, as the number of time periods (and correspondingly, the number of observations per parameter) increases, the rationale for the use of conditional logistic regression (the incidental parameters problem) becomes less of a concern (the number of time-specific observations increases without increasing the number of parameters).

In the first part of Table 13.1, the only predictors are exposure (EDF) and belief that it is wrong to violate the law (BELIEF). The influence of exposure is unexpectedly negative, but not statistically significant; the influence of belief is, as expected, negative and statistically significant, with a standardized coefficient of $-.421$. $R_L^2 = .02$, marginally significant at $p = .0751$, but $R_O^2 = .13$, suggesting a slightly stronger relationship (and a larger discrepancy than one would normally expect in the conclusions to be derived from these two measures of explained variation). In the second part of Table 13.1, age is added as a predictor, with some curious results. R_L^2 increases to .05 and is statistically significant at $p = .002$, but R_O^2 actually decreases to .07. The standardized coefficients for exposure and belief are substantially decreased in magnitude, and belief is only marginally significant

TABLE 13.1   Unconditional Change, Conditional Logistic Regression Model for Change in Marijuana Use

Dependent Variable	$R_L^2/$ R_O^2	Independent Variables	b^*	b	$p(b)(Wald)$
Change in marijuana use	.016/ .133	Change in exposure Change in belief	−.128 −.421	.029 −.099	.403 .027
	.047/ .071	Change in exposure Change in belief Age	.040 −.090 .236	.032 −.082 .424	.360 .069 .002

with $p = .069$, even though the unstandardized coefficients are very little changed from the model without age in the equation. Despite the restricted age range used here, age itself is a substantively and statistically significant predictor of marijuana use with $b^* = .236$ and $p = .002$.

One source of these differences, evident from further examination of predicted values of the two models, is the increased estimated variance for the predicted value of the prevalence of marijuana use (from $\hat{\sigma} = .342$ to $\hat{\sigma} = .959$, where $\hat{\sigma}$ is the estimated standard deviation), a change that reduces the magnitude of the standardized coefficients in the model. Similar results are obtained when the model is extended to four waves of data. These results are distinctly at odds with other findings that exposure is the strongest predictor of marijuana use. Why the difference? Part of the explanation lies in the fact that individuals with very high levels of exposure who use marijuana at both times, and individuals with very low levels of exposure who use marijuana at neither time, have been eliminated from the analysis because the dependent variable is a constant. Calculating a standard logistic regression model on the same data produces statistically significant influences of both exposure and belief on marijuana use, higher values of R_L^2, and increasing values of R_O^2 as variables are added to the equation. Broadly, then, these results suggest caution when applying and interpreting the fixed effects model using conditional logistic regression to the analysis of longitudinal data. The exclusion of cases that do not change on the dependent variable is potentially highly problematic, as these may be the cases that contribute the most to the association between the dependent variable and the predictors.

STANDARD LOGISTIC REGRESSION FOR THE UNCONDITIONAL CHANGE MODEL

Using standard (as opposed to conditional) logistic regression for the unconditional change model, four models were calculated for change in marijuana use as the dependent variable. In all four models, change in marijuana use is measured by subtracting marijuana use in 1979 from marijuana use in 1980, resulting in an ordinal dependent variable coded −1 for change from use to nonuse, +1 for change from nonuse to use, and 0 for no change (both users and nonusers). In the first model, constructed to parallel as closely as possible the conditional logistic regression analysis above, change in exposure and change in belief are the predictors, calculated as 1980 exposure or belief minus 1979 exposure or belief. Here, the choice is made to consider changes in the independent variables that occur contemporaneously with the change in the dependent variable. The alternative, measuring change in the independent variables strictly prior to change in the dependent variable (i.e., measuring change in the predictors from 1978 to 1979) would result in a model in which the time ordering was clearly correct between predictor and outcome, but in which the lag time might be too long, resulting in lower levels of explained variation and smaller standardized and unstandardized coefficients for the predictors. In the second model, age is added to the equation. In the third model, age is dropped and gender and ethnicity are added to the equation, producing the same set of predictors that has been used in previous analyses of marijuana use in this book. The fourth and final analysis includes change in exposure, change in belief, age, gender, and ethnicity as predictors. Analysis is performed using the cumulative logit model, and the results are presented in Table 13.2. Note that we have now moved from a fixed effects to a marginal model.

TABLE 13.2	**Unconditional Change Models for Marijuana Use**				
Dependent Variable	R_L^2 / R_O^2/ τ_b/τ_b^2	*Independent Variables*	b^*	b	*p(b) (Wald)*
Change in marijuana use	.026 .028 .003/.000	Change in exposure Change in belief Threshold 1 Threshold 2	.146 −.057 — —	0.114 −0.051 −2.798 2.306	.000 .030 .000 .000
	.033 .034 .034/.001	Change in exposure Change in belief Age Threshold 1 Threshold 2	.142 −.054 −.082 — —	0.113 −0.048 −0.082 −4.788 0.361	.000 .039 .002 .000 .566
	.034 .036 −.043/(−).001	Change in exposure Change in belief Gender (Male) Ethnicity: African American Other Threshold 1 Threshold 2	.155 −.058 .005 .087 .033 — —	0.120 −0.051 0.026 0.656 0.381 −3.750 1.401	.000 .029 .855 .001 .214 .000 .000
	.039 .042 .001/.000	Change in exposure Change in belief Age Gender (Male) Ethnicity: African American Other Threshold 1 Threshold 2	.151 −.054 −.080 .008 .083 .027 — —	0.119 −0.049 −0.113 0.045 0.638 0.319 −5.600 −0.406	.000 .038 .003 .755 .001 .299 .000 .565

In Table 13.2, each successive model explains a little more of the variation in the dependent variable than the previous model, although the overall level of explanation is low, according to R_L^2 and R_O^2. Categorical prediction is very weak and not statistically significant. In the third model, it is even negative ($\tau_b = -.043$). This appears to be because the cases are heavily clustered in the "no change" category of the dependent variable. For all the models, the test for nonparallel slopes was not statistically significant, indicating that the parallel slopes model fits well (small consolation, especially for applied researchers, in a model with such weak accuracy of prediction). Turning to the individual predictors, change in exposure is consistently statistically significant and the strongest predictor, based on the standardized coefficient. An increase in exposure is associated with higher change scores for marijuana use. When they are included in the model, the effects of age and African American ethnicity are also statistically significant and nearly equal in magnitude. Increasing age is negatively associated, and African American ethnicity is positively associated, with the change score for marijuana use. Further exploration of these relationships suggest that (a) marijuana use tends to be initiated at younger ages, and to decline at older ages, producing the pattern of results with age, and (b) African American respondents tend to initiate marijuana use later than non–African American respondents, with the result that they are more likely than non–African American respondents to be increasing their marijuana use at the ages (14 to 21 years) covered in these waves of the NYS. Fourth in magnitude of effect is change in belief, with the expected negative relationship between stronger beliefs that it is wrong to violate the law and higher change scores for marijuana use. Gender and other ethnicity are not statistically significant predictors of marijuana use. Males are no more likely than females, and other ethnic groups no more likely than White non-Hispanic Europeans, to have higher change scores on marijuana use.

A few comments on these results are in order. First, the relatively low levels of explained variation when using change scores (for exposure and belief) as predictors of change scores are not uncommon in social science research. Second, the use of change scores as predictors typically introduces one of two problems, excessively long lag between change in independent variables and change in dependent variables or else ambiguous temporal (and hence causal) ordering between changes in independent variables and changes in the dependent variable. Third, even though African American ethnicity does not change, it does have an impact on change in marijuana use, reinforcing the observation that the exclusion of time-constant variables from the conditional logistic regression model described in the previous section may be problematic. Fourth, apart from the influence of African American ethnicity on change in marijuana use and the sheer magnitude of the standardized coefficients and explained variation, these results are fairly similar to the cross-sectional models for marijuana use described in previous chapters. Using raw scores instead of change scores for exposure and belief in the present example merely produces worse results compared with using change scores. The model predicting change in marijuana use from change, rather than level, of exposure and belief appears to be reasonably well specified; it just does not explain a great deal of variation in the change in marijuana use. Fifth, as noted earlier in this chapter, there are other codings that could be used for change in marijuana use; for all of them, the unconditional change model seems best suited to analysis of change from one time period to a subsequent period, that is, to the analysis of only two periods rather than multiple periods. With data from multiple periods, however, one could use a pooled TSCS data structure with logistic regression for the unconditional change model, possibly incorporating chronological or calendar time in addition to or instead of age as a control variable.

Finally, despite their apparent similarities, the models in Table 13.1 and the first row of Table 13.2 are different in a very important way. The model in Table 13.1 assumes (correctly or incorrectly) that (1) there is unmeasured heterogeneity in the respondents, (2) the form taken by this unobserved heterogeneity is adequately reflected in differences in intercepts, representing unmeasured interindividual differences in the distribution of the probability of marijuana use, and not in the coefficients, which would represent unmeasured interindividual differences in the *effects* of exposure and belief on marijuana use; and (3) the exclusion of cases with no change and predictors that are either constant over time (gender and ethnicity) or whose changes are invariant across individuals (age) does not bias the results. In contrast, the models in Table 13.2 assume either that there is no significant unmeasured heterogeneity among the respondents that would be reflected in either intercept or slope parameters (equal slopes are also assumed in the model in Table 13.1), or that we are not concerned with such individual variation (e.g., because we are planning an intervention at the population rather than the individual level, and it is the average effects across individuals, not the individual-level effects that count). Even given this, the results from the conditional logistic regression fixed effects model render it suspect, given past research in this area. Better resolution of this issue might be possible with additional waves of data, allowing the modeling of individual trajectories (not just intercepts) and perhaps random slope coefficients; that possibility is addressed to some extent in the present chapter, with the consideration of multiwave panel models, and even further in the next chapter, with the use of multilevel longitudinal analysis of categorical dependent variables.

STANDARD LOGISTIC REGRESSION FOR THE LAGGED ENDOGENOUS VARIABLE MODEL

For the lagged endogenous variable model, four models were calculated, paralleling the models for the unconditional change model. The dependent variable is current marijuana use in Wave 5 (1980) of the NYS. The predictors are exposure (not change in exposure), belief (not change in belief), age, gender, and ethnicity, plus prior marijuana use. In this analysis, exposure and belief are measured at the same time as *prior* marijuana use (1979), temporally prior to the dependent variable, current (1980) marijuana use. The temporal ordering of the presumed cause and effect is thus relatively unambiguous. It would be possible to include change scores for exposure and belief from 1979 to 1980 in place of levels of exposure and belief in 1979, but as noted earlier, the use of the levels as opposed to the change scores is the more common practice in lagged endogenous variable models. The lagged endogenous variable model is presented in Table 13.3. The model is a straightforward application of the standard dichotomous dependent variable logistic regression model covered in previous chapters, and like the conditional change model in the previous section, it is a marginal rather than a case-specific model.

The first column in Table 13.3 specifies the dependent variable. The second column includes R_L^2, ΔR_L^2, and R_O^2, where ΔR_L^2 is the change in R_L^2 that occurs when the other predictors are added to a model that already includes prior marijuana use. In effect, ΔR_L^2 is the *likelihood ratio partial multiple squared correlation:* (a) likelihood ratio (using R_L^2); (b) partial (controlling for prior marijuana use); (c) multiple (since it involves two or more predictors); and (d) squared correlation (really explained variation) between the set of predictors and current marijuana use, controlling for prior

TABLE 13.3 Lagged Endogenous Variable Models for Marijuana Use

Dependent Variable	R^2_L / ΔR^2_L / R^2_O	Independent Variables	b^*	b	$p(b)$ (Wald)
Marijuana use	.401	Exposure	.144	0.088	.000
	.042	Belief	−.187	−0.129	.000
	.482	Prior marijuana use	.402	2.270	.000
		Intercept	—	0.960	.192
	.402	Exposure	.143	0.087	.000
	.042	Belief	−.194	−0.133	.000
	.482	Age	−.025	−0.036	.368
		Prior marijuana use	.489	2.749	.000
		Intercept	—	1.657	.121
	.404	Exposure	.146	0.088	.000
	.043	Belief	−.199	−0.136	.000
	.482	Gender (Male)	−.027	−0.151	.327
		Ethnicity:			
		African American	.045	0.345	.092
		Other	.017	0.195	.536
		Prior marijuana use	.489	2.737	.000
		Intercept	—	1.155	.121
	.404	Exposure	.144	0.087	.000
	.044	Belief	−.205	−0.140	.000
	.482	Age	−.026	−0.037	.358
		Gender (Male)	−.028	−0.152	.323
		Ethnicity:			
		African American	.045	0.348	.089
		Other	.015	0.182	.567
		Prior marijuana use	.495	2.766	.000
		Intercept	—	1.870	.083

marijuana use. Comparing ΔR^2_L in Table 13.3 with R^2_L in Table 13.2, the two are of a similar order of magnitude, with ΔR^2_L being very slightly larger, a common result in comparing unconditional change and lagged endogenous variable models. As a partial correlation, ΔR^2_L is a very conservative estimate of the impact of the predictors on the dependent variable.

Turning to the individual predictors, the substantive results are similar but not identical to the results for the unconditional change model. First, prior marijuana use is the strongest influence in each of the models in Table 13.3, followed by belief (with standardized coefficients $b^* = -.187$ to $-.205$), then exposure ($b^* = .143$ to .146), all three of which are statistically significant in all four models. Being African American is the only other influence to attain even marginal significance, with $b^* = .083$ to .087, $p = .089$ to .092. In contrast to the results for the unconditional change model, age does not appear to be a statistically significant influence on marijuana use. Note, however, that age was a very weak ($b^* < .100$) influence in the unconditional change model, and would have been regarded as substantively nonsignificant, even though it was statistically significant. The coefficients for exposure are comparable for the unconditional change and lagged endogenous variable models, but the lagged endogenous variable model suggests that the influence of belief is substantively as well as statistically significant (and stronger than the influence of exposure), while the unconditional change model indicates that the influence of belief is substantively nonsignificant and weaker than the influence not only of exposure but also of being African American.

There are a couple of possible reasons for the differences in results between the unconditional change model and the lagged endogenous variable model. First, the dependent and independent variables are different, change scores in the unconditional change model and levels in the lagged endogenous variable model. Note, moreover, that the change scores used for the dependent variable in the unconditional change model are calculated in the original metric of the dependent variable (direct measurement of change), but the lagged endogenous variable model measures change only in the metric of standard deviation units. Second, the time lag between dependent and independent variables is different, with no lag for the unconditional change model and a lag of 1 year for the lagged endogenous variable model. Also, as indicated earlier, the results of the unconditional change model are similar regardless of whether levels or changes in belief and exposure are used as predictors, with slightly lower explained variation using levels as opposed to changes in belief and exposure in the unconditional change model. It seems more likely that it is not the differences in how the predictors are measured but rather the difference in the operationalization of change in the dependent variable that makes the difference between the lagged endogenous variable and unconditional change models here.

EXTENSIONS TO POLYTOMOUS DEPENDENT VARIABLES

The unconditional change and lagged endogenous variable models are readily extended to the analysis of polytomous dependent variables, and to the analysis of multiple waves or panels of data. In Table 13.4, the variable drug user type (nonusers; alcohol users; marijuana users; and polydrug users) measured in 1980, previously introduced in Chapter 10, is the dependent variable, here treated as a nominal variable, this time with prior drug user type (operationalized as the dummy variables prior nonuse, prior alcohol use, and prior marijuana use as predictors; the reference category is prior polydrug use) as a predictor, along with exposure, belief, gender, and ethnicity. Note that the reference category for the dependent variable is nonuse in Table 13.4, so some caution is necessary in interpreting the coefficients of the predictors. For the first logistic function, R_O^2 and the standardized coefficients are small, indicating that the model is not particularly strong in predicting the difference between nonusers and alcohol users; but both R_O^2 and the average magnitude of the coefficients increase successively for the second and third logistic functions, indicating that the model does a better job of predicting the difference between nonusers and marijuana users, and the best job (of the three logistic functions) in predicting the difference between nonusers and polydrug users. This result is what we might expect if the ordering of the categories is meaningful. In each of the logistic functions, prior drug user type is the strongest predictor of the outcome.

For the first logistic function, prior nonuse is negatively associated with being an alcohol user as opposed to a nonuser; for this logistic function, the effects of prior alcohol and marijuana use are

TABLE 13.4 Nominal Logistic Regression With Lagged Endogenous Variable

Logistic Function	Predictor	Standardized Coefficient	Unstandardized Coefficient	p(Wald) for Unstandardized Coefficients Separately by Logistic Function
Function 1:	Prior nonuse	−.168	−2.450	.000
	Prior alcohol	.011	0.182	.638
Nonuser vs.	Prior marijuana	.041	0.979	.195
Alcohol user	Prior exposure	.002	0.004	.890
	Prior belief	−.072	−0.129	.000
$R_O^2 = .051$	Male	−.020	−0.285	.082
	African American	−.061	−1.222	.000
	Other	−.015	−.467	.149
	Intercept	—	4.452	.000
Function 2:	Prior nonuse	−.330	−4.184	.000
	Prior alcohol	−.150	−2.132	.000
Nonuser vs.	Prior marijuana	.057	1.200	.089
Marijuana user	Prior exposure	.063	0.088	.002
	Prior belief	−.128	−0.200	.000
$R_O^2 = .146$	Male	−.044	−0.548	.007
	African American	−.021	−0.422	.115
	Other	.004	0.113	.773
	Intercept	—	5.902	.000
Function 3:	Prior nonuse	−.372	−4.765	.000
	Prior alcohol	−.190	−2.736	.000
Nonuser vs.	Prior marijuana	−.052	−1.103	.115
Polydrug user	Prior exposure	.122	0.170	.000
	Prior belief	−.159	−0.251	.000
$R_O^2 = .298$	Male	−.039	−0.497	.085
	African American	−.087	−1.543	.002
	Other	−.001	−.031	.959
	Intercept	—	7.028	.000

$G_M = 1382.27$, 24 df, $p = .000$; $R_L^2 = .362$.

Observed	Predicted			
	1: Nonuse	2: Alcohol	3: Marijuana	4: Polydrug
1: Nonuse	416	144	48	7
2: Alcohol	42	279	63	7
3: Marijuana	15	61	176	52
4: Polydrug	16	25	35	110

$\lambda_p = .477$, $p = .000$; $\tau_p = .518$, $p = .000$; proportion correctly classified = .66.

not statistically significant. For the second logistic function, prior nonuse and prior alcohol use are negatively associated with being a marijuana user (as opposed to being a nonuser), while prior marijuana use is marginally significantly associated with being a current marijuana user. For the third logistic function, prior nonuse, alcohol use, and marijuana use are all negatively associated with being a polydrug user as opposed to a nonuser. The result for prior marijuana use may seem counterintuitive, but bear in mind that the reference category for prior drug user type is prior polydrug use, and it is relative to this category that prior marijuana use has its negative impact on current polydrug use. Exposure has no statistically significant impact on being an alcohol user (as opposed to a nonuser), but has the expected positive impact on being a marijuana or polydrug user, with the strongest impact on polydrug use. Belief has the expected negative impact on higher levels of substance use in all three logistic functions, and like exposure, its impact increases from the first to the third logistic function. The impact of gender is greater for marijuana and polydrug use than for alcohol use (it is statistically significant for marijuana use, but only marginally significant for alcohol and polydrug use). Being African American is statistically significantly negatively associated with alcohol use and polydrug use, but not statistically significant for marijuana use. Other ethnicity is not statistically significant in any of the logistic functions. The prediction table associated with Table 13.4 indicates good prediction of drug user type, with $\lambda_p = .477$ and $\tau_p = .518$, both statistically significant with $p = .000$. Overall, this model indicates results consistent with prior models of drug user type, and suggests that a polytomous ordinal logistic regression model may be appropriate.

Ordinal polytomous models for drug user type are presented in Table 13.5. The first three models are lagged endogenous variable models, and the last model is an unconditional change model. The very first model includes only the prior value of drug user type as a predictor and provides a baseline for comparison with the other two lagged endogenous variable models. As indicated in the first row of Table 13.4, prior drug user type is a good predictor of current drug user type, with τ_b^2 indicating 41% explained variation, and the standardized coefficient of .746 is equal to the Pearson correlation between drug user type in 1980 (current) and 1979 (prior). Model 2 presents the same model with the predictors exposure, belief, gender, and ethnicity added. There is practically no increase in explained variation based on τ_b^2, and an increase of only 3% in explained variation according to R_L^2. Still, in Model 1, the coefficients for exposure, belief, gender, and African American ethnicity (but not other ethnicity) are all statistically significant, and the standardized coefficients for belief (the second strongest influence in the model, after prior drug user type) and exposure (the third strongest influence in the model) are also substantively significant (greater than .100).

Nearly identical results are obtained in Model 2, with dummy variables for nonuse, alcohol use, and marijuana use replacing the single ordinal (and treated as interval in Model 1) variable for prior substance user type. All three of the dummy variables for prior drug user type are statistically significant, and the standardized coefficients indicate that they are the strongest predictors in the model, followed again by belief that it is wrong to violate the law and exposure to delinquent or criminal friends, in that order. On one hand, then, including the other predictors has little impact beyond what we could already get from prior drug user type (and, comparing these results with the results in Chapter 10, adding prior drug user type does increase our accuracy of prediction of current drug user type). On the other hand, because it incorporates effects of prior influences of the measured variables in the model and also of unmeasured variables that may influence the dependent variable, the magnitude of the coefficient for the lagged endogenous variable may be overstated, and the magnitudes of the coefficients for the other variables in the model may be understated. The inclusion of the lagged endogenous variable provides a conservative test of the impact of the other

TABLE 13.5 Polytomous Ordinal Panel Models

DV: Drug User Type (1980) Predictors:	b^*	b	SE(b)	Wald z (1 df)	p
Model 0: Prior drug type only	.746	2.145	.077	27.85	.000
$\tau_b^2 = .414\ (p = .000),\ R_L^2 = .297\ (p = .000)$					
Model 1: Lagged ordinal variable					
Prior drug type	.331	1.767	.085	20.90	.000
Exposure	.132	0.089	.016	5.48	.000
Belief	−.145	−0.111	.018	−6.07	.000
Gender (Male)	−.041	−0.253	.112	−2.27	.023
Ethnicity (African American)	−.064	−0.545	.164	−3.31	.001
Ethnicity (Other)	.001	0.007	.233	0.03	.976
Cutpoint/Threshold (1)	—	−0.077	—	—	—
Cutpoint/Threshold (2)	—	2.588	—	—	—
Cutpoint/Threshold (3)	—	5.154	—	—	—
$\tau_b^2 = .415\ (p = .000),\ R_L^2 = .324\ (p = .000)$					
Model 2: Lagged dummy variables					
Nonuse	.277	1.721	.144	11.93	.000
Alcohol use	.265	1.773	.166	10.67	.000
Marijuana use	.182	1.875	.240	7.81	.000
Exposure	.131	0.089	.016	5.42	.000
Belief	−.145	−0.111	.018	−6.06	.000
Gender (Male)	−.041	−0.255	.112	−2.28	.023
Ethnicity (African American)	−.063	−0.545	.165	−3.31	.001
Ethnicity (Other)	.000	0.003	.233	0.01	.989
Cutpoint/Threshold (1)	—	−1.871	—	—	—
Cutpoint/Threshold (2)	—	0.781	—	—	—
Cutpoint/Threshold (3)	—	3.368	—	—	—
$\tau_b^2 = .415\ (p=.000),\ R_L^2 = .324\ (p = .000)$					
Model 3: Unconditional change (DV=change in drug use type)	.026	0.086	.017	5.06	.000
Change in exposure	−.026	−0.097	.019	−5.11	.000
Change in belief	−.005	−0.108	.111	−0.97	.333
Gender (Male)	−.001	−0.042	.159	−0.27	.790
Ethnicity (African American)	.002	0.094	.234	0.40	.689
Ethnicity (Other)	—	−2.265	—	—	—
Cutpoint/Threshold (1)	—	1.257	—	—	—
Cutpoint/Threshold (2)					
$\tau_b^2 = .002\ (p = .091),\ R_L^2 = .027\ (p = .000)$					

variables in the model; by implication, then, if other variables are both statistically and substantively significant in the presence of a lagged endogenous variable, it is reasonable to conclude that they do have an impact on the dependent variable, even if this is not reflected in the summary measures of explained variation for the model.

Model 3 is an unconditional change model. The dependent variable is change in drug user type, coded −1 for movement from a higher to a lower category, 0 for no change, and +1 for movement from a lower to a higher category (option c from the beginning of the chapter for measuring change in a polytomous dependent variable); included as predictors are contemporaneous change in exposure and change in belief, plus gender and ethnicity. The magnitude of τ_b^2 and R_L^2 for the unconditional change model are, as has been the case before, of the same order of magnitude (actually, within rounding error) as the *change* in those coefficients from the baseline (lagged endogenous variable only, with no other predictors in the model) to the full (lagged endogenous variable plus the other predictors) model. In the unconditional change model, however, neither gender nor ethnicity is statistically significant, and none of the predictors is substantively significant (standardized coefficients are all less than .03) as a predictor of drug user type.

There are valid differences in perspective on how to interpret these results. One approach would be to suggest that prior behavior is not only the most but really the *only* useful predictor of current behavior, and the other variables in the model can be safely ignored. This would be problematic, however, for both technical considerations (the probable exaggeration of the impact of the lagged endogenous variable and minimization of the impact of the other variables in the model) and logical considerations (the behavior had to start somehow, so something else must have some influence beyond mere behavioral inertia). As a practical matter, too, we may have a concern not only with identifying the best and most parsimonious predictive model but also with identifying potential points of intervention to change (either increase or reduce) the behavior in question. From this latter perspective, exposure and belief would certainly be considered important in the model, both for theoretical and practical reasons. Finally, note that although the explained variation in the ordinal lagged endogenous variable models (1 and 2) is less than the explained variation in the nominal lagged endogenous variable model, the difference is slight, and the results are more easily interpretable for drug user type as an ordinal rather than a nominal dependent variable. Again, however, one can validly argue for a preference for either, depending on the criteria one chooses to emphasize (e.g., precision vs. parsimony).

MULTIWAVE LOGISTIC REGRESSION PANEL MODELS

So far, we have been dealing only with two-wave panel models, models in which measurement of the dependent variable (and possibly the predictors) occurs at two distinct times. It is also possible to have a two-wave panel model in which more than one variable is treated as a dependent variable, at least with respect to some of the other variables in the model. For example, it is possible that marijuana use not only is influenced by but also influences exposure to delinquent friends and belief that it is wrong to violate the law. Returning to the terminology of path analysis from Chapter 8, belief, exposure, and marijuana use may all be treated as endogenous variables not only with respect to gender and ethnicity but also with respect to one another, in a two-wave or multiwave panel model. As with any other path analytic model, we must be concerned with method of estimation and model identification. As described in Chapter 8, if we build all possible influences into the model, the model will be underidentified, and we will not be able to calculate the path coefficients for the model until we impose some constraints on the model.

One common constraint is to limit the influence of an independent variable to the wave immediately following the wave for which the independent variable was measured, and to assume that any impact of the independent variable on subsequent waves occurs as a result of, or in a sense is filtered through, the variables in the immediately following wave on which the independent variable has an effect. For example, if exposure has an effect on marijuana use, it may be assumed that exposure at Time 1 directly affects marijuana use at Time 2, but does not affect marijuana use at Time 3, independent of its effect on exposure at Time 2 and marijuana use at Time 2 (which in turn may affect marijuana use at Time 3). This approach would be appropriate for the model illustrated in Figure 13.3. Another commonly imposed constraint for a small number of waves (e.g., 1–5) is to constrain the effect of one variable (e.g., belief) on another variable (e.g., exposure) to be constant regardless of for which adjacent waves the variables are measured. Alternatively, one can allow for the possibility that the impact of an independent variable on a dependent variable varies over time or age, either by building interaction terms between time or age and other variables into a pooled TSCS model, or if none of the coefficients is constrained to be equal over time or age, by using separate equations for the same variable measured at different times, as is common in structural equation panel models.

To estimate the model in Figure 13.3, the data were arranged in a pooled TSCS file. Each panel included (1) the endogenous variables: prevalence of marijuana use, exposure to delinquent friends, and belief that it is wrong to violate the law; (2) the lagged endogenous variables: prior year prevalence of marijuana use, exposure to delinquent friends, and belief that it is wrong to violate the law; and (3) the exogenous variables, gender (male) and ethnicity (dummy variables for African American and Other ethnicity). The model was estimated for three waves of data, with prevalence of marijuana use in Waves 3 to 5 (1978, 1979, 1980) of the NYS as the endogenous variable in which we are primarily interested. A single equation constant coefficients model was estimated, pooling the three waves, in effect constraining the coefficients in the model to be equal across the three waves. The use of a constant coefficients model with a pooled TSCS data structure raises two questions: (1) Can we really treat observations within individuals as though they contributed information independently to the analysis? (2) Can we really assume that the relationships among the variables are, as implied by the use of the TSCS data structure without interactions between time and the predictors in each equation, constant over the time span for which the model is estimated?

To address the first question, a diagnostic was run to see to what extent the use of robust estimates or inclusion of random effects at the individual level affected the inferential statistics for the model. Testing for the random effects[4] indicated no statistically significant random effects ($p =$ .498). The estimated standard errors and statistical significance levels are practically identical for the logistic regression model without consideration of clustering within cases across time and for the random effects model, and the results for estimation with robust standard errors (without explicit consideration of clustering within cases across time) are very similar as well. It appears that a logistic regression model without explicit adjustment for clustering within cases across time would be reasonable in this instance. For comparison, a population-averaged model was also estimated; some of the coefficients for the population-averaged model were different from the coefficients for the standard logistic regression model with and without random effects, but the statistical significance of the predictors and substantive conclusions were still highly similar. For the standard logistic regression and random effects models, with or without robust standard errors, the equation for prevalence of marijuana use was logit(Marijuana use) = 1.177 + 2.752(Prior marijuana use) + .075(Exposure) − .127(Belief) − .079(Male) − .122(African American) − .174(Other ethnicity), and for the population-averaged model the equation is logit(Marijuana use) = 1.118 + 2.839(Prior marijuana use) + .075(Exposure) − .126(Belief) − .080(Male) − .117(African American) − .165 (Other ethnicity). The unstandardized coefficients are the same within rounding error to two significant digits, and in both models, the effects of prior use, exposure, and belief are statistically significant, while the effects of gender and ethnicity are not.

The question of whether we can assume the relationships are constant over the time span for which the model is estimated can be addressed using the model building techniques described in Chapter 6. To test for the possibility of variation over time, a comparison was made between the model with only the predictors (prior use, exposure, belief, gender, ethnicity), and a model in which an interaction term was constructed between each of the predictors and time. This was done by coding the variable for year or wave of data as −1 for 1978, 0 for 1979, and +1 for 1980, producing a variable by which we can multiply the predictors in the model and at the same time avoid collinearity. For prevalence of marijuana use, comparison of the G_M statistics for the two models produced a likelihood ratio $\chi^2 = (G_{M1} - G_{M2}) = 9.42$, where G_{M1} here refers to the model including the interaction terms and G_{M2} refers to the model without the interaction terms. With 6 degrees of freedom (corresponding to the six interaction terms) for the difference in the two models, $p = .17$, indicating no statistically significant difference across waves in the coefficients with marijuana use as the dependent variable. For belief that it is wrong to violate the law, estimation was done using OLS multiple linear regression, and the F test for the difference between the models with and without the interaction terms was not statistically significant ($p = .316$); but the F test for the difference in models with and without the interaction terms for exposure to delinquent and criminal friends was statistically significant ($p = .000$), indicating that the coefficients for exposure do vary over time in this analysis, *if* each observation is considered independent and no adjustment is made for the fact that there are 4,410 observations, but only 1,470 cases.

Given the differences in the coefficients over time, we can either calculate separate models for each wave, or we can be more selective and include only those interaction terms that appear to be statistically and substantively significant. Exploring the latter approach, backward stepwise linear regression analysis was used to eliminate the statistically nonsignificant interaction terms from the equation for exposure.[5] In both the equation with all the interaction terms, and in the reduced equation with the statistically nonsignificant interaction terms eliminated, the only statistically significant interaction ($p = .024$ in the full model, $p = .000$ in the reduced model) was the interaction between belief and year as a predictor of exposure. The effect is very weak (standardized coefficient $b* = -.061$ in the full model, $b* = -.054$ in the reduced model; unstandardized $b = -.012$ in the full model, $b = -.054$ in the reduced model). The change in R^2 is a negligible .003 (.474 in the full model, .471 in the reduced model). This is a judgment call, but this appears to be a good example of how statistical significance can suggest exaggerated importance for a minuscule effect given a large enough sample size (here 1,470 cases, 4,410 observations). If we repeat the F test, but weight each case by 1/3 (because each case contributes three observations) when we test for significance of the interactions, the F test for the change in R^2 that results from adding the interaction terms is no longer statistically significant ($p = .208$). Based on this more conservative test, and on the weakness of the belief/year interaction effect indicated by the standardized regression coefficient, constraining the estimated parameters to be constant across the three waves appears to be reasonable, and the resulting model is presented in Table 13.6.

TABLE 13.6	Three-Wave Panel Model: Constant Predictors Across Waves				
Dependent Variable	*Explained Variation*	*Independent Variables*	b^*	b	*p(b) (Wald)*
Marijuana use	$R_L^2 = .39$ $R_O^2 = .48$	Prior marijuana use	.490	2.752	.000
		Prior exposure	.125	0.075	.000
		Prior belief	−.189	−0.127	.000
		Male	−.015	−0.079	.366
		African American	−.016	−0.122	.316
		Other ethnicity	−.015	−0.174	.351
		Intercept	—	1.177	.007
Exposure	Waves 3–5 $R^2 = .47$	Prior exposure	.532	0.531	.000
		Prior belief	−.106	−0.119	.000
		Prior marijuana use	.118	1.094	.000
		Male	.070	0.617	.000
		African American	.003	0.037	.790
		Other ethnicity	−.002	−0.041	.846
		Intercept	—	8.187	.000
Belief	Waves 3–5 $R^2 = .50$	Prior belief	.582	.590	.000
		Prior exposure	−.095	−.801	.000
		Prior marijuana use	−.085	−.078	.000
		Male	−.061	−.491	.000
		African American	.060	.694	.000
		Other ethnicity	.009	.158	.392
		Intercept	—	11.856	.000

In Table 13.6, explained variance (R_O^2; denoted only R^2 for the OLS linear regression equations for exposure and marijuana use) is close to 50% for all three endogenous variables, but bear in mind that much of this is attributable to the inclusion of the lagged endogenous variable in the equation. The lagged endogenous variable alone explains 45% of the 48% explained variance in marijuana use (35% of the 39% explained variation as indicated by R_L^2), 44% of the 47% explained variance in exposure, and 48% of the 50% explained variance in belief. As discussed earlier, these are liberal estimates of the explained variance attributable to the lagged endogenous variables and very conservative estimates of the variance explained by the other predictors. A more reasonable estimate of the percentage of explained variance directly attributable to the lagged endogenous variable may be the product of the standardized coefficient with the zero-order correlation coefficient, $(b^*)(r)$, which as described in Chapter 8 and in Menard (2004a) can be considered an estimate of the variance in the dependent variable directly but not uniquely attributable to the predictor. Using this formula, the lagged endogenous variable accounts for approximately $(.45)(.49) = 22\%$ of the variance in prevalence of marijuana use, $(.44)(.53) = 23\%$ of the variance in exposure, and $(.48)(.58) = 28\%$ of the variance in belief.

The structure of this model can be summarized graphically either by adding arrows from ethnicity and gender to the endogenous variables at later waves, or by presenting the model without specific reference to the waves in which the variables were measured, only to the variables themselves. The result of the latter approach is the model diagrammed in Figure 13.4. Note the inclusion in Figure 13.4 of curved arrows from each of the endogenous variables to itself, representing the effect of the lagged endogenous variable. At first glance, this appears to be a highly nonrecursive underidentified cross-sectional model. We can, however, fill in the coefficients for each of the paths (with some difficulty, given the density of the arrows) from the coefficients in Table 13.6. Using these coefficients, it becomes possible (but complicated, given the nonrecursive paths in the model) to estimate indirect as well as direct effects. As an example, consider the impact of being male on marijuana use. The direct effect is $b^* = -.015$, which is not statistically significant. The other paths are: Male to Belief to Marijuana use: $(-.061)(-.189) = .012$; Male to Belief to Exposure to Marijuana use: $(-.061)(-.106)(.125) = .001$; Male to Exposure to Marijuana use: $(.070)(.125) = .009$; and Male to Exposure to Belief to Marijuana use: $(.070)(-.095)(-.189) = .001$, for a direct plus indirect effect of $-.015 + .012 + .001 + .009 + .001 = .008$. The total direct plus indirect effect is thus positive instead of negative, but not substantively significant.[6]

Overall, the coefficients in Table 13.6 indicate that (1) the impact of exposure on marijuana use is slightly stronger than the impact of marijuana use on exposure, (2) the impact of exposure on

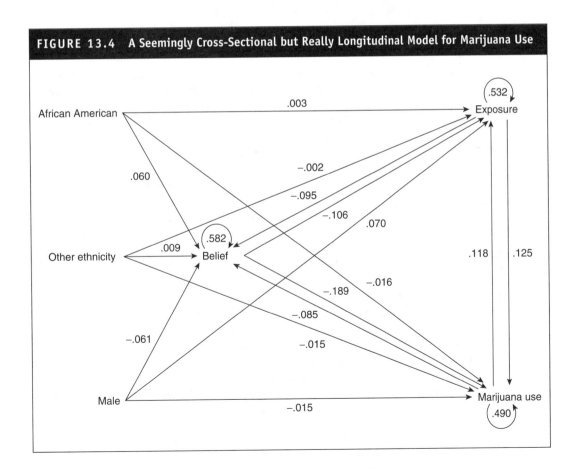

FIGURE 13.4   A Seemingly Cross-Sectional but Really Longitudinal Model for Marijuana Use

belief is slightly weaker than the impact of belief on exposure, (3) the impact of belief on marijuana use is about twice as strong as the impact of marijuana use on belief, (4) the lagged endogenous variables are the strongest predictors of each of the endogenous variables in the model (frequently but not always the case in models with lagged endogenous variables), (5) apart from the lagged endogenous variables, belief has a stronger influence than exposure on marijuana use, marijuana use has a stronger impact than belief on exposure, and exposure has a stronger impact than marijuana use than belief; (6) ethnicity has no direct impact on marijuana use or exposure, but a very weak impact on belief, and (7) gender has a weak impact on belief and exposure, but no direct impact on marijuana use. The approach used in Figure 13.4 and Table 13.6 can readily be extended to the analysis of polytomous nominal dependent variables and to ordinal dependent variables using a polytomous nominal variable with an ordinal contrast such as the cumulative logit contrast plus separate estimation of the logistic functions for ordinal dependent variables in the unequal slopes model. Use of a statistical routine for the equal slopes model is also possible with an ordinal dependent variable, but requires some decision on how to code the lagged endogenous variable as a predictor, and may suggest the use of an alternative to logistic regression analysis. Diagnostics are the same as described in previous chapters for the respective models.

CONCLUSION

The use of logistic regression in longitudinal panel analysis poses all the problems associated with the use of OLS linear regression or related techniques in longitudinal analysis, plus a few more. As with linear regression, there are questions of (1) whether to use a lagged endogenous variable or an unconditional change model and (2) whether to measure predictors as levels (the predictor measured at a single time) or change scores. In addition, for longitudinal logistic regression models, we must decide how to measure change in qualitative dependent variables, as dichotomies, trichotomies, considering each possible change separately, and whether to consider each possible type of continuity separately. For much the same reasons that the lagged endogenous variable model is more generally applicable in linear panel analysis, and for other reasons as well, the lagged endogenous variable model seems generally to be the best option for data involving a large number of cases and relatively few time periods, either dichotomous or polytomous nominal or polytomous ordinal data with relatively few categories, and the use of logistic regression analysis. As will be discussed in Chapter 15, lagged endogenous variable models for dichotomous and ordinal variables can also be implemented in the structural equation modeling framework, using weighted least squares, as an alternative to the logistic regression framework.

In addition to the general reasons for preferring the lagged endogenous variable model described earlier in this chapter, the use of the lagged endogenous variable model allows us to resolve the issue of measuring qualitative change relatively easily and in a way that makes intuitive sense, keeping both independent and lagged endogenous variable predictors in their measurement scales (unless there is good reason to do otherwise) and allowing for a variable impact of prior levels of the dependent variable on current levels of the dependent variable. This approach works equally well for dichotomous and polytomous nominal dependent variables, but as is often the case, for polytomous ordinal dependent variables, it may be appropriate to consider alternatives to logistic regression analysis. The lagged endogenous variable model is also consistent with approaches taken in analyzing data with a larger number of periods, particularly multilevel change models, to be described in the next chapter. This is not to say that one should avoid the use of other models for longitudinal analysis of data with a small number of periods, only that one should probably begin with the lagged endogenous variable model and consider whether the data, model assumptions, or other factors provide sufficient reason for selecting a different model for longitudinal panel analysis using logistic regression.

NOTES

1. The discussion in this section draws heavily on Menard (2002b). Now that we will no longer be dealing with case-control studies, we will drop the use of the term *subjects*; the term *cases* (or in some instances, *units*) will be used as in Chapters 1 to 11 to refer to the units from which the data are collected.

2. To add to the confusion, as seen in the last chapter, the term *panel data* is also used for panels of interdependent data not defined by repeated measurement over time. Note that for longitudinal data, some statistical packages have specialized commands (the menu command **restructure** in SPSS and the Stata **reshape** command) that, if data are arranged and named properly, can make the process of constructing a pooled time series cross-sectional data file easier.

3. Adding a single case adds T observations and 1 parameter, where T is small for longitudinal panel analysis; adding a single period adds N observations and 1 parameter, where N is usually large; so the incidental parameters problem is greater for the addition of cases than periods. The number of observations per parameter in the typical longitudinal panel data will be just less than the number of time periods. To illustrate, start with 1,000 cases and 2, 3, or 4 time periods, and calculate the number of observations per parameter, $NT/(N + T)$; then see what happens when you add 100 cases (a small fractional increase in observations per parameter), and what happens when you add 1 time period (an increase of approximately 1 in the number of observations per parameter).

4. Software Note: The test for random effects was done using the Stata **xtlogit** procedure (which was also used to calculate the population-averaged model). The likelihood ratio test for random effects produced a nonsignificant $\chi^2 = .000033$, $df = 1$, $p = .498$.

5. Software Note: To test the interaction effects in the model, SPSS **logistic** was used with backward elimination for the statistically nonsignificant interaction terms.

6. Spurious effects can also be calculated, using the same procedures described in Chapter 8, based on the correlation of being male with being African American or Other ethnicity in the sample, by multiplying the correlation between being male and being, respectively, African American and Other.

Logistic Regression for Historical and Developmental Change Models

Multilevel Logistic Regression and Discrete Time Event History Analysis

The models in the last chapter had in common the features that (1) they are typically used for relatively short time series of data, usually two to three periods, often as many as five, but rarely as many as 10 and (2) in part because of the small number of periods, time does not necessarily enter explicitly into the models. Instead, the inclusion of a time dimension, either age or period, is optional, depending on whether there was reason to believe that age or historical time is a predictor of change in the outcome variable. In addition, it is assumed that all cases are measured for all periods, and if cases have missing data on one or more periods, they are typically dropped from the analysis. An alternative for three or more periods is to interpolate missing data for cases for which the missing data are not in the first or last waves to be analyzed, or to otherwise impute data missing for any particular case at any particular wave. With any method for imputing missing data, the result is only as good as the underlying model, but for short series, linear interpolation may be reasonable. Listwise deletion of all cases with any missing data is, however, the more common practice.

When there are many cases (typically more than 100) and many periods (at least 5, often more than 10), the interest is often in the pattern of change over several periods (historical change) or ages (developmental change). The most common applications involve individuals as cases, and may be called intraindividual change models, but the same principles apply to more aggregated cases such as neighborhoods, cities, and nations. It is possible to construct models that involve neither a time dimension nor a change dimension, but this would imply that (1) there is no interest in the timing of an outcome, in the ages or periods at which the outcome is most or least prevalent, (2) there is no interest in change from one period to the next, and (3) there is an assumption that the relationship between the outcome and the predictors is invariant over time, either because there are only two periods (hence no possibility that the impact of a predictor will differ over time because the timing of the impact of the predictor on the outcome never varies) or because the relationship between the predictor and the outcome (as opposed to the predictor itself) does not change over time or age, but is the same at every age and time. This is essentially Model A from the last chapter, $X \rightarrow Y$, and would be the same as the models illustrated in Tables 13.3 through 13.6 (pp. 280–288) only with potentially more waves of data and with prior marijuana use excluded.

Adding prior marijuana use would make this a lagged endogenous variable model. Adding a function (possibly linear, possibly nonlinear) of age or time, without adding prior marijuana use, would imply an interest in the *pattern* of change in the outcome, when it was more or less prevalent. In other words, we would be modeling age or period as one predictor of *whether* $Y = 1$ as opposed to $Y = 0$, and interpret the coefficient of the time dimension to indicate *when* $P(Y = 1)$ was higher or lower. This in itself is a form of change model. If the time dimension is chronological time, the periods for which the repeated measurements of the outcome variable and the time-dependent covariates were measured, it implies that we are interested in a pattern of historical change. If instead age is used as the time dimension, it implies that we are interested in a pattern of developmental change, change over the life course of an individual or other case (city, country, organization, etc.), at what ages the prevalence of the outcome is higher or lower. The time dimension may be independent of, or interactive with, the other predictors in the model. If, in addition to the inclusion of a time dimension, the dependent variable is itself a change variable, either in the unconditional change model (a difference variable) or a conditional change model (with a lagged dependent variable), the implication is that we are interested in the *timing* (as opposed to the pattern) of change. In other words, age or period would be modeled as a predictor, not only of *whether* $Y = 1$ or *when* $P(Y = 1)$ was highest or lowest, but also of *when the change occurred* in Y from 0 to 1 (or from 1 to 0), that is, when $P(\Delta Y = 1)$ or $P(\Delta Y = -1)$ was highest or lowest. In models for either the pattern or the timing of change, it is possible to assess the impact of two different types of predictors, predictors which are constant over time (e.g., an individual's gender or ethnicity) and predictors which vary over time, the latter often described as *time-varying covariates* (e.g., income or attitudes).

The *timing* of change is most commonly modeled using event history analysis, in which the dependent variable is measured as a dichotomous dependent variable representing whether the specific change being modeled has occurred. For continuous interval/ratio dependent variables, two approaches, *latent growth curve* modeling and *multilevel growth curve* modeling, have been used to attempt to describe the *pattern* of change over time. In the context of analyzing ordinal dependent variables, the terminology of *growth* models may be appropriate, with "growth" defined as an increase in rank. Following this logic, a dichotomous dependent variable may be considered as a special case of an ordinal variable, and "growth" can be defined as a change from the category coded 0 to the category coded 1, with the obvious qualification that which category is coded 0 and which is coded 1 may be arbitrary. With a dichotomous dependent variable, moreover, instead of a potential progression through a series of higher or lower categories, one can have at most oscillation between two categories. For a polytomous nominal dependent variable, given the absence of ordinal direction in changes among categories, it is really not possible to define "growth" in a meaningful way.

For categorical variables generally, a more appropriate concern may be not with "growth" models but with models of change more generically. The question is whether one can reasonably extend latent growth curve and multilevel growth curve models for continuous interval/ratio dependent variables to *latent change* and *multilevel change* models for categorical dependent variables. In the present chapter, for models of the *pattern* of change over time, the focus is on multilevel as opposed to latent change models; latent change models are considered in Chapter 15. This is done for two reasons. First, it seems useful to consider latent change models along with structural equation models for multiwave panel data within the more general framework of SEM. As with conditional logistic regression in Chapter 12, the latent change and multiwave panel structural equation models for dichotomous and polytomous dependent variables share a common estimation technique, and certain comments about structural equation models apply to both types of change models. Second, while both multilevel analysis and SEM accommodate the use of categorical dependent variables, problems of estimation are more severe in the SEM framework, as will be discussed in Chapter 15.

PRELIMINARY SCREENING OF THE TIME DIMENSION

For any model involving the pattern or timing of change in a categorical dependent variable, a useful step in constructing logistic regression change models consists of screening the data to determine the zero-order relationship between the dependent variable and time. For a dichotomous dependent variable, it may be informative to plot the mean of the dependent variable (the mean probability of a response of 1 as opposed to a response of 0) with respect to the time dimension (age or chronological time). Polytomous nominal dependent variables are problematic in this respect, because there is no "increase" or "decrease" in the dependent variable, only change. Here, for manageably short series, a contingency table of the dependent variable with time may be useful for exploring the data, but for longer series (e.g., more than 20 or so periods or ages) this becomes unwieldy. A polytomous ordinal dependent variable can, for this purpose, be treated as an interval variable, and the average (mean or median) rank can be plotted against age or chronological time. Such plots, however, may not by themselves be adequate, particularly when the focus is on change *within* cases. One approach to examining patterns of intraindividual change is to plot the values of the dependent variable along the time dimension for each individual separately, possibly overlaying the plots. For a small number of cases, this may produce distinct and distinguishable patterns, but with more than 1,000 cases, the plot is likely to be an indistinct blob, possibly obscuring even outlying cases.

With large numbers of cases and a focus on change within cases, therefore, initial screening may best be done using a model with a polynomial function of time as a predictor. For age (A) or time (T) in their original metrics, the different powers of the polynomial will be highly correlated, for example, A with A^2 and A^3, producing collinearity among the powers of A and making it difficult or impossible to separate linear (A) from quadratic (A^2) and cubic (A^3) effects. Centering A by subtracting the mean eliminates the correlation between the linear and quadratic effects: $(A - \mu_A)$ should be uncorrelated with $(A - \mu_A)^2$. For higher powers, however, centering is generally not sufficient, and more complex methods of calculating orthogonal polynomials may be required. An orthogonal polynomial contrast can be automatically implemented in some existing software (e.g., SAS or SPSS). The equation being modeled can be expressed as $\text{logit}(Y) = \alpha + \beta_1 f_1(t) + \beta_2 f_2(t^2) + \cdots + \beta_{c-1} f_{c-1}(t^{c-1})$, where t is again the time dimension (age or chronological time) and $f(t)$ is a transformation designed to make the contrast involving time orthogonal.

The degree of the polynomial (the highest power included in the function) needs to be at least one less than the number of time points (period or age) against which the dependent variable is plotted and as a practical matter should probably be about three less than the number of time points. The model would then be $\text{logit}(Y) = \alpha + \beta_1 \tau + \beta_2 \tau^2 + \cdots + \beta_{T-3} \tau^{T-3}$, where τ is the time variable (age or period), and there are a total of $t = 1, 2, \ldots, T$ distinct periods for which the model is being estimated. This procedure, although especially informative for explaining intracase change for a large number of cases, can be informative for deciding the function of time to be used, at least initially, in the full model. For dichotomous dependent variables, estimating a bivariate model with age or time as the only predictor can be estimated using an *orthogonal polynomial* contrast. For a polytomous dependent variable, the same procedure can be followed by first selecting an appropriate contrast, then using that contrast to dichotomize the dependent variable into $c - 1$ dichotomous variables, where c is the number of categories in the dependent variable. The $c - 1$ dichotomous variables will correspond to the $c - 1$ logistic functions to be modeled. For a nominal polytomous dependent variable, an indicator contrast corresponding to the baseline category logit model would be most appropriate; for an ordinal polytomous dependent variable, a contrast corresponding to the type of ordinal logistic regression (e.g., cumulative or continuation ratio logit) should be used. Once again, an orthogonal polynomial contrast for the predictor (age or time) should be used, but there will be $c - 1$ separate logistic regression equations to estimate.

By examining the statistical significance of the categorical time dimension variable as a whole, it is possible to see whether age or time has any statistically significant *bivariate* influence on the dependent variable, but given the possibility of a suppressor effect, statistical nonsignificance of the time dimension in the bivariate analysis is *not* a sufficient basis for eliminating the time dimension from the full model. A slightly different approach may be followed, however, in examining the statistical significance of the specific powers of the time dimension. As a general observation, it is rare in both the social and the physical sciences to find a relationship that requires higher than a cubic power between a predictor and an outcome. For powers higher than 4, there is a danger that the model may be overfitted and that the additional variation being explained by the higher powers of the polynomial may be random rather than systematic variation in the dependent variable. For this reason, it is generally reasonable to eliminate all powers higher than the last statistically significant power of age or time from the model for further estimation.

If it is the case that there are statistically nonsignificant coefficients for powers of τ *lower* than the highest power of τ for which there is a statistically significant coefficient, there are three options: (1) stepwise elimination of statistically nonsignificant powers of τ using backward elimination, regardless of whether the nonsignificant powers of τ thus eliminated are lower than the highest power of τ for which a statistically significant coefficient is obtained; (2) hierarchical elimination, in which all powers of τ *lower* than the highest power of τ for which there is a statistically significant coefficient are retained; or (3) forward inclusion, stopping when the next power of τ is statistically nonsignificant. The danger of using Option 3 is the same as the danger of using forward stepwise inclusion generally, misspecification by the omission of effects that would be discovered as statistically significant in a full model or a reduced model using backward elimination. Option 2 is probably the safest option in the sense of avoiding misspecification, but it runs the risk of inefficiency by the inclusion of unnecessary parameters in the model. Option 1 seems like a reasonable balance between the two. In general, hierarchical elimination (Option 2) seems to be the preferred option in practice, but there is generally little reason to expect the function of time expressed as a higher-order polynomial (greater than 3) to be hierarchical in nature. Bear in mind, too, that the polynomial form of the function of time may only be an approximation to another function of time, not a representation of the true function of time, and a higher-order polynomial may reflect this.

Further insight on this may be attained when other predictors are added into the model, if coefficients for higher-order functions of τ are no longer statistically significant in the presence of statistical control for other predictors. The initial results regarding the powers of τ that are statistically significant, however, do give us a starting point for estimating the model with a particular function of time. It may not be the case, however, that higher powers of time are necessary in the full model. Instead, the apparent influence of the higher powers of time may instead reflect the interaction between the time dimension and one or more *time-varying covariates,* predictors whose values, like that of the dependent variable, can change over time. This can be tested by comparing models (1) having *both* the higher-order powers of the time dimension *plus* the time-covariate interactions in the model, with models having (2) the time-covariate interactions but not the higher powers of the time dimension, and (3) the higher-order powers of the time dimension but not the time-covariate interactions. This may be relevant in models of either historical or developmental change but seems to be more typical of developmental change.

MULTILEVEL LOGISTIC REGRESSION
CHANGE MODELS FOR REPEATED MEASURES DATA

Multilevel change models of intraindividual (or more generally intracase) change are discussed in Bijleveld et al. (1998, chap. 5), Raudenbush and Bryk (2002, chap. 6), and Snijders and Bosker (1999, chap. 12). Raudenbush et al. (2000) and Snijders and Bosker (1999) include chapters on analysis of categorical (dichotomous, nominal, ordinal, and count) dependent variables. The basic model for multilevel analysis of longitudinal data involves two levels, the individual or case level (Level 2), with data that describe characteristics of the case that do not vary over time, and the observation level (Level 1), with data on repeated measurements of time-varying individual characteristics, including the dependent variable. A simple descriptive growth curve model would include no Level 2 predictors, and only a measure of time or age (or both) as a predictor (e.g., $X_1 =$ time) in the Level 1 model. In this case, the effect of time on the dependent variable is said to be fixed (as opposed to random, i.e., variable). More complex models could include more complex functions of time (e.g., quadratic or cubic polynomials) and additional time-invariant covariates at Level 2 plus time-varying covariates at Level 1.

To recast the material from Chapter 11 in the context of the longitudinal multilevel change model, the general form of the two-level logistic regression model again consists of two equations. The *Level 1 equation* now represents the *repeated observations* nested within individuals or cases, and has the form

$$\eta_{tj} = \text{logit}(Y_{tj}) = \beta_0 + \beta_{1j}X_{1tj} + \beta_{2j}X_{2tj} + \cdots + \beta_{Kj}X_{Ktj}, \tag{14.1}$$

where the subscript $t = 1, 2, \ldots, T$ refers to the measurement times (replacing the subscript i, referring to individual cases), $k = 1, 2, \ldots, K$ refers as usual to the predictors $X_1, X_2, \ldots, X_K$, and $j = 1, 2, \ldots, J$ now refers to the specific cases (typically individuals) for which the parameters $\beta_0, \beta_1, \ldots, \beta_J$ are calculated; and once again β_0 is the intercept (instead of α) to simplify the multilevel notation. The dependent variable η is, as before, a function of Y in a generalized linear model, and our specific concern is with $\eta_{tj} = \text{logit}(Y_{tj})$ or a parallel transformation for the nominal and ordinal polytomous logistic regression models. The predictors $X_1, X_2, \ldots, X_K$ are now *time-varying covariates*, predictors which like the dependent variable represent repeated observations or measurements nested within the cases. The Level 2 predictors $W_1, W_2, \ldots, W_Q$ are now *time-constant* covariates—stable characteristics of the cases on which the repeated measurements (of at least the dependent variable) are taken over time. At Level 2 (now the *case* or, most often, the *individual* level), we can model the Level 1 coefficients as a function of an intercept (an individual or case mean value) and the $q = 1,$ $2, \ldots, Q$ time-constant covariates:

$$\beta_{kj} = \gamma_{k0} + \gamma_{k1}W_{k1} + \gamma_{k2}W_{k2} + \cdots + \gamma_{kQ}W_{kQ} + u_{kj}, \tag{14.2}$$

where u_{kj} is the Level 2 random effect. Combining the Level 1 and Level 2 models,

$$\eta_{tj} = (\gamma_{00} + u_{0j}) + [\Sigma_k \, \Sigma_q \, (\gamma_{kq}W_{kq} + u_{kj})]X_{ktj}, \tag{14.3}$$

where the respective Level 1 β coefficients have been replaced by their Level 2 equations. Possible models again include pure fixed effect models (all $u_{kj} = 0$ by definition), *random intercept* models with fixed coefficients ($u_{0j} \neq 0$ but all other $u_{kj} = 0$ by definition), and more broadly *random coefficient* or *random effects* (random slope plus random intercept) models (random components u_{kj} are included in at least some of the β coefficients).[1]

For dichotomous or orthogonal polynomial predictors (discussed below), one will typically want to enter the variables into the model uncentered. For continuous predictors, the principal reason for centering or not centering the predictors is one of interpretation: Do you want the intercept to represent the predicted value of the dependent variable when the predictor is 0, or when the predictor is at its grand mean, or when the predictor for each Level 2 unit is at the mean for that Level 2 unit? Whatever option one chooses for centering the predictors, one should keep it in mind when generating the predicted values of the dependent variable and related statistics such as R_O^2 and standardized coefficients. If the predictor has been centered at its grand mean in the model, then one should use the centered predictor (subtracting the grand mean) when the coefficients are used to generate the predicted values of the dependent variable.

For both conceptual and practical reasons involving limitations in existing software, the time-explicit analysis of change in the logistic regression framework at present must depart from some of the standard models used in the time-explicit analysis of change for continuous interval/ratio dependent variables. This is not, however, to say that time-explicit models of change in the logistic regression framework must be uninformative. Instead, we can analyze *whether* change occurs over time, the *timing* of change, and *explanations* or *predictions* of whether and when change occurs, using *population-averaged*, *random effects*, and *event history analysis* models. All three models will be based on what should now be a familiar data structure, the pooling of time series and cross-sectional data (the TSCS data structure), with adjustments for the fact that observations are nested within individuals. Unlike multilevel growth curve models for interval/ratio dependent variables, however, the use of multilevel change modeling in the context of logistic regression analysis will typically involve less of a concern with variance components, and particularly with the allocation of variance in the dependent variable between the Level 1 and Level 2 components of the model, than is the usual practice using multilevel modeling. Instead, the focus will generally be on (a) how well we can explain the variation in the dependent variable and (b) the statistical and substantive significance of different predictors as predictive or explanatory variables. With respect to the two foundations of logistic regression analysis, these concerns more closely parallel those of linear regression analysis (as reviewed in Chapter 1) than log-linear analysis (as reviewed in Chapter 2), and this is in part at least a consequence of the focus on partitioning of variance rather than model fit in the development of multilevel modeling.

MULTILEVEL LOGISTIC REGRESSION
FOR PREVALENCE OF MARIJUANA USE

To illustrate the application of the unit-specific and population-averaged multilevel models in logistic regression for a dichotomous dependent variable, we turn once again to the prevalence of marijuana use as our dependent variable, with exposure, belief, gender, and ethnicity as predictors, using data from the National Youth Survey (NYS). Exposure and belief are both time-varying covariates on which we have repeated measures across the different ages and periods, and thus will be included in the Level 1 model. Gender and ethnicity are time-invariant covariates, unchanging characteristics of the individuals within which the observations are nested, and will be included in the Level 2 model. In addition to the usual predictors, however, we also want to model the relationship between marijuana use and age. Here, we begin by examining the mean age-specific prevalence of marijuana use plus the relationship between prevalence of marijuana use and age with an orthogonal polynomial contrast for age. Figure 14.1 shows the pattern of the mean prevalence of marijuana use with age. (A plot of the mean of the logit of marijuana use with age has a similar shape but different numerical values.) It appears from the plot that marijuana use peaks around ages 17 to 19, then

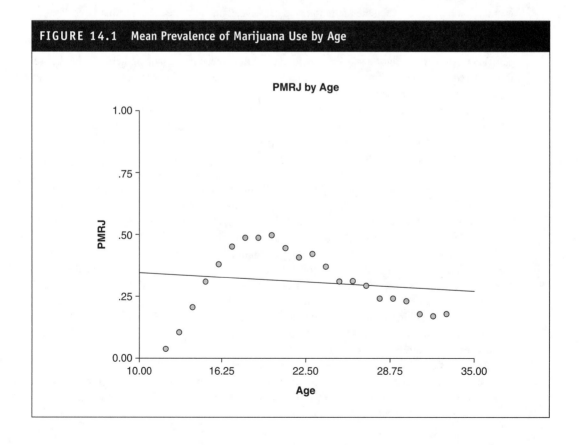

FIGURE 14.1   Mean Prevalence of Marijuana Use by Age

declines (a little irregularly) up to age 33, the oldest age included here. The pattern suggests that there is at least a quadratic relationship involving (Age)^2, and possibly higher powers of age.

For the analysis of the relationship between marijuana use and the orthogonal polynomial contrast[2] of age, marijuana use for the first wave of data was omitted, consistent with the intention to maintain appropriate temporal ordering between the dependent variable and the predictors, and as a result, no estimate for age 11 (present only in the first wave of the data) was produced. The linear coefficient of Age, or the coefficient of (Age)^1, was not statistically significant, but the coefficients for the second, third, and fourth powers of Age were statistically significant as predictors of marijuana use. Based on these results, a fourth-order orthogonal polynomial coding for age was used. A word of caution: The fourth-order polynomial function of age appears to be appropriate for the age range included in the sample, but it would generally be inappropriate to try to generalize the results beyond the ages included in the sample. In particular, projecting the fourth-order polynomial function of age below age 11 or above age 33 to predict prevalence of marijuana use at earlier or later ages would be inappropriate, and such projections, taken far enough beyond the age ranges for which they were estimated, typically produce nonsensical results. Using only the fourth-order orthogonal polynomial function of age as a predictor of marijuana use produces predicted mean prevalences that closely resemble the curve for the observed mean prevalences, as shown in Figure 14.2, which plots the predicted age-specific mean prevalences of marijuana use (PPMRJ1) with age.

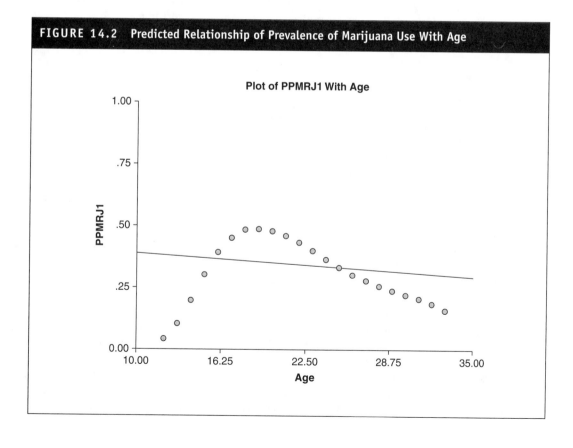

FIGURE 14.2   Predicted Relationship of Prevalence of Marijuana Use With Age

We also need to contend with a feature of the NYS data that may occur in other data sets as well: unequal measurement intervals. For the data used here, measurements were taken for the years 1976, 1977, 1978, 1979, 1980, 1983, 1986, 1989, and 1992. Also, as noted earlier, marijuana use and exposure are measured for the interval spanning the entire year for which measurement occurs, but belief is measured for a point in time at the end of that measurement period. For the three-wave panel model in the previous chapter, we lagged both exposure and belief as predictors of marijuana use, but if we do that here, we have a lag of 3 years between belief and exposure as predictors and marijuana use as an outcome. Possible solutions to this problem include (1) ignoring the length of the measurement period, risking misspecification and underestimation of the impact of exposure and belief in the later waves of the model; (2) ignoring the incorrect temporal order of belief relative to exposure and marijuana use, risking overestimation of the relationship of belief to marijuana use and calling into question the causal direction of the relationship; or (3) using a 1-year lag for each wave, and where necessary imputing the values of the lagged predictors, belief and possibly exposure as well. There are several possible implementations of this last approach. The simplest would be linear interpolation, calculating the change per year and then subtracting that amount from the values for exposure and belief as measured for 1983, 1986, 1989, and 1992. A more complex alternative would be to use information about the distribution of exposure and belief over time, plus information about *all* of the waves of data (instead of just using the information for the current and previous wave) to estimate the missing values. Rather than focus on the issues involved in missing value imputation, linear interpolation is used here to produce estimates of the lagged values of the predictors exposure and belief.[3]

THE POPULATION-AVERAGED MODEL
FOR PREVALENCE OF MARIJUANA USE

As described in Chapter 11, in a population-averaged model, the concern is with rates or averages in the population, with how much an increase in *average* exposure or *average* belief would have on the *average* prevalence of marijuana use in the population. This model would typically be more appropriate for (1) historical change, when all of the cases in the population experienced the same historical influences, and (2) broadly based population level as opposed to individual level interventions, when all of the cases received the same intervention. The population averaged or marginal model includes within-cluster dependence by averaging effects across all clusters. Table 14.1 presents the results of calculating a population-averaged model for the prevalence of marijuana use with exposure and belief (both lagged to be measured temporally prior to the measurement of marijuana use), gender, ethnicity, and the orthogonal fourth power polynomial function of age. Not shown here are tests for collinearity, which indicated that collinearity among the predictors was not a problem. The first row presents summary statistics for the model, including R_O^2 and the number of degrees of freedom for Level 2 (individual respondents) and Level 1 (observations nested within respondents), used in calculating the statistical significance of the Student's t statistics for the coefficients. Note that the usual likelihood-based statistics for the maximum likelihood standard logistic regression model are not presented here. As noted in Chapter 11, the use of likelihood-based statistics with the population-averaged generalized estimating equation (GEE) model is inappropriate, because there is no likelihood underlying the model (Hardin and Hilbe 2001; 2003). In Table 14.1, $R_O^2 = .28$, $p = .000$, indicating a moderate level of explained variation.

	b^*	b	SE(b)	t	p	Mean	Standard Deviation
TABLE 14.1 Population-Averaged Model for Prevalence of Marijuana Use							
Penalized Quasi-Likelihood Estimation (PQL) in Hierarchical Linear Modeling							
$R_O^2 = .28\ p = .000$							
$df = 1{,}672$ Level 2							
$df = 10{,}950$ Level 1							
Logit(Marijuana use)	—	—	—	—	—	−0.852	1.091
Predicted marijuana use	—	—	—	—	—	0.329	0.207
Marijuana use prevalence	—	—	—	—	—	0.353	0.478
Male	.002	0.008	.108	0.08	.938	0.511	0.500
Black	−.035	−0.221	.153	−1.44	.149	0.136	0.343
Other	−.023	−0.224	.231	−0.97	.334	0.053	0.225
Exposure (lagged)	.248	0.137	.009	14.62	.000	11.691	3.910
Belief (lagged)	−.221	−.130	.010	−12.64	.000	26.940	3.653
Age	−.026	−.307	.195	−1.57	.116	−0.069	0.181
Age^2	−.189	−2.343	.198	−11.82	.000	−0.042	0.174
Age^3	.148	1.646	.165	9.96	.000	0.045	0.194
Age^4	−.039	−0.440	.161	−2.73	.007	−0.045	0.191
Intercept/constant	—	−0.971	.085	−11.49	.000	—	—

The dependent variable (logit, predicted, and observed) is listed along with the predictors in the first column in Table 14.1. The second column presents the standardized logistic regression coefficient, b^*. The third column presents unstandardized logistic regression coefficients for the predictors, followed in the fourth column by the estimated standard errors of the unstandardized logistic regression coefficients. The fifth column presents Student's t, the test statistic used to find the statistical significance of each predictor, and the sixth column presents the statistical significance of each predictor.[4] The t statistic is based on the estimated coefficient and its standard error, from which the p value is found based on the number of degrees of freedom, in this instance, 1,672 for the intercept, gender, and ethnicity, and 10,950 for the other predictors in the model. The last two columns list the means and standard deviations of logit(Y) and the predicted prevalence (probability) of marijuana use, plus the means and standard deviations of the dependent variable and the predictors. Based on these standard deviations for logit(Y) and the predictors, the correlation between the observed and predicted values of the dependent variable, and the unstandardized coefficients, the standardized coefficients presented in the second column of the table are calculated using the usual formula $b^* = (b)(s_x)(R)/s_{logit(\hat{y})}$.

The strongest predictor of marijuana use appears to be exposure, followed by belief that it is wrong to violate the law. Because age is split into four components, two of which have substantial standardized coefficients, the question arises, what is the contribution of age relative to other variables in the model, particularly exposure and belief, to the explanation of marijuana use? One possible approach to answering this question is to use the technique described in Chapter 8 and in Menard (2004a) of multiplying each standardized coefficient by the corresponding zero-order correlation to estimate the direct contribution to the explained variance of each predictor. Using the results in Table 14.1 and multiplying the zero-order correlations between marijuana use and each power of age by the standardized coefficients and summing the results gives us $(-.032)(-.026) + (-.201)(-.189) + (.169)(.148) + (.027)(-.039) = .063$. Note that the last of the four components of the sum is negative (but very small, $-.001$), not uncommon with correlations and standardized coefficients that are small in magnitude. It is possible, as described in Menard (2007), to normalize the contributions to the explained variance so all the components are positive, but in this instance, the difference would be less than .001. For exposure, the direct contribution to the explained variance is $(.447)(.248) = .111$, and for belief it is $(-.439)(-.221) = .097$. Similarly, the direct contribution of ethnicity is $(-.032)(-.035) + (-.027)(-.023) = .002$, and for gender it is $(.083)(.002) = .0001$, a negligible effect. It appears that, in descending order, exposure, then belief, then age have the strongest influences on marijuana use. The impacts of gender and ethnicity are not statistically significant.

THE RANDOM EFFECTS MODEL FOR PREVALENCE OF MARIJUANA USE

In contrast to the population-averaged model, in the unit-specific model, the concern is with the extent to which a change in an independent variable for a particular observation is associated with a change in the dependent variable for that same case. For example, how much of an impact would an increase in exposure or belief for a particular individual have on that individual's marijuana use? This model would typically be more appropriate for (1) developmental change, when different cases in the population had different individual experiences (e.g., different changes in belief) over time, and (2) narrowly based individual level as opposed to population level interventions, when different cases were subjected to different interventions or different levels of intervention. The random effects model includes specific random components for the clusters that are not actually estimated, but the parameters (the variance components) of the assumed distribution of the random effects are incorporated into the model (Hardin and Hilbe 2003:42–49). As a practical matter, results from estimating population-averaged and random effects models are often quite similar, but in some instances there may be interesting differences. Table 14.2, parallel in structure to Table 14.1, presents the results of estimating random effects models for the prevalence of marijuana use. The variance attributable to the random intercept is statistically significant ($p = .000$), and the intraclass correlation (the proportion of the total variance attributable to the variance between Level 2 units, in this case individual respondents) $\rho = .518, p = .000$. In other words, roughly half of the total variance (remember, ρ is a proportion) between *observations* actually occurs between *individuals* (the Level 2 units).

A random effects model may include a random intercept β_0, random slopes $\beta_1, \beta_2, \ldots, \beta_K$, or both. In the present analysis, the model was tested separately for random effects in the coefficients for age and the coefficients for exposure and belief, but the random effects for these coefficients were not statistically significant, and thus they are excluded from the model.[5] The variance attributable to the random intercept is statistically significant ($p = .000$), and the intraclass correlation (the proportion of the total variance attributable to the variance between Level 2 units, in this case individual respondents) $\rho = .518, p = .000$. In other words, roughly half of the total variance between observations actually occurs between individuals (the Level 2 units).

TABLE 14.2   Random Effects Model for Prevalence of Marijuana Use

	b^*	b	$SE(b)$	t	p	Mean	Standard Deviation
Laplace estimation in HLM							
$R_O^2 = .29, p = .000$							
$df = 1,672$ Level 2							
$df = 10,950$ Level 1							
$D_M = 29,565.17$							
$D_{0(\text{random effects included})} = 31,691.19; D_{0(\text{fixed effects only})} = 14.678.19$							
$G_M = 2,126.02, df = 9, p = .000$							
$R_L^2 = .14$, (based on $D_{0(\text{fixed effects only})}$ and G_M), $R_L^2 = .07$, (based on $D_{0(\text{random effects included})}$ and G_M)							
Logit(Marijuana use)	—	—	—	—	—	−1.183	1.810
Predicted marijuana use	—	—	—	—	—	0.303	0.273
Marijuana use prevalence	—	—	—	—	—	0.353	0.478
Male	−.010	−0.066	.122	−0.54	.587	0.511	0.500
Black	−.037	−0.366	.160	−2.29	.022	0.136	0.343
Other	−.024	−0.358	.250	−1.43	.152	0.054	0.225
Exposure (lagged)	.266	0.229	.010	23.78	.000	11.691	3.910
Belief (lagged)	−.229	−0.212	.012	−18.19	.000	26.940	3.653
Age	−.030	−0.560	.232	−2.41	.016	−0.069	0.181
Age^2	−.172	−3.348	.249	−13.44	.000	−0.042	0.174
Age^3	.138	2.407	.217	11.08	.000	0.045	0.194
Age^4	−.035	−0.612	.202	−3.04	.000	−0.045	0.191
Intercept/constant	—	−1.394	.100	−13.90	.000	—	—

For the model in Table 14.2, $R_O^2 = .29, p = .000$. $G_M = 2,126.02$ with 0 degrees of freedom, $p = .000$. Recall from Chapter 11 that R_L^2 calculated based on the inclusion of the random effects in D_0 will appear to be low, compared with its calculation based on the inclusion of only fixed effects in D_0. Including random effects in D_0, $R_L^2 = .07$; including only fixed effects in D_0, $R_L^2 = .14$, twice as large. (See Chapter 11 for the more extended discussion of calculating R_L^2 for random effects models.) Once again, exposure, belief, and age are statistically significant, and gender is not statistically significant as a predictor of marijuana use, but this time ethnicity is also a statistically significant predictor. Substantively, the results are similar to the results from the population-averaged model. Based on calculation of the direct contribution of each predictor to the explained variance in the dependent variable, using the same technique described above, the strongest predictors are exposure and belief, followed by age. The effect of ethnicity is statistically significant, with African Americans in particular being less likely to use marijuana across this part of the life span, but substantively the effect is weak, with ethnicity (both Black and Other) accounting for little more than 0.1% of the variance in marijuana use. The effect of gender is not statistically significant.[6] If we plot the mean predicted values of marijuana use with age, we obtain the result in Figure 14.2. Note that by projecting the plot past age 10, we would obtain a negative predicted probability of marijuana use, illustrating the danger of projecting predicted values using polynomial functions past the range for which the polynomial function was calculated. Since the fourth power of age is negatively signed and dominates the function after about age 30, the same would occur for older ages. Broadly, one can think of the model as (a) describing the pattern of marijuana use across the life cycle from age 12 to age 33 and (b) explaining some of the error in prediction one would obtain using age alone as a predictor in terms of gender, ethnicity, belief, and exposure.

POLYTOMOUS MULTILEVEL LOGISTIC REGRESSION CHANGE MODELS

Extension of the multilevel logistic regression model for dichotomous dependent variables to polytomous dependent variables is, in principle, straightforward. One attractive option is to use existing multilevel analysis software that permits polytomous nominal and ordinal dependent variables.[7] Table 14.3 presents the model for drug user type as a polytomous nominal dependent variable with the appropriate summary statistics. The first row indicates the dependent variable and the overall $R_O^2 = .23$ for the model in the first column; then in three blocks of two columns identifies the logistic functions (nonuse, alcohol, and marijuana use, with polydrug use as the reference category), and indicates the explained variation R_O^2 associated with each separate logistic function. Calculation of R_O^2, descriptive statistics, a prediction table, and standardized coefficients for Table 14.3 follow the same procedure detailed in Chapter 9 for a polytomous ordinal dependent variable.[8] The coefficients for the predictors in Table 14.3 were estimated using full penalized quasi-likelihood (PQL) estimation, for which it is not clear in the context of a polytomous nominal dependent variable that likelihood-based statistics are appropriate, so R_O^2 is used here. In the second set of rows, the standardized and unstandardized coefficients are presented for each model, and in the third set of rows, the predictors are listed with their respective degrees of freedom (1,673 for the predictors measured at Level 2, 10,943 for the predictors measured at Level 1), t statistics, and statistical significance. In the last row, the tests for the random effects on each of the intercepts is presented, and it appears that the random effects are statistically significant for the first and second but not the third logistic function, indicating random effects on changes from the lowest to the highest levels of substance use, but not between marijuana and polydrug use. Another way of phrasing this is that the predictors in the model appear to be adequate to explain any individual differences in propensity to move between marijuana and polydrug use, but not for individual differences in nonuse or alcohol use versus polydrug use.

Because the last category (polydrug use) is the reference category, the coefficients for the individual predictors need to be interpreted as predictive of *lower* levels of drug use. Thus, the positive coefficients (all of them statistically significant) for belief in all three logistic functions indicate that belief is positively related to lower levels of drug use (or to put it in more familiar terms, negatively related to higher levels of drug use), and the negative coefficients for exposure (all statistically significant) in all three logistic functions indicates that exposure is negatively related to being in a lower category of drug user type (or again, in more familiar terms, positively related to higher levels of drug use). In Table 14.3, all the predictors except gender (male) appear to be statistically significant in at least one of the logistic functions. In particular, African American ethnicity is associated

TABLE 14.3   Polytomous Nominal HLM Logistic Regression

Dependent Variable: Drug User Type

Dependent Variable: *Drug User Type* $R_O^2 = .231, p = .000$	*Function 1: Nonuse* $R_O^2 = .255, p = .000$		*Function 2: Alcohol* $R_O^2 = .129, p = .000$		*Function 3:* *Marijuana* $R_O^2 = .092, p = .000$	
Predictors	b^*	b	b^*	b	b^*	b
Intercept	—	−4.633	—	0.157	—	0.023
Gender (Male)	.020	0.205	.024	0.209	.031	0.165
Ethnicity (African American)	.106	1.518	.025	0.303	.093	0.693
Ethnicity (Other)	.001	0.028	−.022	−0.411	−.046	−0.518
Exposure	−.241	−0.298	−.235	−0.249	−.141	−0.090
Belief	.271	0.363	.174	0.199	.114	0.079
Age	−.172	−4.799	−.040	−0.948	−.167	−2.400
Age^2	.036	5.369	.016	2.073	.013	0.970
Age^3	−.009	−2.676	−.007	−1.903	−.004	−0.562
Age^4	−.000	−0.350	−.000	−0.039	−.001	−0.604
Predictor (Degrees of Freedom)	t	p	t	p	t	p
Intercept (1,673)	−7.224	.000	0.299	.765	0.054	.957
Gender (1,673)	1.374	.170	1.626	.104	1.541	.123
Ethnicity (1,673)	6.456	.000	1.495	.135	4.148	.000
Ethnicity (1,673)	0.085	.933	−1.416	.157	−2.370	.018
Exposure (10,943)	−14.596	.000	−15.666	.000	−8.833	.000
Belief (10,943)	17.267	.000	11.575	.000	5.419	.000
Age (10,943)	−8.725	.000	−1.793	.072	−4.572	.000
Age^2 (10,943)	10.512	.000	4.207	.000	1.974	.048
Age^3 (10,943)	−6.660	.000	−5.002	.000	−1.495	.135
Age^4 (10,943)	−0.991	.322	−0.116	.908	−1.803	.071
Random effect: (1,673 *df*)	$\chi^2 = 9187.901,$ $p = .000$		$\chi^2 = 2432.026,$ $p = .000$		$\chi^2 = 1532.696,$ $p > .500$	

	Predicted			
Observed	*1: Nonuse*	*2: Alcohol*	*3: Marijuana*	*4: Polydrug*
1: Nonuse	2,448	1,087	82	20
2: Alcohol	1,166	3,159	153	45
3: Marijuana	377	1,151	281	73
4: Polydrug	88	566	253	149

NOTE: $\lambda_p = .230$, $p = .000$; $\tau_p = .338$, $p = .000$; Percent correctly classified = 54.

with lower levels of substance use (nonuse and marijuana use as opposed to polydrug use), but Other ethnicity is, very weakly ($b^* = -.046$) associated with polydrug as opposed to marijuana use. The pattern of the coefficients for age indicates that (a) initially there is an increase in substance use with age, as indicated by the negative coefficient (negative with lower substance use, hence positive with higher substance use) for Age, the linear component; (b) but at some point there is a decrease, indicated by the positive coefficient for Age^2, followed by either an increase or at least a slower rate of decline, as indicated by the negative coefficients for Age^3 and Age^4. The pattern suggested by the coefficients is reflected in Figure 14.2. Overall, the strongest predictors of drug user type, consistent with past results, are exposure and belief, but ethnicity also has an impact, and age has a statistically and substantively significant impact in all three logistic functions. (Age^4 comes into play only marginally in the third logistic function for marijuana vs. polydrug use, and Age^3 is statistically significant in the first and second but not the third logistic function; but the point here is that polynomial transformation of age is an important predictor of substance use.)

The ordinal multilevel logistic regression change model is presented in Table 14.4. The first column lists the predictors along with their degrees of freedom (1,673 for the Level 2 predictors, 10,961 for the Level 1 predictors). The standardized logistic regression coefficient is presented in the second column, the unstandardized logistic regression coefficient in the third, the standard error of the unstandardized logistic regression coefficient in the fourth, the t statistic for the coefficient in the fifth, and the statistical significance of the unstandardized logistic regression coefficient in the last column. As with the polytomous nominal multilevel logistic regression model, there is insufficient justification for using likelihood-based statistics even with full PQL estimation, and as indicated in Chapter 10, with ordinal logistic regression models, our interest is more likely to be focused on the categorical prediction table than on the continuous predicted values of the outcome. For the prediction table, Kendall's τ_b^2 indicates that 20% of the variation in drug user type is explained by the model. Comparing the nominal indices of predictive efficiency, the ordinal model with a single logistic function is only about 1% less accurate in the percentage of cases correctly classified, and only 2% lower for λ_p (.23 vs. .21) and τ_p (.34 vs. .32).

With polydrug use once again as the reference category (so the coefficients should again be interpreted as predicting *lower* levels of drug use), in Table 14.4, all of the predictors except male (including ethnicity, since even though the coefficient for Other ethnicity is not statistically significant, the coefficient for African American is) are statistically significant. As in the polytomous nominal multilevel change model, the age trend is dominated by a general positive trend in substance use (as indicated by negative coefficient of the linear term, Age, with *lower* substance use), followed by a decrease, then either an increase or at least a slower rate of decline. Of the variables in the ordinal multilevel change model, exposure and belief have the strongest impacts on change in drug user type (and the relationships are in the usual direction), followed by age, with the pattern just described, and finally African American ethnicity, which is associated with lower levels of substance use. With little reduction in predictive ability despite a more parsimonious model with only one-third as many parameters to estimate, the ordinal polytomous multilevel logistic regression change model leads to the same substantive conclusions as the nominal polytomous multilevel change logistic regression model. In the last row of the table, the test for random effects indicates that the random effects on the intercept for this model are statistically significant, indicating as before that these predictors do not fully explain individual differences in trajectories of substance use.

TABLE 14.4   Polytomous Ordinal Hierarchical Linear Modeling Logistic Regression Model

Dependent Variable: Drug User Type

Predictors	b^*	b	SE(b)	t	p
Intercept	—	−4.392	.319	13.764	.000
Gender (Male)	.001	0.003	.081	0.041	.968
Ethnicity (African American)	.119	0.904	.136	6.767	.000
Ethnicity (Other)	.022	0.252	.198	1.272	.204
Exposure	−.271	−0.178	.010	−18.376	.000
Belief	.268	0.190	.010	19.042	.000
Age	−.208	−3.070	.182	−16.910	.000
Age^2	.044	3.455	.177	19.565	.000
Age^3	.013	−2.013	.142	−14.192	.000
Age^4	.000	0.275	.132	2.080	.037
Threshold (2)	—	3.069	.057	54.112	.000
Threshold (3)	—	5.119	.078	65.315	.000
Random effect for intercept			$\chi^2 = 6152.529,$		$p = .000$

	Predicted			
Observed	1: Nonuse	2: Alcohol	3: Marijuana	4: Polydrug
1: Nonuse	2,202	1,384	42	9
2: Alcohol	944	3,426	142	11
3: Marijuana	193	1,465	194	30
4: Polydrug	47	685	251	73

NOTE: Kendall's τ_b = .452, Kendall's τ_b^2 = .204, p =.000; Percent correctly classified = 53; λ_p = .209, p = .000; τ_p = .319, p = .000.

CONCLUSION: MULTILEVEL LOGISTIC
REGRESSION FOR LONGITUDINAL DATA ANALYSIS

Most of the existing literature on multilevel modeling treats the analysis of discrete dependent variables generally, and logistic regression in particular, as an afterthought or a secondary issue, assuming a focus on interval/ratio dependent variables, partitioning of variance, and by the way, if you are unfortunate enough to have to deal with discrete dependent variables, here is something that may help. Here, the focus has been somewhat different, attempting to strengthen the bridge between multilevel modeling and modeling discrete dependent variables. In this light, greater emphasis has been given than is usual in the multilevel modeling literature to the calculation of explained variation (and, given the existing methods for estimating multilevel logistic regression models, this means a greater focus on explained variance, R_O^2, than has been the case elsewhere in this book) and standardized coefficients for assessing the relative impact within a model of predictors measured on different scales. The good news is that for the simplest (e.g., random intercept) models, one can obtain relatively consistent estimates across different software packages.

The bad news is that (a) in order to know for sure whether the simpler model is adequate, it may be necessary to first examine the more complex models, (b) the statistical routines in general purpose statistical software packages are not up to the task of estimating the more complex models, and one may instead need to rely on more specialized multilevel statistical software (an observation also made by Luke 2004:73), and (c) for more complex models, it may not be possible to obtain maximum likelihood estimates, with all that implies for assessing the relative fit of different models and explained variation based on the criterion actually being maximized in a logistic regression approach. The principal strength and importance of multilevel logistic regression modeling for longitudinal data is that it takes into account dependencies in the data occasioned by repeated measurement of the same cases (Level 2 units) in modeling the relationship of the outcome with chronological age or time and with time-varying and time-constant covariates, including the use of appropriate degrees of freedom for Level 2 units in calculating inferential statistics.

EVENT HISTORY ANALYSIS USING LOGISTIC REGRESSION[9]

The interest in the timing (as opposed to the pattern) of qualitative changes or events over time or age has led to the development of a set of techniques that link regression analysis and the analysis of transition matrices for data that include measurements at several periods, variously described as event history analysis, survival analysis, hazard analysis, analysis of failure time data, analysis of lifetime data, and transition rate (or simply rate) models (e.g., Allison 1995; Blossfeld et al. 1989; Cox and Oakes 1984; Hosmer and Lemeshow 1999; Kalbfleisch and Prentice 2002; Lawless 2003; Namboodiri and Suchindran 1987; Powers and Xie 2008; Yamaguchi 1991). Terms like survival analysis typically are used, for example, in the study of mortality rates in demography, while terms like hazard analysis and failure time analysis are more commonly applied in industrial applications, for example modeling time to failure of machine components. The term *event history analysis,* perhaps the most general term, is commonly used in the social sciences, and will be the term used in the remainder of this chapter. Event history analysis allows the use of either age or chronological time as the underlying time continuum or dimension, and optionally the use of the other time variable as an independent variable, so that both historical and developmental trends may be examined.

Different techniques are used in event history analysis models, depending on how precisely the time dimension is measured. The principal distinction is between *continuous time* event history analysis, in which the occurrence of an event can be precisely located along a time dimension, and each event typically occurs at a unique time, with few if any ties in the time of occurrence; and *discrete time* (or *grouped time, grouped duration,* or *interval censored*) event history analysis (variations in the terminology described, for example, by Beck et al. 1998 and Hosmer and Lemeshow 1999:257–269), in which time is measured more imprecisely relative to the timing of events, there are typically many ties in time of occurrence, and what we know is whether an event occurred within a specified time interval, rather than the precise time of occurrence. For example, in a study of mortality over a 10-year period, continuous time data would specify the day and perhaps even the hour and minute of death, thus providing a (usually if not always) unique time of death for each individual, while discrete time data might only specify the year of death, thus involving many individuals dying within the same time interval. In some instances, the nature of the phenomenon under study may force the use of discrete time event history analysis because the event in question can only occur at a specific time. For example, if one wanted to examine the onset of voting behavior by examining the timing of the first vote in a national or local election, voting only occurs within a relatively narrow period of time, and many individuals will cast their first votes at exactly the same time (for any reasonable level of precision in the measurement of time). More often, potentially precise time periods will be aggregated into larger, less precise intervals because data are only collected monthly or annually. An example of the use of aggregation over broad intervals would be whether an individual had experienced certain events such as being a victim of crime or getting married in a 1-year or perhaps a 1-month time span. In contrast, in continuous time event history analysis, the precise time of victimization or marriage would be recorded, along with any time-varying characteristics thought to influence the event.

The *hazard rate* for an event at a particular time t is $\lambda_t = h(t)$, that is, the hazard rate λ at time t is a function h of the time t. The hazard rate is the probability that an "event" or a qualitative change occurs at a given time, usually given that it has not occurred prior to that time (the exception here is the analysis of repeated or repeatable events). In equation format, $h(t)$ = (Number of cases experiencing an event in the interval beginning at time = t)/[(Number of individuals entering the interval beginning at time = t without previously having experienced an event)(length of interval beginning at time = t)]. Life table models, including multistate life table models, may in a sense be regarded as a *nonparametric* form of event history analysis. They analyze stage-state transitions without making any assumptions about the underlying temporal distribution of those transitions (as in event history analysis), and in that sense are more flexible than event history analysis, but they also have greater difficulty handling large numbers of independent variables. In *parametric event history analysis* for continuous time data, the hazard rate is assumed to have a particular distribution such as the exponential, Weibull, or log-logistic distribution.

The natural logarithm of the hazard rate, $\ln(\lambda_t)$, is written as a function of an intercept, an error term with a specified distribution (again, e.g., exponential, Weibull, log-logistic), and a set of predictors or covariates along with their coefficients: $\ln(\lambda_t) = \alpha + \beta_1 X_{1it} + \beta_2 X_{2it} + \cdots + \beta_K X_{Kit} + \varepsilon_{it}$. If the errors are distributed according to an exponential or a Weibull function, the ratio of hazard functions for different individuals is constant over time, and we have a *proportional hazards* model. For other distributions, the proportional hazards property does not hold. An alternative to parametric event history analysis for continuous data, in which the distribution is assumed to be known, is *semiparametric event history analysis*, in which it is not assumed that the distribution is known, but proportional hazards are assumed. In this model, we obtain the equation $\ln(\lambda_t) = \lambda_0 + \beta_1 X_{1it} + \beta_2 X_{2it} + \cdots + \beta_K X_{Kit}$, in which the *baseline hazard rate,* λ_0, replaces the intercept, and the error term is not explicitly included in the model. The baseline hazard rate is unobserved and assumed to be the same for all cases. In comparing two log hazard rates (e.g., for individuals $i = 1$ and $i = 2$), we obtain the difference $\ln(\lambda_{1t}) - \ln(\lambda_{2t}) = [\lambda_0 + \Sigma_K \beta_K X_{1tk}] - [\lambda_0 + \Sigma_K \beta_K X_{2tk}] = \Sigma_K \beta_K X_{1tk} - \Sigma_K \beta_K X_{2tk}$, and the baseline hazard rate drops out of the result. This property allows the estimation of the semiparametric proportional hazards model even though the baseline hazard rate is unobserved and of unknown distribution.

For short time series, *discrete time event history analysis* models require only a few (often four or five) periods, and can be estimated using logistic regression (for proportional odds) or complementary log-log models (for proportional hazards), or other distributions. The short time series may result from events really occurring at discrete intervals (the voting example given above) or from crude measurement of time. In discrete time event history analysis, the two principal alternatives are the *proportional hazards* model and the *proportional odds* model, the latter being the logistic regression model with the usual logit link. In the proportional odds model, the dependent variable is logit$(\lambda_t) = \ln[\lambda_t/(1 - \lambda_t)]$, and the model is written logit$(\lambda_t) = \ln[\lambda_t/(1 - \lambda_t)] = \alpha + \beta_1 X_{1it} + \beta_2 X_{2it} + \cdots + \beta_K X_{Kit}$. The *complementary log-log* link, in which the dependent variable is cloglog$(\lambda_t) = \ln[-\ln(1 - \lambda_t)]$, produces a proportional hazards model, written cloglog$(\lambda_t) = \ln[-\ln(1 - \lambda_t)] = \alpha + \beta_1 X_{1it} + \beta_2 X_{2it} + \cdots + \beta_K X_{Kit}$. As described in Hosmer and Lemeshow (1999:268), the logit and the cloglog links produce similar results for outcomes with low hazard rates, but tend to diverge for outcomes with higher hazard rates. The use of logistic regression (or the logit model) is increasingly being abandoned in favor of the complementary log-log model for discrete time event history analysis. The principal attraction for doing so is the preference for the proportional hazards model, which is also used in both parametric and semiparametric event history analysis, over the proportional odds model, which is not. In choosing between the two models, however, one should consider whether there is any substantive reason (as opposed to general popularity) to prefer one over the other, and if not, then which of the two models better fits the data or explains the variation in the dependent variable.

PROPORTIONAL ODDS DISCRETE TIME EVENT HISTORY ANALYSIS

Had enough examples with marijuana use as the dependent variable? OK, let's try one with perpetration of serious assault as the dependent variable instead. Criminologists have a long-standing interest in what causes the onset or initiation of different types of criminal behavior, including serious assaults. More recently, as longitudinal data on individuals over the life course have become more readily available, that interest has been extended to include temporary or permanent suspension as well as initiation of criminal behaviors. In light of this substantive interest, both onset and suspension of serious assault are included as dependent variables here, in part to compare whether the influences on one are the same as the influences on the other.

As predictors, we continue to use exposure and belief (lagged so the measurement of exposure and belief occurs prior to the change or continuity in serious violent offending), plus gender and ethnicity. Also included as predictors are age (for developmental effects), the year in which the measurement was taken (for historical effects), and the interval since the last measurement. The measurement interval is equal to 1 for Waves 1 to 5, which were collected annually, and 3 for Waves 6 to 9, which were collected at 3-year intervals, as described earlier in this chapter. The incorporation of the interval since the last measurement allows us to adjust for the length of time over which a change could have occurred. If, for example, the annual rate of change is the same across the years (1976–1993) in which measurements were taken for the sample, then we would expect the rate of change to be higher over a longer interval (3 years for the later waves) than over a shorter interval (1 year for the earlier waves). The *variable* INTERVAL is coded as a dichotomy, 0 for the earlier waves and 1 for the later waves, to allow construction of two sets of equations, one for the earlier and one for the later waves, should the time interval and its interaction with other variables prove to be statistically significant. A potential problem in interpretation is unavoidable, however, since the longer measurement interval occurs for later years and thus also (since this is a longitudinal cohort study) for older respondents. Collinearity diagnostics confirm the problem: The tolerance statistics for all of the predictors in the model other than age, year, and interval are greater than .650; for interval, tolerance is an acceptable .227; for age, it is a potentially problematic .127; and for year, it is .087, suggesting that if the coefficients appear to be seriously affected, we might want to drop the variable year from the model.

To decide whether the interactions between measurement interval and the other variables in the model were statistically significant, two models were estimated for each dependent variable, one with and one without the interaction terms. The differences in the G_M (model χ^2) statistics and their statistical significance were calculated. The results indicated that the model with the interaction terms was statistically significantly better for both initiation and suspension of serious assault perpetration, so the interaction terms with the measurement interval are included in both models. For each dependent variable, initiation and suspension, then, there will be two equations, one for the earlier waves (1976–1980, ages 11–21) and one for the later waves (1983–1992, ages 18–33). Table 14.5 presents the results of the analysis with onset of serious assault as the dependent variable. In Table 14.5, instead of presenting the interaction terms as such, they have been used instead to construct the equation for the later waves of the data. This has been accomplished by running the models twice, the second time with the dummy variable coding of interval reversed. Note that interval does not appear as a predictor in the table, although it and its interactions with the other variables are used in the model. Interval is only used as an interaction term to provide the separate slopes and intercepts for the earlier and later waves of data.

Overall, the relationship between the predictors and the onset of serious assault is weak ($R_L^2 = .12$, $R_O^2 = .04$) but statistically significant. Year is not a statistically significant predictor, even though the standardized coefficient for year is as large as coefficients for other predictors that are statistically significant, suggesting that collinearity is leading us to fail to reject the null hypothesis of no relationship when it may in fact be false. Substantively, however, almost all the standardized coefficients in the model indicate weak and arguably substantively nonsignificant ($b^* < .100$) relationships. The primary exceptions are age for Waves 1 to 5 ($b^* = -.218$) and exposure ($b^* = .116$) and being male ($b^* = .101$) for Waves 6 to 9. The coefficient for age is not statistically significant for Waves 6 to 9, and the difference in the coefficients for age between the earlier and later waves is marginally statistically significant ($.05 < p < .10$ for Waves 1–5 vs. Waves 6–9). Although the coefficients for belief are not statistically different between Waves 1 to 5 and Waves 6 to 9, belief appears to have a statistically significant effect in the expected direction (negative) in the earlier but not the later waves. All of the other coefficients are at least marginally statistically significant. Turning to the odds ratios for the dichotomous predictors, being male doubles or triples the odds of onset of serious assault, as does being African American. The impact of being other than majority or African American ethnicity increases the odds of onset of serious assault by two-thirds in the earlier waves, but by a factor of 4 in the later waves (although this difference is not statistically significant). The odds ratios for the dichotomous predictors, then, suggest a somewhat stronger relationship than is indicated by the standardized coefficients. For belief and exposure, a one-unit change has a small impact on the odds of initiation of serious assault (about a 6% change for belief and 9% for exposure in Waves 1 to 5, and about 22% for exposure in Waves 6 to 9), but the odds ratio is less informative here.

TABLE 14.5 Initiation of Serious Assault

Predictor	b^*	Odds Ratio	b	SE(b)	Wald χ^2	p(Wald)
Waves 1–5						
Age*	−.218	0.797	−0.226	0.043	27.401	.000
Year	−.054	0.941	−0.061	0.079	0.597	.440
Male	.089	2.663	0.980	0.162	36.492	.000
Black	.037	1.874	0.628	0.190	10.937	.001
Other	.019	1.625	0.486	0.291	2.793	.095
Exposure***	.048	1.085	0.082	0.019	19.541	.000
Belief	−.040	0.939	−0.063	0.022	8.002	.005
Intercept***	—	2.171	0.775	1.074	0.521	.470
Waves 6–9						
Age*	−.063	0.937	−0.065	0.074	0.772	.380
Year	−.016	0.982	−0.018	0.086	0.042	.837
Male	.101	3.044	1.113	0.310	12.871	.000
Black	.061	2.843	1.045	0.351	8.841	.003
Other	.054	3.954	1.375	0.472	8.475	.004
Exposure***	.116	1.216	0.196	0.037	28.317	.000
Belief	−.010	0.984	−0.016	0.046	0.120	.729
Intercept***	—	0.007	−5.018	1.893	7.029	.008

NOTE: $R_L^2 = .12$, $G_M = 262.834$, $df = 15$, $p = .000$; $R_O^2 = .04$, $p = .000$.

Statistical significance of difference of coefficients between Waves 1 to 5 and Waves 6 to 9:

*$.05 < p < .10$.

**$.01 < p < .05$.

***$.001 < p < .01$.

****$p < .001$.

Suspension of serious assault is better explained by the model than initiation, as indicated in Table 14.6, with $R_L^2 = .21$ and $R_O^2 = .19$. The impact of history (year), being African American, and once again exposure, all are statistically significantly different in the earlier compared with the later waves, and the difference in the impact of age from the earlier to the later waves is marginally significant. In the earlier waves, being older increases the odds of suspension of serious assault; in the later waves, the impact of age is not statistically significant. The impact of historical time, represented by year, is strong and statistically significant in the earlier waves, but not statistically significant (even though it appears to be substantively significant) in the later waves. Once again, collinearity poses the risk of a false negative finding with respect to the impact of historical time. Incidentally, this finding of increased suspension of serious assault over time is consistent with declines in rates of serious assault and other offenses based on other national statistics during the years 1976 to 1980 and 1983 to 1992 (e.g., Covey et al. 1997:38–43), and the finding of increased suspension with age is consistent with research on illegal behavior over the life course (e.g., Elliott et al. 1989). For each calendar year from 1976 to 1993, the odds that an active offender will discontinue involvement in serious assault increase by nearly half; for each year of age in the earlier but not the later waves, the odds increase by about 9%.

Being male is not quite statistically significant as a predictor of suspension of serious assault. Being African American has a statistically significantly different effect in the earlier waves (no statistically significant effect) as opposed to the later waves (a statistically significant negative effect; of those already involved in serious assaultive behavior, African Americans are only a little

TABLE 14.6 Suspension of Serious Assault

Predictors	b^*	Odds Ratio	b	SE(b)	Wald χ^2	p(Wald)
Waves 1–5						
Age	.138	1.093	0.089	0.038	5.552	.018
Year***	.560	1.461	0.379	0.069	30.050	.000
Male	−.035	0.769	−0.263	0.161	2.659	.103
Black***	.005	1.043	0.042	0.183	0.052	.819
Other	−.046	0.533	−0.630	0.247	6.508	.011
Exposure****	−.101	0.933	−0.070	0.014	25.970	.000
Belief	.080	1.070	0.068	0.018	13.337	.000
Intercept**	—	0.104	−2.265	0.912	6.173	.013
Waves 6–9						
Age	.017	1.011	0.011	0.064	0.031	.861
Year***	.174	1.125	0.118	0.075	2.451	.117
Male	−.059	0.644	−0.441	0.297	2.199	.138
Black***	−.109	0.387	−0.948	0.272	12.128	.000
Other	−.012	0.852	−0.160	0.496	.104	.747
Exposure****	−.266	0.832	−0.184	0.024	59.580	.000
Belief	.112	1.100	0.096	0.036	7.225	.007
Intercept**	—	6.214	1.827	1.368	1.782	.182

NOTE: $R_L^2 = .21$; $G_M = 487.341$, $df = 15$, $p = .000$; $R_O^2 = .19$, $p = .000$.

Statistical significance of difference of coefficients between Waves 1 to 5 and Waves 6 to 9:

*.05 < p < .10.

**.01 < p < .05.

***.001 < p < .01.

****p < .001.

more than a third as likely as majority group members to suspend their involvement in serious assaults). The difference between earlier and later waves for "Other" ethnic group members is practically the opposite of that for African Americans, with a statistically significant negative effect in the earlier waves (about half as likely to suspend serious assaultive behavior as majority group members) but no statistically significant effect in the later waves. Despite the apparent difference, the difference in the impact of other ethnicity between earlier and later waves is not statistically significant. As one would expect, those with more exposure to delinquent or criminal friends are less likely to suspend their involvement in serious assault, more so in the later than the earlier waves ($b^* = -.101$ for the earlier waves, $-.266$ for the later waves, difference statistically significant at $p = .000$). Also as expected, belief that it is wrong to violate the law increases the odds of suspension of serious assault perpetration.

Substantively, comparing the results for initiation and suspension of serious violence, we can interpret the coefficients and global statistics to indicate the following points: (1) We are better able to predict which individuals involved in serious assault perpetration will suspend their involvement, than we are to predict which individuals who are *not* involved in serious assaults will become perpetrators. (2) In the earlier waves (adolescence to early adulthood), older individuals are less likely to initiate and more likely to suspend serious assault perpetration, but age does not appear to matter in the later waves (with older respondents, ages 18–33). (3) Exposure and belief consistently have the expected effects on serious assault (although the effect of belief on initiation is not statistically significant for the later waves). (4) Gender matters for initiation (males are more likely to initiate serious assault perpetration) but not for suspension (differences in the odds of suspension are in the expected direction, with males less likely to suspend serious assault perpetration, but the differences are not statistically significant). (5) The impact of ethnicity is statistically significant for both initiation and suspension, with minority group members more likely to initiate and less likely to suspend involvement in serious assaultive behavior, with the exception of two statistically nonsignificant coefficients (African American ethnicity on suspension in the earlier waves, other ethnicity on suspension in the later waves). (6) The distinction between the earlier waves, with 1-year measurement intervals, and later waves, with 3-year measurement intervals, may not reflect the measurement interval itself so much as differences between different historical periods or different age spans in the sample.

CONCLUSION

Developmental change in individuals is an area of long-standing interest in the behavioral sciences, and research in this area has become more extensive with the increased availability of long-term longitudinal data on individuals. Techniques used in studying developmental changes in individuals can also, in principle, be used on more aggregated cases (cities, counties, nations, formal organizations). Adapting the technology of multilevel growth curve modeling to the study of discrete dependent variables moves us from multilevel *growth* models to multilevel *change* models. Ideally, beginning with a multilevel model incorporating a time dimension (age or period), one could incorporate other predictors that would explain the relationship of time or age to the dependent variable (and, by implication, successful explanation would mean that controlling for these other predictors would reduce the relationship between the time dimension and the dependent variable to statistical and substantive nonsignificance). Short of a full explanation of the relationship between the time dimension and the dependent variable, the use of multilevel logistic regression models allows us to model the pattern of the relationship between the dependent variable and the time dimension using repeated measures for the predictors and the dependent variables on the same set of cases while adjusting for the inherent dependency in data collected repeatedly from the same subjects. Although multilevel modeling was developed from a perspective emphasizing the analysis of variance, including the partitioning of variance between the individual observations and the larger contexts or clusters within which those observations were nested, some multilevel statistical software makes it reasonably easy to estimate simple multilevel logistic regression models for longitudinal, repeated measures data. More complex models, ironically, may be problematic for the more sophisticated multilevel statistical packages, and in some instances, the best solution may be to rely on simpler statistical models and routines, perhaps sacrificing some specificity in accounting for the nature of the clustering of the observations in the data, in exchange for being able to reasonably estimate the model.

Multilevel change modeling for categorical dependent variables, event history analysis, and, from the last chapter, longitudinal panel analysis of categorical dependent variables, differ from one another in important ways. Multilevel logistic regression modeling may be seen as a straightforward extension of the basic logistic regression model to account for the clustering of observations within individuals, most typically modeling the pattern of change over time and, if the dependent variable is itself a change variable, also being able to model the timing of change. Event history analysis models, in contrast, are explicitly models of the timing of change, as reflected in the dependent variable (which represents a change of state), which cases are included (cases not eligible for the change in question are excluded from the analysis), and a time dimension as a predictor. Panel analysis with logistic regression typically involves fewer than five separate time points and does not necessarily include a time dimension in the model. For example, several of the models in the previous chapter included no time dimension at all, and when they did include age as a time dimension, because there were only two or three waves of data, the age comparisons really involved between-individual rather than within-individual differences in marijuana use associated with age.

A time dimension is one of the defining features of event history analysis, and although not absolutely necessary in a multilevel model (age and time may prove to have no statistically significant impacts on the outcome variable), we typically begin in multilevel longitudinal modeling by examining the relationship of the outcome with at least one time dimension. Where multilevel change modeling and (usually) panel analysis differ from event history analysis is in not restricting the analysis to cases defined as being "at risk" of change in the direction of interest. In event history analysis, *initiation* (whether someone who has not previously used marijuana begins to do so, for which only nonusers are at risk) or *suspension* (whether someone who has been using marijuana ceases to do so, for which only users are at risk) would typically be the variables of interest, each with its own separate at risk set of cases. In multilevel analysis and panel analysis, it is more typically *prevalence* (simply whether one does or does not use marijuana) that is the dependent variable of interest, and the risk set is typically defined as all respondents. Multilevel analysis, panel analysis, and event history analysis thus present a complementary set of approaches for the analysis of longitudinal categorical data. In some cases, they may be combined: For example, lagged endogenous variables may be incorporated into multilevel modeling; multilevel models may be used to provide the separate estimation of the different components of a path model when we are dealing with a combination of clustered data and categorical outcomes. Roberts (2008) provides an example combining multilevel analysis and event history analysis (proportional odds model) to analyze clearance rates (whether a criminal case was solved, and if so, when) for nonlethal violent crimes. The proportional odds event history analysis, operating at Level 1 answers the questions of whether and when cases are cleared; Level 2 consists of cities, for which random intercepts and city characteristics including social organization and police resources are used to account for nonindependence within cities in whether and when cases are cleared.

For both multilevel logistic regression models and discrete time event history analysis models using logistic regression, there are alternatives which do not involve the use of the logistic regression framework. To a large extent, the alternatives involve a very similar approach, but based on different distributional assumptions, as in probit or discriminant analysis, or the use of the complementary log-log link for discrete time event history analysis. These approaches can be regarded as minor variations on the theme offered by logistic regression analysis. In other instances, however, the differences are more pronounced, as in the use of polychoric correlations with weighted least squares to estimate latent change models for discrete dependent variables with repeated measurement. It is to these alternative approaches to logistic regression that we turn in the next and final chapter.

NOTES

1. Software Note: If the only random coefficient is the random intercept, then as seen in Chapter 11 it is possible to estimate the model using Stata **xtlogit** for a dichotomous dependent variable (and, by extension, one can use separate estimation with Stata **xtlogit** for polytomous dependent variables). More complex models with additional random coefficients can be estimated using a multilevel analysis package such as HLM. One could also use the user-supplied Stata procedure **gllamm**, but the long time required to calculate any but the simplest models using quadrature (an issue exacerbated by the large number of cases, more than 1,000, constituting the Level 2 units for the analysis in this chapter) was noted Chapter 11.

2. Software Note: This was performed using both SAS and SPSS **logistic**, and the results were similar but not identical for the two packages; the results reported in the text use the SPSS contrast, which had better success in constructing a complete set of orthogonal polynomials for ages 12 to 33.

3. For a general discussion of missing value imputation, see Little and Rubin (2002); and specific to wave-missing panel data, see, for example, Lepkowski (1989).

4. Software Note: HLM was used for the estimates in Table 14.1; Stata **xtlogit** could also be used in the present context. For HLM, the predicted values of logit(Y) and the predicted probability of marijuana use must be calculated separately. For **xtlogit**, the predicted values are obtained using the standard prediction options available in Stata. Stata **xtlogit** provides the Wald z statistic; HLM calculates a Student's t statistic based on the estimated coefficient and its standard error, from which the p value is found based on the number of degrees of freedom, in this instance 1,672 for the intercept, gender, and ethnicity, and 10,950 for the other predictors in the model.

5. Software Note: Separately, the model was tested using HLM for random effects in the coefficients for age and the coefficients for exposure and belief, but the random effects for these coefficients were not statistically significant, and thus (a) they are excluded from the model and (b) **xtlogit** can be used to estimate the random effects model. Comparing the maximum likelihood Laplace model from HLM and the model from **xtlogit**, levels of explained variance are the same, unstandardized coefficients are similar, and standardized coefficients appear to be even more similar than the unstandardized coefficients for the two models. Substantively, the results are similar to the results from the population-averaged model.

6. Software Note: While not shown here in detail, models were also calculated using Stata **logit** and **gllamm**. In Stata **logit**, the impact of being male on marijuana use was negative and statistically significant with the same set of predictors in the model, and the impact of ethnicity was not statistically significant. The **gllamm** model produced substantially larger coefficients that were generally at odds with the findings from the other random intercept models.

7. Software Note: There may, however, be limitations to this approach. Specific to HLM, for example, only the unit-specific model is calculated. There is no provision for estimating the population-averaged model, and it is not possible with existing software to calculate Laplace-type maximum likelihood estimates, for polytomous nominal or ordinal dependent variables. At best, with HLM, we can use full PQL estimation, but as indicated in the text, this may not be sufficient to justify the use of likelihood-based statistics to assess the model.

8. Software Note: HLM was used in constructing Tables 14.3 and 14.4, but it requires a fair amount of supplementation by a general purpose statistical package (SAS, SPSS, or Stata) to calculate the logistic functions, correlations between observed and predicted values as described in Chapters 9 and 10, and calculation of descriptive statistics for use in constructing the fully standardized logistic regression coefficients, which were calculated by hand. The HLM default of excluding the last category was implemented here for illustration, but it is possible to recode the outcome variable to have a different reference category (and for most of us, having the lowest category as the reference category and talking about positive coefficients indicating increases in levels of substance use is probably much more intuitively appealing). Alternatives to using HLM or comparable multilevel software to calculate the multilevel polytomous logistic regression model include using a procedure such as **xtlogit** for separate estimation of the logistic functions in a polytomous nominal or ordinal model, the latter with unequal slopes and using procedures such as Stata **mlogit** and **ologit** with the "cluster" specification to try to account for the dependencies in the data that result from repeated observations on the same cases.

9. Event history analysis is itself a book-length topic, and the reader is referred to the numerous texts available on the topic (e.g., Hosmer and Lemeshow 1999; Kalbfleisch and Prentice 2002; Lawless 2003; Yamaguchi 1991) for more detail than is provided here. The purpose in this chapter is to give a general overview of event history analysis, then illustrate how logistic regression analysis has been and can be used to analyze discrete time event history data. In the example that follows, orthogonal polynomials were used to test for a nonlinear relationship between the dependent variable and age but no evidence of nonlinearity was found.

CHAPTER 15

Comparisons

Logistic Regression and Alternative Models

 T his book began by noting the difficulties in ordinary least squares linear regression (Chapter 1) and log-linear analysis (Chapter 2) for modeling dichotomous dependent variables as functions of a mixture of continuous and categorical predictors, and the emergence of the logistic regression model, which blended the analysis of dichotomous (or more generally discrete) dependent variables from log-linear analysis and the incorporation of continuous predictors from linear regression analysis. The logistic regression model is based on the assumption that the distribution of the probabilities of "success" for each value of the predictor follows the S-shaped logistic curve in Figure 1.3 on page 12. The logistic distribution, however, is by no means the only distribution to produce this type of curve. The first, and perhaps conceptually the simplest, alternatives to logistic regression involve distributions other than the logistic distribution as the basis for estimating the relationship between the predictors and the dependent variable. Two of the more common alternatives are the probit and complementary log-log distributions.

In the probit model, like the logit model in the context of log-linear analysis, cases are typically aggregated into covariate patterns, groups of cases having the same values on the independent variables. Each covariate pattern is viewed as a *cell* in a contingency table, with an observed frequency (the number of cases in the cell) and an expected frequency (the number of cases that would be in the cell if the variables that define the cell were unrelated or independent of one another). For categorical variables with few values (e.g., ethnicity, with only three categories), there may be many cases in a single covariate pattern. For a continuous variable, there may be no more than one case with a particular value. If there are several continuous variables, each with a large (relative to the sample size) number of possible values, each covariate pattern may, as is so often the case in logistic regression analysis, represent a single case.

In the logistic regression model, the unstandardized coefficients could be interpreted as the change in logit(Y) associated with a one-unit change in the independent variable. In logit analysis, if the variables are scaled in the same way as in logistic regression, the coefficients and their interpretation will be the same, but the model fit will be based on predicted and observed frequencies within covariate patterns, rather than predicted probabilities. For probit models, the coefficients may be interpreted as the change in probit(Y) associated with a one-unit change in the independent variable, where

$$\text{probit}(Y) = \Phi^{-1}\left[P(Y=1)\right] \tag{15.1}$$

and

$$\Phi(X) = (1/\sqrt{2\pi}) \int_{-\infty}^{X} e^{-z^2/2}\, dz. \tag{15.2}$$

The coefficients in the probit model are commonly multiplied by 2, and a constant of 5 is commonly added. Probit coefficients are therefore typically about twice as large as logit coefficients for the same model. Probit models can accommodate polytomous dependent variables, particularly polytomous ordinal variables in the ordered probit model, but are most often used with dichotomous dependent variables.

The logistic regression model is based on the equation $\eta = \text{logit}(Y) = \ln\{P(Y=1)/[1-P(Y=1)]\} = \alpha + \beta_1 X_1 + \beta_2 X_2 + \cdots + \beta_K X_K$, where $\eta = \text{logit}(Y)$ is the link function used to transform Y to a form that allows the right-hand side of the equation $(\alpha + \beta_1 X_1 + \beta_2 X_2 + \cdots + \beta_K X_K)$ to be expressed in linear form. In parallel fashion, the complementary log-log model is based on the transformation $\eta = \text{cloglog}(Y) = \ln\{-\ln[1-P(Y=1)]\} = \alpha + \beta_1 X_1 + \beta_2 X_2 + \cdots + \beta_K X_K$. If e is the exponential function, then reversing the transformation for the logistic regression model requires us to calculate $P(Y=1) = \exp(\eta)/[1 + \exp(\eta)]$; for the complementary log-log model, the reverse transformation is $P(Y=1) = \{\exp[\exp(\eta)] -1\}/\{\exp[\exp(\eta)]\}$. The logistic regression model can be interpreted as a proportional odds model; the complementary log-log regression model can be interpreted as a proportional hazards model, a point which makes it of interest in event history analysis, where several of the more common models make the proportional hazards rather than the proportional odds assumption. Like the probit model, the complementary log-log model can readily handle dichotomous and ordinal polytomous dependent variables, but for nominal polytomous dependent variables, logistic regression is much more commonly used.[1] In most instances, results from using probit or cloglog in place of logit transformations will have little impact on the substantive results, but particularly for event history analysis, the cloglog proportional hazards model deserves consideration as an alternative. It will very likely be preferred to the logistic regression proportional odds model.

DISCRIMINANT ANALYSIS

Discriminant analysis (Klecka 1980), like linear regression, assumes continuous independent variables, but a binary or categorical dependent variable. A linear relationship is assumed, not between the dependent and independent variables, but between the independent variables and the *discriminant functions,* linear combinations of predictors used to classify cases. Discriminant analysis also assumes a multivariate normal distribution for the predictors, and that covariance matrices among the predictors are equal for each group. As noted by Hosmer and Lemeshow (1989) and Ryan (1997), discriminant analysis is highly sensitive to the assumption of normality of the predictors, but this assumption is rarely correct in practice, with the result, particularly if there are dichotomous predictors in the model, that discriminant function coefficients (which are analogous to linear regression coefficients) are biased away from zero when the true coefficient is nonzero. When the condition of multivariate normality is satisfied, discriminant analysis is the true maximum likelihood estimator, and is more efficient than logistic regression in estimating the parameters of the model (Maddala 1983), but the condition of multivariate normality is rarely satisfied, and unless there are good reasons to believe that the assumptions for using discriminant analysis are satisfied, there appears to be a general consensus that probit or log-linear/logit/logistic regression models are preferable (Hosmer and Lemeshow 1989; Maddala 1983; Ryan 1997).

With respect to empirical considerations, in discriminant analysis, rather than selecting a reference category prior to the analysis and comparing all of the other categories of the dependent variable to the reference category, the standard practice is to maximize the discrimination among the different possible combinations of categories of the dependent variables by selecting (usually automatically, through the software routine) to first split the variable into categories or combinations of categories that are the most different from one another, then selecting subsequent splits to be orthogonal to (statistically independent of) the first split, and subject to that orthogonality, to maximize the difference between the categories or groups of categories. This continues until a total of $(M - 1)$ design variables for the unordered polytomous dependent variable have been created. In discriminant analysis, the criterion for deciding where to make the first and subsequent splits to construct the contrasts for the dependent variable is based on maximizing the ability of the independent variables in the model to discriminate among the categories of the dependent variable, as indicated by the canonical correlation coefficient for each discriminant function. In other words, the first split, on which subsequent splits depend (because they must be orthogonal), is the one which produces the highest canonical correlation coefficient between the dependent variable contrast and the predictors in the model.

The discriminant analysis model is similar to the linear probability model, described in Chapter 1, insofar as the dependent variable is modeled as a linear function of the independent variables, but in discriminant analysis, the categorical nature of the dependent variable is explicitly recognized, and discriminant analysis easily allows analysis of nominal polytomous dependent variables. For a dependent variable with h categories, $h - 1$ separate equations are calculated, representing the distinctions among $h - 1$ independent subsets of the values of the dependent variable. In this respect, the discriminant analysis model is similar to the polytomous logistic regression model. The coefficients in the discriminant analysis model represent the change in the value of the *discriminant function* associated with a one-unit change in the independent variable. The discriminant function is simply a linear combination of the independent variables used to predict the value of the dependent variable. For a dichotomous dependent variable, the discriminant function coefficients are a constant multiple of the linear regression coefficients in the linear probability model.

AN EMPIRICAL COMPARISON OF LOGISTIC REGRESSION, PROBIT, LINEAR PROBABILITY, AND DISCRIMINANT ANALYSIS

Table 15.1 presents the results of analyzing the prevalence of marijuana use at Wave 5 (PMRJ5) of the National Youth Survey (NYS) with exposure to delinquent friends at Wave 5 (EDF5), belief that it is wrong to violate the law at Wave 4 (BELIEF4), gender (MALE), and ethnicity (BLACK, OTHER) using (a) logistic regression and logit models, whose coefficients are the same, (b) a probit model, (c) a linear probability model, and (d) a discriminant analysis model. The logistic

TABLE 15.1	Alternative Models for a Dichotomous Dependent Variable				
		Model (Standardized Coefficients)			
Dependent Variable	*Independent Variables*	*Logistic Regression or Logit*	*Probit*	*Linear Probability (Linear Regression)*	*Discriminant Analysis*
PMRJ5	EDF5	.955	1.007	.503	.841
	BELIEF4	−.257	−.203	−.148	−.275
	MALE	−.418	−.431	−.208	−.417
	Ethnicity:				
	BLACK	.050	.050	.015	.030
	OTHER	.106	.108	.035	.072
	R^2	.435	.394 unweighted .411 weighted	.394	.394
	R^2_L	.367	—	—	—

regression model is evaluated using both R^2_L and R^2_O (here simply designated R^2); the other models are all evaluated using R^2 (the canonical correlation squared, R^2_C, for discriminant analysis). For the probit analysis, R^2 is calculated using the aggregated data, without weighting for the number of cases in each covariate pattern, and for disaggregated data, weighting each covariate pattern by the number of cases having that pattern. The linear probability, discriminant analysis, and unweighted probit models all have an R^2 of .394. For the probit model with covariate patterns weighted by number of cases, $R^2 = .411$. In the logistic regression model, $R^2 = .435$ (the appropriate standard of comparison with the other models) and $R^2_L = .367$. It will by no means always be the case that the logistic regression model produces the strongest relationship between the predictors and the dependent variable, but in this instance, it appears to explain 2% to 4% more of the variation in prevalence of marijuana use than the alternative models.

After multiplying the probit coefficients by two, the coefficients produced by the different models may be compared. The *unstandardized* regression coefficients are equal to .2345 multiplied by the *unstandardized* discriminant function coefficients, but the ratio of the standardized regression and discriminant function coefficients is not (and would not be expected to be) constant. The discriminant function coefficients are very similar to the logistic regression coefficients. The coefficients for ethnicity in the probit model are almost identical to the coefficients in the logistic regression model, and the coefficient for EDF5 is also close (within .05), but for BELIEF4 and GENDER, the probit model coefficients are not as close as the coefficients in the discriminant analysis model are to the logistic regression coefficients. From all four models, the substantive conclusions are the same: The dependent variable, prevalence of marijuana use, is most strongly related to exposure to delinquent friends (EDF5), followed by gender, then belief that it is wrong to violate the law. The effect of ethnicity is not statistically significant in any of the models. In addition, in the probit model, the effect of belief on prevalence of marijuana use is not statistically significant ($p = .121$). In all the other models, the effect of belief is statistically significant.

For polytomous models, discriminant analysis automatically searches for the combination of groups that results in the largest difference between groups for the first discriminant function, unlike logistic regression, in which the contrasts must be specified by the researcher. For the second function, it attempts to maximize the differences between groups again, subject to the constraint that the second function must be *orthogonal* to or independent of the first. The third function is selected to be orthogonal to the other two, and again, discriminant analysis calculates parameters that maximize the differences between groups. The value of the canonical discriminant function at the group centroids indicates which groups are being separated. The group centroid is the mean of the discriminant function for all the variables in the discriminant function at once, not combined, but taken separately in multidimensional space, with each variable in the discriminant function representing one dimension. Typically, there is no one reference group in discriminant analysis as there is in polytomous logistic regression or multinomial logit models.

In terms of sheer convenience, discriminant analysis is easier to use for a polytomous dependent variable than logistic regression or the multinomial logit model. Like logistic regression, it calculates $h - 1$ equations, where h is the number of categories in the dependent variable. Unlike logistic regression, statistical packages for discriminant analysis commonly provide summary statistics for each equation separately: a test for the statistical significance of the relationship between the dependent variable and the independent variables, and a measure of association (the canonical correlation) for each equation separately. In this respect, discriminant analysis is more like the separate logistic regressions approach than the multinomial logit model for analyzing a polytomous dependent variable. The principal problems with discriminant analysis of polytomous dependent variables are the arbitrary nature of the contrasts discriminant analysis selects, and the very strong likelihood of violating the assumptions underlying the use of discriminant analysis, especially the assumption that the independent variables are similarly related to one another for each of the groups defined by the dependent variable. This can be illustrated by comparing a discriminant analysis model with logistic regression models with drug user type (DRGTYPE) as a dependent variable.

Table 15.2 provides a summary of results from discriminant analysis with DRGTYPE as the dependent variable. The first half of the table presents the discriminant analysis results. The second half presents results of a separate regressions logistic regression analysis designed to parallel the discriminant analysis contrasts. The *canonical discriminant function evaluated at group centroids* (bottom of table) indicates which contrasts are made for each function. In Table 15.2, the first function appears to be an ordinal function of the seriousness of drug use. It distinguishes nonusers (value of the discriminant function at the group centroid for nonusers $C_1 = -.957$) from alcohol users ($C_2 = -.380$), alcohol users from marijuana users ($C_3 = .709$), and marijuana users from polydrug users ($C_4 = 1.744$), and a little more loosely nonusers and alcohol users (negative) from marijuana and polydrug users (positive). The second function appears to distinguish alcohol users (positive) from the combination of nonusers and marijuana users (negative), and to be largely unrelated to polydrug use. This is not a grouping or contrast that we would be likely to make based on theory or intuition, but it is the contrast that maximizes the separation between groups for the second discriminant function, subject to the constraint of orthogonality with the first function. The third function distinguishes marijuana users (positive) from polydrug users (negative), and appears to be largely unrelated to nonuse or alcohol use. Although this makes more sense intuitively, the function is not statistically significant ($p = .252$), and the strength of association between the canonical discriminant function and the two groups is weak ($R_{C3}^2 = .012$).

TABLE 15.2   Polytomous Discriminant Analysis and Separate Logistic Regressions

Dependent Variable	Model Fit	Independent Variables	Unstandardized Coefficients	Standardized Coefficients
Discriminant				
Function 1: Nonusers vs. alcohol, marijuana, and polydrug users	$\chi^2 = 165.39$, 12 df ($p = .000$) $R_C^2 = .455$	EDF5 BELIEF4 MALE WHITE Constant	0.232 −0.106 −0.793 0.405 0.206	.789 −.365 −.386 .163 —
Function 2: Alcohol users vs. marijuana users and nonusers	$\chi^2 = 30.78$, 6 df ($p = .000$) $R_C^2 = .119$	EDF5 BELIEF4 MALE WHITE Constant	−0.104 −0.128 1.022 1.910 2.775	−.355 −.441 .497 .770 —
Function 3: Marijuana users vs. polydrug users	$\chi^2 = 2.76$, 2 df ($p = .252$) $R_C^2 = .012$	EDF5 BELIEF4 MALE WHITE Constant	0.070 −0.024 1.626 −1.063 −0.144	.239 −.083 .791 −.428 —
Logistic				
Equation 1: Nonusers vs. alcohol, marijuana, and polydrug users	$G_M = 107.306$ ($p = .000$) $R^2 = .428$ $R_L^2 = .363$	EDF5 BELIEF4 MALE WHITE Constant	.410 −0.107 −1.558 −0.341 −1.687	.963 −.233 −.429 −.145 —
Equation 2: Alcohol users vs. marijuana users and nonusers	$G_M = 29.717$ ($p = .000$) $R^2 = .144$ $R_L^2 = .110$	EDF5 BELIEF4 MALE WHITE Constant	−0.151 −0.106 0.917 1.403 2.816	−.355 −.231 .253 .596 —
Equation 3: Marijuana users vs. polydrug users	$G_M = 19.113$ ($p = .001$) $R^2 = .221$ $R_L^2 = .177$	EDF5 BELIEF4 MALE WHITE Constant	0.115 −0.118 −1.141 1.729 −0.404	.270 −.257 −.315 .182 —

Canonical Discriminant Functions Evaluated at Group Centroids	Function 1	Function 2	Function 3
Group 1 (Nonusers)	−0.957	−0.406	−0.077
Group 2 (Alcohol users)	−0.380	0.430	0.019
Group 3 (Marijuana users)	0.709	−0.288	0.168
Group 4 (Polydrug users)	1.744	0.028	−0.179

On the first function, polydrug users are most different from nonusers, followed by marijuana users and alcohol users. The *standardized canonical discriminant function coefficients,* which are like standardized regression coefficients, indicate that being in a higher category of drug user type is strongly positively associated with exposure to delinquent friends and weakly positively associated with being White, and moderately negatively associated with gender and belief that it is wrong to violate the law. The logistic regression model for this contrast produces similar results, except that being White is negatively, but not statistically significantly, associated with being a drug user as opposed to a nonuser. More consistent with the first discriminant function is the ordinal, parallel slopes model for DRGTYPE in Chapter 10 (e.g., Figure 10.2, p. 199, or Figure 10.3 p. 201). The coefficients in the cumulative logit model in Chapter 10 are all statistically significant, all have the same sign as the coefficients for the first discriminant function, and the relative strengths of the relationships are similar, with the exception that BELIEF4 appears to be more strongly related than GENDER to type of drug use in the ordinal polytomous model.

On the second canonical discriminant function, alcohol users are contrasted with nonusers and marijuana users. The low value of the canonical discriminant function for polydrug users indicates that they are not distinguished from other groups by this discriminant function. Low values of both exposure and belief, along with being White and male, characterize respondents who use alcohol, as opposed to being nonusers or using marijuana. The logistic regression model contrasting alcohol users with marijuana users and with nonusers produces similar results with respect to the sign of each coefficient but not with respect to the magnitude of the standardized logistic regression coefficients. In the logistic regression model, being White has the strongest effect, but this is followed by the effect of exposure to delinquent friends, the weakest predictor in the discriminant analysis model.

The third discriminant function is not statistically significant; it attempts to discriminate between marijuana users and polydrug users, but the squared canonical correlation $R_C^2 = .012$, and $\chi^2 = 2.76$ with 2 degrees of freedom ($p = .252$), indicating that this difference is essentially unexplained by the model. The logistic regression model is more successful ($G_M = 19.113$, $p = .0007$; $R_L^2 = .177$; $R^2 = .221$), and indicates that respondents who have high exposure to delinquent friends, low belief that it is wrong to violate the law, are female, and are White, are more likely to be polydrug users as opposed to marijuana users. In this instance, both the signs and the magnitudes of the logistic regression coefficients are inconsistent with the discriminant analysis coefficients.

Logistic regression and discriminant analysis appear to generate different results in two ways. If we compare the polytomous logistic regression model to the discriminant analysis model in Table 15.2, the contrasts that we would naturally make for the logistic regression model are not the contrasts made in the discriminant analysis model. In particular, the contrast between alcohol users on one hand and both nonusers and marijuana users on the other is counterintuitive, has no basis in theory or past research, and appears to have no advantage other than satisfying the purely numerical criterion of maximizing separation between groups, subject to the constraint that it be orthogonal to the first canonical discriminant function. Alternatively, constructing separate logistic regressions to parallel the contrasts made in the discriminant analysis model, the results of the logistic regression are somewhat, but not overwhelmingly, consistent with the discriminant analysis results. Acknowledging the discrepancy between the logistic regression and discriminant analysis results, which set of results is better?

Technically, the discriminant analysis model violated the assumption of equal covariances among the predictors for the different groups (Box's $M = 104.3$, $p = .000$), and the ordinal logistic regression model based on the parallel slopes assumption violated the assumption of parallel slopes (Score test $\chi^2 = 32.066$, $p = .000$). The separate regressions approach to polytomous logistic regression appears to be fairly but not completely consistent with the polytomous logistic regression model. In the purely categorical model, the relationships between the dependent variable and the independent variables vary, depending on the groups being compared. In general, if the coefficients are statistically significant (and usually when they are not), increases in exposure, decreases in belief, being female, and being White are predictive of higher levels or seriousness of drug use, but the numerical values of the slopes (unstandardized coefficients of .165 to .633 for exposure, $-.271$ to $-.360$ for belief, -2.224 to $+0.505$ for gender, .357 to 2.209 for ethnicity) are so different that it appears best to treat type of drug use as an unordered categorical variable. Based on purely technical considerations, the polytomous logistic regression model with unordered categories seems most appropriate in this instance. For other samples and other variables, the conclusions may be quite different.

EVENT HISTORY ANALYSIS

As noted in the previous chapter, although logistic regression analysis was commonly used to estimate the proportional odds discrete time event history analysis model in the past, with the increased availability of statistical routines that can calculate the proportional hazards discrete time event history analysis model using the complementary log-log (cloglog) link, the suggestion has been made that the proportional hazards model is preferable, and that the reasons for using logistic regression for discrete time event history analysis in the past were (a) the greater accessibility of logistic regression as opposed to cloglog regression and (b) the fact that the logit and cloglog links typically produced similar results for low-probability outcomes (e.g., Hosmer and Lemeshow 1999:268). Hosmer and Lemeshow cite the work of Kalbfleisch and Prentice (1980), which indicated that if the discrete-time data arose from grouping continuous-time data, estimates of the parameters using the proportional odds (logistic regression) discrete time event history analysis model were not consistent. They also note that when one estimates both models, logistic regression and cloglog regression produce coefficients that are different from one another. This last point is hardly surprising; after all, with different transformations for the dependent variable, one essentially has the dependent variable measured on two different scales, a logit scale and a cloglog scale, and although the two may be similar, one would not expect the coefficient estimates from the two to be identical.

To illustrate the comparison between the proportional odds logit link used in logistic regression and the proportional hazards cloglog link used in cloglog regression, initiation and suspension of serious assault are once again considered as the dependent variables. For purposes of this illustration, to avoid getting bogged down in detail, the model from the last chapter has been simplified by omitting the measurement interval and the interaction terms associated with it from the present model, and odds ratios are not presented since they are essentially redundant with the unstandardized coefficients. Table 15.3 presents the results for initiation of serious assault, paralleling the analysis in Table 14.5 (p. 312), but this time with the first half of the table showing the results for the logit link, and the second half of the table showing the results for the cloglog link. As summary statistics, G_M and its statistical significance are included, along with R_O^2 (and its square root, R_O, used in calculating the standardized coefficients), R_L^2 and R_N^2. As mentioned in Chapter 3 (remember back that far?), it has been suggested that R_N^2 is the more appropriate measure of explained variation for the proportional hazards model, so it is included here as an additional point of comparison between the logit and cloglog link models for event history analysis. The three measures of explained variation

TABLE 15.3   Initiation of Serious Assault

Predictor	b^*	b	SE(b)	Wald χ^2 (df = 1)	p(Wald)
Logit link (Proportional Odds)					
Age	−.181	−0.192	.037	27.278	.000
Year	.063	0.072	.040	3.289	.070*
Male	.090	1.018	.143	50.470	.000
Black	.040	0.701	.166	17.788	.000
Other	.026	0.669	.247	7.350	.007
Exposure	.058	0.100	.016	37.626	.000
Belief	−.027	−0.044	.020	4.945	.026*
Intercept	—	−0.985	.892	1.218	.270*

$G_M = 244.324$, $df = 7$, $p = .000$

$R_L^2 = .109$

$R_N^2 = .124$

$R_O^2 = .035$; $R_O = .188$

	b^*	b	SE(b)	Wald χ^2 (df = 1)	p(Wald)
Cloglog link (Proportional hazards)					
Age	−.180	−0.055	.011	25.182	.000
Year	.076	0.025	.012	4.520	.034*
Male	.091	0.295	.041	51.948	.000
Black	.051	0.256	.055	21.692	.000
Other	.029	0.221	.083	7.120	.008
Exposure	.076	0.038	.006	38.656	.000
Belief	−.038	−0.018	.007	2.753	.097*
Intercept	—	0.704	.288	5.977	.014*

$G_M = 248.828$, $df = 7$, $p = .000$

$R_L^2 = .111$

$R_N^2 = .174$

$R_O^2 = .037$; $R_O = .193$

* Significance levels substantially different between the two models.

tell a similar story: Explained variation is very slightly better for the proportional hazards model than for the proportional odds model, and the difference is greater using R_N^2 than the other measures of explained variation.

If one examines the unstandardized coefficients in the model, they are indeed different for the two models. The standardized coefficients, however, are quite similar, in both cases indicating that the strongest predictor of initiation of serious assault (without controlling for measurement interval) is age, followed by being male, then chronological time, then exposure to delinquent friends.

Younger respondents, males, and individuals with more exposure to delinquent friends are more likely to initiate involvement in serious assault perpetration, and more likely to do so in later than in earlier years. The impacts of age and year here run counter to one another, since younger ages (with higher initiation rates) occur in earlier years (with lower initiation rates). There are some relatively minor differences in the statistical significance of the coefficients for the two models: For the variable YEAR, $p = .070$ with the logit link, .034 with the cloglog link; for the variable BELIEF $p = .026$ with the logit link and .097 with the cloglog link; and for the intercept, $p = .270$ for the logit link and .014 for the cloglog link. Substantively, however, the two models paint a similar picture, based on the standardized coefficients.

Table 15.4 presents the results of the two models for suspension of serious assault. This time, according to R^2_L and R^2_N, the proportional odds model is very slightly better than the proportional hazards model, but according to R^2_O, the proportional hazards model is very slightly better. Comparing both models for both initiation and suspension, there is little in the summary statistics to recommend one model over the other. The unstandardized coefficients are more similar across the two models for suspension than they were for initiation of serious assault. The effect of being African American (BLACK) is marginally significant with the logit link, but not statistically significant with the cloglog link; the intercept is not statistically significant in either model; and all of the other predictors are statistically significant ($p < .05$) in both models. The standardized coefficients for both models indicate that the strongest influence on suspension is chronological time, followed by exposure to delinquent friends, then age, with suspension being more likely for later years, older ages, and individuals having less exposure to delinquent friends. This time the age and time trends reinforce one another, in contrast to the finding for initiation.

There are other distributions that could be used in event history analysis models for discrete time data that involve neither the proportional hazards nor the proportional odds assumption. Usually, there is little theoretical reason to choose one distribution over another (although there may be a certain aesthetic appeal to having proportional hazards or proportional odds, other things being equal). As a practical matter, unless one has strong theoretical reason to do otherwise, it would be reasonable to compare the results of different distributions and select the one that produces the best predictions of the dependent variable. Alternatively, if data dredging and playing with different distributional assumptions does not appeal to you, the cloglog proportional hazards model seems generally reasonable, is unlikely to produce results greatly different from those produced by the proportional odds model, and is the distribution least likely to be questioned by journal editors—the last not a great reason for its selection, but often as not there are really no better reasons for the selection of one distribution over another. If nothing else, comparison of results across different assumed distributions can be used as a diagnostic tool to indicate how sensitive the results are to the distributional assumptions used in the model. Speaking of diagnostics, the literature on diagnostics for the cloglog link is not nearly as well developed as the literature on diagnostics for the logistic regression model, something that, until this situation changes, might be considered a point in favor of the logit over the cloglog link for event history analysis. If one is going to compare results for different distributions, results in this chapter seem to repeatedly reinforce the point that standardized coefficients are most useful for comparisons across models. This is because the models are calculated on the same data, using the same model structure, with the only difference being the transformation applied to the dependent variable (and hence the scale on which the dependent variable is measured). Comparisons of unstandardized coefficients in these circumstances are not as informative because they are contaminated by differences in the scale of measurement for the dependent variable.

TABLE 15.4 Suspension of Serious Assault

Predictors	b^*	b	$SE(b)$	$Wald\ \chi2$	$p(Wald)$
Logit Link (Proportional Odds)					
Age	.105	.065	.032	4.182	.041
Year	.219	.142	.034	17.319	.000
Male	−.045	−.320	.139	5.295	.021
Black	−.030	−.251	.151	2.772	.096*
Other	−.040	−.530	.212	6.214	.013
Exposure	−.151	−.100	.012	68.480	.000
Belief	.062	.051	.016	10.619	.001
Intercept	—	.093	.719	.017	.898
$G_M = 429.027, df = 7, p = .000$					
$R_L^2 = .181$					
$R_N^2 = .256$					
$R_O^2 = .167; R_O = .409$					
Cloglog Link (Proportional Hazards)					
Age	.109	.059	.027	4.801	.028
Year	.232	.131	.029	20.000	.000
Male	−.045	−.282	.120	5.498	.019
Black	−.019	−.135	.129	1.089	.297*
Other	−.042	−.477	.168	8.097	.004
Exposure	−.124	−.072	.009	60.058	.000
Belief	.067	.048	.013	13.939	.000
Intercept	—	.126	.593	.045	.831
$G_M = 423.524, df = 7, p = .000$					
$R_L^2 = .178$					
$R_N^2 = .253$					
$R_O^2 = .168; R_O = .410$					

* Significance levels substantially different between the two models.

LATENT VARIABLE STRUCTURAL EQUATION MODELS AND LATENT CHANGE MODELS

Latent variable structural equation models (Bollen 1989; Hayduk 1987; Kaplan 2000; Kline 2005; Raykov and Marcoulides 2006) are a general class of models in which the assumption is made that for at least some of the measured variables in the data, the measured variables constitute no better than indirect measurement of the underlying concepts they represent. For example, the measure of belief that it is wrong to violate the law is based on a series of questions about whether specific law violations were very wrong, wrong, somewhat wrong, or not wrong at all. These responses were simply added together for the set of questions, and used to represent the underlying concept, belief that it is wrong to violate the law. In latent variable structural equation modeling (SEM), the answers to these questions would more likely have been combined using a factor analysis model, weighting the questions differently, depending on how much variance they shared with other questions in the set. In addition to multiple indicator variables, in which the multiple indicators are combined into a single variable via factor analysis, it is also possible to have single indicator variables, such as gender and ethnicity, in a latent variable structural equation model, resulting in a mix of latent and manifest (single indicator, assumed to directly measure the concept) variables. Once the measurement model has been specified, the relationships among the variables are hypothesized and tested, using simultaneous estimation of all the structural relationships at once in a model like the path analytical models described in Chapter 8, where it was noted that simultaneous estimation of path models is generally the preferred approach.

Latent variable structural equation models are a general class of models, of which structural equation models without latent variables constitute a proper subset. Technically, all the models used in this book up to this point are structural equation models; they just have not been described as such in the latent variable SEM context. Likewise, while simultaneous estimation is the generally preferred approach to SEM, separate estimation of the components of the structural equation model may also be performed. For continuous interval/ratio variables, there are numerous options for latent variable SEM, including EQS, LISREL, AMOS, SAS **calis**, Mplus, and provisions for latent variable analysis in software designed primarily for multilevel analysis such as HLM and Stata **gllamm**. In Mplus, logistic regression for a dependent dichotomous, polytomous nominal, or polytomous ordinal dependent variable is explicitly included as an option, and produces estimates consistent with logistic regression routines in general purpose statistical software. The polytomous nominal option in Mplus essentially uses separate estimation of the logistic functions for a repeatedly dichotomized dependent variable. In LISREL, it has long been possible to analyze ordinal variables using polychoric correlations with weighted least squares estimation; more recently, the ability to use polychoric correlations has been incorporated into EQS. By extension, one can treat a dichotomous variable as an ordinal variable with only two categories, and by further extension, one can dichotomize a polytomous nominal dependent variable and use separate estimation of the logistic functions, again using polychoric correlation with weighted least squares estimation (Jöreskog and Sörbom 1988), or using weighted least squares with mean- and variance-adjusted χ^2 statistics (WLSMV; Muthén and Muthén 2007). These approaches allow the inclusion of multiple categorical endogenous variables in the model.

The SEM approach has little to offer over standard logistic regression for a single equation model, but it does allow simultaneous estimation of multiple equation models like the three-wave panel model in Chapter 13. Table 15.5 presents an example comparing the results for a three-wave panel model using SEM with WLSMV estimation to results using generalized estimating equations (GEE) for the same model.[2] The three endogenous variables are prevalence of marijuana use, exposure to delinquent or criminal friends, and belief that it is wrong to violate the law; exogenous variables are gender (male) and ethnicity (here a single dichotomous variable, non-White). Intercepts are irrelevant here and have been dropped from Table 15.5. The first column lists the dependent variable; the second presents the explained variance (the usual R^2 statistic for all except prevalence of marijuana use in the GEE model, R_O^2 for the GEE model), and the third lists the predictors. In the fourth, fifth, and sixth columns, the results of the SEM model are presented; first the unstandardized coefficients, then the standardized coefficients, then the statistical significance of the unstandardized coefficients. In the SEM model, the unstandardized coefficients are estimated for each wave but have been constrained to be equal. This constraint, however, does not constrain the standardized coefficients, which are estimated separately for each wave, to be equal, and in fact they vary across waves because the variance in the endogenous variables and the predictors varies across waves. For that reason, the mean of the three standardized coefficients for the three waves is presented in Table 15.5. Also, the standardized coefficients in the SEM model are (see Note 2) not fully standardized coefficients, while the standardized coefficients in the GEE model are fully standardized. This should affect the magnitude of the standardized coefficients but should not affect which independent variables are identified as having stronger or weaker effects on the dependent variable. The last three

TABLE 15.5   Three-Wave Panel Models: SEM and GEE

Dependent Variable	Explained Variation	Independent Variables	Structural Equation Modeling: Weighted Least Squares, Mean and Variance Adjusted			Linear or Logistic Regression: Generalized Estimating Equations		
			b	b^* (Mean)	$p(b)$	b	b^*	$p(b)$
Marijuana use	SEM:	Prior marijuana use	.939	.627	.000	2.752	.505	.000
	R^2 .49 to .82	Prior exposure	.067	.162	.000	.075	.129	.000
		Prior belief	−.056	−.124	.000	−.127	−.183	.000
	Logistic	Male	−.091	−.026	.032	−.079	−.018	.368
	Regression $R_O^2 = .47$	Non-White	−.107	−.025	.055	−.137	−.010	.200
Exposure	SEM:	Prior exposure	.626	.623	.000	.531	.465	.000
	R^2 .51 to .68	Prior belief	−.079	−.071	.000	−.118	−.124	.000
		Prior marijuana use	.480	.143	.000	1.095	.141	.000
	Linear	Male	.439	.050	.000	.618	.092	.000
	Regression $R^2 = .43$	Non-White	.079	.007	.464	.015	.003	.904
Belief	SEM:	Prior belief	.535	.517	.000	.591	.548	.000
	R^2 .54 to .60	Prior exposure	−.193	−.213	.000	−.077	−.087	.000
		Prior marijuana use	−.385	−.127	.000	−.800	−.109	.000
	Linear	Male	−.294	−.037	.000	−.485	−.070	.000
	Regression $R^2 = .44$	Non-White	.558	.058	.000	.540	.030	.000

columns present the unstandardized and standardized coefficients, plus the statistical significance of the unstandardized coefficients, for the GEE model. For this model, the unstandardized coefficients are first calculated for all three waves combined; then the standardized coefficients were computed by hand, using the procedure described in Chapter 5.

Comparison of the unstandardized coefficients and their statistical significance in Table 15.5 indicates that both may differ across the two models. Most striking is the difference in the estimated statistical significance of gender and ethnicity in the model for marijuana use: statistically significant (marginally so for ethnicity) in the WLSMV model, not statistically significant in the GEE model. The coefficients themselves may be extremely close or may differ by as much as a factor of five. When we turn to the standardized coefficients, there are still differences not only in the standardized coefficients for marijuana use (which we would expect, given the different methods of estimation used in the SEM and the GEE models)[3] but also for exposure and belief; but not so great (less than a factor of three) as for the unstandardized coefficients. In the model for marijuana use, exposure appears to have a stronger effect than belief in the WLSMV model, but the order is reversed in the GEE model. In both models, prior marijuana use has the strongest effect, gender has the second weakest effect, and ethnicity has the weakest effect. In the model for exposure to delinquent/criminal friends, the ordering of the predictors based on the standardized coefficients is identical. In the model for belief that it is wrong to violate the law, prior belief has the strongest effect; it is followed by exposure then belief in the WLSMV model but by belief then exposure in the GEE model; and by ethnicity and then gender in the WLSMV model but by gender and then ethnicity in the GEE model.

Substantively, then, the differences between the two models are (a) whether gender and ethnicity are statistically significant predictors of marijuana use; (b) whether belief or exposure is the better predictor of marijuana use; (c) whether exposure or marijuana use is the better predictor of belief; and (d) whether gender or ethnicity is the better predictor of belief. Although the results of the two models are in many respects fairly similar, these differences in substantive conclusions are not trivial from either a theoretical or a practical perspective (Are there sociodemographic differences in risk of marijuana use; and what is the best variable to target for intervention?). Bear in mind that the estimation strategies are a bit different here: one pooling time series and cross-sectional data to produce a single estimate of each coefficient, the other in principle estimating each coefficient separately and constrained to produce equal coefficients only for the unstandardized coefficients. In the present context, neither approach is obviously better than the other. The fact that different substantive results are obtained should alert us to the sensitivity of our conclusions to the specific methods of estimation used in calculating the impacts of the independent variables on the dependent variables.

Latent change models are discussed in Bijleveld et al. (1998, chap. 4), Kaplan (2000, chap. 8), McArdle and Bell (2000), and Stoolmiller (1995). Adapting (but not quite adopting) the simplified notation from Bijleveld et al. (1998:250), the latent growth curve model without covariates can be written as $\hat{Y}_t = Z_1 + Z_2$, where $\hat{Y}_t$ is the observed value of Y at time t, $t = 0, 1, 2, \ldots, T$; t is the index of time (or age); Z_1 is a latent variable parameter representing the Y-intercept or the initial value (at $t = 0$) of Y; and Z_2 is a latent variable parameter representing the growth rate or slope of the growth curve indicated by the pattern of values of Y over time. In this equation, Z_1 has taken the place of the usual Y-intercept, the fixed parameter estimate a, and Z_2 replaces the usual fixed parameter estimate b as the slope of the growth curve (the coefficient of time). Covariates may be added to the model to explain either the dependent variable Y or the parameters of the latent growth curve, Z_1 and Z_2; if the latter, the structure of the model parallels the usual structure of the multilevel growth curve model, discussed on the next page. There are details excluded from the above equation, including any measurement model for the predictors, and the model for any correlations among errors. A fully detailed model, however, might prove a bit unwieldy in the present context. For example, Stoolmiller (1995) used 27 equations to provide a detailed specification of a single four-period latent growth curve model for intelligence. In both textbook treatments and empirical research applications of SEM latent growth curve models, the number of periods is typically 2 to 7, and it seems that 4 or 5 waves of data are both the modal and the recommended pattern (Bijleveld et al. 1998:265–268; McCallum and Kim 2000).

As described in Muthén and Muthén (2007:87), Mplus (and this is also true of other SEM software packages) SEM growth curve modeling differs from multilevel growth curve modeling in its treatment of the dependent variable. Multilevel modeling, as described by Muthén and Muthén, takes a univariate approach, regarding the dependent variable as a single variable with multiple measurements nested (clustered) within a single case. Mplus (and SEM more generally) treats the dependent variable as a multivariate vector, rather than a single variable. Additionally, multilevel modeling allows time to be a (manifest, measured) variable that reflects times of observations that may vary across individuals and for which slopes may be different for different individuals; SEM allows time scores to be latent parameters to be estimated, rather than fixed variables to be measured. It is instructive that in Muthén and Muthén, as elsewhere, examples of latent growth curve models generally and latent change models in particular are limited to four or five time periods. Larger numbers of time periods can lead to problems in the estimation of the model, including failure of the model to converge; inability of the model to estimate standard errors; and nonpositive definite residual covariance matrices (i.e., variances that are estimated to be less than zero, technically impossible) for a model no more complicated than the multilevel change model in the previous chapter.[4] One issue may be whether the latent change model is restricted to observed variables or includes multiple indicator latent variables in the model; part of the problem may be the sensitivity of SEM software to minor departures from the underlying assumptions; but a major part of the problem may also be that the latent *growth* model as implemented in SEM, with its assumption of an underlying continuous pattern of change, may simply not adequately reflect the true nature of discrete, oscillatory *change* in a truly dichotomous or categorical dependent variable.

CONCLUSION

Logistic regression analysis is a highly flexible approach to analyzing discrete (dichotomous, nominal polytomous, and ordinal polytomous) dependent variables. Limitations on its use lie primarily in the software available to implement the logistic regression model. Still, in some instances, alternatives to the logistic regression framework may be preferable. Other statistical distributions or transformations such as the probit or cloglog may produce a better fit or explanation of the dependent variable than the logistic distribution. Discriminant analysis, once relatively popular in the social sciences for the analysis of nominal and dichotomous dependent variables, may also be a more appropriate model under certain specific conditions, but discriminant analysis seems to have been largely abandoned in favor of logistic regression analysis because the assumptions underlying the logistic regression model are generally more realistic than those underlying the discriminant analysis model. Logistic regression models may be implemented using standard routines in general purpose statistical packages, and also in more specialized software for SEM and multilevel modeling. In the context of SEM, the use of weighted least squares estimation does allow the estimation of models involving multiple discrete endogenous variables, including repeated measurement of discrete variables in longitudinal models such as the latent growth curve model, but this lies outside the focus on the logistic regression model.

When I first started writing about logistic regression analysis nearly 15 years ago, I commented on the limitations of existing software, and the need to work around those limitations to obtain the information one really wanted for logistic regression analysis. Fifteen years does not seem like such a long time now, and some of the same comments that applied then still apply, particularly with respect to measures of explained variation, standardized logistic regression coefficients, and now with a concern for longitudinal analysis using logistic regression, the incorporation of repeated measures of discrete variables into statistical packages for multilevel and latent variable analysis. I would add that no single software package is presently, in my estimation, deserving of exclusive loyalty when it comes to logistic regression analysis; different packages have different desirable (and undesirable) features for different types of analysis within the logistic regression framework, and I hope that this has been evident without any obvious advocacy on my part. I think there are distinct, specific improvements possible in the implementation of logistic regression software, and my hope is that some of my comments on software limitations will quickly become obsolete. For the present, logistic regression remains a powerful and flexible tool for the analysis of discrete data, and I hope this book will assist readers in making better use of this tool in their own research.

NOTES

1. Software Note: The probit and cloglog distributions can easily be implemented in SAS **logistic** by specifying "link=probit" or "link=cloglog." In SPSS, there is a separate **probit** command, designed primarily for data with several cases per covariate pattern. For mixed categorical and continuous predictors with potentially many covariate patterns having only a single case, however, SPSS **plum** allows specification of a probit or cloglog link and provides output very similar to the output for logistic regression. Because **plum** is designed for the analysis of ordinal polytomous dependent variables, it readily accommodates dichotomous dependent variables (treating them as ordinal variables with only two categories), but the thresholds produced in SPSS **plum** will be opposite in sign to the intercepts produced by other methods of estimating the probit and cloglog models for dichotomous dependent variables. In Stata, a separate **probit** and a separate **cloglog** command are available for estimating probit and cloglog models with dichotomous dependent variables, and **oprobit** can be used to estimate probit models for ordinal polytomous dependent variables.

2. Software Note: The WLSMV model was estimated using Mplus; the GEE model was estimated using Stata **xtlogit**. Computation of the standardized coefficients in Mplus parallels the calculation of standardized coefficients in SAS, norming by $(\pi/\sqrt{3}$; www.statmodel.com/discussion/messages/11/16.html?1214239116, accessed August 2008); standardized coefficients in **xtlogit** were computed by hand and are the fully standardized coefficients described in Chapter 5.

3. Software Note: Moreover, standardized coefficients for Stata **xtlogit** calculated as $b^*_{SAS} = b/(\pi/\sqrt{3})$, consistent with the approach in Mplus, produce standardized coefficients that differ even more, in terms of absolute or squared differences, from the standardized coefficients produced by Mplus.

4. Software Note: And in fact, using year instead of age as the time dimension and calculating a linear, quadratic, or cubic latent change model with prevalence of marijuana use as the dependent variable, all of these problems were encountered; and when they were absent, standard error estimates were so large that none of the coefficients in the model was statistically significant, despite high fit indices (cumulative fit index CFI = .944, Tucker-Lewis index TLI = .936, root mean square error of approximation RMSEA = .042; R^2 approximately equal to 1, and reasonable estimates for standardized coefficients). This example, moreover, is by no means unique, but reflects past experience in estimating any but the conceptually simplest models using SEM.

APPENDIX A

Estimation for Logistic Regression Models[1]

As described by Coleman (1981:226–228), the general idea underlying maximum likelihood estimation is that if the data are hypothesized to have been generated under a particular model, it is possible to write the likelihood that a particular observation will have occurred. The likelihood of observing the whole set of values in the data is the product of the likelihoods. Maximum likelihood methods obtain estimates of parameter values that maximize the likelihood that the particular data will have been generated, given the hypothesized model. When the number of parameters is less than the number of observations, maximizing the likelihood is ordinarily carried out by setting equal to zero the *first* partial derivatives of the likelihood with respect to each of the parameters and solving the resulting set of simultaneous equations for the parameters. Because the maximum of the natural logarithm of the likelihood function occurs at the same point as the maximum of the likelihood function itself, it is possible to maximize the natural logarithm of the likelihood function, or the log likelihood, instead of the likelihood. Because the likelihood is a *product* of several terms, while its logarithm is the *sum* of a corresponding set of terms, it is easier to find the partial derivative of the log likelihood than of the likelihood itself. In addition, the negative of the expected values of the *second* derivatives of the log likelihood with respect to all pairs of parameters is equal to the *Fisher information matrix,* which is the inverse of the covariance matrix of the parameters. Thus the same process used in selecting the parameters can usually be readily extended to obtain variance and covariance estimates for the parameters. Coleman (1981) succinctly describes the advantages of maximum likelihood estimation: Because it allows the use of a single estimation procedure across different data types and model types, it increases comparability of the estimates from different forms of data by eliminating differences attributable to the estimation method, and it makes comparison between different forms of model structure (e.g., the outcome as a linear function of the predictors versus the outcome as an exponential function of the predictors) more feasible.

Maximum likelihood (ML) estimation begins with two assumptions: (1) We have data that consist of n randomly sampled observations $y_1, y_2, \ldots, y_n$. (2) The observations are independently and identically distributed, and can be described in terms of a function, f, and a set of one or more parameters (which may include the mean, standard deviation, regression coefficients, etc.), $\theta = \{\theta_1, \theta_2, \ldots, \theta_m\}$. If the observations are drawn from a continuous distribution (e.g., a distribution that can

334

take any integer value or any fractional value between the integers), the function f is called a probability density function or PDF, but if the observations are drawn from a discrete distribution (e.g., only the integers between 1 and 20), f is called a probability function. The principle of ML is to find an estimate for θ that maximizes the likelihood of obtaining the observed values of the data. The likelihood of the observed data depends on the specific distribution of f, the parameter vector θ, and the observed values. Since the observations are independently and identically (they all have the same function f) distributed, the likelihood of obtaining *all* the values observed in the data is equal to the product of the probabilities of obtaining each of the observed values: $L(\theta) = f(y_1; \theta) \times f(y_2; \theta) \times \cdots \times f(y_n; \theta)$.

To find the value at which $L(\theta)$ reaches its maximum, we find the values of $\theta_1, \theta_2, \ldots, \theta_m$ for which, using calculus, the first derivative of $L(\theta)$ is 0 and the second derivative of $L(\theta)$ is negative. As noted in Gould and Sribney (1999), however, there are two reasons for not working with the product $f(y_1; \theta) \times f(y_2; \theta) \times \cdots \times f(y_n; \theta)$. Statistically, it is easier to calculate expectations and variances of sums than of products; numerically, the actual value of the product, which approaches 0 (because each term in the product is a probability, between 0 and 1) as the number of observations increases, may generate numbers too small for the typical computer to handle. To deal with these considerations, we can take the natural logarithm of the likelihood, or the *log likelihood,* which has the form $\ln[L(\theta)] = \ln[f(y_1; \theta)] + \ln[f(y_2; \theta)] + \cdots + \ln[f(y_n; \theta)]$. The solution that maximizes the log likelihood $\ln[L(\theta)]$ also maximizes the likelihood $L(\theta)$, and is called the *maximum likelihood estimator,* or MLE. The sum of the terms in the log likelihood will result in a number between $-\infty$ (a negative number of infinitely large magnitude) and 0. Because the individual terms in the log likelihood are the natural logarithms of fractions less than 1 (probabilities between 0 and 1), the sum will be a negative number (unless all the individual terms are equal to 1, and hence their natural logarithms are equal to 0). As more observations are added, the magnitude of the (negatively signed) likelihood can only increase. The increase is not so large that it runs up against the numerical limitations of modern computers.

PROPERTIES OF MAXIMUM LIKELIHOOD ESTIMATORS

If they satisfy certain *regularity conditions*[2] maximum likelihood estimators have certain desirable properties. First, they are invariant to reparameterization, meaning that one can estimate either the parameter of interest or a function of that parameter, and transform as needed. With application to logistic regression, for example, we can obtain an ML estimate of an unstandardized logistic regression coefficient, transform that coefficient to an odds ratio, and know that the estimate of the odds ratio is also an MLE for the odds ratio. Second, ML estimates are invariant to sampling plans, in the sense that they do not depend on the rules for selecting the sample size. Third, *"If an unbiased minimum variance estimator exists, then the method of ML chooses it"* (King 1989:77). It is possible, however, that no unbiased estimator exists; or that, a biased estimator may be more intuitively reasonable. (The latter situation can arise, e.g., in ordinary least squares (OLS) regression in the presence of high multicollinearity, when a biased estimate based on ridge regression may be more reasonable than an unbiased estimate based on OLS; see, e.g., Ryan 1997, chap. 12.)

For increasingly large samples, MLEs are consistent, asymptotically normal, and asymptotically efficient. Consistency refers to the property that as the sample size increases, the estimated value of the parameter gets closer and closer to the true value of the parameter. This does not, however, mean that the estimator is unbiased. For example, the parameter estimate may be positively biased, and approach the true parameter only from the positive direction, as the sample size increases. Asymptotic normality means that when the parameter estimate is standardized (i.e., when we divide it by its standard error) it comes closer and closer to being normally distributed as the sample size increases. As King (1989) notes, the key regularity condition for this property is that the likelihood function be differentiable, although the property sometimes holds even if the likelihood function is not differentiable. Asymptotic normality provides the bases for some inferential tests regarding parameters and their modification in logistic regression and other procedures based on maximum likelihood. Finally, asymptotic efficiency means that for large samples, the standardized distribution of the parameter has the minimum variance of all possible consistent MLEs. Taken together, these three asymptotic properties mean, practically, that as the sample size gets larger, our estimates of the population parameters become more accurate, more efficient, and we are able to draw inferences about parameters and differences in parameters with greater confidence that the inferences are valid.

MAXIMUM LIKELIHOOD ESTIMATION PROCEDURE AND TERMINOLOGY

Maximum likelihood parameter estimates may be obtained either analytically or numerically. For an analytical solution, it must be possible to calculate the first and second derivatives of the log likelihood function with respect to an unknown parameter θ or more generally with respect to a vector of unknown parameters $\theta = \{\theta_1, \theta_2, \ldots, \theta_m\}$. The vector of first derivatives $S(\theta) = \partial\{\ln[L(\theta)]\}/\partial\theta$ is called the *Score vector*. The matrix of partial second derivatives $H(\theta) = \partial^2\{\ln[L(\theta)]\}/\partial\theta\partial\theta'$ is called the *Hessian matrix*. To obtain the MLE, we must choose each θ_m to satisfy the condition $s_m = \partial\{\ln[L(\theta)]\}/\partial\theta_m = 0$, where s_m is an element of the Score vector; and $h_{m1m2} = \partial^2\{\ln[L(\theta)]\}/\partial\theta_{m1}\theta_{m2} < 0$ where h_{m1m2} is an element of the Hessian matrix. When a *closed form* solution exists, we have M equations with M unknowns (parameters), and we can solve directly for θ. This is possible, for example, when the unknown parameters represent regression coefficients, the dependent variable is linearly related to the predictors, and $f(\mathbf{y}; \theta)$ has a normal distribution. In this case, the MLEs for the regression coefficients can be shown (with a little calculus) to be the familiar OLS estimates for the regression coefficients.

Alternatively, we may have a likelihood function that is nonlinear in the unknown parameters and for which no closed form solution is known. In this instance, we begin by substituting tentative parameter estimates in the likelihood equations, calculating the resulting likelihood function, calculating the Score vector and the Hessian matrix based on the initial estimates, then modifying parameter estimates according to some rule and calculating a new likelihood function, Score vector, and Hessian matrix. We select the better estimate (based on the larger likelihood or log likelihood, remembering that the log likelihood will be negative, so for the log likelihood we select the negative number which is smaller in magnitude) and repeating the process until there is, to some predefined level of precision, no change from one step to the next. This process of repeated estimation, modification, and testing, is called *iteration*, and there are several techniques for obtaining iterative maximum likelihood estimates of parameters. At the first step, we may use 0 as our tentative estimate for all the parameters, but it is sometimes possible to make the process faster and more efficient (fewer steps before the likelihood stops changing from one step to the next) by using estimates other than zero, for example,

OLS estimates for a binary logistic regression model, or empirical probabilities for a log-linear model, on the first step. Note that these are initial estimates only, and while they may be inappropriate as final estimates, they may produce a reasonable initial estimate to begin the iteration process.

Methods of iterative estimation of parameters that produce MLEs include the Newton-Raphson algorithm and the Fisher scoring procedure. The *Newton-Raphson* algorithm begins with a vector of initial parameter estimates $\theta^{(1)}$, the Score vector $S^{(1)}$, and the Hessian matrix $H^{(1)}$, then produces a new set of parameter estimates $\theta^{(2)}$ by calculating $\theta^{(2)} = \theta^{(1)} + c[-H^{(t)}]^{-1}[S^{(t)}]$, where c is a step function, often but not necessarily set to 1. This process is repeated to calculate third, fourth, and so on, estimates of the parameter vector θ until the solution *converges*. Convergence is determined by a predefined criterion, such as (a) no change (to some predetermined degree of precision, the *tolerance*) in the parameter vector (i.e., $\theta^{(t+1)} = \theta^{(t)}$ to some degree of precision), (b) no change in the Score vector $S^{(t)} = 0$ to some predefined degree of precision, or (c) the criterion most commonly available in computer output from packages such as SAS, SPSS, and Stata, no change in the log likelihood function, $\ln[L^{(t+1)}] - \ln[L^{(t)}] = 0$, again to some degree of precision. As this is a numerical solution, not an analytical solution, the first derivative, as represented by the Score vector, or the change in the parameter vector or the log likelihood, may not be exactly equal to 0, but must be "close enough" (within .01, or .0001, or some other predetermined tolerance) to conclude that there is little or no purpose in continuing the iteration process. The Newton-Raphson algorithm is most appropriate when it is possible to calculate the first and second derivatives of the likelihood function. The Fisher scoring procedure is appropriate when the first derivative can be calculated, but the second derivative must be estimated from the Score vector. Other procedures are available when neither the first nor the second derivative is available (see, e.g., Eliason 1993:43–45). As noted by Allison (1999:72), the Newton-Raphson and Fisher scoring procedures produce the same results for logistic regression, but the standard errors for the two procedures may be different when used with other link functions such as probit and complementary log-log functions.

ITERATIVELY REWEIGHTED LEAST SQUARES ESTIMATION

Another procedure used by some software packages to estimate parameters for logistic regression or logit models is *iteratively reweighted least squares* (IRLS) estimation. IRLS estimation is derived from the Generalized Linear Model approach (McCullagh and Nelder 1989), rather than from ML. IRLS estimation proceeds similarly to the Newton-Raphson and Fisher scoring procedures, but instead of adding or subtracting a quantity based explicitly on the Score vector and the Hessian matrix, IRLS uses a vector of responses (the dependent variable) y, a vector of conditional means for the response variable at a given step, $m^{(t)}$, a matrix of predictors, X, the transpose of X, X', and a matrix of weights for the current step, $W^{(t)}$. At each step, the vector of parameters $\theta^{(t)}$ is updated: $\theta^{(t+1)} = \theta^{(t)} + [X'W^{(t)}X]^{-1}X'[y - m^{(t)}]$, where $[X'W^{(t)}X]$ is the estimate for the negative of the Hessian matrix and $X'[y - m^{(t)}]$ is the estimate for the Score vector, relative to the Newton-Raphson procedure. The contents of the weight matrix W depend on the model (log-linear, logit, probit) being estimated. Powers and Xie (2008:290) note that IRLS usually converges to ML estimates in a few iterations, but my own experience comparing IRLS estimates with Newton-Raphson ML estimates indicates that they are not always identical to the degree of precision commonly used by mainstream statistical packages on personal computers.

ROBUST STANDARD ERRORS AND
GENERALIZED ESTIMATING EQUATIONS[3]

Variance and covariance estimates for the estimated coefficients under simple random sampling are obtained by taking the inverse of the Hessian matrix. For polytomous dependent variables, if there is evidence of underdispersion or overdispersion, the estimates may be adjusted by incorporating a scaling factor. More generally, when the assumption that the observations are independent appears to be violated, some adjustment may be made to either (a) only the variance-covariance matrix or (b) both the variance-covariance matrix and the coefficients. Adjustments to only the variance-covariance matrix may be made using bootstrap or jackknife estimation of standard errors, or by using robust standard error estimates. Bootstrap and jackknife estimation involve resampling techniques and are mathematically simple. The details of bootstrap and jackknife estimation for standard errors are presented in Chapter 11, along with a general description of the use of robust standard errors. In more detail, elements included in the adjustment using robust estimates of standard errors for the coefficients include (1) the vector of observed values of the predictors for each case, $\mathbf{x}_i$; (2) an estimator of the dispersion parameter (an ancillary parameter), $\hat{\varphi}$; (3) μ, the expected value of the dependent variable; (4) the estimating equation for the expected value, $\eta = \sum X_k \beta_k + \omega$, where ω is an offset to normalize the equation; (5) $\partial\mu/\partial\eta$, the derivative of the expected value with respect to the estimating equation; (6) the variance of the expected value, $V(\hat{\mu})$; and (6) the ratio of the difference between each observed value of Y, y_i, and its expected value, $\hat{\mu}$, divided by the variance in the expected value of Y, where the expected values are model-based or empirical: $(y_i - \hat{\mu})/V(\hat{\mu})$, possibly with an additional adjustment factor which varies by the type of sandwich estimator. For clustered data, the equation for the middle factor in the "sandwich" is $\hat{B}_{MS} = \sum_i\{\sum_j w_{ij}\mathbf{x}'_{ij}[(y_{ij} - \hat{\mu}_{ij})/V(\hat{\mu}_{ij})](\partial\mu/\partial\eta)_{ij}\hat{\varphi}\}\ \{\sum_j[(y_{ij} - \hat{\mu}_{ij})/V(\hat{\mu}_{ij})](\partial\mu/\partial\eta)_{ij}\hat{\varphi}\mathbf{x}'_{ij}w_{ij}\}$, where $\mathbf{x}'_{ij}$ is the transpose of the vector $\mathbf{x}_{ij}$ described above; the outer sum is taken over all cases $I = 1, 2, \ldots, n$; the inner sums are taken over the cases within a given cluster, $j = 1, 2, \ldots, n_i$; and the w_{ij} are weights applied as a result of clustering (and the w_{ij} may be equal to one for a self-weighting sample). The sandwich estimate of the variance is then $\hat{V}_{MS} = \hat{V}_H^{-1}\hat{B}_{MS}\hat{V}_H^{-1}$ where $\hat{V}_H^{-1}$ is the variance estimate based on the inverse of the Hessian matrix (Hardin and Hilbe 2001:28). As noted by Hardin and Hilbe (2001:31), the sandwich estimate of variance is asymptotically equivalent to some jackknife estimates.

Adjustments to both the coefficients and their variance-covariance matrix may be made using jackknife estimates or generalized estimating equations. Generalized estimating equations (GEEs) are an extension of the generalized linear model (GLM) to estimate parameters for correlated data. GEEs provide consistent estimators of logistic regression coefficients (or coefficients for other types of regression) and their standard errors are based on relatively weak assumptions about the actual correlations among observations. Following the notation used in Littell et al. (1996), for the exponential family of distributions, the log likelihood has the general form $LL(\theta, \varphi; y) = [y\theta - b(\theta)]/a(\varphi) + c(y, \varphi)$, where θ is the parameter we are interested in estimating and is a function of the mean denoted $\theta(\mu)$, φ is a scale parameter; and the variance of y, $V(y)$, is a function of the mean and $a(\varphi)$ such that $V(y) = V(\mu)a(\varphi)$. Members of the exponential family include the normal, binomial, and Poisson distributions, and for the binomial distribution, which is used in logistic regression, $\mu = \pi$ where π is the probability of a positive or "success" outcome on Y; $\theta(\mu) = \ln[\pi/(1 - \pi)]$; $a(\varphi) = 1/n$; $V(\mu) = \pi(1 - \pi)$; and $V(y) = [\pi(1 - \pi)]/n$.

Suppose $E(y_i) = \mu_i$ and the variance of y_i, $V(y_i)$, is proportional to the variance of μ_i, $V = V(\mu_i)$, where $V(\mu)$ is a known function and μ_i is a function of a set of predictors and associated parameters, such that $\mu_i = h(\eta_i) = \sum_k X_{ik}\beta_i$, and $h(\eta)$ in the inverse link function of the general linear model. The maximum likelihood estimator of the parameter vector β is obtained by solving the Score equations $\sum[\partial\mu_i/\partial\beta]V^{-1}[y_i - \mu_i(\beta)] = 0$. Solving these equations maximizes the log likelihood. The log likelihood function is a special case of the *quasi-likelihood* function, which allows the GLM to be applied to *any* dependent variable, whose mean and variance can be described, not just members of the exponential family. The quasi-likelihood function $Q(\mu_i, y_i)$ is defined as $[\partial Q(\mu_i, y_i)]/\mu_i = (y_i - \mu_i)/V(\mu_i)$. Parallel to the log likelihood function for the exponential family of distributions, $Q(\mu_i, y_i) = [y_i\theta_i - b(\theta_i)]/a(\varphi_i)$, but the term $c(y_i, \varphi_i)$ is dropped. The generalized estimating equation for estimating β based on the quasi-likelihood function is $\sum[\partial\mu/\partial\beta]V^{-1}[y_i - \mu_i(\beta)] = 0$. Compared with the estimating equation for the GLM model, we now have a vector of means instead of a single mean, and a variance-covariance matrix instead of a scalar variance. It is possible to use the quasi-likelihood function for the GLM whenever the mean μ, the mean function $\theta(\mu)$, the variance function $V(\mu)$, and the scale parameter $a(\varphi)$ are all known.

In the generalized estimating equation using quasi-likelihood estimation, the estimated variance-covariance matrix depends on both the *model-based* covariance and the *empirical* correlation, the known, hypothesized, or estimated covariance or correlation among different observations within the same cluster or stratum. The variance-covariance matrix of $\mathbf{Y}_i$ is specified as the estimator $\mathbf{V}_i = \varphi\mathbf{A}_j^{.5}\mathbf{R}_j(\alpha)\mathbf{A}_j^{.5}$, where $\mathbf{A}$ is a $T \times T$ diagonal matrix (where T is the number of clusters in the data) with $V(\mu_{ij})$ as the jth diagonal element and $\mathbf{R}_i(\alpha)$ is the *working correlation matrix*. Each element of $\mathbf{R}_i(\alpha)$ is the empirical correlation between pairs of observations within the same cluster or stratum. The structure of the working correlation matrix depends on the nature of the dependence among observations. If the observations are independent, $\mathbf{R}_i(\alpha)$ should be the identity matrix, a diagonal matrix with main diagonal entries equal to one and zeros elsewhere. (All the working correlation matrices discussed here will have main diagonal entries equal to 1.) In this case, there is no distinction between GEE and GLM estimation. *Exchangeable* correlations are often appropriate for cross-sectional complex sample data in which observations are clustered within PSUs; $\mathbf{R}_i(\alpha)$ has a constant correlation coefficient, α, for all entries off the main diagonal, indicating that the correlations among observations should be constant within a cluster. This requires the estimation of only a single parameter α. For longitudinal data with repeated observations on the same cases, the *autoregressive* correlation structure, in which the magnitude of the correlation depends on the closeness of the observations, is often appropriate. This requires the estimation of a single parameter, but the correlation is squared for observations separated by a distance of 2 (typically two measurement intervals), cubed for observations separated by an interval of 3, and so forth. The autoregressive correlation structure is a special case of a correlation structure in which the correlation between observations depends on the distance or time between the observations, but in which separate estimation of the correlation for each possible distance may be required. In an *unstructured* correlation matrix, no assumptions are made about the correlations, and all $T(T-1)$ possible unique correlations must be calculated. This makes heavy demands on the data, but produces the most efficient estimates of β. Once the working correlation matrix has been selected, the variance-covariance matrix of β is estimated using the robust estimator as described above. For logistic regression, if $V(\beta)$ is the variance-covariance matrix for β, then $V(\beta) = \mathbf{H}^{-1}\mathbf{V}_i\mathbf{H}^{-1}$, where $\mathbf{H}^{-1}$ is the inverse of the Hessian matrix and $\mathbf{V}_i = \varphi\mathbf{A}_i^{.5}\mathbf{R}_i(\alpha)\mathbf{A}_i^{.5}$ as described above.

Misspecification of the working correlation matrix results in inefficiency but not inconsistency in the estimation of β. GEE is thus robust to errors in the selection of the structure of the working correlation matrix. As the number of clusters becomes large, so long as the model for the means is correct, the estimates of the parameters and for the estimated variance-covariance matrix $\mathbf{V}_i$ are consistent, even if the working correlation matrix is misspecified. For $T = 1$ (only one general cluster), GEE reduces to GLM estimation. Stokes et al. (2000:479) suggest that the minimum number of clusters needed for very few predictors is about 25; for 5 to 12 predictors at least 100; and it would generally be best to have more than 200 clusters. Finally, as noted by several authors (e.g., Hardin and Hilbe 2001, 2003; Hosmer and Lemeshow 2000; Stokes et al. 2000), because GEE uses quasi-likelihood rather than maximum likelihood estimation, maximum likelihood statistics such as D_0, D_M, and G_M are no longer valid. An alternative to G_M for GEE is the multivariate Wald statistic, $W = (\boldsymbol{\beta})'[\mathbf{S}(\boldsymbol{\beta})]^{-1}(\boldsymbol{\beta})$, distributed as a χ^2 statistic, where $\mathbf{S}(\boldsymbol{\beta})$ is the variance-covariance matrix for the estimated values of $\boldsymbol{\beta}$ in the full model and the equation is the same whether that variance-covariance matrix has been estimated by maximum likelihood or not. An adjusted Wald statistic with an F distribution has also been suggested: $F_{K,J-K+1} = (J - K + 1)W/JK$, where J is the total number of sampled PSUs minus the total number of strata and K = number of parameters (excluding the constant term) estimated by the model. The F statistic parallels G_M and the Wald χ^2 output by other routines, but Hosmer and Lemeshow (2000:213) express some reservations about its use, suggesting that insufficient theory and simulation evidence support its use. Stokes et al. (2000; see also LaVange et al. 2001; Shah et al. 1977) have suggested that the unadjusted Wald χ^2 and the adjusted Wald F statistics may be used as upper and lower bounds for judging the robustness of the attained statistical significance, and the adjusted and unadjusted multivariate Wald statistics should produce very similar results as the number of clusters becomes large.

EXACT CONDITIONAL LOGISTIC REGRESSION

While maximum likelihood estimates and, to the extent that they are consistent with maximum likelihood estimates, IRLS estimates have certain desirable properties for large samples, as noted earlier, these asymptotic properties may not hold for small samples. In fact, not only small samples but also other conditions, including extremely unbalanced data (very few cases in one of the two categories of the dichotomous dependent variable) or complete separation (some combination of the predictors perfectly predicts the values of the dependent variable) may render inferences unreliable or result in the inability of the iterative process to converge (Mehta and Patel 1995; Santner and Duffy 1989). An alternative approach suggested by Cox (1970) is to base the estimation and inference on exact permutational distributions (as opposed to the theoretical distributions assumed in maximum likelihood estimation) of *sufficient statistics* for the logistic regression parameters in which we are interested, *conditional* on fixing the sufficient statistics of the remaining parameters at their observed values. A *sufficient statistic* is a statistic that summarizes all the information contained in a particular sample of observations about a particular parameter. Estimation of parameters of interest *conditional* on sufficient statistics about some parameters means that the parameters that are not of interest (*nuisance* parameters) need not be estimated, but that the estimates of the parameters of interest depend (are conditional) on the sufficient statistics for the nuisance parameters.

Exact conditional logistic regression (ECLR, sometimes shortened to *exact logistic regression*) is based on consideration of all possible vectors of values for the dependent variable. For a binary dependent variable Y with a sample size of N, this means 2^N distinct permutations. To paraphrase two-time third-party presidential candidate Ross Perot, the loud sucking sound you hear is your CPU time and memory space going into the exact logistic regression algorithm. (OK, the original had more punch, but you get the idea.) The four-variable model for prevalence of marijuana use with 227 cases presented in Chapter 3 would require the calculation of more than 2×10^{68} permutations, hours of computer time, and gigabytes of memory using the exact logistic regression algorithm in SAS **logistic**. Because the number of permutations increases exponentially with the sample size, the method was initially not considered to be feasible, but improvements in statistical algorithms (Hirji et al. 1987) have made it possible to apply the method at least to the small samples for which the method is most appropriate. Relatedly, a Monte Carlo network sampling approach (Mehta et al. 2000) appears to produce results similar to ECLR in samples for which both the exact and Monte Carlo approaches can be used, suggesting that the Monte Carlo approach may yield results similar to what would be obtained if it were feasible to apply the exact conditional approach to larger samples with highly unbalanced data. ECLR, as noted earlier, is available in SAS **logistic** as well as in the standalone package LogXact.

As described in Mehta and Patel (1995) and King and Ryan (2002), the vector of sufficient statistics for $\beta = (\beta_0, \beta_1, \beta_2, \ldots, \beta_K)$ for a binary logistic regression model is $t_k = \Sigma_j(y_j x_{jk})$, where t_k is the sufficient statistic, y_j is the value of Y for case $j = 1, 2, \ldots, N$, and x_{jk} is the value of predictor X_k, $k = 1, 2, \ldots, K$ for case j. For β_0 (the intercept), $t = \Sigma_j y_j$ (since the predictors do not affect the intercept). The distribution of the vector of sufficient statistics is $P(T_1 = t_1, T_2 = t_2, \ldots, T_K = t_K) = [c(\mathbf{t})e^{t'\beta}]/[\Sigma_u c(\mathbf{u}) \, e^{u'\beta}]$, where $c(\mathbf{t}) = |S(\mathbf{t})|$, $S(\mathbf{t}) = \{(y_1, y_2, \ldots, y_N), t_0,(t_1, \ldots, t_K)\}$, $|S|$ $c(\mathbf{t}) = |S(\mathbf{t})|$, $S(\mathbf{t}) = \{(y_1, y_2, \ldots, y_N), t_0,(t_1, \ldots, t_K)\}$, $|S|$ denotes the number of distinct elements in the set S, and the summation in the denominator is over all $\mathbf{u}$ for which $c(\mathbf{u}) \geq 1$. In other words, as described by Mehta and Patel (1995:2145), $c(\mathbf{t})$ is a count of the number of binary sequences of the form $(y_1, y_2, \ldots, y_N)$ such that $\Sigma_j y_j = t_0$ and $\Sigma_j y_j x_{jk} = t_k$, and exact inference about the vector of coefficients β requires computation of coefficients such as $c(\mathbf{t})$ in which some of the sufficient statistics are fixed at their observed values and others are required to vary over their permissible ranges. Inferences are based on the proportion of outcomes that are at least as extreme, relative to the null hypothesis, as the observed outcome.

Issues raised about the use of ECLR include the justification for regarding the specific parameters not being estimated as being fixed at their observed values (King and Ryan 2002) and the computational intensity required for larger samples. Although King and Ryan (2002) suggest that ECLR may be useful for data involving complete or near-complete separation, because ECLR makes it possible to estimate logistic regression coefficients when maximum likelihood estimation cannot, Rindskopf (2002) dissents, suggesting that the infinite or very large logistic regression coefficients produced by maximum likelihood estimation are actually more informative and more accurate than the ECLR estimates, a position echoed by Webber (2003; see also Wang and Brady 2003 for further support of the use of maximum likelihood as opposed to exact logistic regression). The general consensus seems to be that maximum likelihood estimation is to be preferred except when the sample is small (examples used for ECLR routinely use samples less than 100) or when the data are seriously unbalanced (few cases in one of the two categories of the dependent variable), although for large samples, maximum likelihood estimation may be feasible even when more than 90% of the cases are in one of the two categories.

CONCLUSION

Table A.1 summarizes the differences between OLS estimation for linear regression and ML estimation for logistic regression. As indicated in the table, the exact nature of what the model is trying to

TABLE A.1 Ordinary Least Squares and Maximum Likelihood Estimation

	Ordinary Least Squares/Linear Regression	*Maximum Likelihood/Logistic Regression*
What the model is trying to predict	*Exact observed value of dependent variable*	*Probability of obtaining observed value of dependent variable*
Criterion for selecting model parameters $(a, b_1, b_2, \ldots, b_K)$	Select parameters to minimize the sum of squared errors, $\sum(e_j)^2 = \sum(Y_j - \hat{Y}_j)^2 =$ $\sum[Y_j - (a + b_1 X_{1j} + \cdots + b_K X_{Kj})]^2$	Select parameters to maximize the likelihood of obtaining the observed values of the dependent variable, given the independent variables: (Equation here in bivariate form) $l(Y) = \prod P(Y_j \mid X_j) = \prod [P(Y_j = 1 \mid X_j)]^{[P(Y_j=1)]} [1 - P(Y_j = 1 \mid X_j)]^{[1-P(Y_j=1)]}$ $= \prod [e^{a+bX_j}/(1 + e^{a+bX_j})]^{[P(Y_j=1)]} [1/(1 + e^{a+bX_j})]^{[1-P(Y_j=1)]}$ Equivalently, select parameters to maximize the natural logarithm of the likelihood, $\ln[l(Y)]$: $L(Y) = \ln[l(Y)] = \sum[P(Y_j = 1 \mid X_j)$ $= \sum \{P(Y_j = 1)\ln[e^{a+bX_j}/(1 + e^{a+bX_j})] + [1 - P(Y_j = 1)]\ln[1/(1 + e^{a+bX_j})]\}$
Process of estimating parameters	Solve directly for parameters using calculus and linear algebra	Solve for parameters iteratively, using calculus, linear algebra, and numerical algorithms that propose, test, and modify tentative solutions until the solutions converge
Form of the function	Linear	Logistic
Properties of coefficients (if assumptions are correct)	Best linear unbiased estimates for $a, b_1, b_2, \ldots, b_K$	Asymptotically efficient, unbiased estimates for $a, b_1, b_2, \ldots, b_K$

predict, the criteria for selecting model parameters, the estimation process, the form of the function relating the predictors to the dependent variable, and the properties of the coefficients (if the model assumptions are correct) are parallel but not identical for OLS and ML. Note, too, that when the usual assumptions underlying the OLS multiple regression model are satisfied, OLS estimates are identical to ML estimates. Because those assumptions are violated with dichotomous or categorical dependent variables, however, OLS cannot provide ML estimates for dichotomous or categorical dependent variables, and logistic regression using a maximum likelihood or generalized least squares estimation procedure for large samples, and possibly an exact conditional estimation procedure for small samples, is more appropriate.

NOTES

1. This appendix is intended to provide a brief discussion of maximum likelihood estimation and exact conditional estimation as they are used to estimate logistic regression models. For a more extended but still accessible treatment of maximum likelihood estimation, see the monograph by Eliason (1993) or Part I, especially Chapter 4, of King (1989). Appendix B of Powers and Xie (2008) also provides a brief, general introduction to maximum likelihood estimation. Gould and Sribney (1999) provide a good introduction to maximum likelihood estimation and its implementation in Stata. For exact conditional logistic regression, see Mehta and Patel (1995) for a description, and King and Ryan (2002) for a comparison between maximum likelihood and exact conditional logistic regression. In this appendix, **boldface** type is used to indicate vectors and matrices. Other than this, there is no universally accepted standard notation for maximum likelihood estimation or exact conditional estimation.

2. King (1989:75) offers the following set of sufficient regularity conditions: (a) the values of y for which $f(y; \theta) > 0$ (i.e., the sample space) do not depend on θ; (b) $f(y; \theta)$ is "twice differentiable," that is, it has a second derivative, for all observations in the sample space and all parameters in the parameter space; (c) the information matrix $I_n \equiv E\{\partial \ln[f(y; \theta)]/\partial\theta\}\{\partial \ln[f(y; \theta)]/\partial\theta\}'$ is positive definite and finitely bounded; and (d) $|\partial \ln[f(y; \theta)]/\partial\theta| \le h_1(y)$, $|\partial^2 \ln[f(y; \theta)]/\partial\theta^2| \le h_2(y)$, and $|\partial^3 \ln[f(y; \theta)]/\partial\theta^3| \le h_3(y)$, where $E[h_j(y)] < \infty$ for $j = 1$, 2 and $E[h_3(y)]$ does not depend on θ. As King notes, the topic of regularity conditions is fairly complex, and it is not treated in detail here. The principal point is that the properties described in this appendix do *not* always apply to MLEs, even though MLEs are sometimes treated as if they did, and appropriate tests for regularity conditions should be applied when substantive conclusions depend on the assumption or inference that the regularity conditions do apply. Even when the regularity conditions do not apply, however, the MLE is still the estimator that maximizes the likelihood of observing the data, given f and θ.

3. For a book-length treatment of GEEs, including robust standard errors, see Hardin and Hilbe (2003). Similar coverage of these topics may also be found in Hardin and Hilbe (2001), and more abbreviated coverage in some of the SAS manuals (Littell et al. 1996; Stokes et al. 2000). The original treatment of GEE is credited to Liang and Zeger (1986); see also Diggle et al. (1994). Hosmer and Lemeshow (2000:211–222) also discuss GEE in the context of logistic regression models for complex sample data.

Proofs Related to Indices of Predictive Efficiency

MINIMUM POSSIBLE VALUES OF λ_p AND τ_p

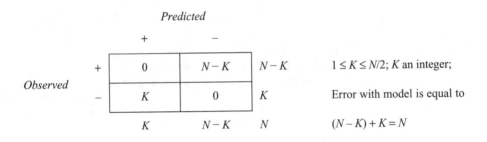

1. Minimum value for λ_p:

For λ_p, the error without the model is the number of cases in the nonmodal category, K. Therefore,

$$\lambda_p = (\text{Error without model} - \text{Error with model})/(\text{Error without model})$$

$$= 1 - (\text{Error with model})/(\text{Error without model}) = 1 - N/K;$$

and λ_p is a minimum when K is a minimum, that is, when $K = 1$ and $\lambda_p = 1 - N$.

2. Minimum value for τ_p:

For τ_p, error without the model is $(N - K)K/N + K(N - K)/N = 2K(N - K)/N$.

In general,

$$\tau_p = (\text{Error without model} - \text{Error with model})/(\text{Error without model})$$

$$= 1 - (\text{Error with model})/(\text{Error without model}) = 1 - N/[2K(N - K)/N].$$

For $K = 1$, $\tau_p = 1 - N/[2(N-1)/N]$.

    (a) Now, suppose that for some K such that $1 < K < N/2$, $\tau_p < 1 - N/[2(N-1)/N]$ (i.e., $K \geq 2$, since $K \in I$); then

$$1 - N/[2K(N-K)/N] < 1 - N/[2(N-1)/N];$$

$$-1/[K(N-K)] < -1/[N-1];$$

multiplying by -1 (thus reversing the inequality)

$$1/[K(N-K)] > 1/[N-1];$$

$$[N-1]/[K(N-K)] > 1;$$

$$(N-1)/(N-K) > K.$$

Now, since $K < N/2$, $(N-K) < (N-N/2)$ which is equal to $N/2$, and therefore $(N-1)/(N-K) < (N-1)/(N/2)$ which is equal to $2(N-1)/N$, which is less than 2.

Therefore, if $(N-1)/(N-K) > K$, then $2 > K$, which contradicts the condition in (a).

Thus, it is not possible to obtain a smaller value for τ_p than the value obtained when $K = 1$, and the minimum value of τ_p is $\tau_p = 1 - N/[2(N-1)/N] = 1 - N^2/[2(N-1)]$.

MINIMUM VALUE OF τ_p WITH CONSISTENT MARGINAL DISTRIBUTION

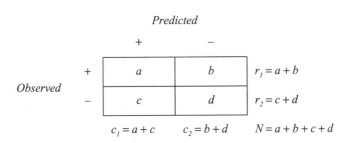

1. Assume $r_1 \geq r_2$ and $c_1 \geq c_2$ (consistent order); then $r_1 \geq .5N$, $r_2 \leq .5N$, $c_1 \geq .5N$, and $c_2 \leq .5N$.

    (a) At maximum possible error, if $a \geq d$, $d = 0$ (i.e., all the correctly classified cases are in the row with the larger marginal total); thus $c_2 = b + d = b$ and $r_2 = c + d = c$; since $c_2 \leq .5N$ and $r_2 \leq .5N$, $b \leq .5N$ and $c \leq .5N$; Maximum error occurs when $b = .5N$ and $c = .5N$ (and $a = 0$), that is, all cases are incorrectly classified.

    (b) At maximum possible error, if $d \geq a$, $a = 0$; thus, $c_1 = a + c = c$ and $r_1 = a + b = b$; since $c_1 \geq .5N$ and $r_1 \geq .5N$, $b \geq .5N$ and $c \geq .5N$; maximum error occurs when $a = 0$, implying $b = c = .5N$, because of $b < .5N$, $r_1 < .5N$, which contradicts the initial conditions (1).

Given (from the above) $a = d = 0$ and $b = c = .5N$,

$$\tau_p = (\text{Error without model} - \text{Error with model})/(\text{Error without model})$$
$$= \{[r_1(r_2/\langle r_1 + r_2 \rangle) + r_2(r_1/\langle r_1 + r_2 \rangle)] - (b + c)\}/\{r_1[r_2/(r_1 + r_2)] + r_2[r_1/(r_1 + r_2)]\}$$
$$= [2r_1r_2/(r_1 + r_2) - (b + c)]/[2r_1r_2/(r_1 + r_2)]$$
$$= [2(.5N)(.5N)/(.5N+.5N)] - (.5N + .5N)]/[2(.5N)(.5N)/(.5N + .5N)]$$
$$= [2(.25NN)/N - N]/[2(.25NN)/N]$$
$$= [.5N - N]/.5N$$
$$= -.5N/.5N$$
$$= -1.$$

2. Assume $r_2 \geq r_1$ and $c_2 \geq c_1$ (consistent order); then $r_2 \geq .5N$, $r_1 \leq .5N$, $c_2 \geq .5N$, and $c_1 \leq .5N$.

   (a) At maximum possible error, if $a \geq d$, $d = 0$ (i.e., all the correctly classified cases are in the row with the larger marginal total); thus, $c_2 = b + d = b$ and $r_2 = c + d = c$; since $c_2 \geq .5N$ and $r_2 \geq .5N$, $b \geq .5N$ and $c \geq .5N$; Maximum error occurs when $a = 0$, implying $b = c = .5N$; all cases are incorrectly classified.

   (b) At maximum possible error, if $d \geq a$, $a = 0$; thus $c_1 = a + c = c$ and $r_1 = a + b = b$; since $c_1 \leq .5N$ and $r_1 \leq .5N$, $b \leq .5N$ and $c \leq .5N$; maximum error occurs $c = .5N$ and $b = .5N$, implying $a = 0$.

   (c) Computation is the same as in (1) above.

3. If $r_1 > r_2$ and $c_1 > c_2$ (consistency), let $r_1 = .5N + K$, $0 < K < .5N$; $r_2 = .5N - K$; $c_1 = .5N + J$,
$$0 < J < .5N; \text{ and } c_2 = .5N - J.$$

   (a) Minimum correct occurs when $d = 0$ (all the correct cases are in the row with the larger marginal total), $r_2 = c + d = c = .5N - K$, $c_2 = b + d = b = .5N - J$, and
$$A = N - b - c - d = N - b - c = N - (.5N - J) - (.5N - K) = J + K.$$

   (b) Minimum $\tau_p = [2r_1r_2/N - (b + c)]/[2r_1r_2/N]$
$$= [4r_1r_2 - 2N(b + c)]/[4r_1r_2]$$
$$= [4(.5N + K)(.5N - K) - 2N(N - K - J)]/[4(.5N + K)(.5N - K)]$$
$$= [4(.25N^2 + .5K - .5K - K^2) - 2N(N - J - K)]/[4((.25N^2 + .5K - .5K - K^2)]$$
$$= [N^2 - 4K^2 - 2N^2 + 2NK + 2NJ]/[N^2 - 4K^2]$$
$$= [-N^2 + 2KN + 2JN - 4K^2]/[(N - 2K)(N + 2K)]$$

   (c) If $J > K$,

$$[-N^2 + 2KN + 2JN - 4K^2]/[(N - 2K)(N + 2K)] > [-N^2 + 2KN + 2KN - 4K^2]/[(N - 2K)(N + 2K)];$$
$$[-N^2 + 2KN + 2JN - 4K^2]/[(N - 2K)(N + 2K)] > [(-N + 2K)(N - 2K)]/[(N - 2K)(N + 2K)];$$
$$[-N^2 + 2KN + 2JN - 4K^2]/[(N - 2K)(N + 2K)] > -(N - 2K)/(N + 2K);$$

   since $(N - 2K) < (N + 2K)$,

$$- (N - 2K)/(N + 2K) > -1,$$

   so minimum $\tau_p > -1$ if $J > K$.

Predicted

		+	−	
	+	60	30	90
Observed				
	−	10	0	10
		70	30	100

(d) If $J < K$, it is possible for minimum τ_p to be less than −1; for example, in the table above, $\tau_p = [2(90)(10)/100 − (40)]/[2(90)(10)/100] = −1.22$; but it will not always be the case that minimum τ_p will be less than −1. In the table below, $\tau_p = −0.66$.

Predicted

		+	−	
	+	30	40	70
Observed				
	−	30	0	30
		60	40	100

The Range of λ_p

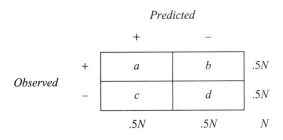

Predicted

		+	−	
	+	a	b	$.5N$
Observed				
	−	c	d	$.5N$
		$.5N$	$.5N$	N

1. For a table with symmetric, equal marginal totals,

$$\lambda_p = [(c + d) - (b + c)]/(c + d) = 1 - (b + c)/(c + d) = 1 - (b + c)/.5N = 1 - 2(b + c)/N.$$

Now the maximum for $b + c$ occurs when $b = c = .5N$ and $a = d = 0$, and the minimum for $b + c$ occurs when $b = c = 0$ and $a = d = .5N$; therefore

$$\text{Maximum}(\lambda_p) - \text{Minimum}(\lambda_p) = [1 - 2(0)/N] - [1 - 2(.5N + .5N)/N] = 1 - (-1) = 2.$$

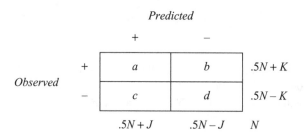

2. For a table with nonsymmetric marginals that may be unequal, but for which the order of the marginals is consistent,

$$\lambda_p = [(c + d) - (b + c)]/(c + d) = 1 - (b + c)/(.5N - K) = 1 - 2(b + c)/(N - 2K).$$

(a) For $K \geq J$, the minimum of $(b + c)$ occurs when a and d are equal to the lesser of their two marginal sums: $a = .5N - J$ and $d = .5N - K$, in which case $c = 0$ and $b = K - J$. The maximum of $(b + c)$ occurs when b and c are equal to the lesser of their two marginal sums: $b = .5N - J$, $c = .5N - K$, in which case $d = 0$ and $a = K + J$. Therefore, for $K \geq J$,

$$\begin{aligned}
\text{Maximum}(\lambda_p) - \text{Minimum}(\lambda_p) &= [1 - 2(K - J)/(N - 2K)] - [1 - 2(N - K - J)/(N - 2K)] \\
&= 1 - 2(K - J)/(N - 2K) - 1 + 2(N - K - J)/(N - 2K) \\
&= 2(N - K - J - K + J)/(N - 2K) \\
&= 2(N - 2K)/(N - 2K) = 2.
\end{aligned}$$

(b) For $K \leq J$, the minimum of $(b + c)$ occurs when $a = .5N + K$, $d = .5N - J$, $b = 0$, and $c = J - K$; the maximum of $(b + c)$ occurs when $b = .5N - J$, $c = .5N - K$, $d = 0$, and $a = K + J$. Therefore, for $K \leq J$,

$$\begin{aligned}
\text{Maximum}(\lambda_p) - \text{Minimum}(\lambda_p) &= [1 - 2(J - K)/(N - 2K)] - [1 - 2(.5N - J + .5N - K)/(N - 2K)] \\
&= 1 - 2(J - K)/(N - 2K) - 1 + 2(N - J - K)/(N - 2K) \\
&= 2(N - J - K)/(N - 2K) - 2(J - K)/(N - 2K) \\
&= 2(N - J - K - J + K)/(N - 2K) \\
&= 2(N - 2J)/(N - 2K);
\end{aligned}$$

and since $J \leq K$, $2(N - 2J)/(N - 2K) \leq 2$.

Predicted

	+	−	
+	a	b	$.5N + K$
−	c	d	$.5N - K$
	$.5N - J$	$.5N + J$	N

Observed (row label, left of table)

3. For a table with nonsymmetric and unequal marginals in which the order of the marginals is inconsistent,

$$\lambda_p = [(c + d) - (b + c)]/(c + d) = 1 - (b + c)/(.5N - K) = 1 - 2(b + c)/(N - 2K).$$

(a) The minimum of $(b + c)$ occurs when a and d are equal to the lesser of their two marginal sums: $a = .5N - J$, $d = .5N - K$, in which case $c = 0$ and $b = K + J$.

(b) The maximum of $(b + c)$ occurs when b and c are equal to the lesser of their two marginal sums: for $K \geq J$, $b = .5N + J$, $c = .5N - K$, $d = 0$, and $a = K + J$; for $K \leq J$, $b = .5N + K$, $c = .5N - J$, $a = 0$, and $d = K + J$.

(c) Therefore, for $K \geq J$,

$$\begin{aligned}
\text{Maximum}(\lambda_p) - \text{Minimum}(\lambda_p) &= [1 - 2(K + J)/(N - 2K)] - [1 - 2(N - J - K)/(N - 2K)] \\
&= 1 - 2(K + J)/(N - 2K) - 1 + 2(N + K + J)/(N - 2K) \\
&= 2(N + J - K - K - J)/(N - 2K) \\
&= 2(N - 2K)/(N - 2K) \\
&= 2.
\end{aligned}$$

(d) For $K < J$,

$$\begin{aligned}
\text{Maximum}(\lambda_p) - \text{Minimum}(\lambda_p) &= [1 - 2(K + J)/(N - 2K)] - [1 - 2(N + K - J)/(N - 2K)] \\
&= 1 - 2(K + J)/(N - 2K) - 1 + 2(N + K - J)/(N - 2K) \\
&= 2(N + K - J - K - J)/(N - 2K) \\
&= 2(N - 2J)/(N - 2K);
\end{aligned}$$

and since $K < J$,

$$\text{Maximum}(\lambda_p) - \text{Minimum}(\lambda_p) = 2(N - 2J)/(N - 2K) < 2.$$

ERRORS FOR λ_p AND τ_p

Referring only to errors without the model (as errors with the model = $b + c$):

Let N = number of cases in sample, K = number of cases in the modal category, k, and $N - K$ = number of cases in all categories other than the mode; let the categories be $a, b, c, \ldots, i, j, k$ with associated frequencies $A, B, C, \ldots, I, J, K$.

1. The error without the model for λ_p is simply $N - K$.

2. The error for τ_p is $A(N - A)/N + B(N - B)/N + \ldots + J(N - J)/N + K(N - K)/N$.

Let J be the maximum of $(A, B, C, \ldots, I, J)$; but $J \leq K$ since K is the mode; therefore, error for $\tau_p \geq A(N - J)/N + B(N - J)/N + \ldots + J(N - J)/N + K(N - K)/N = (N - K)(N - J + K)/N$.

Since $J \leq K$, $(N - J + K) \geq N$; therefore, $(N - J + K)/N \geq 1$ and $(N - K)(N - J + K)/N \geq N - K$; therefore, the error without the model for $\tau_p \geq N - K$, which is the error without the model for λ_p. For the same table, then,

$$\text{(Error without model} - \text{Error with model)}/\text{(Error with model)} =$$
$$1 - \text{(Error with model)}/\text{(Error without model)}$$

will be equal or larger for τ_p than for λ_p, because the second term (the part subtracted from 1) will be smaller for τ_p than for λ_p. *Hence, τ_p will always be greater than or equal to λ_p.*

φ_p AND φ

$$|\varphi_p| \leq |\varphi| \Rightarrow |(ad - bc)/.5[(a + b)(b + d) + (a + c)(c + d)]| \leq$$
$$|(ad - bc)/[(a + b)(a + c)(b + d)(c + d)]^{.5}|$$

$$\Rightarrow |2/[(a + b)(b + d) + (a + c)(c + d)]| \leq$$
$$|1/[(a + b)(b + d)(a + c)(c + d)]^{.5}|$$

Since a, b, c, and d all represent nonnegative cell frequencies, $|2/[(a + b)(b + d) + (a + c)(c + d)]| = 2/[(a + b)(b + d) + (a + c)(c + d)]$ and $|1/[(a + b)(b + d)(a + c)(c + d)]^{.5}| = 1/[(a + b)(b + d)(a + c)(c + d)]^{.5}$, so the absolute value signs can be removed. Let $a + b = w$, $b + d = x$, $a + c = y$, and $c + d = z$. Since a, b, c, and d are all nonnegative, sums involving a, b, c, and d must also be nonnegative. Continuing,

$$|\varphi_p| \leq |\varphi| \Rightarrow 2/[wx + yz] \leq 1/[wxyz]^{.5};$$

squaring

$$\Rightarrow 4/[w^2x^2 + y^2z^2 + 2wxyz] \leq 1/wxyz;$$

assuming $wxyz \neq 0$

$$\Rightarrow 4wxyz \leq w^2x^2 + y^2z^2 + 2wxyz;$$

subtracting $4wxyz$ from each side,

$$\Rightarrow 0 \leq w^2x^2 + y^2z^2 - 2wxyz = (wx - yz)^2.$$

Now, if $w = x = y = z = 0$, or if $wx = yz = 0$ (contrary to the assumption above and implying either an empty contingency table with $a = b = c = d = 0$; or a table with a single nonzero cell; or a table in which there is only one nonzero row or column), then we either have an empty contingency table (no cases in any of the cells), in which case neither φ_p nor φ can be calculated; or a single nonzero cell, in which case it makes no sense to calculate φ_p or φ; or a table in which either one row or one column has no cases, in which case it again makes no sense to calculate φ_p or φ. If $wx = yz$, then $0 = (wx - yz)^2$, consistent with the proposed inequality. As noted above, because a, b, c, and d are all nonnegative frequency counts, the sums w, x, y, and z must also be nonnegative, and thus the product of any two of w, x, y, and z must also be nonnegative. If $wx \neq yz$ (including the case in which either one but not both of wx or yz equals zero), then $0 < (wx - yz)^2$, consistent with the hypothesis. Hence, for all possible w, x, y, and z (hence all possible a, b, c, and d) for which we would calculate φ_p or φ, it must be the case that $|\varphi_p| \leq |\varphi|$. Since the numerator, equal to $(ad - bc)$ for both φ_p and φ, may be either positive or negative, however, it is not necessarily the case that $\varphi_p \leq \varphi$ (i.e., without the absolute value signs).

APPENDIX C

Ordinal Measures of Explained Variation

$\mathbf{I}$n ordinal regression models generally, and in ordinal logistic regression models in particular, we may want to compare the observed and predicted ranks of the dependent variable. The classification table will be similar to the classification table produced for polytomous nominal logistic regression, possibly but not necessarily with a larger number of categories than is the usual case for polytomous nominal logistic regression. In principle, it is possible to use the nominal measures of predictive efficiency (λ_p, τ_p, and φ_p), because the assumptions for nominal measures of association are satisfied by ordinal variables, but nominal measures of association ignore the information provided by the ordering of the categories of the dependent variable. There are several commonly used ordinal measures of association that have a proportional reduction in error (PRE) interpretation and that do take the ordering of the categories into account. The principal measures of ordinal association are Kendall's τ_a, τ_b, and τ_c (tau-a, tau-b, and tau-c); Goodman and Kruskal's γ (gamma); Somers' d_{yx} and d_{xy} (Somers' d, an asymmetric measure, d_{yx} with Y as the dependent variable or d_{xy} with X as the dependent variable); and Spearman's ρ_s (rho-s).[1]

Spearman's ρ_s actually treats the variables as interval variables by assuming that (a) each variable is fully ranked, that is, there are no tied ranks on either variable, and (b) that the actual distance between any adjacent pair of ranked categories is exactly the same as the distance between any other adjacent pair of ranked categories. The assumption of equal distance between adjacent pairs of categories is the defining feature of an interval scale. All the other ordinal measures of association are based on comparisons of all possible pairs of cases to see whether the cases are *concordant* (they have the same order on the two variables) or *discordant* (they have the opposite order on the two variables), or for some but not all the other measures, whether they are *tied* on at least one of the variables. Kendall's τ_a, like Spearman's ρ_s, assumes that the data are fully ranked. Goodman and Kruskal's γ excludes ties altogether from the calculation. Somers' d_{yx} and d_{xy} adjust for ties on the predictor but not the dependent variable, and Kendall's τ_b and τ_c, which do not make a distinction between independent and dependent variables, adjust for ties on both variables. For any of these ordinal coefficients of association, all possible comparisons between cases are made, and the total number of possible comparisons is $N(N-1)/2 = .5(N^2 - N)$, where N is the sample size.

SPEARMAN'S ρ_s

Spearman's ρ_s (sometimes written r_s by authors who wish to reserve the use of Greek letters for parameters and Roman letters for parameter estimates), as noted above, assumes fully ranked data with equal intervals between the ranks, and is based on calculating differences between ranks for the two variables being compared. Note once again that subtraction is an operation defined for interval but not for ordinal variables, so Spearman's ρ_s is really an interval measure of association. When there are tied ranks, the mean of the ranks is used. Thus, for 10 cases initially assigned ranks 1, 2, 3, 3, 3, 4, 4, 5, 6, 7 the ranks would be recoded as 1, 2, 4, 4, 4, 6.5, 6.5, 8, 9, 10 for purposes of calculating ρ_s. If the difference between the rank on X and the rank on Y is written $\delta = Y - X$, the formula for ρ_s is then $\rho_s = 1 - [6\Sigma\delta^2/(N^3 - N)]$; see Siegel (1956:202–204) for the derivation of this formula. Siegel also describes a method for correcting ρ_s for ties, but this method seems to be rarely if ever applied in practice. Conover (1999) recommends the use of the Pearson correlation coefficient r in place of ρ_s when the number of ties is large. The statistical significance of ρ_s can be tested using a t statistic calculated as $t = \rho_s\sqrt{(N-2)/(1-\rho_s^2)}$.

At least two different PRE interpretations have been offered for ρ_s. One, described in Ott et al. (1992; see also Mueller et al. 1977) assigns each observation of the predicted variable a rank equal to the mean rank for fully ranked data for n pairs, $(n + 1)/2$, when no information is used from the predictor. When the values of the ranks for the predictor variable are known, the PRE interpretation depends on assigning not the rank on the predictor variable, r_x, but instead estimates the rank on the dependent variable $r_y = r_x(\rho_s) + [(N + 1)/2](1 - \rho_s)$. In other words, the rank on the dependent variable is estimated to be the Spearman correlation multiplied by the rank on the dependent variable, plus the average rank on the dependent variable multiplied by 1 minus Spearman's ρ_s. If these rules for prediction are applied, then Mueller et al. (1977) show that ρ_s^2 is a PRE measure. Alternatively, a PRE interpretation for ρ_s has been proposed based on triples rather than pairs of observations. This interpretation is detailed in Hildebrand et al. (1977; see also Kruskal 1958), and based on this interpretation, it is ρ_s rather than ρ_s^2 that is the PRE measure. Both these interpretations seem somewhat strained. The use of triples is not as intuitively plausible as the use of pairs of cases to establish the existence of a PRE relationship in the second interpretation, and in the first interpretation, the prediction of the rank of the dependent variable as something other than the rank of the predictor seems less reasonable than simply predicting that the ranks will be the same on the predictor and the dependent variable. To summarize, then, issues that arise with the use of ρ_s as a PRE measure for the relationship between predicted and observed outcomes in ordinal logistic regression include (1) ρ_s is really an interval measure of association, insofar as it assumes equal intervals between adjacent ranks; (2) it is unclear whether ρ_s^2 or ρ_s should be used as the PRE measure of association and also whether the PRE interpretation of either ρ_s^2 or ρ_s is entirely satisfactory.

CONCORDANCE, DISCORDANCE, AND TIES

Several measures depend on the comparison of pairs of cases, in which the ranks of the two variables being compared for the two cases are either *concordant, discordant,* or *tied.* The pair of cases is said to be concordant if the ordering of the cases is the same on the two variables; that is, if Case 1 has a lower rank than Case 2 on X, Case 1 also has a lower rank than Case 2 on Y, and if Case 1 has a higher rank than Case 2 on X, Case 1 also has a higher rank than Case 2 on Y. The pair is said to be discordant if the ordering of the cases is opposite on the two variables; that is, if Case 1 has a lower rank than Case 2 on X, Case 1 has a higher rank than Case 2 on Y, and vice versa. A tie occurs when Case 1 and Case 2 have the same rank; that is, a tie occurs on X if both cases have the same rank on X, a tie occurs on Y if both cases have the same rank on Y, and (trivially) a tie occurs on both X and Y when both cases have the same rank on each variable (but not necessarily the same rank on X as on Y). Symbolically, let C represent the number of concordant pairs, D represent the number of discordant pairs, T_x the number of pairs tied on X, T_y the number of pairs tied on Y (there is no need to separately represent the number of pairs tied on both X and Y), and the total number of possible pairs is, as noted earlier, $.5N(N-1)$, where N is the sample size. All the measures to be discussed in the following section depend on these five quantities.

The simplest measure based on concordance and discordance is Goodman and Kruskal's γ (gamma, sometimes represented by "G" or "g," again by authors who wish to reserve Greek letters for parameters and Roman letters for parameter estimates), calculated as $\gamma = (C - D)/(C + D)$. This measure excludes all pairs tied on either X or Y (and hence all pairs tied on both) from the calculation. With these pairs excluded, $C + D$ is the total number of pairs considered. The PRE interpretation for γ is as follows. If we use no information about the predictor, then we would predict concordance or discordance at random, with an expected error rate of 50% or an expected number of errors equal to $.5(C + D)$; that is, we would be right at random about half the time. If instead, however, we used the information about the predictor to predict that all pairs are concordant, then the number of errors is equal to the number of discordant pairs divided by the total number of pairs, or D. The difference between these two error rates is $.5(C + D) - D = .5C + .5D - D = .5C - .5D = .5 (C - D)$. The proportional change in error is thus equal to the expected number of errors ignoring the predictor, minus the expected number of errors using the information from the predictor, divided by the expected number of errors using the predictor, or $[.5(C + D) - D]/.5(C + D) = (C - D)/(C + D) = \gamma$. If the number of concordant pairs is greater than the number of discordant pairs, then γ is the proportional reduction in error we obtain when we always predict that one variable will have the same ordering as the other. If, however, the number of discordant pairs is greater than the number of concordant pairs, then γ is the proportional reduction in error we would obtain when we always predict that one variable will have the ordering that is the opposite of the other variable. The problems with γ are widely known. Most important, it may ignore the majority of the possible pairs in the data, and may produce a numerical value of 1, indicating "perfect" correlation, when the actual pattern of values in a contingency table appears to represent an association that we would intuitively regard as a good deal less than perfect, a point nicely illustrated in Loether and McTavish (1993:226).

Statistical significance for γ can be tested using the statistic $z = \gamma\sqrt{(C+D)/2N(1-\gamma^2)}$, which has an approximate normal distribution.

Somers' d_{yx} and d_{xy} (collectively, Somers' d) are asymmetric measures, d_{yx} treating X as the predictor and Y as the dependent variable, and d_{xy} treating Y as the predictor and X as the dependent variable, having identical properties and nearly identical construction. In calculating d_{yx} and d_{xy}, instead of dividing the quantity $(C - D)$ by the sum of the concordant plus discordant cases $(C + D)$, we divide by the total number of cases, minus the number of cases tied on the predictor[2]: $d_{yx} = (C - D)/[.5N(N - 1) - T_x]$ and, with a difference only between T_x and T_y in the denominator, $d_{xy} = (C - D)/[.5N(N - 1) - T_y]$. Somers' d_{yx} and d_{xy} can be interpreted as the proportional reduction in error that occurs under the following conditions. Error without using the predictor is calculated as the error that occurs by predicting concordance or discordance at random for pairs not tied on the predictor. Errors with the predictor are the errors that occur by always predicting concordance (if the relationship is positive) or discordance (if the relationship is negative) between the predictor and the dependent variable for those same cases. As with gamma, if there are more discordant than concordant pairs, the proportional reduction in error is obtained by always predicting discordance rather than concordance, while if there are more concordant than discordant pairs, the proportional reduction in error is obtained by always predicting concordance. The difference between gamma and Somers' d is that the calculation of proportional change in error for Somers' d is calculated over a larger denominator, one that includes cases tied on Y but not cases tied on X, so ties on Y are counted as errors, but with less weight than errors involving a prediction of concordance when the actual result is discordance (or vice versa, in the case of a negative relationship).[3] Somers' d_{yx} and d_{xy} are, in the present context, primarily of interest for comparison with γ, above, and Kendall's τ_b, below.

There are three Kendall's τ measures, τ_a, τ_b, and τ_c. Kendall's τ_a is based on all possible pairs, and assumes fully ranked data (no ties): $\tau_a = (C - D)/[.5N(N - 1)]$. The case of no ties is rare in practice, and rarer still in the sort of data likely to be analyzed using polytomous ordinal logistic regression, and in practice τ_a is almost always ignored. Instead, $\tau_b = (C - D)/\sqrt{[.5N(N - 1) - T_y][.5N(N - 1) - T_x]}$, which is equal to τ_a when there are no ties ($T_y = T_x = 0$), is usually calculated. Kendall's τ_c is an adjusted version of τ_b for tables with unequal numbers of rows and columns (i.e., unequal numbers of different ranks on the two variables). Because our interest is in calculating the predicted and observed ranks on the same variable, the number of rows and columns (or ranks on the observed and predicted variable) will be equal, and τ_c need not be considered further. Kendall's τ_b is equal to the geometric mean of Somers' d_{yx} and d_{xy}, or squaring both, $\tau_b^2 = (d_{yx})(d_{xy})$, and thus represents a symmetric measure closely related to d_{yx} and d_{xy}. Kendall's τ_b, unlike γ, d_{yx}, and d_{xy}, can only indicate perfect (positive or negative) correlation when, in a table in which the cells are defined by the ranks on the two variables, all the cases lie on the positive (for $\tau_b = 1$) or negative ($\tau_b = -1$) diagonal.

For Kendall's τ_b, errors of prediction can be measured on a strictly ordinal scale, with three ordered symbols (0, 1, 2 or a, b, c). If the pair of cases is ordered on both X and Y and the ordering is the same, we assign the first symbol (0 or a). If the pair of cases is tied on one of the two variables and ordered on the other, we assign the second symbol (1 or b), indicating that it would take us one step or transformation (eliminating the tie) to bring the pair into concordance. If the pair of cases is ordered on both X and Y and the ordering is opposite on the two variables, we assign the third symbol (2 or c), indicating a larger error than if one of the variables is tied, and two steps or transformations (first from discordant to tied, then from tied to concordant) to transform the discordant pair to a concordant pair. If the cases are tied on both variables, the pair is ignored (effectively, as will be seen in a moment, assigning the first symbol). The assignment of ordered symbols recognizes that the instance of two orderings that are opposite each other is more different from the instance of two orderings that are identical to each other than either is from the instance in which the two orderings are not opposite but also not identical. The statistical significance of τ_b can be tested using the statistic $z = 3\tau_b\sqrt{N(N - 1)/[2(2N + 5)]}$, which has an approximate normal distribution for large ($N > 40$) samples.

The error of prediction can be quantified as the number of steps or transformations, from zero (identical ordering) to one (ordered on one variable, tied on the other) to two (opposite ordering) required to make the orderings for any pair of cases on X and Y concordant. As Siegel (1956) describes Kendall's τ_b, "One may think of τ as a function of the minimum number of inversions or interchanges between neighbors which is required to transform one ranking into another. That is, τ is a sort of coefficient of disarray" (p. 215). Thus, the error categories are not just *arbitrarily* represented by zero, one, and two, but these numbers actually represent a quantity, the number of changes required to achieve concordance. We can thus take a sum of the errors, or a sum of the squared errors (squared error = 0 if the error is zero, 1 if the error is one, and 4 if the error is two). Because pairs of cases tied on both X and Y are ignored, the case of a tie on both X and Y contributes nothing to the sum of the errors or squared errors, and hence is treated as a concordant case for purposes of calculating errors. As described by Wilson (1969; see also Hildebrand et al. 1977), when this scoring is used for the errors in predicting concordance and discordance, τ_b^2 is a proportional reduction in error measure. Compared with γ, d_{yx} and d_{xy}, τ_b is the most conservative measure of association, in the sense that it has the most restrictive definition of a "perfect" correlation (predicted rank must equal observed rank exactly), and numerically it is usually the case that $\tau_b < d_{yx}$ (or d_{xy}) $< \gamma$. When $\tau_b = 1$, it is also the case that $\gamma = d_{yx} = d_{xy} = 1$. Another useful property of τ_b in other contexts is that it is straightforward to interpret and compute a partial τ_b for the correlation between two ordinal variables, controlling for a third ordinal variable.

In more detail, following Wilson (1969), consider two cases with an observed ordering on an ordinal variable Y and a predicted ordering based on knowledge of another variable, X, in which the ordering on Y is predicted to be the same as the ordering on X if τ_b is positive (if there are more concordant than discordant pairs), but the ordering on Y is predicted to be the opposite of the ordering on X if τ_b is negative (if there are more discordant than concordant pairs). If the observed and predicted ordering are the same, the error is scored as zero. If the two cases are tied and any ordering is predicted, or if the two cases have some order and a tie is predicted, the error is scored as one. If the observed ordering of the two cases is the opposite of the predicted ordering, the error is scored as a two. The score thus represents the degree of error measured on an integer scale, and the corresponding squared errors are (1) zero for agreement, including agreement that the two cases are tied, (2) one for an error involving a tie when a particular ordering is observed or predicted, and (3) $2^2 = 4$ when the observed and predicted ordering are opposite.

The expected error in the absence of information about X is $2u_y$, where u_y is the proportion of pairs not tied on Y. Expected error using information about X is $2u_y - 2d_{yx} u_x^2$, where d_{yx} is the Somers' d statistic with Y as the dependent variable and X as the predictor, and u_x is the number of cases not tied on X. When these expressions are substituted into the definition of proportional reduction in error, the result is exactly τ_b^2 : $[2u_y - (2u_y - 2d_{yx}^2 u_x)]/2u_y = d_{yx}^2 u_x/u_y = (\tau_b^2 u_y/u_x)(u_x/u_y) = \tau_b^2$, because $d_{yx}^2 = \tau_b^2 u_y/u_x$. Wilson (1969:342) notes that the prediction rules are in a reasonable sense unbiased (the expected value of the prediction using the rules for τ_b is equal to the expected value of the actual distribution or order), but they do not minimize the expected error. For example, the expected error can be reduced to just u_y instead of $2u_y$ by simply predicting a tie in every pair. If, however, unbiased prediction rules that actually minimize error are used, it can be shown that the proportional change in error is negative whenever the absolute value of d_{yx} is less than .5. In other words, the error using information about X is greater than when information about X is ignored. As Wilson notes, continuing, this is not merely an artifact of the particular definition of error used here (note the parallel here to the possible negative values of τ_p, λ_p, and φ_p), but can be shown to hold for any definition of error.

Costner (1965) asserts that any measure that includes ties of any kind in its pool is not properly a PRE measure, because a tie cannot clearly be counted as either a correct or an erroneous prediction, and only these two categories are permissible for PRE measures. Loether and McTavish (1993) counter that if one takes the position that the pool of potential errors should include all those instances for which a prediction is likely to be made, then it is reasonable to include ties. Daniel (1978:306) notes that an important difference between Kendall's τ (both τ_a and τ_b) is that the τ measures provide an unbiased estimator of a population parameter, while the sample statistic ρ_s does not provide an estimate of a population coefficient of rank correlation. The parameter estimated by τ_b may be defined as the probability of concordance minus the probability of discordance. Daniel (1978:314) also notes that the distribution of τ_b approaches the normal distribution more rapidly than does the distribution of ρ_s, so when the normal approximation is used to calculate statistical significance with samples of intermediate size, τ_b may provide a more reliable test statistic. As noted by Siegel (1956), τ_b can also be used to calculate partial correlations (and, coincidentally, the formula for the partial τ_b, $\tau_{xy.z}$ is the same as the formula for the Pearson partial correlation coefficient, $r_{xy.z}$, with τ_b substituted for r), but the sampling distribution of the partial τ_b is not known, so its significance cannot be tested by conventional methods (although resampling methods may be used to estimate statistical significance).

RANK CORRELATION IN POLYTOMOUS ORDINAL LOGISTIC REGRESSION

Based on the above considerations, τ_b^2 seems to be the natural choice for an ordinal measure of explained variation. (1) It is a PRE measure, involving only ordinal comparisons and an intuitively reasonable scoring system for calculating errors; (2) unlike ρ_s it does not assume equal distances between adjacent ranks; (3) unlike γ, d_{yx}, and d_{xy}, it has an intuitively appealing definition of a "perfect" correlation, which requires the predicted rank to be equal to the observed rank; (4) unlike γ, d_{yx}, and d_{xy}, it incorporates all pairs of cases into the calculation; and (5) unlike ρ_s (and τ_a), it has no difficulty in handling tied ranks. In addition, as noted by Daniel (1978:314), unlike ρ_s, τ_b provides an unbiased estimator of a population parameter, the probability of concordance minus the probability of discordance (ρ_s does not provide an estimate of a population coefficient of rank correlation), and also the distribution of τ_b approaches the normal distribution more quickly than does the distribution of ρ_s, so for samples of intermediate size, the test for the statistical significance of τ_b may be more reliable than the corresponding test for ρ_s.

NOTES

1. Useful general discussions of ordinal measures of association are given in Siegel (1956), Hildebrand et al. (1977), Daniel (1978), Ott et al. (1992), Loether and McTavish (1993), and Conover (1999), all of which were used in the preparation of this appendix.

2. Alternatively, Loether and McTavish (1993:224) use the quantity $(C + D + T_y)$ as the denominator for Somers' d_{yx}, and similarly (see the discussion of Kendall's τ_b) use $C + D$ in the denominator of Kendall's τ_b, adding ties to the sum of the concordant and discordant pairs rather than subtracting ties from the total number of pairs.

3. This PRE interpretation is noted in Loether and McTavish (1993) and Ott et al. (1992), and provided in a little more detail by Hildebrand et al. (1977).

References

Achen, C. H. (1982). *Interpreting and Using Regression*. Beverly Hills, CA: Sage.

Agresti, A. (1990). *Categorical Data Analysis*. New York: Wiley.

Agresti, A. (1996). *An Introduction to Categorical Data Analysis*. New York: Wiley.

Agresti, A. (2002). *Categorical Data Analysis*, second edition. New York: Wiley.

Agresti, A., and Finlay, B. (1997). *Statistical Methods for the Social Sciences,* third edition. Upper Saddle River, NJ: Prentice Hall.

Aldrich, J. H., and Nelson, F. D. (1984). *Linear Probability, Logit, and Probit Models*. Beverly Hills, CA: Sage.

Allen, J. and Le, H. (2008). An additional measure of overall effect size for logistic regression models. *Journal of Educational and Behavioral Statistics* 33:416–441.

Allison, P. D. (1978). Measures of inequality. *American Sociological Review* 43:865–880.

Allison, P. D. (1995). *Survival Analysis Using the SAS System: A Practical Guide*. Cary, NC: SAS Institute.

Allison, P. D. (1999). *Logistic Regression Using the SAS System*. Cary, NC: SAS Institute.

Allison, P. D. (2005). *Fixed Effects Regression Methods for Longitudinal Data Using SAS*. Cary, NC: SAS Institute.

Andersen, E. B. (1970). Asymptotic properties of conditional maximum-likelihood estimators. *Journal of the Royal Statistical Society, Series B* 32:283–301.

Anderson, J. A. (1984). Regression and ordered categorical variables (with discussion). *Journal of the Royal Statistical Society, Series B* 54:781–791.

Apisarnthanarak, A., Holzmann-Pazgal, G., Hamvas, A., Olsen, M. A., and Fraser, V. (2003). Ventilator-associated pneumonia in extremely preterm neonates in a neonatal intensive care unit: Characteristics, risk factors, and outcomes. *Pediatrics* 112: 1283–1289.

Asher, H. B. (1983). *Causal Modeling*. Beverly Hills, CA: Sage.

Babbie, E. (2001). *The Practice of Social Research*. Belmont, CA: Wadsworth.

Beck, N., Katz, J., and Tucker, R. (1998). Taking time seriously: Time-series cross-section analysis with a binary dependent variable. *American Journal of Political Science* 42:1260–1288.

Begg, C. B., and Grey, R. (1984). Calculation of polychotomous logistic regression parameters using individualized regressions. *Biometrika* 71:11–18.

Belsley, D. A., Kuh, E., and Welsch, R. E. (1980). *Regression Diagnostics: Identifying Influential Data and Sources of Collinearity*. New York: Wiley.

Ben-Akiva, M., and Lerman, S. R. (1985). *Discrete Choice Analysis: Theory and Application to Travel Demand*. Cambridge: MIT Press.

Bendel, R. B., and Afifi, A. A. (1977). Comparison of stopping rules in forward regression. *Journal of the American Statistical Association* 72:46–53.

Berry, W. D. (1984). *Nonrecursive Causal Models*. Beverly Hills, CA: Sage.

Berry, W. D. (1993). *Understanding Regression Assumptions*. Newbury Park, CA: Sage.

Berry, W. D., and Feldman, S. (1985). *Multiple Regression in Practice.* Beverly Hills, CA: Sage.

Biagotti, R., Desii, C., Vanzi, E., and Gacci, G. (1999). Predicting ovarian malignancy: Application of artificial neural networks to transvaginal and color Doppler flow US. *Radiology* 210:399–403.

Bijleveld, C. C. J. H., and Van Der Kamp, L. J. T. (with Mooijaart, A., Van Der Kloot, W. A., Van Der Leeden, R., and Van Der Burg, E.). (1998). *Longitudinal Data Analysis: Designs, Models, and Methods.* London: Sage.

Blair, J., and Lacy, M. G. (2000). Statistics of ordinal variation. *Sociological Methods and Research* 28:251–279.

Blalock, H. M., Jr. (1964). *Causal Inferences in Nonexperimental Research.* Chapel Hill: University of North Carolina Press.

Blalock, H. M., Jr. (1971a). *Causal Models in the Social Sciences.* Chicago: Aldine.

Blalock, H. M., Jr. (1971b). Causal inferences, closed populations, and measures of association. In H. M. Blalock, Jr. (ed.), *Causal Models in the Social Sciences.* Chicago: Aldine, pp. 139–151.

Blau, P. M., and Duncan, O. D. (1967). *The American Occupational Structure.* New York: Wiley.

Blossfeld, H., Hamerle, A., and Mayer, K. U. (1989). *Event History Analysis: Statistical Theory and Application in the Social Sciences.* Hillsdale, NJ: Lawrence Erlbaum.

Bohrnstedt, G. W., and Knoke, D. (1994). *Statistics for Social Data Analysis,* third edition. Itasca, IL: F. E. Peacock.

Bollen, K. A. (1989). *Structural Equation Models With Latent Variables.* New York: Wiley.

Bollen, K. A., and Barb, K. H. (1981). Pearsons' r and coarsely categorized measures. *American Sociological Review* 46:232–239.

Bollen, K. A., and Stine, R. A. (1993). Bootstrapping goodness-of-fit measures in structural equation models. In K. A. Bollen and J. S. Long (eds.), *Testing Structural Equation Models.* Newbury Park, CA: Sage, pp. 111–135.

Box-Steffensmeier, J. M., and Jones, B. S. (2004). *Event History Modeling: A Guide for Social Scientists.* Cambridge, UK: Cambridge University Press.

Breslow, N. E. (1996). Statistics in epidemiology: The case-control study. *Journal of the American Statistical Association* 91:14–28.

Breslow, N., and Clayton, D. G. (1993). Approximate inference in generalized linear mixed models. *Journal of the American Statistical Association* 88:9–25.

Breslow, N. E., and Day, N. E. (1980). *Statistical Methods in Cancer Research I: The Analysis of Case-Control Studies.* Lyon, France: International Agency for Research on Cancer.

Breslow, N., and Lin, X. (1995). Bias correction in generalized linear mixed models with a single component of dispersion. *Biometrika* 82:81–91.

Brier, G. W. (1950). Verification of forecasts expressed in terms of probability. *Monthly Weather Review* 75:1–3.

Browne, M. W. (1984). Asymptotically distribution-free methods for the analysis of covariance structures. *British Journal of Mathematical and Statistical Psychology* 37:62–83.

Bulmer, M. G. (1979). *Principles of Statistics.* New York: Dover.

Chamberlain, G. (1980). Analysis of covariance with qualitative data. *Review of Economic Studies* 47:225–238.

Chamberlain, G. (1984). Panel data. In Z. Griliches and M. D. Intriligator (eds.), *Handbook of Econometrics, Vol. 2.* Amsterdam: Elsevier, pp. 1247–1318.

Chen, P. Y., and Popovich, P. M. (2002). *Correlation: Parametric and Nonparametric Measures.* Thousand Oaks, CA: Sage.

Clogg, C. C., and Shihadeh, E. S. (1994). *Statistical Models for Ordinal Variables.* Thousand Oaks, CA: Sage.

Cohen, J. (1968). Multiple regression as a general data-analytic system. *Psychological Bulletin* 70:426–443.

Coleman, J. S. (1981). *Longitudinal Data Analysis.* New York: Basic Books.

Conover, W. J. (1999). *Practical Nonparametric Statistics,* third edition. New York: Wiley.

Copas, J. B., and Loeber, R. (1990). Relative improvement over chance (RIOC) for 2 × 2 tables. *British Journal of Mathematical and Statistical Psychology* 43:293–307.

Costner, H. L. (1965). Criteria for measures of association. *American Sociological Review* 30:341–353.

Covey, H. C., Menard, S., and Franzese, R. J. (1997). *Juvenile Gangs,* second edition. Springfield, IL: Charles C. Thomas.

Cox, D. R. (1970). *The Analysis of Binary Data.* London: Chapman & Hall.

Cox, D. R., and Oakes, D. (1984). *Analysis of Survival Data.* London: Chapman & Hall.

Cox, D. R., and Snell, E. J. (1989). *The Analysis of Binary Data,* second edition. London: Chapman & Hall.

Cox, D. R., and Wermuth, N. (1992). A comment on the coefficient of determination for binary responses. *The American Statistician* 46:1–4.

Cragg, J. G., and Uhler, R. (1970). The demand for automobiles. *Canadian Journal of Economics* 3:386–406.

Cramer, J. S. (1999). Predictive performance of the binary logit model in unbalanced samples. *The Statistician* 48(Part 1):85–94.

Cramer, J. S. (2003). *Logit Models From Economics and Other Fields.* Cambridge, UK: Cambridge University Press.

Cronbach, L. J., and Furby, L. (1970). How should we measure change: Or should we? *Psychological Bulletin* 72:68–80.

Daniel, W. W. (1978). *Applied Nonparametric Statistics.* Boston: Houghton Mifflin.

Davies, R. B. (1994). From cross-sectional to longitudinal analysis. In A. Dale and R. B. Davies (eds.), *Analyzing Social and Political Change: A Casebook of Methods.* London: Sage, pp. 20–40.

Davis, J. A. (1985). *The Logic of Causal Order.* Beverly Hills, CA: Sage.

Davis, J. A., and Smith, T. W. (1992). *The NORC General Social Survey.* Newbury Park, CA: Sage.

Davis, J. A., Smith, T. W., and Marsden, P. V. (2000). *General Social Surveys, 1972–2000: Cumulative Codebook* [and machine-readable data file]. Chicago: National Opinion Research Center.

Davis, J. A., Smith, T. W., and Marsden, P. (2005). *General Social Surveys, 1972–2004: Cumulative Codebook.* Chicago: National Opinion Research Center.

DeMaris, A. (1992). *Logit Modeling.* Newbury Park, CA: Sage.

DeMaris, A. (2002). Explained variance in logistic regression: A Monte Carlo study of proposed measures. *Sociological Methods and Research* 31:27–74.

Diggle, P. J., Liang, K., and Zeger, S. L. (1994). *Analysis of Longitudinal Data.* Oxford, UK: Oxford University Press.

Duncan, O. D. (1971). Path analysis: Sociological examples. In H. M. Blalock, Jr. (ed.), *Causal Models in the Social Sciences.* Chicago: Aldine, pp. 115–138.

Duncan, O. D. (1975). *Introduction to Structural Equation Models.* New York: Academic Press.

Efron, B. (1978). Regression and ANOVA with zero-one data: Measures of residual variation. *Journal of the American Statistical Association* 73:113–121.

Efron, B. (1979). Bootstrap methods: Another look at the jackknife. *Annals of Statistics* 7:1–26.

Eliason, S. R. (1993). *Maximum Likelihood Estimation: Logic and Practice.* Newbury Park, CA: Sage.

Elliott, D. S., Huizinga, D., and Ageton, S. S. (1985). *Explaining Delinquency and Drug Use.* Beverly Hills, CA: Sage.

Elliott, D. S., Huizinga, D., and Menard, S. (1989). *Multiple Problem Youth: Delinquency, Substance Use, and Mental Health Problems.* New York: Springer-Verlag.

Elliott, D. S., and Menard, S. (1996). Delinquent friends and delinquent behavior: Temporal and developmental patterns. In J. D. Hawkins (ed.) *Delinquency and Crime: Current Theories.* Cambridge, UK: Cambridge University Press, pp. 28–67.

Elliott, D. S., Menard, S., Rankin, B., Elliott, A., Wilson, W. J., and Huizinga, D. (2006). *Good Kids From Bad Neighborhoods: Successful Development in Social Context.* Cambridge, UK: Cambridge University Press.

Elliott, D. S., Wilson, W. J., Huizinga, D., Sampson, R. J., Elliott, A., and Rankin, B. (1996). The effects of neighborhood disadvantage on adolescent development. *Journal of Research in Crime and Delinquency* 33:389–426.

Elward, A. M., Warren, D. K., and Fraser, V. J. (2002). Ventilator-associated pneumonia in pediatric intensive care unit patients: Risk factors and outcomes. *Pediatrics* 109:758–764.

Eshima, N., Tabata, M., and Zhi, G. (2001). Path analysis with logistic regression models: Effect analysis of fully recursive causal systems of categorical variables. *Journal of the Japan Statistical Society* 31:1–14.

Farrington, D. P., and Loeber, R. (1989). Relative improvement over chance (RIOC) and phi as measures of predictive efficiency and strength of association in 2 × 2 tables. *Journal of Quantitative Criminology* 5:201–213.

Fiegener, M. K., Brown, B. M., Dreux, D. R., and Dennis, W. J., Jr. (2000). The adoption of outside boards by small private U.S. firms. *Entrepreneurship and Regional Development* 12:291–309.

Fienberg, S. E. (1980). *The Analysis of Cross-Classified Categorical Data,* second edition. Cambridge: MIT Press.

Finkel, S. E. (1995). *Causal Analysis With Panel Data.* Thousand Oaks, CA: Sage.

Fox, J. (1991). *Regression Diagnostics.* Newbury Park, CA: Sage.

Frankel, M. R. (1971). *Inference From Survey Samples.* Ann Arbor, MI: Institute of Social Research.

Goldstein, H. (1991). Nonlinear multilevel models, with an application to discrete response data. *Biometrika* 78:45–51.

Goldstein, H. (1995). *Multilevel Statistical Models.* New York: Halsted.

Goldstein, H., Rashbash, J., Plewis, I., Draper, D., Browne, W., Yang, M., Woodhouse, G., and Healy, M. (1998). *A user's guide to MLwiN.* London: Multilevel Models Project, Institute of Education, University of London.

Goodman, L. A. (1972). A modified multiple regression approach to the analysis of dichotomous variables. *American Sociological Review* 37:28–46.

Goodman, L. A. (1973a). Causal analysis of data from panel studies and other kinds of surveys. *American Journal of Sociology* 78:1135–1191.

Goodman, L. A. (1973b). The analysis of multidimensional contingency tables when some variables are posterior to others: A modified path analysis approach. *Biometrika* 60:179–192.

Gould, W., and Sribney, W. (1999). *Maximum likelihood estimation with Stata.* College Station, TX: Stata Press.

Grömping, U. (2007). Estimators of relative importance in linear regression based on variance decomposition. *The American Statistician* 61:139–147.

Gunson, K. E., Chruszcz, B., and Clevenger, A. P. (2003). Large animal-vehicle collisions in the Central Canadian Rocky Mountains: Patterns and characteristics. *Road Ecology Center eScholarship Repository, John Muir Institute of the Environment, University of California, Davis.* Retrieved July 6, 2008, from http://repositories.cdlib.org/jmie/roadeco/Gunson2003a

Haberman, S. J. (1982). Analysis of dispersion of multinomial responses. *Journal of the American Statistical Association* 77:568–580.

Hagle, T. M., and Mitchell, G. E., II (1992). Goodness-of-fit measures for probit and logit. *American Journal of Political Science* 36:762–784.

Hamerle, A., and Ronning, G. (1995). Panel analysis for qualitative variables. In G. Arminger, C. C. Clogg, and M. E. Sobel (eds.), *Handbook of Statistical Modeling for the Social and Behavioral Sciences.* New York: Plenum Press, pp. 401–451.

Hardin, J., and Hilbe, J. (2001). *Generalized Linear Models and Extensions.* College Station, TX: Stata Press.

Hardin, J. W., and Hilbe, J. M. (2003). *Generalized Estimating Equations.* Boca Raton, FL: Chapman & Hall.

Hardy, M. (1993). *Regression With Dummy Variables.* Newbury Park, CA: Sage.

Harrell, F. E., Jr. (1986). The LOGIST procedure. In SAS Institute, Inc. (ed.), *SUGI Supplemental Library User's Guide,* Version 5 edition. Cary, NC: SAS Institute, Inc., pp. 269–293.

Hauck, W. W., and Donner, A. (1977). Wald's test as applied to hypotheses in logit analysis. *Journal of the American Statistical Association* 72:851–853; with correction in W. W. Hauck and A. Donner (1980), *Journal of the American Statistical Association* 75:482.

Hauser, J. R. (1978). Testing the accuracy, usefulness, and significance of probabilistic choice models: An information-theoretic approach. *Operations Research 26:406–421.*

Hausman, J. A., and McFadden, D. (1984). Specification tests for the multinomial logit model. Econometrica 52:1219–1240.

Hayduk, L. A. (1987). *Structural Modeling With LISREL: Essentials and Advances.* Baltimore: Johns Hopkins University Press.

Heise, D. R. (1975). *Causal Analysis.* New York: Wiley.

Henry, F. (1982). Multivariate analysis and ordinal data. *American Sociological Review* 47:229–307.

Hildebrand, D. K., Laing, J. D., and Rosenthal, H. (1977). *Analysis of Ordinal Data.* Beverly Hills, CA: Sage.

Hill, M. S. (1992). *The Panel Study of Income Dynamics: A User's Guide.* Newbury Park, CA: Sage.

Hirji, K. F., Mehta, C. R., and Patel, N. R. (1987). Computing distributions for exact logistic regression. *Journal of the American Statistical Association* 82:1110–1117.

Hosmer, D. W., and Lemeshow, S. (1989). *Applied Logistic Regression.* New York: Wiley.

Hosmer, D. W., and Lemeshow, S. (1999). *Applied Survival Analysis: Regression Modeling of Time to Event Data.* New York: Wiley.

Hosmer, D. W., and Lemeshow, S. (2000). *Applied Logistic Regression,* second edition. New York: Wiley.

Hox, J. (2002). *Multilevel Analysis: Techniques and Applications.* Mahwah, NJ: Lawrence Erlbaum.

Hsieh, F. Y., Bloch, D. A., and Larsen, M. D. (1998). A simple method for sample size calculation for linear and logistic regression. *Statistics in Medicine* 17:1623–1634.

Hu, L., Bentler, P. M., and Kano, Y. (1992). Can test statistics in covariance structure analysis be trusted? *Psychological Bulletin* 112:351–362.

Hutcheson, G., and Sofroniou, N. (1999). *The multivariate social scientist: Introductory statistics using generalized linear models.* London: Sage.

Ishii-Kuntz, M. (1994). *Ordinal Log-Linear Models.* Thousand Oaks, CA: Sage.

Jaccard, J. (2001). *Interaction Effects in Logistic Regression.* Thousand Oaks, CA: Sage.

Jennings, D. E. (1986). Judging inference adequacy in logistic regression. *Journal of the American Statistical Association* 81:471–476.

Jöreskog, K. G., and Sörbom, D. (1988). *PRELIS: A Program for Multivariate Data Screening and Data Summarization,* second edition. Chicago: Scientific Software.

Jöreskog, K. G., and Sörbom, D. (1993). *LISREL 8: Structural Equation Modeling With the SIMPLIS Command Language.* Chicago: Scientific Software.

Kalbfleisch, J. D., and Prentice, R. L. (1980). *The Statistical Analysis of Failure Time Data.* New York: Wiley.

Kalbfleisch, J. D., and Prentice, R. L. (2002). *The Statistical Analysis of Failure Time Data,* second edition. New York: Wiley.

Kalbfleisch, J. D., and Sprott, D. A. (1970). Application of likelihood methods to models involving large numbers of parameters. *Journal of the Royal Statistical Society, Series B (Methodological)* 32:175–208.

Kalton, G. (1983). *Introduction to Survey Sampling.* Beverly Hills, CA: Sage.

Kandel, D. B., and Faust, R. (1975). Sequences and states in patterns of adolescent drug use. *Archives of General Psychiatry* 32:923–932.

Kaplan, D. (2000). *Structural Equation Modeling: Foundations and Extensions.* Thousand Oaks, CA: Sage.

Kaufman, R. L. (1996). Comparing effects in dichotomous logistic regression: A variety of standardized coefficients. *Social Science Quarterly* 77:90–109.

Kessler, R. C., and Greenberg, D. G. (1981). *Linear Panel Analysis: Models of Quantitative Change.* New York: Wiley.

King, E. N., and Ryan, T. P. (2002). A preliminary investigation of maximum likelihood logistic regression versus exact logistic regression. *The American Statistician* 56:163–170.

King, G. (1989). *Unifying Political Methodology: The Likelihood Theory of Statistical Inference.* Cambridge, UK: Cambridge University Press.

Kish, L. (1965). *Survey Sampling.* New York: Wiley.

Klecka, W. R. (1980). *Discriminant Analysis.* Beverly Hills, CA: Sage.

Kleinbaum, D. G., and Klein, M. (2002). *Logistic Regression: A Self-Learning Text,* second edition. New York: Springer.

Kline, R. B. (2005). *Principles and Practice of Structural Equation Modeling,* second edition. New York: Guilford Press.

Knoke, D., and Burke, P. J. (1980). *Log-Linear Models.* Beverly Hills, CA: Sage.

Korn, E. L., and Simon, R. (1991). Explained residual variation, explained risk, and goodness of fit. *The American Statistician* 45:201–206.

Kracman, K. (1996). The effect of school-based arts instruction on attendance at museums and the performing arts. *Poetics* 24:203–218.

Kreft, I., and De Leeuw, J. (1998). *Introducing Multilevel Modeling.* London: Sage.

Krippendorf, K. (1986). *Information Theory.* Beverly Hills, CA: Sage.

Kritzer, H. M. (1976). Problems in the use of two stage least squares: Standardization of coefficients and multicollinearity. *Political Methodology, 3,* 71–93.

Kruskal, W. H. (1958). Ordinal measures of association. *Journal of the American Statistical Association* 53:814–861.

Kupek, E. (2005). Log-linear transformation of binary variables: A suitable input for structural equation modeling. *Structural Equation Modeling: A Multidisciplinary Journal* 12:35–47.

Kupek, E. (2006). Beyond logistic regression: Structural equations modelling for binary variables and its application to investigating unobserved confounders. *BMC Medical Research Methodology* 6. Retrieved July 6, 2008, from www.biomedcentral.com/1471-2288/6/13

Kvålseth, T. O. (1985). Cautionary note about R^2. *The American Statistician* 39:279–285.

Lambert, W. (2007). *Objective Lightning Probability Forecasting for Kennedy Space Center and Cape Canaveral Air Force Station, Phase II.* NASA Contractor Report NASA/CR-2007–214732. Hanover, MD: NASA Center for AeroSpace Information. Retrieved August 2, 2008, from http://science.ksc.nasa.gov/amu

Lambert, W., and Wheeler, M. (2005). *Objective Lightning Probability Forecasting for Kennedy Space Center and Cape Canaveral Air Force Station.* NASA Contractor Report NASA/CR-2005–212564. Hanover, MD: NASA Center for AeroSpace Information. Retrieved August 2, 2008, from http://science.ksc.nasa.gov/amu

Landwehr, J. M., Pregibon, D., and Shoemaker, A. C. (1984). Graphical methods for assessing logistic regression models. *Journal of the American Statistical Association* 79:61–71.

LaVange, L. M., Koch, G. G., and Schwartz, T. A. (2001). Applying sample survey methods to clinical trials data. *Statistics in Medicine* 20:2609–2623.

Lawless, J. F. (2003). *Statistical Models and Methods for Lifetime Data,* second edition. New York: Wiley.

Lee, C., and Moudon, A. V. (2006). Correlates of walking for transportation or recreation purposes. *Journal of Physical Activity and Health* 3(Suppl. 1):S77–S98.

Lee, E. S., Forthofer, R. N., and Lorimor, R. J. (1989). *Analyzing Complex Survey Data.* Newbury Park, CA: Sage.

Lepkowski, J. M. (1989). Treatment of wave nonresponse in panel surveys. In D. G. Kasprzyk, G. Duncan, G. Kalton, and M. P. Singh (eds.), *Panel Surveys.* New York: Wiley, pp. 348–374.

Levy, P. S., and Lemeshow, S. (1999). *Sampling of Populations: Methods and Applications,* third edition. New York: Wiley.

Lewis-Beck, M. S. (1980). *Applied Regression: An Introduction.* Beverly Hills, CA: Sage.

Liang, K., and Zeger, S. L. (1986). Longitudinal data analysis using generalized linear models. *Biometrika* 73:13–22.

Liao, J. G., and McGee, D. (2003). Adjusted coefficients of determination for logistic regression. *The American Statistician* 57:161–165.

Liebetrau, A. M. (1983). *Measures of Association.* Newbury Park, CA: Sage.

Liker, J. K., Augustyniak, S., and Duncan, G. J. (1985). Panel data and models of change: A comparison of first difference and conventional two-wave models. *Social Science Research* 12:80–101.

Lindeman, R. H., Merenda, P. F., and Gold, R. Z. (1980). *Introduction to Bivariate and Multivariate Analysis.* Glenview, IL: Scott, Foresman.

Lipsey, M. W. (1998). Design sensitivity: Statistical power for applied experimental research. In L. Bickman and D. J. Rog (eds.), *Handbook of Applied Social Research Methods.* Thousand Oaks, CA: Sage.

Littell, R. C., Milliken, G. A., Stroup, W. W., and Wolfinger, R. D. (1996). *SAS system for Mixed Models.* Cary, NC: SAS Institute.

Little, R. J. A., and Rubin, D. B. (2002). *Statistical Analysis With Missing Data,* second edition. New York: Wiley.

Livezey, R. E. (1995). The evaluation of forecasts. In H. von Storch and A. Navarra (eds.), *Analysis of Climate Variability.* Berlin, Germany: Springer-Verlag, pp. 177–196.

Loeber, R., and Dishion, T. (1983). Early predictors of male delinquency: A review. *Psychological Bulletin* 94:68–99.

Loether, H. J., and McTavish, D. G. (1993). *Descriptive and Inferential Statistics: An Introduction.* Boston: Allyn & Bacon.

Long, J. S. (1997). *Regression Models for Categorical and Limited Dependent Variables.* Thousand Oaks, CA: Sage.

Luke, D. A. (2004). *Multilevel Modeling.* Thousand Oaks, CA: Sage.

Maddala, G. S. (1983). *Limited-Dependent and Qualitative Variables in Econometrics.* Cambridge, UK: Cambridge University Press.

Maddigan, S. L., Farris, K. B., Keating, N., Wiens, C. A., and Johnson, J. A. (2003). Predictors of older adults' capacity for medication management in a self-medication program. *Journal of Aging and Health* 15:332–352.

Magee, L. (1990). R^2 measures based on Wald and likelihood ratio joint significance tests. *The American Statistician* 44:250–253.

Magidson, J. (1981). Qualitative variance, entropy, and correlation ratios for nominal dependent variables. *Social Science Research* 10:177–194.

Maruyama, G. M. (1998). *Basics of Structural Equation Modeling.* Thousand Oaks, CA: Sage.

McArdle, J. J., and Bell, R. Q. (2000). An introduction to latent growth models for developmental data analysis. In T. D. Little, K. U. Schnabel, and J. Baumert (eds.), *Modeling Longitudinal and Multilevel Data: Practical Issues, Applied Approaches, and Specific Examples.* Mahwah, NJ: Lawrence Erlbaum, pp. 69–107.

McCallum, R. C., and Kim, C. (2000). Modeling multivariate change. In T. D. Little, K. U. Schnabel, and J. Baumert (eds.), *Modeling Longitudinal and Multilevel Data: Practical Issues, Applied Approaches, and Specific Examples.* Mahwah, NJ: Lawrence Erlbaum, pp. 51–68.

McCullagh, P. (1980). Regression models for ordinal data (with discussion). *Journal of the Royal Statistical Society, Series B* 42:109–142.

McCullagh, P., and Nelder, J. A. (1989). *Generalized Linear Models,* second edition. London: Chapman & Hall.

McFadden, D. (1974). The measurement of urban travel demand. *Journal of Public Economics* 3:303–328.

McKelvey, R., and Zavoina, W. (1975). A statistical model for the analysis of ordinal level dependent variables. *Journal of Mathematical Sociology* 4:103–120.

Mehta, C. R., and Patel, N. R. (1995). Exact logistic regression: Theory and examples. *Statistics in Medicine* 14:2143–2160.

Mehta, C. R., Patel, N. R., and Senchaudhuri, P. (2000). Efficient Monte Carlo methods for conditional logistic regression. *Journal of the American Statistical Association* 95:99–108.

Mehta, J. N., and Heinen, J. T. (2001). Does community-based conservation shape favorable attitudes among locals? An empirical study from Nepal. *Environmental Management* 28:165–177.

Menard, S. (1995). *Applied Logistic Regression Analysis.* Thousand Oaks, CA: Sage.

Menard, S. (2000). Coefficients of determination for multiple logistic regression analysis. *The American Statistician* 54:17–24.

Menard, S. (2002a). *Applied Logistic Regression Analysis,* second edition. Thousand Oaks, CA: Sage.

Menard, S. (2002b). *Longitudinal Research,* second edition. Thousand Oaks, CA: Sage.

Menard, S. (2004a). Six approaches to calculating standardized logistic regression coefficients. *The American Statistician* 58:218–223.

Menard, S. (2004b, July). *Path Analysis With Logistic Regression.* Paper presented at the Joint Statistical Meetings of the American Statistical Association, Toronto, Ontario, Canada.

Menard, S. (2007). Two simple estimators of relative importance in linear regression based on variance decomposition. *The American Statistician* 61:280–282.

Menard, S. (2008a). Panel analysis with logistic regression. In S. Menard (ed.), *Handbook of Longitudinal Research: Design, Measurement, and Analysis.* San Diego, CA: Academic Press, pp. 505–522.

Menard, S. (2008b). Multilevel analysis with categorical outcomes. In S. Menard (ed.), *Handbook of Longitudinal Research: Design, Measurement, and Analysis.* San Diego, CA: Academic Press, pp. 565–576.

Mieczkowski, T. (1990). The accuracy of self-reported drug use: An evaluation and analysis of new data. In R. Weisheit (ed.), *Drugs, Crime, and the Criminal Justice System.* Cincinnati, OH: Anderson, pp. 275–302.

Milot, J., Rodriguez, M. J., and Sérodes, J. B. (2000). Modeling the susceptibility of drinking water utilities to form high concentrations of trihalomethanes. *Journal of Environmental Management* 60:155–171.

Mittlböck, M., and Schemper, M. (1996). Explained variation for logistic regression. *Statistics in Medicine* 15:1987–1997.

Mooney, C. Z., and Duval, R. D. (1993). *Bootstrapping: A Nonparametric Approach to Statistical Inference.* Newbury Park, CA: Sage.

Mueller, J. H., Schuessler, K. F., and Costner, H. L. (1977). *Statistical Reasoning in Sociology,* third edition. Boston: Houghton Mifflin.

Muthén, B. O. (1995). Goodness of fit with categorical and other nonnormal variables. In K. A. Bollen and J. S. Long (eds.), *Testing Structural Equation Models.* Newbury Park, CA: Sage, pp. 205–234.

Muthén, L. K., and Muthén, B. O. (2007). *MPlus: Statistical Analysis With Latent Variables, User's Guide,* Version 5. Los Angeles, CA: Muthén & Muthén.

Nagelkerke, N. J. D. (1991). A note on a general definition of the coefficient of determination. *Biometrika* 78:691–692.

Namboodiri, K., and Suchindran, C. M. (1987). *Life Table Techniques and Their Applications.* Orlando, FL: Academic Press.

Neyman, J., and Scott, E. L. (1948). Consistent estimates based on partially consistent observations. *Econometrika* 16:1–32.

Norusis, M. J. (1999). *SPSS Regression Models 10.0.* Chicago: SPSS, Inc.

O'Brien, R. (1979). The use of Pearson's *r* with ordinal data. *American Sociological Review* 44:851–857.

O'Neill, T. J., and Barry, S. C. (1995). Truncated logistic regression. *Biometrics* 51:533–541.

Ohlin, L. E., and Duncan, O. D. (1949). The efficiency of prediction in criminology. *American Journal of Sociology* 54:441–451.

Ohlmacher, G. C., and Davis, J. C. (2003). Using multiple logistic regression and GIS technology to predict landslide hazard in northeast Kansas, USA. *Engineering Geology* 69:331–343.

Ott, R. L., Larson, R., Rexroat, C., and Mendenhall, W. (1992). *Statistics: A tool for the social sciences.* Boston: PWS-Kent.

Patrick, W. J. (2001). Estimating first-year student attrition rates: An application of multilevel modeling using categorical variables. *Research in Higher Education* 42:151–170.

Pearl, J. (2000). *Causality: Models, reasoning, and inference.* Cambridge, UK: Cambridge University Press.

Pepe, M. S. (2002). Receiver operating characteristic methodology. In A. E. Raftery, M. A. Tanner, and M. T. Wells (eds.), *Statistics in the 21st Century.* Boca Raton, FL: Chapman Hall.

Peterson, B., and Harrell, F. (1990). Partial proportional odds models for ordinal response variables. *Applied Statistics* 39:205–217.

Powers, D. A., and Xie, Y. (2008). *Statistical Methods for Categorical Data Analysis,* second edition. London: Emerald Insight.

Pregibon, D. (1981). Logistic regression diagnostics. *Annals of Statistics* 9:705–724.

Prentice, R. L., and Pyke, R. (1979). Logistic disease incidence models and case-control studies. *Biometrika* 66:403–411.

Raudenbush, S. W. (2001). Toward a coherent framework for comparing trajectories of individual change. In L. M. Collins and A. G. Sayer (eds.), *New Methods for the Analysis of Change.* Washington, DC: American Psychological Association, pp. 35–64.

Raudenbush, S. W., and Bryk, A. S. (2002). *Hierarchical Linear Models: Applications and Data Analysis Methods,* second edition. Thousand Oaks, CA: Sage.

Raudenbush, S. W., Bryk, A. S., Cheong, Y. F., and Congdon, R. T., Jr. (2000). *HLM5: Hierarchical Linear and Nonlinear Modeling.* Lincolnwood, IL: Scientific Software, Inc.

Raudenbush, S. W., Bryk, A. S., Cheong, Y. F., and Congdon, R. T., Jr. (2004). *HLM6: Hierarchical Linear and Nonlinear Modeling.* Lincolnwood, IL: Scientific Software, Inc.

Raykov, T. A., and Marcoulides, G. A. (2006). A *First Course in Structural Equation Modeling,* second edition. Mahwah, NJ: Erlbaum.

Reynolds, H. T. (1984). *Analysis of Nominal Data,* second edition. Newbury Park, CA: Sage.

Rindskopf, D. (2002). Infinite parameter estimates in logistic regression: Opportunities, not problems. *Journal of Educational and Behavioral Statistics* 27:147–161.

Roberts, A. (2008). The influences of incident and contextual characteristics on crime clearance of nonlethal violence: A multilevel event history analysis. *Journal of Criminal Justice* 36:61–71.

Rogosa, D. (1995). Myths and methods: "Myths about longitudinal research" plus supplemental questions. In J. M. Gottman (ed.), *The Analysis of Change.* Mahwah, NJ: Lawrence Erlbaum, pp. 3–66.

Rosenthal, R., Rosnow, R. L., and Rubin, D. B. (2000). *Contrasts and Effect Sizes in Behavioral Research: A Correlational Approach.* Cambridge, UK: Cambridge University Press.

Rudas, T. (1998). *Odds Ratios in the Analysis of Contingency Tables.* Thousand Oaks, CA: Sage.

Ryan, T. P. (1997). *Modern Regression Methods.* New York: Wiley.

Santner, T. J., and Duffy, D. E. (1989). *The Statistical Analysis of Discrete Data.* New York: Springer-Verlag.

SAS Institute, Inc. (1989). *SAS/STAT User's Guide,* Version 6, fourth edition, Volumes 1 and 2. Cary, NC: SAS Institute, Inc.

SAS Institute, Inc. (1995). *Logistic Regression Examples Using the SAS System.* Cary, NC: SAS Institute, Inc.

SAS Institute, Inc. (1999). *SAS/STAT User's Guide,* Version 8, Volumes 1–3. Cary, NC: SAS Institute, Inc.

Sayrs, L. W. (1989). *Pooled Time Series Analysis.* Newbury Park, CA: Sage.

Schaefer, R. L. (1986). Alternative estimators in logistic regression when the data are collinear. *Journal of Statistical Computation and Simulation* 25:75–91.

Schemper, M. (1990). The explained variation in proportional hazards regression. *Biometrika* 77:216–218.

Schemper, M. (1992). Further results on the explained variation in proportional hazards regression. *Biometrika* 79:202–204.

Schroeder, L. D., Sjoquist, D. L., and Stephan, P. E. (1986). *Understanding Regression Analysis: An Introductory Guide.* Beverly Hills, CA: Sage.

Shah, B. V., Holt, M. M., and Folsom, R. E. (1977). Inference about regression models from sample survey data. *Bulletin of the International Statistical Institute* 47:43–57.

Shannon, C. E. (1948). A mathematical theory of communication. *Bell Systems Technical Journal* 27:379–423 and 623–656.

Shtatland, E. S., Kleinman, K., and Cain, E. M. (2002). *One More Time About R^2 Measures of Fit in Logistic Regression.* NESUG 15 Proceedings Paper. Cary, NC: SAS Institute, Inc. Retrieved July 6, 2008, from http://nesug.org/proceedings/nesug02/st/st004.pdf

Siegel, S. (1956). *Nonparametric Statistics for the Behavioral Sciences.* New York: McGraw-Hill.

Simonoff, J. S. (1998). Logistic regression, categorical predictors, and goodness of fit: It depends on who you ask. *The American Statistician* 52:10–14.

Singer, J. D., and Willett, J. B. (2003). *Applied Longitudinal Data Analysis: Modeling Change and Event Occurrence.* Oxford, UK: Oxford University Press.

Smith, T. W. (2008). Repeated cross-sectional research: General Social Surveys. In S. Menard (ed.), *Handbook of Longitudinal Research: Design, Measurement, and Analysis.* San Diego, CA: Academic Press, pp. 33–48.

Snijders, T., and Bosker, R. (1999). *Multilevel Analysis: An Introduction to Basic and Advanced Multilevel Modeling.* London: Sage.

Soderstrom, I., and Leitner, D. (1997, October). *The Effects of Base Rate, Selection Ratio, Sample Size, and Reliability of Predictors on Predictive Efficiency Indices Associated With Logistic Regression Models.* Paper presented at the annual meeting of the Mid-Western Educational Research Association, Chicago.

Spathis, C. T. (2002). Detecting false financial statements using published data: Some evidence from Greece. *Managerial Auditing Journal* 17:179–191.

SPSS, Inc. (1991). *SPSS Statistical Algorithms,* second edition. Chicago: SPSS, Inc.

SPSS, Inc. (1999a). *SPSS Advanced Models 10.0.* Chicago: SPSS, Inc.

SPSS, Inc. (1999b). *SPSS Base 10.0 Applications Guide.* Chicago: SPSS, Inc.

Stata (2003). *Stata Reference Manual,* Release 8, Volumes 1–4. College Station, TX: Stata Press.

Stokes, M. E., Davis, C. S., and Koch, G. G. (2000). *Categorical Data Analysis Using the SAS System,* second edition. Cary, NC: SAS Institute.

Stoolmiller, M. (1995). Using latent growth curve models to study developmental processes. In J. M. Gottman (ed.), *The Analysis of Change.* Mahwah, NJ: Lawrence Erlbaum Associates, pp. 103–138.

Studenmund, A. H., and Cassidy, H. J. (1987). *Using Econometrics: A Practical Guide.* Boston: Little, Brown.

Sudman, S. (1976). *Applied Sampling.* New York: Academic Press.

Tatsuoka, M. M. (1971). *Multivariate Analysis: Techniques for Educational and Psychological Research.* New York: Wiley.

Thompson, S. K. (2002). *Sampling,* second edition. New York: Wiley.

Trusty, J., and Harris, M. B. C. (1999). Lost talent. *Journal of Adolescent Research* 14:359–382.

van Zuijlen, P. (1999). The prognostic factors regarding long-term functional outcome of full-thickness hand burns. *Burns* 25:709–714.

Veall, M. R., and Zimmerman, K. F. (1996). Pseudo-R^2 measures for come common limited dependent variable models. *Journal of Economic Surveys* 10:241–260.

Wang, J. and Brady, M. F. (2003). Comment on King and Ryan (2002). *The American Statistician* 57:148.

Webber, W. F. (2003). Comment on King and Ryan (2002). *The American Statistician* 57:147–148.

Weisberg, H. F. (1992). *Central Tendency and Variability.* Thousand Oaks, CA: Sage.

Westat. (2000). *WesVar 4.0 User's Guide.* Rockville, MD: Westat.

Wiggins, J. S. (1973). *Personality and Prediction: Principles of Personality Assessment.* Reading, MA: Addison-Wesley.

Wilson, T. P. (1969). A proportional reduction in error interpretation for Kendall's tau-b. *Social Forces* 47:340–342.

Wofford, S., Elliott, D. S., and Menard, S. (1994). Continuities in marital violence. *Journal of Family Violence* 9:195–225.

Wong, G. Y., and Mason, W. M. (1985). The hierarchical logistic regression model for multilevel analysis. *Journal of the American Statistical Association* 80:513–524.

Wooldridge, J. M. (2002). *Econometric Analysis of Cross Section and Panel Data.* Cambridge: MIT Press.

Wright, S. (1918). On the nature of size factors. *Genetics* 3:367–374.

Wright, S. (1921). Correlation and causation. *Journal of Agricultural Research* 20:557–585.

Wright, S. (1934). The method of path coefficients. *Annals of Mathematical Statistics* 5:161–215.

Wright, S. (1971). Path coefficients and path regressions: Alternative or complementary concepts. *Biometric* 16:189–202.

Yamaguchi, K. (1991). *Event History Analysis.* Newbury Park, CA: Sage.

Zheng, B., and Agresti, A. (2000). Summarizing the predictive power of a generalized linear model. *Statistics in Medicine* 19:1771–1781.

Author Index

Davis, J. C., 1, 365
Day, N. E., 260, 359
De Leeuw, J., 243, 363
De Maris, A., 35, 48–49, 58, 61, 360
Dennis, W. J., Jr., 1, 361
Desii, C., 51, 359
Diggle, P. J., 228, 343, 360
Dishion, T., 71, 364
Donner, A., 99, 361
Draper, D., 243, 361
Dreux, D. R., 1, 361
Duffy, D. E., 340, 366
Duncan, G. J., 269, 363, 364
Duncan, O. D., 66, 68, 92, 145, 169, 359–360, 365
Duval, R. D., 227, 235, 365

Efron, B., 43, 52, 55, 73, 227, 360
Eliason, S. R., 16, 29, 48, 337, 343, 360
Elliott, A., 3, 238, 360
Elliott, D. S., 3, 117–119, 213, 215, 238, 313, 360, 367
Elward, A. M., 1, 361
Eshima, N., 153, 361

Farrington, D. P., 66, 71, 361
Farris, K. B., 1, 364
Faust, R., 213, 362
Feldman, S., vi, viii, 7–8, 13, 107, 129, 359
Fiegener, M. K., 1, 361
Fienberg, S. E., vi, 19, 153, 361
Finkel, S. E., x, 246, 261, 267, 269, 361
Finlay, B., vii, 1, 5, 8, 19, 51, 117, 134, 169, 358
Folsom, R. E., 340, 366
Forthofer, R. N., 225–228, 243, 363
Fox, J., viii, 108, 129, 135, 144, 361
Frankel, M. R., 227, 361
Fraser, V., 1, 358
Fraser, V. J., 1, 361
Furby, L., 269, 360

Gacci, G., 51, 359
Gold, R. Z., 25, 364
Goldstein, H., 243, 361
Goodman, L. A., 24, 28, 152–153, 361
Gottman, J. M., 366, 367
Gould, W., 335, 343, 361
Greenberg, D. G., x, 246, 261, 267, 362
Gray, R., 174, 358
Grömping, U., 150, 361
Gunson, K. E., 1, 361

Haberman, S. J., 32, 48, 54, 361
Hagle, T. M., 45, 49, 51, 361

Hamerle, A., 273, 308, 359, 361
Hamvas, A., 1, 358
Hardin, J., 132, 192, 226, 228–229, 231–232, 243, 251, 261, 300, 302, 338, 340, 343, 361
Hardy, M., 8, 40, 84, 96, 361, 366
Harrell, F. E., Jr., 48, 56, 82, 204, 211, 219, 361, 366
Harris, M. B. C., 1, 367
Hauck, W. W., 99, 361
Hauser, J. R., 48, 362
Hayduk, L. A., 169, 328, 362
Healy, M., 243, 361
Heinen, J. T., 1, 365
Heise, D. R., 92, 152, 164, 169, 362
Henry, F., 196, 362
Hilbe, J., 132, 192, 226, 228–229, 231–232, 243, 251, 261, 300, 302, 338, 340, 343, 361
Hildebrand, D. K., 353, 356–357, 362
Hill, M. S., 222, 362
Hirji, K. F., 341, 362
Holt, M. M., 340, 366
Holzmann-Pazgal, G., 1, 358
Hosmer, D. W., vii, 48–49, 57–59, 77, 82, 94, 98–100, 102, 106, 117, 120, 130, 132–135, 139, 144, 181, 201, 260, 308, 310, 317, 319–320, 325, 340, 343, 362
Hox, J., 248, 362
Hsieh, F. Y., 102, 362
Hu, L., 196, 362
Huizinga, D., 3, 213, 238, 313, 360
Hutcheson, G., 25, 28, 33, 36, 48, 143, 170, 194, 362

Ishii-Kuntz, M., 33, 362

Jaccard, J., 116, 362
Jennings, D. E., 99, 362
Johnson, J. A., 1, 364
Jones, B. S., x, 359
Jöreskog, K. G., 45, 153, 196, 329, 362

Kalbfleisch, J. D., 248, 308, 317, 325, 362
Kalton, G., 225–227, 243, 362–363
Kandel, D. B., 213, 362
Kano, Y., 196, 362
Kaplan, D., 169, 328, 331, 362
Kaufman, R. L., 90, 362
Keating, N., 1, 364
Kessler, R. C., x, 246, 261, 267, 362
Kim, C., 332, 364
King, E. N., 341, 343, 362, 367
King, G., 29, 268, 335–336, 343, 362
Kish, L., 226, 243, 363
Klecka, W. R., 68, 195, 319, 363
Kleinman, K., 48–50, 57, 367

Subject Index

NOTE: Bold terms indicate statistical software commands.

Supporting researchers for more than 40 years

Research methods have always been at the core of SAGE's publishing program. Founder Sara Miller McCune published SAGE's first methods book, *Public Policy Evaluation*, in 1970. Soon after, she launched the *Quantitative Applications in the Social Sciences* series—affectionately known as the "little green books."

Always at the forefront of developing and supporting new approaches in methods, SAGE published early groundbreaking texts and journals in the fields of qualitative methods and evaluation.

Today, more than 40 years and two million little green books later, SAGE continues to push the boundaries with a growing list of more than 1,200 research methods books, journals, and reference works across the social, behavioral, and health sciences. Its imprints—Pine Forge Press, home of innovative textbooks in sociology, and Corwin, publisher of PreK–12 resources for teachers and administrators—broaden SAGE's range of offerings in methods. SAGE further extended its impact in 2008 when it acquired CQ Press and its best-selling and highly respected political science research methods list.

From qualitative, quantitative, and mixed methods to evaluation, SAGE is the essential resource for academics and practitioners looking for the latest methods by leading scholars.

For more information, visit **www.sagepub.com**.